THE DESIGN COLLECTION: ADOBE®
INDESIGN® CS3, PHOTOSHOP® CS3,
AND ILLUSTRATOR® CS3
REVEALED

THE DESIGN COLLECTION: ADOBE®
INDESIGN® CS3, PHOTOSHOP® CS3,
AND ILLUSTRATOR® CS3
REVEALED

Botello/Reding

COURSE TECHNOLOGY
CENGAGE Learning™

The Design Collection—Revealed

Botello/Reding

Vice President, Technology and Trades ABU: David Garza

Director of Learning Solutions: Sandy Clark

Managing Editor: Larry Main

Senior Acquisitions Editor: James Gish

Product Managers: Jane Hosie-Bounar, Nicole Bruno

Editorial Assistant: Sarah Timm

Marketing Director: Deborah Yarnell

Marketing Manager: Kevin Rivenburg

Marketing Specialist: Victoria Ortiz

Content Product Managers: Cathie DiMassa, Tintu Thomas

Developmental Editors: Ann Fisher, Rachel Bunin

Technical Editors: Tara Botelho, Elizabeth Gorman

Art Director: Bruce Bond

Cover Design: Lisa Kuhn, Curio Press, LLC

Cover Photo: © Paul Springett / Royalty-Free/ALAMY

Text Designer: Ann Small

Proofreader: Wendy Benedetto, Kim Kosmatka, Harold Johnson

Indexer: Alexandra Nickerson

For product information and technology assistance, contact us at
Cengage Learning Customer & Sales Support, 1-800-354-9706

For permission to use material from this text or product, submit all requests online at cengage.com/permissions. Further permissions questions can be emailed to **permissionrequest@cengage.com**

Some of the product names and company names used in this book have been used for identification purposes only and may be trademarks or registered trademarks of their respective manufacturers and sellers.

Adobe® InDesign®, Adobe® Photoshop®, Adobe® Illustrator®, Adobe® Flash®, Adobe® Dreamweaver®, and Adobe® Creative Suite® are trademarks or registered trademarks of Adobe Systems, Inc. in the United States and/or other countries. Third party products, services, company names, logos, design, titles, words, or phrases within these materials may be trademarks of their respective owners.

The Adobe Approved Certification Courseware logo is a proprietary trademark of Adobe. All rights reserved.

ISBN-13: 978-1-4283-1962-2

ISBN-10: 1-4283-1962-X

Course Technology
25 Thomson Place,
Boston, Massachusetts, 02210.

Cengage Learning is a leading provider of customized learning solutions with office locations around the globe, including Singapore, the United Kingdom, Australia, Mexico, Brazil and Japan. Locate your local office at: **international.cengage.com/region**

Cengage Learning products are represented in Canada by Nelson Education, Ltd.

For your lifelong learning solutions, visit **course.cengage.com**
Visit our corporate website at **cengage.com**

Course Technology, a part of Cengage Learning, and *The Design Collection—Revealed* are independent from ProCert Labs, LLC and Adobe Systems Incorporated, and are not affiliated with ProCert Labs and Adobe in any manner. This publication may assist students to prepare for an Adobe Certified Expert exam, however, neither ProCert Labs nor Adobe warrant that use of this material will ensure success in connection with any exam.

Printed in China
2 3 4 5 6 7 8 9 11 10 09 08

Revealed Series Vision

The Revealed Series is your guide to today's hottest multimedia applications. These comprehensive books teach the skills behind the application, showing you how to apply smart design principles to multimedia products such as dynamic graphics, animation, Web sites, software authoring tools, and digital video.

A team of design professionals including multimedia instructors, students, authors, and editors worked together to create this series. We recognized the unique learning environment of the multimedia classroom and created a series that:

- Gives you comprehensive step-by-step instructions
- Offers in-depth explanation of the "Why" behind a skill
- Includes creative projects for additional practice
- Explains concepts clearly using full-color visuals

It was our goal to create a book that speaks directly to the multimedia and design community—one of the most rapidly growing computer fields today. We think we've done just that, with a sophisticated and instructive book design.

—The Revealed Series

Authors' Visions

Hands-on is the best way to explore any software application. You can study every chapter of an instruction manual, but reading about Adobe InDesign, Photoshop, and Illustrator and actually using InDesign, Photoshop, and Illustrator are two very different things indeed. This book is a series of exercises that will take you on a fully guided tour of these three Adobe products—from basic concepts to intermediate techniques—all with a hands-on approach. You will learn by doing, and you'll have fun, which is an essential skill not covered in any instruction manual.

I had fun writing this, and that was possible because of the focus and hard work of my editor and long-time friend Ann Fisher. Ann kept the Illustrator and InDesign books on track but left me enough room to bounce around the applications and share with you some of my favorite tips and tricks. Her dedication—combined with a great capacity for laughter—brought out the best in both of us. Special thanks also to Jim Gish, Senior Acquisitions Editor for this series, Jane Hosie-Bounar, Product Manager, and Tara Botelho, Technical Editor.

—Chris Botello

While this is not the first revision of this book, it is the first time working with slightly different crews with slightly different ways of doing things, all while meeting ridiculous deadlines (which we're used to). Rachel Bunin, Cathie DiMassa, Jane Hosie-Bounar and I have all worked together before on a variety of projects that has spanned more than 10 years. Added to the mix is Jim Gish, Larry Main, Nicole Bruno, Sarah Timm, Kim Ryttel, Tintu Thomas, and Elizabeth Gorman. The majority of us have never met face-to-face, yet we managed to finish this project in a professional manner, while defying the time-space continuum.

I would also like to thank my husband, Michael, who is used to my disappearing acts when I'm facing deadlines, and Phoebe, Bix, and Jet, who know when it's time to take a break for some good old-fashioned head-scratching.

—Elizabeth Eisner Reding

SERIES & AUTHORS' VISIONS

v

Introduction to The Design Collection

Welcome to *The Design Collection: Adobe InDesign CS3, Photoshop CS3, and Illustrator CS3 Revealed.* This book offers creative projects, concise instructions, and coverage of basic to intermediate InDesign, Photoshop, and Illustrator skills, helping you to create polished, professional-looking layouts, photographs, and illustrations. Use this book both in the classroom and as your own reference guide.

This text is organized into 15 chapters. In these chapters, you will learn many skills, including how to move amongst the Creative Suite applications, which, in this release, provide familiar functionality from one application to the next. The first five chapters cover InDesign, where you'll work extensively with InDesign features and use both Illustrator and Photoshop files as you create quality layouts. The next five chapters cover additional Photoshop-specific skills, and the last five chapters

teach you some of the finer points of illustrating with Adobe Illustrator.

What You'll Do

A What You'll Do figure begins every lesson. This figure gives you an at-a-glance look at what you'll do in the chapter, either by showing you a file from the current project or a tool you'll be using.

Comprehensive Conceptual Lessons

Before jumping into instructions, in-depth conceptual information tells you "why" skills are applied. This book provides the "how" and "why" through the use of professional examples. Also included in the text are tips and sidebars to help you work more efficiently and creatively, or to teach you a bit about the history or design philosophy behind the skill you are using.

Step-by-Step Instructions

This book combines in-depth conceptual information with concise steps to help you learn CS3. Each set of steps guides you through a lesson where you will create, modify, or enhance a CS3 file. Step references to large colorful images and quick step summaries round out the lessons. The Data Files for the steps are provided on the CD at the back of this book.

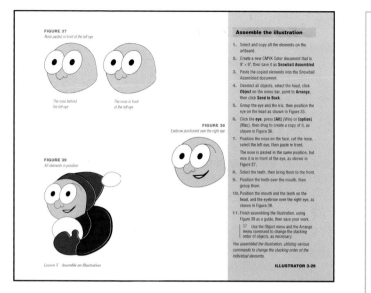

Projects

This book contains a variety of end-of-chapter materials for additional practice and reinforcement. The Skills Review contains hands-on practice exercises that mirror the progressive nature of the lesson material. The chapter concludes with four projects; two Project Builders, one Design Project, and one Group Project. The Project Builders and the Design Project require you to apply the skills you've learned in the chapter. The Group Project encourages group activity as students use the resources of a team to address and solve challenges based on the content explored in the chapter.

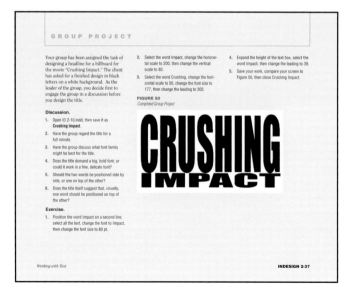

BRIEF CONTENTS

InDesign

Chapter 1   Exploring the InDesign Workspace
Lesson 1   Explore the InDesign Workspace 1-4
2   Change Document Views 1-10
3   Navigate Through a Document 1-16
4   Use InDesign Help 1-22

Chapter 2   Working with Text
Lesson 1   Format Text 2-4
2   Format Paragraphs 2-12
3   Create and Apply Styles 2-20
4   Edit Text 2-26

Chapter 3   Setting up a Document
Lesson 1   Create a New Document 3-4
2   Create Master Pages 3-18
3   Apply Master Pages to Document Pages 3-32
4   Place Text and Thread Text 3-36
5   Modify Master Pages and Document Pages 3-42
6   Create New Sections and Wrap Text 3-46

Chapter 4   Working with Frames
Lesson 1   Align and Distribute Objects on a Page 4-4
2   Stack and Layer Objects 4-14
3   Work with Graphics Frames 4-24
4   Work with Text Frames 4-38

Chapter 5   Working with Color
Lesson 1   Work with Process Colors 5-4
2   Apply Color 5-12
3   Work with Spot Colors 5-24
4   Work with Gradients 5-30

Photoshop

Chapter 1   Getting Started with Adobe Photoshop CS3
Lesson 1   Start Adobe Photoshop CS3 1-4
2   Learn How to Open and Save an Image 1-8
3   Use Organizational and Management Features 1-14
4   Examine the Photoshop Window 1-16
5   Use the Layers and History Palettes 1-24
6   Learn About Photoshop by Using Help 1-28
7   View and Print an Image 1-32
8   Close a File and Exit Photoshop 1-36

Chapter 2   Working with Layers
Lesson 1   Examine and Convert Layers 2-4
2   Add and Delete Layers 2-8
3   Add a Selection from One Image to Another 2-12
4   Organize Layers with Layer groups and Colors 2-16

Chapter 3   Making Selections
Lesson 1   Make a Selection Using Shapes 3-4
2   Modify a Marquee 3-12
3   Select Using Color and Modify a Selection 3-16
4   Add a Vignette Effect to a Selection 3-23

Chapter 4   Incorporating Color Techniques
Lesson 1   Work with Color to Transform an Image 4-4
2   Use the Color Picker and the Swatches Palette 4-10
3   Place a Border Around an Image 4-14
4   Blend Colors Using the Gradient Tool 4-16
5   Add Color to a Grayscale Image 4-20
6   Use Filters, Opacity and Blending Modes 4-24
7   Match Colors 4-30

Chapter 5   Placing Type in an Image
Lesson 1   Learn About Type and How It is Created 5-4
2   Change Spacing and Adjust Baseline Shift 5-8
3   Use the Drop Shadow Style 5-12
4   Apply Anti-Aliasing to Type 17-16
5   Modify Type with the Bevel and Emboss Style 5-20
6   Apply Special Effects to Type using Filters 5-24
7   Create Text on a Path 5-28

Illustrator

Chapter 1   Getting Started with Illustrator
Lesson 1   Create a New Document 1-4
2   Explore the Illustrator Window 1-8
3   Create Basic Shapes 1-18
4   Apply Fill and Stroke Colors to Objects 1-22
5   Select, Move, and Align Objects 1-26
6   Transform Objects 1-30
7   Make Direct Selections 1-36

Chapter 2   Creating Text and Gradients
Lesson 1   Create and Format Text 2-4
2   Flow Text into an Object 2-10
3   Position Text on a Path 2-16
4   Create Colors and Gradients 2-20

5   Apply Colors and Gradients
to Text 2-26
6   Adjust a Gradient and Create a Drop
Shadow 2-30

Chapter 3   **Drawing and Composing an
Illustrator**
Lesson 1   Draw Straight Lines 3-4
2   Draw Curved Lines 3-10
3   Draw Elements of an
Illustration 3-18
4   Apply Attributes to Objects 3-24
5   Assemble an Illustration 3-28

6   Stroke Objects for Artistic
Effect 3-30
7   Use Live Trace and the Live Paint
Bucket Tool 3-36

Chapter 4   **Transforming and Distorting
Objects**
Lesson 1   Transform Objects 4-4
2   Offset and Outline Paths 4-12
3   Create Compound Paths 4-16
4   Work with the Pathfinder
Panel 4-20
5   Create Clipping Masks 4-30

Chapter 5   **Working with Layers**
Lesson 1   Create and Modify Layers 5-4
2   Manipulate Layered Artwork 5-12
3   Work with Layered Artwork 5-20
4   Create a Clipping Set 5-26

Data Files   1

Glossary   8

Index   21

InDesign

CHAPTER 1 — EXPLORING THE INDESIGN WORKSPACE

INTRODUCTION
Exploring the InDesign Workspace 1-2

LESSON 1
Explore the InDesign Workspace 1-4
Looking at the InDesign Workspace 1-4
Exploring the Toolbox 1-5
Working with Panels 1-6
Tasks   Explore the Toolbox 1-8
        Work with panels 1-9

LESSON 2
Change Document Views 1-10
Using the Zoom Tool 1-10
Accessing the Zoom Tool 1-10
Using the Hand Tool 1-11
Creating Multiple Views of a Document 1-12
Tasks   Use the Zoom Tool and the Hand Tool 1-13
        Create a new window 1-14

LESSON 3
Navigate Through a Document 1-16
Navigating to Pages in a Document 1-16
Using the Navigator Panel 1-18
Tasks   Navigate to Pages in a Document 1-19
        Use the Navigator panel 1-20

LESSON 4
Use InDesign Help 1-22
Accessing InDesign Help 1-22

CHAPTER 2 — WORKING WITH TEXT

INTRODUCTION
Working with Text 2-2

LESSON 1
Format Text 2-4
Using the Character Panel 2-4
Understanding Leading 2-4
Scaling Text Horizontally and Vertically 2-6
Kerning and Tracking Text 2-6
Creating Superscript Characters 2-7
Creating Subscript Characters 2-7
Underlining Text 2-7
Tasks   Modify text attributes 2-8
        Track and kern text 2-9
        Create superscript characters 2-10
        Underline text 2-11

LESSON 2
Format Paragraphs 2-12
Using the Paragraph Panel 2-12
Understanding Returns and Soft Returns 2-15
Tasks   Use the Paragraph panel and Character
        panel to modify leading and alignment 2-16
        Apply vertical spacing between
        paragraphs 2-17
        Apply paragraph indents 2-18
        Apply drop caps and soft returns 2-19

LESSON 3
Create and Apply Styles 2-20
Working with Character and
Paragraph Styles 2-20
Tasks   Create character styles 2-22
        Apply character styles 2-23
        Create paragraph styles 2-24
        Apply paragraph styles 2-25

LESSON 4
Edit Text 2-26
Using the Find/Change Command 2-26
Checking Spelling 2-26
Tasks   Use the Find/Change command 2-28
        Check Spelling 2-29

CONTENTS

CHAPTER 3   SETTING UP A DOCUMENT

INTRODUCTION
Setting up a Document 3-2

LESSON 1
Create a New Document 3-4
Creating a New Document 3-4
Understanding Master Pages 3-5
Creating Master Items on Master Pages 3-6
Understanding Guides 3-6
Creating Guides 3-6
Changing the Color of Guides, Margins, and
Columns 3-7
Choosing Default Colors for Guides, Margins,
and Columns 3-7
Using the Transform Panel 3-7
Using the Control Panel 3-8
Using the Transform Panel to Transform
Objects 3-9
Tasks   Create a new document 3-10
         Rename and modify the default master
         page 3-11
         Add guides to a master page 3-12
         Create placeholder text frames 3-14
         Change the color of guides, margins, and
         columns 3-15
         Use the Transform Panel to transform
         text frames 3-16

LESSON 2
Create Master Pages 3-18
Creating a New Master Page 3-18
Loading Master Pages 3-19
Creating Automatic Page Numbering 3-19
Inserting White Space Between Text
Characters 3-20
Inserting Em Dashes and En Dashes 3-20
Creating a New Master Page Based on
Another Master Page 3-21

Tasks   Create a new master page 3-22
         Create text frames on a master page 3-24
         Create automatic page numbering and
         insert white space between characters 3-26
         Create master items on a master page 3-28
         Create a new master page based on
         another master page 3-30

LESSON 3
Apply Master Pages to Document Pages 3-32
Applying Master Pages to Document Pages 3-32
Task   Apply master pages to document pages 3-34

LESSON 4
Place Text and Thread Text 3-36
Placing Text 3-36
Threading Text 3-38
Tasks   Place text on document pages 3-40
         Thread text 3-41

LESSON 5
**Modify Master Pages and Document
Pages** 3-42
Modifying Master Pages 3-42
Overriding Master Items on Document
Pages 3-42
Detaching Master Items 3-42
Tasks   Override master items on a document
         page 3-43
         Modify master pages 3-44

LESSON 6
Create New Sections and Wrap Text 3-46
Creating Sections in a Document 3-46
Wrapping Text Around a Frame 3-47
Tasks   Create sections in a document 3-48
         Wrap text around a frame 3-49

CONTENTS

CHAPTER 4   WORKING WITH FRAMES

INTRODUCTION
Working with Frames 4-2

LESSON 1
Align and Distribute Objects on a Page 4-4
Applying Fills and Strokes 4-4
Using the Step and Repeat Command 4-6
Aligning Objects 4-7
Distributing Objects 4-8
Tasks   Apply fills and strokes 4-9
        Use the Step and Repeat command 4-10
        Align objects 4-12
        Distribute objects 4-13

LESSON 2
Stack and Layer Objects 4-14
Understanding the Stacking Order 4-14
Understanding Layers 4-14
Working with Layers 4-15
Manipulating Layers and Objects on Layers 4-16
Selecting Artwork on Layers 4-17
Selecting Objects Behind Other Objects 4-17
Tasks   Use the Arrange commands to change the
        stacking order of objects 4-18
        Create new layers in the Layers panel 4-19
        Position objects on layers 4-20
        Change the order of layers in the Layers
        panel 4-22

LESSON 3
Work with Graphics Frames 4-24
Placing Graphics in a Document 4-24
Understanding the Difference Between the
Graphics Frame and the Graphic 4-25
Understanding the Difference Between the
Selection Tool and the Direct Selection Tool 4-25
Moving a Graphic Within a Graphics Frame 4-27
Resizing a Graphic 4-27
Using the Fitting Commands 4-28
Wrapping Text Around an Imported
Photoshop Graphic Saved with a Named
Clipping Path 4-28
Tasks   Place graphics in a document 4-30
        Move a graphic in a graphics frame 4-31
        Resize graphics frames and graphics 4-33
        Wrap text around a graphic 4-35

LESSON 4
Work with Text Frames 4-38
Semi-Autoflowing Text 4-38
Autoflowing Text 4-38
Inserting a Column Break 4-39
Inserting a "Continued on page..." Notation 4-40
Tasks   Autoflow text 4-41
        Reflow text 4-42
        Add a column break 4-43
        Insert a page continuation notation 4-44

INTRODUCTION
Working with Color 5-2

LESSON 1
Work with Process Colors 5-4
Understanding Process Colors 5-4
Understanding Tints 5-4
Creating Tint Swatches 5-6
Working with Unnamed Colors 5-6
Tasks　Create process color swatches 5-8
　　　　Create a tint swatch and modify the original
　　　　color swatch 5-9
　　　　Use the Color panel 5-10
　　　　Save an unnamed color in the Swatches
　　　　panel 5-11

LESSON 2
Apply Color 5-12
Applying Color to Objects 5-12
Understanding the Paper Swatch 5-14
Applying Color to Text 5-15
Creating Black Shadow Text 5-16
Modifying and Deleting Swatches 5-16
Tasks　Drag and drop colors onto objects 5-18
　　　　Use the Swap Fill and Stroke and Default
　　　　Fill and Stroke buttons 5-19
　　　　Apply color to text 5-20
　　　　Create black shadow text 5-21
　　　　Modify and delete swatches 5-23

LESSON 3
Work with Spot Colors 5-24
Understanding Spot Colors 5-24
Creating Spot Colors 5-25
Importing Graphics with Spot Colors 5-25
Tasks　Create a spot color swatch 5-26
　　　　Import graphics with spot colors 5-27

LESSON 4
Work with Gradients 5-30
Creating Gradients 5-30
Applying Gradients 5-32
Modifying a Gradient Fill Using the Gradient
Panel 32
Tasks　Create a linear gradient swatch 5-33
　　　　Create a radial gradient swatch 5-34
　　　　Apply gradient swatches and use the
　　　　Gradient Swatch Tool 5-35
　　　　Use the Gradient Swatch Tool to extend
　　　　a gradient across multiple objects and
　　　　modify a gradient 5-36

CONTENTS

Photoshop

CHAPTER 1 — GETTING STARTED WITH ADOBE PHOTOSHOP CS3

INTRODUCTION

Getting Started with Adobe Photoshop CS3 1-2
Using Photoshop 1-2
Understanding Platform Interfaces 1-2
Understanding Sources 1-2

LESSON 1

Start Adobe Photoshop CS3 1-4
Starting Photoshop and Creating a File 1-5
Defining Image-Editing Software 1-4
Understanding Images 1-4
Using Photoshop Features 1-4
Tasks Start Photoshop (Windows) 1-6
Start Photoshop (Macintosh) 1-7

LESSON 2

Learn How to Open and Save an Image 1-8
Opening and Saving Files 1-8
Customizing How You Open Files 1-8
Browsing Through Files 1-9
Understanding the Power of Bridge 1-10
Creating a PDF Presentation 1-10
Using Save As Versus Save 1-10
Tasks Open a file using the File menu 1-11
Open a file using Folders palette in
Adobe Bridge 1-11
Use the Save As command 1-12
Rate and filter with Bridge 1-13

LESSON 3

Use Organizational and Management Features 1-14
Learning about Version Cue 1-14
Understanding Version Cue
Workspaces 1-14
Using Version Cue's Administrative
Functions 1-15
Making Use of Bridge 1-15

LESSON 4

Examine the Photoshop Window 1-16
Learning About the Workspace 1-16
Finding Tools Everywhere 1-16
Using Tool Shortcut Keys 1-18
Customizing Your Environment 1-18
Tasks Select a tool 1-19
Select a tool from the Tool Preset
picker 1-20
Add a tool to the Tool Preset picker 1-21
Show and hide palettes 1-22
Create a customized workspace 1-23

LESSON 5

Use the Layers and History Palettes 1-24
Learning About Layers 1-24
Understanding the Layers Palette 1-25
Displaying and Hiding Layers 1-25
Using the History Palette 1-25

Tasks Hide and display a layer 1-26
Move a layer on the Layers palette
and delete a state on the
History palette 1-27

LESSON 6

Learn About Photoshop by Using Help 1-28
Understanding the Power of Help 1-28
Using Help Topics 1-28
Tasks Find information in Contents 1-29
Find information in the Index 1-30
Find information using Search 1-31

LESSON 7

View and Print an Image 1-32
Getting a Closer Look 1-32
Printing Your Image 1-32
Understanding Color Handling in
Printing 1-33
Viewing an Image in Multiple Views 1-33
Tasks Use the Zoom Tool 1-34
Modify print settings 1-35

LESSON 8

Close a File and Exit Photoshop 1-36
Concluding Your Work Session 1-36
Closing Versus Exiting 1-36
Task Close a file and exit Photoshop 1-37

CHAPTER 2 WORKING WITH LAYERS

INTRODUCTION
Working with Layers 2-2
Layers Are Everything 2-2
Understanding the Importance of Layers 2-2
Using Layers to Modify an Image 2-2

LESSON 1
Examine and Convert Layers 2-4
Learning About the Layers Palette 2-4
Recognizing Layer Types 2-4
Organizing Layers 2-5
Converting Layers 2-6
Task   Convert an image layer into
          a Background layer 2-7

LESSON 2
Add and Delete Layers 2-8
Adding Layers to an Image 2-8
Naming a Layer 2-9
Deleting Layers From an Image 2-9
Tasks   Add a layer using the Layer menu 2-10
          Delete a layer 2-11
          Add a layer using the Layers palette 2-11

LESSON 3
**Add a Selection from One Image
to Another** 2-12
Understanding Selections 2-12
Understanding the Extract and Color
Range Commands 2-12
Making a Selection and Moving
a Selection 2-13
Defringing Layer Contents 2-13
Tasks   Make a color range selection 2-14
          Move a selection to another image 2-15
          Defringe the selection 2-15

LESSON 4
**Organize Layers with Layer groups
and Colors** 2-16
Understanding Layer Groups 2-16
Organizing Layers into Groups 2-16
Adding Color to a Layer 2-17
Flattening an Image 2-17

Understanding Layer Comps 2-18
Using Layer Comps 2-18
Tasks   Create a layer group 2-19
          Move layers to the layer group 2-19
          Rename a layer and adjust opacity 2-20
          Create layer comps 2-20
          Flatten an image 2-2

CHAPTER 3 MAKING SELECTIONS

INTRODUCTION
Making Selections 3-2
Combining Images 3-2
Understanding Selection Tools 3-2
Understanding Which Selection Tool
to Use 3-2
Combining Imagery 3-2

LESSON 1
Make a Selection Using Shapes 3-4
Selecting by Shape 3-4
Creating a Selection 3-4
Using Fastening Points 3-4
Selecting, Deselecting, and Reselecting 3-5
Placing a Selection 3-6
Using Guides 3-6
Tasks   Create a selection with the
          Rectangular Marquee Tool 3-7
          Position a selection with the
          Move Tool 3-8
          Deselect a selection 3-9
          Create a selection with the
          Magnetic Lasso Tool 3-10
          Move a complex selection to an
          existing image 3-11

LESSON 2
Modify a Marquee 3-12
Changing the Size of a Marquee 3-12

Modifying a Marquee 3-12
Moving a Marquee 3-13
Using the Quick Selection Tool 3-13
Tasks   Move and enlarge a marquee 3-14
          Use the Quick Selection Tool 3-15

LESSON 3
**Select Using Color and
Modify a Selection** 3-16
Selecting with Color 3-16
Using the Magic Wand Tool 3-16
Using the Color Range Command 3-17
Transforming a Selection 3-17
Understanding the Healing Brush Tool 3-17
Using the Healing Brush Tool 3-17
Tasks   Select using color range 3-18
          Select using the Magic Wand Tool 3-19
          Flip a selection 3-20
          Fix imperfections with the
          Healing Brush Tool 3-21

LESSON 4
**Add a Vignette Effect to a
Selection** 3-23
Understanding Vignettes 3-22
Creating a Vignette 3-22
Task   Create a vignette 3-23

CHAPTER 4   INCORPORATING COLOR TECHNIQUES

INTRODUCTION
Incorporating Color Techniques 4-2
Using Color 4-2
Understanding Color Modes and Color
Models 4-2
Displaying and Printing Images 4-2

LESSON 1
**Work with Color to Transform
an Image** 4-4
Learning About Color Models 4-4
L*a*b Model 4-5
HSB Model 4-5
RGB Mode 4-5
CMYK Mode 4-6
Understanding the Bitmap and
Grayscale Modes 4-6
Changing Foreground and
Background Colors 4-6
Task   Set the default foreground
and background colors 4-7
Change the background color using the
Color palette 4-8
Change the background color using the
Eyedropper Tool 4-9

LESSON 2
**Use the Color Picker and
the Swatches Palette** 4-10
Making Selections from the
Color Picker 4-10
Using the Swatches Palette 4-11

Tasks   Select a color using the
Color Picker dialog box 4-12
Select a color using the
Swatches palette 4-12
Add a new color to the
Swatches palette 4-13

LESSON 3
Place a Border Around an Image 4-14
Emphasizing an Image 4-14
Locking Transparent Pixels 4-14
Task   Create a border 4-15
Understanding Gradients 4-16

LESSON 4
Blend Colors Using the Gradient Tool 4-16
Using the Gradient Tool 4-17
Customizing Gradients 4-17
Tasks   Create a gradient from a
sample color 4-18
Apply a gradient fill 4-19

LESSON 5
Add Color to a Grayscale Image 4-20
Colorizing Options 4-20
Converting Grayscale and Color Modes 4-20
Colorizing a Grayscale Image 4-21
Tweaking adjustments 4-21
Tasks   Change the color mode 4-22
Colorize a grayscale image 4-23

LESSON 6
**Use Filters, Opacity and
Blending Modes** 4-24
Manipulating an Image 4-24
Understanding Filters 4-24
Choosing Blending Modes 4-25
Understanding Blending
Mode Components 4-25
Softening Filter Effects 4-25
Balancing Colors 4-25
Tasks   Adjust brightness and contrast 4-27
Work with a filter, a blending
mode, and an opacity setting 4-28
Adjust color balance 4-29

LESSON 7
Match Colors 4-30
Finding the Right Color 4-30
Using Selections to Match Colors 4-30
Task   Match a color 4-31

CONTENTS

INTRODUCTION

Placing Type in an Image 5-2
Learning About Type 5-2
Understanding the Purpose of Type 5-2
Getting the Most Out of Type 5-2

LESSON 1

**Learn About Type and
How It is Created** 5-4
Introducing Type Types 5-4
Getting to Know Font Families 5-4
Measuring Type Size 5-5
Acquiring Fonts 5-5
Tasks   Create and modify type 5-6
          Change type color using an
          existing image color 5-7

LESSON 2

**Change Spacing and
Adjust Baseline Shift** 5-8
Adjusting Spacing 5-8
Understanding Character and
Line Spacing 5-8
Using the Character Palette 5-9
Adjusting the Baseline Shift 5-9
Tasks   Kern characters 5-10
          Shift the baseline 5-11

LESSON 3

Use the Drop Shadow Style 5-12
Adding Effects to Type 5-12
Using the Drop Shadow 5-12
Applying a Style 5-12
Controlling a Drop Shadow 5-13
Tasks   Add a drop shadow 5-14
          Modify drop shadow settings 5-15

LESSON 4

Apply Anti-Aliasing to Type 17-16
Eliminating the "Jaggies" 5-16
Knowing When to Apply Anti-Aliasing 5-16
Understanding Anti-Aliasing 5-17
Tasks   Apply anti-aliasing 5-18
          Undo anti-aliasing 5-19

LESSON 5

**Modify Type with the Bevel and
Emboss Style** 5-20
Using the Bevel and Emboss Style 5-20
Understanding Bevel and
Emboss Settings 5-20
Tasks   Add the Bevel and Emboss style
          with the Layer menu 5-22
          Modify Bevel and Emboss
          settings 5-23

LESSON 6

**Apply Special Effects to Type
using Filters** 5-24
Understanding Filters 5-24
Creating Special Effects 5-24
Producing Distortions 5-24
Using Textures and Relief 5-25
Blurring Imagery 5-25
Tasks   Rasterize a type layer 5-26
          Modify filter settings 5-27

LESSON 7

Create Text on a Path 5-28
Understanding Text on a Path 5-28
Creating Text on a Path 5-28
Task   Create a path and add type 5-29

CONTENTS

Illustrator

CHAPTER 1 GETTING STARTED WITH ILLUSTRATOR

INTRODUCTION
Getting Started with Illustrator 1-2
Getting to Know Illustrator 1-2

LESSON 1
Create a New Document 1-4
Creating a New Document 1-4
Choosing Color Modes and Document
Size 1-4
Choosing a Unit of Measure 1-5
Tasks   Create a new document (Windows) 1-6
         Create a new document (Macintosh) 1-7

LESSON 2
Explore the Illustrator Window 1-8
Touring the Illustrator Window 1-8
Using Quick Keys in Illustrator 1-11
Tasks   Navigate the Illustrator artboard 1-14
         Work with objects 1-16

LESSON 3
Create Basic Shapes 1-18
Getting Ready to Draw 1-18
Understanding Bitmap Images and
Vector Graphics 1-18

Tasks   Use the Rectangle Tool 1-20
         Use the Rectangle dialog box 1-21

LESSON 4
Apply Fill and Stroke Colors to Objects 1-22
Activating the Fill or Stroke 1-22
Applying Color with the Swatches Panel 1-23
Task   Apply fill and stroke colors 1-24

LESSON 5
Select, Move, and Align Objects 1-26
Selecting and Moving Objects 1-26
Grouping Objects 1-26
Making a Marquee Selection with the
Selection Tool 1-26
Working with Smart Guides 1-27
Tasks   Select and move an object using Smart
         Guides 1-28
         Duplicate objects using drag and
         drop 1-29

LESSON 6
Transform Objects 1-30
Transforming Objects 1-30
Repeating Transformations 1-31

Tasks   Use the Scale and Rotate Tools 1-32
         Use the Transform Again command 1-33
         Create a star and a triangle, and use the
         Reflect Tool 1-34

LESSON 7
Make Direct Selections 1-36
Using the Direct Selection Tool 1-36
Adding Anchor Points 1-36
Turning Objects into Guides 1-36
Tasks   Make guides and direct selections 1-38
         Add anchor points 1-39
         Select paths 1-40
         Create a simple special effect utilizing a
         direct selection 1-41

CHAPTER 2 | CREATING TEXT AND GRADIENTS

INTRODUCTION
Creating Text and Gradients 2-2
Working with Text 2-2
Creating and Applying Gradient Fills 2-2

LESSON 1
Create and Format Text 2-4
Creating Type 2-4
Formatting Text 2-4
Hiding Objects 2-5
Tasks   Create text 2-6
            Format text 2-7
            Track and kern text 2-8
            Create vertical type 2-9

LESSON 2
Flow Text into an Object 2-10
Filling an Object with Text 2-10
Locking Objects 2-11
Using Rulers, Guides, and the Grid 2-11
Making Guides 2-11
Tasks   Fill an object with text 2-12

Format text in an object 2-13
Make guides and use the Lock
command 2-14

LESSON 3
Position Text on a Path 2-16
Using the Path Type Tools 2-16
Tasks   Flow text on a path 2-18
            Move text along a path 2-19

LESSON 4
Create Colors and Gradients 2-20
Using the Gradient Panel 2-20
Using the Color Panel 2-21
Adding Colors and Gradients to the
Swatches Panel 2-21
Tasks   Create a gradient and a color 2-22
            Add gradients and colors to the Swatches
            panel 2-24

LESSON 5
Apply Colors and Gradients to Text 2-26
Applying Fills and Strokes to Text 2-26

Converting Text to Outlines 2-26
Tasks   Apply color to text 2-28
            Create outlines and apply a gradient
            fill 2-29

LESSON 6
**Adjust a Gradient and Create a Drop
Dhadow** 2-30
Using the Gradient Tool 2-30
Adding a Drop Shadow 2-31
Tasks   Use the Gradient Tool 2-32
            Add a drop shadow to text 2-33

CONTENTS

CHAPTER 3 DRAWING AND COMPOSING AN ILLUSTRATION

INTRODUCTION
Drawing and Composing an Illustration 3-2
Drawing in Illustrator 3-2

LESSON 1
Draw Straight Lines 3-4
Viewing Objects on the Artboard 3-4
Drawing Straight Segments with the
Pen Tool 3-4
Aligning and Joining Anchor Points 3-5
Tasks   Create new views 3-6
         Draw straight lines 3-7
         Close a path and align the anchor
         points 3-8
         Join anchor points 3-9

LESSON 2
Draw Curved Lines 3-10
Defining Properties of Curved Lines 3-10
Converting Anchor Points 3-12
Tasks   Draw and edit a curved line 3-14
         Convert anchor points 3-15
         Draw a line with curved and straight
         segments 3-16
         Reverse direction while drawing 3-17

LESSON 3
Draw Elements of an Illustration 3-18
Starting an Illustration 3-18
Drawing from Scratch 3-18
Tracing a Scanned Image 3-18

Tasks   Draw a closed path using smooth
         points 3-20
         Begin and end a path with a corner
         point 3-21
         Redirect a path while drawing 3-22
         Place a scanned image 3-23

LESSON 4
Apply Attributes to Objects 3-24
Using the Eyedropper Tool 3-24
Adding a Fill to an Open Path 3-25
Tasks   Apply new attributes to open and closed
         paths 3-26
         Copy attributes with the Eyedropper
         Tool 3-27

LESSON 5
Assemble an Illustration 3-28
Assembling an Illustration 3-28
Task   Assemble the illustration 3-29

LESSON 6
Stroke Objects for Artistic Effect 3-30
Defining Joins and Caps 3-30
Defining the Miter Limit 3-31
Creating a Dashed Stroke 3-32
Creating Pseudo-Stroke Effects 3-32
Tasks   Modify stroke attributes 3-33
         Create a dashed stroke 3-34
         Create pseudo-strokes 3-35

LESSON 7
**Use Live Trace and the Live Paint Bucket
Tool** 3-36
Introducing Live Trace 3-36
Tracing a Line-Art Sketch 3-37
Expanding a Traced Graphic 3-37
Tracing a Photograph 3-38
Introducing Live Paint 3-39
Live Painting Regions 3-40
Painting Virtual Regions 3-41
Inserting an Object into a Live
Paint Group 3-42
Expanding a Live Paint Group 3-43
Live Painting Edges 3-43
Tasks   Use Live Trace to trace a sketch 3-44
         Use Live Trace to trace a photo 3-45
         Use the Live Paint Bucket Tool 3-47
         Use the Live Paint Bucket Tool to paint
         an illustration 3-49

CHAPTER 4   TRANSFORMING AND DISTORTING OBJECTS

INTRODUCTION
Transforming and Distorting Objects 4-2
Putting It All Together 4-2

LESSON 1
Transform Objects 4-4
Defining the Transform Tools 4-4
Defining the Point of Origin 4-4
Working with the Transform Again
Command 4-6
Using the Transform Each Command 4-6
Using the Free Transform Tool 4-7
Using the Transform Panel 4-7
Tasks   Rotate an object around a defined point 4-8
         Use the Shear Tool 4-10
         Use the Reflect Tool 4-11

LESSON 2
Offset and Outline Paths 4-12
Using the Offset Path Command 4-12
Using the Outline Stroke Command 4-13
Tasks   Offset a path 4-14
         Convert a stroked path to a closed path 4-15

LESSON 3
Create Compound Paths 4-16
Defining a Compound Path 4-16
Tasks   Create compound paths 4-18
         Create special effects with compound
         paths 4-19

LESSON 4
Work with the Pathfinder Panel 4-20
Defining a Compound Shape 4-20
Understanding Essential Pathfinder
Filters 4-20
Using the Pathfinder Panel 4-22
Applying Shape Modes 4-23
Tasks   Apply the Add shape mode 4-24
         Apply the Subtract shape mode 4-25
         Apply the Intersect shape mode 4-26
         Apply the Divide pathfinder 4-27
         Create compound shapes using the
         Pathfinder panel 4-28
         Create special effects with compound
         shapes 4-29

LESSON 5
Create Clipping Masks 4-30
Defining a Clipping Mask 4-30
Using Multiple Objects as a Clipping
Mask 4-31
Creating Masked Effects 4-31
Tasks   Create a clipping mask 4-32
         Apply a fill to a clipping mask 4-33
         Use text as a clipping mask 4-34
         Use a clipping mask for special
         effects 4-35

CHAPTER 5   WORKING WITH LAYERS

INTRODUCTION
Working with Layers 5-2
Designing with Layers 5-2

LESSON 1
Create and Modify Layers 5-4
Creating Layers and Sublayers 5-4
Duplicating Layers 5-5
Setting Layer Options 5-6
Selecting Artwork on Layers and Sublayers 5-7
Selecting All Artwork on a Layer 5-7
Tasks   Create a new layer 5-8
     Name a layer and change a layer's selection color 5-9
     Select items on a layer and lock a layer 5-10
     Show and hide layers 5-11

LESSON 2
Manipulate Layered Artwork 5-12
Changing the Order of Layers and Sublayers 5-12

Merging Layers 5-12
Defining Sublayers 5-12
Working with Sublayers 5-13
Dragging Objects Between Layers 5-13
Tasks   Change the hierarchy of layers 5-14
     Merge layers 5-15
     Work with sublayers 5-16
     Create new sublayers 5-17
     Move objects between layers 5-18

LESSON 3
Work with Layered Artwork 5-20
Using the View Buttons in the Layers Panel 5-20
Locating an Object in the Layers Panel 5-21
Reversing the Order of Layers 5-21
Making Layers Nonprintable 5-21
Tasks   Explore view options in the Layers panel 5-22

Locate, duplicate, and delete layers 5-23
Dim placed images 5-24
Exclude specific layers from printing 5-25

LESSON 4
Create a Clipping Set 5-26
Working with Clipping Sets 5-26
Flattening Artwork 5-26
Tasks   Create clipping sets 5-27
     Copy a clipping mask and flatten artwork 5-28

Data Files 1

Glossary 8

Index 21

What Instructor Resources Are Available with This Book?

The Instructor Resources CD-ROM is Course Technology's way of putting the resources and information needed to teach and learn effectively into your hands. All the resources are available for both Macintosh and Windows operating systems.

Instructor's Manual

Available as an electronic file, the Instructor's Manual includes chapter overviews and detailed lecture topics for each chapter, with teaching tips. The Instructor's Manual is available on the Instructor Resources CD-ROM.

PowerPoint Presentations

Each chapter has a corresponding PowerPoint presentation that you can use in lectures, distribute to your students, or customize to suit your course.

Data Files for Students

To complete most of the chapters in this book, your students will need Data Files. The Data Files are available on the CD at the back of this text book. Instruct students to use the Data Files List at the end of this book. This list gives instructions on organizing files.

Solutions to Exercises

Solution Files are Data Files completed with comprehensive sample answers. Use these files to evaluate your students' work. Or distribute them electronically so students can verify their work. Sample solutions to all lessons and end-of-chapter material are provided.

Test Bank and Test Engine

ExamView is a powerful testing software package that allows instructors to create and administer printed, computer (LAN-based), and Internet exams. ExamView includes hundreds of questions that correspond to the topics covered in this text, enabling students to generate detailed study guides that include page references for further review. The computer-based and Internet testing components allow students to take exams at their computers, and also save the instructor time by grading each exam automatically.

INSTRUCTOR RESOURCES

Intended Audience

This text is designed for the beginner or intermediate user who wants to learn how to use InDesign CS3, Photoshop CS3, and Illustrator CS3. The book is designed to provide basic and in-depth material that not only educates, but also encourages you to explore the nuances of these exciting programs.

Approach

The text allows you to work at your own pace through step-by-step tutorials. A concept is presented and the process is explained, followed by the actual steps. To learn the most from the use of the text, you should adopt the following habits:

- Proceed slowly: Accuracy and comprehension are more important than speed.
- Understand what is happening with each step before you continue to the next step.
- After finishing a skill, ask yourself if you could do it on your own, without referring to the steps. If the answer is no, review the steps.

Icons, Buttons, and Pointers

Symbols for icons, buttons, and pointers are shown in the step each time they are used. Icons may look different in the files panel depending on the file association settings on your computer.

Fonts

The Data Files contain a variety of commonly used fonts, but there is no guarantee that these fonts will be available on your computer. In a few cases, fonts other than those common to a PC or a Macintosh are used. If any of the fonts in use is not available on your computer, you can make a substitution, realizing that the results may vary from those in the book.

Windows and Macintosh

Adobe Creative Suite works virtually the same on Windows and Macintosh operating systems. In those cases where there is a significant difference, the abbreviations (Win) and (Mac) are used.

Data Files

To complete the lessons in this book, you need the Data Files on the CD in the back of this book. Your instructor will tell you where to store the files as you work, such as the hard drive, a network server, or a USB storage device. The instructions in the lessons will refer to "where you store your Data Files" when referring to the Data Files for the book.

InDesign

Units and Increments

The page layout measurements for the documents in this book are given in inches, not points or picas. In order to follow these exercises, it is important that the horizontal and vertical ruler units are set to inches. To verify this, click Edit (Win) or InDesign (Mac) on the menu bar, point to Preferences, then click Units & Increments.

All text sizes and rule weights are expressed in points.

You may or may not prefer to work with rulers showing. You can make rulers visible by clicking View on the menu bar, then clicking Show Rulers. You can make rulers invisible by clicking View on the menu bar, then clicking Hide Rulers. Having rulers visible or invisible will not affect your ability to follow the exercises in this book in any way, unless a step specifically refers to a measurement on the ruler.

Fonts

Because InDesign is a page layout program, text is involved in almost every exercise in the book, even those that focus on placed graphics. The fonts used in the exercises in this book were chosen from a set of very common typefaces that you are likely to have available on your computer. In most cases, the fonts used are either Impact or Garamond. If any of the fonts in use is not available on your computer, please make a substitution with another typeface that has a similar look. Also, please note that because Garamond is such a common typeface, it is possible that the Garamond font on your computer will be that of a different manufacturer than the Garamond used in the exercises, particularly if you are using a Macintosh computer. If that is the case, simply replace the "missing" Garamond in the exercises with the Garamond font on your computer. The following tip, which explains how to substitute fonts, appears in Chapter 1.

> **QUICK**TIP
>
> If you see the Missing Fonts dialog box, you can use the font chosen by InDesign by clicking OK, or click Find Font and choose another font in the Find Font dialog box. If you see a Missing Links dialog box, click Fix Links Automatically.

When you open an InDesign Data File, if any fonts used in the file are not available on your computer, the usages of that font will be highlighted in pink. Once you substitute the missing font with an available font, the pink highlight disappears.

Working with Guides

Chapter 3 focuses on creating and setting up a new document, which includes a thorough exploration of creating and positioning guides and changing the color of guides. Throughout the remainder of the book, the steps in the lessons will direct you to make guides visible or invisible when necessary. However, when guides are inconsequential to the lesson, the steps do not instruct you to make guides visible or not. Therefore, your document may differ from the figures in the book in terms of guides. For example, your document may have guides visible, whereas the figures in the book may not show guides.

Panels

Chapter 1 explains panels in depth. You are shown how to group, ungroup, dock, and undock panels. Like guides, the way that you choose to display panels may differ from the figures in the book.

Hiding and Showing Frame Edges / Normal View Mode and Preview Mode

Objects on an InDesign page appear with frame edges. When an object is selected, the frame edges are more prominent, but even when the object is not selected, the frame edges are visible. Sometimes the frame edges can be distracting, especially at the end of a lesson when you want to view the final result of your work. You can choose to hide frame edges, so that an object's frame is visible only when the object is selected. An alternative to hiding frame edges is to switch from Normal view to Preview using the appropriate buttons on the Toolbox. In Preview, all guides and frame edges are hidden.

The lessons in the book offer specific instruction for hiding and showing frame edges and for switching between Normal view and Preview. Once you learn these commands, you can work with the settings that are most comfortable. Because this is a personal choice, you may find that your work differs from the figures in the book. For example, you may be working in Preview, whereas the figures in the book may be in Normal view.

File Formats for Placed Graphics

Because InDesign is an Adobe product, it interfaces naturally with Adobe Photoshop and Adobe Illustrator. Therefore, Photoshop and Illustrator files can be placed in InDesign as "native" Photoshop and Illustrator files—it is not necessary to save them as TIFF or EPS files. For this reason, in the exercises that include placed images, the placed images are sometimes native Photoshop files, sometimes native Illustrator files, sometimes Photoshop TIFF files, and sometimes they are EPS files from Photoshop or Illustrator. The point is to understand that InDesign works with a variety of file formats, including native Photoshop and Illustrator files.

Working with Process Colors and Spot Colors

Chapter 5 focuses on creating colors in the Swatches panel. Some of these colors will be process colors, some will be spot colors. The narrative in this chapter provides substantial information on the offset printing process and the role of CMYK inks vs. non-process inks. Nevertheless, comprehensive coverage of the myriad concepts involved in offset printing is beyond the scope of this book. The author presumes that readers already have some familiarity with the basic concepts of 4-color process printing and/or can consult a resource specifically devoted to covering that topic in detail.

Updating Placed Graphics

You will be working with Data Files that contain placed graphics throughout the book. These support files are stored in the same folder as the InDesign Data File they are placed in. Normally, there are no issues for opening files with placed graphics; nevertheless, for a

number of reasons, a warning dialog box may appear stating that the placed graphics have been modified and the link needs to be updated. In most cases, the placed graphics themselves have not been modified—only their location has been modified. Because the placed graphics are now on a new computer, InDesign may determine that the link needs to be updated. When this occurs, click the button that says Fix Links Automatically.

After clicking the Fix Links Automatically button, an additional warning dialog box may appear stating that "Edits have been made to this object. You will lose these edits by updating. Update anyway?" This dialog box refers to a handful of text documents used throughout the book. Make sure you click No in this dialog box so that the text file is not updated. Otherwise, the formatting applied to the text will be lost.

Quick Keys

Quick keys are keyboard shortcuts that you can use in place of clicking a command in a pull-down menu. [Ctrl][X] (Win) or ⌘ [X] (Mac), for example, are basic quick keys for the Cut command. After you become familiar with InDesign basics, you will find that learning and using quick keys will speed up your work considerably.

Photoshop

File Identification

Instead of printing a file, the owner of a Photoshop image can be identified by reading the File Info dialog box.
Use the following instructions to add your name to an image:

1. Click File on the menu bar, then click File Info.
2. Click the Description, if necessary.
3. Click the Author text box.
4. Type your name, course number, or other identifying information.
5. Click OK.

There are no instructions with this text to use the File Info feature other than when it is introduced in Chapter 1. It is up to each user to use this feature so that his or her work can be identified.

Measurements

When measurements are shown, needed, or discussed, they are given in pixels. Use the following instructions to change the units of measurement to pixels:

1. Click Edit on the menu bar, point to Preferences, then click Units & Rulers.
2. Click the Rulers list arrow, then click pixels.
3. Click OK.

You can display rulers by clicking View on the menu bar, then clicking Rulers, or by pressing [Ctrl][R] (Win) or ⌘[R] (Mac). A check mark to the left of the Rulers command indicates that the Rulers are displayed. You can hide visible rulers by clicking View on the menu bar, then clicking Rulers, or by pressing [Ctrl][R] (Win) or ⌘[R] (Mac).

Icons, Buttons, and Pointers

Symbols for icons, buttons, and pointers are shown each time they are used.

Fonts

Data and Solution Files contain a variety of fonts, and there is no guarantee that all of these fonts will be available on your computer. The fonts are identified in cases where less common fonts are used in the files. Every effort has been made to use commonly available fonts in the lessons. If any of the fonts in use are not available on your computer, please make a substitution.

Menu Commands in Tables

In tables, menu commands are abbreviated using the following format: Edit ➤ Preferences ➤ Units & Rulers. This command translates as follows: Click Edit on the menu bar, point to Preferences, then click Units & Rulers.

Skills Reference

As a bonus, a Power User Shortcuts table is included at the end of every chapter. This table contains the quickest method of completing tasks covered in the chapter. It is meant for the more experienced user, or for the user who wants to become more experienced. Tools are shown, not named.

Grading Tips

Many students have Web-ready accounts where they can post their completed assignments. The instructor can access the student accounts using a browser and view the images online. Using this method, it is not necessary for the student to include his/her name on a type layer, because all of their assignments are in an individual password-protected account.

Creating a Portfolio

One method for students to submit and keep a copy of all of their work is to create a portfolio of their projects that is linked to a simple Web page that can be saved on a CD-ROM. If it is necessary for students to print completed projects, work can be printed and mounted at a local copy shop; a student's name can be printed on the back of the image.

Illustrator

Measurements

Measurements on the artboard and measurements referring to an object are given in inches, not points or picas. In order to follow the exercises, it's important that the General Units Preference in the Preferences dialog box be set to Inches. To set this preference, click Edit on the menu bar, point to Preferences, and then click Units & Display Performance.

Text attributes are given in points. You may or may not prefer to work with rulers showing. You can make rulers visible by clicking View on the menu bar, then clicking Show Rulers, or by pressing [Ctrl][R](Win) or ⌘ [R] (Mac). You can hide visible rulers by clicking View on the menu bar, then clicking Hide Rulers or by pressing [Ctrl][R](Win) or ⌘[R](Mac).

Document Color Mode

Documents in Adobe Illustrator CS3 can be created in one of two color modes—RGB or CMYK. You can determine the color mode in the New dialog box when you create a document. You can also change a document's color mode by clicking File on the menu bar, then clicking Document Color Mode. The color mode for each document is identified in the title bar at the top of the Illustrator window.

Whenever you are asked to create a new document, the color mode will be specified. Many menu commands, such as those under the Effect menu, are available only in RGB mode. If you run into a situation in which a specified menu command is not available, first check the color mode.

Fonts

Whenever fonts are used in Data and Solution Files, they are chosen from a set of very common typefaces that you will most likely have available on your computer. If any of the fonts in use are not available on your computer, please make a substitution.

For variety and typographic appeal, we have used other typefaces in Data and Solution Files that are not standard; however, we have converted those fonts to outlines. When a font is converted to an outline, the letterform is simply a vector graphic, like all other vector graphics.

Quick Keys

Quick keys are keyboard shortcuts that can be used in place of clicking the command on the menu. [Ctrl][X], for example, is the quick key for Cut on the PC platform. Mastering basic quick keys is essential for a smooth work flow in Illustrator. It's a good idea to start with the commands on the Edit and Object menus as candidates for quick keys.

EXPLORING THE
INDESIGN WORKSPACE

1. Explore the InDesign workspace

2. Change document views

3. Navigate through a document

4. Use InDesign Help

1 EXPLORING THE
INDESIGN WORKSPACE

Introduction

Welcome to Adobe InDesign! InDesign is a comprehensive software program that allows you to create output-ready layouts for anything from a simple coupon to an 8-page newsletter to a 120-page full-color magazine. What's even better is that, with InDesign, Adobe Systems has created a layout program that interfaces seamlessly with Adobe Photoshop and Illustrator.

If you love those two applications, you'll love InDesign too. In terms of its concept and its intuitive design, InDesign is pure Adobe. You'll feel right at home. In fact, at times, you may need to remind yourself that you're working in InDesign, not Photoshop or Illustrator.

The key word to keep in mind is layout: That's InDesign's primary function. Everything you need is here along with some pleasant surprises. With InDesign, you can build tables quickly and easily. You'll also find that the table of contents and index features are fun and easy to learn. And try to remember that you're not using Illustrator when you're positioning that text on a curved path!

Best of all, you'll never have to leave the world of Adobe. The interface of InDesign with Photoshop and Illustrator allows them to work together as something of a trinity. From that combination, InDesign emerges as one of the most powerful layout utilities ever devised.

Tools You'll Use

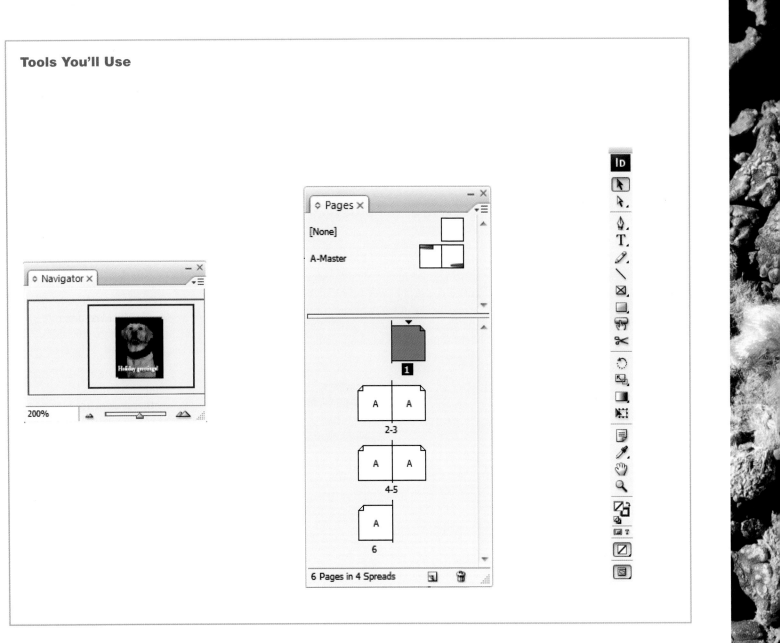

EXPLORE THE
INDESIGN WORKSPACE

What You'll Do

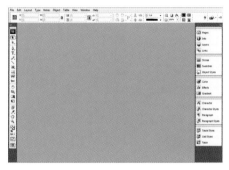

 In this lesson, you will start Adobe InDesign and explore the workspace.

Looking at the InDesign Workspace

The arrangement of windows and panels that you see on your monitor after starting InDesign is called the **workspace**. InDesign's default workspace features four areas: the document window, the Toolbox, the pasteboard, and the panels along the right edge of the document window, as shown in Figure 1.

You can customize the workspace to suit your working preferences; for example, you can change the location of the Toolbox, the document window, and other panels in relation to each other.

Of these workspace elements, the role of the pasteboard is perhaps the least obvious. The **pasteboard** is the area

FIGURE 1
InDesign workspace

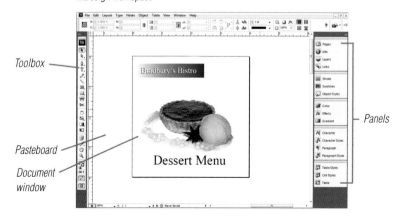

Toolbox

Pasteboard

Document window

Panels

surrounding the document. The pasteboard provides space for extending objects past the edge of the page (known as creating a bleed), and it also provides space for storing objects that you may or may not use in the document. Objects that are positioned wholly on the pasteboard, as shown in Figure 2, do not print.

Exploring the Toolbox

As its name implies, the Toolbox houses all the tools that you will work with in InDesign. The first thing that you should note about the Toolbox is that not all tools are visible; many are hidden. Look closely and you will see that nine tools have small black triangles beside them. These triangles indicate that other tools are hidden behind them. To access hidden tools, point to the visible tool in the Toolbox, then press and hold the mouse button; this will reveal a menu of hidden tools. The small black square to the left of a tool name in the menu indicates the tool that is currently visible in the Toolbox, as shown in Figure 3. The Toolbox contains 32 tools, as shown in Figure 4.

QUICKTIP

You can view the Toolbox as a single column, a double column or even as a horizontal row of tools. Click Edit on the menu bar (Win) or InDesign on the menu bar (Mac), point to Preferences then click Interface. Click the Floating Tools Panel list arrow in the Tools section, then experiment with the three different orientations.

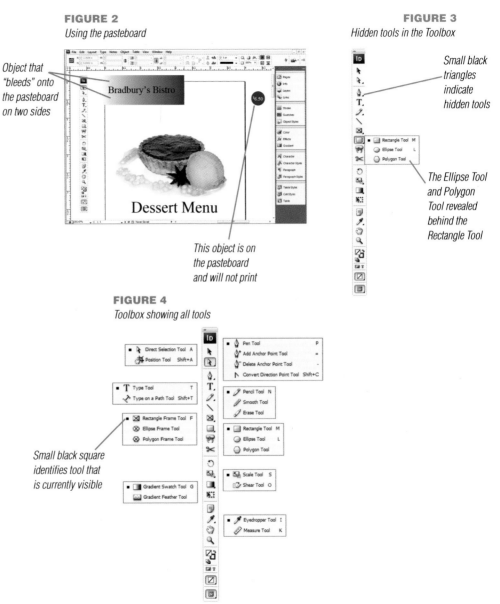

FIGURE 2
Using the pasteboard

Object that "bleeds" onto the pasteboard on two sides

Bradbury's Bistro

Dessert Menu

This object is on the pasteboard and will not print

FIGURE 3
Hidden tools in the Toolbox

Small black triangles indicate hidden tools

The Ellipse Tool and Polygon Tool revealed behind the Rectangle Tool

FIGURE 4
Toolbox showing all tools

Small black square identifies tool that is currently visible

Horizontal lines divide the Toolbox into eight sections. The top section contains the selection tools. The section beneath that contains item creation tools—drawing tools, shape tools, and type tools. Next is a section that contains transform tools, such as the Rotate Tool and the Scale Tool. You can think of the next section as the navigation section, which houses the Hand Tool—used for scrolling through the document—and the Zoom Tool—used for magnifying your view of the document.

The bottommost sections of the Toolbox contain functions for applying colors and gradients to objects and choices for viewing modes used to display the page on your screen. The Preview mode is probably used most often since it allows you to view your document without the guides being visible.

To choose a tool, simply click it; you can also press a single key to access a tool. For example, pressing [p] selects the Pen Tool. To learn the shortcut key for each tool, point to a tool until a tooltip appears with the tool's name and its shortcut key in parentheses. Figure 5 shows the tooltip for the Type Tool.

QUICKTIP

Shortcut keys are not case-sensitive. In other words, if you press [p], you'll switch to the Pen Tool regardless of whether the Caps Lock key is pressed.

Working with Panels

InDesign features 41 panels, all of which are listed and can be accessed from the Window menu. Some panels are placed within categories on the Window menu. For example, all of the text and table-related panels, such as the Character panel and the Table panel, are listed in the Type & Tables category on the Window menu. Panels offer controls for you to modify and manipulate your work; for example, the Character panel offers controls for changing the font, font size, and leading, as shown in Figure 6.

By default, panels appear in groups along the right side of the document window—this is necessary to conserve space on your monitor. The default groupings of panels are designed so that panels with similar functions are grouped together.

QUICKTIP

Feel free to drag and drop panels anywhere you want them to go.

FIGURE 5

Viewing a tool name and shortcut key

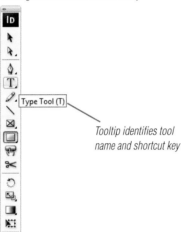

Tooltip identifies tool
name and shortcut key

FIGURE 6

Character panel

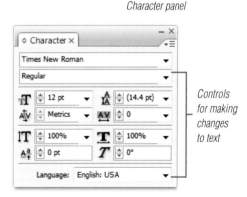

Controls
for making
changes
to text

Figure 7 shows three panels grouped together. The Paragraph panel is the active panel—it is in front of the others in the group and available for use. To activate a panel in a group, simply click its name tab. In the default workspace, many of the panels are collapsed along the right side of the workspace. Clicking the active panel name tab will expand that panel. The other panels in the group will appear in the expanded panel as tabs. Once expanded, you can activate other panels in the group by clicking the appropriate panel name tab; clicking it again will collapse the group of panels. When you choose a panel from the Window menu, the panel will be displayed in its expanded view.

To ungroup panels, simply drag a panel's name tab away from the other panels. When you release the mouse button, the panel is no longer part of a group. To add a panel to a group, simply drag and drop the panel into the group.

QUICKTIP

You can restore the default arrangement of panels by clicking Window on the menu bar, pointing to Workspace, then clicking [Default Workspace].

Don't confuse grouping panels with docking panels. Docking panels is a different function. When you dock panels, you connect the bottom edge of one panel to the top edge of another panel, so that both move together. Drag a panel's name tab to the bottom edge of another panel. When the bottom edge of the other panel is highlighted in bright blue, release the mouse button and the two panels will be docked. Figure 8 shows docked panels. To undock a panel, simply drag it away from its group.

QUICKTIP

You can temporarily hide all open panels and the Toolbox simply by pressing [Tab]. Press [Tab] again to show the panels and the Toolbox.

FIGURE 7
Three grouped panels

Paragraph panel

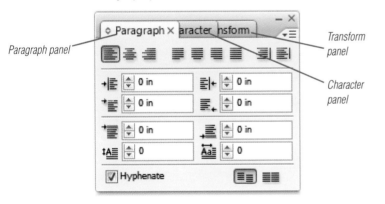

Transform panel

Character panel

FIGURE 8
Docked panels

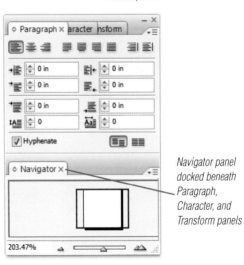

Navigator panel docked beneath Paragraph, Character, and Transform panels

Explore the Toolbox

1. Click **Start** 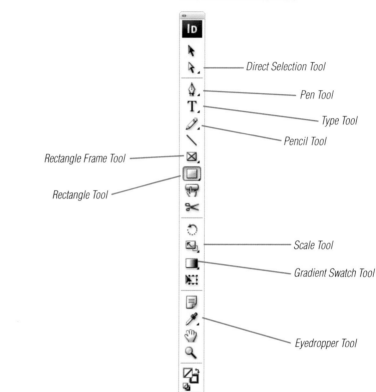 on the taskbar, point to **All Programs**, then click **Adobe InDesign CS3** (Win) or double-click **the hard drive icon**, double-click the **Adobe InDesign CS3 folder**, then double-click **Adobe InDesign CS3** (Mac). If you see a startup screen, click the **Don't show again check box** in the lower-left corner.

2. Click **File** on the menu bar, click **Open**, navigate to the drive and folder where your Chapter 1 Data Files are stored, click **ID 1-1.indd**, then click **Open**.

   TIP   If you see the Missing Fonts dialog box, you can use the font chosen by InDesign by clicking OK, or click Find Font and choose another font in the Find Font dialog box. If you see a warning about missing links, click Fix Links Automatically.

3. Point to the **Type Tool** T , then press and hold the mouse button to see the Type on a Path Tool.

4. Using the same method, view the hidden tools behind the other tools with small black triangles, shown in Figure 9.

   Your visible tools may differ from the figure.

5. Point to the **Selection Tool** until its tooltip appears.

6. Press the following keys: **[v]**, **[a]**, and **[p]**.

   The associated tools are selected.

7. Press **[Tab]** to temporarily hide all open panels, then press **[Tab]** again.

   The panels reappear.

You explored the Toolbox, revealed hidden tools, used shortcut keys to access tools quickly, hid the panels, then displayed them again.

FIGURE 9
Tools that contain hidden tools

Direct Selection Tool

Pen Tool

Type Tool

Pencil Tool

Rectangle Frame Tool

Rectangle Tool

Scale Tool

Gradient Swatch Tool

Eyedropper Tool

Responding to the Links dialog box

When you open a file, you may see a dialog box saying that this file contains links to missing or modified files. If so, click Fix Links Automatically. If necessary, do this whenever this dialog box appears, with one exception: Chapter 6 is about linking support files, and the Data Files have been provided with intentionally missing links.

FIGURE 10

Removing the Paragraph panel from the group

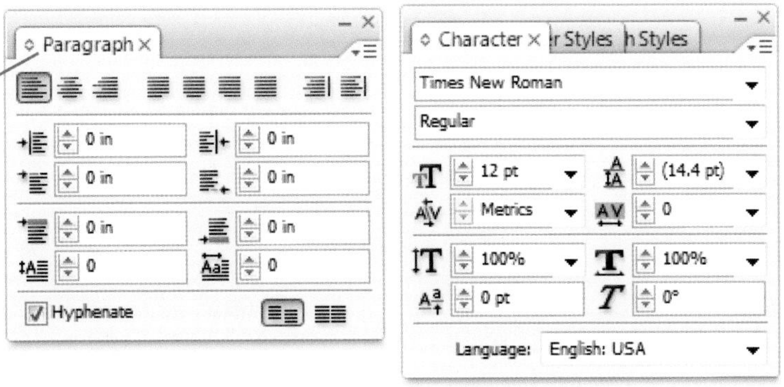

Drag a panel by its name tab

FIGURE 11

Grouping the Character panel with the Paragraph panel

FIGURE 12

Docking the Transform panel

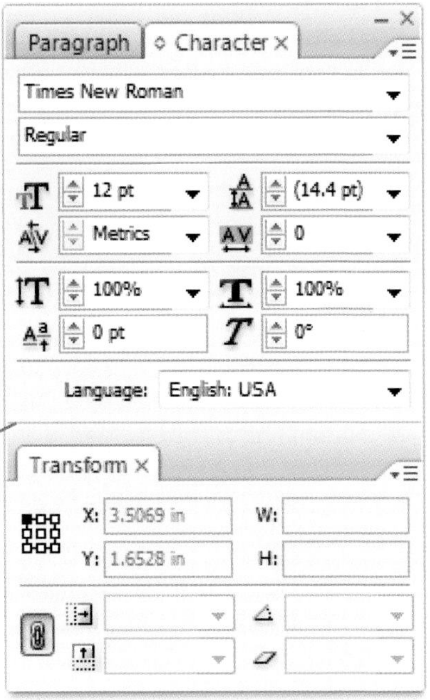

Drag a panel to the bottom edge of another to dock it

Work with panels

1. Click **Window** on the menu bar, point to **Type & Tables**, then click **Paragraph**.

2. Drag the **Paragraph panel name tab** to the left, away from the group, as shown in Figure 10.

3. Drag the **Character panel name tab** next to the Paragraph panel name tab, then release the mouse.

   The Character panel is grouped with the Paragraph panel, as shown in Figure 11. Note that the order—from left to right—of panels within the group on your computer may differ from the figure.

4. Click **Window** on the menu bar, point to **Object and Layout**, then click **Transform**.

5. Drag the **Transform panel name tab** to the bottom edge of the Character and Paragraph panels group, then release the mouse when they snap together.

   The Transform panel is docked, as shown in Figure 12.

6. Click the **Transform panel name tab**, then drag it away from the other two panels.

   The Transform panel is undocked.

7. Press **[Tab]** to hide all panels and the Toolbox, then press **[Tab]** again to show them.

You explored methods for grouping and ungrouping panels, and you docked and undocked a panel.

CHANGE DOCUMENT VIEWS

What You'll Do

In this lesson, you will explore various methods for changing the magnification of your document.

Using the Zoom Tool

Imagine creating a layout on a traditional pasteboard—not on your computer. For precise work, you would bring your nose closer to the pasteboard so that you could better see what you were doing. At other times, you would hold the pasteboard away from you, say at arms' length, so that you could get a larger perspective of the artwork. When you're working in InDesign, the Zoom Tool performs these functions for you.

When you click the Zoom Tool and move the pointer over the document window, the pointer becomes the Zoom pointer with a plus sign; when you click the document with the Zoom pointer, the document area you clicked is enlarged. To reduce the view of the document, press and hold [Alt] (Win) or [option] (Mac). The plus sign changes to a minus sign; when you click the document with this Zoom pointer, the document size is reduced.

Using the Zoom Tool, you can reduce or enlarge the view of the document from 5% to 4000%. Note that the current percentage appears in two places: in the title bar next to the filename and in the Zoom text box in the lower-left corner of the document window, as shown in Figure 13.

Accessing the Zoom Tool

As you work, you can expect to zoom in and out of the document more times than you can count. The most basic way of accessing the Zoom Tool is simply to click its icon in the Toolbox, however this can get very tiring if you have to access it often. Another method for accessing the Zoom Tool is to use keyboard shortcuts. When you are using any tool, for example the Selection Tool, don't switch to the Zoom Tool. Instead, press and hold [Ctrl][Spacebar] (Win) or ⌘ [Spacebar] (Mac). This keyboard combination changes the Selection Tool into the Zoom Tool (in the enlarge mode). Click the document to enlarge the view; when you release the keys, the Zoom Tool changes back to the Selection Tool.

To access the Zoom Tool in reduction mode, press and hold [Ctrl][Alt][Spacebar] (Win) or ⌘ [option][Spacebar] (Mac).

In addition to the Zoom Tool, InDesign offers other ways to zoom in and out of your document. You can choose a preset percentage from the Zoom menu in the lower-left corner of the document window, or you can double-click the current percentage in the Zoom text box, then type a new percentage.

You can also use the Zoom In and Zoom Out commands on the View menu.

Using the Hand Tool

When you zoom in on a document—when you make it appear larger—eventually the document will be too large to fit in the window. Therefore, you will need to scroll to see other areas of it. You can use the scroll bars along the bottom and the right sides of the document window. You can also use the Hand Tool to scroll through the document, as shown in Figure 14.

The best way to understand the concept of the Hand Tool is to think of it as your own hand. Imagine that you could put your hand up to the document on your monitor, then move the document left, right, up, or down, like a paper on a table or against a wall. This is analogous to how the Hand Tool works.

FIGURE 13

A reduced view of the document

FIGURE 14

Scrolling through a document

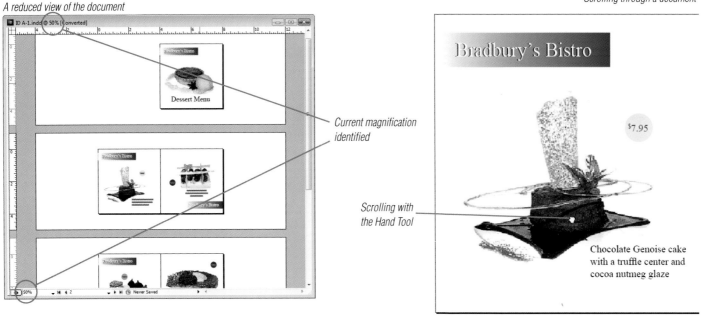

Current magnification identified

Scrolling with the Hand Tool

The Hand Tool is often a better choice for scrolling than the scroll bars. Why? You can access the Hand Tool using a keyboard shortcut. Regardless of whatever tool you are using, simply press and hold [Spacebar] to access the Hand Tool. Release [Spacebar] to return to whatever tool you were using, without having to choose it again.

QUICKTIP

When you are using the Type Tool, don't use the [Spacebar] shortcut to access the Hand Tool because it will add spaces to the text you are working with. Instead, use the scroll bar.

Creating Multiple Views of a Document

You can create more than one view of a single document using multiple windows. A dual view is the most common—view the document at 100% in one window, then create another window to enlarge or reduce the document. In this method of working, you maintain a view of your document at actual size (100%) at all times.

Click Window on the menu bar, point to Arrange, then click New Window to create a new window. To view both windows simultaneously, click Window on the menu bar, point to Arrange, then click Tile Vertically. The document in the new window will have the number 2 in the title bar. Figure 15 shows two tiled documents with different magnification settings.

QUICKTIP

(Macintosh) The commands for accessing the Zoom Tool are also the same shortcut commands for accessing Spotlight. For the purposes of this chapter you should deactivate the Spotlight feature by clicking the Apple icon on the menu bar, clicking System Preferences, then clicking Spotlight. Remove the check marks in the Spotlight menu keyboard shortcut and the Spotlight window keyboard shortcut checkboxes.

FIGURE 15
Two views of the same document

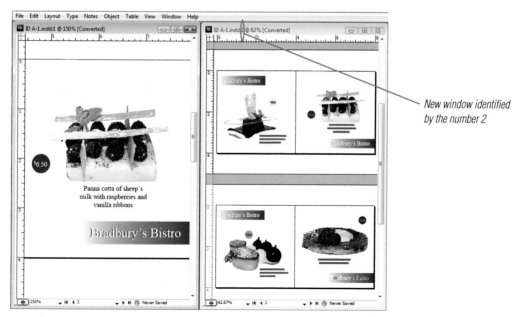

New window identified by the number 2

FIGURE 16
Scrolling with the Hand Tool

The Hand Tool becomes a fist when clicked and dragged

1. If the Toolbox is not already visible, click **Window** on the menu bar, then click **Tools**.

2. Press **[z]** to access the Zoom Tool 🔍.

3. Position the Zoom Tool over the document window, click twice to enlarge the document, press **[Alt]** (Win) or **[option]** (Mac), then click twice to reduce the document.

4. Click the **Zoom menu list arrow** in the lower-left corner of the document window, then click **800%**.

   Note that 800% is listed in the title bar at the top of the document window.

5. Double-click **800%** in the Zoom text box, type **400**, then press **[Enter]** (Win) or **[return]** (Mac).

6. Click the **Hand Tool** 🖐 in the Toolbox, then click and drag the **document window** so that the image in the window appears as shown in Figure 16.

7. Double-click the **Zoom Tool** 🔍 in the Toolbox.

   The magnification changes to 100% (actual size).

8. Click the **Selection Tool** ▶, point to the **center** of the document window, then press and hold **[Ctrl][Spacebar]** (Win) or ⌘ **[Spacebar]** (Mac).

   The Selection Tool changes to the Zoom Tool.

9. Click three times, then release [Ctrl][Spacebar] (Win) or ⌘ [Spacebar] (Mac).

(continued)

10. Press and hold **[Spacebar]** to access the Hand Tool, then scroll around the image.

11. Press and hold **[Ctrl][Alt][Spacebar]** (Win) or ⌘**[option][Spacebar]** (Mac), then click the mouse six times.

Your document window should resemble Figure 17.

You explored various methods for accessing and using the Zoom Tool for enlarging and reducing the document. You also used the Hand Tool to scroll around an enlarged document.

Create a new window

1. Click **View** on the menu bar, then click **Fit Page in Window**.

> TIP Make it a point to memorize the keyboard shortcuts for Fit Page in Window—[Ctrl][0] (Win) or ⌘ [0] (Mac)—and Fit Spread in Window—[Ctrl][Alt][0] (Win) or ⌘ [option][0] (Mac). (Be sure to press the zero key, not the letter O.)

2. Click **Window** on the menu bar, point to **Arrange**, then click **New Window**.

3. Click **Window** on the menu bar, point to **Arrange**, then click **Tile Vertically**.

The two windows are positioned side-by-side, as shown in Figure 18.

(continued)

FIGURE 17
A reduced view of the document

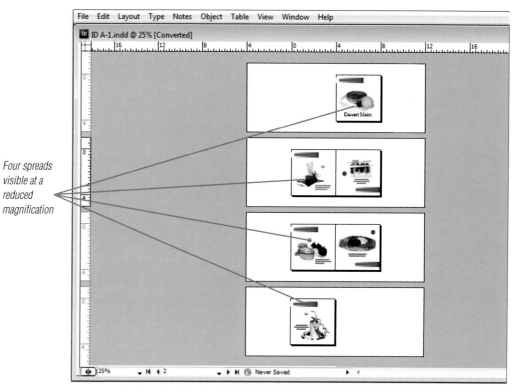

Four spreads visible at a reduced magnification

FIGURE 18

Two views of the same document

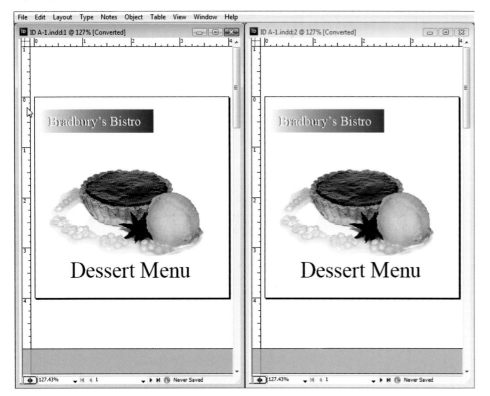

4. Click the title bar of the new window to make it the active window.
5. Press and hold **[Ctrl][Spacebar]** (Win) or ⌘ **[Spacebar]** (Mac), position the Zoom pointer over the center of the new window, then click twice.
6. Close the new window.
7. Click the **Maximize button** (Win) or the **Resize button** (Mac) on the title bar to maximize the document window.

You created a new window and used the Zoom Tool to enlarge the view of the new document.

NAVIGATE THROUGH A DOCUMENT

What You'll Do

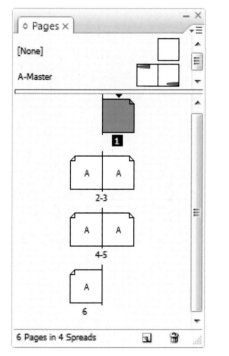

6 Pages in 4 Spreads

In this lesson, you will use various methods for viewing individual pages and navigating through a multiple page document.

Navigating to Pages in a Document

When you are creating a layout for a magazine, a book, or a brochure, by definition you will create a document that has multiple pages. **Spreads** are two pages that face each other; a left page and a right page in a multi-page document.

You have a variety of methods at your disposal for navigating to pages or spreads in your document. You can use the scroll bars on the bottom and right sides of the document window or choose a page from the Page menu in the lower-left corner of the document window. You can also use the First Spread, Previous Spread, Next Spread, and Last Spread buttons at the bottom of the document window, as shown in Figure 19. These navigation buttons have corresponding menu commands on the Layout menu.

FIGURE 19
Page buttons and the Page menu

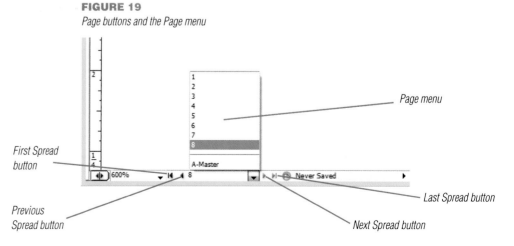

First Spread button

Previous Spread button

Page menu

Next Spread button

Last Spread button

Exploring the InDesign Workspace

The Pages panel, shown in Figure 20, is a comprehensive solution for moving from page to page in your document. The Pages panel shows icons for all of the pages in the document. Double-clicking a single page icon brings that page into view. The icon representing the currently visible page appears in blue in the panel.

Double-clicking the numbers under the page icons representing a spread, as

shown in Figure 21, centers the spread in the document window. In this case, both icons representing the spread will appear as blue in the Pages panel. Click the Pages panel list arrow, also shown in Figure 21, to display the Pages panel menu. This menu contains a number of powerful commands that you can use to control all of your page navigation in InDesign.

QUICKTIP
Click the Panel Options command at the bottom of the menu to choose various display options for the Pages panel.

FIGURE 20
Pages panel

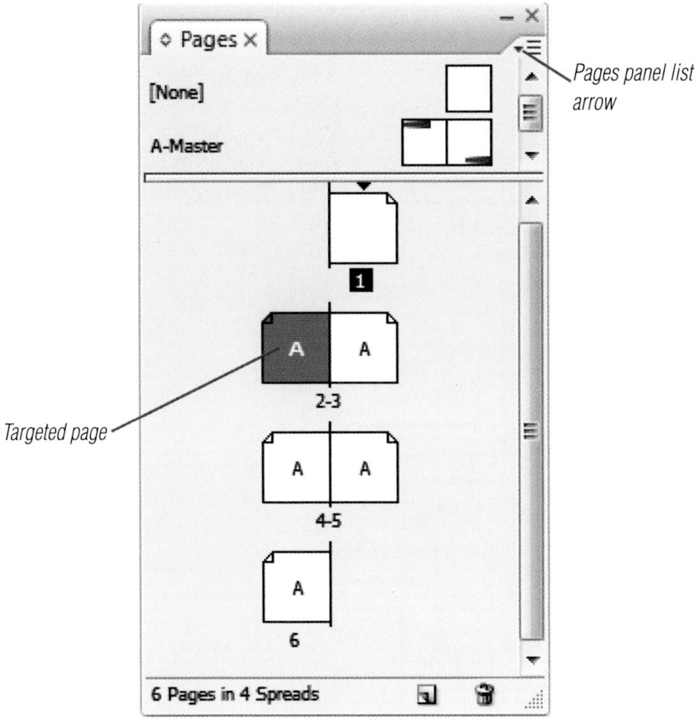

Pages panel list arrow

Targeted page

FIGURE 21
A two-page spread selected in the Pages panel

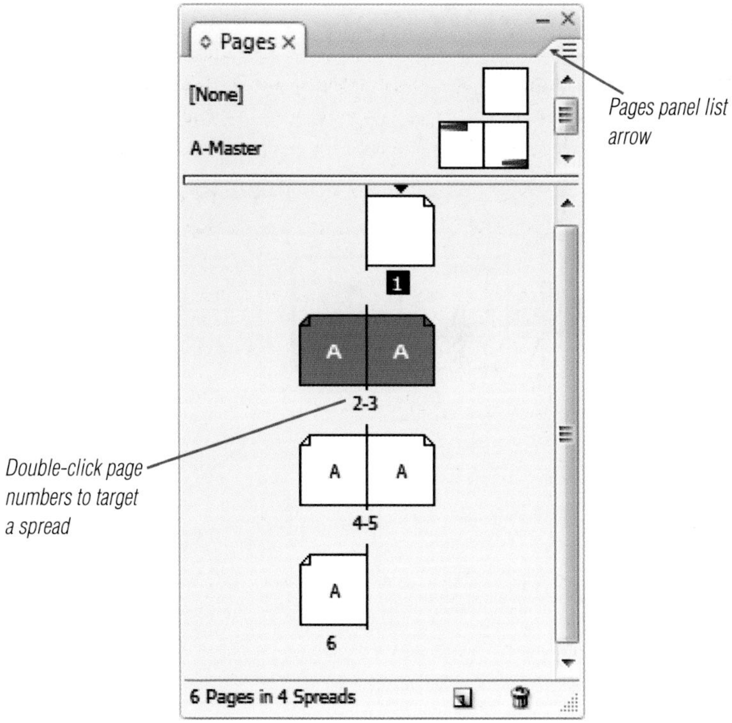

Pages panel list arrow

Double-click page numbers to target a spread

Using the Navigator Panel

The Navigator panel, shown in Figure 22, is an excellent resource for moving through a document. Though you certainly can use the Navigator panel to move from page to page, many designers use the Pages panel for that function and use the Navigator panel to move around a single page. This is why it's a great idea to group the Navigator panel with the Pages panel.

The red box in the Navigator panel is called the View Box and identifies the area of the page currently being viewed in the document window. Moving the View Box is akin to scrolling—moving it to a different area of the page moves the view to that area of the page.

QUICKTIP

You can change the color of the View Box by clicking the Navigator panel list arrow, clicking Panel Options, then choosing a new color from the Color list.

Additionally, you can use the Zoom Slider and the Zoom In and Zoom Out buttons in the Navigator panel to change the view of the document. You can also enter a percentage in the Zoom text box at the lower-left corner of the panel.

As stated above, you can move from page to page by dragging the View Box up or down. You can also use the View Box to move from spread to spread. To do so, first choose View All Spreads from the Navigator panel menu, then drag the View Box to move from spread to spread, as shown in Figure 23.

FIGURE 22
Navigator panel

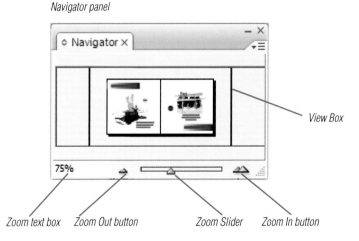

Zoom text box   Zoom Out button   Zoom Slider   Zoom In button

FIGURE 23
Viewing all spreads in a document

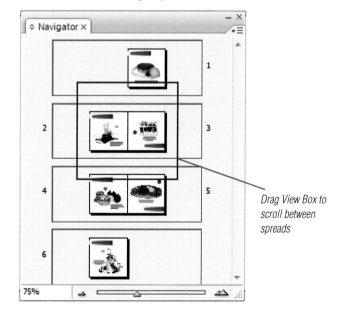

Drag View Box to scroll between spreads

INDESIGN 1-18

Exploring the InDesign Workspace

FIGURE 24
Page menu and the Previous Spread and Next Spread buttons

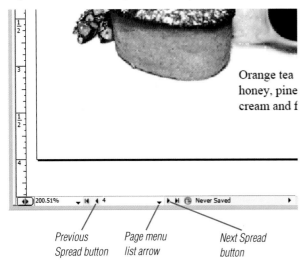

Orange tea
honey, pine
cream and f

Previous
Spread button

Page menu
list arrow

Next Spread
button

FIGURE 25
Targeting page 6 in the Pages panel

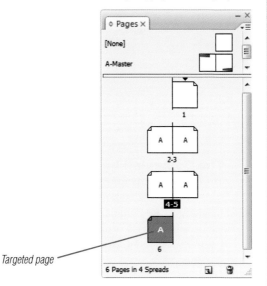

Targeted page

Navigate to pages in a document

1. Click the **Page menu list arrow** at the bottom of the document window, then click **3**.

   The document view changes to page 3.

2. Click **View** on the menu bar, then click **Fit Spread in Window**.

3. Click the **Next Spread button** ▶.

   Your screen should resemble Figure 24.

4. Click the **Previous Spread button** ◀ twice.

5. Click the **Pages panel name tab** to display the Pages panel, if necessary.

   TIP   If you do not see the Pages panel name tab on the right side of the document window, click Window on the menu bar, then click Pages. Checked items in the Window menu indicate panels that are already displayed and those that are the active panels within their groups.

6. Double-click the **page 6 icon** in the Pages panel.

   The document view changes to page 6, and the page 6 icon in the Pages panel changes to blue, as shown in Figure 25.

7. Double-click the **page 3 icon** in the Pages panel.

   The right half of the spread—page 3—is centered in the document window.

   (continued)

8. Double-click the numbers **2-3** beneath the page 2 and page 3 icons in the Pages panel.

   TIP Double-clicking numbers below the icons in the Pages panel centers the full spread in the document window.

9. Click **Layout** on the menu bar, then click **First Page**.

You explored various methods for moving from one page to another. You chose a page from the Page menu, you clicked the Next Spread and Previous Spread buttons, you selected page icons in the Pages panel, and you used the Layout menu.

Use the Navigator panel

1. Click **Window** on the menu bar, point to **Object & Layout**, then click **Navigator**.

   TIP Clicking a panel's name in the Window menu makes that panel the active panel.

2. Drag the **Zoom Slider** to the right until the Zoom text box is somewhere between 500% and 550%.

3. Double-click the percentage in the Zoom text box to select it, type **500**, press **[Enter]** (Win) or **[return]** (Mac), then compare your screen to Figure 26.

4. Click the **Zoom In button** ◬ once.

   The magnification increases to 600%.

   (continued)

FIGURE 26
Dragging the Zoom Slider in the Navigator panel

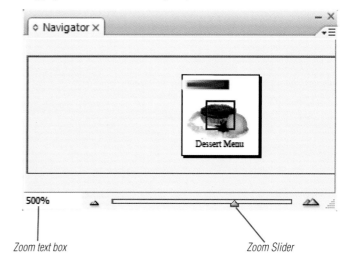

Zoom text box

Zoom Slider

The Command bar

The Command bar (formerly known as the PageMaker toolbar) provides easy access to commonly used tasks, such as opening, saving, printing, and checking spelling. In addition, the Command bar includes buttons for opening the Character and Paragraph panels as well as launching Adobe Illustrator and Photoshop. To view the Command bar, click Window on the menu bar, point to Object & Layout, then click Command Bar.

FIGURE 27

Navigator panel showing all spreads

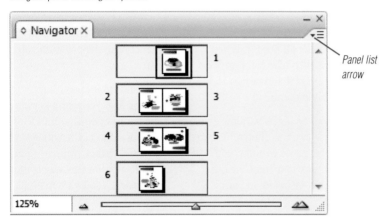

Panel list
arrow

5. Drag the **View Box** in the Navigator panel to scroll around the page.

6. Click the **Zoom Out button** five times.

   The magnification is reduced to 125%.

7. Click the **Navigator panel list arrow**, then click **View All Spreads**.

   The panel now shows all spreads, as shown in Figure 27.

8. Click **File** on the menu bar, then click **Close**.

You used the Navigator panel to enlarge and reduce the view of the document and to scroll around the document.

Creating custom workspaces

With InDesign CS3, you can customize the workspace as you like it—opening and dragging panels wherever you want them—and wherever they help make your workflow the most efficient. When you are happy with the way that you have customized your workspace, click Window on the menu bar, point to Workspace, then click Custom Workspace. Assign a descriptive name to your workspace, then click OK. To choose your workspace, click Window on the menu bar, then point to Workspace. You'll see your custom-named workspace in the list of commands.

USE
INDESIGN HELP

What You'll Do

 In this lesson, you will access help using Adobe Help Viewer.

Accessing InDesign Help

Help! At some point we all need it. When you do, you can use it to search for answers to your questions using the InDesign Help command on the Help menu.

InDesign Help opens in a new window called Adobe Help Viewer, as shown in Figure 28. From this same window, you can access help for any and all of the other Adobe CS3 programs installed on your

computer. Just click the Browse list arrow, then choose the program you need help with.

You can find information quickly by conducting a search using keywords. To do so, type your keyword(s) into the Search text box at the top of the window, then press [Enter] (Win) or [return] (Mac). Searching for information this way is more powerful than using a software manual.

Opening files in InDesign CS2

InDesign CS2 cannot open InDesign CS3 documents. To open an InDesign CS3 document in InDesign CS2, you must export the CS3 document as the InDesign Interchange (INX) format. Click File on the menu bar, click Export, then choose InDesign Interchange from the Save as type menu. The exported document will be saved with the .inx file extension and can be opened in InDesign CS2. Note, however, that any new CS3 features applied to your document may be lost when the file is converted to the older format.

Adobe Help Viewer offers you the power to do much broader searches and to view a number of different topics at a glance that relate to your search. For example, if you search for information about guides, you are given a very thorough list of topics relating to guides, as shown in Figure 29. Compare that to using the traditional index in a book and you will probably agree that this is a much more comprehensive and effective solution for accessing information.

FIGURE 28
Adobe Help Viewer

FIGURE 29
Search results for "guides"

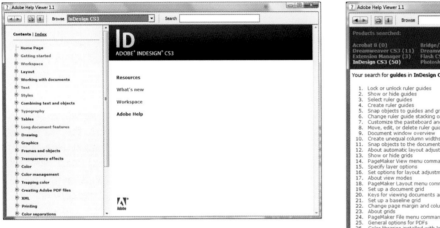

New features in CS3

When Adobe Help Viewer opens, you'll see a "What's new" link in the right pane. You should take some time to read about the new features in Adobe InDesign CS3. Don't rely on just poking around the application to see what's new; this list includes creativity and productivity enhancements, support for long documents, and customizable user interface information. Here you can read about every new feature in InDesign CS3 — many of which you'll never find on your own. While you're at it, check out the new features for Illustrator and Photoshop CS3 too!

Explore the InDesign workspace.

1. Start Adobe InDesign, then open ID 1-2.indd. (*Hint*: You may see the Missing Fonts dialog box which lets you know that one or more fonts used in the document you are opening are not available on your computer. You can either use the substitute font chosen by InDesign by clicking OK, or click Find Font and choose another font of your choice in the Find Font dialog box. Also, if you see a dialog box about modified links, click Fix Links Automatically.)

2. Point to the Type Tool, and press and hold the mouse button until you see the hidden tool beneath it.

3. Using the same method, view the hidden tools behind the other tools with small black triangles.

4. Click Window on the menu bar, point to Workspace, then click Default Workspace.

5. Drag the Pages panel away from its group on the right side of the workspace to the center of the document window.

6. Drag the Layers panel away from its group, then dock it beneath the Pages panel.

7. Drag the Layers panel away from the Pages panel, so that it is no longer docked.

8. Drag the Layers panel name tab next to the Pages panel name tab so that the two panels are grouped.

Change document views.

1. Click the Zoom Tool, then click inside the document window twice to enlarge the document, press and hold [Alt] (Win) or [option] (Mac), then click twice to reduce the document.

2. Click the Zoom menu list arrow, then click 600%.

3. Double-click 600% in the Zoom text box, type **800**, then press [Enter] (Win) or [return] (Mac).

4. Double-click the Zoom Tool in the Toolbox.

5. Click the Selection Tool, position it over the center of the document window, then press and hold [Ctrl][Spacebar] (Win) or $\mathcal{H}$[Spacebar] (Mac).

6. Click the mouse once, then release [Ctrl][Spacebar] (Win) or $\mathcal{H}$[Spacebar] (Mac).

7. Press [Spacebar] to access the Hand Tool, then scroll around the document.

8. Press and hold [Ctrl][Alt][Spacebar] (Win) or $\mathcal{H}$[option][Spacebar] (Mac), then click the mouse three times.

Navigate through a document.

1. Click the Page menu list arrow, then click 3.

2. Click View on the menu bar, then click Fit Spread in Window.

3. Click the Previous Spread button.

4. Click the Next Spread button two times.

5. In the Pages panel, double-click the page 5 icon.

6. Double-click the numbers 2-3 beneath the page 2 and page 3 icons in the Pages panel.

7. Click Layout on the menu bar, then click First Page.

8. Click Window on the menu bar, point to Object & Layout, then click Navigator.

9. Drag the Zoom Slider to the right until the Zoom text box is approximately at 300%.
10. Double-click the percentage in the Navigator's Zoom text box to select it, type **400**, then press [Enter] (Win) or [return] (Mac).
11. Click the Navigator's Zoom In button once.
12. Drag the View Box in the Navigator panel to scroll around the page.
13. Click the Zoom Out button five times. Close ID 1-2.indd without saving any changes.

FIGURE 30
Skills Review

You work at a local design studio. Your boss has informed you that the studio will be switching to Adobe InDesign for its layout software. She tells you that she wants you to spend the day investigating the software and creating simple layouts. You decide first to group and dock panels in a way that you think will be best for working with type and simple layouts.

1. Start Adobe InDesign.
2. Without creating a new document, group the Paragraph and Character panels together, then click the Paragraph panel name tab so that it is the active panel. (*Hint*: The Character and Paragraph panels can be found on the Window menu under Type & Tables.)
3. Dock the Pages panel to the bottom of the Paragraph panel group.
4. Group the Navigator and Layers panels with the Pages panel, then click the Navigator panel name tab so that it is the active panel.
5. Dock the Swatches panel below the Navigator panel group.
6. Group the Color, Stroke, and Gradient panels with the Swatches panel, then click the Gradient panel name tab so that it is the active panel.
7. Dock the Align panel below the Gradient panel group.
8. Group the Transform and the Effects panels with the Align panel, then click the Transform panel name tab so that it is the active panel.
9. Compare your panels with Figure 31. (If any of your panels are larger than those shown, click the panel's list arrow, then click Hide Options.)

FIGURE 31
Completed Project Builder 1

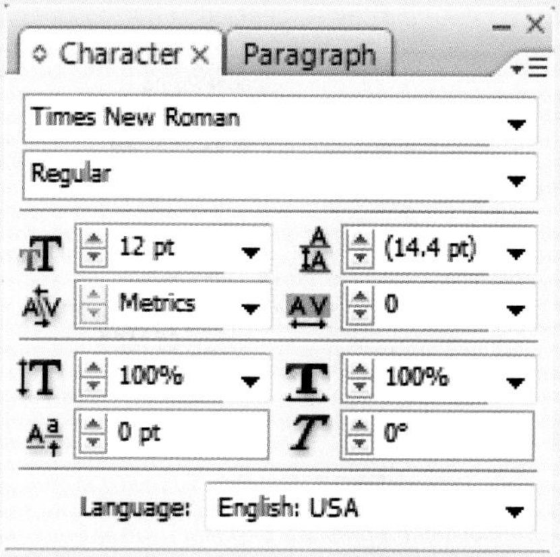

Exploring the InDesign Workspace

You are the creative director at a design studio. The studio has recently switched to Adobe InDesign for its layout software. You will be conducting a series of in-house classes to teach the junior designers how to use InDesign. Before your first class, you decide to practice some basic skills for viewing a document.

1. Open ID 1-3.indd. (*Hint*: If you see a dialog box about missing fonts, click OK to use the substitute font chosen by InDesign. If you see a dialog box about modified links, click Fix Links Automatically.)

2. Click Window on the menu bar, point to Workspace, then click Default Workspace.

3. Click the Selection Tool if necessary, then press [Ctrl][Spacebar] (Win) or [⌘] [Spacebar] (Mac) to access the Zoom Tool.

4. Position the Zoom Tool slightly above and to the left of the left eye, click and drag the Zoom Tool pointer to draw a dotted rectangle around the eye, then release the mouse button.

5. Press [Spacebar], then scroll with the Hand Tool to the right eye.

6. Press [Ctrl][Alt][Spacebar] (Win) or [⌘][option][Spacebar] (Mac), then click the Zoom Tool five times on the dog's right eye.

7. Drag the View Box in the Navigator panel so that both of the dog's eyes and his snout are visible in the window and your screen

resembles Figure 32. (Your magnification may differ from that shown in the figure.)

8. Close ID 1-3.indd without saving any changes.

FIGURE 32
Completed Project Builder 2

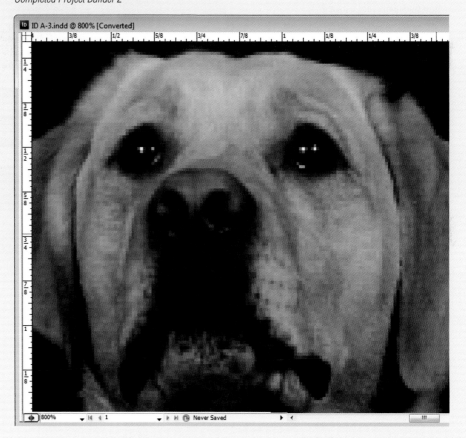

You will be teaching a small, in-house class on InDesign, and you will need to design handouts for students to take away from your lecture. To get ideas, you decide to visit a site created by a local design firm and look at solutions devised by other users of Adobe InDesign.

1. Connect to the Internet, go to www.bostonchefs.com.
2. Click through the Web site, shown in Figure 33, looking at a variety of pages.
3. Regard each layout from a design perspective: note the use of typography, imagery, color, and layout.
4. Write a brief summary stating why you like or dislike the design of this Web site, then save it as **Web Notes**.

FIGURE 33
Completed Design Project

In this project, your group will examine the layout that they worked with in the lessons of this chapter. The group is encouraged to critique the layout from a design perspective, to comment on the elements that they think are effective, and to suggest ways that the presentation may be improved.

1. Open ID 1-4.indd. (*Hint*: If necessary, click OK to accept a substitute font, then click Fix Links Automatically.)
2. Click View on the menu bar, point to Display Performance, then click High Quality Display.
3. Use the Pages panel to move from page to page, so that the group has seen each of the six pages at least one time. You may also refer to Figure 34 during the discussion.
4. What does the group think of the photographs? Are they effective? Does the fact that they are "silhouetted" against a white background make them more effective, or does the group think it would be better if they were photographed in context, such as on a plate or on a table in a restaurant setting?
5. How does the clean white background add to the look and feel of the piece, given that this is a layout about food?
6. Move through all the pages again. The layout changes from page to page. Though the restaurant's name doesn't move from one spread to another and the desserts are all positioned at the center of the page, the location of the menu descriptions changes, as does the location of the prices. Also, the circle behind the prices changes color. What does the group think about these changes from page to page? Would the layout be improved if all items were consistent from page to page?
7. Should the prices be in a bold typeface?
8. None of the pages features a title of the food item; the food is described only in the menu description. Does the group think it would be better if a title appeared on every page? If so, would the group be willing to discard the restaurant's name in the upper-left corner in favor of a title?
9. Submit your answers to these three questions in a document called **Design Critique**.
10. Close ID 1-4.indd without saving any changes.

FIGURE 34
Completed Group Project

chapter

2

WORKING WITH
TEXT

1. Format text

2. Format paragraphs

3. Create and apply styles

4. Edit text

2 WORKING WITH
TEXT

Earth, air, fire, and water—it is said that these are the four essential elements of our world. A different quartet establishes itself as the four main elements of any layout: text, color, illustration, and imagery. Take a moment to read them again, and make a mental note of them. We will use these four elements—text, color, illustration, and imagery—throughout this book to reduce the myriad features of InDesign into four simple categories.

In this chapter, we will focus on working with text. Like Proteus, the mythological figure who could change his outer form at will, text in a layout can appear in a variety of ways. It is *protean*—it is versatile. It can be display text—a bold, dramatic headline at the center of a page, for example, or a miniscule footnote tucked away unobtrusively. It can be flowed as body copy—paragraphs of text; or it can appear as simple page numbers at the lower corner of a page.

You will be pleased to find that InDesign is a first-rate application for generating and editing text. Everything that you want to do—you can do. With InDesign, your ability to generate functional, readable text and beautiful typographic artwork is limited only by your imagination.

Tools You'll Use

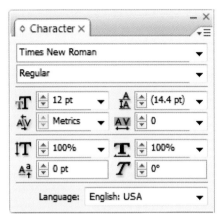

FORMAT TEXT

What You'll Do

Introducing the Min-Pin
by Christopher Smith

In this lesson, you will use the Character panel and various keyboard commands to modify text attributes.

Using the Character Panel

The Character panel, shown in Figure 1, is the command center for modifying text. The Character panel works hand in hand with the Paragraph panel, which is why they are grouped together. Where the Paragraph panel, as its name implies, focuses on manipulating paragraphs or blocks of text, the Character panel focuses on more specific modifications, such as font, font style, and font size.

In addition to these basic modifications, the Character panel offers other controls for manipulating text. You use the panel to modify leading; to track and kern text; to apply a horizontal scale or a vertical scale to text; to perform a baseline shift; or to skew text. To select text for editing, you can use the methods shown in the table on the next page.

Understanding Leading

Leading is the term used to describe the vertical space between lines of text. This space is measured from the baseline of one line of text to the baseline of the next line of text. As shown in Figure 2, the **baseline** is the invisible line on which a line of text sits. As with font size, leading is measured in points.

Pasting text without formatting

A great feature in InDesign CS3 is the ability to paste text with or without formatting. When you copy text, then paste it, it is by default pasted with all of its formatting—its type-face, type style, type size, and any other formatting that has been applied. Sometimes, this can be undesirable. For example, if you were pasting text into a text block that had different formatting, you would then need to edit the pasted text to conform to the new formatting. This is where the Paste without Formatting command comes into play: It strips the copied text of all its original formatting, then reformats it to match the formatting of the text where it is pasted. This is a very useful feature. Make a mental note of it, because when you need it, it will be very handy.

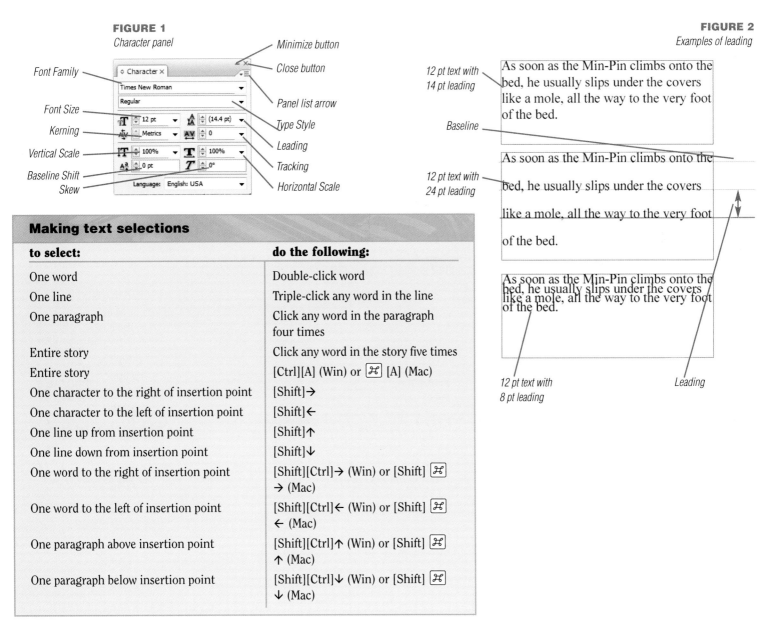

FIGURE 1
Character panel

Minimize button
Close button
Font Family
Panel list arrow
Font Size
Type Style
Kerning
Vertical Scale
Leading
Baseline Shift
Tracking
Skew
Horizontal Scale

FIGURE 2
Examples of leading

12 pt text with 14 pt leading

As soon as the Min-Pin climbs onto the bed, he usually slips under the covers like a mole, all the way to the very foot of the bed.

Baseline

12 pt text with 24 pt leading

As soon as the Min-Pin climbs onto the bed, he usually slips under the covers like a mole, all the way to the very foot of the bed.

As soon as the Min-Pin climbs onto the bed, he usually slips under the covers like a mole, all the way to the very foot of the bed.

12 pt text with 8 pt leading

Leading

Making text selections

to select:	do the following:
One word	Double-click word
One line	Triple-click any word in the line
One paragraph	Click any word in the paragraph four times
Entire story	Click any word in the story five times
Entire story	[Ctrl][A] (Win) or ⌘ [A] (Mac)
One character to the right of insertion point	[Shift]→
One character to the left of insertion point	[Shift]←
One line up from insertion point	[Shift]↑
One line down from insertion point	[Shift]↓
One word to the right of insertion point	[Shift][Ctrl]→ (Win) or [Shift] ⌘ → (Mac)
One word to the left of insertion point	[Shift][Ctrl]← (Win) or [Shift] ⌘ ← (Mac)
One paragraph above insertion point	[Shift][Ctrl]↑ (Win) or [Shift] ⌘ ↑ (Mac)
One paragraph below insertion point	[Shift][Ctrl]↓ (Win) or [Shift] ⌘ ↓ (Mac)

Scaling Text Horizontally and Vertically

When you format text, your most basic choice is which font you want to use and at what size you want to use it. Once you've chosen a font and a font size, you can further manipulate the appearance of the text with a horizontal or vertical scale.

In the Character panel, horizontal and vertical scales are expressed as percentages. By default, text is generated at a 100% horizontal and 100% vertical scale, meaning that the text is not scaled at all. Decreasing the horizontal scale only, for example, maintains the height of the characters but decreases the width—on the horizontal axis. Conversely, increasing the horizontal scale again maintains the height but increases the width of the characters on the horizontal axis. Figure 3 shows four examples of horizontal and vertical scales.

Kerning and Tracking Text

Though your computer is a magnificent instrument for generating text in myriad fonts and font sizes, you will often want to manipulate the appearance of text after you have created it—especially if you have the meticulous eye of a designer. **Kerning** is a long-standing process of increasing or decreasing space between a pair of characters. **Tracking** is more global. Like kerning, tracking affects the spaces between letters, but it is applied globally to an entire word or paragraph.

Kerning and tracking are standard features in most word processing applications, but they are more about typography than word processing—that is, they are used for setting text in a way that is pleasing to the eye. Spacing problems with text are usually more prominent with large size headlines than with smaller body copy—this is why many designers will spend great amounts of time tracking and kerning a headline. Figures 4 and 5 show examples of kerning and tracking applied to a headline. Note, though, that kerning and tracking are also used often on body copy as a simple solution for fitting text within an allotted space.

FIGURE 3

Scaling text horizontally and vertically

original text

50% horizontal scale

150% horizontal scale

50% vertical scale

150% vertical scale

FIGURE 4

Kerning text

Without kerning, some letters are spaced further apart

Wonderful

Wonderful

After Kerning, all letters are evenly spaced

Without kerning, some letters are very close

Kerned text with no tracking

FIGURE 5

Tracking text

Wonderful

Wonderful

Tracked text with greater space between characters

InDesign measures both kerning and tracking in increments of 1/1000 em, a unit of measure that is determined by the current type size. In a 6-point font, 1 em equals 6 points; in a 12-point font, 1 em equals 12 points. It's good to know this, but you don't need to have this information in mind when kerning and tracking text. Just remember that the increments are small enough to provide you with the specificity that you desire for creating eye-pleasing text.

Creating Superscript Characters

You are already familiar with superscript characters, even if you don't know them by that term. When you see a footnote in a book or document, the superscripted character is the footnote itself, the small number positioned to the upper-right of a word. Figure 6 shows a superscripted character.

The only tricky thing about applying a superscript is remembering how to do it. The Superscript command, as shown in Figure 7, is listed in the Character panel menu. Wait—there's one more tricky thing you need to remember about superscripts. If, for example, you select a 12-point character and then apply the Superscript command, by definition the character will be smaller in size. However, its point size will still be identified in the Character panel as 12 points.

Creating Subscript Characters

The Character panel menu also offers a command for Subscript. You can think of Subscript as the opposite of Superscript. Instead of raising the baseline of the selected text, the Subscript command

positions the text below its original baseline. As with Superscript, the Subscript command makes the selected text appear smaller.

Of the two, Subscript is used less often. Though it is seldom used for footnotes, many designers use Subscript for trademarks and register marks.

Underlining Text

InDesign offers different methods for creating **rules**—horizontal, vertical, or diagonal lines—and for underlining text. When you want simply to underline selected text, the most basic method is to use the Underline command in the Character panel menu. With this command, the weight of the underline is determined by the point size of the selected text. The greater the point size, the greater the weight of the line.

FIGURE 7
Locating the Superscript command

FIGURE 6
Identifying a superscripted character

Superscripted character

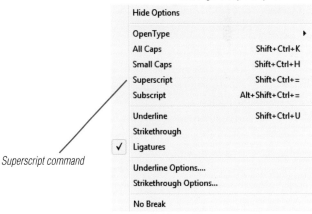

Superscript command

Modify text attributes

1. Open ID 2-1.indd, then save it as **Min-Pin Intro**.

2. Click **Edit** (Win) or **InDesign** (Mac) on the menu bar, point to **Preferences**, then click **Units & Increments**.

3. In the Keyboard Increments section, change the Size/Leading value to 1 pt (if necessary), as shown in Figure 8.

4. Click **OK**, click the **Type Tool**, then double-click the word **Introducing** at the top of the page.

5. Click the **Character panel name tab** on the right side of the document window to open the Character panel, if necessary.

6. Triple-click **Introducing** to select the entire line.

7. In the Character panel, click the **Font Family list arrow**, click **Impact**, click the **Font Size list arrow**, click **48 pt**, then verify that the Leading text box contains **57.6** pt, as shown in Figure 9.

   TIP   You can set the font list in the Character panel to show font names or font names and samples of each font. To enable or disable this feature, click Edit on the menu bar, point to Preferences, click Type on the left, then add or remove a check mark in the Font Preview Size check box. Notice also, that you can click the Font Preview Size list arrow and choose Small, Medium, or Large.

8. Press and hold **[Shift][Ctrl]** (Win) or **[Shift]** ⌘ (Mac), then press **[<]** ten times. The point size is reduced by one point size every time you press **[<]**.

9. Press and hold **[Shift][Ctrl]** (Win) or **[Shift]** ⌘ (Mac), then press **[>]** two times. The point size is increased by two points.

10. Triple-click **by** on the second line, change the font to Garamond or a similar font, click

   (continued)

FIGURE 8

Units & Increments section of the Preferences dialog box

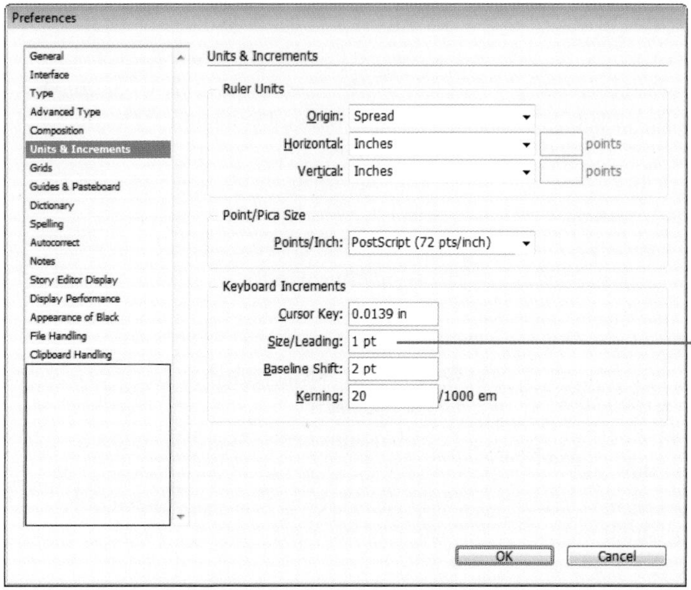

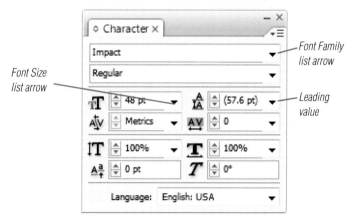

FIGURE 9

Character panel

FIGURE 10

Text frame indicates a selected text box

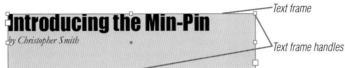

Introducing the Min-Pin
by Christopher Smith
Text frame
Text frame handles

FIGURE 11

Increasing the tracking value of selected text

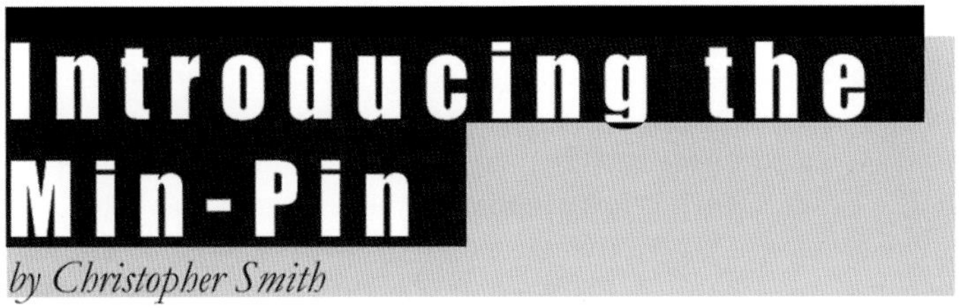

Introducing the
Min-Pin
by Christopher Smith

FIGURE 12

Decreasing the kerning value between two letters

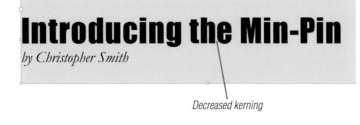

Introducing the Min-Pin
by Christopher Smith
Decreased kerning

the **Type Style list arrow**, click **Italic**, click the **Font Size list arrow**, then click **18 pt**.

> TIP If the Garamond font is not available to you, use a similar font.

11. Click the **Selection Tool**, then note that the text frame is highlighted, as shown in Figure 10.
12. Click **Object** on the menu bar, click **Text Frame Options**, click the **Align list arrow**, click **Center**, then click **OK**.

You used keyboard commands and the Character panel to modify text.

Track and kern text

1. Click the **Zoom Tool**, click and drag the **Zoom Tool pointer** around the light green frame that encompasses the entire headline, then release the mouse button.

   When you drag the Zoom Tool pointer, a dotted-lined selection rectangle appears. When you release the mouse, the contents within the rectangle are magnified.
2. Click the **Type Tool** T, then triple-click the word **Introducing**.
3. Click the **Tracking list arrow** in the Character panel, then click **200**.

   The horizontal width of each word increases, as a consistent amount of space is applied between each letter, as shown in Figure 11.
4. Change the tracking value to **25**.
5. Click between the letters h and e in the word the, click the **Kerning list arrow**, then click **-50**.

   The space between the two letters decreases.
6. Click the **Kerning up arrow** twice to change the kerning value to -30.

(continued)

7. Click the **Selection Tool** .

   Your headline should resemble Figure 12.

   You used the Character panel to modify tracking and kerning values applied to text.

Create superscript characters

1. Click **View** on the menu bar, click **Fit Page in Window**, click the **Zoom Tool** , then drag a selection box that encompasses all of the body copy on the page.

2. Click the **Type Tool** , then select the number **1** after the words Doberman Pinscher at the end of the fourth paragraph.

3. Click the **Character panel list arrow**, then click **Superscript**.

   The character's size is reduced and it is positioned higher than the characters that precede it, as shown in an enlarged view in Figure 13.

4. Select the number **2** after the word cows in the last paragraph, then apply the Superscript command.

   | TIP   When the Superscript command is applied to text, its designated font size remains the same.

5. Select the number **1** beside the footnote at the bottom of the page, apply the Superscript command, select the number **2** below, apply the Superscript command again, then deselect the text.

   Your footnotes should resemble Figure 14.

   You applied the Superscript command to format selected text as footnotes.

FIGURE 13
Applying the Superscript command

Pinscher[1].

Superscript character

Inserting footnotes automatically

While you can insert footnotes using the techniques in this lesson, if you have many footnotes in a document, you can use the InDesign CS3 enhanced footnote feature to insert them quickly and easily. In InDesign, a footnote consists of a **reference number** that appears in document text, and the **footnote text** that appears at the bottom of the page or column. To add a footnote, place the insertion point in the document location where you want the reference number to appear. Click Type on the menu bar, then click Insert Footnote. The insertion point moves to the footnote area at the bottom of the page or column. Type the footnote text; the footnote area expands as you type. If the text containing a footnote moves to another page, its footnote moves with it.

FIGURE 14
Using the Superscript command to format footnotes

Superscript characters

[1] Montag, Scott: In Love with the Min-Pin, All Breeds Publishing, 1997
[2] Miltenberger, William: Working Toy Breeds, CJP Press, 2002

FIGURE 15
Underlining text

¹ Montag, Scott: In Love with the Min-Pin, All Breeds
² Miltenberger, William: Working Toy Breeds, CJP Pre

Formatting footnotes

If you use the Insert Footnote command to enter footnotes in a document, you can specify a number of formatting attributes. Click Type on the menu bar, then click Document Footnote Options. On the Numbering and Formatting tab, you can select the numbering style, starting number, prefix, position, character style, or separator. The Layout tab lets you set the spacing above and between footnotes, as well as the rule that appears above them. Formatting changes you make to footnotes affect all existing and new footnotes.

FIGURE 16
Formatting footnotes

¹ Montag, Scott: In Love with the Min-Pin, All Breeds Publishing, 1997
² Miltenberger, William: Working Toy Breeds, CJP Press, 2002

8 pt text

Underline text

1. Click **View** on the menu bar, click **Fit Page in Window**, click the **Zoom Tool** 🔍, then drag a selection box that encompasses both footnotes at the bottom of the page.

2. Click the **Type Tool** T, then select **In Love with the Min-Pin** in the first footnote.

3. Click the **Character panel list arrow**, then click **Underline**.

   Only the selected text is underlined, as shown in Figure 15.

   TIP The weight of the line is automatically determined, based on the point size of the selected text.

4. Select **Working Toy Breeds** in the second footnote, then apply the Underline command.

5. Select the entire first footnote except the number 1, double-click the **Font Size text box**, type **8**, then press **[Enter]** (Win) or **[return]** (Mac).

6. Select the entire second footnote except the number 2, change its font size to 8 pt, then click to deselect the text.

   Your footnotes should resemble Figure 16.

   TIP To specify how far below the baseline the underline is positioned, click the Underline Options command on the Character panel menu, then increase or decrease the Offset value.

You selected text, then applied the Underline command from the Character panel menu.

FORMAT
PARAGRAPHS

What You'll Do

Introducing the Min-Pin
by Christopher Smith

The Miniature Pinscher is a smooth coated dog in the Toy Group. He is frequently - and incorrectly - referred to as a Miniature Doberman. The characteristics that distinguish the Miniature Pinscher are his size (ten to twelve and a half inches), his racy elegance, and the gait which he exhibits in a self-possessed, animated and cocky manner.

The Miniature Pinscher is part of the larger German Pinscher family, which belonged to a prehistoric group that dates back to 3000 B.C. One of the clear-cut traits present in the ancient Pinschers was that of the two opposing size tendencies: one toward the medium to larger size and the other toward the smaller "dwarf" of miniature size. This ancient miniature-sized Pinscher was the forerunner of today's Miniature pinscher.

"Is the Miniature Pinscher bred down from the Doberman Pinscher?"

The answer is a definite "No." Since ancient times, the Min Pin was developing with its natrual tendency to smallness in stature. In fact, as a recognized breed, the Miniature Pinscher predates the development of the well-known Doberman Pinscher[1].

The Min Pin is an excellent choice as a family pet. The breed tends to attach itself very quickly to children and really delights in joining a youngster in bed. As soon as the Min-Pin climbs onto the bed, he usually slips under the covers like a mole, all the way to the foot of the bed.

The Min Pin is intelligent and easily trained. He has a tendency to be clean in all respects, the shedding of the short coat constitutes minimal, if any, problems to the apartment dweller. On the other hand, the Miniature Pinscher certainly is not out of his element on the farm and has been trained to tree squirrels, chase rabbits, and even help herd cows[2]. It is not unusual for the Miniature Pinscher on a farm to catch a rabbit that is equal to or larger than the size of the dog.

[1] Manning, Scott: In Love with the Min-Pin, All Breeds Publishing, 1997
[2] Miltenberger, William: Working Toy Breeds, CJP Press, 2002

In this lesson, you will use the Paragraph panel and various keyboard commands to modify paragraph attributes.

Using the Paragraph Panel

The **Paragraph panel,** shown in Figure 17, is the command center for modifying paragraphs or blocks of text also known as body copy. The Paragraph panel works hand in hand with the Character panel, which is why they are grouped together.

The Paragraph panel is divided into three main sections. The top section controls alignment. Of the nine icons offering

FIGURE 17
Paragraph panel

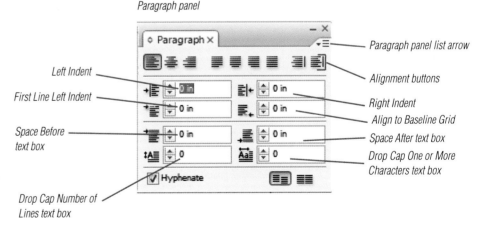

Left Indent

First Line Left Indent

Space Before text box

Drop Cap Number of Lines text box

Paragraph panel list arrow

Alignment buttons

Right Indent

Align to Baseline Grid

Space After text box

Drop Cap One or More Characters text box

options for aligning text, the first four—Align left, Align center, Align right, and Justify with last line aligned left—are the most common. The remaining five are subtle modifications of justified text and are used less often.

QUICKTIP

Optical Margin Alignment controls the alignment of punctuation marks for all paragraphs within a block of type. Optical margin alignment forces punctuation marks, as well as the edges of some letters, to hang outside the text margins so that the type appears aligned. To override this feature, click the text box or type object, click the Paragraph panel list arrow, then click Ignore Optical Margin. You can also click the Paragraph Styles panel list arrow, click Style Options, click the Indents and Spacing category, then click the Ignore Optical Margin check box.

The next section offers controls for indents. Use an indent when you want the first line of each paragraph to start further to the right than the other lines of text, as shown in Figure 18. This figure also shows what is commonly referred to as a **pull quote**. You have probably seen pull quotes in most magazines. They are a typographical design solution in which text is used at a larger point size and positioned prominently on the page. Note the left and right indents applied to the pull quote in Figure 18. They were created using the Left Indent and Right Indent buttons in the Paragraph panel.

The third section of the Paragraph panel controls vertical spacing between paragraphs and applying drop caps. For large blocks of text, it is often most pleasing to the eye to create either a subtle or distinct space after every paragraph. In InDesign, you create these by entering values in the

FIGURE 18

First line indent and left and right indents

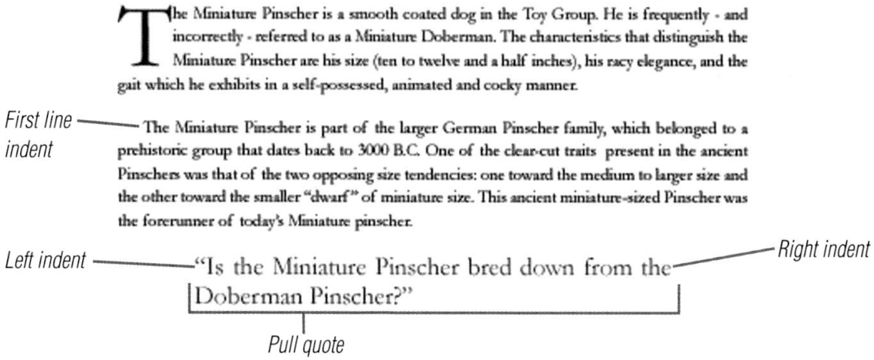
The Miniature Pinscher is a smooth coated dog in the Toy Group. He is frequently - and incorrectly - referred to as a Miniature Doberman. The characteristics that distinguish the Miniature Pinscher are his size (ten to twelve and a half inches), his racy elegance, and the gait which he exhibits in a self-possessed, animated and cocky manner.
First line indent
The Miniature Pinscher is part of the larger German Pinscher family, which belonged to a prehistoric group that dates back to 3000 B.C. One of the clear-cut traits present in the ancient Pinschers was that of the two opposing size tendencies: one toward the medium to larger size and the other toward the smaller "dwarf" of miniature size. This ancient miniature-sized Pinscher was the forerunner of today's Miniature pinscher.
Left indent
"Is the Miniature Pinscher bred down from the Doberman Pinscher?"
Right indent
Pull quote

Space After or the Space Before text boxes in the Paragraph panel. Of the two, the Space After text box is more commonly used. The Space Before text box, when it is used, is often used in conjunction with the Space After text box to offset special page elements, such as a pull quote.

A **drop cap** is a design element in which the first letter or letters of a paragraph are increased in size to create a visual effect. In the figure, the drop cap is measured as being three text lines in height. If you click to place the cursor to the right of the drop cap then increase the kerning value in the

Character panel, the space between the drop cap and all three lines of text will be increased. Figure 19 shows a document with a drop cap and a .25 inch space after every paragraph.

FIGURE 19

A drop cap and paragraphs with vertical space applied after every paragraph

Drop cap ——

The Miniature Pinscher is a smooth coated dog in the Toy Group. He is frequently - and incorrectly - referred to as a Miniature Doberman. The characteristics that distinguish the Miniature Pinscher are his size (ten to twelve and a half inches), his racy elegance, and the gait which he exhibits in a self-possessed, animated and cocky manner.

The Miniature Pinscher is part of the larger German Pinscher family, which belonged to a prehistoric group that dates back to 3000 B.C. One of the clear-cut traits present in the ancient Pinscher was that of the two opposing size tendencies: one toward the medium to larger size and the other toward the smaller "dwarf" of miniature size. This ancient miniature-sized Pinscher was the forerunner of today's Miniature pinscher.

"Is the Miniature Pinscher bred down from the Doberman Pinscher?"

The answer is a definite "No." Since ancient times, the Min Pin was developing with its natrual tendency to smallness in stature. In fact, as a recognized breed, the Miniature Pinscher predates the development of the well-known Doberman Pinscher[i].

Vertical space applied after every paragraph ——

The Min Pin is an excellent choice as a family pet. The breed tends to attach itself very quickly to children and really delights in joining a youngster in bed. As soon as the Min-Pin climbs onto

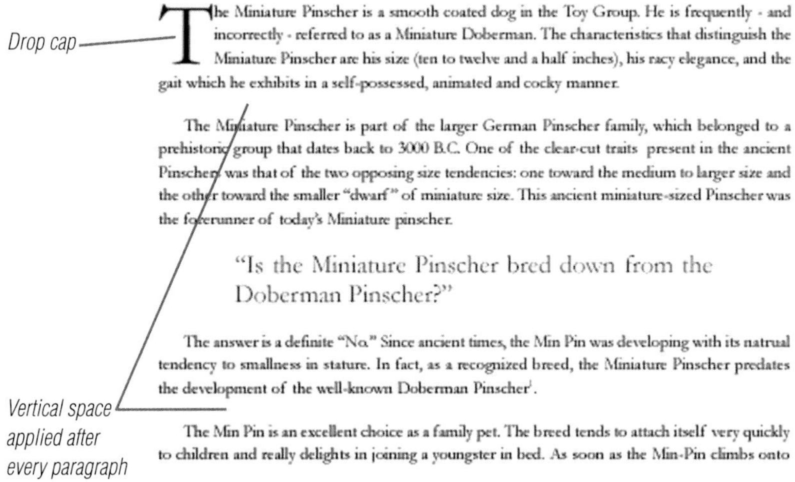

Understanding Returns and Soft Returns

A paragraph is a block of text, a line of text, or even a single word, that is followed by a paragraph return. A **paragraph return**, also called a **hard return**, is inserted into the text formatting by pressing [Enter] (Win) or [return] (Mac). For example, if I type my first name and then enter a paragraph return, that one word—my first name—is a paragraph. You are more familiar with paragraphs as blocks of text, which is fine. But the definition doesn't change. When working with body copy, paragraphs appear as blocks of text, each separated by a single paragraph return.

Here's an example of incorrect formatting. When typing body copy, often many designers will want a space after each paragraph because it is visually pleasing and helps to keep paragraphs visually distinct. The mistake many designers make is that they press [Enter] (Win) or [return] (Mac) twice to create that space after the paragraph. Wrong! What they've done is created two paragraphs. The correct way to insert space between paragraphs is to enter a value in the Space After text box in the Paragraph panel.

Here's a similar problem: When creating a first line paragraph indent, many users will press [Spacebar] 5 or 10 times and then start typing. This too is incorrect formatting. Paragraph indents are created using the First Line Left Indent setting in the Paragraph panel, not by inserting multiple spaces.

Why is this a problem? For one thing, it's an example of not using the features of the software properly. Also, space characters are not always consistent. If you press [Spacebar] 5 times to indent every paragraph in a document, you might be surprised to find that your indents will not necessarily be consistent from paragraph to paragraph.

Untold numbers of formatting problems occur from these incorrect typesetting behaviors, especially from misusing paragraph returns. "But," you may ask, "what if I need to move a word down to the next line?"

As you edit text, you may encounter a "bad line break" at the end of a line, such as an oddly hyphenated word or a phrase that is split from one line to the next. In many cases, you will want to move a word or phrase to the next line. You can do this by entering a **soft return**. A soft return moves words down to the next baseline but does not create a new paragraph. You enter a soft return by pressing and holding [Shift] and then pressing [Enter] (Win) or [return] (Mac).

Creating bulleted and numbered lists

A great feature in InDesign CS3 lets you create lists with bullets or numbers. Simply select text, then choose Bullets and Numbering from the Paragraph panel menu which opens the Bullets and Numbering dialog box. Depending on the list type you choose, InDesign will place a bullet or a number after every return in the selected text. You can also specify that a glyph—an asterisk, for example—be used in place of the bullet. Remember that bullets and numbers applied this way aren't text characters; InDesign regards them more as adornments that can be turned on or off. However, you can convert the bullets or numbers to text by choosing Convert Bullets to Text from the Paragraph panel menu. Once they are converted, InDesign no longer regards the paragraph as being part of a bulleted or numbered list and lets you treat the bullets as characters. Be sure to experiment with this feature—it is useful, powerful, and one you are likely to use often.

Use the Paragraph panel and Character panel to modify leading and alignment

1. Click **View** on the menu bar, click **Fit Page in Window**, then click the first instance of **The** in the first paragraph four times.

   TIP Clicking a word four times selects the entire paragraph.

2. Click the same word five times.

   TIP Clicking a word five times selects all the text in the text frame.

3. Click the **Leading list arrow** in the Character panel, then click **30 pt**.

   The vertical space between each line of text is increased, as shown in Figure 20.

   TIP Because leading can be applied to a single selected word as well as to an entire paragraph, the Leading setting is in the Character panel (as opposed to the Paragraph panel).

4. Double-click the **Leading text box**, type **16**, then press **[Enter]** (Win) or **[return]** (Mac).

5. Click the **Paragraph panel name tab** to display the Paragraph panel, then click the **Justify with last line aligned left button** ▤.

6. Click **Introducing** at the top of the document three times, then click the **Align center button** ▤ in the Paragraph panel.

7. Click **Edit** on the menu bar, then click **Deselect All**.

   Your document should resemble Figure 21.

You modified the leading and alignment of a block of selected text.

FIGURE 20
Modifying leading

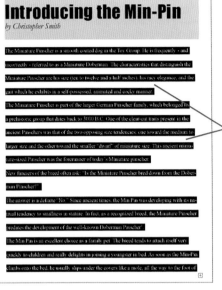

Increased leading adds more vertical space between lines of text

FIGURE 21
Modifying alignment

Text justified with last line aligned left

FIGURE 22

Increasing the Space After value

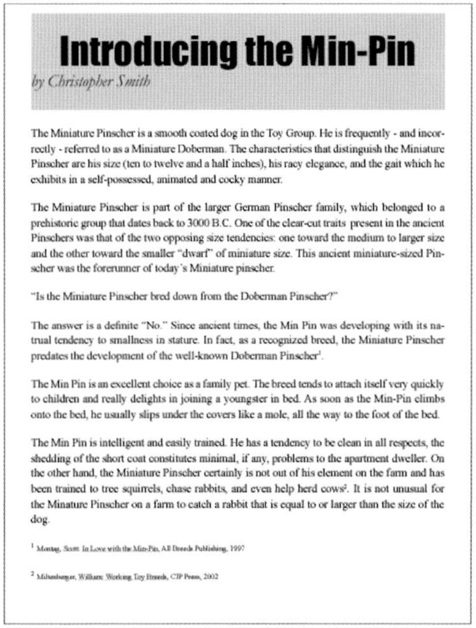

Introducing the Min-Pin
by Christopher Smith

The Miniature Pinscher is a smooth coated dog in the Toy Group. He is frequently - and incorrectly - referred to as a Miniature Doberman. The characteristics that distinguish the Miniature Pinscher are his size (ten to twelve and a half inches), his racy elegance, and the gait which he exhibits in a self-possessed, animated and cocky manner.

The Miniature Pinscher is part of the larger German Pinscher family, which belonged to a prehistoric group that dates back to 3000 B.C. One of the clear-cut traits present in the ancient Pinschers was that of the two opposing size tendencies: one toward the medium to larger size and the other toward the smaller "dwarf" of miniature size. This ancient miniature-sized Pinscher was the forerunner of today's Miniature pinscher.

"Is the Miniature Pinscher bred down from the Doberman Pinscher?"

The answer is a definite "No." Since ancient times, the Min Pin was developing with its natural tendency to smallness in stature. In fact, as a recognized breed, the Miniature Pinscher predates the development of the well-known Doberman Pinscher[1].

The Min Pin is an excellent choice as a family pet. The breed tends to attach itself very quickly to children and really delights in joining a youngster in bed. As soon as the Min-Pin climbs onto the bed, he usually slips under the covers like a mole, all the way to the foot of the bed.

The Min Pin is intelligent and easily trained. He has a tendency to be clean in all respects, the shedding of the short coat constitutes minimal, if any, problems to the apartment dweller. On the other hand, the Miniature Pinscher certainly is not out of his element on the farm and has been trained to tree squirrels, chase rabbits, and even help herd cows[2]. It is not unusual for the Miniature Pinscher on a farm to catch a rabbit that is equal to or larger than the size of the dog.

[1] Morring, Scott: In Love with the Min-Pin, All Breeds Publishing, 1997

[2] Milsenberger, William: Working Toy Breeds, CIP Press, 2002

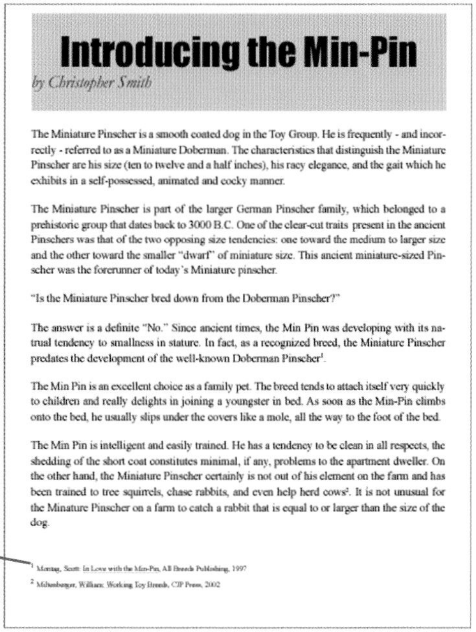

Introducing the Min-Pin
by Christopher Smith

The Miniature Pinscher is a smooth coated dog in the Toy Group. He is frequently - and incorrectly - referred to as a Miniature Doberman. The characteristics that distinguish the Miniature Pinscher are his size (ten to twelve and a half inches), his racy elegance, and the gait which he exhibits in a self-possessed, animated and cocky manner.

The Miniature Pinscher is part of the larger German Pinscher family, which belonged to a prehistoric group that dates back to 3000 B.C. One of the clear-cut traits present in the ancient Pinschers was that of the two opposing size tendencies: one toward the medium to larger size and the other toward the smaller "dwarf" of miniature size. This ancient miniature-sized Pinscher was the forerunner of today's Miniature pinscher.

"Is the Miniature Pinscher bred down from the Doberman Pinscher?"

The answer is a definite "No." Since ancient times, the Min Pin was developing with its natural tendency to smallness in stature. In fact, as a recognized breed, the Miniature Pinscher predates the development of the well-known Doberman Pinscher[1].

The Min Pin is an excellent choice as a family pet. The breed tends to attach itself very quickly to children and really delights in joining a youngster in bed. As soon as the Min-Pin climbs onto the bed, he usually slips under the covers like a mole, all the way to the foot of the bed.

The Min Pin is intelligent and easily trained. He has a tendency to be clean in all respects, the shedding of the short coat constitutes minimal, if any, problems to the apartment dweller. On the other hand, the Miniature Pinscher certainly is not out of his element on the farm and has been trained to tree squirrels, chase rabbits, and even help herd cows[2]. It is not unusual for the Miniature Pinscher on a farm to catch a rabbit that is equal to or larger than the size of the dog.

[1] Morring, Scott: In Love with the Min-Pin, All Breeds Publishing, 1997

[2] Milsenberger, William: Working Toy Breeds, CIP Press, 2002

Space before
value increased

Apply vertical spacing between paragraphs

1. Click the **Type Tool** T, , click anywhere in the body copy, click **Edit** on the menu bar, then click **Select All**.

   TIP The keyboard shortcut for Select All is [Ctrl][A] (Win) or ⌘[A] (Mac).

2. Click the **Space After up arrow** in the Paragraph panel three times, so that the value reads .1875 in, then deselect all.

   .1875 inches of vertical space is applied after every paragraph, as shown in Figure 22.

   TIP You may need to click the Paragraph panel list arrow, then click Show Options to expand the panel.

3. Select only the two footnotes at the bottom of the document, double-click the **Space After text box** in the Paragraph panel, type **0**, then press [Enter] (Win) or [return] (Mac).

4. Select only the first of the two footnotes, double-click the **Space Before text box** in the Paragraph panel, type **.25**, then press [Enter] (Win) or [return] (Mac).

   .25 inches of vertical space is positioned above the first footnote.

5. Click **Edit** on the menu bar, then click **Deselect All**.

   Your document should resemble Figure 23.

You used the Space After and Space Before text boxes in the Paragraph panel to apply vertical spacing between paragraphs.

Apply paragraph indents

1. Click **Type** on the menu bar, then click **Show Hidden Characters**.

   As shown in Figure 24, hidden characters appear in blue, showing blue dots for spaces, created by pressing [Spacebar], and paragraph marks for paragraph returns.

2. Select all the body copy on the page except the two footnotes, then click the **First Line Left Indent up arrow** in the Paragraph panel four times to change the value to .25 in, as shown in Figure 25.

   The first line of each paragraph is indented .25 in.

3. Select **by Christopher Smith**, then change the left indent value to .5 in.

4. Click anywhere in the third paragraph, change the First Line Left Indent value to 0 in, change the Left Indent value to .75 in, then change the Right Indent value to .75 in.

5. Click any word in the third paragraph three times to select the entire line, click the **Character panel name tab**, change the font size to 18 pt, change the leading to 20 pt, then deselect the paragraph.

   Your document should resemble Figure 26.

You showed hidden characters so that you could better identify each paragraph. You indented the first lines of every paragraph, and then you added substantial left and right indents to a paragraph and increased its point size to create a "pull quote."

FIGURE 24
Showing hidden characters

The · characteristics · that — *Space symbol*
lf · inches), · his · racy · elegan
ocky · manner.¶ ——————— *Paragraph return symbol*

FIGURE 25
Applying a first line left indent

First Line Left Indent up arrow

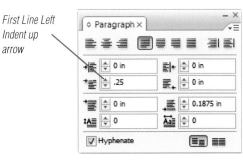

FIGURE 26
Using indents to format text as a pull quote

Introducing the Min-Pin¶
by Christopher Smith¶

The Miniature Pinscher is a smooth coated dog in the Toy Group. He is frequently - and incorrectly - referred to as a Miniature Doberman. The characteristics that distinguish the Miniature Pinscher are his size (ten to twelve and a half inches), his racy elegance, and the gait which he exhibits in a self-possessed, animated and cocky manner.¶

The Miniature Pinscher is part of the larger German Pinscher family, which belonged to a prehistoric group that dates back to 3000 B.C. One of the clear-cut traits present in the ancient Pinschers was that of the two opposing size tendencies: one toward the medium to larger size and the other toward the smaller "dwarf" of miniature size. This ancient miniature-sized Pinscher was the forerunner of today's Miniature pinscher.¶

"Is the Miniature Pinscher bred down from the Doberman Pinscher?" ¶ ——— *Pull quote formatted with increased left and right indents*

The answer is a definite "No." Since ancient times, the Min Pin was developing with its natrual tendency to smallness in stature. In fact, as a recognized breed, the Miniature Pinscher predates the development of the well-known Doberman Pinscher[1].¶

The Min Pin is an excellent choice as a family pet. The breed tends to attach itself very quickly to children and really delights in joining a youngster in bed. As soon as the Min-Pin climbs onto the bed, he usually slips under the covers like a mole, all the way to the foot of the bed. ¶

The Min Pin is intelligent and easily trained. He has a tendency to be clean in all respects, the shedding of the short coat constitutes minimal, if any, problems to the apartment dweller. On the other hand, the Miniature Pinscher certainly is not out of his element on the farm and has been trained to tree squirrels, chase rabbits, and even help herd cows[2]. It is not unusual for the Minature Pinscher on a farm to catch a rabbit that is equal to or larger than the size of the dog.¶

[1] Mantag, Scott. In Love with the Min-Pin, All Breeds Publishing, 1997¶
[2] Mehlenburger, William. Working Toy Breeds, CTP Press, 2002¶

Working with Text

FIGURE 27

Creating a drop cap

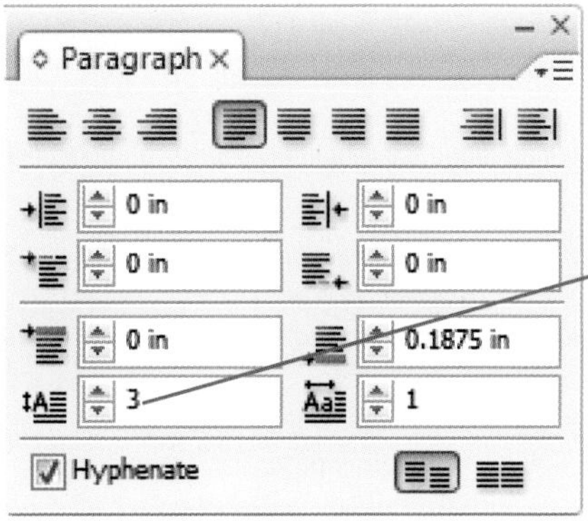

Drop Cap Number
of Lines value

FIGURE 28

Viewing the finished document

Introducing the Min-Pin

by Christopher Smith

The Miniature Pinscher is a smooth coated dog in the Toy Group. He is frequently - and incorrectly - referred to as a Miniature Doberman. The characteristics that distinguish the Miniature Pinscher are his size (ten to twelve and a half inches), his racy elegance, and the gait which he exhibits in a self-possessed, animated and cocky manner.

The Miniature Pinscher is part of the larger German Pinscher family, which belonged to a prehistoric group that dates back to 3000 B.C. One of the clear-cut traits present in the ancient Pinschers was that of the two opposing size tendencies: one toward the medium to larger size and the other toward the smaller "dwarf" of miniature size. This ancient miniature-sized Pinscher was the forerunner of today's Miniature pinscher.

"Is the Miniature Pinscher bred down from the Doberman Pinscher?"

The answer is a definite "No." Since ancient times, the Min Pin was developing with its natural tendency to smallness in stature. In fact, as a recognized breed, the Miniature Pinscher predates the development of the well-known Doberman Pinscher[1].

The Min Pin is an excellent choice as a family pet. The breed tends to attach itself very quickly to children and really delights in joining a youngster in bed. As soon as the Min-Pin climbs onto the bed, he usually slips under the covers like a mole, all the way to the foot of the bed.

The Min Pin is intelligent and easily trained. He has a tendency to be clean in all respects, the shedding of the short coat constitutes minimal, if any, problems to the apartment dweller. On the other hand, the Miniature Pinscher certainly is not out of his element on the farm and has been trained to tree squirrels, chase rabbits, and even help herd cows[2]. It is not unusual for the Miniature Pinscher on a farm to catch a rabbit that is equal to or larger than the size of the dog.

No new
paragraph

[1] Montag, Scott: *In Love with the Min-Pin*, All Breeds Publishing, 1997

[2] Miltenberger, William: *Working Toy Breeds*, CJF Press, 2002

1. Click the **Paragraph panel name tab**, click anywhere in the first paragraph, then change the First Line Left Indent value to 0.

2. Click the **Drop Cap Number of Lines up arrow** three times, so that the text box displays a 3, as shown in Figure 27.

   A drop cap with the height of three text lines is added to the first paragraph.

3. Select all the body copy text, including the two footnotes, then change the font to Garamond or a similar font.

4. Click the **Zoom Tool** 🔍 , then drag a selection box around the entire last paragraph.

5. Click the **Type Tool** T, click to insert the cursor immediately before the capital letter O of the word On in the third sentence of the last paragraph.

6. Press and hold **[Shift]**, then press **[Enter]** (Win) or **[return]** (Mac) to create a soft return.

7. Click **Type** on the menu bar, click **Hide Hidden Characters**, click **View** on the menu bar, point to **Grids & Guides,** then click **Hide Guides,** if necessary.

8. Click **View** on the menu bar, then click **Fit Page in Window**.

   Your document should resemble Figure 28.

9. Click **File** on the menu bar, click **Save**, then close Min-Pin Intro.

You created a drop cap and a soft return, which moved text to the next line without creating a new paragraph.

CREATE AND
APPLY STYLES

What You'll Do

Jake's Diner
Early Bird Breakfast Menu

Eggs and Bacon	**French Toast**
Two eggs any style, two strips of lean bacon, one biscuit with our homestyle gravy, and home fries.	*Four triangles of thick peasant bread dipped in a cinnamon-egg batter. Served with French Fries.*
$5.95	$6.95
Egg Sandwich	**Biscuits and Gravy**
One egg over easy, served with American or Jack cheese on a soft French croissant.	*Light fluffy southern biscuits served with a hearty sausage gravy.*
$5.25	$3.95
Belgian Waffle	**Eggs Hollandaise**
A golden brown buttery waffle served with fresh-picked strawberries, raspberries and blueberries. Whipped fresh cream on request.	*Three eggs lightly poached served on a bed of romaine lettuce and topped with a rich Hollandaise sauce.*
$4.95	$6.95
Silver Dollar Pancakes	**Steak and Eggs**
A stack of eight golden pancakes served with fresh creamery butter and warm maple syrup.	*A 6 oz. strip of peppered breakfast steak cooked to your liking, served with two eggs, any style.*
$4.95	$7.95

In this lesson, you will use the Character Styles and Paragraph Styles panels to create and apply styles to text.

Working with Character and Paragraph Styles

Imagine that you are writing a book—let's say a user's manual for how to care for houseplants. This book will contain seven chapters. In each chapter, different sections will be preceded by a headline that is the same font as the chapter title, but a smaller font size. Within those sections would be subheads—same font, smaller size. This would be a perfect scenario for using styles.

A **style** is a group of formatting attributes, such as font, font size, color, and tracking, that is applied to text—whenever and wherever you want it to appear—throughout a document or multiple documents. Using styles saves you time, and it keeps your work consistent. Styles are given descriptive names for the type of text they are applied to. Figure 29 shows three styles in the Character Styles panel. You use the Character Styles panel to create styles for individual words or characters, such as a footnote, and you use the Paragraph Styles panel to apply a style to a paragraph. Paragraph styles include formatting options such as indents and drop caps. The Paragraph Styles panel is shown in Figure 30.

QUICKTIP

You can easily import character and paragraph styles from other InDesign documents. Click the Character Styles or Paragraph Styles panel list arrow, then click Load Character Styles or Load Paragraph Styles. You'll be prompted to navigate to the documents that have the styles you wish to import.

In the scenario of the houseplant book, if you weren't using styles, you would be required to format those chapter headlines one at time, for all seven chapter heads. You'd need to remember the font size, the font style, and any tracking, kerning, scaling, or other formatting. Then you'd need to do the same for every section headline, then every sub-headline. For any body copy, you'd risk inconsistent spacing, indents, and other formatting options. Using styles, you define those formats one time and one time only. A much better solution, don't you think?

Another important feature about styles is that they are very useful when you change your mind and want to modify text. Simply modify the style, and all the text that is assigned to that style will be automatically updated—throughout the document!

QUICKTIP

Glyphs are type characters that you won't find on your keyboard—characters such as trademark and register mark signs, arrows, cent signs, boxes, and so forth. InDesign makes it easy to find and use glyphs. Click Type on the menu bar, then click Glyphs to display the Glyphs panel. Click the document window with the Type Tool, then double-click the glyph in the Glyphs panel that you wish to insert.

FIGURE 29
Character Styles panel

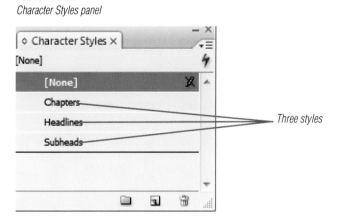

Three styles

FIGURE 30
Paragraph Styles panel

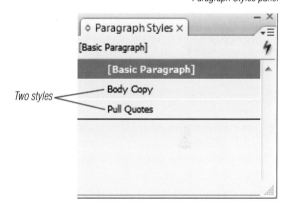

Two styles

Create character styles

1. Open ID 2-2.indd, then save it as **Jake's Diner**.

2. Drag the **Character Styles panel** away from its group.

   TIP The Character Styles panel is grouped with the Character, Paragraph, and Paragraph Styles panels.

3. Click the **Character Styles panel list arrow**, then click **New Character Style**.

4. Type **Dishes** in the Style Name text box of the New Character Style dialog box, then click **Basic Character Formats** in the left column, as shown in Figure 31.

5. Click the **Font Family list arrow**, click **Impact**, click the **Size list arrow**, click **14 pt**, click the **Leading text box**, type **16 pt**, then click **Advanced Character Formats** in the left column.

6. Type **85** in the Horizontal Scale text box, then click **OK**.

   The style "Dishes" now appears in the Character Styles panel.

7. Click the **Character Styles panel list arrow**, click **New Character Style**, type **Descriptions** in the Style Name text box, then click **Basic Character Formats** in the left column.

8. Click the **Font Family list arrow**, click **Garamond** or a similar font, click the **Font Style list arrow**, click **Italic**, change the font size to 10 pt, change the leading to 12 pt, then click **OK**.

   The style "Descriptions" now appears in the Character Styles panel.

   (continued)

FIGURE 31
New Character Style dialog box

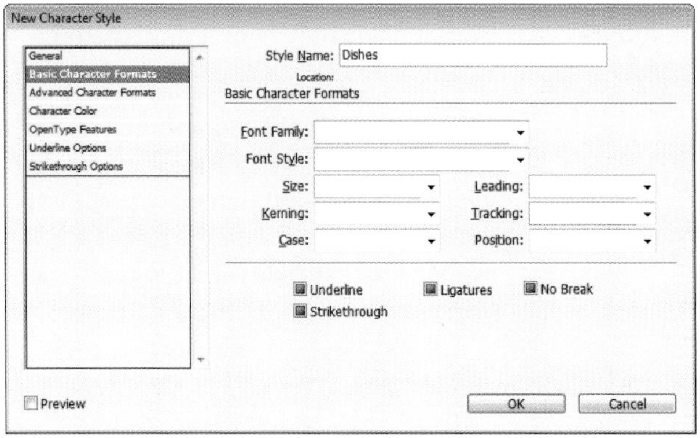

Using Data Merge

InDesign lets you create documents that are customized for each recipient, much like a mail merge in a word processing program, that you can use for letters, name labels, postcards, and the like. In a **data merge**, you use a data source (usually a text file) that contains **fields** (labels such as "First Name") and **records** (rows representing information for each recipient, such as "Bob Jones"). A **target document** is an InDesign file containing the text that will be seen by all recipients, such as a letter, as well as placeholders representing fields, such as <<First Name>>. In a data merge, InDesign places information from each record in the appropriate places in the target document, as many times as necessary. The result is a **merged document** containing the personalized letters.

To perform a data merge, select a data source from the Data Merge panel, available by clicking Window on the menu bar, then pointing to Automation. Click the Data Merge panel list arrow, click Select Data Source, locate the data source file, then click Open. This displays the merge fields in the Data Merge panel. Click in a text frame and click field names to enter them in the frame. If you place placeholders on master pages, the merged document is connected to the data source, and you can automatically update the merged document with the most recent version of your data source.

To merge the document, click the Data Merge panel list arrow, then click Create Merged Document. Select the records to include, then click OK.

FIGURE 32
Character Styles panel

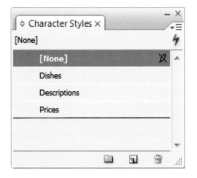

FIGURE 33

Applying three different character styles

Dishes style ——— **Eggs and Bacon**

Descriptions style — *Two eggs any style, two strips of lean bacon, one biscuit with our homestyle gravy, and home fries.*

$5.95

Prices style

FIGURE 34

Viewing the document with all character styles applied

Jake's Diner
Early Bird Breakfast Menu

Eggs and Bacon
Two eggs any style, two strips of lean bacon, one biscuit with our homestyle gravy, and home fries.
$5.95

Egg Sandwich
One egg over easy, served with American or Jack cheese on a soft French croissant.
$5.25

Belgian Waffle
A golden brown buttery waffle served with fresh-picked strawberries, raspberries and blueberries. Whipped fresh cream on request.
$4.95

Silver Dollar Pancakes
A stack of eight golden pancakes served with fresh creamery butter and warm maple syrup.
$4.95

French Toast
Four triangles of thick peasant bread dipped in a cinnamon-egg batter. Served with French Fries.
$6.95

Biscuits and Gravy
Light fluffy southern biscuits served with a hearty sausage gravy.
$3.95

Eggs Hollandaise
Three eggs lightly poached served on a bed of romaine lettuce and topped with a rich Hollandaise sauce.
$6.95

Steak and Eggs
A 6 oz. strip of peppered breakfast steak cooked to your liking, served with two eggs, any style.
$7.95

9. Click the **Character Styles panel list arrow**, click **New Character Style**, type **Prices** in the Style Name text box, then click **Basic Character Formats** in the left column.

10. Change the font to Garamond or a similar font, change the font style to Bold, change the font size to 12 pt, change the leading to 14 pt, then click **OK**.

Your Character Styles panel should resemble Figure 32.

You created three new character styles.

Apply character styles

1. Click the **Type Tool**  , triple-click the word **Eggs** in the first title to select the entire title "Eggs and Bacon," then click **Dishes** in the Character Styles panel.

The Dishes character style is applied to the title.

2. Select the entire next paragraph (beginning with the word Two), then click **Descriptions** in the Character Styles panel.

3. Select the first price (**$5.95**), click **Prices** in the Character Styles panel, click **Edit** on the menu bar, then click **Deselect All**.

Your first menu item should resemble Figure 33. If you used a different font, your text may wrap differently.

4. Apply the Dishes style to the remaining seven dish titles.

5. Apply the Descriptions style to the remaining seven descriptions.

6. Apply the Prices style to the remaining seven prices, then deselect so that your document resembles Figure 34.

You applied character styles to format specific areas of a document.

Create paragraph styles

1. Close the Character Styles panel, then drag the **Paragraph Styles panel** away from its group.

   TIP The Paragraph Styles panel is grouped with the Character, Paragraph, and Character Styles panels.

2. Click the **Paragraph Styles panel list arrow**, then click **New Paragraph Style**.

3. Type **Prices** in the Style Name text box, then click **Indents and Spacing** in the left column.

   TIP Note that the New Paragraph Style dialog box contains Basic Character Formats and Advanced Character Formats categories—the same that you find when working in the New Character Style dialog box.

4. Click the **Alignment list arrow**, then click **Center**.

5. Type **.25** in the Space After text box, then click **Paragraph Rules** in the left column.

   TIP The term **rules** is layout jargon for lines. Rules can be positioned on a page as a design element, or text can be underlined with rules.

6. Click the **list arrow** directly beneath Paragraph Rules, click Rule Below, then click the Rule On check box to add a check mark.

7. Type **.125** in the Offset text box, type **.25** in the Left Indent text box, type **.25** in the Right Indent text box, press **[Tab]** so that your dialog box resembles Figure 35, then click **OK**.

   The paragraph style "Prices" now appears in the Paragraph Styles panel as shown in Figure 36.

   You created a paragraph style, which included a center alignment, a space after value, and a paragraph rule.

FIGURE 35
Paragraph Rules window in the New Paragraph Style dialog box

New Paragraph Style

General
Basic Character Formats
Advanced Character Formats
Indents and Spacing
Tabs
Paragraph Rules
Keep Options
Hyphenation
Justification
Drop Caps and Nested Styles
Bullets and Numbering
Character Color
OpenType Features
Underline Options
Strikethrough Options

Style Name: Prices
Location:
Paragraph Rules

Rule Below ☑ Rule On
Weight: 1 pt   Type: ▬▬▬
Color: ■ (Text Color)   Tint:
☐ Overprint Stroke
Gap Color: ■ (Text Color)   Gap Tint:
☐ Overprint Gap
Width: Column   Offset: 0.125 in
Left Indent: 0.25 in   Right Indent: 0.25 in
☐ Keep In Frame

☐ Preview   OK   Cancel

Using Quick Apply

A quick way to apply a character or paragraph style is to use Quick Apply. The Quick Apply button, shown in Figure 36, is available on the Control panel, Character Styles panel, and Paragraph Styles panel. In the Quick Apply dialog box, there is a pull-down menu showing checked items, such as Character Styles. When Character Styles is checked, you can apply a character style quickly by typing its name in the Quick Apply text box. Your style will appear in a list below. Click the name in the list and your style is applied. Quick Apply is not limited to applying styles. You can use Quick Apply to access menu commands and run scripts. Just be sure to click the Quick Apply list arrow in the Quick Apply dialog box and select Include Scripts and Include Menu Commands.

FIGURE 36
Paragraph Styles panel

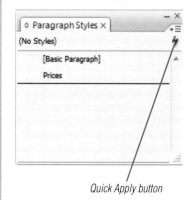

Quick Apply button

FIGURE 37

Applying a paragraph style to two prices

Eggs and Bacon

Two eggs any style, two strips of lean bacon, one biscuit with our homestyle gravy, and home fries.

$5.95

Egg Sandwich

One egg over easy, served with American or Jack cheese on a soft French croissant.

$5.25

Prices paragraph style applied

FIGURE 39

Viewing the final document

Jake's Diner
Early Bird Breakfast Menu

Eggs and Bacon
Two eggs any style, two strips of lean bacon, one biscuit with our homestyle gravy, and home fries.
$5.95

French Toast
Four triangles of thick peasant bread dipped in a cinnamon-egg batter. Served with French Fries.
$6.95

Egg Sandwich
One egg over easy, served with American or Jack cheese on a soft French croissant.
$5.25

Biscuits and Gravy
Light fluffy southern biscuits served with a hearty sausage gravy.
$3.95

Belgian Waffle
A golden brown buttery waffle served with fresh-picked strawberries, raspberries and blueberries. Whipped fresh cream on request.
$4.95

Eggs Hollandaise
Three eggs lightly poached served on a bed of romaine lettuce and topped with a rich Hollandaise sauce.
$6.95

Silver Dollar Pancakes
A stack of eight golden pancakes served with fresh creamery butter and warm maple syrup.
$4.95

Steak and Eggs
A 6 oz. strip of peppered breakfast steak cooked to your liking, served with two eggs, any style.
$7.95

Hollandaise sauce moves to a new line

FIGURE 38

Applying styles to all but the bottom two prices

Jake's Diner
Early Bird Breakfast Menu

Eggs and Bacon
Two eggs any style, two strips of lean bacon, one biscuit with our homestyle gravy, and home fries.
$5.95

French Toast
Four triangles of thick peasant bread dipped in a cinnamon-egg batter. Served with French Fries.
$6.95

Egg Sandwich
One egg over easy, served with American or Jack cheese on a soft French croissant.
$5.25

Biscuits and Gravy
Light fluffy southern biscuits served with a hearty sausage gravy.
$3.95

Belgian Waffle
A golden brown buttery waffle served with fresh-picked strawberries, raspberries and blueberries. Whipped fresh cream on request.
$4.95

Eggs Hollandaise
Three eggs lightly poached served on a bed of romaine lettuce and topped with a rich Hollandaise sauce.
$6.95

Silver Dollar Pancakes
A stack of eight golden pancakes served with fresh creamery butter and warm maple syrup.
$4.95

Steak and Eggs
A 6 oz. strip of peppered breakfast steak cooked to your liking, served with two eggs, any style.
$7.95

You do not need dividing rules at the bottom of the menu

1. Click the **Type Tool** **T.** , then select all the text in the document except for the two headlines at the top of the page.

2. Click the **Align center button** ▤ in the Paragraph panel.

   For this layout, all the menu items will be aligned center. It's not necessary to create a paragraph style for all items to align center, because you can simply use the Align center button in the Paragraph panel.

3. Click the first price (**$5.95**) once, click **Prices** in the Paragraph Styles panel, click the second price (**$5.25**), then click **Prices** in the Paragraph Styles panel again.

   Your first two menu items should resemble Figure 37.

   TIP   When applying paragraph styles, you only need to place the cursor in the paragraph you want to modify.

4. Apply the Prices paragraph style to the remaining prices in the document *except* the Silver Dollar Pancakes and Steak and Eggs prices, then compare your document to Figure 38.

5. Click **View** on the menu bar, point to **Grids & Guides,** then click **Hide Guides.**

6. Click before the second instance of the word Hollandaise, press and hold **[Shift]**, then press **[Enter]** (Win) or **[return]** (Mac).

   Hollandaise sauce is moved to the next line. Using the same method, add soft returns to break any other lines that you think could look better, then compare your work to Figure 39.

7. Save your work, then close Jake's Diner.

You applied a paragraph style to specific areas of the menu.

EDIT TEXT

What You'll Do

In this lesson, you will use the Find/Change and Check Spelling commands to edit the text of a document.

Using the Find/Change Command

One of the great things about creating documents using a computer is the ability to edit text quickly and efficiently. Imagine the days before the personal computer: When you were finished typing a document, you needed to read through it carefully looking for any errors. If you found any, you had only three options: cover it up, cross it out, or type the whole document again.

The Find/Change dialog box, shown in Figure 40, is a very powerful tool for editing a document. With this command, you can search for any word in the document, then change that word to another word or delete it altogether with a click of your mouse. For example, imagine that you have typed an entire document about Abraham Lincoln's early years growing up in Frankfurt, Kentucky. Then the fact checker informs you that Lincoln actually grew up in Hardin County, Kentucky. You could use the Find/Change command to locate every instance of the word "Frankfurt" and change it to "Hardin County." One click

would correct every instance of that error, throughout the entire document. Try that with a typewriter!

QUICKTIP

InDesign CS3 has added a number of new features to the Find/Change dialog box. The Query menu lists pre-defined search options for finding (and changing) common formatting issues. For example, the Query menu has a built-in searches for finding and changing dashes to em dashes, single quotes to double quotes, and double quotes to single quotes. There's a built-in search for 'trailing white space'—useless extra spaces at the end of paragraphs or sentences—and there's even a search for telephone number formatting.

Checking Spelling

Since the earliest days of the personal computer, the ability to check and correct spelling errors automatically has been a much-promoted benefit of creating documents digitally. It has stood the test of time. The spell checker continues to be one of the most powerful features of word processing.

InDesign's Check Spelling dialog box, shown in Figure 41, is a comprehensive utility for locating and correcting typos and other misspellings in a document. If you've done word processing before, you will find yourself on familiar turf. The spell checker identifies words that it doesn't find in its dictionary, offers you a list of suggested corrections, and asks you what you want to do. If it is indeed a misspelling, type the correct spelling or choose the correct word from the suggested corrections list, then click Change to correct that instance or click Change All to correct all instances of the misspelling throughout the document.

Sometimes the spell checker identifies a word that is not actually a misspelling. For example, say you were typing a letter about your dog whose name is Gargantua.

The spell checker is not going to find that word/name in its dictionary, and it is going to ask you what you want to do with it. You have two options. You could click Ignore, which tells the spell checker to make no changes and move on to the next questionable word. However, because in the future you will probably type the dog's name in other documents, you don't want the spell checker always asking you if this word/name is a misspelling. In this case, you'd be better off clicking the Add button. Doing so adds the name Gargantua to the spell checker's dictionary, and in the future, the spell checker will no longer identify Gargantua as a misspelling.

When you click the Add button, the word in question is added to 'eng'—InDesign's

main dictionary. If you use the spell checker often, you will build up a list of words that you've chosen to ignore and a list of words that you've chosen to add to the dictionary. To see those lists—and to modify them—click the Dictionary button in the Check Spelling dialog box.

You can create your own user dictionary in the Dictionary section of the Preferences dialog box. Click the Language list arrow to choose the language you want to associate your dictionary with, then click the New User Dictionary button. To add a list of words to a dictionary, create a Word file, save it in the Plain Text format, then, in InDesign, click Edit on the menu bar, point to Dictionary, then click Import.

FIGURE 40
Find/Change dialog box

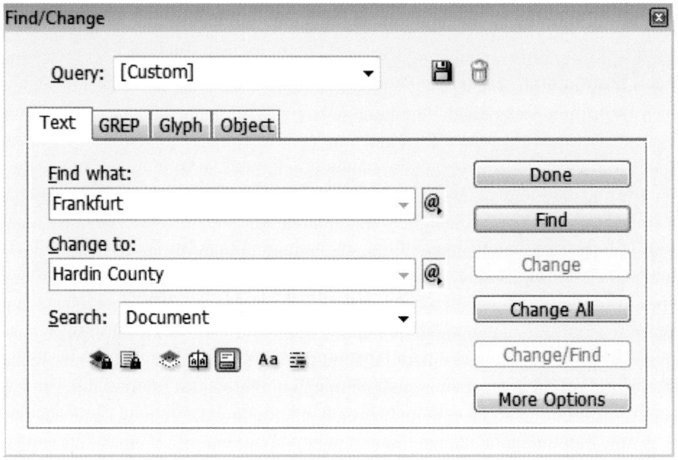

FIGURE 41
Check Spelling dialog box

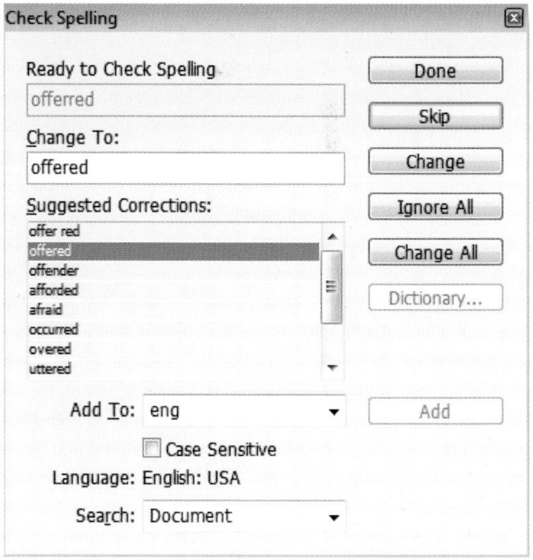

Use the Find/Change command

1. Open ID 2-3.indd, then save it as **Final Edit**.

2. Click **Edit** on the menu bar, then click **Find/Change**.

3. Type **Miniature Pincher** in the Find what text box, then type **Min-Pin** in the Change to text box, as shown in Figure 42.

4. Click **Find**.

   The first use of "Miniature Pincher" in the document is highlighted. As this is the first use of the term, you don't want to change it to a nickname.

   | TIP   Drag the dialog box out of the way if you cannot see your document.

5. Click **Find Next** again, then click **Change**.

   The second use of "Miniature Pincher" is changed to "Min-Pin."

6. Click **Find Next** again, then click **Change**.

7. Click **Find Next** three times.

   You don't want to change *all* instances of Miniature Pincher to Min-Pin.

8. Click **Change**, then click **Done**.

9. Click **Edit** on the menu bar, then click **Find/Change**.

10. Type **Pincher** in the Find what text box, type **Pinscher** in the Change to text box, then click **Change All**.

    A dialog box appears stating that the search is completed and 14 replacements were made.

11. Click **OK**, then click **Done**.

You used the Find/Change command to replace specific words in the document with other words.

FIGURE 42
Find/Change dialog box

Editing text using Drag and Drop

InDesign CS3 has added a Drag and Drop text editing feature that allows you to move text to locations within a document without having to cut and paste. This means that you can select text and simply drag it from one text frame into another text frame. You can drag and drop text between text frames on different pages. You can even drag and drop text between documents. Dragging and dropping text is usually a lot faster and easier than cutting and pasting. You can also drag and drop a copy of selected text by holding [Alt] (Win) or [option] (Mac) down when dragging. You can turn Drag and Drop text on or off in the Type window of the Preferences dialog box. In the Drag and Drop Text Editing section, check both the Enable in Layout View and the Enable in Story Editor check boxes so that the feature is activated for all of your editing methods. Give it a try!

Using dynamic spell checking

InDesign CS3 offers dynamic spell checking, which you may have used in word processing applications. As you type, the program places a squiggly red line under words that its spell checker thinks are misspelled. If you forget to use the spell checker feature when you finish typing a document, the dynamic spell checker has probably already flagged most of the misspellings. To prevent the program from flagging a proper name, you can add that name to your customized dictionary and the program will stop flagging it. To enable dynamic spelling, click Edit on the menu bar, point to Spelling, then click Dynamic Spelling.

FIGURE 43
Check Spelling dialog box

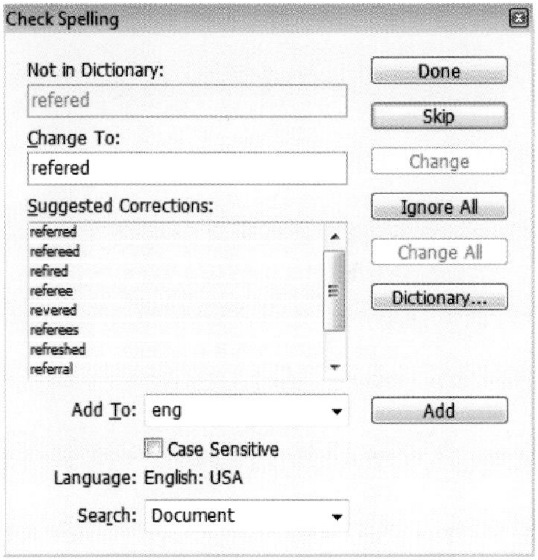

Correcting text automatically

InDesign CS3 offers a feature called Autocorrect, which you can think of as taking dynamic spell checking one step further. Instead of flagging a misspelled word, the Autocorrect feature actually corrects the misspelled word. So if you type the word "refered" and press [Spacebar], Autocorrect changes the word to the correct spelling. Before you use it, though, you need to enter your list of commonly misspelled words in the Autocorrect section of the Preferences dialog box. That might seem like a lot of work, but don't dismiss the Autocorrect feature too quickly! This is a powerful feature. To turn on the Autocorrect feature, click Edit on the menu bar, point to Spelling, then click Autocorrect.

Check spelling

1. Click to the right of the drop cap **T** (between the T and the h) at the top of the page.

   Positioning your cursor at the top of a document forces the spell checker to begin checking for misspellings from the start of the document.

2. Click **Edit** on the menu bar, point to **Spelling**, then click **Check Spelling**.

   As shown in Figure 43, the first word the spell checker can't find in the dictionary—"refered"—is listed and suggested corrections are listed below.

3. Click **referred** in the Suggested Corrections list—then click **Change**.

   The spell checker lists the next word that it can't find in the dictionary—"Min-Pin."

4. Click **Add** to add the word to the dictionary.

   Min-Pin is added to InDesign's main dictionary, which by default is named eng. The spell checker will no longer flag Min-Pin as an unknown word.

5. Click **racy** in the Suggested Corrections list, then click **Change**.

   The spell checker lists "Pinscher1" as not in the dictionary because of the number 1 footnote.

6. Click **Ignore All**, click **Ignore All** for the remaining queries, click **OK**, then click **Done**.

7. Save your work, then close Final Edit.

   TIP Never rely on the spell checker as the sole means for proofreading a document. It cannot determine if you have used the wrong word. For example, the spell checker did not flag the word "gate" in the first paragraph, which should be spelled "gait."

You used the Check Spelling dialog box to proof a document for spelling errors.

Format text.

1. Open ID 2-4.indd, then save it as **Independence**.
2. Click the Type Tool, then triple-click the word Declaration at the top of the page.
3. In the Character panel, type **80** in the Horizontal Scale text box, then press [Enter] (Win) or [return] (Mac).
4. Click the Font Family list arrow, click Impact, click the Font Size list arrow, then click 36 pt.
5. Press and hold [Shift] [Ctrl] (Win) or [Shift] [⌘] (Mac), then press [<] two times.
6. Triple-click the word July on the next line, change the type face to Garamond (if necessary), change the type style to Italic, then click the Font Size up arrow until you change the font size to 18 pt.
7. Click Object on the menu bar, click Text Frame Options, change the Align setting to Center, then click OK.
8. Triple-click the word July (if necessary).
9. Type **100** in the Tracking text box, then press [Enter] (Win) or [return] (Mac).
10. Click between the letters r and a in the word Declaration, click the Kerning list arrow, then click 10.
11. Click View on the menu bar, click Fit Page in Window if necessary, click the Zoom Tool, then drag a selection box that encompasses all of the body copy on the page.
12. Click the Type Tool, then select the number 1 at the end of the first paragraph.
13. Click the Character panel list arrow, then click Superscript.
14. Select the number 1 at the beginning of the last paragraph, then apply the Superscript command.

Format paragraphs.

1. Click View on the menu bar, click Fit Page in Window, then click the first word When in the body copy five times to select all the body copy.
2. Select (12 pt) in the Leading text box in the Character panel, type **13.25**, then press [Enter] (Win) or [return] (Mac).
3. Click the Paragraph panel name tab to display the Paragraph panel, if necessary, then click the Justify with last line aligned left button.
4. Click in the word Independence at the top of the document, then click the Align center button in the Paragraph panel.
5. Click the Type Tool if necessary, click anywhere in the body copy, click Edit on the menu bar, then click Select All.
6. In the Paragraph panel, click the Space After up arrow three times, so that the value reads .1875 in, click Edit on the menu bar, then click Deselect All.
7. Select the footnote (last paragraph of the document), double-click the Space Before text box in the Paragraph panel, type **.5**, then press [Enter] (Win) or [return] (Mac).
8. Apply the Deselect All command.
9. Click Type on the menu bar, then click Show Hidden Characters.
10. Select all the body copy on the page except for the last paragraph (the footnote), double-click the First Line Left Indent text box in the Paragraph panel, type **.25**, then press [Enter] (Win) or [return] (Mac).
11. Select July 4, 1776 beneath the headline, then click the Align right button in the Paragraph panel.
12. Double-click the Right Indent text box in the Paragraph panel, type **.6**, then press [Enter] (Win) or [return] (Mac).
13. Click anywhere in the first paragraph, then change the First Line Left Indent value to 0.
14. Click the Drop Cap Number of Lines up arrow three times, so that the text box displays a 3.

15. Click the Zoom Tool, then drag a selection box that encompasses the entire second to last paragraph in the body copy.

16. Click the Type Tool, position the pointer before the word these—the second to last word in the paragraph.

17. Press and hold [Shift], then press [Enter] (Win) or [return] (Mac).

18. Click Type on the menu bar, click Hide Hidden Characters, click View on the menu bar, point to Grids & Guides, then click Hide Guides.

19. Click View on the menu bar, then click Fit Page in Window.

20. Compare your document to Figure 44, click File on the menu bar, click Save, then close Independence.

FIGURE 44
Completed Skills Review, Part 1

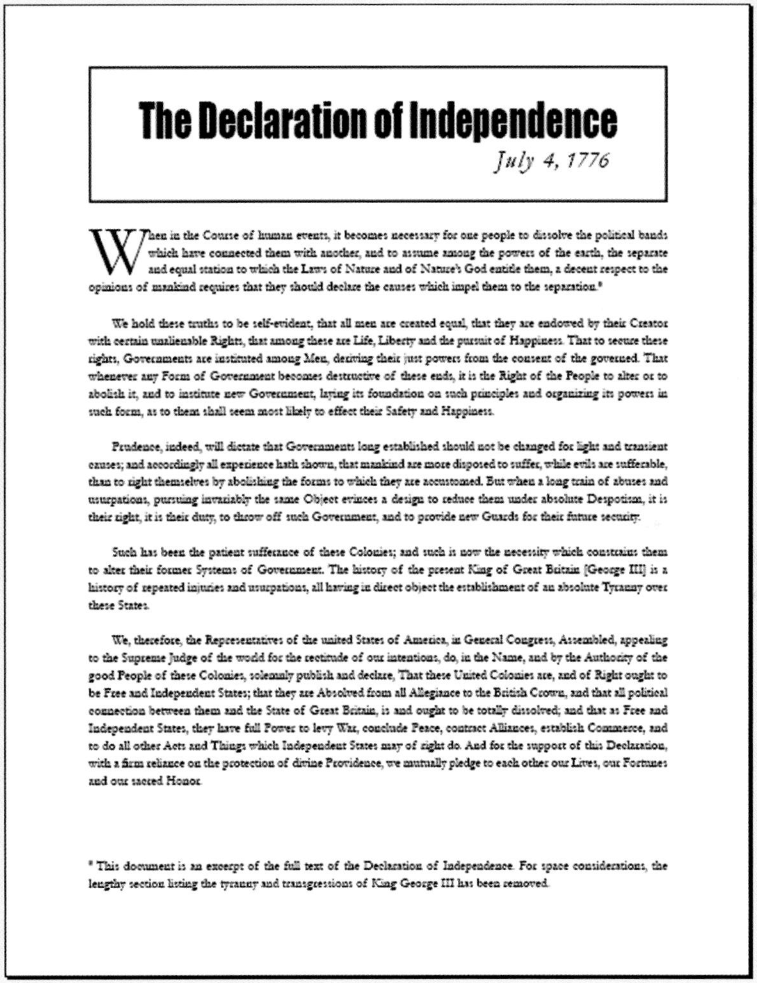

The Declaration of Independence

July 4, 1776

When in the Course of human events, it becomes necessary for one people to dissolve the political bands which have connected them with another, and to assume among the powers of the earth, the separate and equal station to which the Laws of Nature and of Nature's God entitle them, a decent respect to the opinions of mankind requires that they should declare the causes which impel them to the separation.*

We hold these truths to be self-evident, that all men are created equal, that they are endowed by their Creator with certain unalienable Rights, that among these are Life, Liberty and the pursuit of Happiness. That to secure these rights, Governments are instituted among Men, deriving their just powers from the consent of the governed. That whenever any Form of Government becomes destructive of these ends, it is the Right of the People to alter or to abolish it, and to institute new Government, laying its foundation on such principles and organizing its powers in such form, as to them shall seem most likely to effect their Safety and Happiness.

Prudence, indeed, will dictate that Governments long established should not be changed for light and transient causes; and accordingly all experience hath shown, that mankind are more disposed to suffer, while evils are sufferable, than to right themselves by abolishing the forms to which they are accustomed. But when a long train of abuses and usurpations, pursuing invariably the same Object evinces a design to reduce them under absolute Despotism, it is their right, it is their duty, to throw off such Government, and to provide new Guards for their future security.

Such has been the patient sufferance of these Colonies; and such is now the necessity which constrains them to alter their former Systems of Government. The history of the present King of Great Britain [George III] is a history of repeated injuries and usurpations, all having in direct object the establishment of an absolute Tyranny over these States.

We, therefore, the Representatives of the united States of America, in General Congress, Assembled, appealing to the Supreme Judge of the world for the rectitude of our intentions, do, in the Name, and by the Authority of the good People of these Colonies, solemnly publish and declare, That these United Colonies are, and of Right ought to be Free and Independent States; that they are Absolved from all Allegiance to the British Crown, and that all political connection between them and the State of Great Britain, is and ought to be totally dissolved; and that as Free and Independent States, they have full Power to levy War, conclude Peace, contract Alliances, establish Commerce, and to do all other Acts and Things which Independent States may of right do. And for the support of this Declaration, with a firm reliance on the protection of divine Providence, we mutually pledge to each other our Lives, our Fortunes and our sacred Honor.

* This document is an excerpt of the full text of the Declaration of Independence. For space considerations, the lengthy section listing the tyranny and transgressions of King George III has been removed.

Create and apply styles.

1. Open ID 2-5.indd, then save it as **Toy Breeds**.
2. Click the Character Styles panel list arrow, then click New Character Style.
3. Type **Breeds** in the Style Name text box, then click Basic Character Formats in the left column.
4. Change the font to Tahoma, change the size to 14 pt, change the leading to 16 pt, then click OK.
5. Click the Character Styles panel list arrow, click New Character Style, type **Info** in the Style Name text box, then click Basic Character Formats in the left column.
6. Change the font to Garamond, change the style to Italic, change the size to 10 pt, change the leading to 12 pt, then click OK.
7. Select all of the text except for the top two lines, then click Info in the Character Styles panel.
8. Double-click the Affenpinscher headline, then click Breeds in the Character Styles panel.
9. Apply the Breeds character style to the remaining seven breed headlines, then deselect all.
10. Click the Paragraph Styles panel list arrow, then click New Paragraph Style.
11. Type **Info** in the Style Name text box, then click Indents and Spacing in the left column.
12. Click the Alignment list arrow, then click Center.
13. Type **.25** in the Space After text box, then click Paragraph Rules in the left column.
14. Click the list arrow directly below Paragraph Rules, click Rule Below, then click the Rule On check box.
15. Type **.1625** in the Offset text box, type **1** in the Left Indent text box, type **1** in the Right Indent text box, then click OK.
16. Select all of the text except for the top two lines, then click the Align center button in the Paragraph panel.
17. Click in the Affenpinscher description text, then click Info in the Paragraph Styles panel.
18. Apply the Info paragraph style to all the remaining descriptions except for the Pomeranian and the Pug.
19. Click View on the menu bar, point to Grids & Guides, then click Hide Guides.
20. Click before the word bred in the Manchester Terrier description, press and hold [Shift], then press [Enter] (Win) or [return] (Mac).
21. Click before the phrase even-tempered in the "Pug" description, press and hold [Shift], press [Enter] (Win) or [return] (Mac), click before the word and in the "Pug" description, press and hold [Shift], then press [Enter] (Win) or [return] (Mac). (*Hint*: Your text may break differently. Correct any other "bad breaks" you see.)
22. Save your work, compare your screen to Figure 45, then close Toy Breeds.

FIGURE 45
Completed Skills Review, Part 2

TOY BREEDS

A Guide to Small Dog Breeds

Affenpinscher
One of the oldest of the toy breeds, the Affenpinscher originated in Europe. The Affenpinscher is noted for its great loyalty and affection.

Chihuahua
A graceful, alert and swift dog, the Chihuahua is a clannish breed which tends to recognize and prefer its own breed for association.

Maltese
Known as the "ancient dog of Malta," the Maltese has been known as the aristocrat of the canine world for more than 28 centuries.

Manchester Terrier
Dubbed "the gentleman's terrier," this dog was bred in Manchester, England to kill vermin and to hunt small game.

Pekingese
Sacred in China, the Pekingese is a dignified dog who is happy in a rural or urban setting.

Poodle
The national dog of France, Poodles are known for their retrieving capabilities in cold water.

Pomeranian
A descendant of the sled dogs of Iceland and Lapland, the "Pom" is hearty and strong despite his fragile appearance.

Pug
One of the oldest breeds, the Pug is an even-tempered breed who is playful, outgoing and dignified.

Working with Text

Edit text.

1. Open ID 2-6.indd, then save it as **Declaration Edit**.

2. Click at the beginning of the first paragraph.

3. Click Edit on the menu bar, then click Find/Change.

4. Type **IV** in the Find what text box, then type **III** in the Change to text box. (*Hint*: Drag the dialog box out of the way if you cannot see your document.)

5. Click Find. (*Hint*: You want to change the IV in George IV to III, as in George III, however, the spell checker finds all instances of "IV" such as in the word "deriving.")

6. Click the Case Sensitive button in the middle of the Find/Change dialog box (a capital "A" and a lowercase "a" icon), then click Find.

7. Click Change All, click OK in the dialog box that tells you that two replacements were made, then click Done in the Find/Change dialog box.

8. Click before the drop cap in the first paragraph, click Edit on the menu bar, point to Spelling, then click Check Spelling.

9. For the query on the word "Safty," click Safety at the top of the Suggested Corrections list, then click Change.

10. Click Ignore All to ignore the query on hath.

11. Click Ignore All to ignore all instances of III.

12. Click before Assembled in the Change To text box in the Check Spelling dialog box, press [Spacebar] once, then click Change.

13. Click Done.

14. Save your work, deselect, compare your screen to Figure 46, then close Declaration Edit.

FIGURE 46
Completed Skills Review, Part 3

You are a freelance designer. Your client returns a document to you, telling you that she wants you to make a change to a drop cap. She says that, instead of the first letter only being formatted as a drop cap, she wants the entire first word to be more prominent on the page.

1. Open ID 2-7.indd, then save it as **Drop Cap Modifications**.

2. Click the Zoom Tool, then drag a selection box around the first paragraph.

3. Click the Type Tool, click after the W drop cap, double-click the 1 in the Drop Cap One or More Characters text box in the Paragraph panel, then type **4**.

4. Select the letters "hen," click the Character panel list arrow, click All Caps, click the Character panel list arrow again, then click Superscript.

5. Click between the N in WHEN and the I in the word in, then type **100** in the Kerning text box.

6. Select "HEN," then type **–10** in the Baseline Shift text box in the Character panel.

7. Click between the W and H in the word WHEN, then type **–50** in the Kerning text box.

8. Save your work, compare your screen to Figure 47, then close Drop Cap Modifications.

FIGURE 47
Completed Project Builder 1

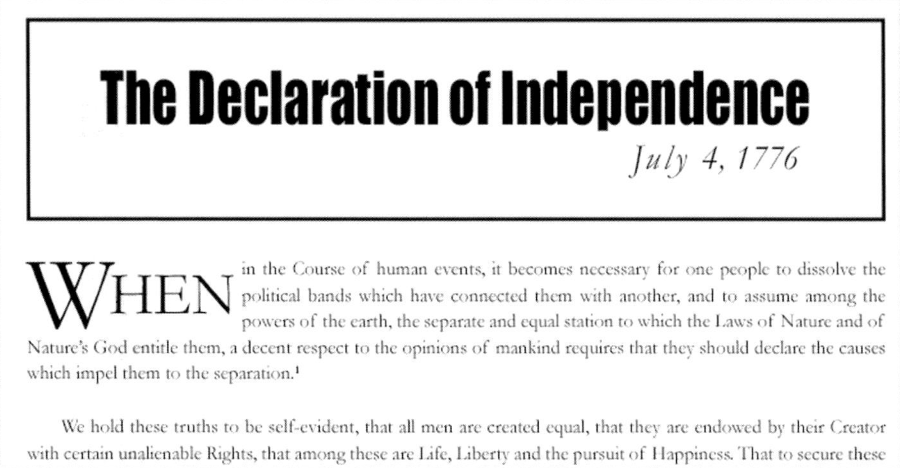

The Declaration of Independence
July 4, 1776

WHEN in the Course of human events, it becomes necessary for one people to dissolve the political bands which have connected them with another, and to assume among the powers of the earth, the separate and equal station to which the Laws of Nature and of Nature's God entitle them, a decent respect to the opinions of mankind requires that they should declare the causes which impel them to the separation.[1]

We hold these truths to be self-evident, that all men are created equal, that they are endowed by their Creator with certain unalienable Rights, that among these are Life, Liberty and the pursuit of Happiness. That to secure these

You have designed a document about miniature pinschers. Your client calls you with changes. He wants to show small pictures of miniature pinschers in the document, one beside each paragraph. He asks you to reformat the document to create space where the small pictures can be inserted.

1. Open ID 2-8.indd, then save it as **Hanging Indents**.

2. Select the four paragraphs of body copy, then change the first line left indent to 0.

3. Change the left indent to 2 in, then change the right indent to .5 in.

4. Create a half-inch space after each paragraph.

5. Type **–1.5** in the First Line Left Indent text box, then deselect all.

6. Select the second paragraph, then type **–10** in the Tracking text box to move the last word Pinscher up to the previous text line.

7. Save your work, deselect all, compare your screen to Figure 48, then close Hanging Indents.

FIGURE 48
Completed Project Builder 2

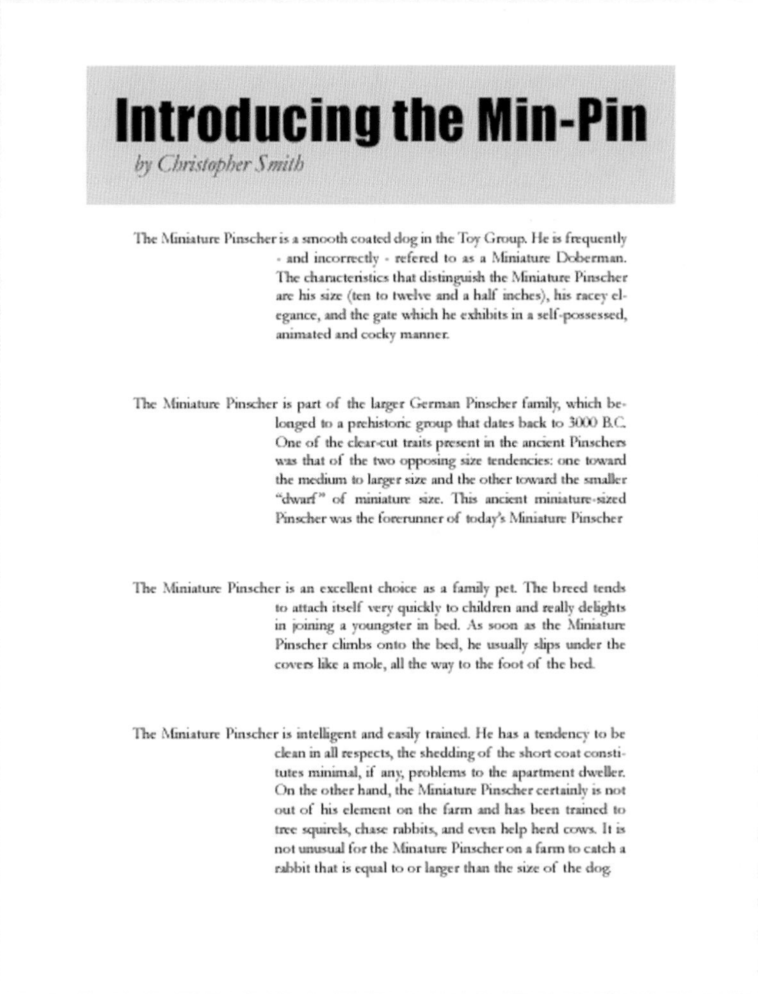

Introducing the Min-Pin
by Christopher Smith

The Miniature Pinscher is a smooth coated dog in the Toy Group. He is frequently - and incorrectly - refered to as a Miniature Doberman. The characteristics that distinguish the Miniature Pinscher are his size (ten to twelve and a half inches), his racey elegance, and the gate which he exhibits in a self-possessed, animated and cocky manner.

The Miniature Pinscher is part of the larger German Pinscher family, which belonged to a prehistoric group that dates back to 3000 B.C. One of the clear-cut traits present in the ancient Pinschers was that of the two opposing size tendencies: one toward the medium to larger size and the other toward the smaller "dwarf" of miniature size. This ancient miniature-sized Pinscher was the forerunner of today's Miniature Pinscher

The Miniature Pinscher is an excellent choice as a family pet. The breed tends to attach itself very quickly to children and really delights in joining a youngster in bed. As soon as the Miniature Pinscher climbs onto the bed, he usually slips under the covers like a mole, all the way to the foot of the bed.

The Miniature Pinscher is intelligent and easily trained. He has a tendency to be clean in all respects, the shedding of the short coat constitutes minimal, if any, problems to the apartment dweller. On the other hand, the Miniature Pinscher certainly is not out of his element on the farm and has been trained to tree squirels, chase rabbits, and even help herd cows. It is not unusual for the Miniature Pinscher on a farm to catch a rabbit that is equal to or larger than the size of the dog.

You are designing a title treatment for a poster for the new music CD titled "Latin Lingo." After typing the title, you realize immediately that the phrase poses obvious kerning challenges. You note that the central letters—TIN LIN—appear close together, but the outer letters are much further apart. You decide to kern the outer letters to bring them closer together.

1. Open ID 2-9.indd, then save it as **Latin Lingo**.

2. Using the Type Tool, click between the A and T, then apply a kerning value of −105.

3. Apply a kerning value of −75 between the N and the G.

4. Apply a kerning value of −30 between the G and the O.

5. Save your work, compare your screen to Figure 49, then close Latin Lingo.

FIGURE 49
Completed Design Project

LATIN LINGO

Your group has been assigned the task of designing a headline for a billboard for the movie "Crushing Impact." The client has asked for a finished design in black letters on a white background. As the leader of the group, you decide first to engage the group in a discussion before you design the title.

Discussion.

1. Open ID 2-10.indd, then save it as **Crushing Impact**.

2. Have the group regard the title for a full minute.

3. Have the group discuss what font family might be best for the title.

4. Does the title demand a big, bold font, or could it work in a fine, delicate font?

5. Should the two words be positioned side by side, or one on top of the other?

6. Does the title itself suggest that, visually, one word should be positioned on top of the other?

Exercise.

1. Position the word Impact on a second line, select all the text, change the font to Impact, then change the font size to 60 pt.

2. Select the word Impact, change the horizontal scale to 200, then change the vertical scale to 80.

3. Select the word Crushing, change the horizontal scale to 50, change the font size to 177, then change the leading to 203.

FIGURE 50
Completed Group Project

4. Expand the height of the text box, select the word Impact, then change the leading to 39.

5. Save your work, compare your screen to Figure 50, then close Crushing Impact.

chapter

3

SETTING UP A
DOCUMENT

1. Create a new document

2. Create master pages

3. Apply master pages to document pages

4. Place text and thread text

5. Modify master pages and document pages

6. Create new sections and wrap text

Starting a new document is often a critical phase, because you will make decisions that determine the fundamental properties of the layout. When you start a new document, you specify the size of the document, the number of pages in the document, and the basic layout of the document. At this stage, you also position columns and guides to help you plan out and work with the layout. Though all of these elements can be modified, it is best if you have already determined these basic properties beforehand, so that you will not need to go back and "retro-fit" the document and its design.

Chapter 3 explores all of the basic principles and features that Adobe InDesign

offers for setting up a new document. You will create a simple layout using master pages, and you will create placeholders for text, graphics, and page numbers. You will also learn how to import or place text into a document and how to "thread" text from page to page.

Keep in mind that this is not a chapter about *design* or designing a layout. Instead, Chapter 3 is an exploration of InDesign's basic tools for setting up and structuring a layout so that you can simplify your work, avoid time-consuming repetition of your efforts, and ensure a consistent layout from page to page.

Tools You'll Use

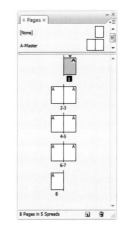

CREATE A NEW
DOCUMENT

What You'll Do

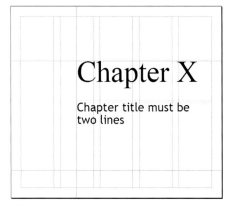

Chapter X

Chapter title must be
two lines

▶ In this lesson, you will create a new document, position guides on a master page,
and create a placeholder for a headline.

Creating a New Document

When you are ready to create a new
document in InDesign, you begin in the
New Document dialog box, shown in
Figure 1. In the New Document dialog
box, you specify the number of pages the
document will contain. You also specify
the **page size** or **trim size**—the width
and height of the finished document. In
addition, you specify whether or not the
document will have **facing pages**. When
you choose this option, the document is
created with left and right pages that *face*
each other in a spread, such as you would
find in a magazine. If this option is not
selected, each page stands alone, like a
stack of pages.

The New Document dialog box also allows
you to specify the width of **margins** on the
outer edges of the page and the number of
columns that will be positioned on the
page. Margins and columns are very useful
as layout guides, and they play an important
role in flowing text. When working with

FIGURE 1
New Document dialog box

*Document Preset
list arrow*

*Enter number of pages
that you want in your
document here*

Page size options

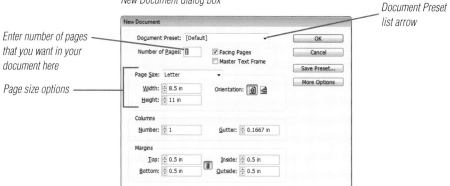

columns, the term **gutter** refers to the space between the columns. Figure 2 shows margins and columns on a typical page.

When creating a document with very specific settings that you plan on using again and again, you can save the settings as a preset by clicking Save Preset in the New Document dialog box. Your named preset will then become available in the Document Preset list in the New Document dialog box.

Understanding Master Pages

Imagine that you are creating a layout for a book and that every chapter title page will have the same layout format. If that book had 20 chapters, you would need to create that chapter title page 20 times. And you'd need to be careful to make the layout consistent every time you created the page. Now imagine that you've finished your layout, but your editor wants you to change the location of the title on the page. That would mean making the same change—20 times!

Not so with master pages. **Master pages** are templates that you create for a page layout. Once created, you apply the master page to the document pages you want to base on that layout. With master pages, you create a layout one time, then use it as many times as you like. Working with master pages saves you from time-consuming repetition of efforts, and it offers consistency between document pages that are meant to have the same layout.

So what happens when your editor asks for that change in location of the title? Simply make the change to the master page, and the change will be reflected on all the document pages based on that master.

When you create a new document, one default master page is created and listed in the Pages panel, shown in Figure 3. The Pages panel is command central for all things relating to pages. You use the Pages panel to add, delete, and reorder document pages. You also use the Pages panel to add, delete, and apply master pages to document pages.

FIGURE 2
Identifying margins and columns

FIGURE 3
Pages panel

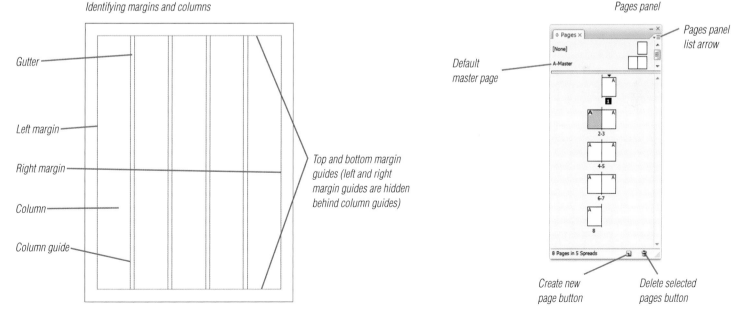

Gutter

Left margin

Right margin

Column

Column guide

Top and bottom margin guides (left and right margin guides are hidden behind column guides)

Default master page

Pages panel list arrow

Create new page button

Delete selected pages button

Creating Master Items on Master Pages

In InDesign, text is positioned in **text frames** and graphics are positioned in **graphics frames**. To create a text frame, you click the Type Tool and then drag it in the document window. You can then type text into the text frame. You use the Rectangle, Ellipse, or Polygon Frame Tools in the same way to create graphics frames.

When you create a frame for text or graphics on a master page, it is referred to as a **master item**. All objects on the master are called master items and function as a place where objects on the document pages are to be positioned. For example, if you had a book broken down into chapters and you created a master page for the chapter title pages, you would create a text frame placeholder for the chapter title text. This text frame would appear on every document page that uses the chapter title master page. Working this way—with the text frame placeholder on the master page—you can feel certain that the location of the chapter title will be consistent on every chapter title page in the book. It is easy to recognize master items on document pages because they are surrounded by a dotted border. Master items on document pages are locked by default. This ensures consistent placement of objects throughout a publication. To select a master item on a document page, press and hold [Shift][Ctrl](Win) or [Shift] ⌘ (Mac), then click the master item.

Understanding Guides

Guides, as shown in Figure 4, are horizontal or vertical lines that you position on a page. As their name suggests, guides are used to help guide you in aligning objects on the page. When the Snap to Guides command is checked, objects adhere more readily to guides. When you position an object near a guide, the object jumps or "snaps" to the guide, making it very easy to align objects with guides.

> **QUICK**TIP
> To turn Snap to Guides on, click View on the menu bar, point to Grids & Guides, then click Snap to Guides to add a check mark, if necessary.

Creating Guides

You have a number of options for creating guides. You can create them manually by "pulling" them out from the horizontal and vertical rulers. You can also use the Create Guides command on the Layout menu. Once created, guides can be selected, moved, and deleted, if necessary. You can also change the color of guides, which sometimes makes it easier to see them, depending on the colors used in your document.

FIGURE 4
Identifying guides

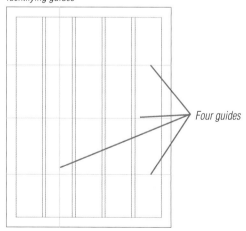

Four guides

Locking column guides

InDesign CS3 lets you lock Column Guides independently from any ruler guides you create. Click View on the menu bar, point to Grids & Guides, and then click Lock Column Guides to add or remove the check mark, which toggles the lock on or off. By default, column guides are locked.

Changing the Color of Guides, Margins, and Columns

By default, guides are cyan, columns are violet, and margins are magenta. Depending on your preferences and on the color of objects in the layout you are creating, you may want to change the color of guides, columns, and margins.

In InDesign, you modify guide colors by selecting them, then clicking the Ruler Guides command on the Layout menu. Choosing a new color in the Ruler Guides dialog box affects only the selected guides. When you create more guides, they will be created in the default color.

You modify the color of margins and columns in the Guides & Pasteboard section of the Preferences dialog box. Once you've modified the color of margins and columns, each new page you create in an existing document will appear with those colors. However, when you create a new document, the margins and columns will appear in their default colors.

Choosing Default Colors for Guides, Margins, and Columns

When you choose colors for guides, margins, and columns, you may want those choices to affect every document you create. You do so by making the color changes in the appropriate dialog boxes without any documents open. The new colors will be applied in all new documents created thereafter. Remember, if you change default colors when a document is open, the changes are only applied to that document.

Using the Transform Panel

The Transform panel identifies a selected object's width and height, and its horizontal and vertical locations on the page. As shown in Figure 5, the width and height of the selected object appears in the Width and Height text boxes of the Transform panel.

When you position an object on a page, you need some way to describe that object's position on the page. InDesign defines the position of an object using X and Y location values in the Transform panel. To work with X and Y locations, you first need to understand that the **zero point** of the page is, by default, at the top left corner of the page. X and Y locations are made in reference to that zero point.

There are nine reference points in the Transform panel that correspond to the

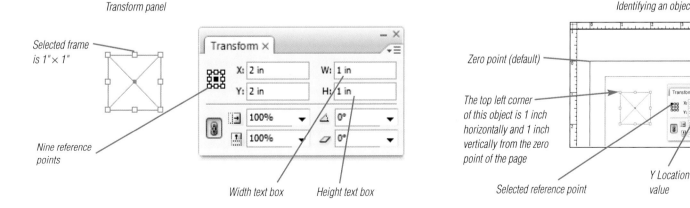

FIGURE 5
Transform panel

Selected frame is 1" × 1"

Nine reference points

Width text box   Height text box

FIGURE 6
Identifying an object's X and Y locations

Zero point (default)

The top left corner of this object is 1 inch horizontally and 1 inch vertically from the zero point of the page

Selected reference point   Y Location value   X Location value

nine points available on a selected item's bounding box. Clicking a reference point tells InDesign that you wish to see the horizontal and vertical locations of that point of the selected object.

When an object is selected, the X Location value is the horizontal location—how far it is across the page—and the Y Location value is the vertical location—how far it is down the page. The selected object in Figure 6 has an X Location of 1 inch and a Y Location of 1 inch. This means that its top left point is 1 inch across the page and 1 inch down. Why the top left point? Because that is the reference point chosen in the Transform panel, also shown in Figure 6.

QUICKTIP

X and Y Location values for circles are determined by the reference points of the bounding box that is placed around circles when they are selected.

Be sure to note that the text boxes in the Transform panel are interactive. For example, if you select an object and find that its X Location value is 2, you can enter 3 in the X Location text box, press [Enter] (Win) or [return] (Mac), and the object will be relocated to the new location on the page. You can also change the width or height of a selected object by changing the value in the Width or Height text boxes.

QUICKTIP

You can perform calculations in the text boxes in the Transform panel. For example, you could select an object whose width is three inches. By typing 3 - .625 in the W text box, you can reduce the object's width to 2.375 inches. What a powerful feature!

Using the Control Panel

The Control panel docked at the top of the document window by default, is similar to the Transform panel. It offers the same settings and ability to modify a selected object. For example, you can change the width and height of a frame using the Control panel, just as you can with the Transform panel.

Unlike the Transform panel, the Control panel offers additional options for frames including changing the frame's stroke weight and stroke style.

The options in the Control panel change based on the type of object selected. For example, if a block of text is selected, the Control panel changes to show all of the type-related options for modifying text, such as changing the font or font size. In Figure 7, the Control panel shows options for a graphics frame.

QUICKTIP

The Info panel displays information about the current document and selected objects, such as text and graphics frames. For example, if you click inside a text frame with the Type Tool, the Info panel displays the number of characters, words, lines, and paragraphs in the frame. If you click the same text frame with the Selection Tool, you can find out the size and location of the text frame. The Info panel is available only for viewing information. You cannot make changes to a selected object using this panel.

FIGURE 7
Control panel

| | X: | 1.5 in | W: | 1.875 in | | | 100% | ▼ | | △ | 0° | ▼ |
| | Y: | 1.9 in | H: | 1.75 in | | | 100% | ▼ | | | 0° | ▼ |

Setting up a Document

Using the Transform Panel to Transform Objects

Transform is a term used to describe the act of moving an object, scaling it, skewing it, or rotating it. You can do all of the above in the Transform or Control panels. Figure 8 shows a rectangular frame positioned between two guides. In Figure 9, the same frame has been rotated 90 degrees—note the 90° value in the Rotation Angle text box in the Transform panel. Note also that the object was rotated at its center point. This is because the center reference

point has been selected as the **point of origin** for the transformation. Think of the point of origin as the point from where the transformation happens. Whichever reference point is selected determines the point of origin for the transformation of the selected object.

Figure 10 shows the frame from Figure 8 rotated 90 degrees. However, this time, the point of origin for the rotation was set at the lower-left corner of the object. Note how differently the rotation affected the object. After the transformation, the

lower-right reference point is selected, because the original lower-left corner of the box is now the lower-right corner.

Don't trouble yourself trying to guess ahead of time how the choice of a point of origin in conjunction with a transformation will affect an object. Sometimes it will be easy to foresee how the object will be transformed; sometimes you'll need to use trial and error. The important thing for you to remember is that the point of origin determines the point where the transformation takes place.

FIGURE 8
A rectangle with its center point identified

FIGURE 9
Rectangle rotated 90 degrees at its center point

FIGURE 10
Rectangle after being rotated 90 degrees from its lower-left point

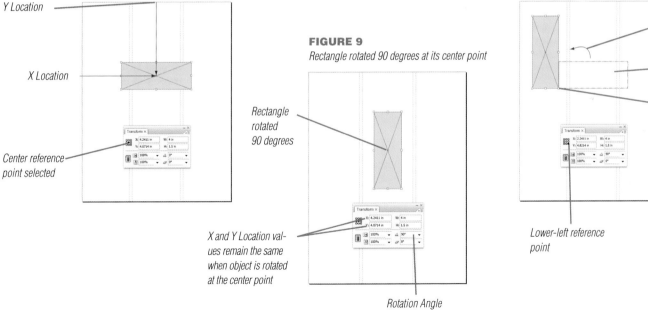

Y Location

X Location

Center reference point selected

Rectangle rotated 90 degrees

X and Y Location values remain the same when object is rotated at the center point

Rotation Angle text box

Rotation angle

Original position of object

Object rotated from its original position 90 degrees from its lower-left point

Lower-left reference point

Create a new document

1. Start InDesign, click **Edit** (Win) or **InDesign** (Mac) on the menu bar, point to **Preferences**, then click **Units & Increments**.

2. Click the **Horizontal list arrow**, click **Inches**, click the **Vertical list arrow**, click **Inches**, then click **OK**.

3. Click **File** on the menu bar, point to **New**, then click **Document**.

4. Type **12** in the Number of Pages text box, then verify that the Facing Pages check box is checked.

5. Type **8** in the Width text box, press **[Tab]**, type **7** in the Height text box, then click the **Landscape Orientation button**.

   TIP Press [Tab] to move your cursor forward from text box to text box in InDesign dialog boxes. Press [Shift][Tab] to move backward from text box to text box.

6. Type **5** in the Number text box in the Columns section, then type **.25** in the Gutter text box.

7. Type **.375** in the Top, Bottom, Inside, and Outside Margin text boxes so that your New Document dialog box resembles Figure 11.

8. Click **OK**, then look at the first page of the document, which should resemble Figure 12.

9. Save the document as **Setup**.

You set the Units & Increments preferences to specify that you will be working with inches for horizontal and vertical measurements. You then created a new document using the New Document dialog box. You specified the number of pages in the document, the page size for each page, and the number of columns on each page.

FIGURE 11
Entering values in the New Document dialog box

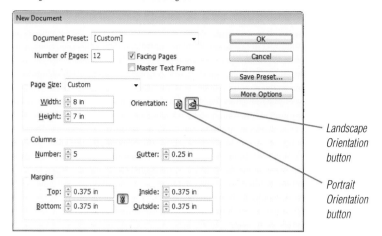

Landscape
Orientation
button

Portrait
Orientation
button

FIGURE 12
Identifying basic elements on a page

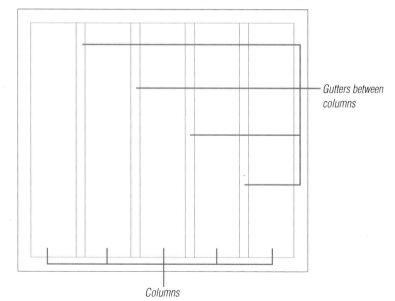

Gutters between
columns

Columns

Setting up a Document

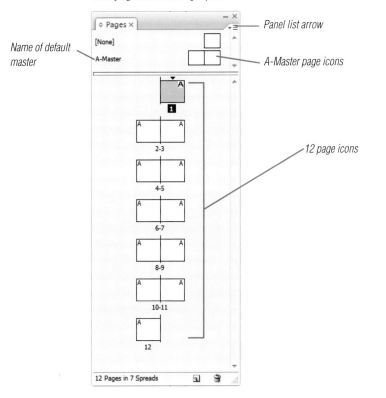

FIGURE 13

Identifying icons in the Pages panel

Name of default master

Panel list arrow

A-Master page icons

12 page icons

Rename and modify the default master page

1. Click **Window** on the menu bar, point to **Workspace**, click **Default Workspace**, then click the **Pages panel name tab** on the right side of the window.

2. Looking at the Pages panel, as shown in Figure 13, note that the document contains the 12 pages that you specified in the New Document dialog box and that the default master page is named A-Master.

   TIP   You may need to resize the Pages panel to see all of the page icons.

3. Click **A-Master** once to select it, click the **Pages panel list arrow**, then click **Master Options for "A-Master"**.

4. Type **Chapter Right Page** in the Name text box of the Master Options dialog box, then type **1** in the Number of Pages text box so that your dialog box resembles Figure 14.

   In this layout design, the chapter title page will always occur on a right-hand page. Therefore, this master needs to be only one page.

5. Click **OK**, then note the changes in the Pages panel.

   The default master page is now named A-Chapter Right Page and listed as a single page.

You renamed the A-Master master page and redefined it as a single page.

FIGURE 14

Master Options dialog box

Master Options

Prefix: A

Name: Chapter Right Page

Based on Master: [None]

Number of Pages: 1

OK

Cancel

Add guides to a master page

1. Double-click **A-Chapter Right Page** in the Pages panel, then note that the page menu at the lower-left corner of the document window lists A-Chapter Right Page.

   A-Chapter Right Page is now the active page.

2. Click **Window** on the menu bar, point to **Object & Layout**, then click **Transform**.

3. If rulers are not visible at the top and left of the document window, click **View** on the menu bar, then click **Show Rulers**.

4. Click the **Selection Tool** ▶, position the pointer over the horizontal ruler, then click and drag a guide from the ruler about 1.5 inches down the page, as shown in Figure 15.

   > TIP As you drag the new guide onto the page, the value in the Y Location text box in the Transform panel continually changes to show the guide's current location.

5. Release the mouse button to position the guide at approximately 1.5 inches down the page.

6. Type **1.9** in the Y Location text box in the Transform panel, then press **[Enter]** (Win) or **[return]** (Mac).

   The guide jumps to the specific vertical location you entered.

7. Drag a second guide from the horizontal ruler, and drop the guide anywhere on the page, then use the Transform panel to position it so that its Y Location value is 5.9 in.

   (continued)

FIGURE 15
Adding a horizontal guide

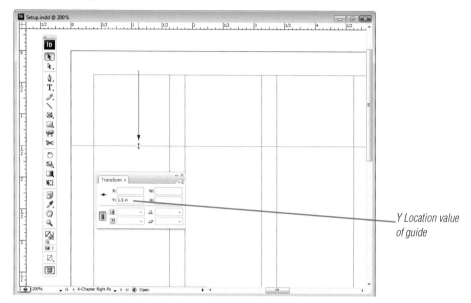

Y Location value of guide

Using the Transform Again commands

InDesign CS3 uses one of the great and classic features of Illustrator: the Transform Again command. When you execute a transformation, you can repeat it. The Transform Again command on the Object menu includes four ways to repeat transformations. Be sure to check out the Transform Sequence Again command. This command goes one step beyond Transform Again—it repeats entire sequences. So if you make a series of transformations to a selected object, as long as you don't change the selection, the Transform Sequence Again command will repeat the entire series of transformations. Experiment with these very important—and fun—commands.

FIGURE 16
Viewing the master page with three guides

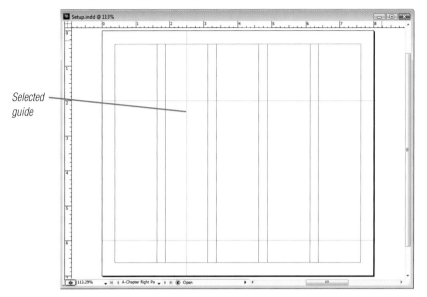

Selected guide

8. Drag a guide from the vertical ruler on the left side of the document window, then use the Transform panel to position it with an X Location value of 2 in.

9. Click the **first horizontal guide** you positioned at 1.9 inches to select it, double-click the **Y Location text box** in the Transform panel, type **2**, then press **[Enter]** (Win) or **[return]** (Mac).

    The guide is moved and positioned exactly two inches from the top of the document.

    TIP Selected guides appear darker blue in color.

10. Change the location of the horizontal guide positioned approximately at 5.9 inches to 6 inches, then change the location of the vertical guide to 2.5 inches.

    As shown in Figure 16, the vertical guide is still selected.

You positioned guides on the master page by dragging them from the horizontal and vertical rulers. You used the Transform panel to position them at precise locations.

Creating baseline grids for text boxes

A **baseline grid** represents the leading for body text in a document. Each text frame can have its own baseline grid, independent of the document's baseline grid. To specify the baseline grid for a text frame, select the text frame, click Object on the menu bar, click Text Frame Options, and then click the Baseline Options tab. Here you can customize the baseline grid for the selected text frame. You can even apply a color for the grid, which will apply to that text frame only. In order to see a document's baseline grid or any grids within text frames, click View on the menu bar, point to Grids & Guides, and then click Show Baseline Grid.

Create placeholder text frames

1. Click the **Type Tool** 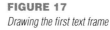, position the cursor approximately where the vertical guide intersects the top horizontal guide, then drag a **text frame** to the right margin.

   Your screen should resemble Figure 17.

2. Type **Chapter X** in the text frame, then select the text.

3. Display the Character panel, set the font to Garamond or a similar font, set the font size to 80 pt, then set the leading to 96 pt (if necessary).

4. Click the **top-left reference point** in the Transform panel, type **1.5** in the Height text box in the Transform panel, then press **[Enter]** (Win) or **[return]** (Mac).

5. Position the Type Tool cursor where the vertical guide intersects the bottom horizontal guide, click and drag toward the top-right corner to create a text frame, then click the **Selection Tool** .

   As shown in Figure 18, the second text frame is selected.

6. Click the **Type Tool** 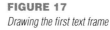, click inside the second text frame, type **Chapter title must be two lines**, then select the text.

7. Set the font to Trebuchet MS or a similar font, set the font size to 32 pt, then set the leading to 33 pt.

8. Click the page to deselect the text so that your page resembles Figure 19.

You created two text frames which will be used as placeholders for chapter numbers and chapter titles in the document.

FIGURE 17
Drawing the first text frame

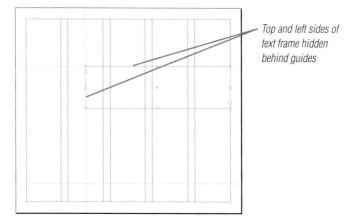

Top and left sides of text frame hidden behind guides

FIGURE 18
Drawing the second text frame

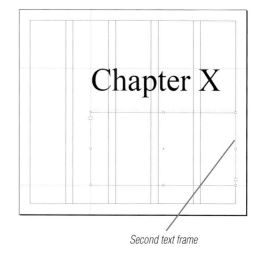

Second text frame

FIGURE 19
Viewing the page with two placeholder text frames

Setting up a Document

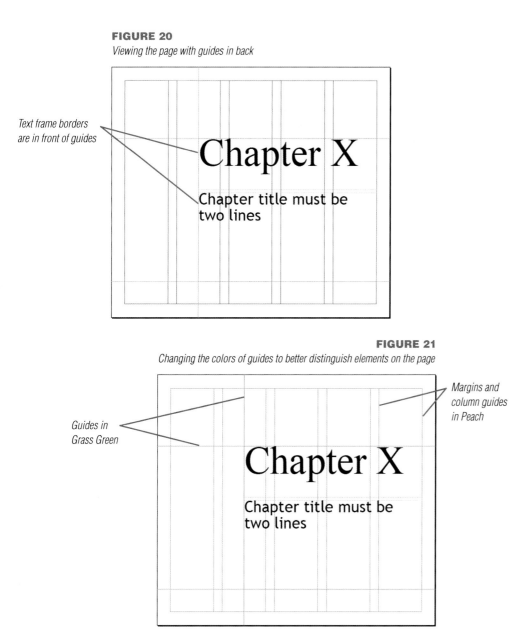

FIGURE 20
Viewing the page with guides in back

Text frame borders
are in front of guides

Chapter X

Chapter title must be
two lines

FIGURE 21
Changing the colors of guides to better distinguish elements on the page

Margins and
column guides
in Peach

Guides in
Grass Green

Chapter X

Chapter title must be
two lines

Change the color of guides, margins, and columns

1. Click **Edit** (Win) or **InDesign** (Mac) on the menu bar, point to **Preferences**, then click **Guides & Pasteboard**.

2. Click the **Guides in Back check box** to select it, then click **OK**.

   As shown in Figure 20, the text frame borders are in front of the guides. Text frame borders are made up of blue dotted lines.

3. Click **Edit** (Win) or **InDesign** (Mac) on the menu bar, point to **Preferences**, then click **Guides & Pasteboard**.

4. In the Color section, click the **Margins list arrow**, then click **Peach**.

5. Click the **Columns list arrow**, click **Peach**, then click **OK**.

6. Click the **Selection Tool**, click the **cyan vertical guide** to select it, press and hold **[Shift]**, click the **top horizontal guide**, then click the **lower horizontal guide**.

   All three cyan guides are selected and appear dark blue.

7. Click **Layout** on the menu bar, then click **Ruler Guides**.

8. Click the **Color list arrow**, click **Grass Green**, then click **OK**.

9. Click the **pasteboard** to deselect the guides, then compare your page to Figure 21.

You changed the color of margins, columns, and guides to improve your ability to distinguish text frames from page guides.

Use the Transform panel to transform text frames

1. Click the **Selection Tool** (if necessary), click anywhere in the lower text frame to select it, click **Object** on the menu bar, then click **Text Frame Options**.

2. In the Vertical Justification section, click the **Align list arrow**, click **Bottom**, then click **OK**.

3. Using Figure 22 as a guide, drag the **top middle handle** of the text frame down to the top of the text.

   TIP   When resizing the text frame, be sure not to make the frame too small to contain the text.

4. With the text frame still selected, click the **middle-left reference point** in the Transform panel, as shown in Figure 23.

   TIP   The selected reference point specifies the point of origin for the transformation.

5. Double-click the **Width (W) text box** in the Transform panel, type **3.875**, then press **[Enter]** (Win) or **[return]** (Mac).

   The width of the selected text frame is reduced to 3.875 inches. Since the point of origin for the transformation was specified as the left edge, only the right side of the text frame moves when the new width is applied.

   (continued)

FIGURE 22
Resizing the height of a text frame

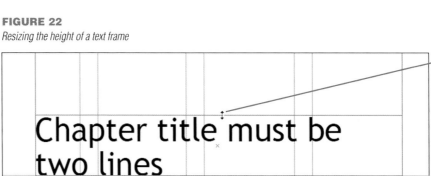

Drag top middle handle to resize text frame

Chapter title must be two lines

FIGURE 23
Selecting a reference point on the Transform panel

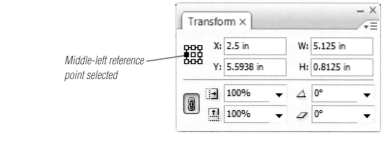

Middle-left reference point selected

Viewing thumbnails on master page
InDesign CS3 provides some very cool and useful new options for viewing the Pages panel. In addition to choosing an icon size for all pages and masters in the Pages panel, you can now choose to show thumbnails of the items on each page and on each master. Click the Pages panel list arrow, click Panel Options, then click the Show Thumbnails check box in the Pages section and/or the Masters section, depending on your needs. Keep in mind, however, that if you view thumbnails, your Pages panel will not match the figures in this book.

FIGURE 24
Repositioning the text frame

FIGURE 25
Viewing the page in Preview mode

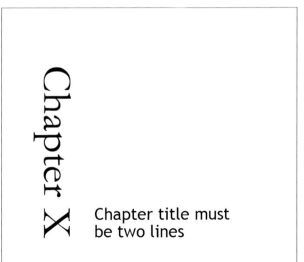

6. Click the **Chapter X text frame**, click the **top-left reference point** on the Transform panel, click the **Transform panel list arrow**, then click **Rotate 90° CW.**

7. Click the **top-left point** on the Transform panel again, change the X Location value to **.375** and the Y Location value to **.875**, then press **[Enter]** (Win) or **[return]** (Mac).

   TIP   When the text frame is repositioned correctly, its lower-left corner will be at the intersection of the left page margin and the bottom horizontal guide, as shown in Figure 24.

8. Display the **Paragraph panel**, then click the **Align right button** .

9. Click **Edit** on the menu bar, click **Deselect All**, click the **Normal button** in the Toolbox, click **Preview**, then press **[Tab]** to hide all panels.

   Your page should resemble Figure 25.

You used the Transform panel to change the width of one text frame and to rotate the other.

CREATE
MASTER PAGES

What You'll Do

Chapter title must
be two lines

In this lesson, you will create two new master pages, create master items for body copy, create automatic page numbering, and create placeholder frames for graphics.

Creating a New Master Page

When you create a new document, a default master page, called A-Master, appears in the top section of the Pages panel. You can use this default master as your first master for the document, and you can also create as many new master pages as you need for the document. You create new master pages by clicking the New Master command on the Pages panel menu.

When you create a new master page, you have the option of giving the master page a new name. This is often very useful for distinguishing one master page from another. For example, you might want to use the name "Body Copy" for master pages that will be used for body copy and then use the name "Chapter Start" for master pages that will be used as a layout for a chapter title page. Figure 26 shows three named master pages in the Pages panel.

When you create a new master page, you have the option of changing the values for the margins and for the number of columns on the new master page.

Loading Master Pages

You can load master pages from one InDesign document to another by simply clicking the Pages panel list arrow, then clicking Load Master Pages. You will be prompted to navigate to the file that has the master pages you wish to load. Select the InDesign document, then click Open. The master pages are added to the Pages panel. You will be prompted to rename master pages that have the same name or replace the existing master pages.

Creating Automatic Page Numbering

When you create a document with multiple pages, chances are you'll want to have page numbers on each page. You could create a text frame on every page, then manually type the page number on every page, but think of what a nightmare that could turn out to be! You would have to create a text frame of the same size and in the same location on every page. Imagine what would happen if you were to remove a page from or add a page to the middle of the document. You'd need to go back and renumber your pages!

Fortunately, InDesign offers a solution for this. You can create placeholders for page numbers on your master pages. Each newly created page will have an automatic page number on it, assuming the page is based on a master page with a page number placeholder. Simply create a text frame on the master page (if you are working with facing pages, create a text frame on both the left and right pages of the spread). Click inside the text frame, click Type on the menu bar, point to Insert Special Character, point to Markers, then click Current Page Number. A letter (that of the master page) will appear in the text frame, as shown in Figure 27.

That letter represents the page number. You can format it using any font, size, and

FIGURE 26
Three master pages in the Pages panel

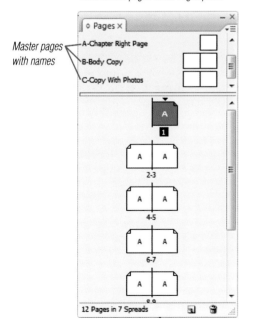

Master pages with names

FIGURE 27
A text frame on a master page containing an auto page number character

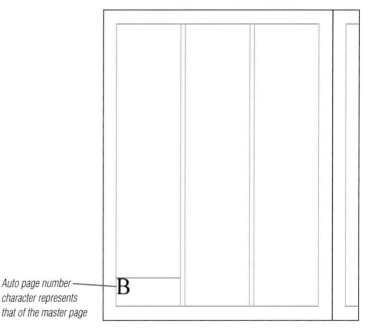

Auto page number character represents that of the master page

alignment that you desire. On the document pages based on that master, the letter in the text frame will appear as the number of the page. The page numbering is automatic. This means that the page number is automatically updated when pages are added to or removed from the document.

When you work with multiple master pages, make sure that each page number placeholder is the same size, in the same location, and formatted the same on each master page. This will make the appearance of page numbers consistent from page to page, regardless of which master a given document page is based on.

Inserting White Space Between Text Characters

In Chapter 2, you learned that you should not press the spacebar more than once to create extra spacing between characters. However, sometimes a single space does not provide enough space between words or characters. You may want to insert additional space to achieve a certain look. In this case, you insert white space.

The Type menu contains commands for inserting white space between words or characters. The two most-used white spaces are **em space** and **en space**. The width of an em space is equivalent to that of the lowercase letter m in the current

typeface at that type size. The width of an en space is narrower—that of the lowercase letter n in that typeface at that type size. Use these commands—not multiple spaces—to insert white space. To insert an em space or an en space, click Type on the menu bar, point to Insert White Space, then click either Em Space or En Space. Figure 28 shows an em space between a page number placeholder and a word.

Inserting Em Dashes and En Dashes

Sometimes you'll want to put a dash between words or characters and you'll find that the dash created by pressing the hyphen

FIGURE 28
Identifying an em space

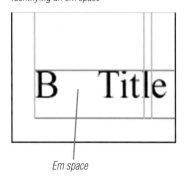

Em space

key is not wide enough. That's because hyphens are shorter than dashes.

InDesign offers two types of dashes—the em dash and the en dash—that you can insert between words or characters. The width of an em dash is equivalent to that of the lowercase letter m in the current typeface at that type size. The width of an en dash is narrower—that of the lowercase letter n in that typeface at that type size. To insert an em dash or an en dash, click Type on the menu bar, point to Insert Special Character, point to Hyphens and Dashes, then click either Em Dash or En Dash. Figure 29 shows an example of an en dash.

Creating a New Master Page Based on Another Master Page

Imagine that you've created a master page for a page in a magazine layout. The master contains master items for the headline, for the body copy, and for the page number. It also contains master items for pictures that will appear on the page. Now imagine that you need to create another master page that will be identical to this master page, with the one exception, that this new master will not contain frames for graphics. You wouldn't want to duplicate all of the work you did to create the first master, would you?

You can create a new master page based on another master page. You do this to avoid repeating efforts and for consistency between masters. In the above example, you would create the new master based on the first master. The new master would appear identical to the first master. You would then modify only the elements that you want to change on the new master, keeping all of the elements that you don't want to change perfectly consistent with the previous master.

Basing a new master on another master is not the same thing as duplicating a master. When one master is based on another, any changes you make to the first master will be updated on the master based on it. Think of how powerful this is. Let's say that your editor tells you to change the type size of the page numbers. If you make that change to the first master, the change will automatically be updated on the master(s) based on it. This offers you a substantial savings in time and effort and provides you with the certainty that the page numbers will be consistent from master to master.

New master pages function in the same manner as the master pages they were based on. Remember that all master items on new master pages will also be locked by default. To unlock a master item, you must press and hold [Shift][Ctrl] (Win) or [Shift]⌘ (Mac) to select those objects on the new master. InDesign does this so that you don't accidentally move or delete objects from the new master or the previous master.

FIGURE 29

Identifying an en dash

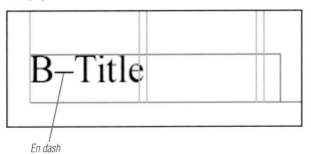

En dash

Create a new master page

1. Press **[Tab]** to show the panels again, click the **Preview button** [▣] on the Toolbox, then click **Normal**.

2. Click the **Pages panel list arrow**, then click **New Master**.

3. Type **Body Copy with Pics** in the Name text box, then type **2** in the Number of Pages text box (if necessary) so that your New Master dialog box resembles Figure 30.

   You need two pages for this master since it will be used for both left and right pages.

4. Click **OK**, note the new master page listing in the Pages panel, click **View** on the menu bar, then click **Fit Spread in Window** (if necessary).

5. Click **Layout** on the menu bar, then click **Margins and Columns**.

6. Click the **Make all settings the same button** [▣] so that you see a broken link icon, double-click the **Inside text box** to select it, type **.5**, then click **OK**.

   The inner margins on both the left and right pages are increased—only on the B-Body Copy with Pics master page.

7. Press and hold **[Ctrl]** (Win) or [⌘] (Mac), then drag a **horizontal guide** onto the spread, positioning it one inch from the top of the page.

   (continued)

FIGURE 30

New Master dialog box

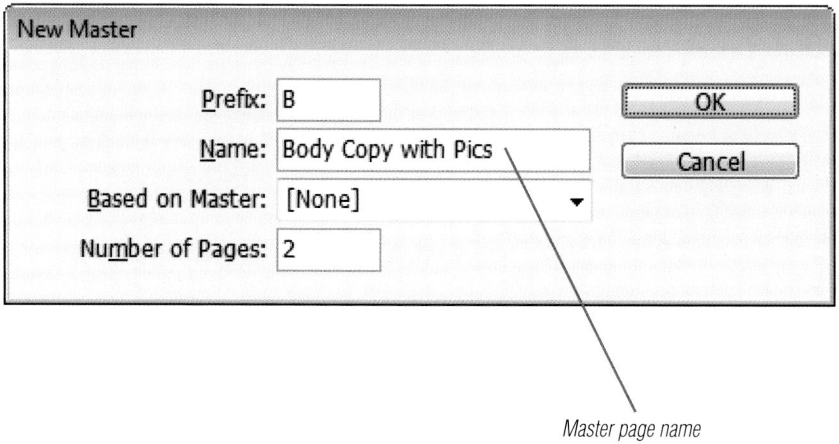

Master page name

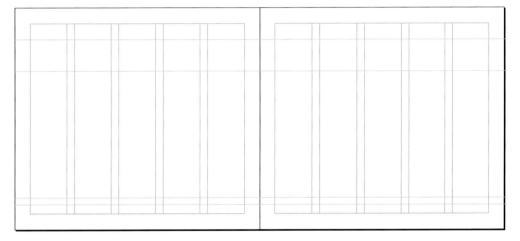

TIP Pressing and holding [Ctrl] (Win) or ⌘ (Mac) creates a spread ruler guide, which extends across both pages of the spread.

8. Using the same method, position three more horizontal guides: one at 2 inches from the top of the page, one at 6 inches from the top of the page, and one at 6.225 inches from the top of the page.

9. Click the page to deselect.

   Because this is a new master page, the guides have reverted to the default cyan color for guides. Your screen should resemble Figure 31.

10. Select all four guides, click **Layout** on the menu bar, click **Ruler Guides**, click the **Color list arrow**, click **Grass Green**, then click **OK**.

    TIP To change the default guide color, open the Ruler Guides dialog box with no InDesign documents open, then select the color you want.

You created and named a new master page, then you modified its margin settings. You also created four spread guides and changed their color.

Create text frames on a master page

1. Click the **Type Tool** , then draw two text frames on the left page of the B-Body Copy with Pics master page in the same locations shown in Figure 32.

2. Click the **Selection Tool** , select the text frame on the right, click **Edit** on the menu bar, then click **Copy**.

3. Click **Edit** on the menu bar, then click **Paste in Place**.

   A copy is pasted exactly above the first text frame.

4. Press and hold **[Shift]**, drag the copy of the text frame to the right page, then position it so that it is aligned with the first two columns on the right page.

   > TIP Pressing and holding [Shift] when dragging an object constrains that object to the axis on which you are moving it.

5. Deselect all, select the smaller text frame on the left page, press and hold **[Shift][Alt]** (Win) or **[Shift][option]** (Mac), then drag a copy to the right page.

   (continued)

FIGURE 32
Positioning two text frames on the left page of the B-Body Copy with Pics master

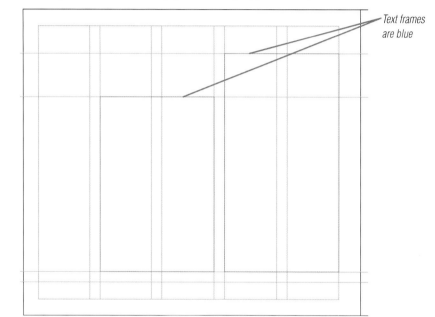

Text frames are blue

FIGURE 33

Positioning two text frames on the right page of the B-Body Copy with Pics master

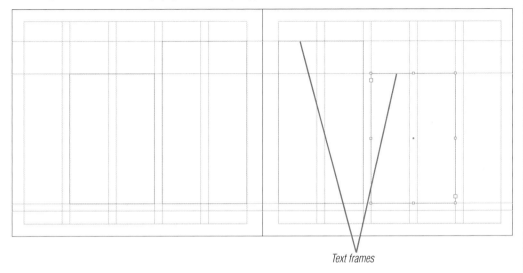

Text frames

FIGURE 34

Positioning a text frame for a headline

Text frame
for headline

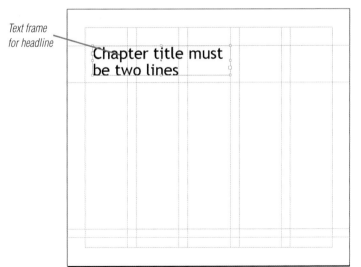

Chapter title must
be two lines

TIP   Pressing and holding [Shift][Alt] (Win)
or [Shift][option] (Mac) when dragging an
object makes a copy of the object.

6. Position the frame so that it is aligned with the third and fourth columns on the right page, as shown in Figure 33.

7. Double-click the **A-Chapter Right Page** title in the Pages panel, select the text frame that includes the text "Chapter title must be two lines," then copy it.

8. Double-click **B-Body Copy with Pics** in the Pages panel, double-click the **left page icon** of the B-Body Copy with Pics master page to center the left page in the window, click **Edit** on the menu bar, then click **Paste**.

9. Position the text frame in the location shown in Figure 34.

10. Display the Paragraph panel (if necessary), then click the **Align right button** 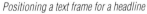 .

You created five text frames on the B master page, which will be used as placeholders for body copy.

Create automatic page numbering and insert white space between characters

1. Click the **Type Tool** T, then draw a text frame on the left page of the B-Body Copy with Pics master, as shown in Figure 35.
2. Click **Type** on the menu bar, point to **Insert Special Character**, point to **Markers**, then click **Current Page Number**.

   The letter B appears in the text frame. This letter will change on document pages to reflect the current document page. For example, on page 4, the B will appear as the number 4.
3. Click **Type** on the menu bar, point to **Insert White Space**, then click **Em Space**.
4. Type the word **Title** so that your text box resembles Figure 36.
5. Click **View** on the menu bar, then click **Fit Spread in Window**.
6. Click the **Selection Tool**, select the text frame, click **Edit** on the menu bar, click **Copy**, click **Edit** on the menu bar again, then click **Paste in Place**.

(continued)

FIGURE 35
Positioning the left page text frame

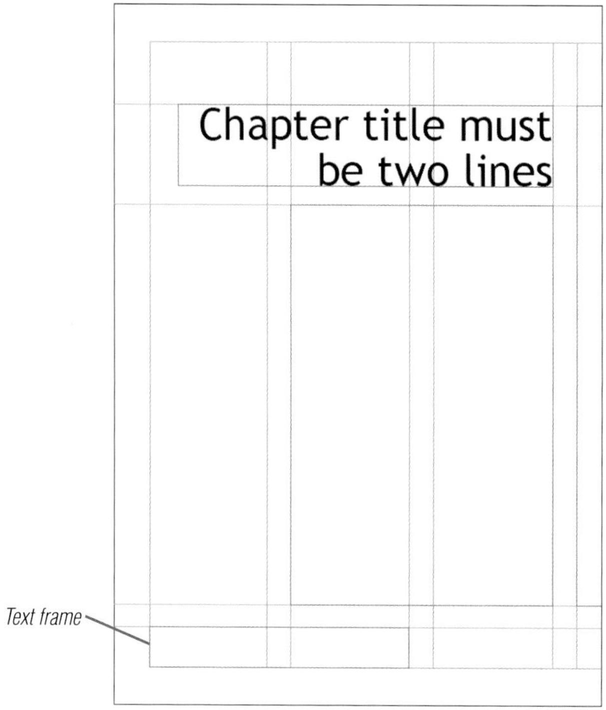
Chapter title must
be two lines
Text frame

FIGURE 36
Viewing the text frame with automatic page numbering

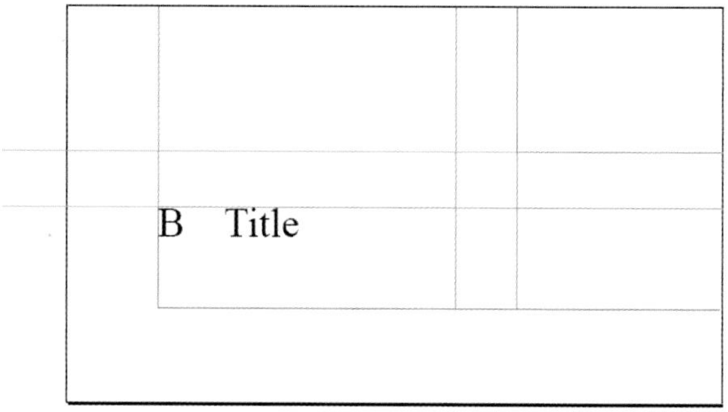
B Title

FIGURE 37
Positioning the right page text frame

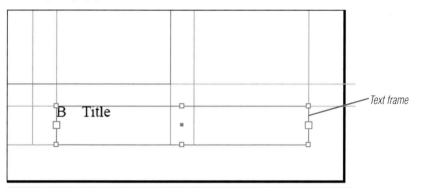

— Text frame

7. Press and hold **[Shift]**, then drag a copy of the text frame so that it is positioned on the right page of the B-Body Copy with Pics master, as shown in Figure 37.

8. Click the **Align right button** ▤ in the Paragraph panel, then delete the B and the white space after the B.

9. Click after the word Title, click **Type** on the menu bar, point to **Insert White Space**, then click **Em Space**.

10. Click **Type** on the menu bar, point to **Insert Special Character**, point to **Markers**, then click **Current Page Number**.

    Your text box should resemble Figure 38.

You created automatic page numbering on the left and right pages of the B-Body Copy with Pics master.

FIGURE 38
Viewing the right text frame with automatic page numbering

Title   B

Create master items on a master page

1. Double-click the **left page icon** of the B-Body Copy with Pics master in the Pages panel to center it in the document window.

2. Click the **Ellipse Frame Tool** , press and hold **[Shift]**, then drag the **pointer** to create an ellipse frame of any size on the left page, as shown in Figure 39.

   Pressing and holding [Shift] constrains the Ellipse Frame Tool to create only a perfect circle.

   TIP   The Ellipse Frame Tool may be hidden beneath the Rectangle Frame Tool or the Polygon Frame Tool.

3. Type **2** in the Width text box in the Transform panel, press **[Tab]**, type **2** in the Height text box, then press **[Enter]** (Win) or **[return]** (Mac).

   The size of the frame changes to a diameter of two inches.

   TIP   You can also use the Control panel to modify the diameter of the circle.

4. Click the **center reference point** in the Transform panel, double-click the **X Location text box**, type **4.65**, press **[Tab]**, type **4** in the Y Location text box, then press **[Enter]** (Win) or **[return]** (Mac).

5. Double-click the **right page icon** of the B-Body Copy with Pics master in the Pages panel to center the page in the window.

6. Click **Edit** (Win) or **InDesign** (Mac) on the menu bar, point to **Preferences**, click **Units & Increments**, click the **Origin list arrow**, click **Page**, then click **OK**.

(continued)

FIGURE 39
Creating an ellipse frame

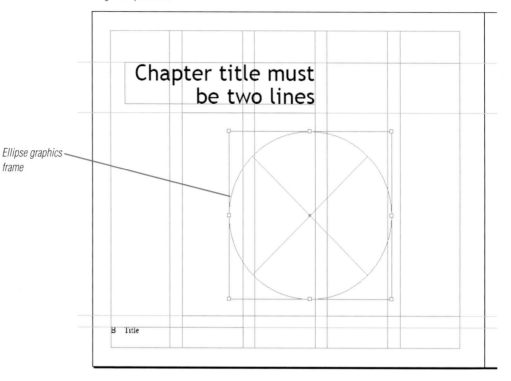

Ellipse graphics frame

Using the Move Pages command

As you have learned, if you have a multiple-page document, you can change the sequence of pages simply by moving them around in the Pages panel. Easy enough. But for documents with more pages—let's say 100 pages—dragging and dropping page icons in the Pages panel isn't so simple. Imagine, for example, trying to drag page 84 so that it follows page 14. Whew! With InDesign CS3's powerful Move Pages command, you can specify which pages you want to move and where you want to move them. Click the Pages panel list arrow, click Move Pages, then choose options in the Move Pages dialog box. Be sure to check it out.

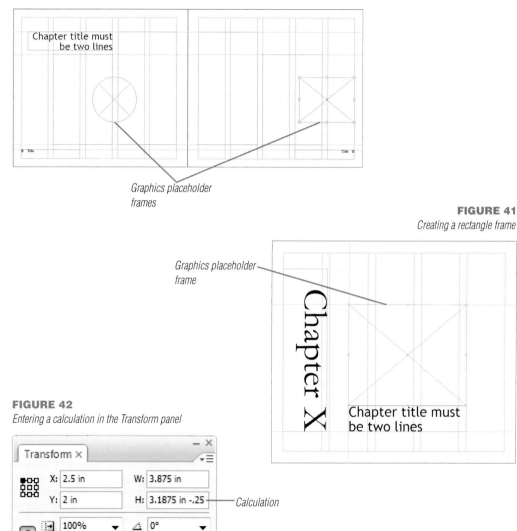

FIGURE 40
Viewing the spread

Chapter title must
be two lines

Graphics placeholder
frames

FIGURE 41
Creating a rectangle frame

Graphics placeholder
frame

Chapter X

Chapter title must
be two lines

FIGURE 42
Entering a calculation in the Transform panel

Transform ×

X: 2.5 in   W: 3.875 in

Y: 2 in   H: 3.1875 in -.25 — Calculation

100%   0°

100%   0°

The horizontal ruler at the top of the window now measures each page, not the entire spread.

7. Using the Hand Tool 👋, move to the right master page, click the **Rectangle Frame Tool** ⊠, draw a rectangle frame of any size anywhere on the right master page, then click the **top-left reference point** in the Transform panel.

8. In the Transform panel, type **5.125** in the X Location text box, type **3** in the Y Location text box, type **2.5** in the Width text box, type **2** in the Height text box, then press **[Enter]** (Win) or **[return]** (Mac).

9. Click **View** on the menu bar, then click **Fit Spread in Window** so that your spread resembles Figure 40.

10. Double-click **A-Chapter Right Page** in the Pages panel, then draw a rectangle frame in the position shown in Figure 41.

    The bottom of the rectangular graphics frame abuts the top of the text frame beneath it.

11. Select the **top-middle reference point** in the Transform panel, click to the right of the value in the Height text box, then type **-.25**, as shown in Figure 42.

    The current value in the Height text box in your Transform panel might differ slightly from the figure.

12. Press **[Enter]** (Win) or **[return]** (Mac).

    The height of the rectangle frame is reduced by .25 inches, and only the bottom edge of the box moves to accommodate the reduction.

You created three frames, which will be used as master items for graphics. You used the Transform panel to specify the sizes of the frames and their locations on the master pages.

Create a new master page based on another master page

1. Click the **Pages panel list arrow**, then click **New Master**.

2. Type **Copy No Pics** in the Name text box of the New Master dialog box.

   The C-Copy No Pics master page will be applied to pages in the document that have no pictures, only text.

3. Click the **Based on Master list arrow**, click **B-Body Copy with Pics**, then click **OK**.

   TIP Since the new master is based on the B-Body Copy with Pics master, it will include everything already positioned on the B-Body Copy with Pics master, such as the automatic page numbering.

   The C-Copy No Pics icons display a B in each of the page icons, as shown in Figure 43. This indicates that the C-Copy No Pics master page is based on the B-Body Copy with Pics master page.

4. Click the **Selection Tool** ▶, press and hold **[Shift][Ctrl]** (Win) or **[Shift]** ⌘ (Mac), click the **ellipse frame**, click the **headline placeholder text frame**, click **Edit** on the menu bar, then click **Cut**.

   The two objects are deleted from the page. Since the ellipse and the headline were master items, you needed to press and hold [Shift][Ctrl] (Win) or [Shift] ⌘ (Mac) to select them before you could cut them from the page.

   (continued)

FIGURE 43
Viewing the new master in the Pages panel

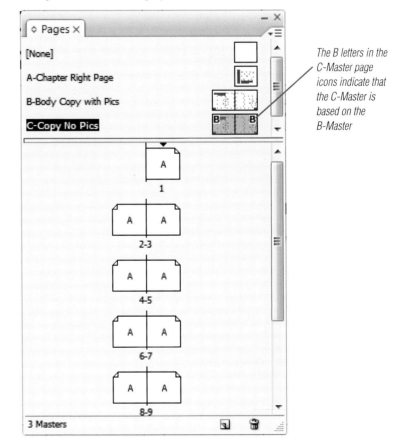

The B letters in the C-Master page icons indicate that the C-Master is based on the B-Master

FIGURE 44

Creating a new text frame

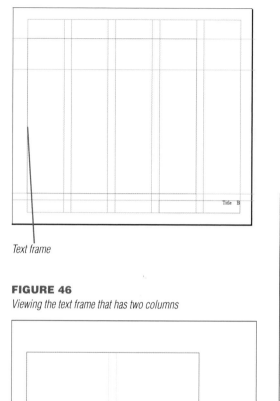

Text frame

FIGURE 46

Viewing the text frame that has two columns

Text frame with
two columns

Columns

Number text box

FIGURE 45

Text Frame Options dialog box

Text Frame Options

General | Baseline Options

Columns

Number: 2   Gutter: 0.25 in

Width: 2.65 in

☐ Fixed Column Width

Inset Spacing

Top: 0 in   Left: 0 in

Bottom: 0 in   Right: 0 in

Vertical Justification

Align: Top ▼

Paragraph Spacing Limit: 0 in

☐ Ignore Text Wrap

☐ Preview   OK   Cancel

Gutter text box

5. Press and hold **[Shift][Ctrl]** (Win) or **[Shift]** ⌘ (Mac), click the **first large text frame** on the right page, click the **second text frame**, then click the **rectangular graphics frame**.

The three master items on the right page are selected and unlocked.

6. Click **Edit** on the menu bar, then click **Cut**.

7. Click the **Type Tool** T, then draw a text frame on the right page in the position shown in Figure 44.

Note that the single text frame covers the width of four columns.

8. Click the **Selection Tool** ▶, click **Object** on the menu bar, then click **Text Frame Options**.

9. Type **2** in the Number text box, double-click the **Gutter text box**, then type **.25**, then press **[Tab]** so that your Text Frame Options dialog box resembles Figure 45.

10. Click **OK**, click the page to deselect all, click **View** on the menu bar, point to **Grids & Guides**, click **Hide Guides**, then save your document and compare your right page to Figure 46.

You created a new master page based on the B-Body Copy with Pics master page. You named the new master C-Copy No Pics and modified it by deleting master items from it and creating a new two-column text frame.

APPLY MASTER PAGES TO
DOCUMENT PAGES

What You'll Do

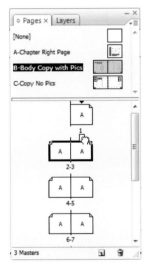

 In this lesson, you will apply master pages to document pages.

Applying Master Pages to Document Pages

Once you have created master pages, you then use the Pages panel to apply them to the document pages. One method for applying master pages is the "drag and drop" method. Using this method, you drag the master page icon or the master page name in the top section of the Pages panel down to the page icons in the lower section of the Pages panel. To apply the master to a single page, you drag the master onto the page icon, as shown in Figure 47. To apply the master to a spread, you drag the master onto one of the four corners of the left and right page icons until you see a dark border around both pages in the spread, as shown in Figure 48.

When you apply a master page to a document page, the document page inherits all of the layout characteristics of the master.

QUICKTIP
You can apply the default None master page to a document page when you want the document page not to be based on any master.

A second method for applying master pages to document pages is to use the Apply Master to Pages command in the Pages panel menu. The Apply Master dialog box, shown in Figure 49, allows you to specify which master you want to apply to which pages. This method is a good choice when you want to apply a master to a series of consecutive pages. When many pages are involved, it's faster than dragging and dropping.

FIGURE 47

Applying the C-Copy No Pics master to page 2

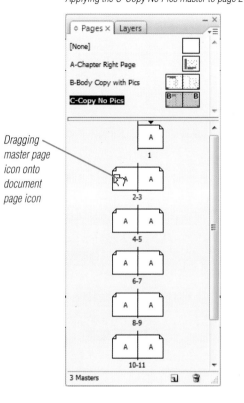

Dragging master page icon onto document page icon

FIGURE 48

Applying the C-Copy No Pics master to pages 2 & 3

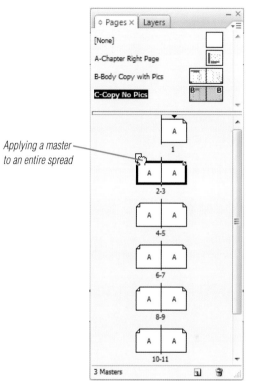

Applying a master to an entire spread

FIGURE 49

Using the Apply Master dialog box

Apply master pages to document pages

1. Double-click **B-Body Copy with Pics** in the Pages panel, drag the corresponding master page icon to the top-right corner of the page 3 icon until a black frame appears around both pages 2 and 3, as shown in Figure 50, then release the mouse button.

   The master is applied to the spread.

2. Double-click **C-Copy No Pics** in the Pages panel, then drag the corresponding master icon on top of the page 4 icon, as shown in Figure 51.

3. Apply the B-Body Copy with Pics master page to page 10, then apply the C-Copy No Pics master page to pages 11 and 12.

   (continued)

FIGURE 50

Applying the B-Body Copy with Pics master page to a spread

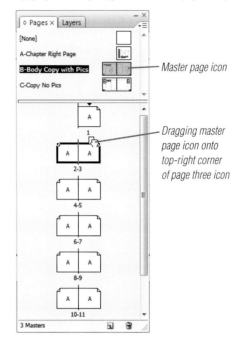

— *Master page icon*

Dragging master page icon onto top-right corner of page three icon

FIGURE 51

Applying the C-Copy No Pics master page to page 4

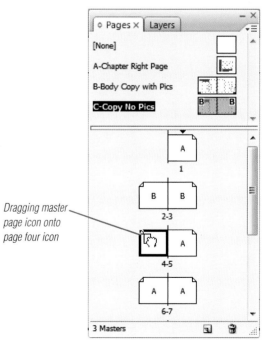

Dragging master page icon onto page four icon

FIGURE 52

Viewing the masters applied to each page

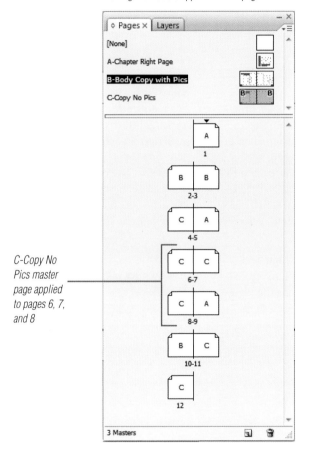

C-Copy No Pics master page applied to pages 6, 7, and 8

4. Click the **Pages panel list arrow**, then click **Apply Master to Pages**.

5. Click the **Apply Master list arrow**, click **C-Copy No Pics** (if necessary), press **[Tab]**, type **6-8** in the To Pages text box, then click **OK**

   As shown in Figure 52, the C-Copy No Pics master page is applied to pages 6, 7, and 8.

You used the Pages panel to explore various ways for applying master pages to document pages and spreads.

PLACE TEXT AND
THREAD TEXT

What You'll Do

In this lesson, you will place text, thread text from frame to frame, then view text threads.

Placing Text

Once you have created a text frame—either on a master page or on a document page—you can type directly into the frame, or you can place text from another document into it. When creating head-lines, you usually type them directly into the text frame. When creating body copy, however, you will often find yourself plac-ing text from another document, usually a word processing document.

Placing text in InDesign is simple and straightforward. Click the Place command on the File menu, which opens the Place dialog box. Find the text document that you want to place, then click Open.

The pointer changes to the loaded text icon. With a loaded text icon, you can drag to create a text frame or click inside an existing text frame. Float the loaded text icon over an existing text frame, and the icon appears in parentheses, as shown in Figure 53. The parentheses indicate that you can click to place the text into the text frame. Do so, and the text flows into the text frame, as shown in Figure 54.

QUICKTIP

The loaded text icon displays a thumbnail image of the first few lines of text that is being placed. This is helpful to make sure you are placing the correct file.

FIGURE 53

Loaded text icon positioned over a text frame

FIGURE 54

Text placed into a text frame

Lorem ipsum dolor sit amet, consect
adipiscing elit, sed diam nonummy nibh
euismod tincidunt ut laoreet dolore magna
aliquam erat volutpat. Ut wisi enim ad
minim veniam, quis nostrud exercitation
ulliam corper suscipit lobortis nisl ut
aliquip exea commodo consequat.

Duis autem veleum iriure dolor in
hendrerit in vulputate velit esse molestie
consequat. Vel willum lunombro dolore
eu feugiat nulla facilisis.

At vero eros et accumsan et iusto odio
dignissim qui blandit praesent luptatum
zzril delenit augue duis dolore te feugait
nulla facilisi.

Li Europan lingues es membres del sam
familie. Lor separat existentie es un myth.
For scientie, musica, sport etc, litot Europa
usa li tam vocabular.

Text placed ———— Li lingues differe solmen in li grammatica, li
in text frame pronunciation e li plu commun vocabules.
Omnicos directe al desirabilite de un nov
lingua franca. On refusa continuar payar
custosi traductores.

It solmen va esser necessi far uniform
grammatica, pronunciation e plu sommun
paroles. Ma quande lingues coalesce, li
grammatica del resultant lingue es plu
simplic e regulari quam ti del coalescent
lingues. Li nov lingua franca va esser plu
simplic.

Regulari quam li existent Europan lingues.
It va esser tam simplic quam Occidental in
fact, it va esser Occidental. A un Angleso
it va semblar un simplificat Angles, quam

Threading Text

InDesign provides many options for **threading text**—linking text from one text frame to another. Text frames have an **in port** and an **out port**. When threading text, you use the text frame ports to establish connections between the text frames.

In Figure 55, the center text frame is selected, and the in port and out port are identified. The in port represents where text would flow into the text frame, and the out port represents where text would flow out from.

In the same figure, note that the out port on the first text frame is red and has a plus sign in its center. This indicates the presence of **overset text**—more text than can fit in the frame.

To thread text manually from the first to the second text frame, first click the Selection Tool, then click the frame with the overset text so that the frame is highlighted. Next, click the out port of the text frame. When you float your cursor over the next text frame, the cursor changes to the link icon, as shown in Figure 56. Click the link icon and the text flows into the frame, as shown in Figure 57. When the Show Text Threads command on the View menu is activated, a blue arrow appears between any two text frames that have been threaded, as shown in Figure 58.

FIGURE 55

Identifying in ports and out ports

FIGURE 56

Link icon

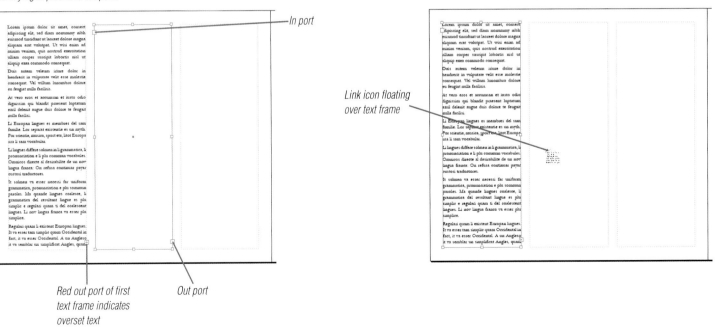

In port

Link icon floating over text frame

Red out port of first text frame indicates overset text

Out port

FIGURE 57

Threading text between frames

FIGURE 58

Showing text threads

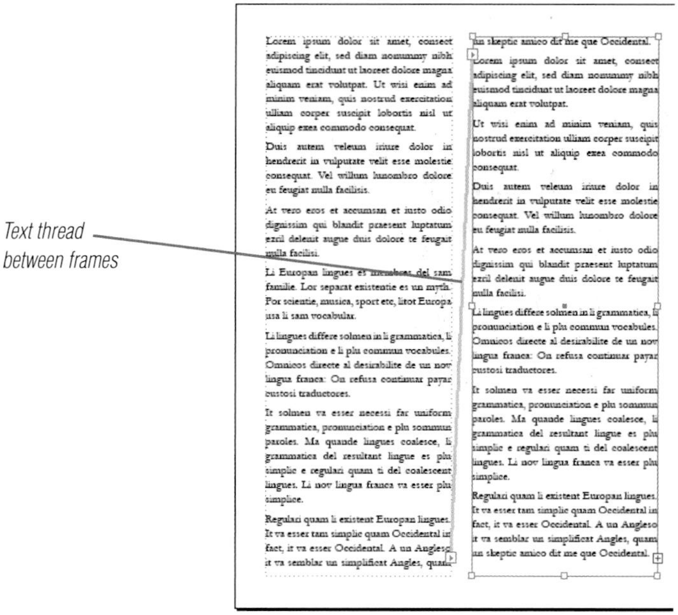

Text thread
between frames

Place text on document pages

1. Double-click the **page 2 icon** in the Pages panel.

   Because the left text frame on page 2 is a master item, it cannot be selected as usual—however, you can place text into the frame without selecting the frame.

2. Click **File** on the menu bar, click **Place**, navigate to the drive and folder where your Chapter 3 Data Files are stored, then double-click **Chapter 1 text**.

3. Point to the **left text frame**.

   The loaded text icon appears in parentheses, signaling you that you can insert the loaded text into the text frame.

4. Click anywhere in the left text frame, then compare your work to Figure 59.

   The red out port with the plus sign indicates that there is overset text—more text than can fit in the text frame.

You used the Place command to load text into a text frame on a document page.

FIGURE 59
Placing text in a text frame

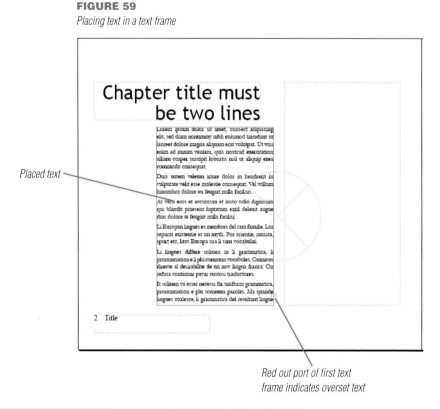

Placed text

Red out port of first text frame indicates overset text

Controlling how text is placed

When you place a Word document or RTF text in InDesign you have a number of options to choose from regarding how text is imported. For example, you can choose to include or not include footnotes, endnotes, table of contents text, and index text. You can also choose to remove any previous styles applied to text, and any table formatting. Conversely you can opt to retain styles and table formatting applied to incoming text. After you click Place on the File menu and find the Word or RTF document that you want to place, click the Show Import Options check box, then click Open. The Import Options dialog box opens. Make your selections in this dialog box, then click OK. The text will be placed with or without the options that you chose.

FIGURE 60
Threading text

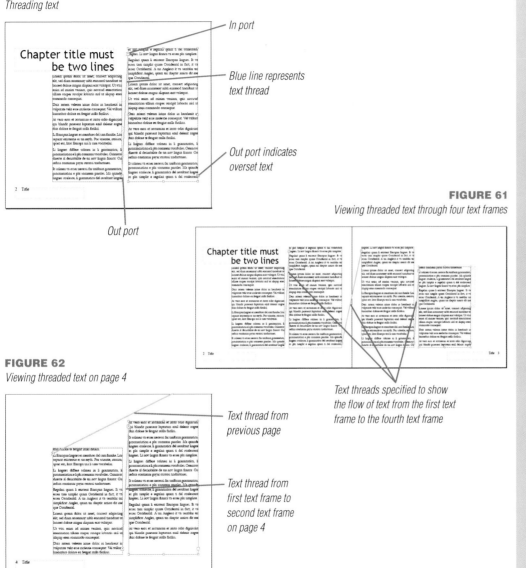

In port

Blue line represents
text thread

Out port indicates
overset text

Out port

FIGURE 61
Viewing threaded text through four text frames

FIGURE 62
Viewing threaded text on page 4

Text thread from
previous page

Text thread from
first text frame to
second text frame
on page 4

Text threads specified to show
the flow of text from the first text
frame to the fourth text frame

Thread text

1. Click **View** on the menu bar, then click **Show Text Threads**.

    With the Show Text Threads command activated, blue arrows will appear between threaded text frames when they are selected.

2. Click the **Selection Tool** , click the **left text frame** to select it, then click the **out port** of the left text frame.

3. Position the pointer on top of the right text frame so that you see the link icon.

4. Click anywhere in the right text frame.

    As shown in Figure 60, a blue text thread appears and the text is threaded from the left to the right text frames.

    TIP   A threaded text frame must be selected for the text threads to be visible.

5. Using the same process, thread text from the second text frame to the third text frame on the spread, then thread text from the third text frame to the fourth text frame, so that your two-page spread resembles Figure 61.

6. Click the **out port** on the fourth text frame, then double-click the **page 4 icon** in the Pages panel.

7. Click anywhere in the first text frame on page 4.

8. Click the **out port** of the first text frame on page 4, then click anywhere in the second text frame.

    Your page 4 should resemble Figure 62.

You threaded text manually on document pages.

MODIFY MASTER PAGES AND
DOCUMENT PAGES

What You'll Do

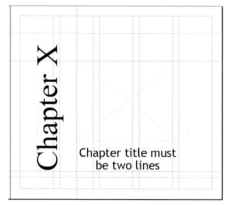

Chapter X

Chapter title must
be two lines

In this lesson, you will make modifications to both master pages and document pages and explore how each affects the other.

Modifying Master Pages

When you modify a master item on a master page, that modification, in theory, will be reflected on all the document pages that are based on that master page. This can be a very powerful option. Let's say that you have created a layout for a 36-page book, and you decide that you want to change the typeface of all the headlines. If they were created on master pages, you could simply reformat the headline in the text frame placeholders on the master pages, and those modifications would be updated on every document page in the book based on those master pages.

Overriding Master Items on Document Pages

Master pages are designed to allow you to lay out the basic elements for a page that will be used repeatedly throughout a document. In most cases, however, you will want to make modifications to the document page once it is created—you will even want to modify some objects on the document page that were created on the master page.

You can override a master item by pressing and holding [Shift][Ctrl] (Win) or [Shift] ⌘ (Mac) while clicking a master item. This unlocks the item making it easily modified. You can change the color, size, rotation angle and so on. Making changes to a document page is often referred to as making a local

change. When you override a master item, that item is still updated with changes to the master page. For example, if you resize a master item on a document page, but you do not change its color, it will retain its new size, but if the color of the master item is changed on the master page, the master item's color will be updated on the document page. In other words, when you override a master item, the document page that contains the master item is still associated with the master page.

You can remove an override and return a master item on a document page back to its original state by selecting the item, clicking the Pages panel list arrow, then clicking Remove All Local Overrides.

Detaching Master Items

When you are sure you no longer want a master item to be affected by updates made to the associated master page, you can detach a master item. Detaching a master item makes it no longer affected by changes to the master. To detach a master item, you must first override it by pressing and holding [Shift][Ctrl] (Win) or [Shift] ⌘ (Mac) while selecting it. Next, click the Pages panel list arrow, then click Detach Selection From Master.

FIGURE 63

Modifying master page items on a document page

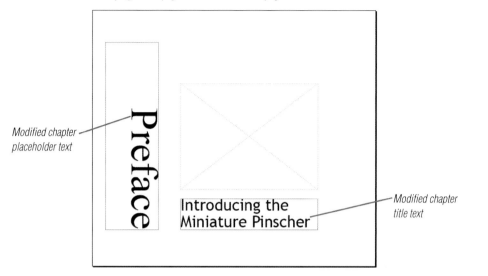

Modified chapter
placeholder text

Introducing the
Miniature Pinscher

Modified chapter
title text

FIGURE 64

Viewing changes made to page 5

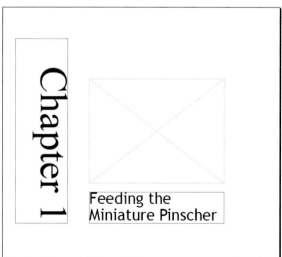

Override master items on a document page

1. Double-click the **page 1 icon** in the Pages panel, click the **Selection Tool** ▶, press and hold **[Shift][Ctrl]** (Win) or **[Shift]** ⌘ (Mac), then click the **Chapter X text frame**.

2. Click the **Type Tool** T, select all the text in the box, type **Preface**, then click the **pasteboard** to deselect.

3. Press and hold **[Shift][Ctrl]** (Win) or **[Shift]** ⌘ (Mac), click the **horizontal text frame**, click the text four times to select all of it, type **Introducing the Miniature Pinscher**, then click the **pasteboard** to deselect so that your page resembles Figure 63.

4. Click the **Selection Tool** ▶, then click the **"Preface" text frame**.

   Since this master item is now unlocked, you no longer need to press and hold [Shift][Ctrl] (Win) or [Shift] ⌘ (Mac).

5. Double-click the **page 5 icon** in the Pages panel, press and hold **[Shift][Ctrl]** (Win) or **[Shift]** ⌘ (Mac), click the **Chapter X text frame**, click the **Type Tool** T, then change the letter X to 1.

6. Change the title on page 5 to read **Feeding the Miniature Pinscher**.

   TIP Use a soft return so that "Miniature Pinscher" is on one line.

   Your document window should resemble Figure 64.

You modified document pages by editing the text within text frames that were created from master items on master pages.

Modify master pages

1. Click **View** on the menu bar, point to **Grids & Guides**, click **Show Guides**, then double-click **A-Chapter Right Page** in the Pages panel.

2. Click the **Selection Tool** 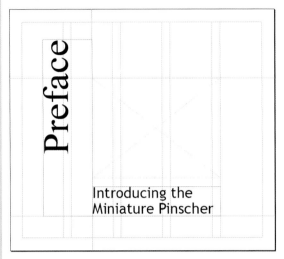 (if necessary), then click the **Chapter X placeholder frame**.

3. Click the **center reference point** in the Transform panel, highlight the contents in the **Rotation Angle text box**, type **90**, then press **[Enter]**(Win) or **[return]**(Mac).

4. Double-click the **X Location text box** in the Transform panel, type **1.75**, then press **[Enter]** (Win) or **[return]** (Mac).

5. Double-click the **page 1 icon** in the Pages panel, then note how the changes made to the A-Chapter Right Page master are reflected on the document page.

   As shown in Figure 65, both the rotation and the relocation of the text frame on the A-Chapter Right Page master are reflected on the document page.

6. View pages 5 and 9 to see the same changes.

7. Double-click **A-Chapter Right Page** in the Pages panel, click the **Chapter X text frame**, click the **Align left button** in the Paragraph panel, click the **horizontal title text frame**, then click the **Align center button** so that your master page resembles Figure 66.

(continued)

FIGURE 65
Viewing changes to page 1

Preface

Introducing the
Miniature Pinscher

FIGURE 66
Viewing text alignment changes to the A-Chapter Right Page master

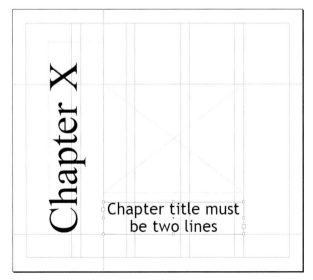

Setting up a Document

FIGURE 67
Viewing changes to page 9

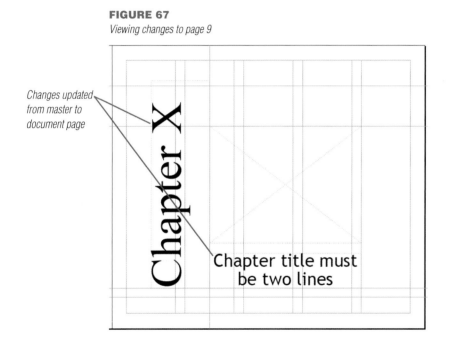

Changes updated from master to document page

Chapter X

Chapter title must be two lines

8. View pages 1 and 5.

Because you have modified the chapter text and the title text on pages 1 and 5, formatting changes to the master have not affected the local formatting.

9. View page 9.

As shown in Figure 67, because you did not modify any text formatting on page 9, the formatting changes you made to the master are reflected on page 9.

10. Double-click **B-Body Copy with Pics** in the Pages panel, then change the typeface for the automatic page numbering text place-holders on both the left and right page to Garamond or a similar font.

> TIP Footer is a term given to information at the bottom of every document page, such as the page number or the date.

11. Double-click **C-Copy No Pics** in the Pages panel.

The footers on both the left and right pages of the C-Copy No Pics master are Garamond because C-Copy No Pics is based on B-Body Copy with Pics.

You modified elements on a master page, then noted which modifications affected corresponding elements on document pages. Next, you modified text on the B-Body Copy with Pics master, and then noted that the C-Copy No Pics master was automatically updated with the modification.

CREATE NEW SECTIONS AND
WRAP TEXT

What You'll Do

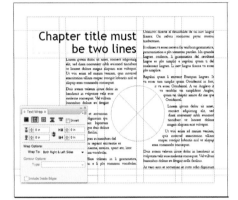

In this lesson, you will create two different numbering sections and create two text wraps around graphics frames.

Creating Sections in a Document

Sections are pages in a document where page numbering changes. For example, sometimes in the front pages of a book, in the introduction or the preface, the pages will be numbered with lowercase Roman numerals, then normal page numbering will begin with the first chapter.

You can create as many sections in a document as you wish. You determine the page on which the new section will start by clicking that page icon in the Pages panel. Choose the Numbering & Section Options command in the Pages panel menu, which opens the New Section dialog box, as shown in Figure 68. In this example, we clicked page 8 in the Pages panel, then opened the New Section dialog box. We then specified that the new section begin with a page numbered 1.

QUICKTIP

The first time you choose a type of page numbering for a document, the Numbering & Section Options dialog box opens instead of the New Section dialog box.

FIGURE 68
New Section dialog box

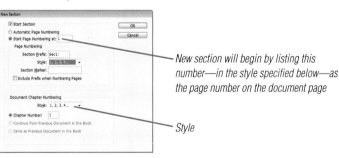

New section will begin by listing this number—in the style specified below—as the page number on the document page

Style

Wrapping Text Around a Frame

When you position a text frame or a graphics frame near another frame that contains text, you can apply a text wrap to the overlapping frame in order to force the underlying text to wrap around it. InDesign offers many options for wrapping text around a frame. One quick method is to click the Wrap around bounding box button in the Text Wrap panel, as shown in Figure 69.

Figure 70 shows a rectangular frame using the No text wrap option in the Text Wrap panel. Figure 71 shows that same frame using the Wrap around bounding box option in the Text Wrap panel.

When you choose the Wrap around bounding box option, you can control the **offset**—the distance that text is repelled by the frame—by entering values in the Top, Bottom, Left, and Right Offset text boxes in the panel. Figure 72 shows the frame with a .125-inch offset applied to all four sides of the frame.

QUICKTIP

The Apply To Master Page Only command is only available when an object on a master page is selected and has a wrap applied to it. If this option is deselected (if there is no check mark next to it), text on both master pages and document pages can wrap around the master page items without the master page items being overridden. If this option is selected, you must override a master page item on a document page to wrap text around it.

FIGURE 69

Text Wrap panel

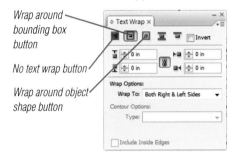

Wrap around bounding box button

No text wrap button

Wrap around object shape button

FIGURE 70

A frame using the No text wrap option

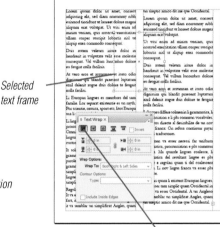

Selected text frame

No text wrap button

FIGURE 71

A frame using the Wrap around bounding box option

Selected text frame

Wrap around bounding box button

FIGURE 72

A frame with a .125-inch offset applied to all sides

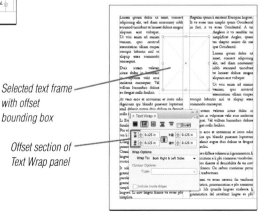

Selected text frame with offset bounding box

Offset section of Text Wrap panel

Create sections in a document

1. Double-click the **page 1 icon** in the Pages panel, click the **Pages panel list arrow**, then click **Numbering & Section Options**.

2. In the Page Numbering section of the dialog box, click the **Style list arrow**, then click the **lower-case Roman numeral style**, as shown in Figure 73.

3. Click **OK**, then view the pages in the document, noting the new style of the page numbering on the pages and in the Pages panel.

4. Double-click the **page v icon** in the Pages panel (page 5), click the **Pages panel list arrow**, then click **Numbering & Section Options**.

5. Click the **Start Page Numbering at option button**, verify that **1** is in the text box, click the **Style list arrow,** then click the **ordinary numerals style**, as shown in Figure 74.

   The fifth page in the document will be designated as page 1. However, the fifth page will not have a page number on it because it's based on the A Chapter Right Page master, which isn't formatted for automatic page numbering.

6. Click **OK**, then view the pages in the document, noting the new style of page numbering beginning on the fifth page of the document.

   Since page 5 is based on the A-Chapter Right Page master, it does not display a page number, even though it begins the new section.

7. Double-click the **page ii icon** in the Pages panel, click the **Selection Tool** 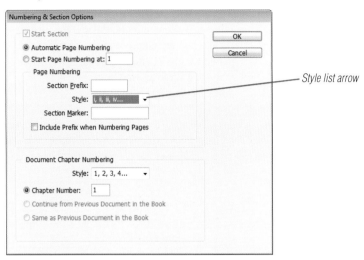, press and hold **[Shift][Ctrl]** (Win) or **[Shift]** ⌘ (Mac), then select the footer text frame.

8. Click the **Type Tool** T, double-click the word **Title**, type **Preface**, then deselect.

(continued)

FIGURE 73
Choosing lower-case Roman numerals

Style list arrow

FIGURE 74
Starting a new section

FIGURE 75

Choosing the Wrap around object shape button

Text wraps
around ellipse

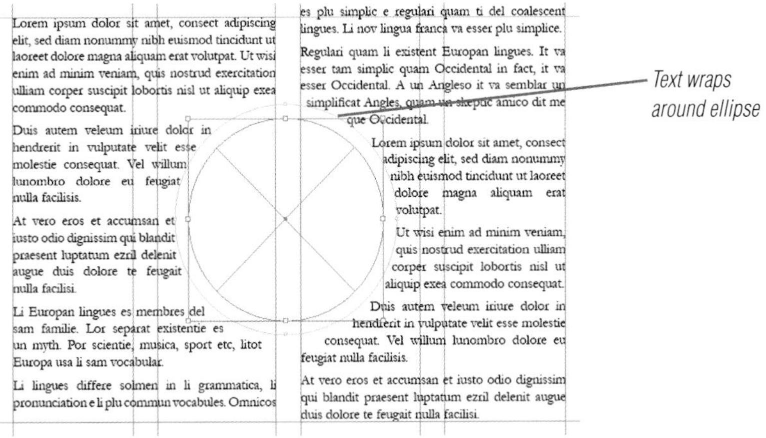

FIGURE 76

Viewing the spread

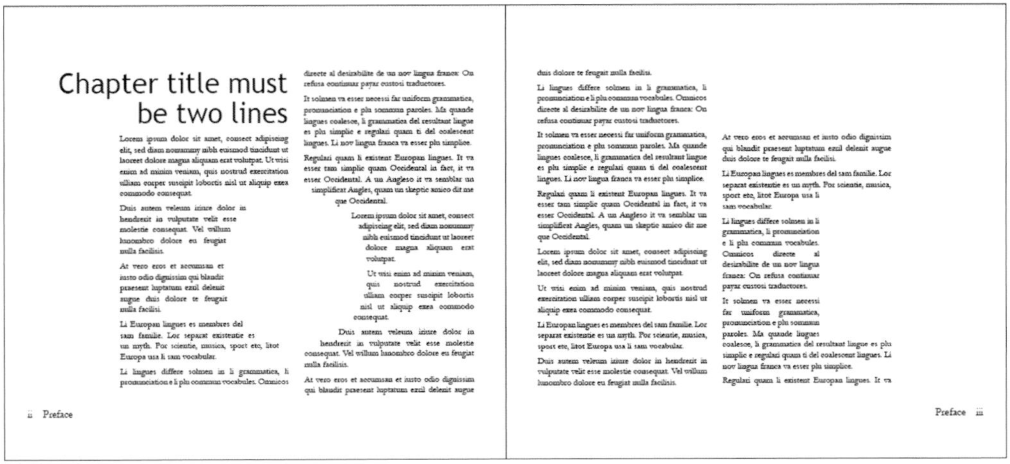

Chapter title must
be two lines

9. Replace the word Title with the word **Preface** on pages iii and iv, then deselect all.

You used the New Section dialog box to change the style of the page numbering in the Preface section of the book, and then again to start numerical page numbering with Chapter 1.

Wrap text around a frame

1. Double-click the **page ii icon** in the Pages panel, click the **Selection Tool** , press and hold [Shift][Ctrl] (Win) or [Shift] ⌘ (Mac), then click the **ellipse frame**.

   TIP Clicking the center point of the ellipse frame is the easiest way to select it.

2. Click **Window** on the menu bar, then click **Text Wrap**.

3. Click the **Wrap around object shape button** .

   The text wraps around the ellipse, as shown in Figure 75.

4. Double-click the **page iii icon** in the Pages panel, select the empty rectangular frame, then click the **Wrap around bounding box button** in the Text Wrap panel.

5. Click the **Make all settings the same button** to deactivate it (if necessary).

6. Double-click the **Top Offset text box** in the Text Wrap panel, type **.125**, press [Tab], type **.125** in the Left Offset text box, then press [Enter] (Win) or [return] (Mac).

7. Click **View** on the menu bar, click **Fit Spread in Window**, then click anywhere to deselect any selected items.

8. Click the **Preview button** in the Toolbox, press [Tab], then deselect all.

   Your spread should resemble Figure 76.

9. Save your work, then close Setup.

You used the Text Wrap panel to flow text around two graphics frames.

Create a new document.

1. Start Adobe InDesign and verify that your rulers display inches instead of picas. (If not, open the Preferences dialog box and choose Inches as the horizontal and vertical ruler units.)

2. Without creating a new document, click Edit (Win) or InDesign (Mac) on the menu bar, point to Preferences, then click Guides & Pasteboard.

3. In the Guide Options section, click the Guides in Back check box to add a check mark, then click OK.

4. Click File on the menu bar, point to New, then click Document.

5. Type **8** in the Number of Pages text box, press [Tab], then verify that the Facing Pages check box is checked.

6. Type **5** in the Width text box, press [Tab], then type **5** in the Height text box.

7. Using [Tab] to move from one text box to another, type **2** in the Number text box in the Columns section, then type **.2** in the Gutter text box.

8. Type **.25** in the Top, Bottom, Inside, and Outside Margins text boxes.

9. Click OK, then save the document as **Skills Review**.

10. Double-click A-Master in the Pages panel to center both pages of the master in your window.

11. Click Window on the menu bar, point to Object & Layout, then click Transform.

12. Click the Selection Tool, press and hold [Ctrl] (Win) or ⌘ (Mac), create a guide on the left page using the horizontal ruler, releasing the mouse pointer when the Y Location text box in the Transform panel reads approximately 2.5 in.

13. Press and hold [Ctrl] (Win) or ⌘ (Mac), create a guide on the left page using the vertical ruler, releasing the mouse pointer when the X Location text box in the Transform panel reads approximately 2.5 in.

14. Click Edit (Win) or InDesign (Mac) on the menu bar, point to Preferences, click Units & Increments, click the Origin list arrow, click Page, then click OK.

15. Press and hold [Ctrl] (Win) or ⌘ (Mac), create a horizontal guide on the right page, releasing the mouse pointer when the X Location text box in the Transform panel reads approximately 2.5 in.

16. Click the horizontal guide, double-click the value in the Y Location text box of the Transform panel, type **2.5**, if necessary, then press [Enter] (Win) or [return] (Mac).

17. Click the vertical guide on the left page, double-click the value in the X Location text box in the Transform panel, type **2.5**, if necessary, then press [Enter] (Win) or [return] (Mac).

18. Click the vertical guide on the right page, double-click the value in the X Location text box in the Transform panel, type **2.5**, then press [Enter] (Win) or [return] (Mac).

19. Click the Rectangle Frame Tool, then draw a rectangle anywhere on the left page.

20. Click the top-left reference point in the Transform panel.

21. With the rectangle frame selected, type **0** in the X Location text box in the Transform panel, type **0** in the Y Location text box, type **5** in the Width text box, type **5** in the Height text box, then press [Enter] (Win) or [return] (Mac).

22. Click Edit on the menu bar, click Copy, click Edit on the menu bar again, then click Paste in Place.

23. Drag the copied box anywhere on the right page, being sure that its top-left corner is on the page.

24. Type **0** in the X Location text box in the Transform panel, type **0** in the Y Location text box, then press [Enter] (Win) or [return] (Mac).

Create master pages.

1. Click the Pages panel list arrow, then click New Master.

2. Type **Body** in the Name text box, click the Based on Master list arrow, click A-Master, then click OK.

3. Click the Selection Tool, press and hold [Shift][Ctrl] (Win) or [Shift]⌘ (Mac), select both rectangle frames, then delete them.

4. Double-click B-Body in the Pages panel to center both pages of the master in your window.

5. Click Layout on the menu bar, then click Margins and Columns.

6. Type **2** in the Number text box in the Columns section (if necessary), then click OK.

7. Click the Type Tool, create a text frame of any size anywhere in the right column on the left page, then click the Selection Tool.

8. Verify that the top-left reference point is selected in the Transform panel, type **2.6** in the X Location text box, type **.25** in the Y Location text box, type **2.15** in the Width text box, type **4.5** in the Height text box, then press [Enter] (Win) or [return] (Mac).

9. Click Edit on the menu bar, click Copy, click Edit on the menu bar again, then click Paste in Place.

10. Press and hold [Shift], then drag the copy of the text frame onto the right page, releasing the mouse button when it "snaps" into the left column on the right page.

11. Click the Type Tool, then draw a small text box anywhere on the left page of the B-Body master.

12. Verify that the top-left reference point is selected in the Transform panel, type **.25** in the X Location text box, type **4.5** in the Y Location text box, type **1.65** in the Width text box, type **.25** in the Height text box, then press [Enter] (Win) or [return] (Mac).

13. Click Type on the menu bar, point to Insert Special Character, point to Markers, then click Current Page Number.

14. Click Type on the menu bar, point to Insert Special Character, point to Hyphens and Dashes, then click En Dash.

15. Type the word **Title**.

16. Click the Selection Tool, select the footer text frame if necessary, click Edit on the menu bar, click Copy, click Edit on the menu bar again, then click Paste in Place.

17. Press and hold [Shift], then drag the copy of the text frame so that it is positioned in the lower-right corner of the right page of the master page.

18. Click the Align right button in the Paragraph panel, then delete the B and the dash after the B.

19. Click after the word Title, click Type on the menu bar, point to Insert Special Character, point to Hyphens and Dashes, then click En Dash.

20. Click Type on the menu bar, point to Insert Special Character, point to Markers, then click Current Page Number.

Apply master pages to document pages.

1. Double-click the page 2 icon in the Pages panel.

2. Drag the B-Body master page title to the bottom-left corner of the page 2 icon until you see a black rectangle around the page 2 and 3 icons, then release the mouse button.

3. Drag the B-Body Copy title to the bottom-left corner of the page 4 icon until you see a black rectangle around the page 4 icon, then release the mouse button.

4. Click the Pages panel list arrow, then click Apply Master to Pages.

5. Click the Apply Master list arrow, click B-Body (if necessary), type **6-8** in the To Pages text box, then click OK.

6. Double-click the page 2 icon in the Pages panel.

Place text and thread text.

1. Click File on the menu bar, click Place, navigate to the drive and folder where your Chapter 3 Data Files are stored, then double-click Skills Review Text.

2. Click anywhere in the text frame on page 2.

3. Click View on the menu bar, then click Show Text Threads.

4. Click the Selection Tool, press and hold [Shift][Ctrl] (Win) or [Shift] ⌘ (Mac), click the text frame on page 2 if necessary to select it, then click the out port of the text frame on page 2.

5. Click the link icon anywhere in the text frame on page 3. (*Hint*: You'll need to press and hold [Shift][Ctrl] (Win) or [Shift] ⌘ (Mac) to select the text box first.)

Modify master pages and document pages.

1. Double-click the page 6 icon in the Pages panel.

2. Click the bottom-middle reference point in the Transform panel.

3. Click the Selection Tool, press and hold [Shift][Ctrl] (Win) or [Shift] ⌘ (Mac), then click the text frame.

4. Type **3** in the Height text box in the Transform panel, then press [Enter] (Win) or [return] (Mac).

5. Double-click A-Master in the Pages panel, then select the graphics placeholder frame on the left page.

6. Click the center reference point in the Transform panel.

7. In the Transform panel, type **3** in the Width text box, type **3** in the Height text box, then press [Enter] (Win) or [return] (Mac).

8. Double-click the right page icon of the A-Master in the Pages panel, then select the graphics placeholder frame on the right page.

9. In the Transform panel, type **2** in the Width text box, type **4** in the Height text box, then press [Enter] (Win) or [return] (Mac).

10. View the two document pages in the Pages panel that are based on the A-Master to verify that the modifications were updated.

11. Double-click B-Body in the Pages panel, click the Rectangle Frame Tool, then create a frame anywhere on the left page of the B-Body master page.

12. Click the top-left reference point in the Transform panel, then type **2** in the X Location text box, type **2.6** in the Y Location text box, type **2.25** in the Width text box, type **1.5** in the Height text box, then press [Enter] (Win) or [return] (Mac).

Create new sections and wrap text.

1. Double-click the page 1 icon in the Pages panel, click the Pages panel list arrow, then click Numbering & Section Options.

2. Click the Style list arrow, click the lower-case style letters (a, b, c, d), click OK, then note the changes to the pages in the Pages panel and in the document.

3. Double-click the page e icon in the Pages panel, click the Pages panel list arrow, then click Numbering & Section Options.

4. Click the Start Page Numbering at option button, type **5** in the text box, then verify that the Style text box shows ordinary numerals (1, 2, 3, 4). (If it does not, click the Style list arrow and select that style.)

5. Click OK, then view the pages in the document noting the new style of the page numbering on the pages and in the Pages panel.

6. Double-click the page b icon in the Pages panel, click the Selection Tool, press and hold [Shift][Ctrl] (Win) or [Shift] ⌘ (Mac), then select the rectangular graphics frame.

7. Click Window on the menu bar, then click Text Wrap.

8. Click the Wrap around bounding box button in the Text Wrap panel.

9. Type **.125** in the Right Offset text box in the Text Wrap panel, then press [Enter] (Win) or [return] (Mac).

10. Click View on the menu bar, click Fit Spread in Window, then click anywhere to deselect any selected items.

11. Compare your screen to Figure 77, save your work, then close Skills Review.

FIGURE 77
Completed Skills Review

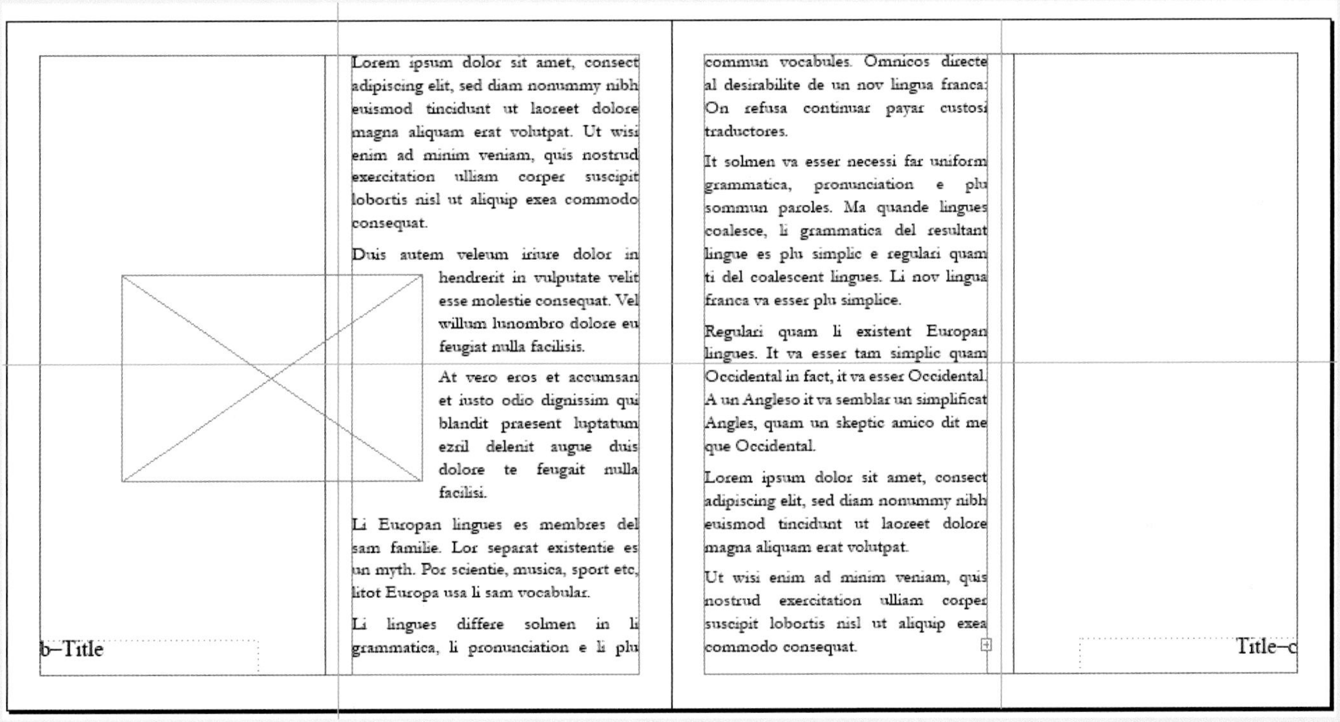

Lorem ipsum dolor sit amet, consect adipiscing elit, sed diam nonummy nibh euismod tincidunt ut laoreet dolore magna aliquam erat volutpat. Ut wisi enim ad minim veniam, quis nostrud exercitation ulliam corper suscipit lobortis nisl ut aliquip exea commodo consequat.

Duis autem veleum iriure dolor in hendrerit in vulputate velit esse molestie consequat. Vel willum lunombro dolore eu feugiat nulla facilisis.

At vero eros et accumsan et iusto odio dignissim qui blandit praesent luptatum ezril delenit augue duis dolore te feugait nulla facilisi.

Li Europan lingues es membres del sam familie. Lor separat existentie es un myth. Por scientie, musica, sport etc, litot Europa usa li sam vocabular.

Li lingues differe solmen in li grammatica, li pronunciation e li plu

commun vocabules. Omnicos directe al desirabilite de un nov lingua franca: On refusa continuar payar custosi traductores.

It solmen va esser necessi far uniform grammatica, pronunciation e plu sommun paroles. Ma quande lingues coalesce, li grammatica del resultant lingue es plu simplic e regulari quam ti del coalescent lingues. Li nov lingua franca va esser plu simplice.

Regulari quam li existent Europan lingues. It va esser tam simplic quam Occidental in fact, it va esser Occidental. A un Angleso it va semblar un simplificat Angles, quam un skeptic amico dit me que Occidental.

Lorem ipsum dolor sit amet, consect adipiscing elit, sed diam nonummy nibh euismod tincidunt ut laoreet dolore magna aliquam erat volutpat.

Ut wisi enim ad minim veniam, quis nostrud exercitation ulliam corper suscipit lobortis nisl ut aliquip exea commodo consequat.

b—Title

Title—c

You are a graphic designer working out of your home office. You have one client—a local investment company who has contracted you to design their monthly 16-page newsletter. You've sketched out a design and created a new document at the correct size, and now you need to add automatic page numbering to the document.

1. Open ID 3-1.indd, then save it as **Newsletter**.
2. Double-click A-Master in the Pages panel.
3. Click the Type Tool, then draw a text frame about one inch tall and one column wide.
4. Position the text frame at the bottom of the center column, being sure that the bottom edge of the text frame snaps to the bottom margin of the page.
5. Set the Preference settings so that the guides are sent to the back of the layout—so that all four sides of the text frame are visible.
6. Click the Type Tool, then click inside the text box.
7. Click Type on the menu bar, point to Insert Special Character, point to Hyphens and Dashes, then click Em Dash.
8. Click Type on the menu bar, point to Insert Special Character, point to Markers, then click Current Page Number.
9. Click Type on the menu bar, point to Insert Special Character, point to Hyphens and Dashes, then click Em Dash.
10. Select all three text elements and change their font size to 20 pt.

11. Click the Align center button in the Paragraph panel.
12. Select the text, then click the dark blue swatch in the Swatches panel.
13. Click the bottom center reference point in the Transform panel, double-click the Height text box in the Transform panel, type .25, then press [Enter] (Win) or [return] (Mac).
14. Double-click the page 5 icon in the Pages panel, compare your page 5 to Figure 78, save your work, then close Newsletter.

FIGURE 78
Completed Project Builder 1

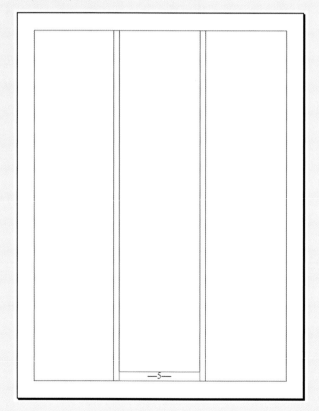

Setting up a Document

You work in the design department for a bank, and you are responsible for creating a new weekly bulletin, which covers various events within the bank's network of branches. You have just finished creating three master pages for the bulletin, and now you are ready to apply the masters to the document pages.

1. Open ID 3-2.indd, then save it as **Bulletin Layout**.
2. Apply the B-Master to pages 2 and 3.
3. Click the Pages panel list arrow, then click Apply Master to Pages.
4. Apply the C-Master to pages 4 through 6, then click OK.
5. Place Bulletin text.doc in the text frame on page 1.
6. Select the text frame, click the out port on the text frame, double-click page 2 in the Pages panel, then click anywhere in the text frame on page 2.
7. Thread the remaining text through each page up to and including page 6 in the document.
8. Click the Preview button, deselect any selected items, then compare your page 6 to Figure 79.
9. Save your work, then close Bulletin Layout.

FIGURE 79
Completed Project Builder 2

Your client has provided you with a page layout that she describes as her design for the background of her page. Knowing that she'll want to use this background design for multiple pages, you decide to "tweak" her document to be sure that the background elements are the same size and are aligned evenly.

1. Open ID 3-3.indd, then save it as **Four Square**.
2. Click File on the menu bar, click Document Setup, note the width and height of the page, then close the Document Setup dialog box.
3. Hide the guides and the frame edges if necessary, then verify that only the Transform panel and the Toolbox are visible.
4. Click the Selection Tool, then click the top-left reference point in the Transform panel.
5. Click the top-left square on the page, type **0** in the X Location text box, type **0** in the Y Location text box, type **7.75** in the Width text box, then press [Enter] (Win) or [return] (Mac).
6. Click to place the insertion point after the number 7.75 in the Width text box, type **/2**, then press [Tab].
7. Type **3.875** in the Height text box, then press [Enter] (Win) or [return] (Mac).
8. Click the top-right square, type **3.875** in the X Location text box, type **0** in the Y Location text box, type **3.875** in the Width and Height text boxes, then press [Enter] (Win) or [return] (Mac).
9. Click the lower-left square, type **0** in the X Location text box, type **3.875** in the Y Location text box, type **3.875** in the Width and Height text boxes, then press [Enter] (Win) or [return] (Mac).
10. Click the lower-right square, type **3.875** in the X Location text box, type **3.875** in the

Y Location text box, type **3.875** in the Width and Height text boxes, press [Enter] (Win) or [return] (Mac), then deselect all.
11. Compare your screen to Figure 80, save your work, then close Four Square.

FIGURE 80
Completed Design Project

Setting up a Document

Your group is going to work on a fun puzzle, which will test your problem-solving skills when using X and Y locations. You will open an InDesign document with two pages. On the first page are four 1-inch squares at each corner of the page. On the second page, the four 1-inch squares appear again—this time forming a large red square that is positioned at the exact center of the 8-inch x 8-inch document page. The challenge is for the group to call out X and Y locations for all four of the squares on the first page so that they will be relocated to the same positions as the four squares on the second page.

Setup.

1. Have one computer set up to display the document so that the entire group can see it. If you can, use a large display projection against the wall.
2. Verify that only the Toolbox and the Transform panel are visible.
3. Have one member sit at the computer display to implement the groups' call-outs in the document, selecting the boxes and entering information in the Transform panel.
4. Explain to the group that, not only is this a challenge to use X and Y Location values to reposition the boxes, it's also a challenge to find what the group will agree is the most straightforward method for doing so using the fewest steps.

5. Divide the group into groups of 4. Have each group choose a spokesperson. Tell the groups that they have exactly one minute to huddle among themselves to come up with a solution for the problem. (Group members should not be in front of computers during this time; they can use pencils and paper and base their calculations on the information given in the introduction.)
6. Have the first group spokesperson call out the changes to the student at the display until the first group spokesperson achieves the objective. Note that the rules of the challenge state that the spokesperson is allowed one try only for each square. This means that the spokesperson can call out a value for any of the X and Y Location text boxes in the Transform panel only one time for each square. The spokesperson is also free to

specify a reference point in the Transform panel. If, at the end, the squares are not aligned, the spokesperson does not get a second chance.
7. Ask the second group spokesperson if he/she thinks she knows a better method. If she says yes, revert the document and let her try. If she says no, her group is out.
8. Proceed in this fashion until all four groups have had the opportunity to try the challenge. At the end, have the groups decide who found the best method.
9. Open ID 3-4.indd, then save it as **Center Squares**.
10. Enter the correct X and Y Location values in the Transform panel for all four squares.
11. Compare your work to Figure 81, then close Center Squares.

FIGURE 81
Completed Group Project

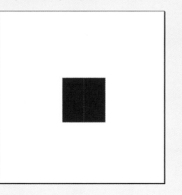

WORKING WITH FRAMES

1. Align and distribute objects on a page

2. Stack and layer objects

3. Work with graphics frames

4. Work with text frames

chapter 4 WORKING WITH
FRAMES

When you position objects on a page, they are positioned in text or graphics frames. Chapter 4 focuses on frames and how you can best work with them.

The first lesson gives you the chance to pause and explore basic options for aligning and distributing frames on the page. In the second lesson, you'll learn how to manipulate the stacking order of frames, and you'll get a thorough tour of the Layers panel. After going through these lessons, you'll feel confident in your ability to position frames precisely on a page and get them to overlap the way you want them to.

The third lesson is an immersion into the world of placing graphics in graphics frames. Put on your thinking caps— there's a lot going on here, all of it interesting. You'll learn the specifics of placing graphics—and the all-important difference between the graphics frame and the graphic itself. Finally, you'll finish by working with text frames and exploring the power of autoflowing text in a document. Watch InDesign create dozens of text frames with a click of a button. Now that's a lot of frames!

Tools You'll Use

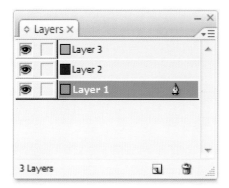

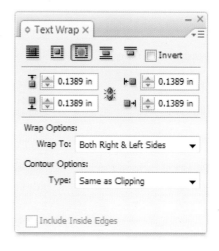

ALIGN AND DISTRIBUTE
OBJECTS ON A PAGE

What You'll Do

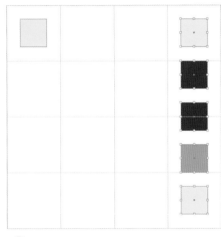

In this lesson, you will explore various techniques for positioning objects in specific locations on the document page.

Applying Fills and Strokes

A **fill** is a color you apply that fills an object. A **stroke** is a color that you apply to the outline of an object. Figure 1 shows an object with a blue fill and a yellow stroke.

InDesign offers you a number of options for filling and stroking objects. The simplest and most direct method for doing so is to select an object and then pick a color from the Swatches panel, shown in Figure 2. The color that you choose in the Swatches panel will be applied to the selected object as a fill or as a stroke, depending on whether the Fill or the Stroke button is activated in the Toolbox.

To activate either the Fill or the Stroke button, simply click it once in the Toolbox.

The Fill button is activated when it is in front of the Stroke button, as shown in Figure 3. When the Fill button is activated, clicking a swatch in the Swatches panel applies that swatch color as a fill to the selected object(s). When the Stroke button is activated, as shown in Figure 4, the swatch color is applied as a stroke.

Once a stroke is applied, you can modify the **stroke weight**—how heavy the outline appears—using the Stroke panel. Figure 5 shows the Stroke panel and an object with a 10-pt red stroke. Note the Stroke panel list arrow, which you can click to display more stroke options in the panel.

FIGURE 1

An object with a fill and a stroke

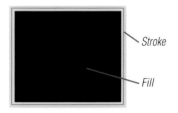

Stroke

Fill

FIGURE 2

Swatches panel

FIGURE 3

Viewing the activated Fill button

Fill button is
in front of the
Stroke button

FIGURE 4

Viewing the activated Stroke button

Stroke button is in
front of the Fill button

FIGURE 5

A 10 pt stroke applied to an object

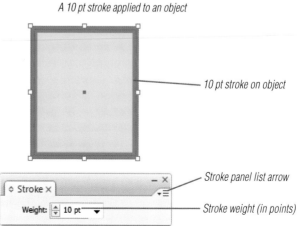

10 pt stroke on object

Stroke panel list arrow

Stroke weight (in points)

Using the Step and Repeat Command

Many times, when laying out a page, you will want to create multiple objects that are evenly spaced. Rather than draw each object one at a time, it's often best to use the Step and Repeat dialog box, as shown in Figure 6.

Before you choose the Step and Repeat command, you need to decide which object you want to make copies of, and how many copies of the object you want to create. After selecting the object, choose Step and Repeat on the Edit menu. In the Step and Repeat dialog box, you choose the number of copies. You also specify the **offset** value for

each successive copy. The offset is easy to understand—it is the distance, horizontally and vertically, that the copy will be from the original. Click the Preview check box to see the transformations before you execute them. Figure 7 shows an original 1-inch square frame and the three copies created using the Step and Repeat command. Note that the horizontal offset is two inches and the vertical offset is two inches. Thus, each copy is two inches to the right and two inches down from the previous copy.

Note that positive and negative offset values create copies in specific directions. On the horizontal axis, a positive value creates copies to the right of the original;

a negative value creates copies to the left of the original. On the vertical axis, a positive value creates copies below the original; a negative value creates copies above the original. Figure 8 is a handy guide for remembering the result of positive and negative offset values.

Use the vertical ruler on the left side of the document page to remember positive and negative values on the vertical axis. You are used to thinking of positive as up and negative as down, but remember that in InDesign, the default (0, 0) coordinate is in the top-left corner of the page. On the ruler, positive numbers *increase* as you move down the ruler.

FIGURE 6
Step and Repeat dialog box

Preview check box

FIGURE 7
Results of the Step and Repeat command

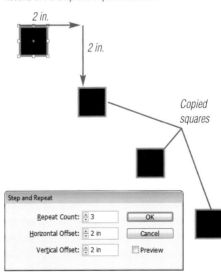

2 in.

2 in.

Copied squares

FIGURE 8
Understanding positive and negative offset values

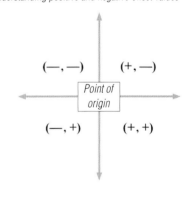

Aligning Objects

The Align panel offers quick and simple solutions for aligning and distributing multiple objects on a page. To **align** objects is to position them by their tops, bottoms, left sides, right sides or centers. To **distribute** objects is to space them equally on a page horizontally, vertically, or both. Using the top section of the Align panel, you can choose from six alignment buttons, shown in Figure 9. Each option includes an icon that represents the resulting layout of the selected objects, after the button has been clicked. Figure 10 shows three objects placed randomly on the page. Figure 11 shows the same three objects after clicking the Align left edges button.

Compare Figure 10 to Figure 11. Only the bottom two objects moved; they moved left to align with the left edge of the top object. This is because the top object was originally the left-most object. Clicking the Align left edges button aligns all selected objects with the left-most object.

Figure 12 shows the same three objects after clicking the Align top edges button. Clicking this button means that the top edges of each object are aligned.

The Align panel is a great feature of InDesign, one that you will use over and over again.

FIGURE 9
Align Objects section of the Align panel

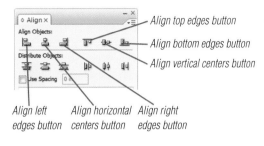

Align top edges button
Align bottom edges button
Align vertical centers button

Align left edges button   Align horizontal centers button   Align right edges button

FIGURE 11
Viewing the results of the Align left edges button

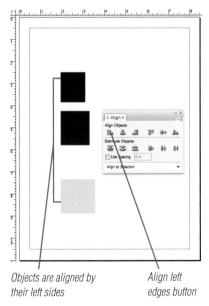

Objects are aligned by their left sides

Align left edges button

FIGURE 10
Three objects not aligned

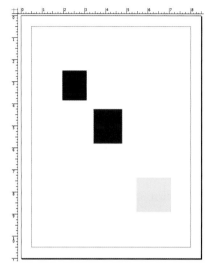

FIGURE 12
Viewing the results of the Align top edges button

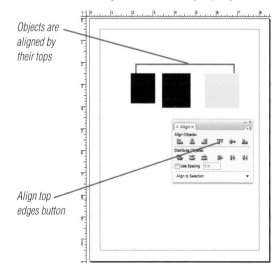

Objects are aligned by their tops

Align top edges button

Distributing Objects

You use the Distribute Objects section of the Align panel to distribute objects. As stated earlier, to distribute objects is to space them equally on a page horizontally, vertically, or both.

Figure 13 shows three objects that are not distributed evenly on either the horizontal or vertical axis. Figure 14 shows the same three objects after clicking the Distribute horizontal centers button. Clicking this button means that—on the horizontal axis—the distance between the center point of the first object and the center point of the second object is the same as the distance between the center point of the second object and the center point of the third object.

Figure 15 shows the same three objects after clicking the Distribute vertical centers button. Clicking this button means that—on the vertical axis—the distance between the center points of the first two objects is the same as the distance between the center points of the second and third objects.

Why are the Align and Distribute buttons in the same panel? Because their power is how they work in conjunction with each other. Figure 16 shows three text frames without any alignment or distribution applied. Figure 17 shows the three frames after clicking the Align top edges button and the Distribute left edges button. Compare the two figures.

FIGURE 13
Three objects, positioned randomly

FIGURE 14
Viewing the results of clicking the Distribute horizontal centers button

FIGURE 15
Viewing the results of clicking the Distribute vertical centers button

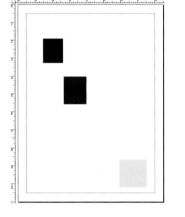

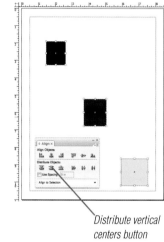

Distribute horizontal
centers button

Distribute vertical
centers button

FIGURE 16
Three text frames, positioned randomly

FIGURE 17
Viewing the results of clicking the Align top edges button and the Distribute left edges button

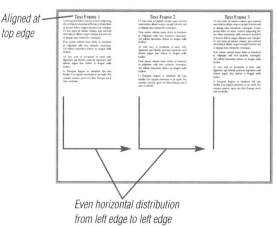

Aligned at
top edge

Even horizontal distribution
from left edge to left edge

FIGURE 18
Positioning the rectangle frame

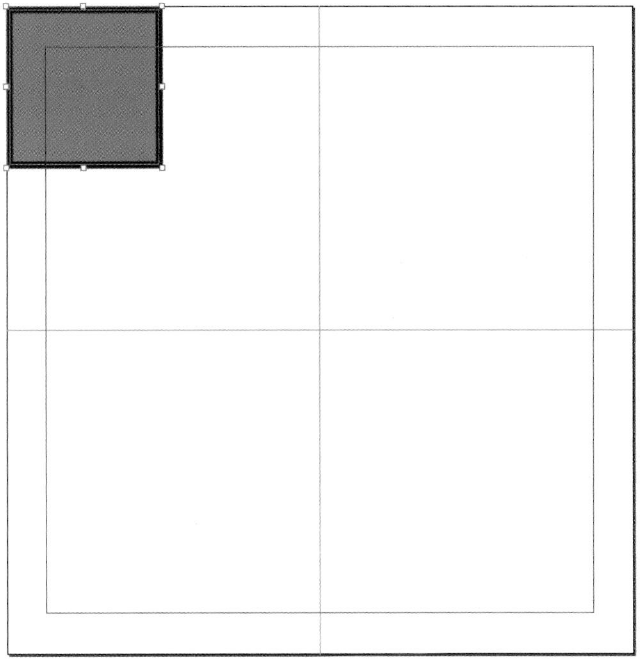

Apply fills and strokes

1. Open ID 4-1.indd, then save it as **Orientation**.

2. Click the **Rectangle Tool** ▣ , then click anywhere on the page.

   TIP When a shape tool is selected in the Toolbox, clicking the document window opens the tool's dialog box, where you can enter values that determine the size of the resulting object.

3. Type **2** in the Width text box, type **2** in the Height text box, then click **OK**.

4. Click the **Swatches panel name tab**.

   TIP If you do not see the Swatches panel name tab, click Window on the menu bar, then click Swatches.

5. Click the **Fill button** in the Toolbox (if necessary) to activate it.

6. Click **Green** in the Swatches panel.

   The rectangle frame fills with green.

7. Click the **Stroke button** in the Toolbox.

8. Click **Brick Red** in the Swatches panel.

9. If the Stroke panel is not visible, click **Window** on the menu bar, click **Stroke**, type **6** in the Weight text box, then press **[Enter]** (Win) or **[return]** (Mac).

10. Press **[V]** to access the Selection Tool, then drag the frame rectangle so that its top-left corner is aligned with the top-left corner of the page, as shown in Figure 18.

11. Click **File** on the menu bar, then click **Save**.

You created a rectangle using the Rectangle dialog box. You then used the Swatches panel to choose a fill color and a stroke color for the rectangle frame. Finally, you increased the weight of the stroke and dragged the rectangle to the top-left corner of the page.

Use the Step and Repeat command

1. Click the **green rectangle**, click the **Stroke button** in the Toolbox, then click the **Apply None button** ⊘, as shown in Figure 19.

   The stroke is removed from the green rectangle. With the loss of the stroke, the rectangle is no longer aligned with the top-left corner.

2. Click the **top-left reference point** in the Transform panel, type **0** in the X Location text box, type **0** in the Y Location text box, then press **[Enter]** (Win) or **[return]** (Mac).

3. Click **Edit** on the menu bar, then click **Step and Repeat**.

4. Type **3** in the Repeat Count text box, type **2** in the Horizontal Offset text box, type **2** in the Vertical Offset text box, then click **OK**.

   Three new rectangles are created, each one two inches to the right and two inches down from the previous one, as shown in Figure 20.

5. Click the **top-left rectangle**, press and hold **[Shift]**, click the **second rectangle**, click **Edit** on the menu bar, then click **Step and Repeat**.

   (continued)

FIGURE 19
Removing the stroke from the rectangle

Apply None button

FIGURE 20
Viewing results of the Step and Repeat command

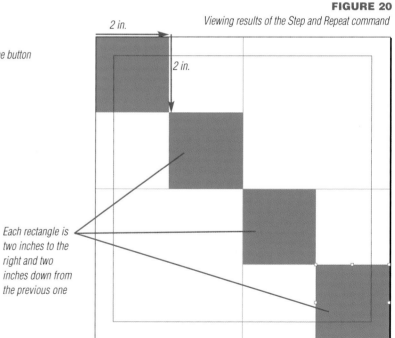

2 in.

2 in.

Each rectangle is two inches to the right and two inches down from the previous one

Working with Frames

FIGURE 21

Viewing a checkerboard created using the Step and Repeat command

6. Type **1** in the Repeat Count text box, type **4** in the Horizontal Offset text box, type **0** in the Vertical Offset text box, then click **OK**.

7. Click the **bottom-right rectangle**, press and hold **[Shift]**, click the **rectangle** that is diagonally above the bottom-right rectangle, click **Edit** on the menu bar, then click **Step and Repeat**.

8. Type **1** in the Repeat Count text box, type **-4** in the Horizontal Offset text box, type **0** in the Vertical Offset text box, then click **OK**.

9. Press **[W]** to switch to Preview, click anywhere to deselect the new rectangles, then compare your page to Figure 21.

10. Click **File** on the menu bar, click **Revert**, then click **Yes** (Win) or **Revert** (Mac) in the dialog box that follows.

 TIP   The Revert command returns the document to its last saved status.

You used the Step and Repeat command to create a checkerboard pattern, duplicating a single rectangle seven times, then reverted the document.

Align objects

1. Press and hold **[Alt]** (Win) or **[option]** (Mac), then click and drag the **square** in the top-left corner down to the bottom-right corner, as shown in Figure 22.

   TIP   Pressing and holding [Alt] (Win) or [option] (Mac) when dragging an object makes a copy of the object.

2. Press and hold **[Alt]** (Win) or **[option]** (Mac), then click and drag the **square** from the bottom-right corner up so that its center point is aligned with the intersection of the two guides, as shown in Figure 23.

3. Click **Window** on the menu bar, point to **Object & Layout**, then click **Align**.

4. Press **[Ctrl][A]** (Win) or ⌘ **[A]** (Mac) to select all the objects on the page, then click the **Align left edges button** 🖿 in the Align Objects section of the Align panel.

5. Click **Edit** on the menu bar, then click **Undo Align**.

6. Click the **Align top edges button** 🎦 in the Align panel.

7. Undo the previous step, then click the **Align horizontal centers button** 🖴.

8. Click the **Align vertical centers button** .

   All three frames are stacked upon one another, their center points aligned both horizontally and vertically.

9. Save your work, then close Orientation.

You used the [Alt] (Win) or [option] (Mac) keyboard shortcut to create two copies of the square. You then used the buttons in the Align Objects section of the Align panel to reposition the frames with various alignments.

INDESIGN 4-12

FIGURE 22
Repositioning a copy

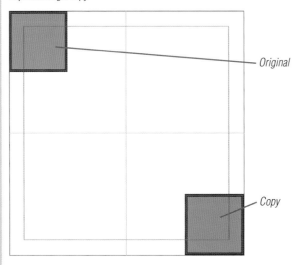

Original

Copy

FIGURE 23
Repositioning a second copy

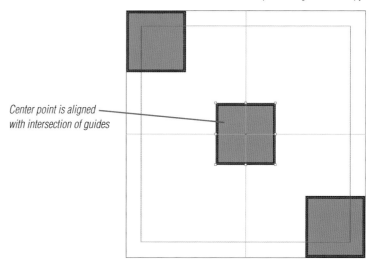

Center point is aligned
with intersection of guides

FIGURE 24
Distributing objects evenly on the horizontal axis

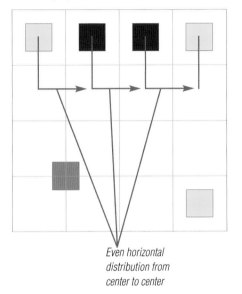

Even horizontal
distribution from
center to center

FIGURE 26
Distributing 5 objects evenly on the vertical axis

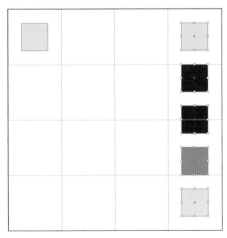

FIGURE 25
Distributing objects evenly on the vertical axis

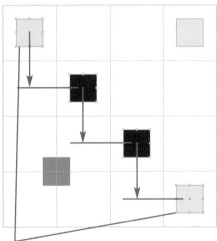

Even vertical distribution
from center to center

Distribute objects

1. Open ID 4-2.indd, then save it as **Distribution**.

2. Select the top two yellow squares and the two red squares, then click the **Align top edges button** 🔳 in the Align Objects section of the Align panel.

    The four objects are aligned at their top edges.

3. Click the **Distribute horizontal centers button** 🔳 in the Distribute Objects section of the Align panel.

    The center points of the two red squares are distributed evenly on the horizontal axis between the center points of the two yellow squares, as shown in Figure 24.

4. Click **Edit** on the menu bar, click **Deselect All**, select the top-left yellow square, select the two red squares, then select the bottom-right yellow square.

5. Click the **Distribute vertical centers button** 🔳, then compare your screen to Figure 25.

6. Select the green square, the two red squares and the bottom yellow square, then click the **Align right edges button** 🔳.

7. Press and hold **[Shift]** then click the **top-right yellow square** to add it to the selection.

8. Click the **Distribute vertical centers button** 🔳.

    The center points of the five squares are distributed evenly on the vertical axis, as shown in Figure 26.

9. Save your work, then close Distribution.

You spaced objects evenly on the horizontal or vertical axis.

STACK AND
LAYER OBJECTS

What You'll Do

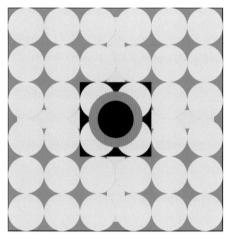

In this lesson, you will use commands to manipulate the stacking order of objects on the page, and you'll use the Layers panel to control how objects are layered.

Understanding the Stacking Order

The **stacking order** refers to how objects are "stacked." When you create multiple objects, it is important for you to remember that every object is on its own hierarchical level. For example, if you draw a square frame, and then draw a circle frame, the circle frame is automatically created one level in front of the square, whether or not they overlap. If they did overlap, the circle would appear in front of the square.

> **QUICK**TIP
> Use the word "level" when discussing the hierarchy of the stacking order, not the word "layer." Layers in InDesign are very different from levels in the stacking order.

You control the stacking order with the four commands on the Arrange menu. The Bring to Front command moves a selected object to the front of the stacking order. The Send to Back command moves a selected object to the back of the stacking order. The Bring Forward command moves

a selected object one level forward in the stacking order, and the Send Backward command moves a selected object one level backward in the stacking order.

Using these four commands, you can control and arrange how every object on the page overlaps other objects.

Understanding Layers

The Layers panel, as shown in Figure 27, is a smart solution for organizing and managing elements of a layout. By default, every document is created with one layer. You can create new layers and give them descriptive names to help you identify a layer's content. For example, if you were working on a layout that contained both text and graphics, you might want to create a layer for all of the text frames called Text and create another layer for all of the graphics called Graphics.

Why would you do this? Well, for one reason, you have the ability to lock layers in the Layers panel. Locking a layer makes its contents non-editable until

you unlock it. In the example, you could lock the Text layer while you work on the graphic elements of the layout. By doing so, you can be certain that you won't make any inadvertent changes to the text elements. Another reason is that you have the ability to hide layers. You could temporarily hide the Text layer, thus allowing you to work on the graphics with a view that is unobstructed by the text elements.

You can also duplicate layers. You do so by clicking the Duplicate Layer command in the Layers panel menu or by dragging a layer on top of the Create new layer icon in the Layers panel. When you duplicate a layer, all of the objects on the original layer are duplicated and will appear in their same locations on the new layer.

Working with Layers

You can create multiple layers in the Layers panel—as many as you need to organize your work. Figure 28 shows the Layers panel with three layers. Notice the padlock icon on Layer 2. This icon, called the Toggles lock button, indicates that this layer cannot be edited. All objects on Layer 2 are locked. Clicking the Toggles lock button will unlock the layer.

Think of layers in the Layers panel as being three-dimensional. The topmost layer is the front layer; the bottommost layer is the back layer. Therefore, it follows logically that objects on the topmost layer are in front of objects on any other layer. Layers themselves are transparent. If you have a layer with no objects on it, you can see through the layer to the objects on the layers behind it.

Note that each layer contains its own stacking order. Let's say that you have three layers, each with five objects on it. Regardless of the stacking order of the top layer, all the objects on that layer are in front of any

FIGURE 27
Layers panel

FIGURE 28
Layers panel with three layers

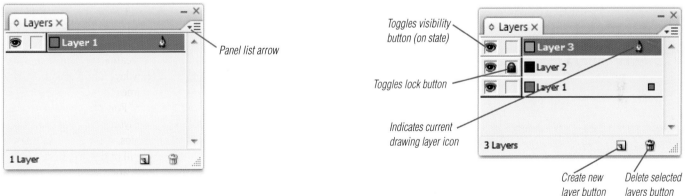

Panel list arrow

Toggles visibility button (on state)

Toggles lock button

Indicates current drawing layer icon

Create new layer button

Delete selected layers button

objects on the other layers. In other words, an object at the back of the stacking order of the top layer is still in front of any object on any layer beneath it.

One great organizational aspect of layers is that you can assign a selection color to a layer. When you select an object, its bounding box appears in the selection color of the layer that it is placed on, as shown in Figure 29. You determine a layer's selection color by selecting the layer, clicking the Layers panel list arrow, clicking Layer Options for the name of the selected layer, then choosing a new color from the Color menu. When you are working with a layout that contains numerous objects, this feature is a great visual aid for keeping track of objects and their relationships to other objects.

Manipulating Layers and Objects on Layers

Once you have created layers in a document, you have many options for manipulating objects on the layers and the layers themselves. You can move objects between layers, and you can reorder the layers in the Layers panel.

QUICKTIP

You can merge the contents of two or more layers by selecting the layers in the Layers panel, clicking the Layers panel list arrow, then clicking Merge Layers. The first layer that you click upon selecting the layers to be merged becomes the resulting merged layer. **Flattening** a document refers to merging all of the layers in the Layers panel.

Clicking a layer in the Layers panel to select it is called **targeting** a layer. The layer that you click is called the **target layer**. When you create a new object, the object will be added to whichever layer is targeted in the Layers panel. The pen tool icon next to a layer's name in the Layers panel is called the **Indicates current drawing layer icon**. This icon will help remind you that anything placed or drawn will become part of that layer.

You can select any object on the page, regardless of which layer is targeted. When you select the object, the layer that the object is on is automatically targeted in the Layers panel. Thus, by clicking an object, you know which layer it is on.

FIGURE 29

Assigning a selection color to a layer

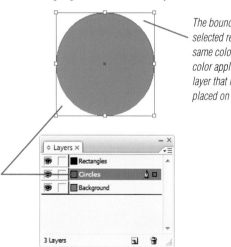

The bounding box of the selected rectangle is the same color as the selection color applied to the Circles layer that it has been placed on

When an object is selected, a small button appears to the right of the name of the layer, as shown in Figure 30. That small button, identified as the **Indicates selected items button**, represents the selected object (or objects). You can click and drag the Indicates selected items button and move it to another layer. When you do so, the selected object(s) moves to that layer. Therefore, you should never feel constrained by which layer you choose for an object; it's easy to move objects from one layer to another.

You can also change the order of layers in the Layers panel by dragging a layer up or down in the panel. As you drag, a heavy black line indicates the new position for the layer when you release the mouse button. In Figure 31, the Rectangles layer is being repositioned under the Circles layer.

Selecting Artwork on Layers

Let's say you have three layers in your document, each with six objects. That means your document has a total of 18 objects. If you apply the Select All command on the Edit menu, all 18 objects will be selected, regardless of which layer is targeted in the Layers panel.

If you want to select only the objects on a single layer, you must use a keyboard shortcut. Press and hold [Alt] (Win) or [option] (Mac), and then click the layer in the Layers panel. Pressing and holding [Alt] (Win) or [option] (Mac) when clicking a layer selects all the objects on that layer.

Selecting Objects Behind Other Objects

When you have multiple overlapping objects on a page, objects behind other objects can sometimes be difficult to select. Pressing and holding [Ctrl] (Win) or ⌘ (Mac) allows you to "click through the stacking order" to select objects behind other objects. Simply click the top object, press and hold [Ctrl] (Win) or ⌘ (Mac), then click the top object again, which will select the object immediately behind it. Click the top object again and the next object down in the stacking order will be selected.

FIGURE 30

Viewing the Indicates selected items button

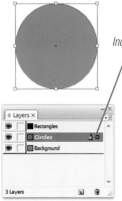

Indicates selected items button

FIGURE 31

Changing the order of two layers in the Layers panel

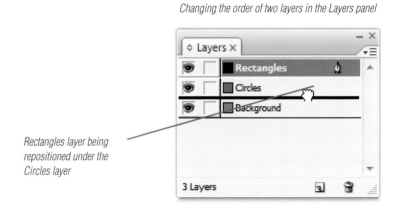

Rectangles layer being repositioned under the Circles layer

Use the Arrange commands to change the stacking order of objects

1. Open ID 4-3.indd, then save it as **Stack and Layer**.
2. Press **[V]** to access the Selection Tool, then click the **yellow rectangle**.
3. Click **Object** on the menu bar, point to **Arrange**, then click **Bring Forward**.

   The yellow rectangle moves forward one level in the stacking order.
4. Click the **red square**, click **Object** on the menu bar, point to **Arrange**, then click **Bring to Front**.
5. Select both the yellow rectangle and the blue circle, click **Object** on the menu bar, point to **Arrange**, then click **Bring to Front.**

   Both objects move in front of the red square, as shown in Figure 32.
6. Click the **green circle**, click **Object** on the menu bar, point to **Arrange**, then click **Bring to Front**.
7. Select all, then click the **Align horizontal centers button** ▲ in the Align panel.
8. Deselect all, click the **green circle**, click **Object** on the menu bar, point to **Arrange**, then click **Send Backward**.

   As shown in Figure 33, the green circle moves backward one level in the stacking order, behind the blue circle.
9. Deselect all, select the **blue circle**, press and hold **[Ctrl]** (Win) or ⌘ (Mac), then click the **blue circle** again to select the green circle behind it.
10. Still pressing and holding **[Ctrl]** (Win) or ⌘ (Mac), click the **blue circle** again to select the yellow rectangle, then click the **blue circle** once more to select the red square.

(continued)

FIGURE 32
Using the Bring to Front command with two objects selected

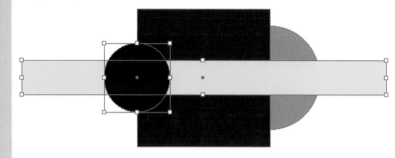

FIGURE 33
Sending the green circle backward one level in the stacking order

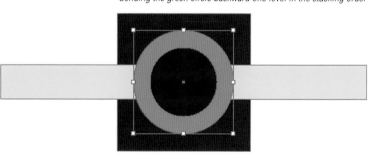

FIGURE 34
Layers panel with Layer 1

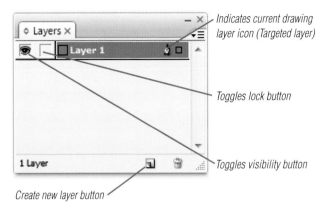

Indicates current drawing
layer icon (Targeted layer)

Toggles lock button

Toggles visibility button

Create new layer button

FIGURE 35
Layers panel with three layers

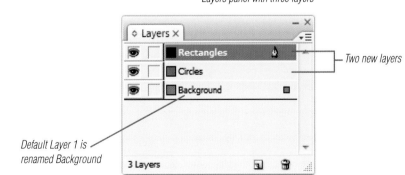

Two new layers

Default Layer 1 is
renamed Background

| TIP Commit this technique to memory, as it is very useful for selecting overlapping objects.

You used the Arrange commands to manipulate the stacking order of four objects.

Create new layers in the Layers panel

1. Deselect all, then click the **Layers panel name tab**.

   As shown in Figure 34, the Layers panel has one default layer named Layer 1.

   | TIP The default location for the Layers panel is along the right side of the document window grouped with the Info, Pages, and Links panels.

2. Double-click **Layer 1** in the Layers panel.

   The Layer Options dialog box opens, which allows you to change settings for Layer 1, such as its name and selection color.

3. Type **Background** in the Name text box, then click **OK**.

4. Click the **Create new layer button** in the Layers panel, then double-click **Layer 2**.

5. Type **Circles** in the Name text box, click the **Color list arrow**, click **Orange**, then click **OK**.

6. Click the **Layers panel list arrow**, then click **New Layer**.

7. Type **Rectangles** in the Name text box, click the **Color list arrow**, click **Purple**, then click **OK**.

   Your Layers panel should resemble Figure 35.

You renamed Layer 1, then created two new layers in the Layers panel.

Position objects on layers

1. Press **[V]** to access the Selection Tool (if necessary), then click the **green circle**.

   As shown in Figure 36, the Background layer on the Layers panel is highlighted and the Indicates selected items button appears next to the Indicates current drawing layer icon.

2. Click and drag the **Indicates selected items button** 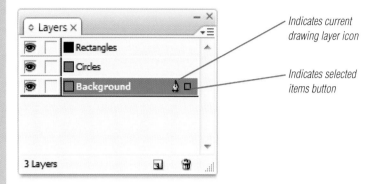 up to the Circles layer.

   The green circle is moved to the Circles layer. The frame around the circle now appears orange, the selection color assigned to the Circles layer.

3. Select both the red square and the yellow rectangle, then drag the **Indicates selected items button** from the Background layer up to the Rectangles layer.

4. Click the **Toggles visibility button** on the Rectangles layer to hide that layer, then click on the Circles layer to hide that layer.

5. Click the **blue circle**, then drag the **Indicates selected items button** from the Background layer up to the Circles layer.

   As shown in Figure 37, you cannot move the circle to the Circles layer because it is hidden.

6. Press and hold **[Ctrl]** (Win) or ⌘ (Mac), then drag the **Indicates selected items button** from the Background layer up to the Circles layer.

   The blue circle disappears because it is moved to the Circles layer, which is hidden.

   (continued)

FIGURE 36
Identifying the Background layer as the targeted layer

Indicates current drawing layer icon

Indicates selected items button

FIGURE 37
Trying to move an object onto a hidden layer

The selected object cannot be placed on a layer that is hidden

Layer not visible

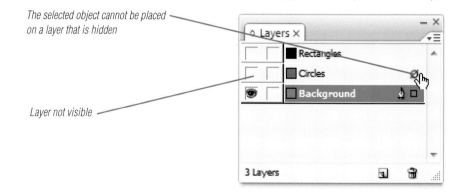

FIGURE 38

Viewing a layered document

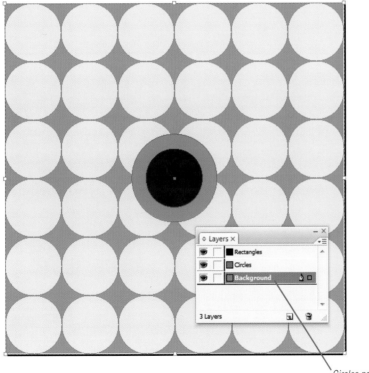

*Circles pasted on
Background layer*

TIP   Pressing and holding [Ctrl] (Win) or
⌘ (Mac) while you drag the Indicates
selected items button allows you to place an
object on a hidden or locked layer.

7. Click the **Background layer**, if necessary, click
the **Rectangle Tool** ▣ , then draw a rectangle that is exactly the same size as the page.

   Because the Background layer was targeted
   in the Layers panel, the new object is positioned on the Background layer.

8. Click the **Fill button** in the Toolbox, click
Light Blue in the Swatches panel, then
remove any stroke if necessary.

9. Click **View** on the menu bar, then click **Fit
Page in Window**.

10. Open ID 4-4.indd, select all the objects on the
page, click **Edit** on the menu bar, click **Copy**,
then close ID 4-4.indd.

11. Verify that the Background layer is still targeted in the Layers panel, click **Edit** on the
menu bar, then click **Paste**.

   The objects are pasted onto the Background
   layer.

12. Click the **Toggles visibility button** ☐ on
the Circles layer so that your Layers panel
and page resemble Figure 38.

*You used the Layers panel to move selected
objects from one layer to another. You targeted a
layer, and then created a new object, which was
added to that layer. You then pasted objects into a
targeted layer.*

Change the order of layers in the Layers panel

1. Switch to the Selection Tool ![pointer], deselect all, click the **Rectangles layer**, then click the **Toggles visibility button** [ ] in its off state in order to make the layer visible.

2. Using Figure 39 as an example, drag the **Rectangles layer** down until you see a heavy black line below the Circles layer, then release the mouse button.

   Since the Rectangles layer is now below the Circles layer, the objects on the Rectangles layer are now beneath the objects on the Circles layer, as shown in Figure 40.

3. Click any of the light blue circles.

   The light blue circles are grouped, so when you click one, you select them all.

4. Click and drag the **Indicates selected items button** [ ] from the Background layer up to the Circles layer.

   Because it is the newest object on the Circles layer, the blue circles group is at the top of the stacking order on that layer.

5. Click **Object** on the menu bar, point to **Arrange**, then click **Send to Back**.

   As shown in Figure 41, the blue circles group is sent to the back of the stacking order on the Circles layer. However, it is in front of the two rectangles, because their layer is beneath the Circles layer.

   (continued)

FIGURE 39
Changing the order of layers

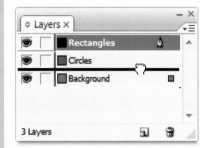

FIGURE 40
Viewing the document after reordering layers

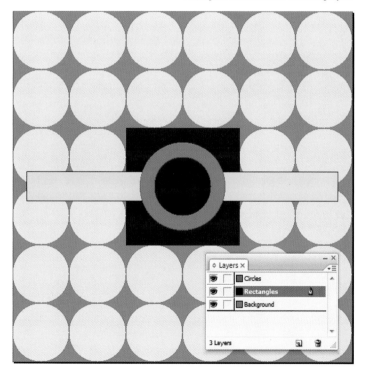

FIGURE 41

Sending the circles to the back of the Circles layer

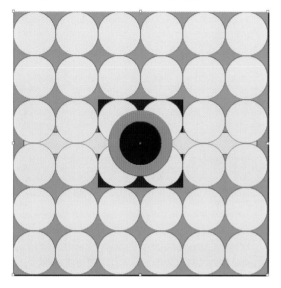

6. Click and drag the **Rectangles layer** down to the Create new layer button 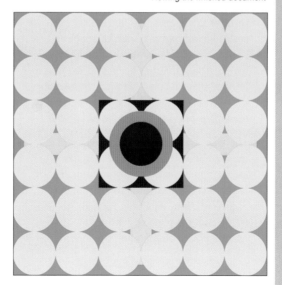 in the Layers panel.

   A duplicate layer named Rectangles copy is created above the original Rectangles layer.

7. Press and hold **[Alt]** (Win) or **[option]** (Mac), then click the **Rectangles copy layer**.

   > TIP Press and hold [Alt] (Win) or [option] (Mac) when clicking a layer in the Layers panel to select all the objects on the layer.

8. Click the **center reference point** in the Transform panel, type **90** in the Rotation Angle text box in the Transform panel, then press **[Enter]** (Win) or **[return]** (Mac).

9. Deselect all, press **[W]** to switch to Preview, press **[V]** to access the Selection Tool, click the **red square**, click **Object** on the menu bar, point to **Arrange**, click **Bring to Front**, then deselect all so that your page resembles Figure 42.

10. Save your work, then close Stack and Layer.

You changed the order of layers, noting the effect on the objects on the page. You also changed the stacking order of objects within layers. You duplicated a layer, and you learned a keyboard shortcut for selecting all the objects on a single layer.

FIGURE 42

Viewing the finished document

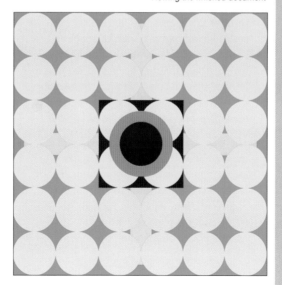

WORK WITH GRAPHICS FRAMES

What You'll Do

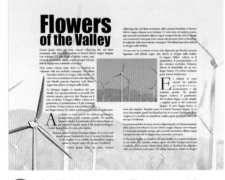

In this lesson, you will create graphics frames, resize them, and manipulate graphics that you import into them.

Placing Graphics in a Document

The term **graphic** is pretty broad. In its most basic definition, a graphic is an element on the page that is not text. A simple square with a fill could be called a graphic. However, when you are talking about placing graphics in an InDesign document, the term graphic usually is referring to bitmap images or vector graphics. **Bitmap images** are images that consist of pixels created in a program, such as Adobe Photoshop. They can also be digital photos. Anything that has been scanned is a bitmap image. Vector graphics are usually illustrations created in and imported from drawing programs like Adobe Illustrator.

There are two essential methods for placing a graphic in a document. You can create a graphics placeholder frame using any of the three shape frame tools, shown in Figure 43. Once you have created the frame and it is selected on the page, you use the Place command on the File menu to select the graphic you want to import into the document. The graphic will appear in the selected graphics frame.

You can also place a graphic without first creating a graphics frame. If you click the Place command and then select the graphic you want to import, you will see the loaded graphics icon when you float the pointer over the page. Click the loaded graphics icon on the page to place the graphic. The graphic will be placed on the page in a graphics frame whose top-left corner will be positioned at the location where you clicked the loaded graphics icon.

Which is the better method? It depends on what you want to do with the graphic. If the size and location of the graphics frame is important, it's probably better to create and position the frame first, then import the graphic and make it fit into the frame. If the size and location of the frame are negotiable, you might want to place the graphic anywhere in the layout and then modify its size and location.

Understanding the Difference Between the Graphics Frame and the Graphic

It is important that you understand that the graphics frame contains the graphic. Think of the graphics frame as a window through which you see the placed graphic. This understanding is important in cases where the graphics frame is smaller than the graphic that it contains. In this case, you can see only the areas of the graphic that can fit in the frame. The other areas of the graphic are still there, you just can't see them because they are outside of the frame.

Understanding the Difference Between the Selection Tool and the Direct Selection Tool

The previous topic is a clear signal that you must differentiate the graphics frame from the graphic itself. This differentiation is reflected in the Toolbox by the Selection Tool and the Direct Selection Tool. Specifically, the Selection Tool addresses the graphics frame while the Direct Selection Tool addresses the *contents* of the frame. Anything you want to do to the frame, you do with the Selection Tool. Anything you want to do to the contents—to the graphic itself—you do

with the Direct Selection Tool. This concept is the key to manipulating graphics within a graphics frame.

Figure 44 shows a selected graphics frame which contains a placed graphic. Note that the frame was selected with the Selection Tool. The Transform panel shows the X and Y locations of the frame and the width and height of the frame.

Figure 45 shows the same object, but this time it has been selected with the Direct Selection Tool. Note that the information in the Transform panel now refers to the graphic itself, not the frame that contains

FIGURE 43
Three graphics frame tools

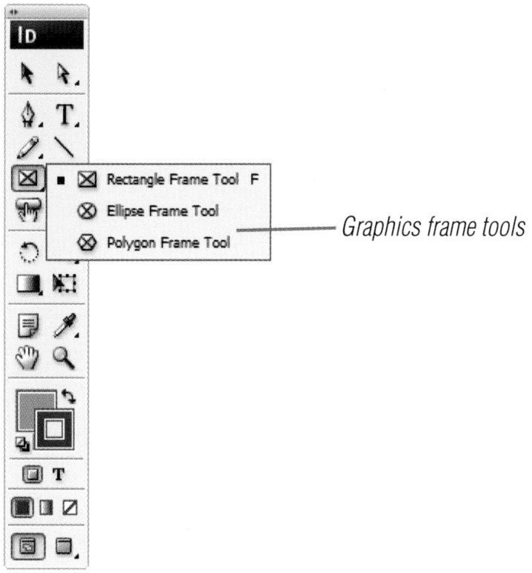

Graphics frame tools

FIGURE 44
Selecting a graphics frame with the Selection Tool

Selection Tool

Graphics frame is selected

Transform panel values refer to selected graphics frame

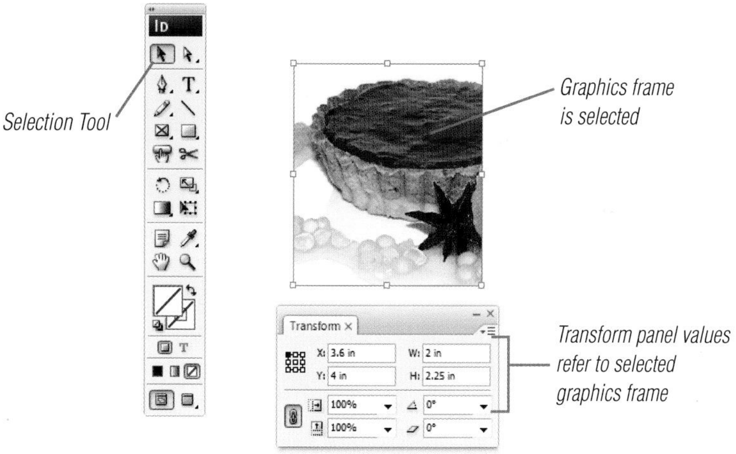

it. Note too that the selection itself appears differently. The selected frame around the image is called the bounding box. The **bounding box**—always rectangular—is the frame that defines the horizontal and vertical dimensions of the graphic. Finally, note that even though you can see the entire bounding box, there are parts of the graphic that you can't see. That's because the graphic is being cropped by the graphics frame.

Hang on. There's a lot of information coming at you all at once here. Let's summarize

the terminology and concepts. The graphics frame contains the graphic. The graphics frame determines how the graphic is cropped. When you click a graphic with the Selection Tool, the graphics frame is selected and the Transform panel displays the physical characteristics of the graphics frame.

When you click a graphic with the Direct Selection Tool, the graphic itself is selected. This selection is indicated by showing you the graphic's bounding box. The bounding box and the graphics frame are completely independent of one another.

They can be, and often are, different sizes. When you click the graphic with the Direct Selection Tool, the Transform panel describes the physical characteristics of the graphic itself.

QUICKTIP

When you click a graphic with the Direct Selection Tool, a small plus sign appears beside the X and Y values in the Transform panel, indicating that the X and Y locations refer to the graphic *within* the graphics frame.

FIGURE 45
Selecting a graphic with the Direct Selection Tool

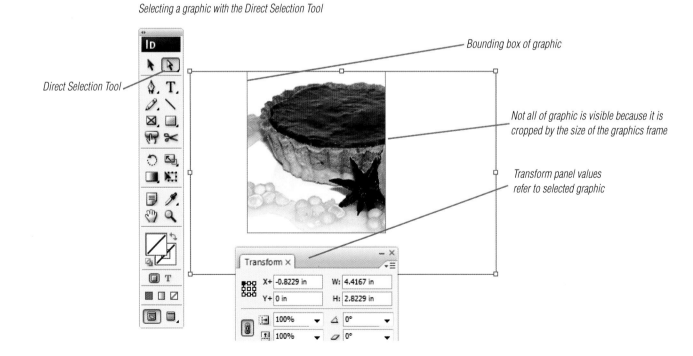

Direct Selection Tool

Bounding box of graphic

Not all of graphic is visible because it is cropped by the size of the graphics frame

Transform panel values refer to selected graphic

Transform ×

X+ -0.8229 in   W: 4.4167 in
Y+ 0 in   H: 2.8229 in

100%   ⌂ 0°
100%   ⌂ 0°

Moving a Graphic Within a Graphics Frame

Once you understand that the Direct Selection Tool selects the graphic itself, it is easy to move a graphic within the graphics frame. Simply click and drag the graphic with the Direct Selection Tool to move the graphic, as shown in Figure 46. But wait... there's a better way to do it. Press and hold the Direct Selection Tool over the graphic until it turns into a black arrow, then drag the black arrow to move the graphic. When you do so, you see a ghosted image of the areas of the graphic that are outside the graphics frame, as shown in Figure 47. The ghosted image is referred to as a **dynamic preview**.

Once you release the mouse button, the graphic will be repositioned within the frame. Remember, though, that regardless of where you move the graphic within the frame, the frame crops the graphic.

Resizing a Graphic

When you select a graphic with the Direct Selection Tool, you can then resize the graphic within the frame. Changes that you make to the size of the graphic do not affect the size of the graphics frame.

One easy way to **scale**, or resize a graphic is to use the Transform panel. With the graphic selected, change the Scale X Percentage and the Scale Y Percentage values in the Transform panel, as shown in Figure 48, to reduce or enlarge the graphic.

You can also use the Transform/Scale command on the Object menu to scale the graphic. Remember, when the graphic is selected with the Direct Selection Tool, only the graphic will be scaled when you use this command.

> **QUICK**TIP
>
> You can resize a graphics frame and the graphic simultaneously by pressing and holding [Ctrl][Shift] (Win) or ⌘ [Shift] (Mac) while dragging the graphics frame bounding box handle.

FIGURE 46
Moving the graphic within the graphics frame

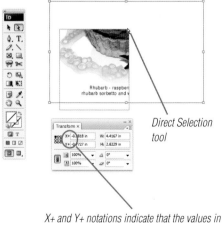

Direct Selection tool

X+ and Y+ notations indicate that the values in the Transform panel refer to the graphic

FIGURE 47
Viewing the dynamic preview

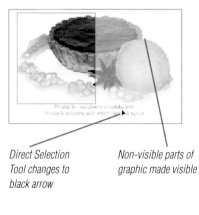

Direct Selection Tool changes to black arrow

Non-visible parts of graphic made visible

FIGURE 48
Scaling a graphic using the Transform panel

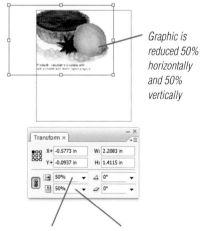

Graphic is reduced 50% horizontally and 50% vertically

Scale X Percentage value   Scale Y Percentage value

Using the Fitting Commands

While it's not difficult to select a graphic with the Direct Selection Tool and then scale it in the Transform panel, there are a lot of steps in the process. "There must be an easier way to resize a graphic," you are thinking. You're right!

For the quick solution, you can use the Fitting commands, located on the Object menu. The Fitting commands refer to the graphic as the content. The Fit Content to Frame command scales the content to fit the frame, and the Fit Frame to Content command scales the frame to fit the content. The Center Content command centers the graphic within the frame.

When you click the Fit Content to Frame command, the content is often distorted to fit the frame. For example, let's say that your content is a two inch square, and it's within a rectangular graphics frame. Applying the Fit Content to Frame command will distort the square's width to fit the full width of the rectangular frame, as shown in Figure 49. You can easily restore the graphic to its normal proportions by clicking the Fit Content

FIGURE 49

Using the Fit Content to Frame command can distort a graphic

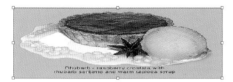

Proportionally command, which is the fourth Fitting command on the Object menu.

QUICKTIP

The Fill Frame Proportionally command resizes the placed graphic to a size that is guaranteed to fit the frame, with no white space around it. This means that some of the graphic may not be visible if it exceeds the size of the frame. In any case, the graphic will *not* be distorted to fit the frame.

Wrapping Text Around an Imported Photoshop Graphic Saved with a Named Clipping Path

In Chapter 3, you learned how to use the Text Wrap panel to wrap text around

a bounding box using the Wrap around bounding box button. You can also wrap text around a graphic inside a graphics frame, as shown in Figure 50.

The Text Wrap panel offers a number of methods for doing so. In this chapter, you will focus on wrapping text around an image that was saved with a named clipping path in Photoshop. Figure 51 shows a Photoshop image with a clipping path drawn around a man. A **clipping path** is a graphic that you draw in Photoshop that outlines the areas of the image that you want to show when the file is placed in a layout program like InDesign. When you save the Photoshop file, you name the clipping path and save it with the file.

FIGURE 50

Wrapping text around a graphic

The text is able to enter the graphics frame to wrap around the picture

FIGURE 51

A Photoshop image with a clipping path

Clipping path created in Photoshop

When you place a graphic that has a named clipping path saved with it into your layout, InDesign is able to recognize the clipping path. With the graphic selected, click the Wrap around object shape button in the Text Wrap panel, click the Type list arrow in the Contour Options section of the panel, and then choose Photoshop Path, as shown in Figure 52. When you do so, the Path menu will list all the paths that were saved with the graphic file (usually, you will save only one path with a file). Choose the path that you want to use for the text wrap.

Remember, in every case, you can always manually adjust the resulting text wrap boundary. Though the clipping path is created in Photoshop, the text wrap itself is created in InDesign—and it is editable. As shown in Figure 53, you can relocate the path's anchor points using the Direct Selection Tool. You can also use the Add Anchor Point and Delete Anchor Point Tools to add or delete points to the path as you find necessary. Click the Add Anchor Point Tool anywhere on the path to add a new point, which gives you further control for manipulating the path. Click any anchor point with the Delete Anchor Point Tool to remove it. Changing the shape of the path changes how text wraps around the path.

FIGURE 52
Choosing the Wrap around object shape button

Wrap around object shape button

Top Offset value (applies to entire path)

Click Type list arrow to choose Photoshop Path

Click Path list arrow to choose a named path saved with the Photoshop file

FIGURE 53
Manipulating the text wrap path

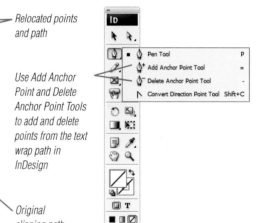

Relocated points and path

Use Add Anchor Point and Delete Anchor Point Tools to add and delete points from the text wrap path in InDesign

Original clipping path

Path created in InDesign

Place graphics in a document

1. Open ID 4-5.indd, click **Fix Links Automatically**, click **No** in the next warning dialog box, then save it as **Flowers**.

2. In the Layers panel, click the **Toggles lock button** on the Text layer to lock the Text layer, as shown in Figure 54.

   TIP   When a layer is locked, the contents of the layer cannot be modified; this is a smart way to protect the contents of any layer from unwanted changes.

3. Click the **Background layer** to target it, click the **Rectangle Frame Tool** , then draw a graphics frame in the center of the page that is approximately the size shown in Figure 55.

   The bounding box of the graphics frame is orange because orange is the selection color applied to the Background layer.

4. Click **File** on the menu bar, click **Place**, navigate to the drive and folder where your Data Files are stored, then double-click **Windmills Ghost.psd**.

   Because the frame was selected, the graphic is placed automatically into the frame, as shown in Figure 56.

5. Click the **Selection Tool** , click anywhere to deselect the frame, click the **Toggles visibility button** on the Background layer to hide it, then click the **Images layer** to target it in the Layers panel.

6. Click **File** on the menu bar, click **Place**, navigate to the drive and folder where your Data Files are stored, click **Windmills Color.psd**, then click **Open**.

   TIP   You can also access the Place command by pressing [Ctrl][D] (Win) or [⌘][D] (Mac).

(continued)

FIGURE 54
Locking the Text layer

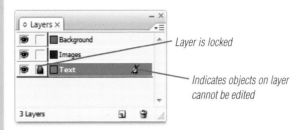

Layer is locked

Indicates objects on layer cannot be edited

FIGURE 55
Drawing a graphics frame

FIGURE 56
Viewing the placed graphic

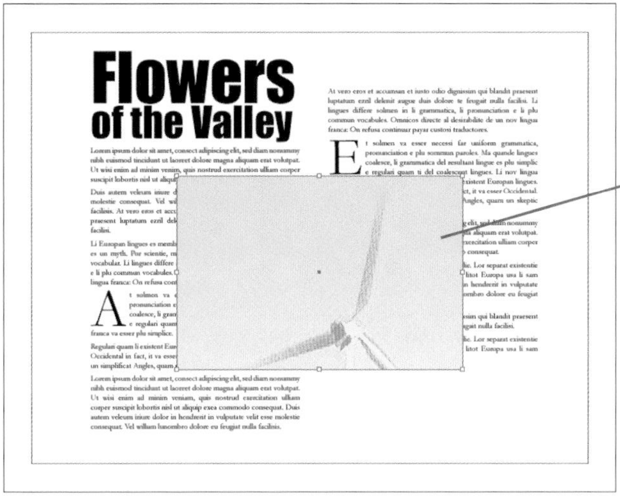

FIGURE 57
Viewing the graphic placed with the loaded graphics icon

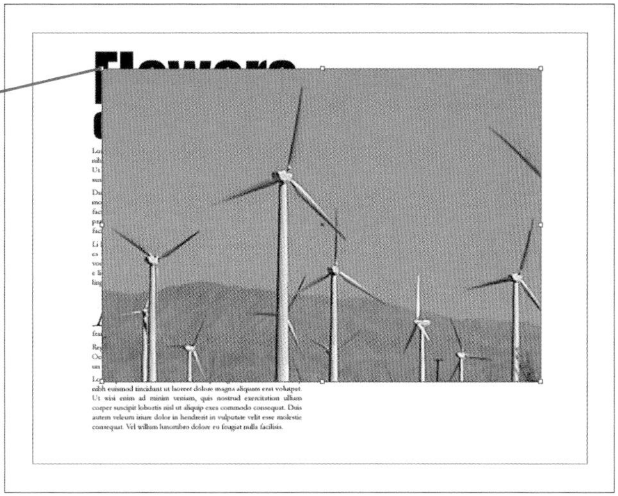

7. Position the pointer over the document.

   The pointer changes to the loaded graphics icon and shows a thumbnail of the graphic.

8. Click the **loaded graphics icon** on the F in the word Flowers.

   As shown in Figure 57, the graphic is placed in a new graphics frame whose top-left corner is located where the loaded graphics icon was clicked.

You imported two graphics using two subtly different methods. You created a graphics frame, and then used the Place command to place a graphic in that frame. Then, you used the Place command to load a graphic file, and finally clicked the loaded graphics icon to create a new frame for the new graphic.

Move a graphic in a graphics frame

1. Hide the Images layer, show and target the Background layer, click the **Selection Tool**, then click the **Windmills Ghost.psd graphic**.
2. Click the **top-left reference point** in the Transform panel.
3. Click the **Direct Selection Tool**, position the tool over the graphic, then click the **graphic.**

   TIP As soon as you position the Direct Selection Tool over the graphic, the pointer becomes a hand pointer.

   The X and Y text boxes in the Transform panel change to X+ and Y+, indicating that the graphic—not the frame—is selected.

4. Note the width and height of the graphic, as listed in the Transform panel.

   The graphic is substantially larger than the frame that contains it, thus there are many areas of the graphic outside the frame that are not visible through the frame.

(continued)

5. Press and hold the **hand icon** on the graphic until the hand icon changes to a black arrow, then drag inside the graphics frame, releasing your mouse when the windmill is centered in the frame, as shown in Figure 58.

   The graphic moves within the frame, but the frame itself does not move. Note that the blue bounding box, now visible, is the bounding box for the graphic within the frame.

6. Click the **Selection Tool**, then click the **graphic**.

   The orange graphics frame appears and the blue bounding box of the graphic disappears. Note that the values in the Transform panel are again specific to the frame only.

7. Click and drag the **top-left selection handle** of the graphics frame so that it is aligned with the top-left corner of the document page.

   As shown in Figure 59, the graphic within the frame does not change size or location.

8. Drag the **bottom-right corner** of the graphics frame so that it is aligned with the bottom-right corner of the document page.

   As the frame is enlarged, more of the graphic within the frame is visible.

9. Click the **Direct Selection Tool**, click the **graphic**, type **0** in the X+ text box in the Transform panel, type **0** in the Y+ text box, then press **[Enter]** (Win) or **[return]** (Mac).

   As shown in Figure 60, the top-left corner of the graphic is aligned with the top-left corner of the frame.

You used the Direct Selection Tool and X+ and Y+ values in the Transform panel to move a graphic within a graphics frame.

FIGURE 58
Viewing the graphic as it is moved in the frame

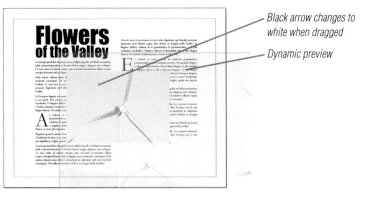

Black arrow changes to white when dragged

Dynamic preview

FIGURE 59
Resizing the graphics frame

Top-left corner of bounding box

Resized frame

Graphic does not change size

FIGURE 60
Viewing the entire graphic in the enlarged frame

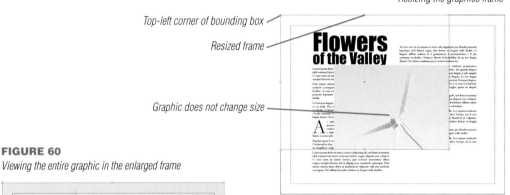

FIGURE 61
Scaling a graphic

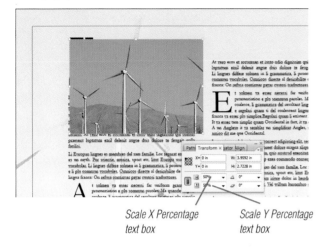

Scale X Percentage
text box

Scale Y Percentage
text box

Placing multiple graphics

With InDesign CS3, you can place multiple graphics, instead of placing them one-at-a-time. Click Place on the menu bar, navigate to the location of your graphics, click the first graphic file, then press [Ctrl](Win) or ⌘ (Mac) while you select the remaining graphic files. After you click Open, the loaded graphics icon appears in the document window. The loaded graphics icon includes a thumbnail of the first loaded image along with the total number of images loaded. In addition, the Links panel displays LP (which stands for "loaded in place cursor") next to the first loaded image. This is a fantastic feature for those of you who need to place multiple images frequently. But wait, there's more: If you [Ctrl](Win) or ⌘ (Mac)-click, all of the images will be loaded cascade-style and you can even press [Esc] to unload the first image without placing it. However, if all of this excitement is too much for your computer to handle, you can deselect the "Show Thumbnails in Place" check box in the Interface section of the Preferences dialog box. Doing so allows you to still place multiple images without the thumbnails—hopefully freeing up computer memory.

Resize graphics frames and graphics

1. Drag the **Background layer** below the Text layer in the Layers panel, then show and target the Images layer.

2. Press **[A]** to access the Direct Selection Tool, then click the **Windmills Color.psd graphic**.

3. Verify that the Constrain proportions for scaling option is activated in the Transform panel—represented by a link icon 🔗 .

   The Constrain proportions for scaling option is activated by default. If you click it, you will deactivate this feature and see a broken link icon.

4. Type **50** in the Scale X Percentage text box in the Transform panel, then press **[Enter]** (Win) or **[return]** (Mac).

   Because the Constrain proportions for scaling option is activated, the graphic is scaled 50% horizontally and 50% vertically, as shown in Figure 61.

5. Press **[V]** to access the Selection Tool, then click the **Windmills Color.psd graphic**.

   The size of the graphics frame was not affected by scaling the graphic itself.

6. Click **Object** on the menu bar, point to **Fitting**, then click **Fit Frame to Content**.

7. Click the **top-left reference point** in the Transform panel.

8. With the frame still selected, type **4.5** in the X Location text box, type **3** in the Y Location text box, type **3.32** in the Width text box, type **2.125** in the Height text box, then press **[Enter]** (Win) or **[return]** (Mac).

(continued)

9. Press **[A]** to access the Direct Selection Tool, click the **graphic**, then note the Scale X Percentage and Scale Y Percentage text boxes in the Transform panel, as shown in Figure 62.

The graphic retains its 50% scale.

TIP   When you resize a graphics frame using the Width and Height text boxes in the Transform panel, the graphic is not resized with the frame.

10. Click **Object** on the menu bar, point to **Fitting**, then click **Fit Content Proportionally**.

The Transform panel shows that the graphic is scaled proportionately to fit the resized frame.

11. Press **[V]**, then click the **graphic**.

12. Click **Object** on the menu bar, point to **Fitting**, then click **Fit Frame to Content**.

As shown in Figure 63, the right edge of the frame moves left to fit to the right edge of the graphic.

You scaled a graphic using the Transform panel, noting that the graphics frame did not change with the scale. You then scaled the graphics frame with the Transform panel, noting that the graphic itself was not scaled. Lastly, you used the Fitting command to fit the graphic proportionally to the new frame size.

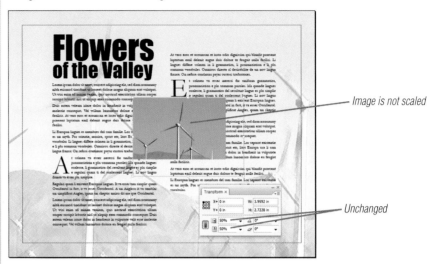

FIGURE 62
Noting the Scale X and Scale Y Percentage values

Image is not scaled

Unchanged

FIGURE 63
Fitting the frame to the content

Working with Frames

FIGURE 64
Wrapping text around a frame's bounding box

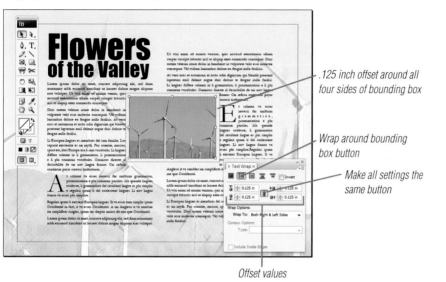

.125 inch offset around all four sides of bounding box

Wrap around bounding box button

Make all settings the same button

Offset values

FIGURE 65
Wrapping text around the graphic

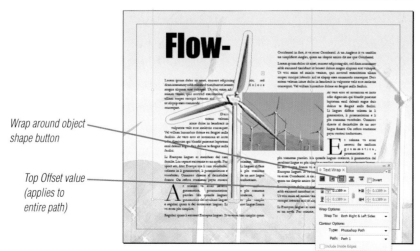

Wrap around object shape button

Top Offset value (applies to entire path)

Wrap text around a graphic

1. Verify that the Selection Tool is selected, click the **graphic**, then click the **Wrap around bounding box button** in the Text Wrap panel.

2. Verify that the Make all settings the same button is active, type **.125** in the Top Offset text box, then press **[Enter]** (Win) or **[return]** (Mac).

    Your page and Text Wrap panel should resemble Figure 64.

3. Deselect all, press **[Ctrl][D]** (Win) or **⌘[D]** (Mac), navigate to the drive and folder where your Data Files are stored, then double-click **Windmills Silhouette.psd**.

4. Click the **loaded graphics icon** on the F in the word Flowers.

    Windmills Silhouette.psd was saved with a clipping path named "Path 1" in Photoshop.

5. Click the **Wrap around object shape button** in the Text Wrap panel, click the **Type list arrow**, click **Photoshop Path**, then note that Path 1 is automatically listed in the Path text box.

    As shown in Figure 65, the text wraps around the graphic's shape. The Text Wrap panel specifies a default offset of .1389 inches for the wrap.

(continued)

6. Deselect, click the **Selection Tool** ![cursor], if necessary, then click the **graphic** to verify that the frame—not the graphic within the frame—is selected.

7. Type **-1.25** in the X Location text box in the Transform panel, type **3.8** in the Y Location text box, then press **[Enter]** (Win) or **[return]** (Mac).

   As shown in Figure 66, because of the shape of the path around the graphic, one word appears in an odd position near the graphic.

8. In the Wrap Options section, click the **Wrap To list arrow**, click **Right Side**, then deselct the graphic.

   As shown in Figure 67, the word is moved to the right because the wrap option forces all items to wrap against the right edge of the graphic.

   TIP Whenever you have a stray word or a stubborn area after applying a text wrap, you can fine-tune the text wrap using the Delete Anchor Point Tool ![tool] to remove unwanted anchor points along the path. You can also move anchor points along the path using the Direct Selection Tool ![tool] .

(continued)

FIGURE 66
Noting a minor problem with the wrap

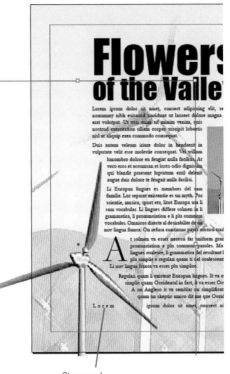

Stray word

FIGURE 67

Identifying results of Wrap To options in the Text Wrap panel

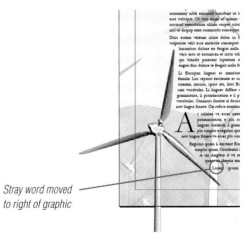

Stray word moved
to right of graphic

Working with Frames

FIGURE 68
Resizing the graphics frame

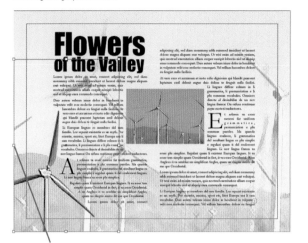

Drag handle right

FIGURE 69
Viewing the completed document

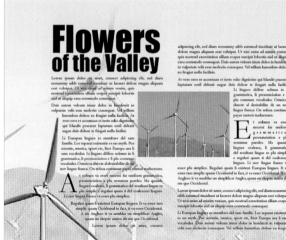

9. Click the **Selection Tool** ![cursor], click the **graphic**, drag the **left-middle handle** of the bounding box to the right so that it abuts the left edge of the page, then drag the **bottom-middle handle** of the bounding box up so that it abuts the bottom of the page, as shown in Figure 68.

   TIP You may need to reduce the page view to see the bottom handles on the bounding box.

10. Click the **pasteboard** to deselect the frame, press **[W]** to change to Preview, then compare your work to Figure 69.

11. Save your work, then close Flowers.

WORK WITH
TEXT FRAMES

What You'll Do

In this lesson, you will explore options for autoflowing text through a document. You will also learn how to add column breaks to text.

Semi-Autoflowing Text

In Chapter 3, you learned how to thread text manually—to make it flow from text frame to text frame. When you click the out port of one text frame with the Selection Tool, the pointer changes to the loaded text icon. When you click the loaded text icon in another text frame, text flows from the first frame to the second frame—and the pointer automatically changes back to the Selection Tool. That's great, but what if you wanted to keep manually threading text? Would you need to repeat the process over and over again?

This is where **semi-autoflowing** text comes in. When you are ready to click the loaded text icon in a text frame where you want text to flow, press and hold [Alt] (Win) or [option] (Mac) and then click the text frame. Text will flow into the text frame, but the loaded text icon will remain active—it will not automatically revert back to the Selection Tool. You can then thread text into another text frame. In a nutshell, semi-autoflowing text is a method for manually threading text through multiple frames.

Autoflowing Text

You can also **autoflow** text, which is a powerful option for quickly adding text to your document. Let's say that you create a six-page document and you specify that each page has three columns. When you create the document, the pages have no text frames on them—they're just blank, with columns and margin guides. To autoflow text into the document, you click the Place command and choose the text document that you want to import. Once you choose the document, the pointer changes to the loaded text icon. If you press and hold [Shift], the loaded text icon becomes the autoflow loaded text icon. When you click the autoflow loaded text icon in a column, InDesign creates text frames within column guides on that page and all subsequent pages, and flows the text into those frames.

Because you specified that each page has three columns when you created the document, InDesign will create three text frames in the columns on every page for the text to flow to. Figure 70 shows a page with three text frames created by autoflowing text. Note that if you autoflow more text than the document can create, InDesign will add as many pages as necessary to autoflow all of the text. Note also that, if your document pages contain objects such as graphics, the text frames added by the autoflow will be positioned in front of the graphics already on the page.

As you may imagine, autoflowing text is a powerful option, but don't be intimidated by it. The text frames that are generated are all editable. You can resize them or delete them. Nevertheless, you should take a few moments to practice autoflowing text to get the hang of it. Like learning how to ride a bicycle, you can read about it all you want, but actually doing it is where the learning happens.

Inserting a Column Break

When you are working with text in columns, you will often want to move text from the bottom of one column to the top of the next. You do this by inserting a column break. A **column break** is a typographic command that forces text to the next column. The Column Break command is located within the Insert Break Character command on the Type menu.

FIGURE 70

Three text frames created in columns by autoflowing text

Using the Story Editor

InDesign has a feature called the Story Editor that makes it easier to edit text in complex documents. Imagine that you are doing a layout for a single magazine article. The text for the article is flowed through numerous text frames across 12 pages. Now imagine that you want to edit the text—maybe you want to proofread it or spell check it. Editing the text within the layout might be difficult—you'd have to scroll from page to page. Instead, you could use the Edit in Story Editor command on the Edit menu. This opens a new window, which contains all the text in a single file—just like a word processing document. Any changes that you make in the Story Editor window will be immediately updated to the text in the layout. It's a great feature!

In Figure 71, the headline near the bottom of the first column would be better positioned at the top of the next column. By inserting a column break, you do exactly that, as shown in Figure 72.

Inserting a "Continued on page..." Notation

When threading text manually or auto-flowing text, you will get to a point where text has filled all the text frames on the page and continues to another page. Usually, the text continues onto the next page—but not always. In many cases, the next page will be reserved for pictures or other publication elements, such as tables or graphs. When the reader gets to the bottom of the page of text, they need to know on which page the text is continued.

You can insert a "Continued on page..." notation to let the reader know where to go to continue reading.

If you've ever read a magazine or newspaper article, you are familiar with "Continued on page..." notations. In InDesign, a page continuation is formatted as a special character. Simply create a text frame, then type the words "Continued on page X." Select the X, then apply the Next Page Number command. The X changes to the page number of the page that contains the text frame that the text flows into. If for any reason you move pages within the Pages panel and page numbers change, the Next Page Number character will automatically update to show the page number where the text continues.

The Next Page Number command is located within the Insert Special Character command on the Type menu.

There's one important point you need to note when creating a "Continued on page..." notation. By definition, body copy will reach the end of a text frame on a given page and be continued on another page. At the end of the text frame on the first page, you will need to create a text frame to contain the "Continued on page..." notation. In order for the notation to work—for it to list the page where the text continues—the top edge of the text frame that contains the notation must be touching the frame that contains the body copy that is to be continued.

FIGURE 71
Viewing text that needs a column break

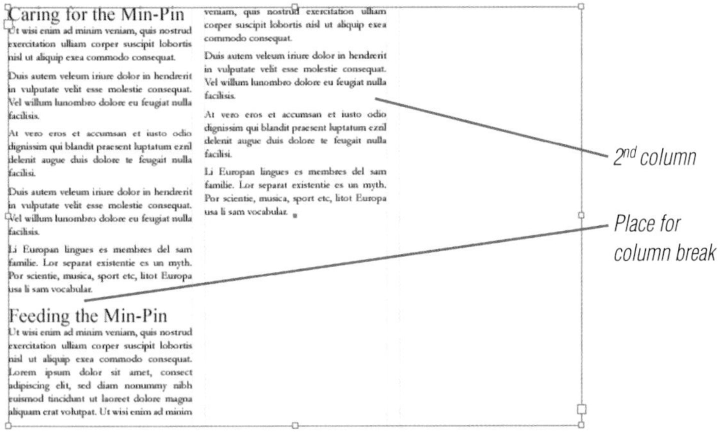

FIGURE 72
Viewing text after inserting a column break

Text is forced to top of next column

2nd column

Place for column break

FIGURE 73

Creating a text frame using the loaded text icon

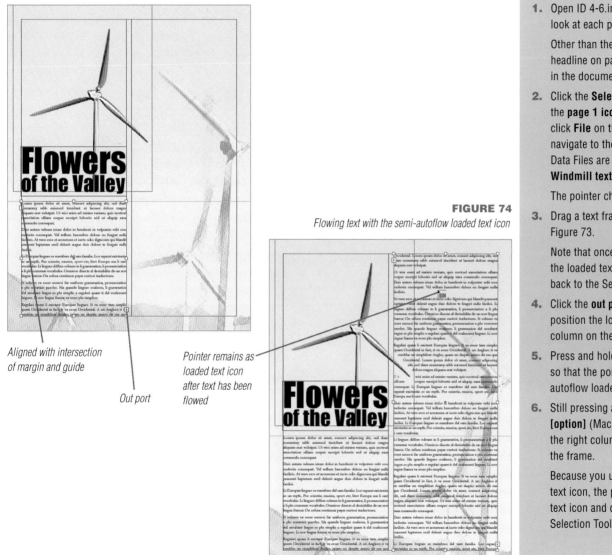

Aligned with intersection
of margin and guide

FIGURE 74

Flowing text with the semi-autoflow loaded text icon

Pointer remains as
loaded text icon
after text has been
flowed

Out port

1. Open ID 4-6.indd, save it as **Autoflow**, then look at each page in the document.

   Other than the text frame that holds the headline on page 1, there are no text frames in the document.

2. Click the **Selection Tool** ▶, double-click the **page 1 icon** in the Pages panel, click **File** on the menu bar, click **Place**, navigate to the drive and folder where your Data Files are stored, then double-click **Windmill text.doc**.

   The pointer changes to the loaded text icon.

3. Drag a text frame in the position shown in Figure 73.

   Note that once you have drawn the frame, the loaded text icon automatically changes back to the Selection Tool.

4. Click the **out port** of the text frame, then position the loaded text icon over the right column on the page.

5. Press and hold **[Alt]** (Win) or **[option]** (Mac) so that the pointer changes to the semi-autoflow loaded text icon.

6. Still pressing and holding **[Alt]** (Win) or **[option]** (Mac), click the **top-left corner** of the right column, so that the text flows into the frame.

   Because you used the semi-autoflow loaded text icon, the pointer remains as a loaded text icon and does not revert back to the Selection Tool, as shown in Figure 74.

(continued)

7. Double-click the **page 2 icon**, then click the **top-left corner** of the left column on the page.

   A new frame is created and text flows into the left column.

8. Click the **out port** of the new text frame on page 2, then position the pointer over the right column on page 2.

9. Press and hold **[Shift]**, note the change to the loaded text icon, then click the **top-left corner** of the second column.

   Because you were pressing [Shift], InDesign creates text frames within column guides on all subsequent pages. InDesign has added new pages to the document to accommodate the autoflow.

You placed text by clicking and dragging the loaded text icon to create a new text frame. You flowed text using the semi-autoflow loaded text icon and the autoflow loaded text icon.

Reflow text

1. Double-click the **page 4 icon** in the Pages panel, then create a horizontal guide at 5.875 in.

2. Click the **left text frame** to select it, drag the **bottom-middle handle** of the text frame's bounding box up until it snaps to the guide, then do the same to the right text frame, so that your page resembles Figure 75.

   The text is reflowed in the document.

3. Double-click the numbers **2-3** in the Pages panel to center the spread in the document window, click **View** on the menu bar, click **Show Text Threads**, then click the **right text frame** on page 2.

(continued)

FIGURE 75
Resizing text frames

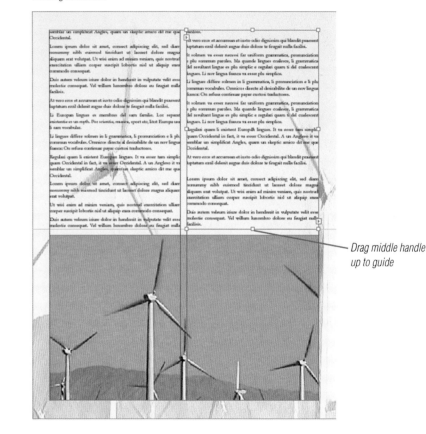

Drag middle handle up to guide

FIGURE 76

Flowing text after deleting a text frame

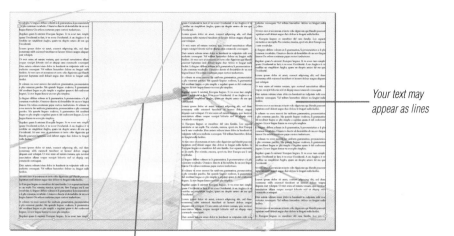

Your text may appear as lines

Text flow continues between remaining text frames

FIGURE 77

Threading text to a new text frame

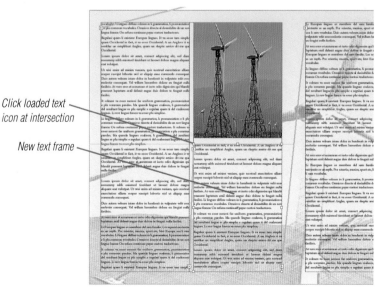

Click loaded text icon at intersection

New text frame

4. With the right frame on page 2 still selected, press **[Delete]** (Win) or **[delete]** (Mac), then click the **text frame** remaining on page 2.

   As shown in Figure 76, the text is reflowed from the first text frame on page 2 to the first text frame on page 3.

5. Press **[Ctrl][D]**(Win) or ⌘ **[D]** (Mac), navigate to the drive and folder where your Data Files are stored, then double-click **2 Windmills.psd**.

6. Click the **top-left corner** of the right column on page 2.

7. Create a horizontal guide at 5.375 in.

8. Click the **text frame** on page 2, then click the **out port**.

9. Click the intersection between the guide you created and the left edge of the right column, beneath the graphic.

   As shown in Figure 77, text is now threaded through the new text frame.

You resized two text frames, noting that text was reflowed through the document. You deleted a text frame, then created a text frame, noting that text continued to flow through the document.

Add a column break

1. Double-click the **page 5 icon** in the Pages panel, then delete the two text frames on page 5.

2. Click **Layout** on the menu bar, click **Margins and Columns**, change the number of columns to 3, then click **OK**.

(continued)

3. Press **[Ctrl][D]**(Win) or ⌘**[D]** (Mac), navigate to the drive and folder where your Chapter 4 Data Files are stored, then double-click **Sidebar copy.doc**.

4. Drag the **loaded text icon** to create a text frame, as shown in Figure 78.

5. Click **Object** on the menu bar, click **Text Frame Options**, change the number of columns to 3, then click **OK**.

6. Click the **Type Tool** T, then click to place the pointer before the W in the Windmill Speeds headline.

7. Click **Type** on the menu bar, point to **Insert Break Character**, then click **Column Break**.

   The Windmill Speeds text is forced into the second column.

8. Click before the W in the Windmill Productivity headline, click **Type** on the menu bar, point to **Insert Break Character**, then click **Column Break**.

   Your page should resemble Figure 79.

You deleted two text frames on a page, then changed the number of columns on that page. You then placed text, formatted the text frame to have three columns, and finally used the Column Break command to create two new column breaks.

Insert a page continuation notation

1. Double-click the **page 4 icon** in the Pages panel, then create a horizontal guide at 5 in.

2. Click the **Selection Tool** ▶, click the text frame in the right column, then drag the

(continued)

FIGURE 78
Creating a text frame with the loaded text icon

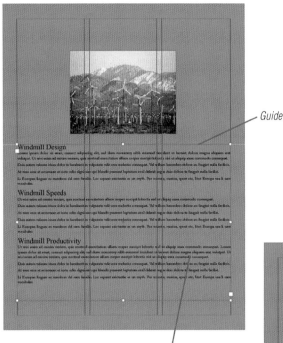

Guide

Text frame

FIGURE 79
Viewing the text frame with column breaks

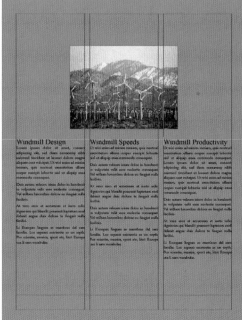

Working with Frames

FIGURE 80

Creating a text frame for the page continuation notation

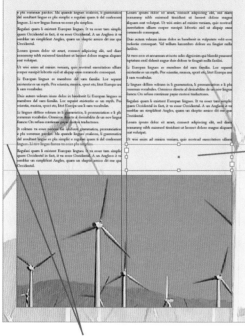

Text frame

Guides

FIGURE 81

Viewing the page continuation notation

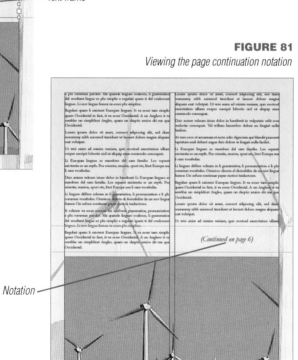

Notation

(Continued on page 6)

bottom middle bounding box handle up until it snaps to the guide at 5 in.

3. Click the **Type Tool** T, then create a text frame between the two guides, as shown in Figure 80.

   The edges of the two text frames abut at the guide, which is critical in order for page continuation notation to work.

4. Click **Object** on the menu bar, click **Text Frame Options**, change the vertical justification to Center, then click **OK**.

5. Click inside the new text box, type **(Continued on Page X)**, click anywhere within the (Continued on Page X) text, show the Paragraph Styles panel, then click the style named **Continued**.

6. Select the letter **X**, click **Type** on the menu bar, point to **Insert Special Character**, point to **Markers**, then click **Next Page Number**.

   The text now reads (Continued on Page 6), as shown in Figure 81.

7. Click the **Selection Tool** , click the **text frame** above the "Continued" text frame, then follow the text thread to verify that the text does indeed continue on page 6.

8. Save your work, then close Autoflow.

   TIP Use the Previous Page Number command along with "Continued from page . . ." text to indicate that a story is continued from a previous page.

You inserted a page continuation notation in the document.

Align and distribute objects on a page.

1. Open ID 4-7.indd, then save it as **Dog Days**.
2. Click the Type Tool, then drag a text frame that fills the left column on the page.
3. Click the Selection Tool, press and hold [Shift][Alt] (Win) or [Shift][option] (Mac), then drag a copy of the text frame and position it in line with the right column.
4. Click the Rectangle Frame Tool, click anywhere on the page, type **1.5** in both the Width and Height text boxes, then click OK.
5. Click the top-left reference point in the Transform panel, type **0** in the X Location text box, type **0** in the Y Location text box, then press [Enter] (Win) or [return] (Mac).
6. Verify that the frame has no fill and no stroke.
7. Click Edit on the menu bar, click Step and Repeat, type **1** in the Repeat Count text box, type **9.5** in the Horizontal Offset text box, type **0** in the Vertical Offset text box, then click OK.
8. Select both graphics frames, click Edit on the menu bar, click Step and Repeat, type **1** in the Repeat Count text box, type **0** in the Horizontal Offset text box, type **7** in the Vertical Offset text box, then click OK.

9. Click the Rectangle Frame Tool, click anywhere in the left column, type **3** in both the Width and Height text boxes, click OK, then verify that the frame has no fill or stroke.
10. Click the Selection Tool, press and hold [Shift], click the top-left graphics frame, then click the top-right graphics frame so that three frames are selected.

FIGURE 82
Completed Skills Review, Part 1

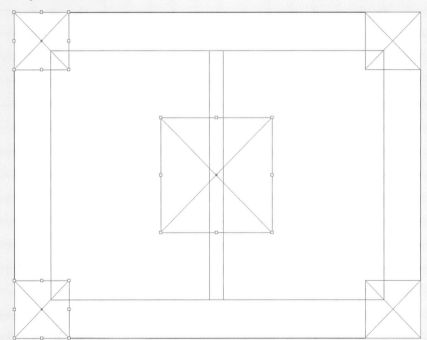

11. In the Align panel, click the Distribute horizontal centers button.
12. Deselect all, select the top-left and bottom-left graphics frames and the 3" x 3" frame, click the Distribute vertical centers button, then compare your page to Figure 82.

Stack and layer objects.

1. Display the Layers panel.
2. Double-click Layer 1, type **Background Graphic** in the Name text box, then click OK.
3. Click the Create new layer button in the Layers panel, double-click the new layer, type **Dog Pics** in the Name text box, then click OK.
4. Click the Layers panel list arrow, click New Layer, type **Body** in the Name text box, then click OK.
5. Click the Selection Tool, select the five graphics frames, then drag the Indicates selected items button from the Background Graphic layer up to the Dog Pics layer.
6. Select the two text frames, then drag the Indicates selected items button from the Background Graphic layer up to the Body layer.
7. Verify that the Body layer is targeted, select only the left text frame, click File on the menu bar, click Place, navigate to the drive and folder where your Chapter 4 Data Files

are stored, then double-click Skills Text.doc.
8. Select all the text, then click the Body Format style in the Paragraph Styles panel. (*Hint*: Click OK in the dialog box that follows if necessary.)
9. Click the Selection Tool, click the out port of the left text frame, then click the loaded text icon anywhere in the right text frame.
10. In the Layers panel, drag the Body layer down below the Dog Pics layer.
11. Save your work.

Work with graphics frames.

1. Click the Selection Tool, select the top-left graphics frame, press [Ctrl][D] (Win) or ⌘[D] (Mac), navigate to the drive and folder where your Chapter 4 Data Files are stored, then double-click Red 1.psd.
2. Select the top-right graphics frame, press [Ctrl][D] (Win) or ⌘[D] (Mac), navigate to the drive and folder where your Chapter 4 Data Files are stored, then double-click Black 1.psd.
3. Select the bottom-left graphics frame, press

[Ctrl][D] (Win) or ⌘[D] (Mac), navigate to the drive and folder where your Chapter 4 Data Files are stored, then double-click Red 2.psd.
4. Select the bottom-right graphics frame, press [Ctrl][D] (Win) or ⌘[D] (Mac), navigate to the drive and folder where your Chapter 4 Data Files are stored, then double-click Black 2.psd.
5. Select the top two graphics frames, click Object on the menu bar, point to Fitting, then click Fit Content to Frame.
6. Deselect all, click the Direct Selection Tool, press and hold your pointer on the bottom-left graphic, then drag until the dog's nose is at the center of the frame.
7. Click the center reference point in the Transform panel, type **40** in both the Scale X Percentage and Scale Y Percentage text boxes, then click and drag to center the dog's head in the frame.

8. Click the Selection Tool, select the four corner graphics frames, click the Wrap around bounding box button in the Text Wrap panel, then type **.125** in all four of the Offset text boxes.
9. Select the center graphics frame, press [Ctrl][D] (Win) or ⌘[D] (Mac), navigate to the drive and folder where your Chapter 4 Data Files are stored, then double-click Dog Silo.psd.
10. Click the Direct Selection Tool, click the new graphic, then click the Wrap around object shape button in the Text Wrap panel.
11. Click the Type list arrow in the Contour Options section, choose Same as Clipping, type **.15** in the Top Offset text box, then press [Enter] (Win) or [return] (Mac).
12. Press [W] to switch to Preview, deselect all, compare your page to Figure 83, save your work, then close Dog Days.

FIGURE 83
Completed Skills Review, Part 2

Lorem ipsum dolor sit amet, consect adipiscing elit, sed diam nonummy nibh euismod tincidunt ut laoreet dolore magna aliquam erat volutpat. Ut wisi enim ad minim venim, quis nostrud exercitation ulliam corper suscipit lobortis nisl ut aliquip exea commodo consequat.

Duis autem veleum iriure dolor in hendrent in vulputate velit esse molestie consequat. Vel willum lunombro dolore eu feugiat nulla facilisis. At vero eros et accumsan et iusto odio dignissim qui blandit praesent luptatum eznil delenit augue duis dolore te feugait nulla facilisi.

Li Europan lingues es membres del sam familie. Lor separat existentie es un myth. Por scientie, musica, sport etc, litot Europa usa li sam vocabular. Li lingues differe solmen in li grammatica, li pronunciation e li plu commun vocables. Omnicos directe al desirabilite de un nov lingua franca: On refusa continuar payar custosi traductores.

At solmen va esser necessi far uniform grammatica, pronunciation e plu sommun paroles. Ma quande lingues coalesce, li grammatica del

resultant lingue es plu simplic e regulari quam ti del coalescent lingues. Li nov lingua franca va esser plu simplice.

Regulari quam li existent Europan lingues. It va esser tam simplic quam Occidental in fact, it va esser Occidental. A un Angleso it va semblar un simplificat Angles, quam un skeptic amico dit me que Occidental.

Lorem ipsum dolor sit amet, consect adipiscing elit, sed diam nonummy nibh euismod tincidunt ut laoreet dolore magna aliquam erat volutpat. Ut wisi enim ad minim veniam, quis nostrud exercitation ulliam corper suscipit lobortis nisl ut aliquip exea commodo consequat. Duis autem veleum iriure dolor in hendrent in vulputate velit esse molestie consequat. Vel willum lunombro dolore eu feugiat nulla facilisis.

At vero eros et accumsan et iusto odio dignissim qui blandit praesent luptatum eznil delenit augue duis dolore te feugait nulla facilisi. Li lingues differe solmen in li grammatica, li pronunciation e li plu commun vocables. Omnicos directe al desirabilite de un nov lingua franca: On refusa continuar payar custosi traductores.

Solmen va esser necessi far uniform grammatica,

Work with text frames.

1. Open ID 4-8.indd, click Fix Links Automatically, click No in the next warning dialog box, then save it as **Dog Days Part 2**. (*Hint*: The first page of the document is identical to the first part of the exercise. Four pages have been added to this document, and a graphic has been placed on page 3.)

2. Click the Selection Tool, click the right text frame on page 1, then click the out port of the text frame.

3. Double-click page 2 in the Pages panel, position the loaded text icon over the left column, press and hold [Shift] so that the autoflow loaded text icon appears, then click the top-left corner of the left column.

4. Click View on the menu bar, click Show Text Threads, double-click page 3 in the Pages panel, then click the Toggles visibility button in the Dog Pics layer in the Layers panel to hide it temporarily. (*Hint*: Autoflowing the text created two text frames on page 3, but they weren't visible because the Body Copy layer is behind the Dog Pics layer.)

5. Verify that the Body Copy layer is targeted, select and delete the two text frames on page 3, then click the Toggles visibility button in the Dog Pics layer so that the layer is visible again.

6. Double-click page 2 in the Pages panel, select the right text frame, then drag the bottom-middle handle of the right text frame up so that it aligns with the top edge of the small text frame at the bottom of the column.

7. Click the Type Tool, click in the small text frame at the bottom of the right column, then type **Turn to page X**.

FIGURE 84
Completed Skills Review, Part 3

8. Click the Continued style in the Paragraph Styles panel, select the letter X, click Type on the menu bar, point to Insert Special Character, point to Markers, then click Next Page Number.

9. Deselect all, compare your screen to Figure 84, save your work, then close Dog Days Part 2.

You work for a design firm, and you are creating a logo for a local shop that sells vintage board games. You decide to create an 8" x 8" checkerboard, which you will later incorporate into your logo.

1. Open ID 4-9.indd, then save it as **Checkerboard**.
2. Click the Rectangle Frame Tool, create a 1" square frame anywhere on the board, fill it with black and no stroke, then position it so that its top-left corner has a (0, 0) coordinate.
3. Use the Step and Repeat command to make one copy, one inch to the right of the original square.
4. Select the new square if necessary, change its fill color to Brick Red, then select both squares.
5. Use the Step and Repeat command again, type **3** in the Repeat Count text box, type **2** in the Horizontal Offset text box, type **0** in the Vertical Offset text box, then click OK.
6. Select all, use the Step and Repeat command again, type **1** in the Repeat Count text box, type **0** in the Horizontal Offset text box, type **1** in the Vertical Offset text box, then click OK.
7. Click the center reference point in the Transform panel, then change the Rotation Angle text box to 180°.

8. Select all, use the Step and Repeat command again, type **3** in the Repeat Count text box, type **0** in the Horizontal Offset text box, type **2** in the Vertical Offset text box, then click OK.

9. Press [W] to switch to Preview, deselect all, then compare your work to Figure 85.
10. Save your work, then close Checkerboard.

FIGURE 85
Completed Project Builder 1

You are a designer at a design firm that specializes in travel. A client comes in with a disk that contains a layout that she created in InDesign. She says that it's the basic layout for a brochure that she wants to create, and that she wants you to use it as a template for future layouts. You open the file and decide that it's best to move the basic elements onto layers.

1. Open ID 4-10.indd, then save it as **Brochure Layers**.
2. In the Layers panel, rename Layer 1 as **Background Colors**.
3. Create a new layer, then name it **Pictures**.
4. Create a new layer, then name it **Text**.
5. Select the four graphics frames, then move them onto the Pictures layer.
6. Select the two text frames, then move them onto the Text layer.
7. Select all the frames on the Pictures layer, then compare your work to Figure 86.
8. Save your work, then close Brochure Layers.

FIGURE 86
Completed Project Builder 2

THE ROAD TO HANA
a visual journey through Maui

DESIGN PROJECT

You head up the layout team for a design firm. Your client has delivered you a Photoshop file with a clipping path. He wants you to use it in the layout he has supplied. He tells you he wants the graphic placed in the middle of the page with text wrapping around it on all four sides. You import the graphic and realize that you will need to modify the path in InDesign that controls the wrap.

1. Open ID 4-11.indd, click Fix Links Automatically, click No in the next dialog box, then save it as **Four Leg Wrap**.
2. Click Edit on the menu bar, then click Place, navigate to the drive and folder where your Chapter 4 Data Files are stored, then double-click Red Silo.psd.
3. Click the loaded graphics icon anywhere on the page, click the Selection Tool, then center the graphic on the page.
4. Verify that you can see the Transform panel, press and hold [Ctrl][Shift] (Win) or ⌘ [Shift] (Mac), then drag the top-left corner of the frame toward the center of the frame, reducing the frame until the Width text box in the Transform panel reads approximately 5 in.
5. Click the center reference point in the Transform panel, type **4.25** in the X Location text box, type **4.2** in the Y Location text box, then press [Enter] (Win) or [return] (Mac).

6. Click the Direct Selection Tool, click the graphic, then click the Wrap around object shape button in the Text Wrap panel.
7. Draw a graphics frame in the position shown in Figure 87, being sure the bottom edges of the two graphics frames are aligned.
8. With only the lower graphics frame selected, click the Wrap around bounding box button in the Text Wrap panel. (*Hint*: Adjust the new frame as necessary to move any stray text.)
9. Deselect all, press [W] to switch to Preview, then compare your work to Figure 88.
10. Save your work, then close Four Leg Wrap.

FIGURE 87
Positioning the graphics frame

FIGURE 88
Completed Design Project

Your group is going to work on a fun puzzle, which will test their problem-solving skills when using the Step and Repeat command and the Align panel. The group will need to recreate the graphic shown in Figure 89. First read the rules and strategize with your group. Then proceed with the exercise steps below.

Rules.

1. You will start by opening an 8" x 8" InDesign document that contains a single red 1.45" square.
2. To recreate the graphic in the figure, you may use only the Step and Repeat command and the Align panel. (*Hint*: You may also drag objects.)
3. In the final graphic, the top-left square must be aligned with the top-left corner of the page. The bottom-right square must be aligned with the bottom-right corner of the page, and the eight squares in between must all be equidistant, forming a perfect staircase.
4. Divide the class into groups of four. Tell each group that they have exactly one minute to strategize. The first group to come up with the simplest solution for recreating the graphic wins.

Exercise.

1. Open ID 4-12.indd, then save it as **Test Your Alignment**.

2. Select the top-left square, click Step and Repeat, type **9** in the Repeat Count text box, type **.5** in the Horizontal Offset text box, type **.5** in the Vertical Offset text box, then click OK.
3. Drag the bottommost square down and align its bottom-right corner with the bottom-right corner of the page.

4. Select all, click the Distribute vertical centers button in the Align panel, then click the Distribute horizontal centers button.
5. Press [W] to switch to Preview.
6. Deselect all, compare your screen to Figure 89, save your work, then close Test Your Alignment.

FIGURE 89
Completed Group Project

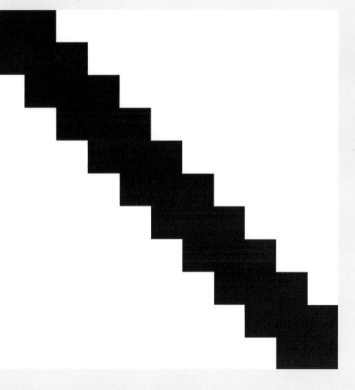

5

WORKING WITH
COLOR

1. Work with process colors

2. Apply color

3. Work with spot colors

4. Work with gradients

chapter 5 WORKING WITH COLOR

In Chapter 5, you will explore InDesign's many methods for creating and applying color. You'll use the Swatches panel to create new colors, and you'll learn a number of tips and tricks for applying color quickly. You'll also use the Color panel to quickly mix colors and modify the color of selected objects.

As a fully functional layout application, InDesign is equipped with a user-friendly interface for creating process tints and spot colors. You'll use the Swatches panel again to create spot colors, and you'll explore the built-in spot color libraries.

Finally, you'll work with gradients. Be prepared to be impressed by InDesign's sophisticated interface for creating, applying, and manipulating gradients.

Tools You'll Use

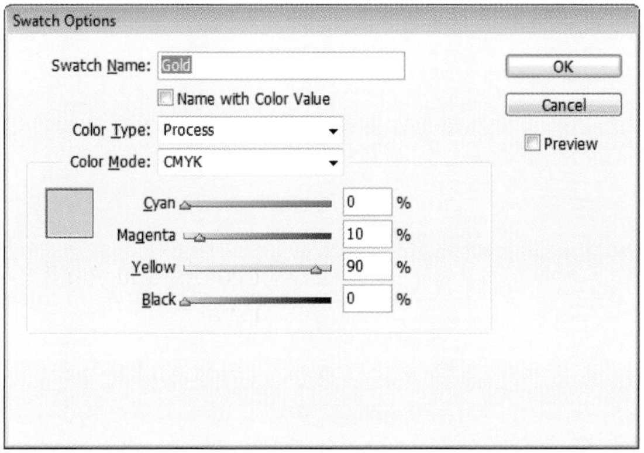

Swatch Options

Swatch Name: Gold

☐ Name with Color Value

Color Type: Process ▼

Color Mode: CMYK ▼

Cyan ——— 0 %
Magenta ——— 10 %
Yellow ——— 90 %
Black ——— 0 %

[OK] [Cancel] ☐ Preview

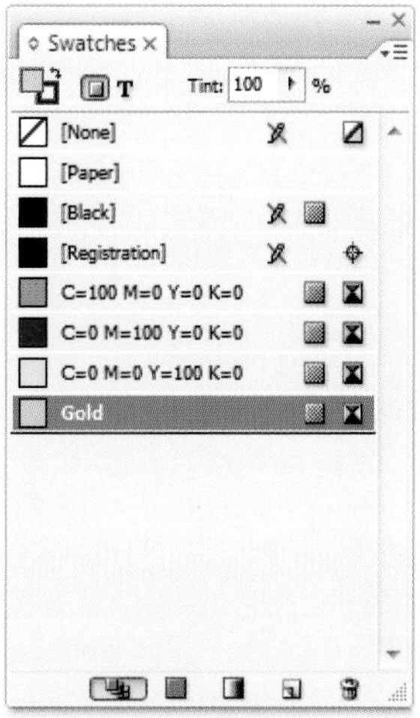

◇ Swatches ×

Tint: 100 ▶ %

☑	[None]	✗	☑
☐	[Paper]		
■	[Black]	✗	■
■	[Registration]	✗	✦
■	C=100 M=0 Y=0 K=0	■	☒
■	C=0 M=100 Y=0 K=0	■	☒
☐	C=0 M=0 Y=100 K=0	■	☒
■	Gold	■	☒

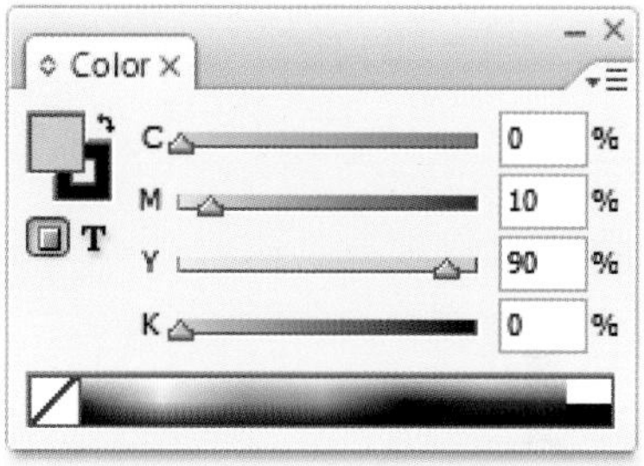

◇ Color ×

C ——— 0 %
M ——— 10 %
Y ——— 90 %
K ——— 0 %

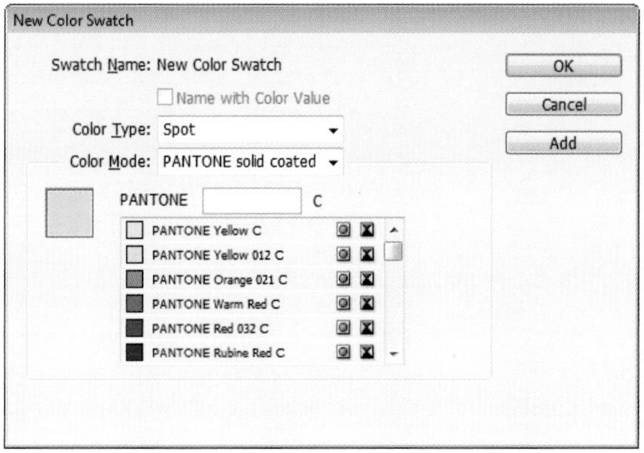

New Color Swatch

Swatch Name: New Color Swatch

☐ Name with Color Value

Color Type: Spot ▼

Color Mode: PANTONE solid coated ▼

PANTONE [ ] C

☐	PANTONE Yellow C	◉	☒
☐	PANTONE Yellow 012 C	◉	☒
■	PANTONE Orange 021 C	◉	☒
■	PANTONE Warm Red C	◉	☒
■	PANTONE Red 032 C	◉	☒
■	PANTONE Rubine Red C	◉	☒

[OK] [Cancel] [Add]

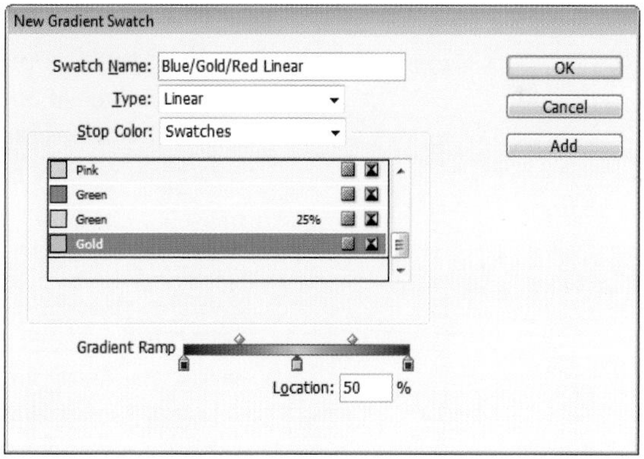

New Gradient Swatch

Swatch Name: Blue/Gold/Red Linear

Type: Linear ▼

Stop Color: Swatches ▼

☐	Pink		■ ☒
☐	Green		■ ☒
☐	Green	25%	■ ☒
■	Gold		■ ☒

Gradient Ramp

Location: 50 %

[OK] [Cancel] [Add]

WORK WITH PROCESS COLORS

What You'll Do

In this lesson, you will create new process colors and a tint swatch.

Understanding Process Colors

Process colors are, quite simply, colors that you create (and eventually print) by mixing varying percentages of cyan, magenta, yellow, and black (CMYK) inks. CMYK inks are called **process inks**. The lightest colors are produced with small percentages of ink, and darker colors with higher percentages. By mixing CMYK inks, you can produce a large variety of colors, and you can even reproduce color photographs. Think about that for a second—when you look at any magazine, most if not all the color photographs you see are created using only four colors!

In Adobe InDesign, you create process colors by creating a new swatch in the Swatches panel. You then mix percentages of CMYK to create the color. Figure 1 shows the New Color Swatch dialog box, where you name and define a color. You can choose Process or Spot as your type of color using the Color Type list arrow in the New Color Swatch dialog box. Choosing Process defines the swatch as a process swatch, meaning that it is created

with percentages of CMYK ink. Any color that you create in this manner is called a **named color** and is added to the Swatches panel, as shown in Figure 2. You can choose to have the color's name defined by CMYK percentages, as shown in the figure, or you can give it another name that you prefer.

One major benefit of working with named colors is that you can update them. For example, let's say you create a color that is 50% cyan and 50% yellow and you name it Warm Green. Let's say that you fill 10 objects on 10 different pages with Warm Green, but your client tells you that she'd prefer the objects to be filled with a darker green. You could simply modify the Warm Green color—change the cyan value to 70% for example—and every object filled with Warm Green would automatically update to show the darker green.

Understanding Tints

In the print world, the term tint is used often to refer to many things. For example, some print professionals refer to all

process colors as tints. In Adobe InDesign, however, the term **tint** refers specifically to a lighter version of a color.

Figure 3 shows four objects, all of them filled with the color cyan. The first is filled with 100% cyan, the second is filled with a 50% tint of cyan, the third 25%, and the fourth 10%. Note the variation in color.

Here's the tricky thing to understand about tints—the four swatches are all filled with the *same* cyan ink. The only difference is

that, in the lighter objects, there's more white space that's not covered with cyan, thus creating the illusion that the object is filled with a lighter blue.

The best way to keep the concept of tints clear in your head is to think of a checkerboard. In a checkerboard, 50% of the squares are black and the other 50% are red. Now imagine that the red squares are filled with solid cyan. Imagine that the other 50% are filled with white. That's exactly what's happening in the 50% cyan swatch in the figure.

It's just that the checkerboard is so small and contains so many squares that your eye perceives the illusion that the object is filled with a light blue.

Tints can also be created from more complex process colors. Figure 4 shows a process color that is C16 Y100 M100. It follows logically that the 50% tint of the color is C8 Y50 M50. A tint of any process color is created by multiplying each of the original colors' CMYK values by the desired tint percentage.

FIGURE 1
New Color Swatch dialog box

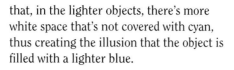

Color Type: Defines whether the color is Process or Spot

FIGURE 2
Swatches panel

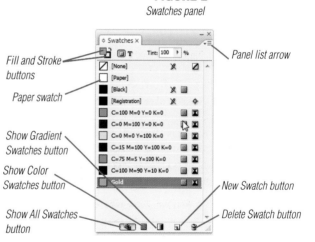

Fill and Stroke buttons

Paper swatch

Show Gradient Swatches button

Show Color Swatches button

Show All Swatches button

Panel list arrow

New Swatch button

Delete Swatch button

FIGURE 3
Four objects filled with cyan

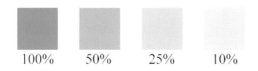

100%   50%   25%   10%

FIGURE 4
A red process color and a 50% tint of that color

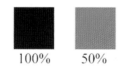

100%   50%

Creating Tint Swatches

Like process colors, you use the Swatches panel to create tint swatches. You can select a swatch in the Swatches panel, and then create a tint based on that original swatch by clicking the Swatches panel list arrow, clicking New Tint Swatch, and then dragging the Tint slider to the desired percentage. The resulting tint swatch is given the same name of the color it was based on plus the tint percentage next to it, as shown in Figure 5.

If you modify the original swatch, any tint swatch that is based on the original will automatically update to reflect that modification. For example, if your client says she wants that Warm Green color to be darker, then any modifications you make to Warm Green will affect all objects filled with Warm Green and all objects filled with tints of Warm Green.

Working with Unnamed Colors

It is not a requirement that you create named swatches for every color that you want to use in your layout. Many designers prefer to use the Color panel, shown in Figure 6, to mix colors and apply them to objects. Using the Color panel, you can apply a color to an object by selecting it, then dragging the sliders in the Color panel until you are happy with the new color. As you drag the sliders, the color is continually updated in the selected object. In this way, you can experiment with different colors and allow the document's color scheme to evolve.

FIGURE 5
Tint swatch in the Swatches panel

FIGURE 6
Color panel

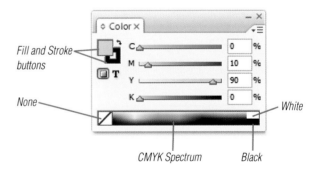

Fill and Stroke buttons

None

CMYK Spectrum

White

Black

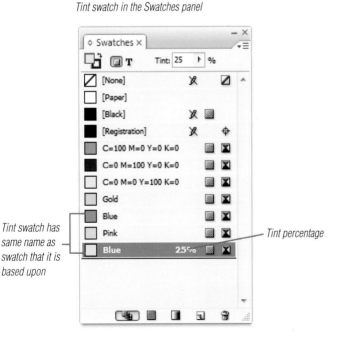

Tint swatch has same name as swatch that it is based upon

Tint percentage

When you create colors using the Color panel, those colors are not saved anywhere. Any colors that you create that aren't saved to the Swatches panel are called **unnamed colors**.

There's nothing wrong, per se, with working with unnamed colors. You can mix a color in the Color panel, then apply it to an object. No problem. But it's important that you understand that the color is not saved anywhere. This can result in problems. For example, let's say that you mix a royal blue color and apply it to a document, then you show the document to your client, who says that he'd prefer it to be green. So you mix a new green color, then the client says he prefers the original blue after all. If you didn't write down the CMYK values of that royal blue, there's no place in InDesign that has recorded it for you.

Other problems can develop. Let's say you used that royal blue to fill multiple objects throughout the document. If you want to modify the color, you would need to modify each individual usage of the color. This could get very time consuming.

Does this mean that you'd be smart not to use the Color panel to mix colors? Not at all. However, once you've decided on a color, save it in the Swatches panel. It couldn't be easier. Simply drag the Fill (or Stroke) button from the Toolbox or the Color panel into the Swatches panel. You can even drag the Fill (or Stroke) button from the top of the Swatches panel down into the Swatches panel. The swatch will instantly be added to the Swatches panel as a process color and its CMYK values will be used as its name, as shown in Figure 7.

FIGURE 7

Viewing a formerly unnamed color dragged into the Swatches panel

Color dragged into
Swatches panel

Create process color swatches

1. Open ID 5-1.indd, click **Fix Links Automatically**, if necessary, then save it as **Oahu Magazine Cover**.

2. Click the **Swatches panel name tab** to display the Swatches panel.

3. Click the **Swatches panel list arrow**, then click **New Color Swatch**.

4. Verify that the Color Type text box displays Process and that the Color Mode text box displays CMYK.

5. Remove the check mark in the Name with Color Value check box, then type **Gold** in the Swatch Name text box.

6. Enter **0**, **10**, **90**, and **0** in the Cyan, Magenta, Yellow, and Black text boxes, as shown in Figure 8.

7. Click **OK**, click the **Swatches panel list arrow**, then click **New Color Swatch**.

8. Remove the check mark in the Name with Color Value check box, then type **Blue** in the Swatch Name text box.

9. Type **85**, **10**, **10**, and **0** in the CMYK text boxes, then click **OK**.

10. Create a new process color named **Pink**, type **20** in the Magenta text box, type **0** in the Cyan, Yellow, and Black text boxes, then click **OK**.

   Your Swatches panel should resemble Figure 9.

You created three new process colors.

FIGURE 8

Creating a process color

New Color Swatch

Swatch Name: Gold

☐ Name with Color Value

Color Type: Process

Color Mode: CMYK

Cyan   0 %
Magenta   10 %
Yellow   90 %
Black   0 %

OK

Cancel

Add

FIGURE 9

Swatches panel

Three new colors

FIGURE 10
Viewing the new tint swatch

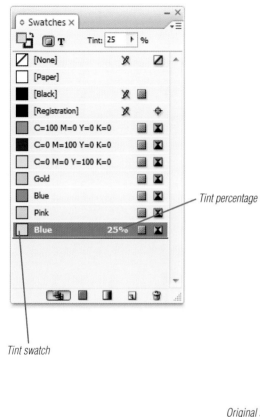

Tint percentage

Tint swatch

FIGURE 11
Viewing changes to the tint swatch

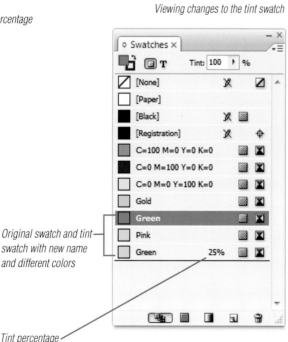

Original swatch and tint swatch with new name and different colors

Tint percentage

1. Click **Blue** in the Swatches panel, click the **Swatches panel list arrow**, then click **New Tint Swatch**.

2. Drag the **Tint slider** to 25%, then click **OK**.

   As shown in Figure 10, a new 25% tint swatch named Blue 25% appears in the Swatches panel.

3. Double-click the original **Blue swatch** that you created in the Swatches panel.

4. Rename it by typing **Green** in the Swatch Name text box, drag the **Yellow slider** to 100%, then click **OK**.

   As shown in Figure 11, the blue swatch is renamed and the 25% tint swatch is renamed Green 25%.

5. Drag the **Green 25% tint swatch** up and relocate it immediately below the Green swatch you just created in the Swatches panel.

6. Drag the **Gold swatch** to the bottom of the panel so that it won't be confused with the Yellow swatch.

7. Click **File** on the menu bar, then click **Save**.

   Be sure to save your work at this step, as you will later revert to this point in the project.

You created a new tint swatch. You then modified the original swatch on which the tint swatch was based, noting that the tint swatch was automatically updated. You also rearranged swatches in the Swatches panel.

Use the Color panel

1. Verify that the Fill button in the Toolbox is activated.

2. Click the **Selection Tool**, if necessary, click the **cyan-filled frame** that surrounds the image on the page, then click the **Color panel name tab**.

3. Click the **Color panel list arrow**, then click **CMYK**.

4. Drag the **Magenta slider** in the Color panel to 50%, then drag the **Cyan slider** to 50%, as shown in Figure 12.

   The fill color of the selected frame changes to purple.

   TIP When you create a new color in the Color panel, it becomes the active fill or stroke color in the Toolbox, depending on which button is active.

5. Drag the **Yellow slider** to 100%, then drag the **Cyan slider** to 0%.

   The purple color that previously filled the frame is gone—there's no swatch for that color in the Swatches panel.

   TIP Colors that you mix in the Colors panel are not automatically saved in the Swatches panel.

6. Click the **green area** of the CMYK Spectrum on the Color panel.

7. Drag the **Cyan slider** to 70%, drag the **Magenta slider** to 20%, then drag the **Yellow** and **Black sliders** to 0%.

You selected an object, then used the Color panel to change its fill to a variety of process colors, none of which were saved in the Swatches panel.

FIGURE 12
Color panel

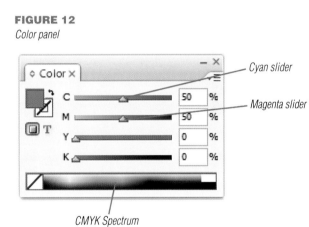

Cyan slider

Magenta slider

CMYK Spectrum

FIGURE 13

Viewing an unnamed color added to the Swatches panel

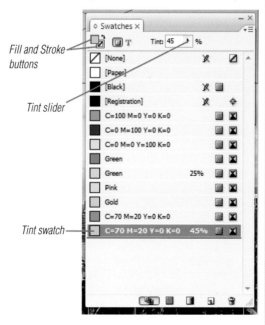

Color dragged into
Swatches panel

FIGURE 14

Viewing a tint swatch added to the Swatches panel

Fill and Stroke
buttons

Tint slider

Tint swatch

Save an unnamed color in the Swatches panel

1. Drag the **Fill color** from the Toolbox into the Swatches panel.

   Your Swatches panel should resemble Figure 13.

2. Drag the **Tint slider** in the Color panel to 45%.

3. Save the new color as a swatch by dragging the **Fill button** from the top of the Swatches panel to the bottom of the list of swatches in the Swatches panel.

   Your Swatches panel should resemble Figure 14.

4. Double-click the **darker blue swatch** in the Swatches panel, remove the check mark in the Name with Color Value check box, type **Purple** in the Name text box, drag the **Magenta slider** to 100%, then click **OK**.

   The darker blue swatch becomes purple, and the tint swatch based on the darker blue swatch is also updated.

5. Click **File** on the menu bar, click **Revert**, then click **Yes** (Win) or **Revert** (Mac) in the dialog box that follows.

   The document is reverted back to its status when you last saved. The new color swatches you created are no longer in the Swatches panel.

You saved an unnamed color in the Swatches panel, created a tint swatch based on that swatch, then reverted the document.

Lesson 1   Work with Process Colors

INDESIGN 5-11

APPLY COLOR

What You'll Do

FALL 2010 · $4.95

A·MAZE·ING
get lost in a
pineapple maze

TWIST & SHOUT
boogie-boarding
daredevils stare down
the north coast waves

MAVERICK
a sizzling interview
with Chef Mavro

In this lesson, you will explore various techniques for applying and modifying color swatches.

Applying Color to Objects

InDesign offers a number of options for applying fills and strokes to objects. The most basic method is to select an object, activate either the Fill or the Stroke button in the Toolbox, then click a color in the Swatches panel or mix a color in the Color panel.

As shown in Figure 15, both the Color panel and the Swatches panel have Fill and Stroke buttons that you can click to activate rather than having to always go back to the Toolbox. When you activate the Fill or Stroke button in any panel, it will be activated in all the panels that have Fill and Stroke buttons.

Keyboard shortcuts also offer useful options. Pressing [X] once toggles the activation between the Fill and the Stroke buttons. In other words, if the Stroke button is activated and you press [X], the Fill button will be activated. Make a note of this. It's extremely useful and practical and

allows you to avoid always having to move the mouse pointer to a panel to activate the fill or the stroke.

Dragging and dropping is also useful. You can drag a swatch from the Swatches panel onto an object and apply the swatch as a fill or a stroke. Drag a swatch over the interior of an object and the swatch will be applied as a fill, as shown in Figure 16. If you position the pointer precisely over the object's edge, it will be applied as a stroke. What's interesting about the drag and drop method is that the object does not need to be selected for you to apply the fill or the stroke.

You can use the drag and drop method with any panel that has Fill and Stroke buttons.

The Toolbox offers useful buttons for working with color, as shown in Figure 17. The **Default Fill and Stroke button** reverts the Fill and Stroke buttons to their

default colors—no fill and a black stroke. Clicking this button will apply a black stroke and no fill to a selected object. The **Swap Fill and Stroke button** swaps the fill color with the stroke color.

Finally, the three "Apply" buttons on the Toolbox are useful for speeding up your work. The **Apply Color** and **Apply Gradient buttons** display the last color and gradient that you've used. This makes for quick and easy access when you are using the same color or gradient repeatedly. The **Apply None button** is available for removing the fill or stroke from a selected object, depending on which button (Fill or Stroke) is active in the Toolbox.

QUICKTIP

If you are viewing your Toolbox as a single column, you will not see all three of these buttons. Press and hold the current button on the Toolbox, then click the desired button.

FIGURE 16
Dragging and dropping a swatch to fill an object

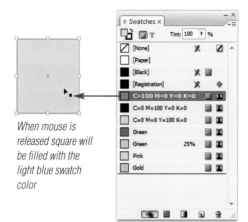

When mouse is released square will be filled with the light blue swatch color

FIGURE 17
Useful color buttons in the Tools panel

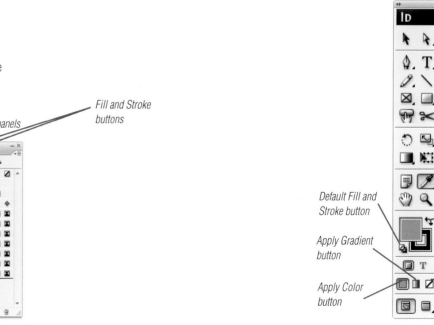

Default Fill and Stroke button

Apply Gradient button

Apply Color button

Swap Fill and Stroke button

Apply None button

FIGURE 15
Fill and Stroke buttons in the Color and Swatches panels

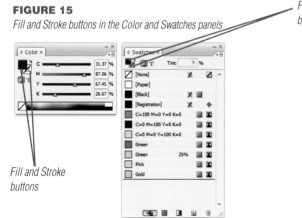

Fill and Stroke buttons

Fill and Stroke buttons

Understanding the Paper Swatch

If I gave you a white piece of paper and a box of crayons and asked you to draw a white star against a blue background, you would probably color all of the page blue except for the star shape, which you would leave blank. The star would appear as white because the paper is white. The Paper swatch, shown in Figure 18, is based on this very concept. Use the Paper swatch whenever you want an object to have a white fill or stroke.

Don't confuse a Paper fill with a None fill. When you fill a frame with Paper, it is filled with white. When you fill it with None, it has no fill—its fill is transparent. Figure 19 illustrates this distinction. In the figure, two text frames are positioned in front of a frame with a yellow fill. The text frame on the left has None as its fill; therefore the yellow frame is visible behind the text. The text frame on the right has Paper as its fill.

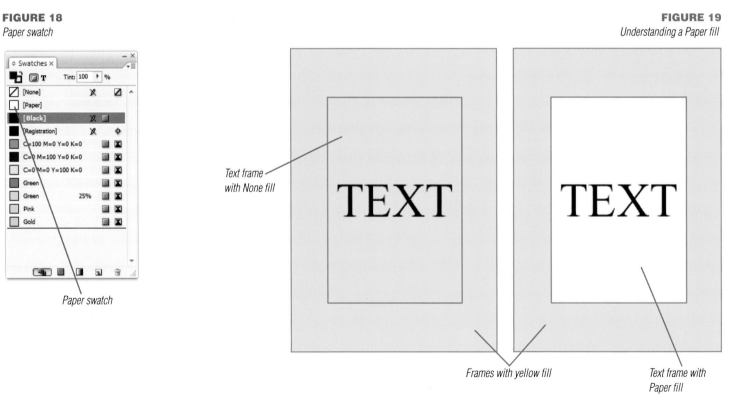

FIGURE 18
Paper swatch

FIGURE 19
Understanding a Paper fill

Paper swatch

Text frame with None fill

TEXT

TEXT

Frames with yellow fill

Text frame with Paper fill

Working with Color

Applying Color to Text

Applying color to text is easy. There are two different methods for applying color to text, depending on which tool you are using to select the text.

When you select text with the Type Tool, the Fill and Stroke buttons in the Toolbox display the letter T, as shown in Figure 20. This is a visual indication that you are filling or stroking text. Click a swatch in the Swatches panel or mix a color in the Color panel and the text will be filled or stroked with that color.

QUICKTIP

The color of the letter T in the Fill and Stroke buttons is the same color as the selected text.

When you select a text frame with a selection tool, you need to tell InDesign what you want to do—apply a fill or stroke to the frame itself or apply a fill or stroke to the text in the frame. If you want to apply color to the text, click the Formatting affects text button in the Toolbox, as shown in Figure 21. If you want to apply color to the frame, click the Formatting affects container button. It's that simple. Note that the two buttons can also be found in the Swatches and Color panels.

FIGURE 20
Fill and Stroke buttons applied to text

Fill and Stroke buttons

FIGURE 21
Formatting buttons

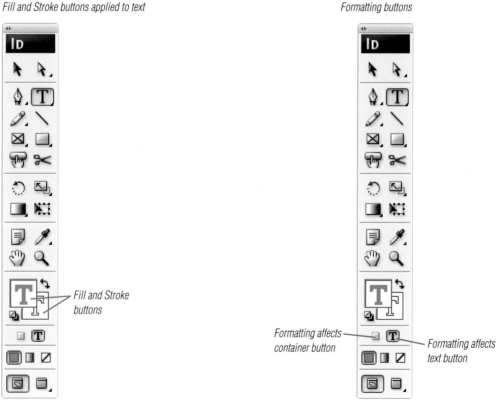

Formatting affects container button

Formatting affects text button

Creating Black Shadow Text

When you position text against a background color or against a photographic image, sometimes it's not easy to see the text, as shown in Figure 22. To remedy this, many designers use the classic technique of placing a black copy of the text behind the original text, as shown in Figure 23. This trick adds much-needed contrast between the text and the image behind it.

QUICKTIP

Placing a black copy of text behind original text produces a different effect than using InDesign's Drop Shadow command.

Modifying and Deleting Swatches

Once you've created a swatch in or added a swatch to the Swatches panel, it is a named color and will be saved with the document. Any swatch can be modified simply by double-clicking it, which opens the Swatch Options dialog box, as shown in Figure 24. Any modifications you make to the swatch will be updated automatically in any frame that uses the color as a fill or a stroke.

You can also delete a swatch from the Swatches panel by selecting the swatch, then clicking the Delete Swatch button in the Swatches panel or clicking the Delete Swatch command on the Swatches panel menu. If you are deleting a swatch that is

Black text placed
behind purple text

used in your document, the Delete Swatch dialog box opens, as shown in Figure 25.

You use the Delete Swatch dialog box to choose a color to replace the deleted swatch. For example, if you've filled (or stroked) a number of objects with the color Warm Green and then you delete the Warm Green swatch, the Delete Swatch dialog box wants to know what color those objects should be changed to. You choose another named color that is already in the Swatches panel by clicking the Defined Swatch list arrow, clicking a color, and then clicking OK. When you do so, all the objects with a Warm Green fill or stroke will change to the named color you chose. Note that this can be a very quick and effective method for changing the fill (or stroke) color of multiple objects simultaneously.

If you click the Unnamed Swatch option button in the Delete Swatch dialog box, all the objects filled or stroked with the deleted color will retain their color. However, since that color is no longer in the Swatches panel, those objects are now filled with an unnamed color.

FIGURE 24
Swatch Options dialog box

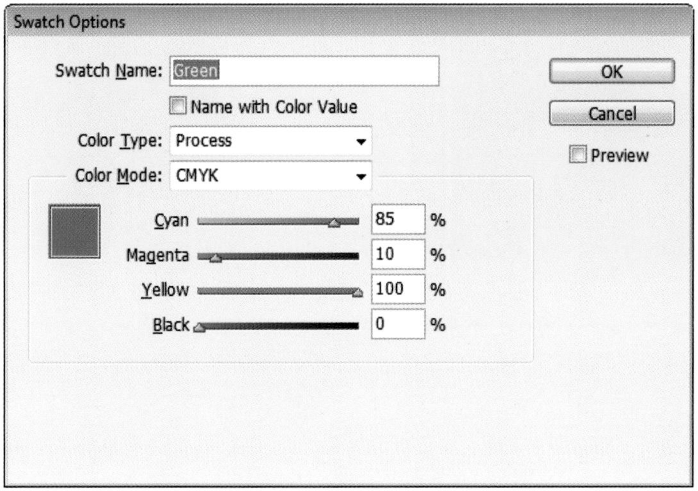

FIGURE 25
Delete Swatch dialog box

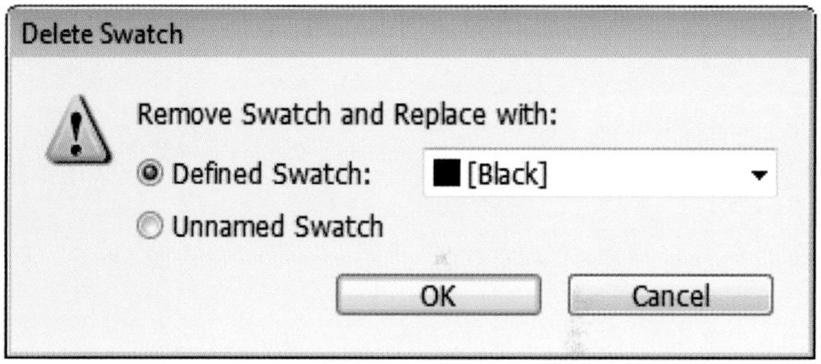

Drag and drop colors onto objects

1. Click **View** on the menu bar, then click **Hide Frame Edges**.

2. Drag and drop the **Green swatch** on top of the blue frame, as shown in Figure 26, then release the mouse button.

   The frame is filled with green.

3. Click the **Toggles visibility button**  on the Photo layer in the Layers panel to hide the background image.

4. Drag the **Pink swatch** to the inside of the white text frame.

   The fill changes to pink.

You dragged and dropped colors from the Swatches panel to objects in the document window.

FIGURE 26
Dragging and dropping a color swatch

Using the Color Picker

In addition to using the Toolbox and the Swatches panel to apply colors, you can use the Color Picker, which lets you choose and mix colors using an interface similar to Photoshop. Select the object you want to fill, then double-click the Fill or Stroke box in the Toolbox to open the Color Picker. In the color spectrum, click or drag to select a color, drag the color slider triangles, or type values in the text boxes. To save the color as a swatch, click Add CMYK Swatch, Add RGB Swatch, or Add Lab Swatch. The color appears in the Swatches panel, displaying its color values as a name.

FIGURE 27
Applying the Default Fill and Stroke button to the frame

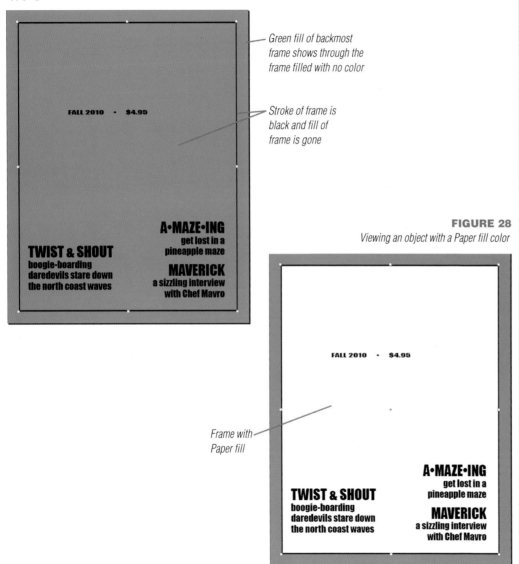

Green fill of backmost
frame shows through the
frame filled with no color

Stroke of frame is
black and fill of
frame is gone

FALL 2010 · $4.95

A·MAZE·ING
get lost in a
pineapple maze

MAVERICK
a sizzling interview
with Chef Mavro

TWIST & SHOUT
boogie-boarding
daredevils stare down
the north coast waves

FIGURE 28
Viewing an object with a Paper fill color

FALL 2010 · $4.95

Frame with
Paper fill

A·MAZE·ING
get lost in a
pineapple maze

MAVERICK
a sizzling interview
with Chef Mavro

TWIST & SHOUT
boogie-boarding
daredevils stare down
the north coast waves

Use the Swap Fill and Stroke and Default Fill and Stroke buttons

1. Click the **Selection Tool** , if necessary, click the center of the pink frame, then note the Fill and Stroke buttons in the Toolbox.

   The Fill button is activated—it is in front of the Stroke button.

2. Press **[X]** to activate the Stroke button in the Toolbox, then click **Gold** in the Swatches panel.

3. Click the **Swap Fill and Stroke button** .

   In the selected frame, the fill and stroke colors are swapped.

4. Click the **Default Fill and Stroke button** .

   The fill color of the selected frame is removed and replaced with no fill, and the stroke changes to black as shown in Figure 27.

5. Press **[X]** to activate the Fill button, click the **Paper swatch** in the Swatches panel, then compare your work to Figure 28.

You used the Swap Fill and Stroke and Default Fill and Stroke buttons to explore ways to modify your document, and then applied the Paper swatch to the center frame.

Apply color to text

1. Click the **Selection Tool** ![selection tool], click the **TWIST & SHOUT text frame**, then click the **Formatting affects text button** **T** in the Toolbox.

   As shown in Figure 29, the Fill and Stroke buttons display the letter T, indicating that any color changes will affect the text in the selected frame, not the frame itself.

2. Click **Gold** in the Swatches panel.

3. Click the **A•MAZE•ING text frame**, then note that the Formatting affects container button is active in the Toolbox because you have selected a frame.

4. Click the **Type Tool** **T.**, then select all of the text in the A•MAZE•ING text frame.

   > TIP   When you select text with the Type Tool, the Formatting affects text button in the Toolbox is automatically activated.

5. Click **Pink** in the Swatches panel.

6. Click the **Selection Tool** ![selection tool], click the **MAVERICK text frame**, then click the **Formatting affects text button** **T** in the Swatches panel.

7. Click the **Green 25% swatch** in the Swatches panel so that your document resembles Figure 30.

You explored two methods for applying color to text, the first by selecting text with the Selection Tool, then clicking the Formatting affects text button before choosing a color, and the second by selecting text with the Type Tool, then choosing a new color.

FIGURE 29
Toolbox with the Formatting affects text button activated

Fill button

Formatting affects text button

FIGURE 30
Viewing the colors applied to text

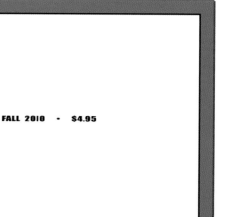

FALL 2010 · $4.95

A•MAZE•ING
get lost in a
pineapple maze

TWIST & SHOUT
boogie-boarding
daredevils stare down
the north coast waves

MAVERICK
a sizzling interview
with Chef Mavre

Working with Color

FIGURE 31

Duplicate Layer dialog box

Duplicate Layer	
Name: Color Headlines	OK
Color: ▓ Orange ▼	Cancel
☑ Show Layer ☑ Show Guides	
☐ Lock Layer ☐ Lock Guides	
☑ Print Layer	
☐ Suppress Text Wrap When Layer is Hidden	

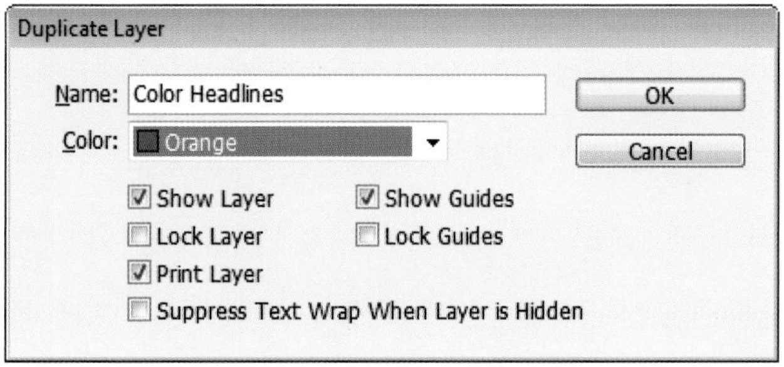

Create black shadow text

1. Click the **Toggles visibility button** ▢ (in its off state) on the Photo layer in the Layers panel, then assess the legibility of the text in the three text frames against the background graphic.

   The text is legible, but some letters like the M in Maverick are more difficult to distinguish from the background.

2. Click the **Original Black Text layer** in the Layers panel, click the **Layers panel list arrow**, then click **Duplicate Layer "Original Black Text"**.

3. Type **Color Headlines** in the Name text box, click the **Color list arrow**, then click **Orange**, so that your Duplicate Layer dialog box resembles Figure 31.

4. Click **OK**, then hide the Original Black Text layer.

5. With the Color Headlines layer still selected, delete the Fall 2010 text frame on the Color Headlines layer since you will not need a duplicate of this text.

6. Hide the Color Headlines layer, then show the Original Black Text layer.

7. Press and hold **[Alt]** (Win) or **[option]** (Mac), then click the **Original Black Text layer** in the Layers panel.

   TIP Pressing and holding [Alt] (Win) or [option] (Mac) when clicking a layer selects all objects on the layer.

(continued)

8. Click the **Formatting affects text button** T in the Swatches panel, then apply a 100% black fill to all the text.

9. Show the Color Headlines layer, press and hold **[Alt]** (Win) or **[option]** (Mac), then click the **Color Headlines layer**.

   The three text frames on the Color Headlines layer are now selected.

10. Click **Object** on the menu bar, point to **Transform**, then click **Move**.

11. Click the **Preview check box** to add a check mark (if necessary), type **-.04** in the Horizontal text box, type **-.04** in the Vertical text box, click **OK**, deselect all, then compare your work to Figure 32.

You duplicated a layer containing text. You changed the fill color of the text on the lower layer to black, then repositioned the colored text on the upper layer so that the black text acts as a shadow. By doing so, you added contrast to the colored text, making it more legible against the picture on the Photo layer.

FIGURE 32
Viewing the colored text with a black shadow

Black text placed behind colored text adds contrast

FIGURE 33
Viewing the modifications to the Gold swatch

FIGURE 35
Viewing the result of replacing gold with pink

FIGURE 34
Delete Swatch dialog box

Delete Swatch

Remove Swatch and Replace with:
⦿ Defined Swatch: ☐ Pink ▼
○ Unnamed Swatch

[OK] [Cancel]

*Gold swatch will be
replaced with Pink*

1. Deselect all, then drag the **Gold swatch** onto the Green frame to change its fill color to Gold.

2. Double-click the **Gold swatch** in the Swatches panel.

3. Click the **Preview check box** to add a check mark (if necessary), then drag the **Black slider** to 20%.

   You may need to move the Swatch Options dialog box to see the effect on the document page.

4. Drag the **Black slider** to 5%, then drag the **Yellow slider** to 50%.

5. Click **OK**, then compare your work to Figure 33.

   All usages of the Gold swatch—the frame and the "Twist & Shout" text—are updated with the modification.

6. Drag the **Gold swatch** to the Delete Swatch button 🗑 in the Swatches panel.

7. Click the **Defined Swatch list arrow**, click **Pink**, as shown in Figure 34, then click **OK**.

   As shown in Figure 35, all usages of the Gold swatch in the document are replaced by the Pink swatch.

You modified a swatch and noted that it updated throughout the document. You then deleted the swatch, replacing all of its usages with a different swatch.

WORK WITH
SPOT COLORS

What You'll Do

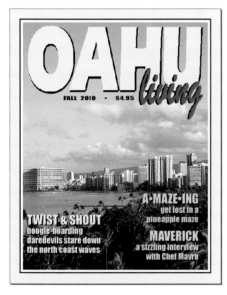

In this lesson, you will create and apply spot colors, and import graphics that contain spot colors.

Understanding Spot Colors

Spot colors are non-process inks that are manufactured by companies. Though printing is based on the four process colors, CMYK, it is not limited to them. It is important to understand that though combinations of CMYK inks can produce a wide variety of colors—enough to reproduce any color photograph quite well—they can't produce every color. For this reason, and others, designers often turn to spot colors.

Imagine that you are an art director designing the masthead for the cover of a new magazine. You have decided that the masthead will be an electric blue, vivid and eye-catching. If you were working with process tints only, you would have a problem. First, you would find that the almost-neon blue that you want to achieve is not within the CMYK range; it can't be printed. Even if it could, you would have an even bigger problem with consistency issues. You would want that blue to be the same blue on every issue of the magazine,

month after month. But offset printing is never perfect; variations in dot size are factored in. As the cover is printed, the blue color in the masthead will certainly vary, sometimes sharply.

Designers and printers use spot colors to solve this problem. **Spot colors** are special pre-mixed inks that are printed separately from process inks. The color range of spot colors far exceeds that of CMYK. Spot colors also offer consistent color throughout a print run.

The design and print worlds refer to spot colors by a number of names:

- Non-process inks: Refers to the fact that spot colors are not created using the process inks—CMYK.
- Fifth color: Refers to the fact that the spot color is often printed in addition to the four process inks. Note, however, that a spot color is not necessarily the "fifth" color. For example, many "two-color" projects call for black plus one spot color.

- PANTONE color: PANTONE is a manufacturer of non-process inks. PANTONE is simply a brand name.
- PMS color: An acronym for PANTONE Matching System.

A good way to think of spot colors is as ink in a bucket. With process inks, if you want red, you must mix some amount of magenta ink with some amount of yellow ink. With spot colors, if you want red, you pick a number from a chart, open the bucket, and there's the red ink—pre-mixed and ready to print.

Creating Spot Colors

You create spot colors in Adobe InDesign using the New Color Swatch dialog box.

Instead of choosing CMYK values, as you would when you create a process color, you choose Spot from the Color Type list, then choose a spot color system from one of 30 systems in the Color Mode list. After you choose a system, the related library of spot colors loads into the New Swatch dialog box allowing you to choose the spot color you want. Figure 36 shows the PANTONE solid coated color system.

Importing Graphics with Spot Colors

When you create graphics in Adobe Illustrator or Adobe Photoshop, you can create and apply spot colors in those applications as well. For example, you can create

a logo in Adobe Illustrator and fill it with a spot color.

Because InDesign, Illustrator, and Photoshop are all made by Adobe, InDesign recognizes the spot colors applied to graphics created in those applications. In the above example, when you place the graphic from Illustrator, InDesign identifies the spot color that was used and that spot color is added to the InDesign Swatches panel. If you double-click the swatch in the Swatches panel, you will see that the swatch is automatically formatted as a spot color.

FIGURE 36

Creating a spot color swatch

Color Type: Defines whether the color is Process or Spot

Color Mode: Defines which type of Spot color system you want to use

PANTONE solid coated color system

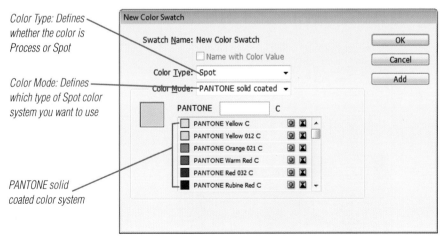

Create a spot color swatch

1. Click the **Swatches panel list arrow**, then click **New Color Swatch**.

2. Click the **Color Type list arrow**, then click **Spot**.

3. Click the **Color Mode list arrow**, then click **PANTONE solid coated**.

4. Type **663** in the PANTONE text box, so that your New Color Swatch dialog box resembles Figure 37.

5. Click **OK**, then compare your Swatches panel with Figure 38.

6. Change the fill of the pink frame to PANTONE 663.

7. Change the fill of the "TWIST & SHOUT" text to PANTONE 663, deselect the "TWIST & SHOUT" text frame, then compare your document to Figure 39.

You created a spot color swatch and then applied it to elements in the layout.

FIGURE 37
Creating a spot color

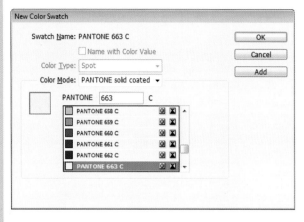

FIGURE 39
Viewing the document with the spot color applied

FIGURE 38
Identifying a spot color in the Swatches panel

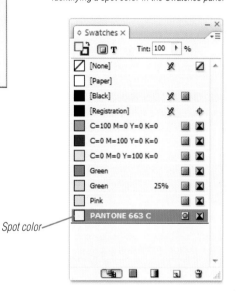

Spot color

FIGURE 40
Selecting a frame for a graphic

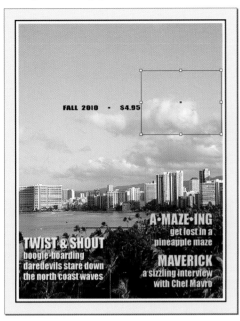

FIGURE 41
Identifying a new spot color in the Swatches panel

PANTONE swatch added
to the Swatches panel
when the Illustrator
graphic was imported

Import graphics with spot colors

1. Click the **Imported Graphics layer** in the Layers panel to target it, click the **Selection Tool** ▶, then select the frame shown in Figure 40.

   TIP Clicking in the general area of the selected frame shown in Figure 40 will select the frame.

2. Click **File** on the menu bar, click **Place**, navigate to the drive and folder where your Data Files are stored, click **Living Graphic.ai**, then click **Open**.

3. Click **Object** on the menu bar, point to **Fitting**, then click **Center Content**.

   The graphic that is placed in the frame was created in Adobe Illustrator.

4. Click **View** on the menu bar, point to **Display Performance**, then click **High Quality Display**.

5. Compare your Swatches panel to Figure 41.

   The PANTONE 159 C swatch was automatically added to the Swatches panel when the graphic was placed, since it was a color used to create the graphic.

6. Deselect the graphics frame, double-click **PANTONE 159 C** in the Swatches panel, note that PANTONE 159 C was imported as a spot color as indicated in the Color Type text box, then click **Cancel**.

   (continued)

7. Select the frame shown in Figure 42.

8. Click **File** on the menu bar, click **Place**, navigate to the drive and folder where your Data Files are stored, then double-click **OAHU graphic.ai**.

OAHU graphic.ai is an Adobe Illustrator file. The fill color of O, A, H, and U is PANTONE 663—the same PANTONE 663 fill that was created in InDesign and applied to the border and the "TWIST & SHOUT" text. For this reason, PANTONE 663 does not need to be added to the Swatches panel.

TIP   If, when you import the graphic, a dialog box appears warning you that the PANTONE color in the graphic is defined differently and asking you if you want to replace it, click No.

(continued)

FIGURE 42
Selecting a frame for a graphic

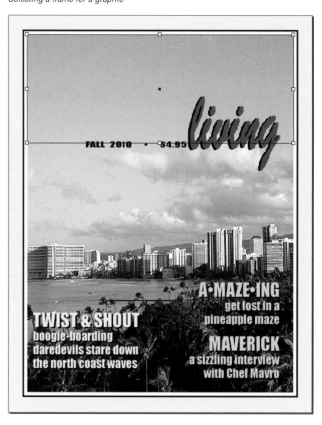

Working with Color

FIGURE 43
Viewing the document page

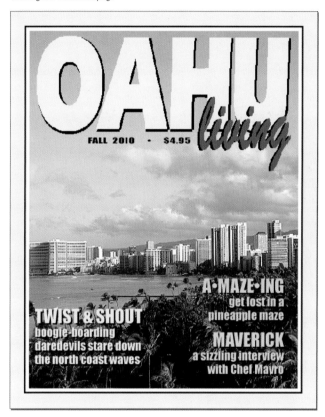

9. Click **Object** on the menu bar, point to **Fitting**, then click **Center Content**.
10. Deselect all, then compare your document with Figure 43.
11. Save your work, then close OAHU Magazine Cover.

You imported a graphic that was created with a spot color in another application, then noted that the spot color was automatically added to the Swatches panel. Next, you imported a graphic that was filled with the same spot color that you had already created in InDesign.

WORK WITH GRADIENTS

What You'll Do

In this lesson, you will create gradients and explore options for applying them to frames.

Creating Gradients

A **gradient** is a graduated blend of two or more colors. By definition, every gradient must have at least two colors, which are commonly referred to as the **starting** and **ending colors** of the gradient. You can add colors to a gradient, colors that come between the starting and ending colors. The colors that you add are called **color stops**.

In InDesign, you create gradients by clicking New Gradient Swatch on the Swatches menu. This opens the New Gradient Swatch dialog box, as shown in Figure 44. In this dialog box, you define all the elements of the gradient. Like new colors, you can give your gradient a descriptive name. You use the Gradient Ramp to define the starting, ending, and any intermediary colors for your gradient. You choose whether your gradient will be radial or linear using the Type list arrow. You can think of a **radial gradient** as a series of concentric circles. With a radial gradient, the starting color appears at the center of the gradient, then radiates out to the ending color.

You can think of a **linear gradient** as a series of straight lines that gradate from one color to another (or through multiple colors). Figure 45 shows a linear and a radial gradient, each composed of three colors.

Figure 46 shows the dialog box used to create the linear gradient. The Gradient Ramp represents the gradient, and the gold color stop is selected. The sliders show the CMYK values that make the gold tint. Note that the Stop Color text box reads CMYK.

You can create gradients using swatches already in the Swatches panel as stop colors. In Figure 47, the selected color stop is a spot color named PANTONE 032 C. Note that the Stop Color text box reads Swatches. When you choose Swatches from the Stop Color menu, all the named colors in the Swatches panel are listed and available to be used in the gradient.

When you close the New Gradient Swatch dialog box, the new gradient swatch appears in the Swatches panel when you click the Show All Swatches button or when you click the Show Gradient Swatches button in the Swatches panel.

Working with Color

FIGURE 44
New Gradient Swatch dialog box

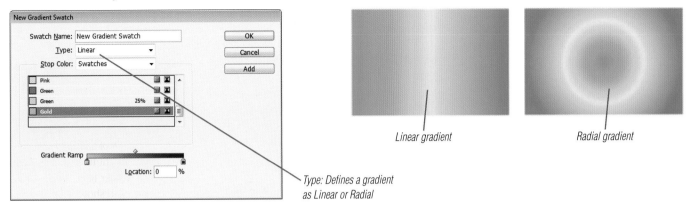

Type: Defines a gradient as Linear or Radial

FIGURE 45
A linear and a radial gradient

Linear gradient

Radial gradient

FIGURE 46
Viewing a linear gradient

Swatch name

Stop Color: Defines a stop color as a named or unnamed process color or a spot color

Starting color

Color stop (selected)

Ending color

Location: Identifies location of color stop on the Gradient Ramp

FIGURE 47
Viewing the formatting of a gradient with a named color

The selected stop color is defined as a named color

Spot color chosen for the selected color stop

Color stop (selected)

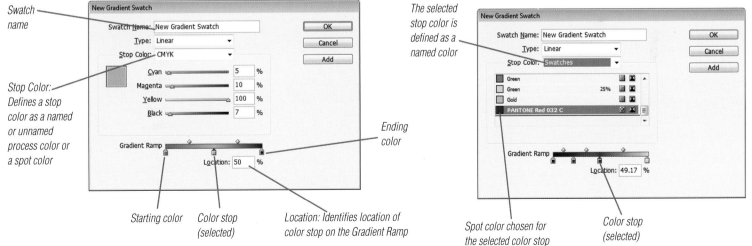

Applying Gradients

You apply a gradient to an object the same way you apply a color to an object. Simply select the object, then click the gradient in the Swatches panel. A gradient swatch can be applied as a fill or as a stroke.

If you use a gradient to fill an object, you can further control how the gradient fills the object using the Gradient Swatch Tool or the Gradient Feather Tool. The Gradient Swatch Tool allows you to change the length and/or direction of a linear or radial gradient. You can also use it to change the angle of a linear gradient and the center point of a radial gradient. To use the Gradient Swatch Tool, you first select an object with a gradient fill, then you drag the Gradient Swatch Tool over the object. For both linear and radial gradients, where you begin dragging and where you stop dragging determines the length of the gradient, from starting color to ending color. The Gradient Feather Tool works exactly like the Gradient Swatch Tool, except that it produces a softer progression of the colors in the gradient.

For linear gradients, the angle that you drag the Gradient Swatch Tool determines the angle that the blend fills the object.

Figure 48 shows six rows of six squares, which are InDesign frames filled with gradients. Each frame is filled with a rainbow gradient. The gradient appears differently in each row as a result of dragging the Gradient Swatch Tool. The black line associated with each example represents the length and direction that the Gradient Swatch Tool was dragged to create each effect.

Modifying a Gradient Fill Using the Gradient Panel

Like color swatches, gradients can be modified. When you modify a gradient, all instances of the gradient used in the document will be automatically updated. Let's say you create a gradient and use it to fill 10 objects. Then you decide that, in only one of those 10 objects, you want to modify the gradient by removing one color. What do you do? If you modify the gradient swatch—remove a color stop—that's going to affect all usages of the gradient. You could, of course, duplicate the gradient swatch, remove the unwanted color stop, then apply the new gradient to the single object. But there's a better way. You can use the Gradient panel, shown in Figure 49.

When you select an object with a gradient fill, the Gradient panel shows the Gradient Ramp that you used to create the gradient in the New Gradient Swatch dialog box. You can manipulate the Gradient Ramp in the Gradient panel. You can add, move, and delete color stops. You can also select color stops and modify their color using the Color panel. And here's the great part: the modifications you make in the Gradient panel only affect the gradient fill of the selected object(s).

FIGURE 48
Using the Gradient Swatch Tool

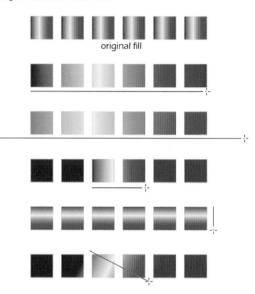

original fill

FIGURE 49
Gradient panel

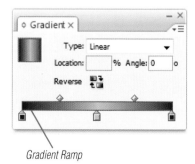

Gradient Ramp

FIGURE 50
New Gradient Swatch dialog box

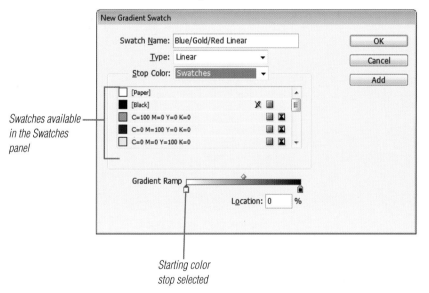

Swatches available
in the Swatches
panel

Starting color
stop selected

1. Open ID 5-2.indd, then save it as **Making the Gradient**.

2. Click the **Swatches panel list arrow**, then click **New Gradient Swatch**.

3. In the Swatch Name text box, type **Blue/Gold/Red Linear**.

4. Click the **left color stop** on the Gradient Ramp, click the **Stop Color list arrow**, then click **Swatches** so that your dialog box resembles Figure 50.

   When you choose Swatches, the colors in the Swatches panel are listed below.

5. Click the swatch named **Blue**.

   The left color stop on the Gradient Ramp changes to blue.

6. Click the **right color stop** on the Gradient Ramp, click the **Stop Color list arrow**, click **Swatches**, then click the swatch named **Red**.

7. Click directly below the Gradient Ramp to add a new color stop.

   TIP   Click anywhere to add the new color stop. You can adjust the location using the Location text box.

8. Type **50** in the Location text box, then press **[Tab]**.

   The new color stop is located at the exact middle of the Gradient Ramp.

(continued)

9. Click the **Stop Color list arrow**, click **Swatches**, then click the swatch named **Gold** so that your New Gradient Swatch dialog box resembles Figure 51.

10. Click **OK**.

The new gradient swatch is added to the Swatches panel.

You created a three-color linear gradient swatch using three named colors.

Create a radial gradient swatch

1. Click the **Swatches panel list arrow**, then click **New Gradient Swatch**.

The New Gradient Swatch dialog box opens with the settings from the last created gradient.

2. In the Swatch Name text box, type **Cyan Radial**.

3. Click the **Type list arrow**, then click **Radial**.

4. Click the **center color stop**, then drag it straight down to remove it from the Gradient Ramp.

5. Click the **left color stop** on the Gradient Ramp, click the **Stop Color list arrow**, then click **CMYK**.

6. Drag each slider to 0% so that your dialog box resembles Figure 52.

7. Click the **right color stop** on the Gradient Ramp, click the **Stop Color list arrow**, then click **CMYK**.

(continued)

FIGURE 51
Creating a linear gradient swatch

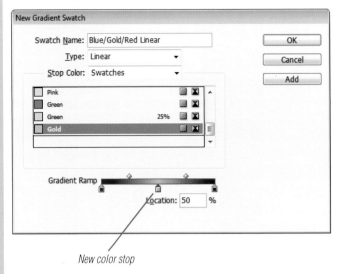

New color stop

FIGURE 52
Formatting the left color stop

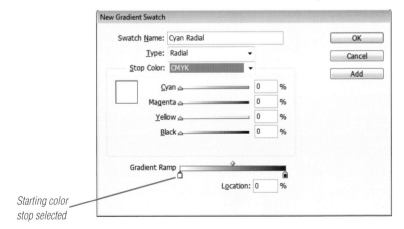

Starting color stop selected

Working with Color

FIGURE 53

Formatting the right color stop

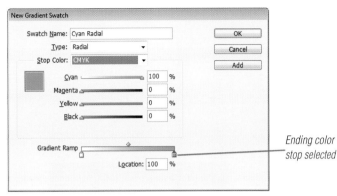

Ending color
stop selected

FIGURE 54

Dragging the Gradient Swatch Tool straight down

Drag Gradient Swatch Tool
cursor straight down

FIGURE 55

Viewing the linear gradient applied vertically to the frame

8. Drag the **Cyan slider** to 100%, then drag the **Magenta, Yellow,** and **Black sliders** to 0% so that your dialog box resembles Figure 53.

9. Click **OK**.

   The new gradient swatch is added to the Swatches panel.

You created a two-color radial gradient swatch using CMYK values.

Apply gradient swatches and use the Gradient Swatch Tool

1. Click the **Show Gradient Swatches button** on the Swatches panel.

2. Click the **Selection Tool** , click the **border** of the top rectangular frame, verify that the Fill button is activated in the Toolbox, then click **Blue/Gold/Red Linear** in the Swatches panel.

   TIP Make sure you are in Normal view and that you are viewing frame edges.

3. Click the **Gradient Swatch Tool** , then, using Figure 54 as a guide, place the mouse pointer anywhere on the top edge of the rectangular frame, click and drag down, and release the mouse button at the bottom edge of the frame.

   Your frame should resemble Figure 55.

   TIP Pressing and holding [Shift] when dragging the Gradient Swatch Tool constrains the movement on a horizontal or vertical axis.

4. Drag the **Gradient Swatch Tool** from the bottom-middle handle of the frame to the top-right handle.

   (continued)

5. Drag the **Gradient Swatch Tool** from the left edge of the document window to the right edge of the document window.

6. Drag the **Gradient Swatch Tool** a short distance from left to right in the center of the frame, as shown in Figure 56.

7. Click the **Selection Tool** ➤ , click the edge of the circular frame, then click **Cyan Radial** in the Swatches panel.

8. Click the **Gradient Swatch Tool** ▱ , press and hold **[Shift]**, then drag the **Gradient Swatch Tool** from the center point of the circle up to the bottom edge of the center rectangle above the circle so that your document resembles Figure 57.

You filled two objects with two different gradients, and you used the Gradient Swatch Tool to manipulate how the gradients filled the objects.

Use the Gradient Swatch Tool to extend a gradient across multiple objects and modify a gradient

1. Click the **Gradient panel name tab** to open the Gradient panel.

2. Deselect all, click the **Selection Tool** ➤ , then select the three rectangular frames above the circle by pressing **[Shift]** and then clicking their edges or dragging a selection box around them.

3. Click **Blue/Gold/Red Linear** in the Swatches panel.

   As shown in Figure 58, the gradient fills each frame individually.

(continued)

FIGURE 56
Dragging the Gradient Swatch Tool from left to right

FIGURE 57
Viewing two gradients applied to two objects

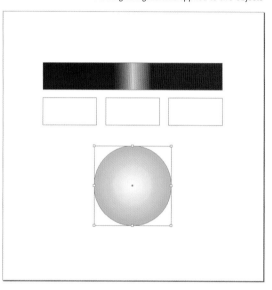

FIGURE 58
A gradient fill applied individually to three objects

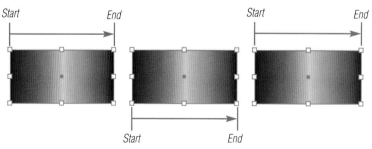

FIGURE 59

A gradient fill gradating across three objects

Start   End

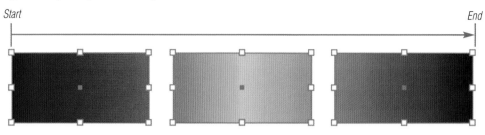

4. Verify that the three objects are still selected, click the **Gradient Swatch Tool** 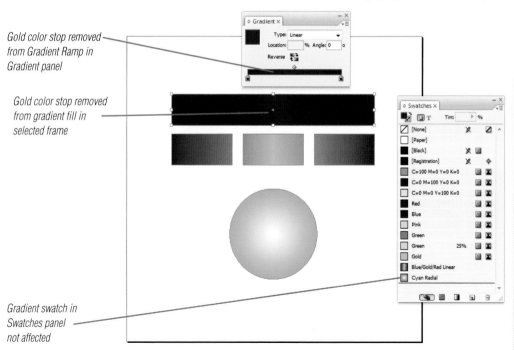, then drag it from the left edge of the leftmost frame to the right edge of the rightmost frame.

   As shown in Figure 59, the gradient gradates across all three selected objects.

5. Click the **Selection Tool** ▶, then click the **rectangular frame** at the top of the document window.

6. Remove the center gold color stop from the Gradient Ramp in the Gradient panel, then click the **Show All Swatches button** ▢ in the Swatches panel.

   As shown in Figure 60, only the gold color is removed from the gradient fill in the selected frame. The original gradient in the Swatches panel (Blue/Gold/Red Linear) is not affected.

7. Save your work, then close Making the Gradient.

You selected three objects, applied a gradient to each of them, then used the Gradient Swatch Tool to extend the gradient across all three selected objects. You then modified the gradient fill of a selected object by removing a color stop from the Gradient panel.

FIGURE 60

Modifying a gradient in the Gradient panel

Gold color stop removed from Gradient Ramp in Gradient panel

Gold color stop removed from gradient fill in selected frame

Gradient swatch in Swatches panel not affected

Work with process colors.

1. Open ID 5-3.indd, then save it as **LAB cover**.
2. Verify that the Swatches panel is open, click the Swatches panel list arrow, then click New Color Swatch.
3. Verify that Process is chosen in the Color Type text box and that CMYK is chosen in the Color Mode text box.
4. Remove the check mark in the Name with Color Value check box, then type **Pink** in the Swatch Name text box.
5. Type **15** in the Cyan text box, press [Tab], type **70** in the Magenta text box, press [Tab], type **10** in the Yellow text box, press [Tab], type **0** in the Black text box, press [Tab], then click OK.
6. Display the Color panel, if necessary.
7. Click the Color panel list arrow, click CMYK, then verify that the Fill button is activated.
8. Drag the Cyan slider in the Color panel to 50%, drag the Magenta slider to 10%, then drag the Yellow and Black sliders to 0%.
9. Drag the color from the Fill button in the Color panel to the Swatches panel.
10. Verify that the C=50 M=10 Y=0 K=0 swatch is still selected in the Swatches panel, click the Swatches panel list arrow, then click New Tint Swatch.
11. Drag the Tint slider to 40%, then click OK.

Apply color.

1. Duplicate the Text layer, then rename it **Colored Text**.

2. Click View on the menu bar, then click Hide Frame Edges.
3. Drag and drop C=50 M=10 Y=0 K=0 from the Swatches panel to the outermost black-filled frame.
4. Click the Selection Tool, click the BRUSH UP text frame, then click the Formatting affects text button in the Toolbox.
5. Click the C=50 M=10 Y=0 K=0 swatch in the Swatches panel.
6. Click the Holiday Issue text frame in the lower left corner of the cover, click the Formatting affects text button in the Swatches panel, then click the Paper swatch in the Swatches panel.
7. Click the Type Tool, select all of the text in the PUPPY LOVE text frame, then click Pink in the Swatches panel.
8. Select all of the text in the FETCH text frame, then click the C=50 M=10 Y=0 K=0 40% tint swatch in the Swatches panel.
9. Click the Selection Tool, press and hold [Alt] (Win) or [option] (Mac), then click the Colored Text layer to select all of the objects on the layer. (Hint: Since you have hidden frame edges, you will not see selection boxes.)
10. Click Object on the menu bar, point to Transform, then click Move.
11. Verify that there is a check mark in the Preview check box, type **-.03** in the Horizontal text box, type **-.03** in the Vertical text box, click OK, then deselect all.

Work with spot colors.

1. Click the Swatches panel list arrow, then click New Color Swatch.
2. Click the Color Type list arrow, then click Spot.
3. Click the Color Mode list arrow, then click PANTONE solid coated.
4. Type **117** in the PANTONE text box, then click OK.
5. Change the fill on the C=50 M=10 border to PANTONE 117 C.
6. Click the Imported Graphics layer in the Layers panel to target it, click the Selection Tool, then click between the dog's eyes to select the frame for placing a new image.
7. Click File on the menu bar, click Place, navigate to the drive and folder where your Chapter 5 Data Files are stored, click LAB.ai, then click Open. (Hint: LAB.ai is an Adobe Illustrator graphic filled with PANTONE 117 C.)
8. Click the Photo layer in the Layers panel, click the dog graphic in the document window, click Edit on the menu bar, click Copy, click Edit on the menu bar, then click Paste In Place.
9. In the Layers panel, drag the Indicates selected items button from the Photo layer up to the Imported Graphics layer.
10. Click File on the menu bar, click Place, navigate to the drive and folder where your Chapter 5 Data Files are stored, then double-click Wally Head Silo.psd. (Hint: Wally Head Silo.psd is identical to the dog photo, with the

exception that it was saved with a clipping path around the dog's head in order to remove the red background.)

11. Deselect all, compare your work to Figure 61, save your work, then close the document.

Work with gradients.

1. Open ID 5-4.indd, then save it as **Gradient Skills Review**.

2. Click the Swatches panel list arrow, then click New Gradient Swatch.

3. In the Swatch Name text box, type **Red/Golden/Green Linear**.

4. Click the left color stop on the Gradient Ramp, click the Stop Color list arrow, then click Swatches.

5. Click the swatch named Red.

6. Click the right color stop on the Gradient Ramp, click the Stop Color list arrow, click Swatches, then click the swatch named Green.

7. Position your pointer anywhere immediately below the Gradient Ramp, then click to add a third color stop.

8. Type **50** in the Location text box, then press [Tab].

9. Click the Stop Color list arrow, choose Swatches, click the swatch named Gold, then click OK.

10. Click the Show Gradient Swatches button on the Swatches panel.

11. Click the Selection Tool, select the border of the top rectangular frame, verify that the Fill button is activated in the Toolbox, then click Red/Golden/Green Linear in the Swatches panel.

12. Click the Gradient Swatch Tool, then drag from the top-middle handle of the rectangle frame down to the bottom-right handle.

13. Display the Gradient panel, if necessary.

14. Click the Selection Tool, deselect the top rectangle frame, then select the three lower rectangular frames.

15. Click Red/Golden/Green Linear in the Swatches panel.

16. Click the Gradient Swatch Tool, and with all three objects still selected, drag the Gradient Swatch Tool from the left edge of the leftmost frame to the right edge of the rightmost frame.

17. Deselect all, then compare your work to Figure 62.

18. Save your work, then close Gradient Skills Review.

FIGURE 61
Completed Skills Review, Part 1

FIGURE 62
Completed Skills Review, Part 2

You are a freelance graphic designer. You have recently been contracted to create a newsletter for a local financial investment company. The newsletter will be 8.5" × 11" and will be printed using the CMYK process inks. You decide on the colors you want to use, open InDesign, create a new document, then, before you start designing, you create a process color and a 40% tint of that color.

1. Open ID 5-5.indd, then save it as **Process Colors**.
2. Display the Swatches panel, if necessary, click the Swatches panel list arrow, then click New Color Swatch.
3. Create a CMYK color named **Tan** using the following values: Cyan: 0%, Magenta: 30%, Yellow: 50%, and Black: 20%.
4. Create a new tint swatch based on Tan, then change the tint amount to 40%.
5. Compare your Swatches panel to Figure 63, save your work, then close Process Colors. (Don't be concerned if your swatch order differs.)

FIGURE 63
Completed Project Builder 1

You are a freelance graphic designer. You have recently been contracted to create a cover for LAB magazine. The magazine is usually published only with one color—in black and white—but the publishers have some extra money for this issue. They want you to create a design for this cover so that it will print as a two-color job. It will be printed with black and one spot color. They provide you with the black and white version of the cover. You are free to choose the spot color and apply it any way that you care to.

1. Open ID 5-6.indd, then save it as **2 Color Cover**.
2. Click the Swatches panel list arrow, then click New Color Swatch.
3. Click the Color Type list arrow, then choose Spot.
4. Click the Color Mode list arrow, then choose PANTONE solid coated.
5. Choose PANTONE 195 C.
6. Click the Swatches panel list arrow, then click New Tint Swatch.
7. Drag the Tint slider to 30%, then click OK.
8. Change the fill of the outermost frame that is filled with black to PANTONE 195 C.
9. Click the inner white border that is filled with Paper and stroked with Black, then change its fill color to 30% PANTONE 195 C.

10. Change the fill color on the three white headlines to 30% PANTONE 195 C.

FIGURE 64
Completed Project Builder 2

11. Compare your cover to Figure 64, save your work, then close 2 Color Cover.

You have recently been contracted to create a logo for the Hypnotists Foundation. Their representative tells you that he wants the logo to be a circle filled with a radial gradient. Starting from the inside of the circle, the colors should go from white to black to white to black to white to black. He tells you that he wants each color to be very distinct—in other words, he doesn't want the white and black colors to blend into each other, creating a lot of gray areas to the logo.

1. Open ID 5-7.indd, then save it as **Concentric Circle Gradient**.
2. Click the Swatches panel list arrow, then click New Gradient Swatch.
3. Create a radial gradient named **Six Ring Radial**.
4. Add four new color stops to the Gradient Ramp, then position them so that they are equally spaced across the ramp.
5. Format the first, third, and fifth color stops as 0% CMYK (White).
6. Format the second, fourth and sixth color stops as 100% Black.
7. Close the New Gradient Swatch dialog box, then apply the new gradient to the circle.
8. Hide the frame edges, then compare your work to Figure 65.
9. Save your work, then close Concentric Circle Gradient.

FIGURE 65
Completed Design Project

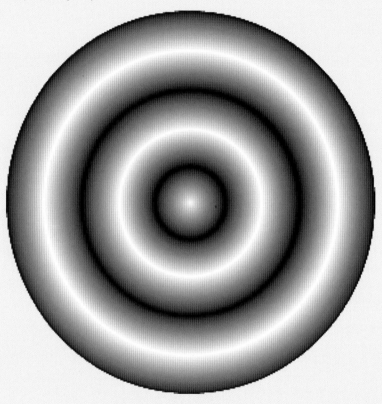

This group project will test the group's familiarity with process colors. The group will open an InDesign document that shows nine process colors. Each process color is numbered, from 1 to 9. All nine colors are very basic mixes. None of the nine is composed of more than two process inks. The inks used to create the nine colors are used at either 100% or 50%. Each member of the group will write down on a piece of paper his or her guess of the percentages of CMYK that were used to make the process color. Once each member has guessed, the instructor will reveal the CMYK percentages of each color.

1. Open ID 5-8.indd, then save it as **Guessing Game**. The color squares are shown in Figure 66.
2. Use the Type Tool to enter your guesses for each process color. You can type directly on top of each of the nine squares or directly below each, for example, **Magenta=100**.
3. When finished, compare your guesses with the group.
4. Enter the total number of your correct answers on your document window, save your work, then close Guessing Game.

FIGURE 66
Group Project Quiz

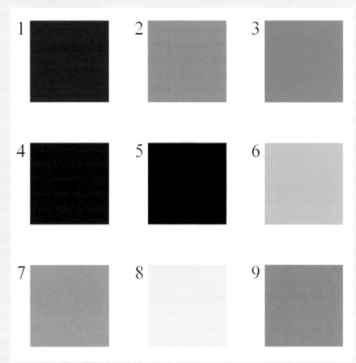

chapter 1

GETTING STARTED WITH
ADOBE
PHOTOSHOP CS3

1. Start Adobe Photoshop CS3

2. Learn how to open and save an image

3. Use organizational and management features

4. Examine the Photoshop window

5. Use the Layers and History palettes

6. Learn about Photoshop by using Help

7. View and print an image

8. Close a file and exit Photoshop

GETTING STARTED WITH
ADOBE
PHOTOSHOP CS3

Using Photoshop

Adobe Photoshop CS3 is an image-editing program that lets you create and modify digital images. 'CS' stands for Creative Suite, a complete design environment. The Adobe® Design Premium Creative Design Suite 3 consists of Adobe Photoshop®, Adobe Dreamweaver®, Adobe InDesign®, and Adobe Flash®. A **digital image** is a picture in electronic form. Using Photoshop, you can create original artwork, manipulate color images, and retouch photographs. In addition to being a robust application popular with graphics professionals, Photoshop is practical for anyone who wants to enhance existing artwork or create new masterpieces. For example, you can repair and restore damaged areas within an image, combine images, and create graphics and special effects for the Web.

QUICKTIP

In Photoshop, a digital image may be referred to as a file, document, graphic, picture, or image.

Understanding Platform Interfaces

Photoshop is available in both Windows and Macintosh platforms. Regardless of which type of computer you use, the features and commands are very similar. Some of the Windows and Macintosh keyboard commands differ in name, but they have equivalent functions. For example, the [Ctrl] and [Alt] keys are used in Windows, and the ⌘ and [option] keys are used on Macintosh computers. There is a visual difference between the two platforms due to the user interface found in each type of computer.

Understanding Sources

Photoshop allows you to work with images from a variety of sources. You can create your own original artwork in Photoshop, use images downloaded from the Web, or use images that have been scanned or created using a digital camera. Whether you create Photoshop images to print in high resolution or optimize them for multimedia presentations, Web-based functions, or animation projects, Photoshop is a powerful tool for communicating your ideas visually.

Tools You'll Use

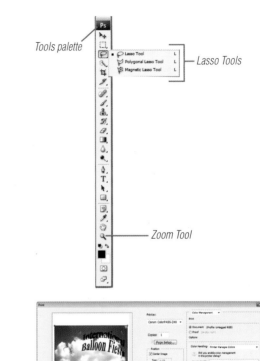

New...	Ctrl+N
Open...	Ctrl+O
Browse...	Alt+Ctrl+O
Open As...	Alt+Shift+Ctrl+O
Open As Smart Object...	
Open Recent	▶
Device Central...	
Close	Ctrl+W
Close All	Alt+Ctrl+W
Close and Go To Bridge...	Shift+Ctrl+W
Save	Ctrl+S
Save As...	Shift+Ctrl+S
Check In...	
Save for Web & Devices...	Alt+Shift+Ctrl+S
Revert	F12
Place...	
Import	▶
Export	▶
Automate	▶
Scripts	▶
File Info...	Alt+Shift+Ctrl+I
Page Setup...	Shift+Ctrl+P
Print...	Ctrl+P
Print One Copy	Alt+Shift+Ctrl+P
Exit	Ctrl+Q

Arrange	▶
Workspace	▶
Actions	Alt+F9
Animation	
Brushes	F5
Channels	
Character	
Clone Source	
✔ Color	F6
Histogram	
History	
Info	F8
Layer Comps	
✔ Layers	F7
Measurement Log	
✔ Navigator	
✔ Options	
Paragraph	
Paths	
Styles	
Swatches	
Tool Presets	
✔ Tools	
✔ 1 PS 1-1.psd	

Tools palette

Lasso Tool L
Polygonal Lasso Tool L
Magnetic Lasso Tool L

Lasso Tools

Zoom Tool

Options bar

START ADOBE
PHOTOSHOP CS3

What You'll Do

In this lesson, you'll start Photoshop for Windows or Macintosh, then create a file.

Defining Image-Editing Software

Photoshop is an image-editing program. An **image-editing** program allows you to manipulate graphic images so that they can be reproduced by professional printers using full-color processes. Using windows, various tools, menus, and a variety of techniques, you can modify a Photoshop image by rotating it, resizing it, changing its colors, or adding text to it. You can also use Photoshop to create and open different kinds of file formats, which enables you to create your own images, import them from a digital camera or scanner, or use files (in other formats) purchased from outside sources. Table 1 lists some of the graphics file formats that Photoshop can open and create.

Understanding Images

Every image is made up of very small squares, which are called **pixels**, and each pixel represents a color or shade. Pixels within an image can be added, deleted, or modified.

QUICKTIP

Photoshop files can become quite large. After a file is complete, you might want to **flatten** it, an irreversible process that combines all layers and reduces the file size.

Using Photoshop Features

Photoshop includes many tools that you can use to manipulate images and text. Within an image, you can add new items and modify existing elements, change colors, and draw shapes. For example, using the Lasso Tool, you can outline a section of an image and drag the section onto another area of the image. You can also isolate a foreground or background image. You can extract all or part of a complex image from nearly any background and use it elsewhere.

QUICKTIP

You can create a logo in Photoshop. A **logo** is a distinctive image that you can create by combining symbols, shapes, colors, and text. Logos give graphic identity to organizations, such as corporations, universities, and retail stores.

You can also create and format text, called **type**, in Photoshop. You can apply a variety of special effects to type; for example, you can change the appearance of type and increase or decrease the distance between characters. You can also edit type after it has been created and formatted.

Adobe Dreamweaver CS3 a Web production software program included in the Design Suite allows you to optimize, preview, and animate images. Because Dreamweaver is part of the same suite as Photoshop, you can jump seamlessly between the two programs.

You can also quickly turn any graphics image into a GIF animation. Photoshop and Dreamweaver let you compress file size (while optimizing image quality) to ensure that your files download quickly from a Web page. Using optimization features, you can view multiple versions of an image and select the one that best suits your needs.

Starting Photoshop and Creating a File

The way that you start Photoshop depends on the computer platform you are using. However, when you start Photoshop in either platform, the computer displays a **splash screen**, a window that displays information about the software, and then the Photoshop window opens.

After you start Photoshop, you can create a file from scratch. You use the New dialog box to create a file. You can also use the New dialog box to set the size of the image you're about to create by typing dimensions in the Width and Height text boxes.

TABLE 1: Examples of Graphic File Formats Supported in Photoshop

file format	filename extension	file format	filename extension
Photoshop	.PSD	Filmstrip	.VLM
Bitmap	.BMP	Kodak PhotoCD	.PCD
PC Paintbrush	.PCX	Pixar	.PXR
Graphics Interchange Format	.GIF	Scitex CT	.SCT
Photoshop Encapsulated PostScript	.EPS	Photoshop PDF	.PDF
Tagged Image Format	.TIF or .TIFF	Targa	.TGA or .VDA
JPEG Picture Format	.JPG, .JPE, or .JPEG	PICT file	.PCT, .PIC, or .PICT
CorelDraw	.CDR	Raw	varies

Start Photoshop (Windows)

1. Click the **Start button** 🔵 on the taskbar.

2. Point to **All Programs**, point to **Adobe Design Premium CS3** as shown in Figure 1, then click **Adobe Photoshop CS3**.

   TIP The Adobe Photoshop CS3 program might be found in the Start menu (in the left pane) or in the Adobe folder, which is in the Program Files folder on the hard drive (Win).

3. Click **File** on the menu bar, then click **New** to open the New dialog box.

4. Double-click the number in the Width text box, type **500**, click the **Width list arrow**, then click **pixels** (if it is not already selected).

5. Double-click the number in the Height text box, type **400**, then specify a resolution of **72** pixels/inch, if necessary.

6. Click **OK**.

7. Click the **arrow** ▶ at the bottom of the image window, point to **Show**, then click **Document Sizes** (if it is not already displayed).

You started Photoshop for Windows, then created a file with custom dimensions. Setting custom dimensions lets you specify the exact size of the image you are creating. You changed the display at the bottom of the image window so the document size is visible.

FIGURE 1

Starting Photoshop CS3 (Windows)

Understanding hardware requirements (Windows)

Adobe Photoshop CS3 has the following minimum system requirements:

- Processor: Intel Based Pentium 4 processor or later
- Operating System: Microsoft® Windows XP SP2 or Windows Vista
- Memory: 512 MB of RAM
- Storage space: 10 GB of available hard-disk space
- Internet connectivity for activation; broadband required for Adobe Stock Photos
- 16-bit video card and Quick Time 7 for Multimedia features

FIGURE 2
Starting Photoshop CS3 (Macintosh)

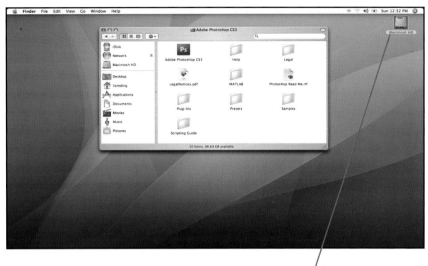

Hard drive icon

Start Photoshop (Macintosh)

1. Double-click the **hard drive icon**, double-click the **Applications folder**, then double-click the **Adobe Photoshop CS3 folder**. Compare your screen to Figure 2.

2. Double-click the **Adobe Photoshop CS3 program icon**.

3. Click **File** on the menu bar, then click **New**.

   TIP If the Color Settings dialog box opens, click No. If a Welcome screen opens, click Close.

4. Double-click the number in the Width text box, type **500**, click the **Width list arrow**, then click **pixels** (if necessary).

5. Double-click the number in the Height text box, type **400**, click the **Height list arrow**, click **pixels** (if necessary), then verify a resolution of **72** pixels/inch.

6. Click **OK**.

7. Click the **arrow** ▶ at the bottom of the image window, click **Show**, then click **Document Sizes** (if is it not already displayed).

You started Photoshop for Macintosh, then created a file with custom dimensions. You changed the display at the bottom of the image window so the document size is visible.

LEARN HOW TO OPEN AND
SAVE AN IMAGE

What You'll Do

 In this lesson, you'll locate and open files using the File menu and Adobe Bridge, flag and sort files, then save a file with a new name.

Opening and Saving Files

Photoshop provides several options for opening and saving a file. Often, the project you're working on determines the techniques you use for opening and saving files. For example, you might want to preserve the original version of a file while you modify a copy. You can open a file, then immediately save it with a different filename, as well as open and save files in many different file formats. When working with graphic images you can open a Photoshop file that has been saved as a bitmap (.bmp) file, then save it as a JPEG (.jpg) file to use on a Web page.

Customizing How You Open Files

You can customize how you open your files by setting preferences. **Preferences** are options you can set that are based on your work habits. For example, you can use the Open Recent command on the File menu to instantly locate and open the files that you recently worked on, or you can allow others to preview your files as thumbnails. Figure 3 shows the Preferences dialog box options for handling your files in Windows.

TIP   In cases when the correct file format is not automatically determined, you can use the Open As command on the File menu (Win).

FIGURE 3
Preferences dialog box

Option for thumbnail preview

Number of files to appear in Open Recent list

Browsing Through Files

You can easily find the files you're looking for by using **Adobe Bridge**: a stand-alone application that serves as the hub for the Adobe Creative Suite. See Figure 4. You can open Adobe Bridge (or just Bridge) by clicking the Go to Bridge button to the left of the Workspace button. You can also open Bridge using the File menu when a Photoshop file is open. When you open Bridge, there are a series of palettes, also called panels, with which you can view the files on your hard drive as hierarchical files and folders. In addition to the Favorites and Folders palettes in the upper-left corner of the Bridge window, there are other important areas. Directly beneath the Favorites and Folders palettes is The Filter panel which allows you to easily change the order of files in the Content panel. Beneath the Preview window is a window containing the Metadata and Keywords palettes, which store information about a selected file that can then be used as search parameters. You can use this tree structure to find the file you are searching for. When you locate a file, you can click its thumbnail to see information about its size, format, and creation and modification dates.

(Clicking a thumbnail selects the image. You can select multiple non-contiguous images by pressing and holding [Ctrl](Win) ⌘ (Mac) each time you click an image.) You can select contiguous images by clicking

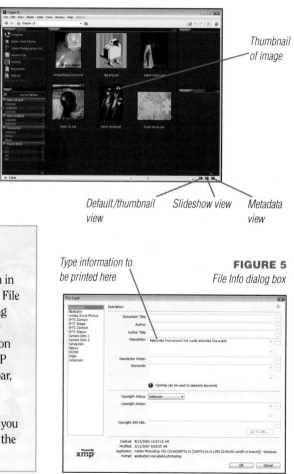

FIGURE 4
Adobe Bridge window

Thumbnail of image

File info

Default/thumbnail view   *Slideshow view*   *Metadata view*

Using the File Info dialog box

You can use the File Info dialog box to identify a file, add a caption or other text, or add a copyright notice. The Description section allows you to enter printable text, as shown in Figure 5. For example, to add your name to an image, click File on the menu bar, click File Info, then click in the Description text box. (You can move from field to field by pressing [Tab] or by clicking in individual text boxes.) Type your name, course number, or other identifying information in the Description text box. You can enter additional information in the other text boxes, then save all the File Info data as a separate file that has an .XMP extension. To print selected data from the File Info dialog box, click File on the menu bar, then click Print. Click the Color Management list arrow, then click Output. Available options are listed in the right panel. To print the filename, select the Labels check box. You can also select checkboxes that let you print crop marks and registration marks. If you choose, you can even add a background color or border to your image. After you select the items you want to print, click Print.

Type information to be printed here

FIGURE 5
File Info dialog box

the first image, then pressing and holding [Shift] and clicking the last image in the group. You can open a file using Bridge by double-clicking its thumbnail, and find out information such as the file's format, and when it was created and edited. You can close Bridge by clicking File (Win) or Bridge CS3 (Mac) on the (Bridge) menu bar, then clicking Exit (Win) or Quit Bridge CS3 (Mac) or by clicking the window's Close button.

Understanding the Power of Bridge

In addition to allowing you to see all your images, Bridge can be used to rate (assign importance), sort (organize by name, rating, and other criteria), and label. Figure 4, on the previous page, contains images that are assigned a rating and shown in Filmstrip view. There are three views in Bridge (Default, Horizontal Filmstrip view, and Metadata Focus view) that are controlled by buttons in the lower-right corner of the window. You can assign a color label or rating to one or more images. Any number of selected images can be assigned a color label by clicking Label on the menu bar, then clicking one of the six options.

Creating a PDF Presentation

Using Bridge you can create a PDF Presentation. Such a presentation can be viewed full-screen on any computer monitor, or in the Adobe Acrobat Reader as a PDF file. You can create such a presentation by opening Bridge, locating and selecting images using the file hierarchy, clicking Tools in the Bridge menu bar, pointing to Photoshop, then clicking PDF Presentation. The PDF Presentation dialog box, shown in Figure 6, opens and lists any figures you have selected. You can add images by clicking the Browse button.

Using Save As Versus Save

Sometimes it's more efficient to create a new image by modifying an existing one, especially if it contains elements and special effects that you want to use again. The Save As command on the File menu creates a copy of the file, prompts you to give the duplicate file a new name, and then displays the new filename in the image's title bar. You use the Save As command to name an unnamed file or to save an existing file with a new name. For example, throughout this book, you will be instructed to open your data files and use the Save As command. Saving your data files with new names keeps them intact in case you have to start the lesson over again or you want to repeat an exercise. When you use the Save command, you save the changes you made to the open file.

FIGURE 6
PDF Presentation dialog box

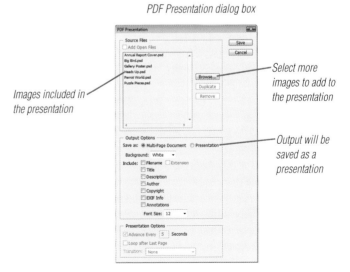

Images included in the presentation

Select more images to add to the presentation

Output will be saved as a presentation

FIGURE 7

Open dialog box for Windows and Macintosh

Look in list arrow
displays list of
available drives

Available folders
and files

Current file location
list arrow

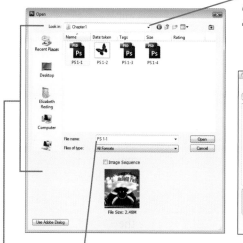

Available folders
and files may differ
from your list

Selected filename

FIGURE 8

Bridge window

Your list may
be different

Click the Keywords
palette tab to assign
keywords to a selected
file, then click any of the
displayed keywords

Drag to resize
thumbnails

Open a file using the File menu

1. Click **File** on the menu bar, then click **Open**.

2. Click the **Look in list arrow** (Win) or the **From list arrow** (Mac), navigate to the drive and folder where you store your Data Files, then click **Open**.

3. Click **PS 1-1.psd** as shown in Figure 7, then click **Open**.

   TIP If you receive a message stating that some text layers need to be updated before they can be used for vector-based output, click Update.

You used the Open command on the File menu to locate and open a file.

Open a file using Folders palette in Adobe Bridge

1. Click the **Go to Bridge button** 🖼 on the options bar, then click the **Folders palette tab** Folders (if necessary).

2. Navigate through the hierarchical tree to the drive and folder where you store your Chapter 1 Data Files.

3. Drag the **slider** (at the bottom of the Bridge window) a third of the way between the Smallest thumbnail size button ▫ and the Largest thumbnail size button ▫. Compare your screen to Figure 8.

4. Double-click the **image of a butterfly**, file **PS 1-2.tif**. The butterfly image opens and Adobe Bridge is no longer visible, but still open.

5. Close the butterfly image in Photoshop.

You used the Folders palette tab in Adobe Bridge to locate and open a file. This feature makes it easy to see which file you want to use.

Use the Save As command

1. Verify that the **PS 1-1.psd window** is active.

2. Click **File** on the menu bar, click **Save As**, then compare your Save As dialog box to Figure 9.

3. If the drive containing your Data Files is not displayed, click the **Save in list arrow** (Win) or the **Where list arrow** (Mac), then navigate to the drive and folder where you store your Chapter 1 Data Files.

4. Select the current filename in the File name text box (Win) or Save As text box (Mac) (if necessary); type **Hot Air Balloons**, then click **Save**. Compare your image to Figure 10.

   TIP   Click OK to close the Maximize Compatibility dialog box (if necessary).

You used the Save As command on the File menu to save the file with a new name. This command makes it possible for you to save a changed version of an image while keeping the original file intact.

FIGURE 9
Save As dialog box

Your list of files might be different

New filename

Changing file formats
In addition to using the Save As command to duplicate an existing file, this is a handy way of changing one format into another. For example, you can open an image you created in a digital camera, then make modifications in the Photoshop format. To do this, open the .jpg file in Photoshop, click File on the menu bar, then click Save As. Name the file, click the Format list arrow, click Photoshop (*.PSD, *.PDD), then click OK.

FIGURE 10
Hot Air Balloons image

Duplicate file has new name

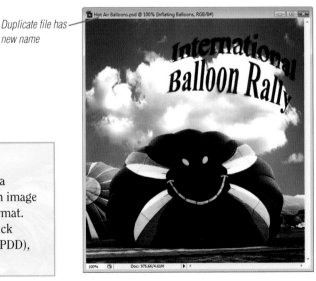

FIGURE 11

Images in Adobe Bridge

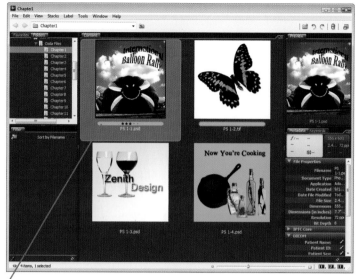

Rated and
Approved file

FIGURE 12

Sorted files

Content panel —

Filter panel —

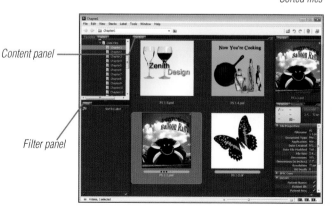

1. Click the **Go to Bridge button** on the options bar.

2. Click the **Folders palette tab** Folders (if necessary), then click the drive and folder where your you store Chapter 1 Data Files on the File Hierarchy tree (if necessary).

3. Click the **butterfly image**, file **PS 1-2.tif** to select it.

4. Press and hold **[Ctrl]** (Win) or **[⌘]** (Mac), click **PS 1-1.psd** (the image of the balloon), then release **[Ctrl]** (Win) or **[⌘]** (Mac).

5. Click **Label** on the menu bar, then click **Approved**.

6. Click **PS 1-1.psd**, click **Label** on the menu bar, then click ★★★. See Figure 11.

7. Click **View** on the menu bar, point to **Sort**, then click **By Label**. Compare your screen to Figure 12.

   The order of the files is changed.

   TIP   You can also change the order of files (in the Content panel) using the Sort by Filename list arrow in the Filter panel. When you click the Sort by Filename list arrow, you'll see a list of sorting options. Click on the option you want and the files in the Content panel will be rearranged.

8. Click **View** on the menu bar, point to **Sort**, then click **Manually**.

   TIP   You can change the Bridge view at any time, depending on the type of information you need to see.

9. Click **File** (Win) or **Bridge CS3** (Mac) on the (Bridge) menu bar, then click **Exit** or **Quit Bridge CS3** (Mac).

You labeled files using Bridge, sorted the files in a folder, then changed the sort order. When finished, you closed Bridge.

USE ORGANIZATIONAL AND
MANAGEMENT FEATURES

What You'll Do

In this lesson, you'll learn how to use Version Cue and Bridge.

Learning about Version Cue

Version Cue is a file versioning and management feature of the Adobe Creative Suite that can be used to organize your work whether you work in groups or by yourself. Version Cue is accessed through Bridge. You can see Version Cue in Bridge in two different locations: the Favorites tab and the Folders tab. Figure 13 shows Version Cue in the Favorites tab of Bridge. You can also view Version Cue in the Folders tab by collapsing the Desktop, as shown in Figure 14.

Understanding Version Cue Workspaces

Regardless of where in Bridge you access it (the Favorites or Folders tab), Version Cue installs a **workspace** in which it stores projects and project files, and keeps track of file versions. The Version Cue Workspace can be installed locally on your own computer and can be made public or kept private. It can also be installed on a server and can be used by many users through a network.

FIGURE 13
Favorites tab in Adobe Bridge

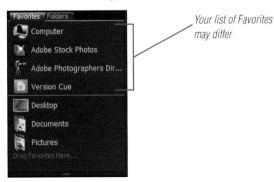

Your list of Favorites may differ

FIGURE 14
Folders tab in Adobe Bridge

Using Version Cue's Administrative Functions

Once you log into Version Cue, you can control who uses the workspace and how it is used with the tabs at the top of the screen. The Content tab, which is shown in Figure 15, lets you open your server, browse projects and other servers, and perform advanced tasks.

Making Use of Bridge

You've already seen how you can use Bridge to find, identify, and sort files. But did you know that you can use Bridge Center to organize, label, and open files as a group? Once you select one or more files, right-click the selection, then click Open, or Open With to display the files in your favorite CS3 program. You can apply label and ratings, or sort the selected files.

QUICKTIP

You can use Bridge to stitch together panoramic photos, rename images in batches, or automate image conversions with the Tools menu. Select the file(s) in Bridge you want to modify, click Tools on the menu bar, point to Photoshop, then click a command and make option modifications.

FIGURE 15
Version Cue CS3 Content tab

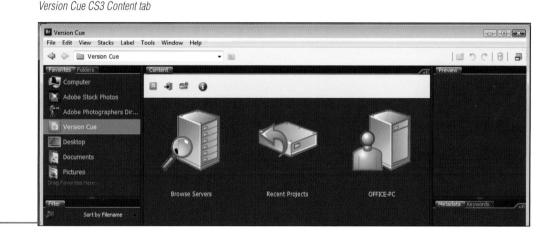

Shortcut key

Using Adobe Stock Photos

You can view and try professional images using Adobe Stock Photos. Available through the Favorites pane in Bridge, an active Internet connection is all you need to browse through a wide variety of images to include in your Photoshop designs. You can download complimentary (comp) low-resolution versions of these images and place them in a Photoshop document to find the perfect fit for your design. Once you find the right image, you can purchase it in a high-resolution format. There are thousands of images to choose from, and you can look at previous downloads and purchases through your Adobe account.

EXAMINE THE PHOTOSHOP WINDOW

What You'll Do

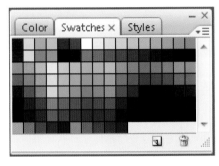

In this lesson, you'll select a tool on the Tools palette, use a shortcut key to cycle through the hidden tools, select and add a tool to the Tool Preset picker, use the Window menu to show and hide palettes in the workspace, and create a customized workspace.

Learning About the Workspace

The Photoshop **workspace** is the area within the program Photoshop window that includes the entire window, from the command menus at the top of your screen to the status bar (Win) at the bottom. Desktop items are visible in this area (Mac). The workspace is shown in Figure 16.

The **title bar** displays the program name (Win) and, if the active image window is maximized, the filename of the open file (for a new file, **Untitled-1**, because it has not been named). The title bar also contains a Close button, and Minimize, Maximize, and Restore buttons (Win).

The **menu bar** contains the program name (Mac) menu from which you can choose Photoshop commands. You can choose a menu command by clicking it or by pressing [Alt] plus the underlined letter in the menu name (Win). Some commands display shortcut keys on the right side of the menu. Shortcut keys provide an alternative way to activate menu commands. Some commands might appear dimmed, which means they are not currently available. An ellipsis after a command indicates additional choices.

Finding Tools Everywhere

The **Tools palette** contains tools associated with frequently used Photoshop commands.

DESIGNTIP **Overcoming information overload**

One of the most common experiences shared by first-time Photoshop users is information overload. There are just too many places and things to look at! When you feel your brain overheating, take a moment and sit back. Remind yourself that the active image area is the central area where you can see a composite of your work. All the tools and palettes are there to help you, not to add to the confusion.

The face of a tool contains a graphical representation of its function; for example, the Zoom Tool shows a magnifying glass. You can place the pointer over each tool to display a tool tip, which tells you the name or function of that tool. Some tools have additional hidden tools, indicated by a small black triangle in the lower-right corner of the tool.

QUICKTIP
You can view the Tools palette in a 2-column format by clicking the Expand arrow in its upper-left corner.

The **options bar**, located directly under the menu bar, displays the current settings for each tool. For example, when you click the Type Tool, the default font and font size appear on the options bar, which can be changed if desired. You can move the options bar anywhere in the workspace for easier access. The options bar also contains the Tool Preset picker. This is the left-most tool on the options bar and displays the active tool. You can click the list arrow on this tool to select another tool without having to use the Tools palette. The options bar also contains the palette well, an area where you can assemble palettes for quick access.

Palettes, also called panels in other CS3 programs, are small windows used to verify settings and modify images. By default, palettes appear in stacked groups at the right side of the window. A collection of palettes usually in a vertical orientation is called a **dock**. The dock is the dark gray bar above the collection of palettes. The arrows in the dock are used to maximize and minimize the palettes. You can display a palette by simply clicking the palette's name tab, which makes it the active palette. Palettes can be separated and moved

FIGURE 16
Workspace

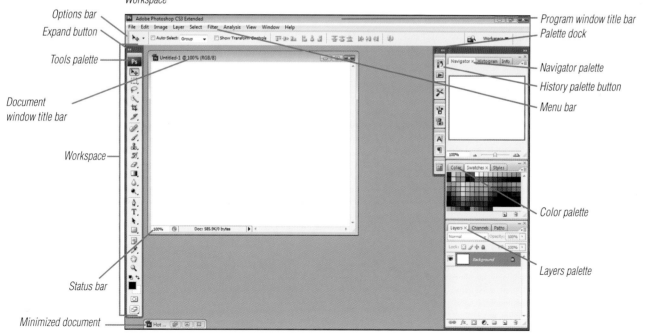

Options bar
Expand button
Tools palette
Document window title bar
Workspace
Status bar
Minimized document

Program window title bar
Palette dock
Navigator palette
History palette button
Menu bar
Color palette
Layers palette

anywhere in the workspace by dragging their name tabs to new locations. You can dock a palette by dragging its tab in or out of a dock. As you move palettes, you'll see blue highlighted drop zones. A **drop zone** is an area where you can move a palette. You can also change the order of tabs by dragging a tab to a new location within its palette. Each palette contains a menu that you can view by clicking the list arrow in the upper-right corner of the palette.

The **status bar** is located at the bottom of the program window (Win) or work area (Mac). It displays information, such as the file size of the active window and a description of the active tool. You can display other information on the status bar, such as the current tool, by clicking the black triangle to view a pull-down menu with more options.

Rulers can help you precisely measure and position an object in the workspace. The rulers do not appear the first time you use Photoshop, but you can display them by clicking Rulers on the View menu.

Using Tool Shortcut Keys
Each tool has a corresponding shortcut key. For example, the shortcut key for the Type Tool is T. After you know a tool's shortcut key, you can select the tool on the Tools palette by pressing its shortcut key. To select and cycle through a tool's hidden tools, you press and hold [Shift], then press the tool's shortcut key until the desired tool appears.

Customizing Your Environment
Photoshop makes it easy for you to position elements you work with just where you want them. If you move elements around to make your environment more convenient, you can always return your workspace to its original appearance by resetting the default palette locations. Once you have your work area arranged the way you want it, you can create a customized workspace by clicking Window on the menu bar, pointing to Workspace, then clicking Save Workspace. If you want to open a named workspace, click Window on the menu bar, point to Workspace, then click the workspace you want to use.

Creating customized keyboard shortcuts
Keyboard shortcuts can make your work with Photoshop images faster and easier. In fact, once you discover the power of keyboard shortcuts, you may never use menus again. In addition to the keyboard shortcuts that are preprogrammed in Photoshop, you can create your own. To do this, click Edit on the menu bar, then click Keyboard Shortcuts. The Keyboard Shortcuts and Menus dialog box opens, as shown in Figure 17.

FIGURE 17
Keyboard Shortcuts and Menus dialog box

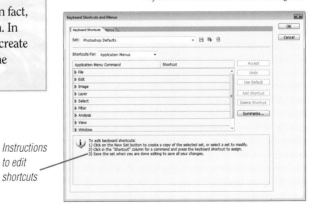

Instructions to edit shortcuts

1. Click the **Lasso Tool** on the Tools palette, press and hold the mouse button until a list of hidden tools appears, then release the mouse button. See Figure 18. Note the shortcut key, L, next to the tool name.

2. Click the **Polygonal Lasso Tool** on the Tools palette.

3. Press and hold **[Shift]**, press **[L]** three times to cycle through the Lasso tools, then release **[Shift]**. Did you notice how the options bar changes for each selected Lasso tool?

   TIP You can return the tools to their default setting by clicking the Click to open the Tool Preset picker list arrow on the options bar, clicking the list arrow, then clicking Reset All Tools.

You selected the Lasso Tool on the Tools palette and used its shortcut key to cycle through the Lasso tools. Becoming familiar with shortcut keys can speed up your work and make you more efficient.

FIGURE 18
Hidden tools

Shortcut key

DESIGNTIP **Learning shortcut keys**

Don't worry about learning shortcut keys. As you become more familiar with Photoshop, you'll gradually pick up shortcuts for menu commands, such as saving a file, or Tools palette tools, such as the Move Tool. You'll notice that as you learn to use shortcut keys, your speed while working with Photoshop will increase and you'll complete tasks with fewer mouse clicks.

Select a tool from the Tool Preset picker

1. Click the **Click to open the Tool Preset picker list arrow** ✌️ ▾ on the options bar.

   The name of a button is displayed in a tool tip, descriptive text that appears when you point to the button. Your Tool Preset picker list will differ, and may contain no entries at all. This list can be customized by each user.

2. Deselect the **Current Tool Only check box** (if necessary). See Figure 19.

3. Double-click **Magnetic Lasso 24 pixels** in the list.

You selected the Magnetic Lasso Tool using the Tool Preset picker. The Tool Preset picker makes it easy to access frequently used tools and their settings.

FIGURE 19
Using the Tool Preset picker

Active tool displays in Tool Preset picker button

List arrow adds new tools and displays more options

File   Edit   Image   Layer   Select   Filter   Anal

Feather: 0 px   ☑ Ant

Healing Brush 21 pixels
Magnetic Lasso 24 pixels
Crop 4 inch x 6 inch 300 ppi
Crop 5 inch x 3 inch 300 ppi
Crop 5 inch x 4 inch 300 ppi

☐ Current Tool Only

Using the Full Screen Mode

By default, Photoshop displays images in the Standard Screen Mode. This means that each image is displayed within its own window. You can choose from three other modes: Maximized Screen Mode, Full Screen Mode with Menu Bar, and Full Screen Mode. And why would you want to stray from the familiar Standard Screen Mode? Perhaps your image is so large that it's difficult to see it all in Standard Mode, or perhaps you want a less cluttered screen. Maybe you just want to try something different. You can switch between modes by clicking the Change Screen Mode button (located near the bottom of the Tools palette) or by pressing the keyboard shortcut F. When you click this button, the screen displays changes. Click the Hand Tool (or press the keyboard shortcut H), and you can reposition the active image, as shown in Figure 20.

FIGURE 20
Full screen mode with menu bar

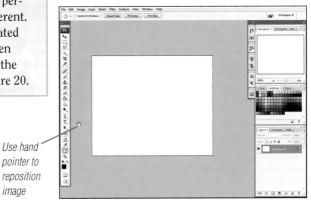

Use hand pointer to reposition image

FIGURE 21
Move Tool added to preset picker

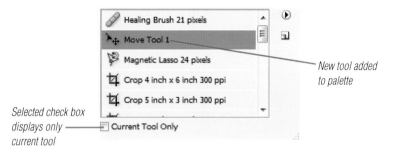

New tool added
to palette

Selected check box
displays only
current tool

FIGURE 22
Tool Preset picker list arrow menu

New Tool Preset...

Rename Tool Preset...
Delete Tool Preset

✔ Sort By Tool
✔ Show All Tool Presets
Show Current Tool Presets

Text Only
✔ Small List
Large List

Reset Tool
Reset All Tools

Preset Manager...

Reset Tool Presets...
Load Tool Presets...
Save Tool Presets...
Replace Tool Presets...

Art History
Brushes
Crop and Marquee
Text

Add a tool to the Tool Preset picker

1. Click the **Move Tool** ⊹ on the Tools palette.
2. Click the **Click to open the Tool Preset picker list arrow** ⊹ ▾ on the options bar.
3. Click the **list arrow** ▾≡ on the Tool Preset picker.
4. Click **New Tool Preset**, then click **OK** to accept the default name (Move Tool 1). Compare your list to Figure 21.

   TIP   You can display the currently selected tool alone by selecting the Current Tool Only check box.

You added the Move Tool to the Tool Preset picker. Once you know how to add tools to the Tool Preset picker, you can quickly and easily customize your work environment.

Modifying a tool preset

Once you've created tool presets, you'll probably want to know how they can be deleted and renamed. To delete any tool preset, select it on the Tool Preset picker palette. Click the list arrow on the Tool Preset picker palette to view the menu, shown in Figure 22, then click Delete Tool Preset. To rename a tool preset, click the same list arrow, then click Rename Tool Preset.

Show and hide palettes

1. Click **Window** on the menu bar, then verify that **Color** has a check mark next to it, then close the menu.

2. Click the **Swatches tab** next to the Color tab to make the Swatches palette active, as shown in Figure 23.

3. Click **Window** on the menu bar, then click **Swatches** to deselect it.

   TIP You can hide all open palettes by pressing [Shift], then [Tab], then show them by pressing [Shift], then [Tab] again. To hide all open palettes, the options bar, and the Tools palette, press [Tab], then show them by pressing [Tab] again.

4. Click **Window** on the menu bar, then click **Swatches** to redisplay the Swatches palette.

You used the Window menu to show and hide the Swatches palette. You might want to hide palettes at times in order to enlarge your work area.

FIGURE 23
Active Swatches palette

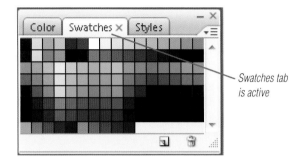

Swatches tab is active

DESIGNTIP **Considering ethical implications**

Because Photoshop enables you to make so many dramatic changes to images, you should consider the ethical ramifications and implications of altering images. Is it proper or appropriate to alter an image just because you have the technical expertise to do so? Are there any legal responsibilities or liabilities involved in making these alterations? Because the general public is more aware about the topic of **intellectual property** (an image or idea that is owned and retained by legal control) with the increased availability of information and content, you should make sure you have the legal right to alter an image, especially if you plan on displaying or distributing the image to others. Know who retains the rights to an image, and if necessary, make sure you have written permission for its use, alteration, and/or distribution. Not taking these precautions could be costly.

FIGURE 24
Save Workspace dialog box

FIGURE 25
Image Size dialog box

Create a customized workspace

1. Click and drag the **Tools palette title bar** so it appears to the right of the image.

2. Click **Window** on the menu bar, point to **Workspace**, then click **Save Workspace**.

3. Type **Sample Workspace** in the Name text box, then verify that only **Palette Locations** has a check mark beside it, as shown in Figure 24.

4. Click **Save**.

5. Click **Window** on the menu bar, then point to **Workspace**.

   The name of the new workspace appears on the Window menu.

6. Click **Reset Palette Locations**.

7. Click **Window** on the menu bar, point to **Workspace**, then click **Sample Workspace**.

8. Click **Window** on the menu bar, point to **Workspace**, then click **Reset Palette Locations**.

You created a customized workspace, reset the palette locations, tested the new workspace, then reset the palette locations again. Customized workspaces provide you with a work area that is always tailored to your needs.

Resizing an image

You may have created the perfect image, but the size may not be correct for your print format. Document size is a combination of the printed dimensions and pixel resolution. With resampling on, you can change the total number of pixels in the image and the print dimensions independently. With resampling off, you can change either the dimensions or the resolution: Photoshop will automatically adjust whichever value you don't ignore. An image designed for a Web site, for example, might be too small for an image that will be printed in a newsletter. You can easily resize an image using the Image Size command on the Image menu. To use this feature, open the file you want to resize, click Image on the menu bar, then click Image Size. The Image Size dialog box, shown in Figure 25, opens. By changing the dimensions in the text boxes, you'll have your image resized in no time.

USE THE LAYERS AND
HISTORY PALETTES

What You'll Do

In this lesson, you'll hide and display a layer, move a layer on the Layers palette, and then undo the move by deleting the Layer Order state on the History palette.

Learning About Layers

A **layer** is a section within an image that can be manipulated independently. Layers allow you to control individual elements within an image and create great dramatic effects and variations of the same image. Layers enable you to easily manipulate individual characteristics within an image. Each Photoshop file has at least one layer, and can contain many individual layers, or groups of layers.

You can think of layers in a Photoshop image as individual sheets of clear plastic that are in a stack. It's possible for your file to quickly accumulate dozens of layers. The **Layers palette** displays all the layers in an open file. You can use the Layers palette to create, copy, delete, display, hide, merge, lock, group or reposition layers.

QUICKTIP

In Photoshop, using and understanding layers is the key to success.

Setting preferences

The Preferences dialog box contains several topics, each with its own settings: General, Interface, File Handling, Performance, Cursors, Transparency & Gamut, Units & Rulers, Guides, Grid, Slices & Count, Plug-Ins, and Type. To open the Preferences dialog box, click Edit (Win) or Photoshop (Mac) on the menu bar, point to Preferences, then click a topic that represents the settings you want to change. If you move palettes around the workspace, or make other changes to them, you can choose to retain those changes the next time you start the program. To always start a new session with default palettes, click Interface on the Preferences menu, deselect the Remember Palette Locations check box, then click OK. Each time you start Photoshop, the palettes will be reset to their default locations and values.

Understanding the Layers Palette

The order in which the layers appear on the Layers palette matches the order in which they appear in the image; the topmost layer in the Layers palette is the topmost layer on the image. You can make a layer active by clicking its name on the Layers palette. When a layer is active, it is highlighted on the Layers palette, the name of the layer appears in parentheses in the image title bar. Only one layer can be active at a time. Figure 26 shows an image with its Layers palette. Do you see that this image contains five layers? Each layer can be moved or modified individually on the palette to give a different effect to the overall image. If you look at the Layers palette, you'll see that the Finger Painting layer is dark, indicating that it is currently active.

QUICKTIP

Get in the habit of shifting your eye from the image in the work area to the Layers palette. Knowing which layer is active will save you time and help you troubleshoot an image.

Displaying and Hiding Layers

You can use the Layers palette to control which layers are visible in an image. You can show or hide a layer by clicking the Indicates layer visibility button next to the layer thumbnail. When a layer is hidden, you are not able to merge it with another, select it, or print it. Hiding some layers can make it easier to focus on particular areas of an image.

Using the History Palette

Photoshop records each task you complete in an image on the **History palette**. This record of events, called states, makes it easy to see what changes occurred and the tools or commands that you used to make the modifications. The History palette, shown in Figure 26, displays up to 20 states and automatically updates the list to display the most recently performed tasks. The list contains the name of the tool or command used to change the image. You can delete a state on the History palette by selecting it and dragging it to the Delete current state button. Deleting a state is equivalent to using the Undo command. You can also use the History palette to create a new image from any state.

QUICKTIP

When you delete a History state, you undo all the events that occurred after that state.

FIGURE 26
Layers and History palettes

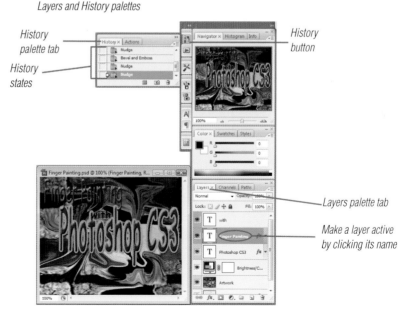

History palette tab

History states

History button

Layers palette tab

Make a layer active by clicking its name

Hide and display a layer

1. Click the **Hot Air Balloon layer** on the Layers palette.

   TIP   Depending on the size of the window, you might only be able to see the initial characters of the layer name.

2. Verify that the **Show Transform Controls check box** on the options bar is not checked, then click the **Indicates layer visibility button** on the Hot Air Balloon layer to display the image, as shown in Figure 27.

   TIP   By default, transparent areas of an image have a checkerboard display on the Layers palette.

3. Click the **Indicates layer visibility button** on the Hot Air Balloon layer to hide the image.

You made the Hot Air Balloon layer active on the Layers palette, then clicked the Indicates layer visibility button to display and hide a layer. Hiding layers is an important skill that can be used to remove distracting elements. Once you've finished working on specific layers, you can display the distracting layers.

FIGURE 27
Hot Air Balloon

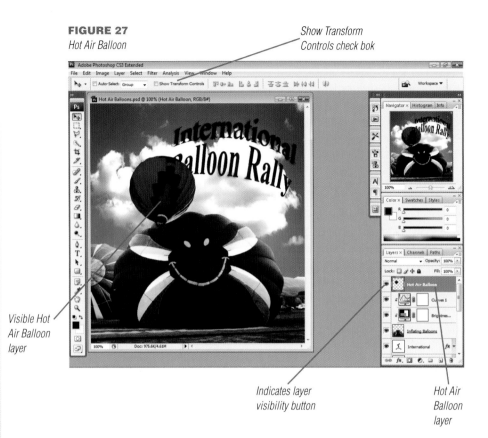

Show Transform Controls check bok

Visible Hot Air Balloon layer

Indicates layer visibility button

Hot Air Balloon layer

FIGURE 28
Layer moved in Layers palette

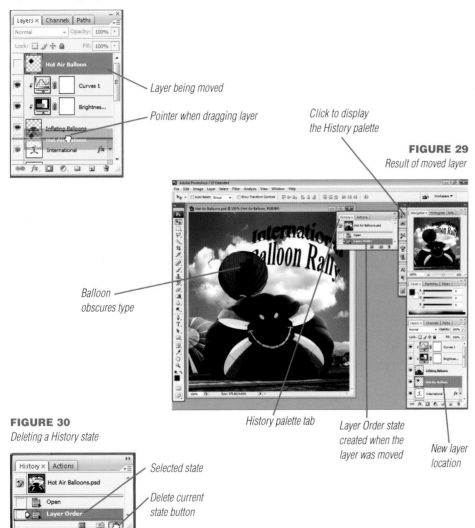

Layer being moved

Pointer when dragging layer

Click to display
the History palette

FIGURE 29
Result of moved layer

Balloon
obscures type

FIGURE 30
Deleting a History state

Selected state

Delete current
state button

Pointer when deleting a history state

History palette tab

Layer Order state
created when the
layer was moved

New layer
location

Move a layer on the Layers palette and delete a state on the History palette

1. Click the **Indicates layer visibility button** on the Hot Air Balloon layer on the Layers palette.

2. Click and drag the **Hot Air Balloon layer** on the Layers palette, beneath the Inflating Balloons layer in the palette, as shown in Figure 28.

   The basket of the Hot Air Balloon is hidden by the Inflating Balloons layer. See Figure 29.

3. Click the **History button** in the Dock to display the History palette.

4. Click **Layer Order** on the History palette, then drag it to the **Delete current state button** on the History palette, as shown in Figure 30.

   TIP   Each time you close and reopen an image, the History palette is cleared.

   The basket of the hot air balloon is now visible.

5. Click **File** on the menu bar, then click **Save**.

You moved the Hot Air Balloon layer so it was behind the Inflating Balloon layer, then returned it to its original position by dragging the Layer Order state to the Delete current state button on the History palette. You can easily undo what you've done using the History palette.

LEARN ABOUT PHOTOSHOP
BY USING HELP

What You'll Do

In this lesson, you'll open Help, then view and find information from the following Help links: Contents, Index, and Search.

Understanding the Power of Help

Photoshop features an extensive Help system that you can use to access definitions, explanations, and useful tips. Help information is displayed in a browser window, so you must have Web browser software installed on your computer to view the information; however, you do not need an Internet connection to use Photoshop Help.

Using Help Topics

The Home page of the Help window has links in the right pane that you can use to retrieve information about Photoshop commands and features. In the left pane, there are two sections: Contents and Index.

The Getting Started link displays the Contents and Index links as shown in Figure 31. The Contents palette tab allows you to browse topics by category; the Index palette tab provides the letters of the alphabet, which you can click to view keywords and topics alphabetically. The Search feature is located on the toolbar (above the left and right panes) in the form of a text box. You can search the Photoshop Help System by entering text in the Type in a word or phrase text box, then click Search.

FIGURE 31
Links in the Getting Started section

Help links

Index link

FIGURE 32

Contents section of the Help window

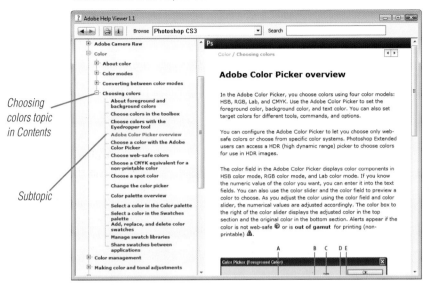

Choosing colors topic in Contents

Subtopic

1. Click **Help** on the menu bar, then click **Photoshop Help**.

    TIP   You can also open the Help window by pressing **[F1]** (Win) or ⌘ **[?]** (Mac).

2. If it's not already selected, click the **Contents link**, scroll down the left pane (if necessary), then click **Color**.

3. Click **Choosing colors**, then click **Adobe Color Picker overview** in the left pane. See Figure 32.

    TIP   You can maximize the window (if you want to take advantage of the full screen display).

You used the Photoshop Help command on the Help menu to open the Help window and viewed a topic in Contents.

Understanding the differences between monitor, images, and device resolution

Image resolution is determined by the number of pixels per inch (ppi) that are printed on a page. Pixel dimensions (the number of pixels along the height and width of a bitmap image) determine the amount of detail in an image, while image resolution controls the amount of space over which the pixels are printed. High resolution images show greater detail and more subtle color transitions than low resolution images. Device resolution or printer resolution is measured by the ink dots per inch (dpi) produced by printers. You can set the resolution of your computer monitor to determine the detail with which images will be displayed. Each monitor should be calibrated to describe how the monitor reproduces colors. Monitor calibration is one of the first things you should do because it determines whether your colors are being accurately represented, which in turn determines how accurately your output will match your design intentions.

Find information in the Index

1. Click the **Index** link in the left pane of the Help window.

2. Click **E**, scroll down, then click **Eyedropper tool**, click **about**, then click **View color values in an image.** Compare your Help window to Figure 33.

You clicked an alphabetical listing and viewed an entry in the Index.

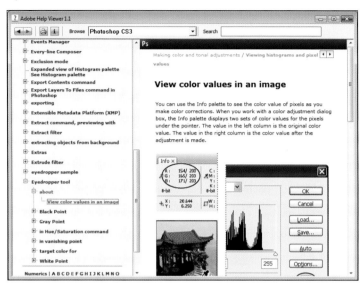

FIGURE 33
Topics in the Index window

Using How-To Help features

Using Help would always be easy if you knew the name of the feature you wanted up look up. To help you find out how to complete common tasks, Photoshop has a listing of "How-To's" in the Help menu. Click Help in the menu bar, point to the How-To you'd like to read, as shown in Figure 34, then click the item you want information about.

FIGURE 34
How-To Help topics

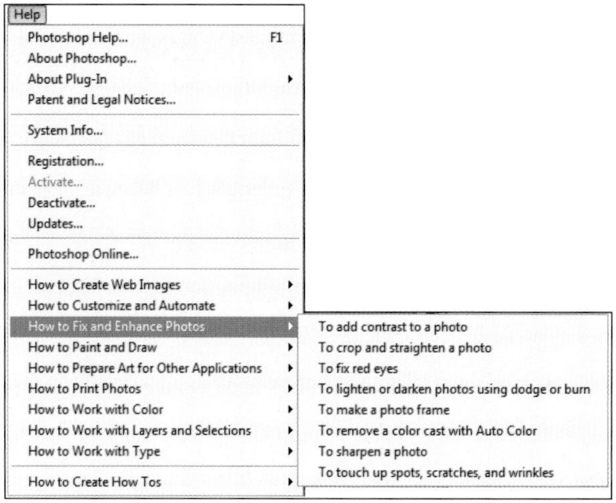

FIGURE 35

Search topic in Help

Search term

FIGURE 36

Create your own How To tips

Find information using Search

1. Click the **Search text box** in the Help window.

2. Type **print quality**, then press **[Enter]** (Win) or **[return]** (Mac).

   TIP   You can search for multiple words by inserting a space; do not use punctuation in the text box.

3. Scroll down the left pane (if necessary), click **Why colors sometimes don't match**, then compare your Help screen to Figure 35.

4. Click the **Close box** when you are finished reading the topic.

You entered a search term, viewed search results, then closed the Help window.

Creating customized How To's

Photoshop Help is pretty helpful, but perhaps there's a technique you've created, only to return later and think 'How did I do this?' Fortunately, you can create your own How To tips so you'll never wonder how you created a cool effect. To find out more, click Help on the menu bar, point to How to Create How Tos, then click Create your own How To tips. The information shown in Figure 36 walks you through the process.

VIEW AND PRINT
AN IMAGE

What You'll Do

In this lesson, you'll use the Zoom Tool on the Tools palette to increase and decrease your views of the image. You'll also change the page orientation settings in the Page Setup dialog box, and print the image.

Getting a Closer Look

When you edit an image in Photoshop, it is important that you have a good view of the area that you are focusing on. Photoshop has a variety of methods that allow you to enlarge or reduce your current view. You can use the Zoom Tool by clicking the image to zoom in on (magnify the view) or zoom out of (reduce the view) areas of your image. Zooming in or out enlarges or reduces your *view*, not the actual image. The maximum zoom factor is 1600%. The current zoom percentage appears in the document's title bar, on the Navigator palette, and on the status bar. When the Zoom Tool is selected, the options bar provides additional choices for changing your view as shown in Figure 37. For example, the Resize Windows To Fit check box automatically resizes the window whenever you magnify or reduce the view. You can also change the zoom percentage using the Navigator palette and the status bar by typing a new value in the zoom text box.

Printing Your Image

In many cases, a professional print shop might be the best option for printing a Photoshop image to get the highest quality. You can print a Photoshop image using a standard black-and-white or color printer. The printed image will be a composite of all visible layers. The quality of your printer and paper will affect the appearance of your output. The Page Setup dialog box displays options for printing, such as paper orientation. **Orientation** is the direction in which an image appears on the page. In **portrait orientation**, the image is printed with the shorter edges of the paper at the top and bottom. In **landscape orientation**, the image is printed with the longer edges of the paper at the top and bottom.

Use the Print command when you want to print multiple copies of an image. Use the Print One Copy command to print a single copy without making dialog box selections, and use the Print dialog box when you want to handle color values using color management.

Understanding Color Handling in Printing

The Print dialog box that opens when you click Print on the File menu lets you determine how colors are output. You can click the Color Handling list arrow to choose whether to use color management, and whether Photoshop or the printing device should control this process. If you let Photoshop determine the colors, Photoshop performs any necessary conversions to color values appropriate for the selected printer. If you choose to let the printer determine the colors, the printer will convert document color values to the corresponding printer color values. In this scenario, Photoshop does not alter the color values. If no color management is selected, no color values will be changed when the image is printed.

Viewing an Image in Multiple Views

You can use the New Window command on the Window ➤ Arrange menu to open multiple views of the same image. You can change the zoom percentage in each view so you can spotlight the areas you want to modify, and then modify the specific area of the image in each view. Because you are working on the same image in multiple views, not in multiple versions, Photoshop automatically applies the changes you make in one view to all views. Although you can close the views you no longer need at any time, Photoshop will not save any changes until you save the file.

FIGURE 37
Zoom Tool options bar

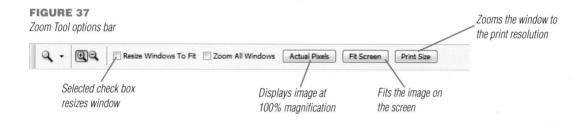

Zooms the window to the print resolution

Selected check box resizes window

Displays image at 100% magnification

Fits the image on the screen

Choosing a Photoshop version

You may have noticed that the title bar on the images in this book say 'Adobe Photoshop CS3 Extended'. What's that about? Well, the release of the Adobe Creative Suite 3 offers two versions of Photoshop: Adobe Photoshop CS3 and Adobe Photoshop CS3 Extended. The Extended version is ideal for multi-media creative professionals, film and video creative professionals, graphic and Web designers who push the limits of 3D and motion, as well as those professionals in the fields of manufacturing, medicine, architecture, engineering and construction, and science and research. Photoshop CS3 is ideal for professional photographers, serious amateur photographers, graphic and Web designers, and print service providers.

Use the Zoom Tool

1. If necessary, click the **Indicates layer visibility button** 👁 on the Layers palette for the Hot Air Balloon layer so the layer is no longer displayed.

2. Click the **Zoom Tool** 🔍 on the Tools palette.

3. Select the **Resize Windows To Fit check box** (if it is not already selected) on the options bar.

4. Position the **Zoom In pointer** ⊕ over the center of the image, then click the **image**.

   TIP Position the pointer over the part of the image you want to keep in view.

5. Press **[Alt]** (Win) or **[option]** (Mac), then when the Zoom Out pointer appears, click the center of the image twice with the **Zoom Out pointer** ⊖.

6. Release **[Alt]** (Win) or **[option]** (Mac), then compare your image to Figure 38.

   The zoom factor for the image is 66.7%. Your zoom factor may differ.

You selected the Zoom Tool on the Tools palette and used it to zoom in to and out of the image. The Zoom Tool makes it possible to see the detail in specific areas of an image, or to see the whole image at once, depending on your needs.

Using the Navigator palette

You can change the magnification factor of an image using the Navigator palette or the Zoom Tool on the Tools palette. By double-clicking the Zoom text box on the Navigator palette, you can enter a new magnification factor, then press [Enter] (Win) or [return] (Mac). The magnification factor—shown as a percentage—is displayed in the lower-left corner of the Navigator palette, as shown in Figure 39. The red border in the palette, called the Proxy Preview Area, defines the area of the image that is magnified. You can drag the Proxy Preview Area inside the Navigator palette to view other areas of the image at the current magnification factor.

FIGURE 38
Reduced image

Zoom Tool options

Zoom percentage changed

Zoom Tool

FIGURE 39
Navigator palette

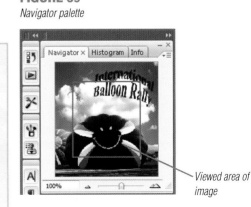

Viewed area of image

FIGURE 40
Page Setup dialog box

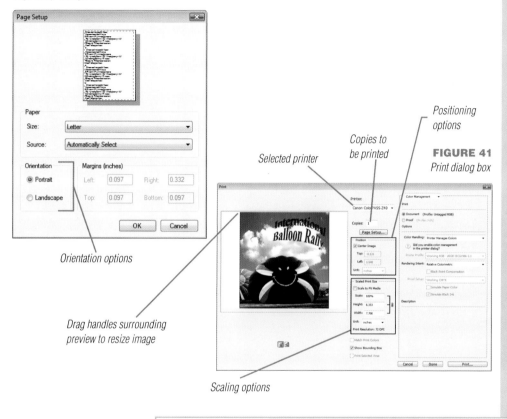

Orientation options

Drag handles surrounding
preview to resize image

Selected printer

Copies to
be printed

Positioning
options

FIGURE 41
Print dialog box

Scaling options

1. Click **File** on the menu bar, then click **Page Setup** to open the Page Setup dialog box, as shown in Figure 40.

   TIP   If you have not selected a printer using the Print Center, a warning box might appear (Mac).

   Page setup and print settings vary slightly in Macintosh.

2. Click the **Landscape option button** in the Orientation section, then click **OK**.

   TIP   Choose either Landscape option (Mac).

3. Click **File** on the menu bar, click **Print**, then click **Proceed** in the message box that opens. If a PostScript dialog box opens, click **OK** (Mac).

4. Make sure that the **All option button** is selected in the Print range section (Win) or Pages section (Mac), and that **1** appears in the Number of copies text box, then click **OK** (Win) or **Print** (Mac). See Figure 41.

You used the Page Setup command on the File menu to open the Page Setup dialog box, changed the page orientation, then printed the image. Changing the page orientation can make an image fit on a printed page better.

Previewing and creating a Proof Setup

You can create and save a Proof Setup, which lets you preview your image to see how it will look when printed on a specific device. This feature lets you see how colors can be interpreted by different devices. By using this feature, you can decrease the chance that colors will vary from what you viewed on your monitor after they are printed. Create a custom proof by clicking View on the menu bar, pointing to Proof Setup, then clicking Custom. Specify the conditions in the Customize Proof Condition dialog box, then click OK. Each proof setup has the .PSF extension and can be loaded by clicking View on the menu bar, pointing to Proof Setup, clicking Custom, then clicking Load. Use the handles on the image preview in the Print dialog box to scale the print size.

CLOSE A FILE
AND EXIT PHOTOSHOP

What You'll Do

New...	Ctrl+N
Open...	Ctrl+O
Browse...	Alt+Ctrl+O
Open As...	Alt+Shift+Ctrl+O
Open As Smart Object...	
Open Recent	▶
Device Central...	
Close	Ctrl+W
Close All	Alt+Ctrl+W
Close and Go To Bridge...	Shift+Ctrl+W
Save	Ctrl+S
Save As...	Shift+Ctrl+S
Check In...	
Save for Web & Devices...	Alt+Shift+Ctrl+S
Revert	F12
Place...	
Import	▶
Export	▶
Automate	▶
Scripts	▶
File Info...	Alt+Shift+Ctrl+I
Page Setup...	Shift+Ctrl+P
Print...	Ctrl+P
Print One Copy	Alt+Shift+Ctrl+P
Exit	Ctrl+Q

▶ *In this lesson, you'll use the Close and Exit (Win) or Quit (Mac) commands to close a file and exit Photoshop.*

Concluding Your Work Session

At the end of your work session, you might have opened several files; you now need to decide which ones you want to save.

QUICKTIP

If you share a computer with other people, it's a good idea to reset Photoshop's preferences back to their default settings. You can do so when you start Photoshop by clicking Window on the menu bar, pointing to Workspace, then clicking Reset Palette Locations.

Closing Versus Exiting

When you are finished working on an image, you need to save and close it. You can close one file at a time, or close all open files at the same time by exiting the program. Closing a file leaves Photoshop open, which allows you to open or create another file. Exiting Photoshop closes the file, closes Photoshop, and returns you to the desktop, where you can choose to open another program or shut down the computer. Photoshop will prompt you to save any changes before it closes the files. If you do not modify a new or existing file, Photoshop will close it automatically when you exit.

QUICKTIP

To close all open files, click File on the menu bar, then click Close All.

Using Adobe online

Periodically, when you start Photoshop, an Update dialog box might appear, prompting you to search for updates or new information on the Adobe Web site. If you click Yes, Photoshop will automatically notify you that a download is available; however, you do not have to select it. You can also obtain information about Photoshop from the Adobe Photoshop Web site (*www.adobe.com/products/photoshop/main.html*), where you can link to downloads, tips, training, galleries, examples, and other support topics.

FIGURE 42

Closing a file using the File menu

Close command —

Exit command —

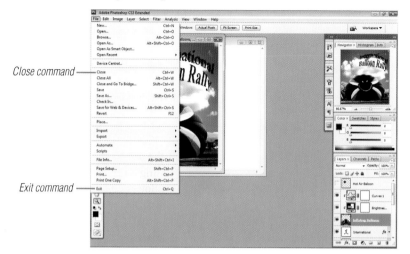

Close a file and exit Photoshop

1. Click **File** on the menu bar, then compare your screen to Figure 42.

2. Click **Close**.

   TIP   You can close an open file (without closing Photoshop) by clicking the Close button in the image window. Photoshop will prompt you to save any unsaved changes before closing the file.

3. If asked to save your work, click **Yes** (Win) or **Save** (Mac).

4. Click **File** on the menu bar, then click **Exit** (Win) or click **Photoshop** on the menu bar, then click **Quit Photoshop** (Mac).

   TIP   To exit Photoshop and close an open file, click the Close button in the program window. Photoshop will prompt you to save any unsaved changes before closing.

5. If asked to save your work, click **No**.

You closed the current file and exited the program by using the Close and Exit (Win) or Quit (Mac) commands.

Power User Shortcuts

Key: Menu items are indicated by ➢ between the menu name and its command. Blue bold letters are shortcuts for selecting tools on the Tools palette.

to do this:	use this method:
Close a file	[Ctrl][W] (Win) ⌘[W] (Mac)
Create a new file	[Ctrl][N] (Win) ⌘[N] (Mac)
Create a workspace	Window ➢ Workspace ➢ Save Workspace
Drag a layer	
Exit Photoshop	[Ctrl][Q] (Win), ⌘[Q] (Mac)
Hide a layer	
Lasso Tool	or L
Modify workspace display	Workspace ▼
Open a file	[Ctrl][O] (Win), ⌘[O] (Mac)
Open Bridge	
Open Help	[F1] (Win)
Open Preferences dialog box	[Ctrl][K] (Win) ⌘[K] (Mac)
Page Setup	[Shift][Ctrl][P] (Win)[Shift] ⌘[P] (Mac)
Print File	File ➢ Print [Ctrl][P], (Win) ⌘[P] (Mac)

to do this:	use this method:
Reset preferences to default settings	[Shift][Alt][Ctrl] (Win) [Shift] option ⌘ (Mac)
Save a file	[Ctrl][S] (Win) ⌘[S] (Mac)
Show a layer	
Show hidden lasso tools	[Shift] L
Show History palette	
Show or hide all open palettes	[Shift][Tab]
Show or hide all open palettes, the options bar, and the Tools palette	[Tab]
Show or hide Swatches palette	Window ➢ Swatches
Use Save As	[Shift][Ctrl][S] (Win) [Shift] ⌘[S] (Mac)
Zoom in	 [⌘][+]
Zoom out	[Alt] (Win) option ⌘ (Mac) [⌘][−]
Zoom Tool	or Z

Start Adobe Photoshop CS3.

1. Start Photoshop.
2. Create a new image that is 500 × 500 pixels, accept the default resolution, then name and save it as **Review**.

Open and save an image.

1. Open PS 1-3.psd from the drive and folder where you store your Data Files, and if prompted, update the text layers.
2. Save it as **Zenith Design Logo**.

Use organizational and management features.

1. Open Adobe Bridge.
2. Click the Folders tab, then locate the folder that contains your Data Files.
3. Close Adobe Bridge.

Examine the Photoshop window.

1. Locate the image title bar and the current zoom percentage.
2. Locate the menu you use to open an image.
3. View the Tools palette, the options bar, and the palettes that are showing.
4. Click the Move Tool on the Tools palette, then view the Move Tool options on the options bar.

Use the Layers and History palettes.

1. Drag the Wine Glasses layer so it is above the Zenith layer, then use the History palette to undo the state.
2. Drag the Wine Glasses layer above the Zenith layer again.

3. Use the Indicates layer visibility button to hide the Wine Glasses layer.
4. Make the Wine Glasses layer visible again.
5. Hide the Zenith layer.
6. Show the Zenith layer.
7. Click the Tag Line layer. Notice that the Tag Line layer is now the active layer.
8. Save your work.

Learn about Photoshop by using Help.

1. Open the Adobe Photoshop CS3 Help window.
2. Using the Index, find information about resetting to the default workspace.
3. Print the information you find.
4. Close the Help window.

View and print an image.

1. Make sure that all the layers are visible in the Layers palette.
2. Click the Zoom Tool, then make sure the setting is selected to resize the window to fit.
3. Zoom in on the wine glasses twice.
4. Zoom out to the original perspective.
5. Print one copy of the image.

Close a file and exit Photoshop.

1. Compare your screen to Figure 43, then close the Zenith Design Logo file.
2. Close the Review file.
3. Exit (Win) or Quit (Mac) Photoshop.

FIGURE 43
Completed Skills Review

As a new Photoshop user, you are comforted knowing that Photoshop's Help system provides definitions, explanations, procedures, and other helpful information. It also includes examples and demonstrations to show how Photoshop features work. You use the Help system to learn about image size and resolution.

1. Open the Photoshop Help window.
2. Click the Workspace topic in the Contents link.
3. Click the Working with pop-up palettes in the Palettes and menus subtopic, in the left pane.
4. After you read this topic, click the Display context menus topic, then read this topic.
5. Click the Opening and importing images topic in the left pane.
6. Click the Image size and resolution topic in the left pane, then click About monitor resolution. Print out this topic, then compare your screen to the sample shown in Figure 44.

FIGURE 44
Sample Project Builder 1

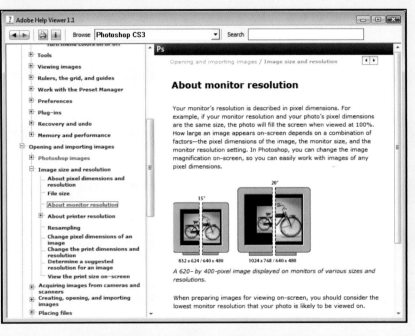

Kitchen Experience, your local specialty cooking shop, has just added herb-infused oils to its product line. They have hired you to draft a flyer that features these new products. You use Photoshop to create this flyer.

1. Open PS 1-4.psd, then save it as **Cooking**.
2. Make the Measuring Spoons layer visible.
3. Drag the Oils layer so the content appears behind the Skillet layer content.
4. Drag the Measuring Spoons layer above the Skillet layer.
5. Save the file, then compare your image to the sample shown in Figure 45.

FIGURE 45
Sample Project Builder 2

As an avid, albeit novice Photoshop user, you have grasped the importance of how layers affect your image. With a little practice, you can examine a single-layer image and guess which objects might display on their own layers. Now, you're ready to examine the images created by Photoshop experts and critique them on their use of layers.

1. Connect to the Internet, and use your browser to find interesting artwork located on at least two Web sites.
2. Review the categories, then download a single-layer image from each Web site.
3. Start Photoshop, then open the downloaded images.
4. Save one image as **Critique-1** and the other as **Critique-2** in the Photoshop format (use the .psd extension).
5. Analyze each image for its potential use of layers.
6. Open the File Info dialog box for Critique-1.psd, then type in the Description section your speculation as to the number of layers there might be in the image, their possible order on the Layers palette, and how moving the layers would affect the image.
7. Close the dialog box.
8. Compare your image to the sample shown in Figure 46, then close the files.

FIGURE 46
Sample Design Project

Depending on the size of your group, you can assign individual elements of the project to group members, or work collectively to create the finished product.

You and a select team of graphic artists are preparing to work together on a series of design projects. You want to see what digital imaging options exist. You decide to see what kind of information on this topic is available on the Adobe Web site. You also want to gain familiarity with the Web site so that you can take advantage of its product information, including user tips and feedback, and become more skillful Photoshop users.

1. Connect to the Internet and go to the Adobe Web site at *www.adobe.com*.
2. Point to Products, then find the link for Digital imaging, as shown in Figure 47.
3. Divide into two groups, and let the first group use the links on the Web page to search for information about digital imaging options.
4. Print the relevant page(s).
5. Let the second group start Photoshop and open the Photoshop Help window.

6. Search for information about Adjusting the Monitor Display, then print the relevant page(s).

FIGURE 47
Completed Group Project

7. Let the entire group evaluate the information in the documents, compare any significant differences, and then discuss your findings.

chapter

2

WORKING
WITH LAYERS

1. Examine and convert layers

2. Add and delete layers

3. Add a selection from one image to another

4. Organize layers with layer groups and colors

chapter 2 **WORKING**
WITH LAYERS

Layers Are Everything

You can use Photoshop to create sophisticated images because a Photoshop image can contain multiple layers. Each object created in Photoshop can exist on its own individual layer, making it easy to control the position and quality of each layer in the stack. Depending on your computer's resources, you can have a maximum of 8000 layers in each Photoshop image with each layer containing as much or as little detail as necessary.

> QUICKTIP
> The transparent areas in a layer do not increase file size.

Understanding the Importance of Layers

Layers make it possible to manipulate the tiniest detail within your image, which gives you tremendous flexibility when you make changes. By placing objects, effects, styles, and type on separate layers, you can modify them individually *without* affecting other layers. The advantage to using multiple layers is that you can isolate effects and images on one layer without affecting the others. The disadvantage of using multiple layers is that your file size might become very large. However, once your image is finished, you can dramatically reduce its file size by combining all the layers into one.

Using Layers to Modify an Image

You can add, delete, and move layers in your image. You can also drag a portion of an image, called a **selection**, from one Photoshop image to another. When you do this, a new layer is automatically created. Copying layers from one image to another makes it easy to transfer a complicated effect, a simple image, or a piece of type. You can also hide and display each layer, or change its opacity. **Opacity** is the ability to see through a layer so that layers beneath it are visible. You can continuously change the overall appearance of your image by changing the order of your layers, until you achieve just the look you want.

2-2

Tools You'll Use

Opacity list arrow

Layer

New	▶
Duplicate Layer...	
Delete	▶
Layer Properties...	
Layer Style	▶
Smart Filter	▶
New Fill Layer	▶
New Adjustment Layer	▶
Change Layer Content	▶
Layer Content Options...	
Layer Mask	▶
Vector Mask	▶
Create Clipping Mask	Alt+Ctrl+G
Smart Objects	▶
Video Layers	▶
3D Layers	▶
Type	▶
Rasterize	▶
New Layer Based Slice	
Group Layers	Ctrl+G
Ungroup Layers	Shift+Ctrl+G
Hide Layers	
Arrange	▶
Align	▶
Distribute	▶
Lock All Layers in Group...	
Link Layers	
Select Linked Layers	
Merge Down	Ctrl+E
Merge Visible	Shift+Ctrl+E
Flatten Image	
Matting	▶

Layer...	Shift+Ctrl+N
Layer From Background...	
Group...	
Group from Layers...	
Layer via Copy	Ctrl+J
Layer via Cut	Shift+Ctrl+J

Layers × | Channels | Paths

Pass Through — Opacity: 100%
Lock: ▢ ◢ ✛ ⬤   Fill: 100%

- 👁 ▶ 📁 Type layers
- 👁 📁 Objects
- 👁 🖼 Autumn Maple Leaves
- 👁 ⬜ Background 🔒

∞ fx. ◨ ⦿. ▢ ⬚ ⊞ 🗑

New Layer...	Shift+Ctrl+N
Duplicate Group...	
Delete Group	
Delete Hidden Layers	
New Group...	
New Group from Layers...	
Lock All Layers in Group...	
Convert to Smart Object	
Edit Contents	
Group Properties...	
Blending Options...	
Create Clipping Mask	Alt+Ctrl+G
Link Layers	
Select Linked Layers	
Merge Group	Ctrl+E
Merge Visible	Shift+Ctrl+E
Flatten Image	
Animation Options	▶
Palette Options...	

Color Range

Select: 🖊 Sampled Colors

Fuzziness: 40

- OK
- Cancel
- Load...
- Save...

🖊 🖊 🖊

☐ Invert

○ Selection ⦿ Image

Selection Preview: None

History × | Actions

- PS 2-1.psd
- ▶ **Open**

📋 📷 🗑

Delete current
state button

New Group

Name: Group 1

- OK
- Cancel

Color: ▨ Violet
Mode: Pass Through   Opacity: 100 %

Layer Properties

Name: Layer 1

- OK
- Cancel

Color: ☐ None

Color list arrow

2-3

EXAMINE AND
CONVERT LAYERS

What You'll Do

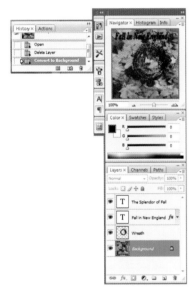

In this lesson, you'll use the Layers palette to delete a Background layer and the Layer menu to create a Background layer from an image layer.

Learning About the Layers Palette

The **Layers palette** lists all the layers within a Photoshop file and makes it possible for you to manipulate one or more layers. By default, this palette is located in the lower-right corner of the screen, but it can be moved to a new location by dragging the palette's tab. In some cases, the entire name of the layer might not appear on the palette. If a layer name is too long, an ellipsis appears, indicating that part of the name is hidden from view. You can view a layer's entire name by holding the pointer over the name until the full name appears. The **layer thumbnail** appears to the left of the layer name and contains a miniature picture of the layer's content, as shown in Figure 1. To the left of the layer thumbnail, you can add color, which allows you to easily identify layers. The Layers palette also contains common buttons, such as the Delete layer button and the Create new layer button.

Recognizing Layer Types

The Layers palette includes several types of layers: Background, type, and image (non-type). The Background layer—whose name appears in italics—is always at the bottom of the stack. Type layers—layers that contain text—contain the type layer icon in the layer thumbnail, and image layers display a thumbnail of their contents. In addition to dragging selections from one Photoshop image to another, you can also drag objects created in other

applications, such as Adobe Dreamweaver, Adobe InDesign, or Adobe Flash, onto a Photoshop image, which creates a layer containing the object you dragged from the other program window.

Organizing Layers

One of the benefits of using layers is that you can create different design effects by rearranging their order. Figure 2 contains the same layers as Figure 1, but they are arranged differently. Did you notice that the wreath is partially obscured by the gourds and the title text? This reorganization was created by dragging the Wreath layer below the Gourds layer and by dragging the Fall in New England layer below the Wreath layer on the Layers palette.

FIGURE 1
Image with multiple layers

Layers palette list arrow

Position mouse over layer name to display full title

Type layer thumbnail

Image layer thumbnail

FIGURE 2
Layers rearranged

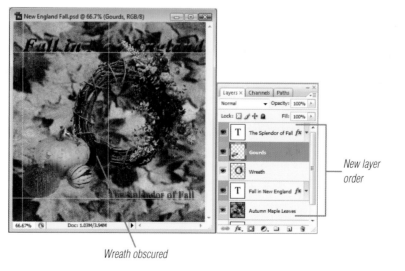

New layer order

Wreath obscured

Converting Layers

When you open an image created with a digital camera, you'll notice that the entire image appears in the Background layer. The Background layer of any image is the initial layer and is always located at the bottom of the stack. You cannot change its position in the stack, nor can you change its opacity or lighten or darken its colors. You can, however, convert a Background layer into an image layer (nontype layer), and you can convert an image layer into a Background layer. You need to modify the image layer *before* converting it to a Background layer. You might want to convert a Background layer into an image layer so that you can use the full range of editing tools on the layer content. You might want to convert an image layer into a Background layer after you have made all your changes and want it to be the bottom layer in the stack.

QUICKTIP

Before converting an image layer to a Background layer, you must first delete the existing Background layer. You can delete a Background layer by clicking it on the Layers palette, then dragging it to the Delete layer button on the Layers palette.

Using rulers and changing units of measurement

You can display horizontal and vertical rulers to help you better position elements. To display or hide rulers, click View on the menu bar, then click Rulers. (A check mark to the left of the Rulers command indicates that the Rulers are displayed.) In addition to displaying or hiding rulers, you can also choose from various units of measurement. Your choices include pixels, inches, centimeters, millimeters, points, picas, and percentages. Pixels, for example, display more tick marks and can make it easier to make tiny adjustments. You can change the units of measurement by clicking Edit [Win] or Photoshop [Mac] on the menu bar, pointing to Preferences, then clicking Units & Rulers. In the Preferences dialog box, click the Rulers list arrow, click the units you want to use, then click OK. The easiest way to change units of measurement, however, is shown in Figure 3. Once the rulers are displayed, right-click (Win) or [Ctrl]-click (Mac) either the vertical or horizontal ruler, then click the unit of measurement you want. The Info palette, located in the upper-right corner of the workspace, also displays your current coordinates. Regardless of the units of measurement in use, the X/Y coordinates are displayed in the Info palette.

FIGURE 3

Changing units of measurement

Right-click (Win) or [Ctrl]-click (Mac) to display measurement choices

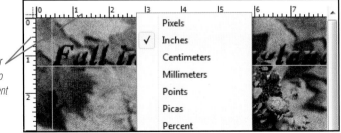

FIGURE 4

Warning box

Adobe Photoshop CS3 Extended

Delete the layer "Background"?

Yes   No

☐ Don't show again

FIGURE 5

Background layer deleted

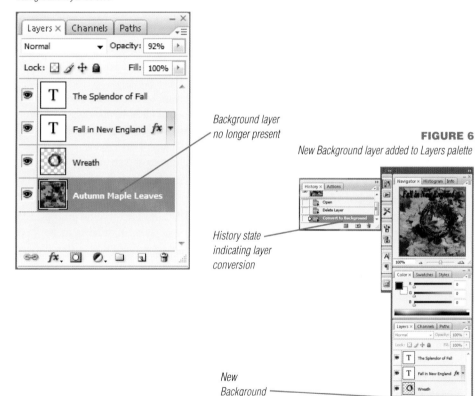

Background layer
no longer present

FIGURE 6

New Background layer added to Layers palette

History state
indicating layer
conversion

New
Background
layer

Convert an image layer into a Background layer

1. Open PS 2-1.psd from the drive and folder where you store your Data Files, then save it as **New England Fall**.

   TIP If you receive a warning box about maximum compatibility, or a message stating that some of the text layers need to be updated before they can be used for vector-based output, click OK or click Update.

2. Click **View** on the menu bar, click **Rulers** if your rulers are not visible, then make sure that your rulers are displayed in pixels.

   TIP If you are unsure which units of measurement are used, right-click (Win) or [Ctrl]-click (Mac) one of the rulers, then verify that Pixels is selected, or click Pixels (if necessary).

3. On the Layers palette, scroll down, click the **Background layer**, then click the **Delete layer button** 🗑.

4. Click **Yes** in the dialog box, as shown in Figure 4, then compare your Layers palette to Figure 5.

5. Click the **History button** 🔄 on the Dock to display the History palette.

6. Click **Layer** on the menu bar, point to **New**, then click **Background From Layer**.

   The Autumn Maple Leaves layer has been converted into the Background layer. Did you notice that in addition to the image layer being converted to the Background layer that a state now appears on the History palette that says Convert to Background? See Figure 6.

7. Save your work.

You displayed the rulers and History palette, deleted the Background layer of an image, then converted an image layer into the Background layer. You can convert any layer into the Background layer, as long as you first delete the existing Background layer.

ADD AND DELETE LAYERS

What You'll Do

 In this lesson, you'll create a new layer using the New command on the Layer menu, delete a layer, create a new layer using buttons on the Layers palette, and relocate a palette tab.

Adding Layers to an Image

Because it's so important to make use of multiple layers, Photoshop makes it easy to add and delete layers. You can create layers in three ways:

- Use the New command on the Layer menu.
- Use the New Layer command on the Layers palette menu.
- Click the Create a new layer button on the Layers palette.

Objects on new layers have a default opacity setting of 100%, which means that objects on lower layers are not visible. Each layer has the Normal (default) blending mode applied to it. (A **blending mode** is a feature that affects a layer's underlying pixels, and is used to lighten or darken colors.)

Merging layers

You can combine multiple image layers into a single layer using the merging process. Merging layers is useful when you want to combine multiple layers in order to make specific edits permanent. (This merging process is different from flattening in that it's selective. Flattening merges *all* visible layers.) In order for layers to be merged, they must be visible and next to each other on the Layers palette. You can merge all visible layers within an image, or just the ones you select. Type layers cannot be merged until they are **rasterized** (turned into a bitmapped image layer), or converted into uneditable text. To merge two layers, make sure that they are next to each other and that the Indicates layer visibility button is visible on each layer, then click the layer in the higher position on the Layers palette. Click Layer on the menu bar, then click Merge Down. The active layer and the layer immediately beneath it will be combined into a single layer. To merge all visible layers, click the Layers palette list arrow, then click Merge Visible. Most layer commands that are available on the Layers menu, such as Merge Down, are also available using the Layers palette list arrow.

Naming a Layer

Photoshop automatically assigns a sequential number to each new layer name, but you can rename a layer at any time. So, if you have four named layers and add a new layer, the default name of the new layer will be Layer 1. After all, calling a layer "Layer 12" is fine, but you might want to use a more descriptive name so it is easier to distinguish one layer from another. If you use the New command on the Layers menu, you can name the layer when you create it. You can rename a layer at any time by using either of these methods:

- Click the Layers palette list arrow, click Layer Properties, type the name in the Name text box, then click OK.
- Double-click the name on the Layers palette, type the new name, then press [Enter] (Win) or [return] (Mac).

Deleting Layers From an Image

You might want to delete an unused or unnecessary layer. You can use four methods to delete a layer:

- Click the name on the Layers palette, click the Layers palette list arrow, then click Delete Layer as shown in Figure 7.
- Click the name on the Layers palette, click the Delete layer button on the Layers palette, then click Yes in the warning box.
- Click the name on the Layers palette, press and hold [Alt] (Win) or [option] (Mac), then click the Delete layer button on the Layers palette.

- Drag the layer name on the Layers palette to the Delete layer button on the Layers palette.

You should be certain that you no longer need a layer before you delete it. If you delete a layer by accident, you can restore it during the current editing session by deleting the Delete Layer state on the History palette.

QUICKTIP

Photoshop always numbers layers sequentially, no matter how many layers you add or delete.

FIGURE 7
Layers palette menu

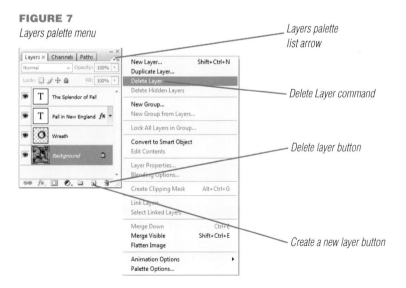

Layers palette list arrow

Delete Layer command

Delete layer button

Create a new layer button

Add a layer using the Layer menu

1. Click the **Fall in New England layer** on the Layers palette.

2. Click **Layer** on the menu bar, point to **New**, then click **Layer** to open the New Layer dialog box, as shown in Figure 8.

   A new layer will be added above the active layer.

   > TIP You can change the layer name in the New Layer dialog box before it appears on the Layers palette.

3. Click **OK**.

4. Drag the **History palette tab** over the Color palette until you see the drop zone (the light blue outline indicating where the palette will be placed), then release the mouse button.

5. Click **Window** on the menu bar, point to **Workspace,** click **Save Workspace** then type **History to Colors palette** (capture Palette Locations), then click **OK**.

6. Click the **Actions close button** in the Dock to close the Actions palette.

   The New Layer dialog box closes and the new layer appears above the Fall in New England layer on the Layers palette. The New Layer state is added to the History palette. See Figure 9.

You created a new layer above the Fall in New England layer using the New command on the Layer menu. The layer does not yet contain any content. You also relocated the History palette to make viewing your progress more convenient.

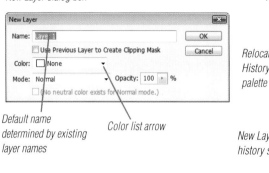

FIGURE 8
New Layer dialog box

Default name
determined by existing
layer names

Color list arrow

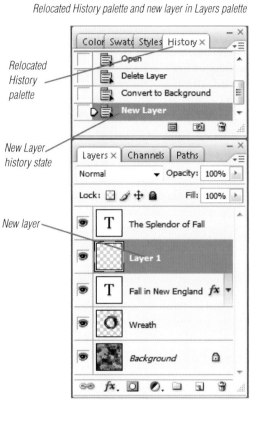

FIGURE 9
Relocated History palette and new layer in Layers palette

Relocated
History
palette

New Layer
history state

New layer

Inserting a layer beneath the active layer

When you add a layer to an image either by using the Layer menu or clicking the Create a new layer button on the Layers palette, the new layer is inserted above the active layer. But there might be times when you want to insert the new layer beneath, or in back of, the active layer. You can do so easily, by pressing [Ctrl] (Win) or [Command] (Mac) while clicking the Create a new layer button on the Layers palette.

FIGURE 10
New layer with default settings

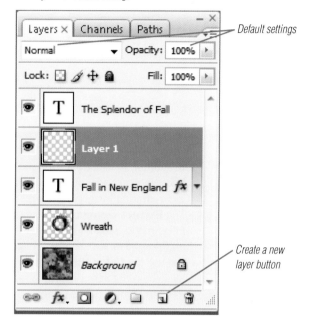

Default settings

Create a new
layer button

Right-clicking for everyone (Mac)

Mac users, are you feeling left out because you can't right-click? If so, you'll welcome this news: anyone (yes, even Mac users!) can right-click simply by replacing the mouse that came with your computer with any two-button mouse that uses a USB connector. OS X was designed to recognize two-button mice without having to add software. Once you've switched mice, just plug and play! You can then right-click using the (Win) instructions in the steps.

Delete a layer

1. Position the **Layer selection pointer** over Layer 1 on the Layers palette.

2. Drag **Layer 1** to the **Delete layer button** on the Layers palette.

   TIP   You can also delete the layer by dragging the New Layer state on the History palette to the Delete current state button.

3. If the Delete the layer "Layer 1" dialog box opens, click the **Don't show again check box**, then click **Yes**.

   TIP   Many dialog boxes let you turn off this reminder feature by selecting the Don't show again check box. Selecting these check boxes can improve your efficiency.

You used the Delete layer button on the Layers palette to delete a layer.

Add a layer using the Layers palette

1. Click the **Fall in New England layer** on the Layers palette, if it is not already selected.

2. Click the **Create a new layer button** on the Layers palette, then compare your Layers palette to Figure 10.

3. Save your work.

You used the Create a new layer button on the Layers palette to add a new layer.

ADD A SELECTION FROM ONE
IMAGE TO ANOTHER

What You'll Do

In this lesson, you'll use the Invert check box in the Color Range dialog box to make a selection, drag the selection to another image, and remove the fringe from a selection using the Defringe command.

Understanding Selections

Often the Photoshop file you want to create involves using an image or part of an image from another file. To use an image or part of an image, you must first select it. Photoshop refers to this as "making a selection." A selection is an area of an image surrounded by a **marquee**, a dashed line that surrounds the area you want to edit or move to another image, as shown in Figure 11. You can drag a marquee around a selection using four marquee tools: Rectangular Marquee, Elliptical Marquee, Single Row Marquee, and Single Column Marquee. Table 1 displays the four marquee tools and other selection tools. You can set options for each tool on the options bar when the tool you want to use is active.

Understanding the Extract and Color Range Commands

In addition to using selection tools, Photoshop provides other methods for incorporating imagery from other files. The **Extract command**, located on the Filter menu, separates an image from a background or surrounding imagery. You can use the **Color Range command**, located on the Select menu, to select a particular color contained in an existing image. Depending on the area you want, you can use the Color Range dialog box to extract a portion of an image.

Cropping an image

You might find an image that you really like, except that it contains a particular portion that you don't need. You can exclude, or **crop**, certain parts of an image by using the Crop Tool on the Tools palette. Cropping hides areas of an image from view *without* losing resolution quality. To crop an image, click the Crop Tool on the Tools palette, drag the pointer around the area you *want to keep*, then press [Enter] (Win) or [return] (Mac).

For example, you can select the Invert check box to choose one color and then select the portion of the image that is every color *except* that one. After you select all the imagery you want from another image, you can drag it into your open file.

Making a Selection and Moving a Selection

You can use a variety of methods and tools to make a selection, which can be used as a specific part of a layer or as the entire layer.

You use selections to isolate an area you want to alter. For example, you can use the Magnetic Lasso Tool to select complex shapes by clicking the starting point, tracing an approximate outline, then clicking the ending point. Later, you can use the Crop Tool to trim areas from a selection. When you use the Move Tool to drag a selection to the destination image, Photoshop places the selection in a new layer above the previously active layer.

Defringing Layer Contents

Sometimes when you make a selection, then move it into another image, the newly selected image can contain unwanted pixels that give the appearance of a fringe, or halo. You can remove this effect using a Matting command called Defringe. This command is available on the Layers menu and allows you to replace fringe pixels with the colors of other nearby pixels. You can determine a width for replacement pixels between 1 and 200. It's magic!

FIGURE 11
Marquee selections

Area selected using the Rectangular Marquee Tool

Specific element selected using the Magnetic Lasso Tool

TABLE 1: Selection Tools

tool	tool name	tool	tool name
☐	Rectangular Marquee Tool	♀.	Lasso Tool
○	Elliptical Marquee Tool	⋈	Polygonal Lasso Tool
⋯	Single Row Marquee Tool	⋟	Magnetic Lasso Tool
┊	Single Column Marquee Tool	⊿.	Eraser Tool
🔲	Crop Tool	🖉	Background Eraser Tool
✻	Magic Wand Tool	🖉	Magic Eraser Tool

Make a color range selection

1. Open PS 2-2.psd from the drive and folder where you store your Data Files, save it as **Gourds**, click the **title bar**, then drag the **window** to an empty area of the workspace so that you can see both images.

   TIP When more than one file is open, each has its own set of rulers.

2. Click **Select** on the menu bar, then click **Color Range**.

   TIP If the background color is solid, you can select the Invert check box to pick only the pixels in the image area.

3. Click the **Image option button**, then type **0** in the Fuzziness text box (or drag the **slider** all the way to the left until you see **0**).

4. Position the **Eyedropper pointer** 🖋 in the **white background** of the image in the Color Range dialog box, then click the **background**.

5. Select the **Invert check box**. Compare your dialog box to Figure 12.

6. Click **OK**, then compare your Gourds.psd image to Figure 13.

You opened a file and used the Color Range dialog box to select the image pixels by selecting the image's inverted colors. Selecting the inverse is an important skill in making selections.

FIGURE 12
Color Range dialog box

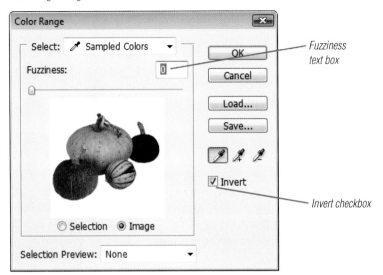

Fuzziness text box

Invert checkbox

Using the Place command
You can add an image from another image to a layer using the Place command. Place an image in a Photoshop layer by clicking File on the menu bar, then clicking Place. The placed artwork appears inside a bounding box at the center of the Photoshop image. The artwork maintains its original aspect ratio; however, if the artwork is larger than the Photoshop image, it is resized to fit.

FIGURE 13
Marquee surrounding selection

Marquee surrounds everything that is the inverse of the white background

FIGURE 14
Gourds image dragged to New England Fall image

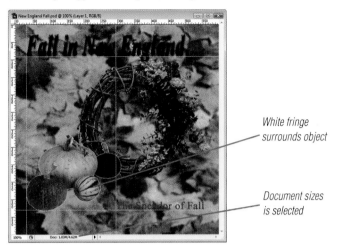

White fringe
surrounds object

Document sizes
is selected

FIGURE 15
Gourds layer defringed

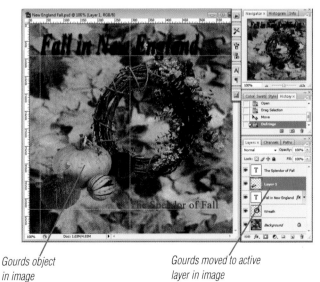

Gourds object
in image

Gourds moved to active
layer in image

Move a selection to another image

1. Click the **Move Tool** ⊹ on the Tools palette.

2. Position the **Move Tool pointer** ⯈⊹ anywhere over the selection in the Gourds image.

3. Drag the **selection** to the New England Fall image, then release the mouse button.

   The Gourds image moves to the New England Fall file appearing on Layer 1.

4. If necessary, use the **Move Tool pointer** ⯈⊹ to drag the **gourds** to the location at the lower-left corner of the wreath.

5. Click the **triangle** ▶ in the document window status bar, point to **Show,** then verify that Document Sizes is selected. Compare your image to Figure 14.

You dragged a selection from one image to another. You verified that the document size is displayed in the window.

Defringe the selection

1. Click **Layer** on the menu bar, point to **Matting,** then click **Defringe**. Defringing a selection gets rid of the halo effect that sometimes occurs when objects are dragged from one image to another.

2. Type **2** in the Width text box, then click **OK.**

3. Save your work.

4. Close **Gourds.psd,** then compare the New England Fall image to Figure 15.

You removed the fringe from a selection.

ORGANIZE LAYERS WITH
LAYER GROUPS AND COLORS

What You'll Do

In this lesson, you'll use the Layers palette menu to create, name, and color a layer group, and then add layers to it. You'll add finishing touches to the image, save it as a copy, then flatten it.

Understanding Layer Groups

A **layer group** is a Photoshop feature that allows you to organize your layers on the Layers palette. A layer group contains individual layers. For example, you can create a layer group that contains all the type layers in your image. To create a layer group, you click the Layers palette list arrow, then click New Group. As with layers, it is helpful to choose a descriptive name for a layer group.

Organizing Layers into Groups

After you create a layer group, you simply drag layers on the Layers palette directly on top of the layer group. You can remove layers from a layer group by dragging them out of the layer group to a new location on the Layers palette or by deleting them. Some changes made to a layer group, such as blending mode or opacity changes, affect every layer in the layer group. You can choose to expand or collapse layer groups, depending on the amount of information you need to see. Expanding a layer group

Duplicating a layer

When you add a new layer by clicking the Create a new layer button on the Layers palette, the new layer contains default settings. However, you might want to create a new layer that has the same settings as an existing layer. You can do so by duplicating an existing layer to create a copy of that layer and its settings. Duplicating a layer is also a good way to preserve your modifications, because you can modify the duplicate layer and not worry about losing your original work. To create a duplicate layer, select the layer you want to copy, click the Layers palette list arrow, click Duplicate Layer, then click OK. The new layer will appear above the original.

shows all of the layers in the layer group, and collapsing a layer group hides all of the layers in a layer group. You can expand or collapse a layer group by clicking the triangle to the left of the layer group icon. Figure 16 shows one expanded layer group and one collapsed layer group.

Adding Color to a Layer

If your image has relatively few layers, it's easy to locate the layers. However, if your image contains many layers, you might need some help in organizing them. You can organize layers by color-coding them, which makes it easy to find the group you want, regardless of its location on the Layers palette. For example, you can put all type layers in red or put the layers associated with a particular portion of an image in blue. To color the Background layer, you must first convert it to a regular layer.

QUICKTIP
You can also color-code a layer group without losing the color-coding you applied to individual layers.

Flattening an Image

After you make all the necessary modifications to your image, you can greatly reduce the file size by flattening the image. **Flattening** merges all visible layers into a single Background layer and discards all hidden layers. Make sure that all layers that you want to display are visible before you flatten the image. Because flattening removes an image's individual layers, it's a good idea to make a copy of the original image *before* it is flattened. The status bar displays the file's current size and the size it will be when flattened. If you work on a Macintosh, you'll find this information in the lower-left corner of the document window.

FIGURE 16
Layer groups

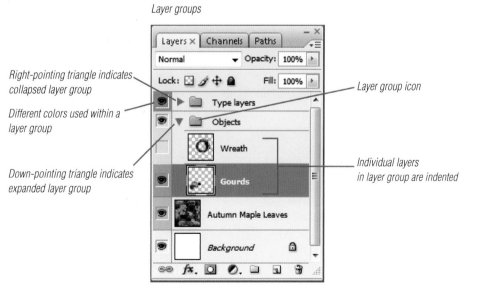

Right-pointing triangle indicates collapsed layer group

Different colors used within a layer group

Down-pointing triangle indicates expanded layer group

Layer group icon

Individual layers in layer group are indented

Understanding Layer Comps

The ability to create a **layer comp**, a variation on the arrangement and visibility of existing layers, is a powerful tool that can make your work more organized. You can create a layer comp by clicking the Layer Comps button on the Dock, then clicking the Create New Layer Comp button on the palette. The New Layer Comp dialog box, shown in Figure 17, opens, allowing you to name the layer comp and set parameters.

Using Layer Comps

Multiple layer comps, shown in Figure 18, make it easy to switch back and forth between variations on an image theme. Say, for example, that you want to show a client multiple arrangements of layers. The layer comp is an ideal tool for this.

FIGURE 17
New Layer Comp dialog box

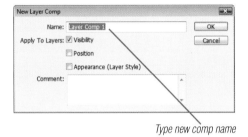

Type new comp name

FIGURE 18
Multiple Layer Comps in image

Layer Comps button

Active layer comp

Layer hidden in active layer comp

FIGURE 19
New Group dialog box

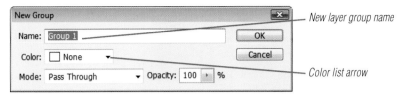

New layer group name

Color list arrow

FIGURE 20
New layer group in Layers palette

New layer group

FIGURE 21
Layers added to the All Type layer group

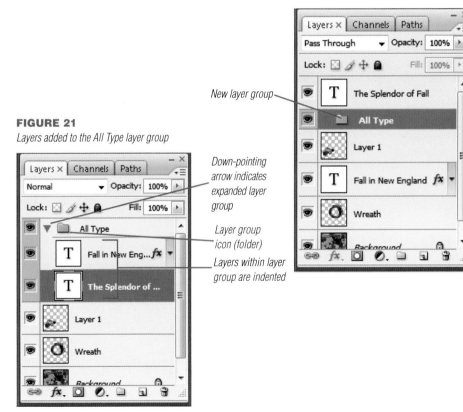

Down-pointing arrow indicates expanded layer group

Layer group icon (folder)

Layers within layer group are indented

Create a layer group

1. Verify that **Layer 1** is active, click the **Layers palette list arrow** ▾≡, then click **New Group**.

   The New Group dialog box opens, as shown in Figure 19.

   | TIP Photoshop automatically places a new layer group above the active layer.

2. Type **All Type** in the Name text box.

3. Click the **Color list arrow**, click **Green**, then click **OK**.

   The New Group dialog box closes. Compare your Layers palette to Figure 20.

You used the Layers palette menu to create a layer group, then named and applied a color to it. This new group will contain all the type layers in the image.

Move layers to the layer group

1. Click the **Fall in New England type layer** on the Layers palette, then drag it on to the **All Type layer group**.

2. Click the **The Splendor of Fall type layer**, drag it on to the **All Type layer group**, then compare your Layers palette to Figure 21.

   | TIP If the Splendor of Fall layer is not below the Fall in New England layer, move the layers to match Figure 21.

3. Click the **triangle** ▽ to the left of the layer group icon (folder) to collapse the layer group.

You created a layer group, then moved two layers into that layer group. Creating layer groups is a great organization tool, especially in complex images with many layers.

Lesson 4   Organize Layers with Layer Groups and Colors

Rename a layer and adjust opacity

1. Double-click **Layer 1**, type **Gourds**, then press **[Enter]** (Win) or **[return]** (Mac).

2. Double-click the **Opacity text box** on the Layers palette, type **75**, then press **[Enter]** (Win) or **[return]** (Mac).

3. Drag the **Gourds layer** beneath the Wreath layer, then compare your image to Figure 22.

4. Save your work.

You renamed the new layer, adjusted opacity, and rearranged layers.

Create layer comps

1. Click the **Layer Comps button** on the Dock.

2. Click the **Create New Layer Comp button** on the Layer Comps palette.

3. Type **Gourds on/Wreath off** in the Name text box, as shown in Figure 23, then click **OK**.

4. Click the **Indicates layer visibility button** on the Wreath layer.

5. Click the **Update Layer Comp button** on the Layer Comps palette. Compare your Layer Comps palette to Figure 24.

6. Save your work, then click the **Layer Comps button** on the Dock to close the Layer Comps palette.

You created a Layer Comp in an existing image.

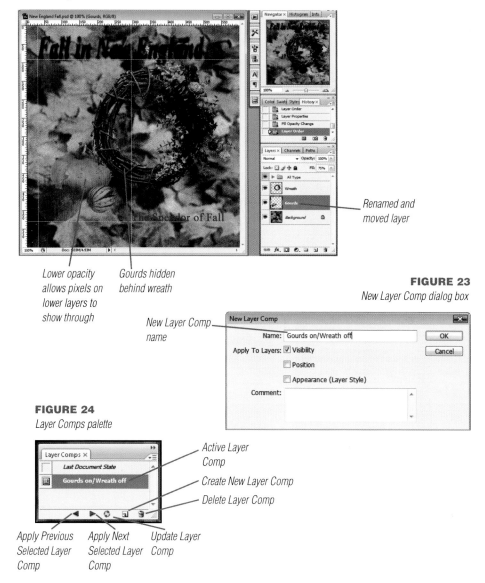

FIGURE 22
Finished image

Renamed and moved layer

Lower opacity allows pixels on lower layers to show through

Gourds hidden behind wreath

FIGURE 23
New Layer Comp dialog box

New Layer Comp name

FIGURE 24
Layer Comps palette

Active Layer Comp

Create New Layer Comp

Delete Layer Comp

Apply Previous Selected Layer Comp

Apply Next Selected Layer Comp

Update Layer Comp

FIGURE 25
Save As dialog box

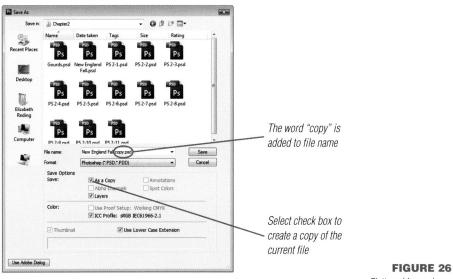

The word "copy" is
added to file name

Select check box to
create a copy of the
current file

FIGURE 26
Flattened image layer

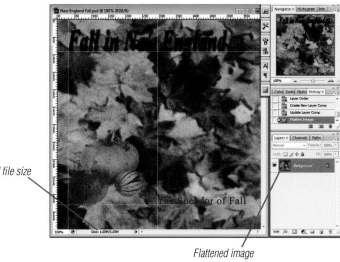

Flattened file size

Flattened image
contains one layer

Flatten an image

1. Click **File** on the menu bar, then click **Save As**.

2. Click the **As a Copy check box** to add a checkmark, then compare your dialog box to Figure 25.

   TIP If "copy" does not display in the File name text box, click this text box and type copy to add it to the name.

3. Click **Save**.

   Photoshop saves and closes a copy of the file containing all the layers and effects.

4. Click **Layer** on the menu bar, then click **Flatten Image**.

5. Click **OK** in the warning box, if necessary, then save your work.

6. Compare your Layers palette to Figure 26.

7. Click **Window** on the menu bar, point to **Workspace,** then click **Reset Palette Locations** to Reset palette locations to the workspace.

8. Close all open images, then exit Photoshop.

You saved the file as a copy, and then flattened the image. The image now has a single layer.

Power User Shortcuts

to do this:	use this method:
Adjust layer opacity	Click Opacity list arrow on Layers palette, drag opacity slider or Double-click Opacity text box, type a percentage
Change measurements	Right-click (Win) or [Ctrl]-click (Mac) ruler
Color a layer	Layers palette list arrow, Layer Properties, Color list arrow
Create a layer comp	Click Layer Comps button
Create a layer group	▾≡, New Group
Delete a layer	
Defringe a selection	Layer ➤ Matting ➤ Defringe

to do this:	use this method:
Flatten an image	Layer ➤ Flatten Image
Move Tool	or V
New Background layer from existing layer	Layer ➤ New ➤ Background From Layer
New layer	Layer ➤ New ➤ Layer or
Rename a layer	Double-click layer name, type new name
Select color range	Select ➤ Color Range
Show/Hide Rulers	View ➤ Rulers [Ctrl][R] (Win) ⌘[R] (Mac)
Update a layer comp	

Key: Menu items are indicated by ➤ between the menu name and its command. Blue bold letters are shortcuts for selecting tools on the Tools palette.

Examine and convert layers.

1. Start Photoshop.
2. Open PS 2-3.psd from the drive and folder where you store your Data Files, update any text layers, if necessary, then save it as **Music Store**.
3. Make sure the rulers appear and that pixels are the unit of measurement.
4. Delete the Background layer.
5. Verify that the Rainbow blend layer is active, then convert the image layer to a Background layer.
6. Save your work.

Add and delete layers.

1. Make Layer 2 active.
2. Create a new layer above this layer using the Layer menu.
3. Accept the default name (Layer 4), and change the color of the layer to Red.
4. Delete Layer 4.
5. Make Layer 2 active (if it is not already the active layer), then create a new layer using the Create a new layer button on the Layers palette.
6. Save your work.

Add a selection from one image to another.

1. Open PS 2-4.psd.
2. Reposition this image of a horn by dragging the window to the right of the Music Store image.
3. Open the Color Range dialog box. (*Hint*: Use the Select menu.)

4. Verify that the Image option button is selected, the Invert check box is selected, and that Fuzziness is set to 0.
5. Sample the white background in the preview window in the dialog box, then close the dialog box.
6. Use the Move Tool to drag the selection into the Music Store image.
7. Position the selection so that the upper-left edge of the instrument matches the sample shown in Figure 27.
8. Defringe the horn selection (in the Music Store image) using a 3 pixel width.
9. Close PS 2-4.psd.
10. Drag Layer 4 above Layer 3.
11. Rename Layer 4 **Horn**.
12. Change the opacity for the Horn layer to 55%.
13. Drag the Horn layer so it is beneath Layer 2.
14. Hide Layer 1.

FIGURE 27
Completed Skills Review

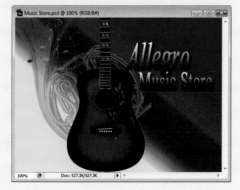

15. Hide the rulers.
16. Save your work.

Organize layers with layer groups and colors.

1. Create a Layer Group called **Type Layers** and assign the color yellow to the group.
2. Drag the following layers into the Type Layers folder: Allegro, Music Store, Layer 2.
3. Delete Layer 2, then collapse the Layer Group folder.
4. Move the Notes layer beneath the Horn layer.
5. Create a layer comp called **Notes layer**.
6. Update the layer comp.
7. Hide the Notes layer.
8. Create a new layer comp called **Notes layer off**, then update the layer comp.
9. Display the previous layer comp, then save your work.
10. Save a copy of the Music Store file using the default naming scheme (add 'copy' to the end of the existing filename).
11. Flatten the original image. (*Hint*: Be sure to discard hidden layers.)
12. Save your work, then compare your image to Figure 27.

A credit union is developing a hotline for members to use to help abate credit card fraud as soon as it occurs. They're going to distribute 10,000 refrigerator magnets over the next three weeks. As part of their effort to build community awareness of the project, they've sponsored a contest for the magnet design. You decide to enter the contest.

1. Open PS 2-5.psd, then save it as **Outlaw Fraud**. The Palatino Linotype font is used in this file. Please make a substitution if this font is not available on your computer.
2. Open PS 2-6.psd, use the Color Range dialog box or any selection tool on the Tools palette to select the cell phone image, then drag it to the Outlaw Fraud image.
3. Rename the newly created layer **Cell Phone**, if necessary, then apply a color to the layer on the Layers palette. Make sure the Cell Phone layer is beneath the type layer.
4. Convert the Background layer to an image layer, then rename it **Banner**.
5. Change the opacity of the Banner layer to any setting you like.
6. Defringe the Cell Phone layer using the pixel width of your choice.
7. Save your work, then compare your image to the sample shown in Figure 28.

FIGURE 28
Completed Project Builder 1

Your local 4-H chapter wants to promote its upcoming fair and has hired you to create a promotional billboard commemorating this event. The Board of Directors decides that the billboard should be humorous.

1. Open PS 2-7.psd, then save it as **4H Billboard**. Substitute any missing fonts.
2. Open PS 2-8.psd, use the Color Range dialog box or any selection tool on the Tools palette to create a marquee around the llama, then drag the selection to the 4-H Billboard image.
3. Name the new layer **Llama**.
4. Change the opacity of the Llama layer to 90%.
5. Save your work, then compare your image to the sample shown in Figure 29.

FIGURE 29
Completed Project Builder 2

A friend of yours has designed a new heat-absorbing coffee cup for take-out orders. She is going to present the prototype to a prospective vendor, but first needs to print a brochure. She's asked you to design an eye-catching cover.

1. Open PS 2-9.psd, update the text layers if necessary, then save it as **Coffee Cover**. The Garamond font is used in this file. Please make a substitution if this font is not available on your computer.
2. Open PS 2-10.psd, then drag the entire image to Coffee Cover.
3. Close PS 2-10.psd.
4. Rename Layer 1 with the name **Mocha**.
5. Delete the Background layer and convert the Mocha layer into a new Background layer.
6. Reposition the layer objects so they look like the sample. (*Hint*: You might have to reorganize the layers in the stack so all layers are visible.)
7. Create a layer group above the Love that coffee layer, name it **Java Text**, apply a color of your choice to the layer group, then drag the type layers to it.
8. Save your work, then compare your image to Figure 30.

FIGURE 30
Completed Design Project

Depending on the size of your group, you can assign individual elements of the project to group members, or work collectively to create the finished product.

Harvest Market, a line of natural food stores, and the trucking associations in your state have formed a coalition to deliver fresh fruit and vegetables to food banks and other food distribution programs. The truckers want to promote the project by displaying a sign on their trucks. The only design requirement is that you use the Harvest Market vegetable logo as the background, keeping in mind that it needs to be seen from a distance.

1. Open PS 2-11.psd, then save it as **Organic Market**. Update the text layers as necessary.
2. Have some members of the group obtain at least two images of different-sized produce. You can obtain images by using what is available on your computer, scanning print media, or connecting to the Internet and downloading images.
3. Other members of the group can open one of the produce files, select it, then drag or copy it to the Organic Market image. (*Hint*: Experiment with some of the other selection tools. Note that some tools require you to copy and paste the image after you select it.)
4. Let other members of the group repeat step 3 then close the two produce image files.

5. Set the opacity of the Market layer to 70%.
6. Arrange the layers so that smaller images appear on top of the larger ones.
7. Create a layer group for the type layers, and apply a color to it.
8. Save your work, then compare your image to Figure 31.

9. Be prepared to discuss the advantages and disadvantages of using multiple images. How would you assess the ease and efficiency of the selection techniques you've learned? Which styles did you apply to the type layers, and why?

FIGURE 31
Completed Group Project

Chapter 2 Working with Layers

chapter

3

MAKING
SELECTIONS

1. Make a selection using shapes

2. Modify a marquee

3. Select using color and modify a selection

4. Add a vignette effect to a selection

Combining Images

Most Photoshop images are created using a technique called **compositing**—combining images from different sources. These sources include other Photoshop images, royalty-free images, pictures taken with digital cameras, and scanned artwork. How you get all that artwork into your Photoshop images is an art unto itself. You can include additional images by using tools on the Tools palette and menu commands. And to work with all these images, you need to know how to select them—or exactly the parts you want to work with.

Understanding Selection Tools

The two basic methods you can use to make selections are using a tool or using color. You can use three freeform tools to create your own unique selections, four fixed area tools to create circular or rec-tangular selections, and a wand tool to make selections using color. In addition, you can use menu commands to increase or decrease selections that you made with these tools, or you can make selections based on color.

Understanding Which Selection Tool to Use

With so many tools available, how do you know which one to use? After you know the different selection options, you'll learn how to look at images and evaluate selection opportunities. With experience, you'll learn how to identify edges that can be used to isolate imagery, and how to spot colors that can be used to isolate a specific object.

Combining Imagery

After you decide on an object that you want to place in a Photoshop image, you can add the object to another image by cutting, copying, and pasting, dragging and dropping objects using the Move Tool, and using the **Clipboard**, the temporary storage area provided by your operating system.

Tools You'll Use

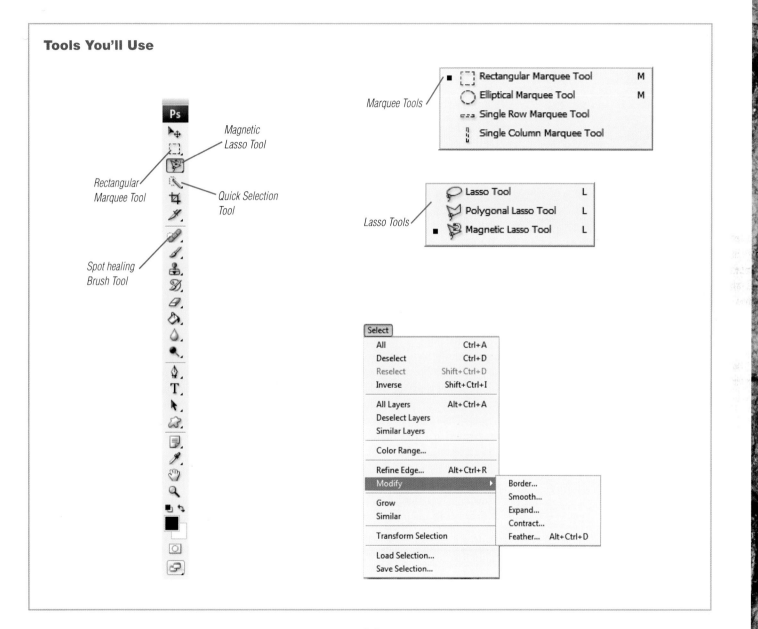

Marquee Tools

- ■ ⬚ Rectangular Marquee Tool   M
- ○ Elliptical Marquee Tool   M
- ⬚ Single Row Marquee Tool
- ▯ Single Column Marquee Tool

Magnetic Lasso Tool

Rectangular Marquee Tool

Quick Selection Tool

Spot healing Brush Tool

Lasso Tools

- ♀ Lasso Tool   L
- ♙ Polygonal Lasso Tool   L
- ■ ♙ Magnetic Lasso Tool   L

Select

All	Ctrl+A
Deselect	Ctrl+D
Reselect	Shift+Ctrl+D
Inverse	Shift+Ctrl+I
All Layers	Alt+Ctrl+A
Deselect Layers	
Similar Layers	
Color Range...	
Refine Edge...	Alt+Ctrl+R
Modify ▶	
Grow	
Similar	
Transform Selection	
Load Selection...	
Save Selection...	

Border...	
Smooth...	
Expand...	
Contract...	
Feather...	Alt+Ctrl+D

MAKE A SELECTION
USING SHAPES

What You'll Do

In this lesson, you'll make selections using a marquee tool and a lasso tool, position a selection with the Move Tool, deselect a selection, and drag a complex selection into another image.

Selecting by Shape

The Photoshop selection tools make it easy to select objects that are rectangular or elliptical in nature. It would be a boring world if every image we wanted fell into one of those categories so fortunately, they don't. While some objects are round or square, most are unusual in shape. Making selections can sometimes be a painstaking process because many objects don't have clearly defined edges. To select an object by shape, you need to click the appropriate tool on the Tools palette, then drag the pointer around the object. The selected area is defined by a **marquee**, or series of dotted lines, as shown in Figure 1.

Creating a Selection

Drawing a rectangular marquee is easier than drawing an elliptical marquee, but with practice, you'll be able to create both types of marquees easily. Table 1 lists the tools you can use to make selections using

shapes. Figure 2 shows a marquee surrounding an irregular shape.

QUICKTIP

A marquee is sometimes referred to as *marching ants* because the dots within the marquee appear to be moving.

Using Fastening Points

Each time you click one of the marquee tools, a fastening point is added to the image. A **fastening point** is an anchor within the marquee. When the marquee pointer reaches the initial fastening point (after making its way around the image), a very small circle appears on the pointer, indicating that you have reached the starting point. Clicking the pointer when this circle appears closes the marquee. Some fastening points, such as those in a circular marquee, are not visible, while others, such as those created by the Polygonal or Magnetic Lasso Tools, are visible.

Selecting, Deselecting, and Reselecting

After a selection is made, you can move, copy, transform, or make adjustments to it. A selection stays selected until you unselect, or **deselect**, it. You can deselect a selection by clicking Select on the menu bar, then clicking Deselect. You can reselect a deselected object by clicking Select on the menu bar, then clicking Reselect.

QUICKTIP

You can select the entire image by clicking Select on the menu bar, then clicking All.

FIGURE 1

Elliptical Marquee Tool used to create marquee

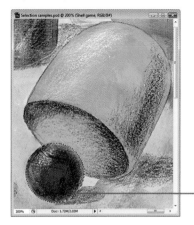

Elliptical Marquee Tool surrounds object

QUICKTIP

Correcting a Selection Error

At some point, you'll spend a lot of time making a complex selection only to realize that the wrong layer was active. Remember the History palette? Every action you do is automatically recorded, and you can use the selection state to retrace your steps and recoup the time spent. Your fix may be as simple as selecting the proper History state and changing the active layer in the Layers palette.

FIGURE 2

Marquee surrounding irregular shape

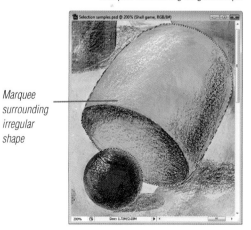

Marquee surrounding irregular shape

TABLE 1: Selection Tools by Shape

tool	button	effect
Rectangular Marquee Tool	⬚	Creates a rectangular selection. Press [Shift] while dragging to create a square.
Elliptical Marquee Tool	○	Creates an elliptical selection. Press [Shift] while dragging to create a circle.
Single Row Marquee Tool	⊏⊐	Creates a 1-pixel-wide row selection.
Single Column Marquee Tool	⌗	Creates a 1-pixel-wide column selection.
Lasso Tool	�	Creates a freehand selection.
Polygonal Lasso Tool	∨	Creates straight line selections. Press [Alt] (Win) or [option] (Mac) to create freehand segments.
Magnetic Lasso Tool	♘	Creates selections that snap to an edge of an object. Press [Alt] (Win) or [option] (Mac) to alternate between freehand and magnetic line segments.

Placing a Selection

You can place a selection in a Photoshop image in many ways. You can copy or cut a selection, then paste it to a different location in the same image or to a different image. You can also use the Move Tool to drag a selection to a new location.

Using Guides

Guides are non-printing horizontal and vertical lines that you can display on top of an image to help you position a selection. You can create an unlimited number of horizontal and vertical guides. You create a guide by displaying the rulers, positioning the pointer on either ruler, then clicking and dragging the guide into position. Figure 3 shows the creation of a vertical guide in a file that contains two existing guides. You delete a guide by selecting the Move Tool on the Tools palette, positioning the pointer over the guide, then clicking and dragging it back

to its ruler. If the Snap feature is enabled, as you drag an object toward a guide, the object will be pulled toward the guide. To turn on the Snap feature, click View on the menu bar, then click Snap. A check mark appears to the left of the command if the feature is enabled.

FIGURE 3
Creating guides in image

FIGURE 4

Rectangular Marquee Tool selection

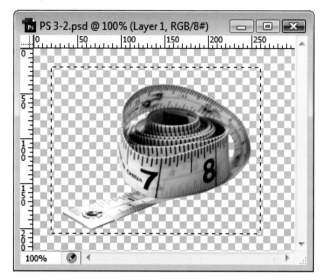

TABLE 2: Working with a Selection

if you want to	then do this
Move a selection (an image) using the mouse	Position the ⊕ over the selection, then drag the marquee and its contents
Copy a selection to the Clipboard	Activate image containing the selection, click Edit ➤ Copy
Cut a selection to the Clipboard	Activate image containing the selection, click Edit ➤ Cut
Paste a selection from the Clipboard	Activate image where you want the selection, click Edit ➤ Paste
Delete a selection	Make selection, then press [Delete] (Win) or [delete] (Mac)
Deselect a selection	Press [Esc] (Win) or [D] (Mac)

Create a selection with the Rectangular Marquee Tool

1. Start Photoshop, open PS 3-1.psd from the drive and folder where you store your Data Files, then save it as **Sewing Box**.

2. Display the rulers (if they are not already displayed) in pixels.

3. Open PS 3-2.psd, then display the rulers in pixels for this image (if they are not displayed).

4. Click the **Rectangular Marquee Tool** ⬚ on the Tools palette.

5. Make sure the value in the Feather text box on the options bar is **0 px**.

   Feathering determines the amount of blur between the selection and the pixels surrounding it.

6. Drag the **Marquee pointer** ┼ to select the tape measure from approximately **20 H/20 V** to **260 H/210 V**. See Figure 4.

   The first measurement refers to the horizontal ruler (H); the second measurement refers to the vertical ruler (V).

   | TIP   You can also use the X/Y coordinates displayed in the Info palette (in the group with the Navigator and Histogram palettes).

7. Click the **Move Tool** ⊕ on the Tools palette, then drag the selection to any location in the Sewing Box image.

   The selection now appears in the Sewing Box image on a new layer (Layer 1).

   | TIP   Table 2 describes methods you can use to work with selections in an image.

Using the Rectangular Marquee Tool, you created a selection in an image, then you dragged that selection into another image. This left the original image intact, and created a copy of the selection in the image you dragged it to.

Position a selection with the Move Tool

1. Verify that the **Move Tool**  is selected on the Tools palette.

2. If you do not see guides in the Sewing Box image, click **View** on the menu bar, point to **Show**, then click **Guides**.

3. Drag the **tape measure** so that the top-right corner snaps to the ruler guides at approximately **1030 H/230 V**. Compare your image to Figure 5.

   Did you feel the snap to effect as you positioned the selection within the guides? This feature makes it easy to properly position objects within an image.

   TIP   If you didn't feel the image snap to the guides, click View on the menu bar, point to Snap To, then click Guides.

4. Rename Layer 1 **Tape Measure**.

You used the Move Tool to reposition a selection in an existing image, then you renamed the layer.

FIGURE 5
Rectangular selection in image

Sewing Box.psd @ 50% (Layer 1, RGB/8#)

50%   Doc: 3.11M/8.76M

Tape measure

Using Smart Guides

Wouldn't it be great to be able to see a vertical or horizontal guide as you move an object? Using Smart Guides, you can do just that. Smart Guides are turned on by clicking View on the menu bar, pointing to Show, then clicking Smart Guides. Once this feature is turned on, horizontal and vertical purple guide lines appear automatically when you draw a shape or move an object. This feature allows you to align layer content as you move it.

FIGURE 6
Deselect command

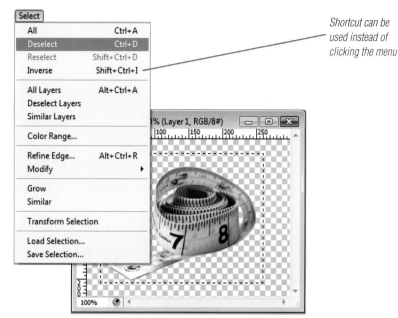

Shortcut can be
used instead of
clicking the menu

1. Click **Window** on the menu bar, then click
   PS 3-2.psd.

   TIP If you can see the window of the
   image you want anywhere on the screen,
   you can just click it to make it active instead
   of using the Window menu.

2. Click **Select** on the menu bar, then click
   Deselect, as shown in Figure 6.

*You hid the active layer, then used the Deselect
command on the Select menu to deselect the
object you had moved into this image. When you
deselect a selection, the marquee no longer
surrounds it.*

FIGURE 7
Save Selection dialog box

Saving and loading a selection

Any selection can be saved independently of the surrounding image, so that if you
want to use it again in the image, you can do so without having to retrace it using one
of the marquee tools. Once a selection is made, you can save it in the image by clicking Select on the menu bar, then clicking Save Selection. The Save Selection dialog
box opens, as shown in Figure 7; be sure to give the selection a meaningful name.
When you want to load a saved selection, click Select on the menu bar, then click Load
Selection. Click the Channel list arrow, click the named selection, then click OK.

Create a selection with the Magnetic Lasso Tool

1. Click the **Magnetic Lasso Tool** on the Tools palette, then change the settings on the options bar so that they are the same as those shown in Figure 8. Table 3 describes Magnetic Lasso Tool settings.

2. Open PS 3-3.psd from the drive and folder where you store your Data Files.

3. Click the **Magnetic Lasso Tool pointer** once anywhere on the edge of the pin cushion, to create your first fastening point.

   TIP If you click on a spot that is not at the edge of the pin cushion, press [Esc] (win) or ⌘ [Z] (Mac) to undo the action, then start again.

4. Drag the **Magnetic Lasso Tool pointer** slowly around the pin cushion (clicking at the top of each pin may be helpful) until it is almost entirely selected, then click directly over the initial fastening point. See Figure 9.

   Don't worry about all the nooks and crannies surrounding the pin cushion: the Magnetic Lasso Tool will select those automatically. You will see a small circle next to the pointer when it is directly over the initial fastening point, indicating that you are closing the selection. The individual segments turn into a marquee.

   TIP If you feel that the Magnetic Lasso Tool is missing some major details while you're tracing, you can insert additional fastening points by clicking the pointer while dragging. For example, click the mouse button at a location where you want to change the selection shape.

You created a selection with the Magnetic Lasso Tool.

FIGURE 8
Options for the Magnetic Lasso Tool

FIGURE 9
Creating a selection with the Magnetic Lasso Tool

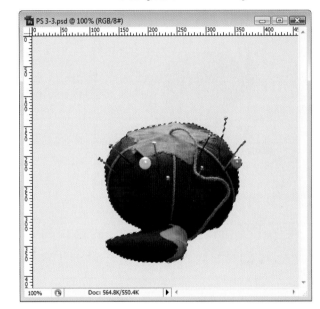

Mastering the art of selections

You might feel that it is difficult when you first start making selections. Making selections is a skill, and like most skills, it takes a lot of practice to become proficient. In addition to practice, make sure that you're comfortable in your work area, that your hands are steady, and that your mouse is working well. A non-optical mouse that is dirty will make selecting an onerous task, so make sure your mouse is well cared for and is functioning correctly.

FIGURE 10
Selection copied into image

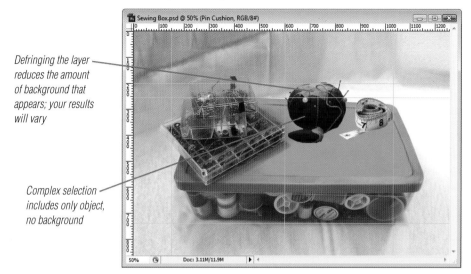

Defringing the layer reduces the amount of background that appears; your results will vary

Complex selection includes only object, no background

TABLE 3: Magnetic Lasso Tool Settings

setting	description
Feather	The amount of blur between the selection and the pixels surrounding it. This setting is measured in pixels and can be a value between 0 and 250.
Anti-alias	The smoothness of the selection, achieved by softening the color transition between edge and background pixels.
Width	The interior width by detecting an edge from the pointer. This setting is measured in pixels and can have a value from 1 to 40.
Edge Contrast	The tool's sensitivity. This setting can be a value between 1% and 100%: higher values detect high-contrast edges.
Frequency	The rate at which fastening points are applied. This setting can be a value between 0 and 100: higher values insert more fastening points.

1. Click the **Move Tool** ⊹ on the Tools palette.

   TIP You can also click the Click to open the Tool Preset picker list arrow on the options bar, then double-click the Move Tool.

2. Use the **Move Tool pointer** ⊹ to drag the pin cushion selection to the Sewing Box image.

   The selection appears on a new layer (Layer 1).

3. Drag the object so that the left edge of the pin cushion snaps to the guide at approximately **600 Y** and the top of the pin cushion snaps to the guide at **200 X** using the coordinates on the info palette.

4. Use the Layer menu to defringe the new Layer 1 at a width of **1** pixel.

5. Close the PS 3-3.psd image without saving your changes.

6. Rename the new layer **Pin Cushion** in the Sewing Box image.

7. Save your work, then compare your image to Figure 10.

8. Click **Window** on the menu bar, then click **PS 3-2.psd.**

9. Close the PS 3-2.psd image without saving your changes.

You dragged a complex selection into an existing Photoshop image. You positioned the object using ruler guides and renamed a layer. You also defringed a selection to eliminate its white border.

MODIFY A
MARQUEE

What You'll Do

In this lesson, you'll move and enlarge a marquee, drag a selection into a Photoshop image, then position a selection using ruler guides.

Changing the Size of a Marquee

Not all objects are easy to select. Sometimes, when you make a selection, you might need to change the size or shape of the marquee.

The options bar contains selection buttons that help you add to and subtract from a marquee, or intersect with a selection. The marquee in Figure 11 was modified into the one shown in Figure 12 by clicking the Add to selection button. After the Add to selection button is active, you can draw an additional marquee (directly adjacent to the selection), and it will be added to the current marquee.

One method you can use to increase the size of a marquee is the Grow command. After you make a selection, you can increase the marquee size by clicking Select on the menu bar, then by clicking Grow. The Grow command selects pixels adjacent to the marquee that have colors

similar to those specified by the Magic Wand Tool. The Similar command selects both adjacent and non-adjacent pixels.

QUICKTIP

While the Grow command selects adjacent pixels that have similar colors, the Expand command increases a selection by a specific number of pixels.

Modifying a Marquee

While a selection is active, you can modify the marquee by expanding or contracting it, smoothing out its edges, or enlarging it to add a border around the selection. These four commands: Border, Smooth, Expand, and Contract are submenus of the Modify command, which is found on the Select menu. For example, you might want to enlarge your selection. Using the Expand command, you can increase the size of the selection, as shown in Figure 13.

Moving a Marquee

After you create a marquee, you can move the marquee to another location in the same image or to another image entirely. You might want to move a marquee if you've drawn it in the wrong image or the wrong location. Sometimes it's easier to draw a marquee elsewhere on the page, and then move it to the desired location.

QUICKTIP

You can always hide and display layers as necessary to facilitate making a selection.

FIGURE 12
Selection with additions

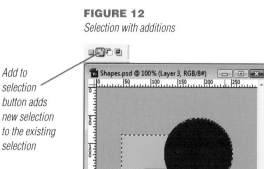

Add to selection button adds new selection to the existing selection

Single marquee surrounds all shapes

Add to selection pointer

FIGURE 11
New selection

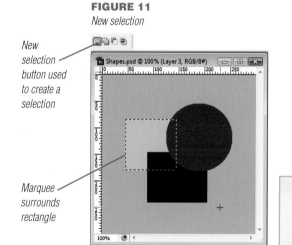

New selection button used to create a selection

Marquee surrounds rectangle

Using the Quick Selection Tool

The Quick Selection Tool lets you paint-to-select an object from the interior using a resizeable brush. As you paint the object, the selection grows. Using the Auto-Enhance check box, rough edges and blockiness are automatically reduced to give you a perfect selection. As with other selection tools, the Quick Selection Tool has options to add and subtract from your selection.

FIGURE 13
Expanded selection

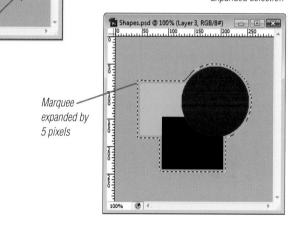

Marquee expanded by 5 pixels

Adding and subtracting from a selection

Of course knowing how to make a selection is important, but it's just as important to know how to make alterations in an existing selection. Sometimes it's almost impossible to create that perfect marquee at first try. Perhaps your hand moved while you were tracing, or you just got distracted. Using the Add to selection, Subtract from selection, and Intersect with selection buttons (which appear with all selection tools), you can alter an existing marquee without having to start from scratch.

Move and enlarge a marquee

1. Open PS 3-4.psd from the drive and folder where you store your Data Files. Change the zoom factor to **200%**.

2. Click the **Elliptical Marquee Tool** on the Tools palette.

   TIP The Elliptical Marquee Tool might be hidden under the Rectangular Marquee Tool.

3. Click the **New selection button** on the options bar (if it is not already selected).

4. Drag the **Marquee pointer** ┼ to select the area from approximately **150 X/50 Y** to **200 X/130 Y**. Compare your image to Figure 14.

5. Position the **pointer** in the center of the selection.

6. Drag the **Move pointer** ► so the marquee covers the thimble, at approximately **100 X/100 Y**, as shown in Figure 15.

   TIP You can also nudge a selection to move it, by pressing the arrow keys. Each time you press an arrow key, the selection moves one pixel in the direction of the arrow.

7. Click the **Magic Wand Tool** on the Tools palette, then select a Tolerance of **16**, and select the **Anti-alias** and **Contiguous checkboxes**.

8. Click **Select** on the menu bar, then click **Similar**.

9. Click **Select** on the menu bar, point to **Modify**, then click **Expand**.

10. Type **1** in the Expand By text box of the Expand Selection dialog box, then click **OK**.

11. Deselect the selection.

You created a marquee, then dragged the marquee to reposition it. You then enlarged a selection marquee by using the Similar and Expand commands.

FIGURE 14
Selection in image

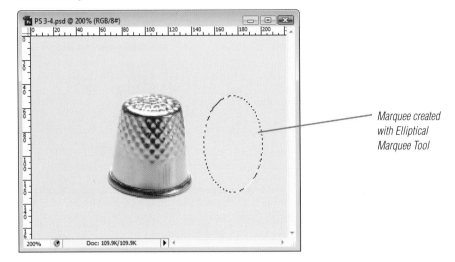

Marquee created
with Elliptical
Marquee Tool

FIGURE 15
Moved selection

New marquee
location

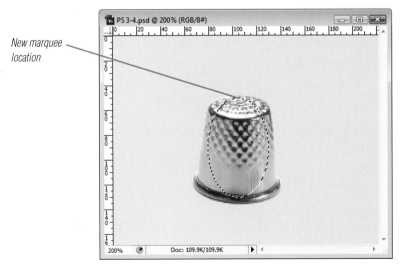

FIGURE 16

Quick Selection Tool settings

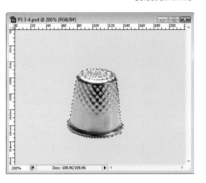

FIGURE 17

Selection in file

FIGURE 18

Selection moved to the Sewing Box image

Use the Quick Selection Tool

1. Click the **Quick Selection Tool** on the Tools palette, then adjust your settings using Figure 16.

2. Position the pointer in the **center of the thimble,** then slowly drag the pointer until the object is selected. See Figure 17.

3. Click the **Move Tool** on the Tools palette.

4. Position the **Move pointer** over the selection, then drag the **thimble** to the Sewing Box image.

5. Drag the **thimble** so that it is to the left of the pin cushion and snaps to the guides at **600 X/200Y**.

6. Defringe the thimble using a setting of **1** pixel.

7. Rename the new layer **Thimble**.

8. Save your work on the sewing box image, then compare your image to Figure 18.

9. Make PS 3-4.psd active.

10. Close PS 3-4.psd without saving your changes.

You selected an object using the Quick Selection Tool, then you dragged the selection into an existing image.

SELECT USING COLOR AND
MODIFY A SELECTION

What You'll Do

In this lesson, you'll make selections using both the Color Range command and the Magic Wand Tool. You'll also flip a selection, then fix an image using the Healing Brush Tool.

Selecting with Color

Selections based on color can be easy to make, especially when the background of an image is different from the image itself. High contrast between colors is an ideal condition for making selections based on color. You can make selections using color with the Color Range command on the Select menu, or you can use the Magic Wand Tool on the Tools palette.

Using the Magic Wand Tool

When you select the Magic Wand Tool, the following options are available on the options bar, as shown in Figure 19:

- The four selection buttons.

- The Tolerance setting, which allows you to specify whether similar pixels will be selected. This setting has a value from 0 to 255, and the lower the value, the closer in color the selected pixels will be.
- The Anti-alias check box, which softens the selection's appearance.
- The Contiguous check box, which lets you select pixels that are next to one another.
- The Sample All Layers check box, which lets you select pixels from multiple layers at once.

Knowing which selection tool to use

The hardest part of making a selection might be determining which selection tool to use. How are you supposed to know if you should use a marquee tool or a lasso tool? The first question you need to ask yourself is, "What do I want to select?" Becoming proficient in making selections means that you need to assess the qualities of the object you want to select, and then decide which method to use. Ask yourself: Does the object have a definable shape? Does it have an identifiable edge? Are there common colors that can be used to create a selection?

Using the Color Range Command

You can use the Color Range command to make the same selections as with the Magic Wand Tool. When you use the Color Range command, the Color Range dialog box opens. This dialog box lets you use the pointer to identify which colors you want to use to make a selection. You can also select the Invert check box to *exclude* the chosen color from the selection. The **fuzziness** setting is similar to tolerance, in that the lower the value, the closer in color pixels must be to be selected.

QUICKTIP

Unlike the Magic Wand Tool, the Color Range command does not give you the option of excluding contiguous pixels.

Transforming a Selection

After you place a selection in a Photoshop image, you can change its size and other qualities by clicking Edit on the menu bar, pointing to Transform, then clicking any of the commands on the submenu. After you select certain commands, small squares called **handles** surround the selection. To complete the command, you drag a handle until the image has the look you want, then press [Enter] (Win) or [return] (Mac). You can also use the Transform submenu to flip a selection horizontally or vertically.

Understanding the Healing Brush Tool

If you place a selection then notice that the image has a few imperfections, you can fix the image. You can fix imperfections such as dirt, scratches, bulging veins on skin, or wrinkles on a face using the Healing Brush Tool on the Tools palette.

QUICKTIP

When correcting someone's portrait, make sure your subject looks the way he or she *thinks* they look. That's not always possible, but strive to get as close as you can to their ideal!

Using the Healing Brush Tool

This tool lets you sample an area, then paint over the imperfections. What is the result? The less-than-desirable pixels seem to disappear into the surrounding image. In addition to matching the sampled pixels, the Healing Brush Tool also matches the texture, lighting, and shading of the sample. This is why the painted pixels blend so effortlessly into the existing image. Corrections can be painted using broad strokes, or using clicks of the mouse.

QUICKTIP

To take a sample, press and hold [Alt] (Win) or [option] (Mac) while dragging the pointer over the area you want to duplicate.

FIGURE 19
Options for the Magic Wand Tool

Select using color range

1. Open PS 3-5.psd from the drive and folder where you store your Data Files.

2. Click **Select** on the menu bar, then click **Color Range**.

3. Click the **Image option button** (if it is not already selected).

4. Click the **Invert check box** to add a check mark.

5. Verify that your settings match those shown in Figure 20, click anywhere in the background area surrounding the sample image, then click **OK**.

   The Color Range dialog box closes and the spool of thread in the image is selected.

6. Click the **Move Tool** on the Tools palette.

7. Drag the selection into Sewing Box.psd, then position the selection as shown in Figure 21.

8. Rename the new layer **Thread**.

9. Activate **PS 3-5.psd**, then close this file without saving any changes.

You made a selection within an image using the Color Range command on the Select menu, and dragged the selection to an existing image.

FIGURE 20
Completed Color Range dialog box

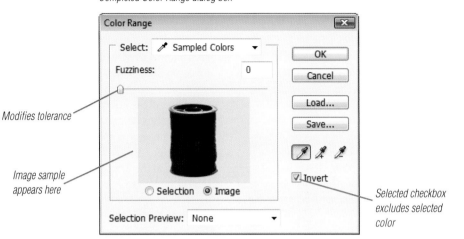

Modifies tolerance

Image sample appears here

Selected checkbox excludes selected color

FIGURE 21
Selection in image

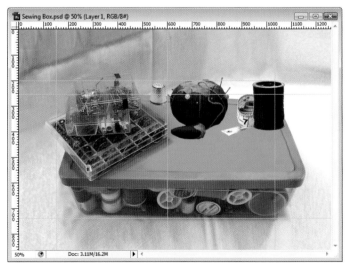

FIGURE 22
Magic Wand Tool settings

FIGURE 23
Selected area

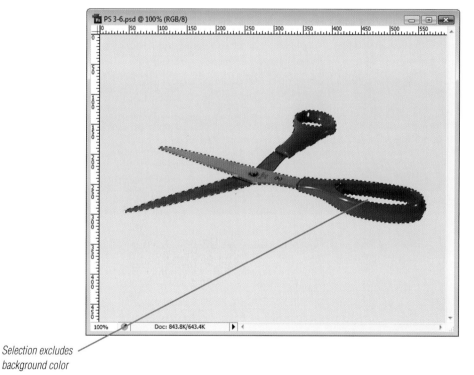

Selection excludes
background color

1. Open PS 3-6.psd from the drive and folder where you store your Data Files.

2. Click the **Magic Wand Tool** ✎ on the Tools palette.

3. Change the settings on the options bar to match those shown in Figure 22.

4. Click anywhere in the background area of the image (such as **50 X/50 Y**).

   TIP   Had you selected the Contiguous check box, the pixels within the handles *would not* have been selected. The Contiguous check box is a powerful feature of the Magic Wand Tool.

5. Click **Select** on the menu bar, then click **Inverse**. Compare your selection to Figure 23.

6. Click the **Move Tool** ⊕ on the Tools palette, then drag the selection into Sewing Box.psd.

You made a selection using the Magic Wand Tool, then dragged it into an existing image. The Magic Wand Tool is just one more way you can make a selection. One advantage of using the Magic Wand Tool is the Contiguous check box, which lets you choose pixels that are next to one another.

Flip a selection

1. Click **Edit** on the menu bar, point to **Transform**, then click **Flip Horizontal**.

2. Rename Layer 1 as **Scissors**.

3. Defringe **Scissors** using a **1** pixel setting.

4. Drag the flipped selection with the **Move Tool pointer** ▶+ so it is positioned as shown in Figure 24.

5. Make **PS 3-6.psd** the active file, then close PS 3-6.psd without saving your changes.

6. Save your work.

You flipped and repositioned a selection. Sometimes it's helpful to flip an object to help direct the viewer's eye to a desired focal point.

FIGURE 24
Flipped and positioned selection

Getting rid of red eye

When digital photos of your favorite people have that annoying red eye, what do you do? You use the Red Eye Tool to eliminate this effect. To do this, select the Red Eye Tool (which is grouped on the Tools palette with the Spot Healing Brush Tool, the Healing Brush Tool, and the Patch Tool), then either click a red area of an eye or draw a selection over one red eye. When you release the mouse button, the red eye effect is removed.

FIGURE 25
Healing Brush Tool options

FIGURE 26
Healed area

Crack removed
from image

FIGURE 27
Image after using the Healing brush

Lesson 3   Select Using Color and Modify a Selection

Fix imperfections with the Healing Brush Tool

1. Click the **Sewing Box layer** on the Layers palette, then click the **Zoom Tool** 🔍 on the Tools palette.

2. Click the image with the **Zoom Tool pointer** ⊕ above the pink spool of thread, (in the box) at **750 X/600 Y** until the zoom factor is **200%** and you can see the crack in the lid of the box.

3. Click the **Healing Brush Tool** 🖉 on the Tools palette. Change the setting on the options bar to match those shown in Figure 25.

    TIP   If you need to change the Brush settings, click the Brush list arrow on the options bar, then drag the sliders so the settings are 10 px diameter, 0% hardness, 1% spacing, 0° angle, 100% roundness, and pen pressure size.

4. Press and hold **[Alt]** (Win) or **[option]** (Mac), click next to the crack at any location on the green lid, such as **700 X/580 Y**, then release **[Alt]** (Win) or **[option]** (Mac).

    You sampled an area of the box that is not cracked so that you can use the Healing Brush Tool to paint a damaged area with the sample.

5. Click the crack (at approximately **720 X/580 Y**).

6. Repeat steps 4 and 5, each time choosing a new source location, then clicking at a parallel location on the crack.

    Compare the repaired area to Figure 26.

7. Click the **Zoom Tool** 🔍 on the Tools palette press and hold **[Alt]** (Win) or **[option]** (Mac), click the center of the image with the **Zoom Tool pointer** ⊖ until the zoom factor is **50%**, then release **[Alt]** (Win) or **[option]** (Mac).

8. Save your work, then compare your image to Figure 27.

You used the Healing Brush Tool to fix an imperfection in an image.

ADD A VIGNETTE EFFECT
TO A SELECTION

What You'll Do

In this lesson, you'll create a vignette effect, using a layer mask and feathering.

Understanding Vignettes

Traditionally, a **vignette** is a picture or portrait whose border fades into the surrounding color at its edges. You can use a vignette effect to give an image an old-world appearance. You can also use a vignette effect to tone down an overwhelming background. You can create a vignette effect in Photoshop by creating a mask with a blurred edge. A **mask** lets you protect or modify a particular area and is created using a marquee.

Creating a Vignette

A **vignette effect** uses feathering to fade a marquee shape. The **feather** setting blurs the area between the selection and the surrounding pixels, which creates a distinctive fade at the edge of the selection. You can create a vignette effect by using a marquee or lasso tool to create a marquee in an image layer. After the selection is created, you can modify the feather setting (a 10- or 20-pixel setting creates a nice fade) to increase the blur effect on the outside edge of the selection.

Getting that Healing feeling

The Spot Healing Brush Tool works in much the same way as the Healing Brush Tool in that it removes blemishes and other imperfections. Unlike the Healing Brush Tool, the Spot Healing Brush Tool does not require you to take a sample. When using the Spot Healing Brush Tool, you must choose whether you want to use a proximity match type (which uses pixels around the edge of the selection as a patch) or a create texture type (which uses all the pixels in the selection to create a texture that is used to fix the area). You also have the option of sampling all the visible layers or only the active layer.

FIGURE 28
Marquee in image

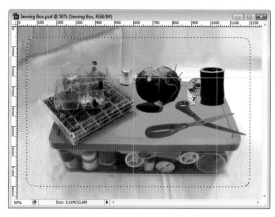

FIGURE 29
Layers palette

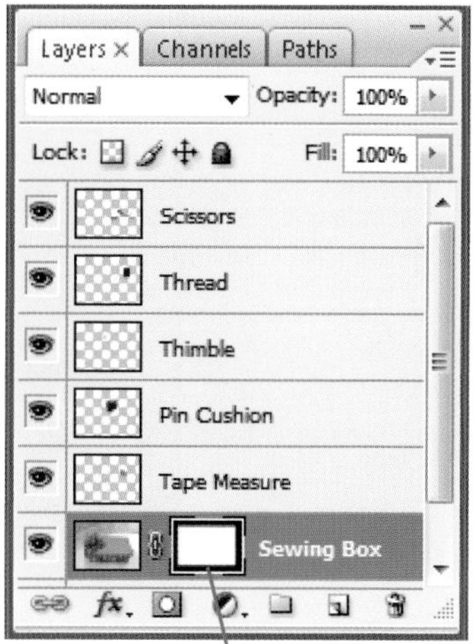

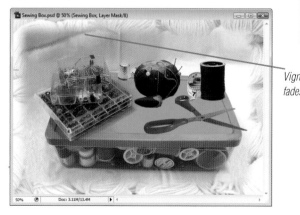

Vignette effect
fades border

Feathered mask creates
vignette effect

FIGURE 30
Vignette in image

1. Verify that the **Sewing Box layer** is selected.

2. Click the **Rectangular Marquee Tool** ⬚ on the Tools palette.

3. Change the **Feather setting** on the options bar to **20px**.

4. Create a selection with the **Marquee pointer** ┼ from **50 X/50 Y** to **1200 X/800 Y**, as shown in Figure 28.

5. Click **Layer** on the menu bar, point to **Layer Mask**, then click **Reveal Selection**.

   The vignette effect is added to the layer.

   Compare your Layers palette to Figure 29.

6. Click **View** on the menu bar, then click **Rulers** to hide them.

7. Click **View** on the menu bar, then click **Clear Guides**.

8. Save your work, then compare your image to Figure 30.

9. Close the Sewing Box image, then exit Photoshop.

You created a vignette effect by adding a feathered layer mask. You also rearranged layers and defringed a selection. Once the image was finished, you hid the rulers and cleared the guides.

SKILLS REFERENCE

Power User Shortcuts

to do this:	use this method:
Copy selection	Click Edit ➤ Copy or [Ctrl][C] (Win) or ⌘[C] (Mac)
Create vignette effect	Marquee or Lasso Tool, create selection, click Layer ➤ Layer Mask ➤ Reveal Selection
Cut selection	Click Edit ➤ Cut or [Ctrl][X] (Win) or ⌘[X] (Mac)
Deselect object	Select ➤ Deselect or [Ctrl][D] (Win) or ⌘[D] (Mac)
Elliptical Marquee Tool	◯ or [Shift] M
Flip image	Edit ➤ Transform ➤ Flip Horizontal
Grow selection	Select ➤ Grow
Increase selection	Select ➤ Similar
Lasso Tool	⟡ or [Shift] L
Magnetic Lasso Tool	⟡ or [Shift] L
Move Tool	⤢ or V

to do this:	use this method:
Move selection marquee	Position pointer in selection, drag ⤢ to new location
Paste selection	Edit ➤ Paste or [Ctrl][V] (Win) or ⌘[V] (Mac)
Polygonal Lasso Tool	⟡ or [Shift] L
Rectangular Marquee Tool	⬚ or [Shift] M
Reselect a deselected object	Select ➤ Reselect, or [Shift][Ctrl][D] (Win) or [Shift]⌘[D] (Mac)
Select all objects	Select ➤ All, or [Ctrl][A] (Win) or ⌘[A] (Mac)
Select using color range	Select ➤ Color Range, click in sample area
Select using Magic Wand Tool	✳ or W, then click image
Select using Quick Selection Tool	⟡ or [Shift] W, then drag pointer over image
Single Column Marquee Tool	▯
Single Row Marquee Tool	▭

Key: Menu items are indicated by ➤ between the menu name and its command. Blue bold letters are shortcuts for selecting tools on the Tools palette.

Make a selection using shapes.

1. Open PS 3-7.psd from the drive and folder where you store your Data Files, substitute any missing fonts, then save it as **All Cats**.
2. Open PS 3-8.tif.
3. Display the rulers in each image window (if necessary).
4. Use the Rectangular Marquee Tool to select the entire image in PS 3-8.tif. (*Hint*: Reset the Feather setting to 0 pixels, if necessary.)
5. Deselect the selection.
6. Use the Magnetic Lasso Tool to create a selection surrounding only the Block cat in the image. (*Hint*: You can use the Zoom Tool to make the image larger.)
7. Drag the selection into the All Cats image, positioning it so the right side of the cat is at 490 X, and the bottom of the right paw is at 450 Y.
8. Save your work.
9. Close PS 3-8.tif without saving any changes.

Modify a marquee.

1. Open PS 3-9.tif.
2. Change the settings on the Magic Wand Tool to Tolerance = 5, and make sure that the Contiguous check box is selected.
3. Create an elliptical marquee from 100 X/50 Y to 200 X/100 Y, using a setting of 0 in the Feather text box.
4. Use the Grow command on the Select menu.
5. Use the Inverse command on the Select menu.

6. Drag the selection into the All Cats image, positioning it so the upper-left corner of the selection is near 0 X/0 Y.
7. Defringe the new layer using a width of 2 pixels.
8. Save your work.
9. Close PS 3-9.tif without saving any changes.

Select using color and modify a selection.

1. Open PS 3-10.tif.
2. Use the Color Range dialog box to select only the kitten.
3. Drag the selection into the All Cats image.
4. Flip the kitten image (in the All Cats image) horizontally.

FIGURE 31
Completed Skills Review project

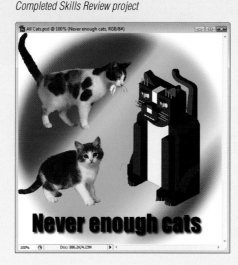

5. Position the kitten image so the bottom right snaps to the ruler guides at 230 X/450 Y.
6. Defringe the kitten using a width of 2 pixels.
7. Save your work.
8. Close PS 3-10.tif without saving any changes.

Add a vignette effect to a selection.

1. Use a 15-pixel feather setting and the Backdrop layer to create an elliptical selection surrounding the contents of the All Cats image.
2. Add a layer mask that reveals the selection.
3. Hide the rulers.
4. Save your work.
5. Compare your image to Figure 31.

As a professional photographer, you often take photos of people for use in various publications. You recently took a photograph of a woman that will be used in a marketing brochure. The client is happy with the overall picture, but wants the facial lines smoothed out. You decide to use the Healing Brush Tool to ensure that the client is happy with the final product.

1. Open PS 3-11.psd, then save it as **Portrait**.
2. Make a copy of the original layer using the default name, or the name of your choice.
3. Use the original copy layer and the Healing Brush Tool to smooth the appearance of facial lines in this image. (*Hint*: You may have greater success if you use short strokes with the Healing Brush Tool than if you paint long strokes.)
4. Save your work, then compare your image to the sample shown in Figure 32.

FIGURE 32
Completed Project Builder 1

The New York Athletic Association, which sponsors the New York Marathon, is holding a contest for artwork to announce the upcoming race. Submissions can be created on paper or computer-generated. You feel you have a good chance at winning this contest, using Photoshop as your tool.

1. Open PS 3-12.psd, then save it as **Marathon Contest**.
2. Locate at least two pieces of appropriate artwork—either on your hard disk, in a royalty-free collection, or from scanned images—that you can use in this file.
3. Use any appropriate methods to select imagery from the artwork.
4. After the selections have been made, copy each selection into Marathon Contest.
5. Arrange the images into a design that you think will be eye-catching and attractive.
6. Deselect the selections in the files you are no longer using, and close them without saving the changes.
7. Add a vignette effect to the Backdrop layer.
8. Display the type layers if they are hidden.
9. Defringe any layers, as necessary.
10. Save your work, then compare your screen to the sample shown in Figure 33.

FIGURE 33
Completed Project Builder 2

You are aware that there will be an open-ing in your firm's design department. Before you can be considered for the job, you need to increase your Photoshop compositing knowledge and experience. You have decided to teach yourself, using informational sources on the Internet and images that can be scanned or purchased.

1. Connect to the Internet and use your browser and favorite search engine to find information on image compositing. (Make a record of the site you found so you can use it for future reference, if necessary.)
2. Create a new Photoshop image, using the dimensions of your choice, then save it as **Sample Compositing**.
3. Locate at least two pieces of artwork— either on your hard disk, in a royalty-free collection, or from scanned images—that you can use.
4. Select the images in the artwork, then copy each into the Sample Compositing image, using the method of your choice.
5. Rename each of the layers using meaningful names.
6. Apply a color to each new layer.
7. Arrange the images in a pleasing design. (*Hint*: Remember that you can flip any image, if necessary.)

8. Deselect the selections in the artwork, then close the files without saving the changes.
9. If desired, create a background layer for the image.
10. If necessary, add a vignette effect to a layer.

11. Defringe any images as you see necessary.
12. Save your work, then compare your screen to the sample shown in Figure 34.

FIGURE 34
Completed Design Project

Depending on the size of your group, you can assign individual elements of the project to group members, or work collectively to create the finished product.

At your design firm, a Fortune 500 client plans to start a 24-hour cable sports network called Total Sportz that will cover any nonprofessional sporting events. You and your team have been asked to create some preliminary designs for the network, using images from multiple sources.

1. Open PS 3-13.psd, then save it as **Total Sportz**. (*Hint*: Click Update to close the warning box regarding missing fonts, if necessary.)
2. Assign a few members of your team to locate several pieces of sports-related artwork—either on your hard disk, in a royalty-free collection, or from scanned images. Remember that the images should not show professional sports figures, if possible.
3. Work together to select imagery from the artwork and move it into the Total Sportz image.
4. Arrange the images in an interesting design. (*Hint*: Remember that you can flip any image, if necessary.)
5. Change each layer name to describe the sport in the layer image.
6. Deselect the selections in the files that you used, then close the files without saving the changes.

7. If necessary, add a vignette effect to a layer and/or adjust opacity. (In the sample, the opacity of the Backdrop layer was adjusted to 100%.)

8. Defringe any images (if necessary).
9. Save your work, then compare your image to the sample shown in Figure 35.

FIGURE 35
Completed Group Project

chapter

4

INCORPORATING COLOR
TECHNIQUES

1. Work with color to transform an image

2. Use the Color Picker and the Swatches palette

3. Place a border around an image

4. Blend colors using the Gradient Tool

5. Add color to a grayscale image

6. Use filters, opacity, and blending modes

7. Match colors

Using Color

Color can make or break an image. Sometimes colors can draw us into an image; other times they can repel us. We all know what colors we like, but when it comes to creating an image, it is helpful to have some knowledge of color theory and be familiar with color terminology.

Understanding how Photoshop measures, displays, and prints color can be valuable when you create new images or modify existing images. Some colors you choose might be difficult for a professional printer to reproduce or might look muddy when printed. As you become more experienced using colors, you will learn which colors can be reproduced well and which ones cannot.

Understanding Color Modes and Color Models

Photoshop displays and prints images using specific color modes. A **mode** is the amount of color data that can be stored in a given file format, based on an established model. A **model** determines how pigments combine to produce resulting colors. This is the way your computer or printer associates a name or numbers with colors. Photoshop uses standard color models as the basis for its color modes.

Displaying and Printing Images

An image displayed on your monitor, such as an icon on your desktop, is a **bitmap**, a geometric arrangement of different color dots on a rectangular grid. Each dot, called a **pixel**, represents a color or shade. Bitmapped images are *resolution-dependent* and can lose detail—often demonstrated by a jagged appearance—when highly magnified. When printed, images with high resolutions tend to show more detail and subtler color transitions than low-resolution images.

Tools You'll Use

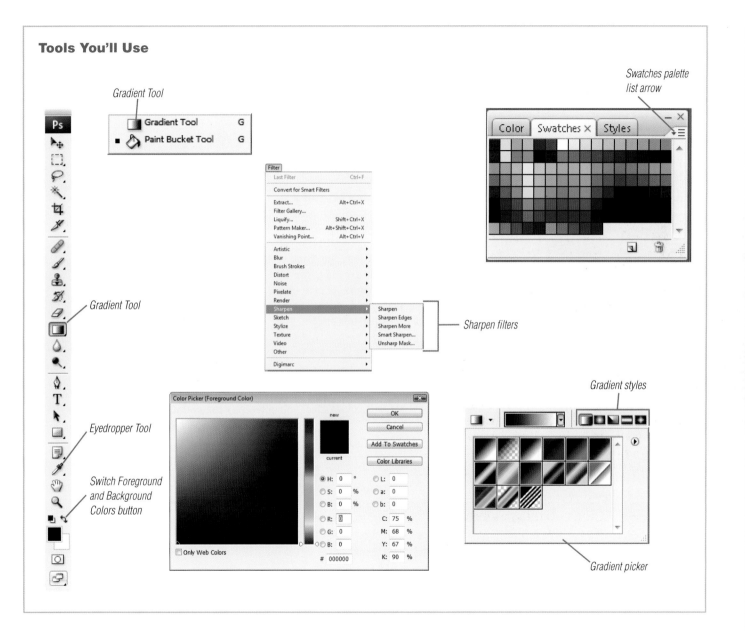

Gradient Tool

▤	Gradient Tool	G
■ ⬧	Paint Bucket Tool	G

Swatches palette list arrow

Color | Swatches ✕ | Styles

Filter

Last Filter	Ctrl+F
Convert for Smart Filters	
Extract...	Alt+Ctrl+X
Filter Gallery...	
Liquify...	Shift+Ctrl+X
Pattern Maker...	Alt+Shift+Ctrl+X
Vanishing Point...	Alt+Ctrl+V
Artistic	▶
Blur	▶
Brush Strokes	▶
Distort	▶
Noise	▶
Pixelate	▶
Render	▶
Sharpen	▶
Sketch	▶
Stylize	▶
Texture	▶
Video	▶
Other	▶
Digimarc	▶

Sharpen filters

Sharpen
Sharpen Edges
Sharpen More
Smart Sharpen...
Unsharp Mask...

Gradient Tool

Gradient styles

Eyedropper Tool

Switch Foreground and Background Colors button

Color Picker (Foreground Color)

new

current

OK
Cancel
Add To Swatches
Color Libraries

◉ H:	0	°	○ L:	0	
○ S:	0	%	○ a:	0	
○ B:	0	%	○ b:	0	
○ R:	0			C:	75	%
○ G:	0			M:	68	%
○ B:	0			Y:	67	%
				K:	90	%

☐ Only Web Colors

000000

Gradient picker

WORK WITH COLOR TO
TRANSFORM AN IMAGE

What You'll Do

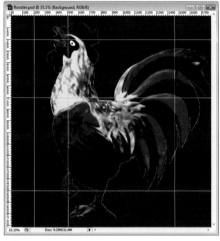

In this lesson, you'll use the Color palette, the Paint Bucket Tool, and the Eyedropper Tool to change the background color of an image.

Learning About Color Models

Photoshop reproduces colors using models of color modes. The range of displayed colors, or **gamut**, for each model available in Photoshop is shown in Figure 1. The shape of each color gamut indicates the range of colors it can display. If a color is out of gamut, it is beyond the color space that your monitor can display or that your printer can print. You select the color mode from the Mode command on the Image menu. The available Photoshop color models are L*a*b, HSB, RGB, CMYK, Bitmap, and Grayscale.

QUICKTIP

A color mode is used to determine which color model will be used to display and print an image.

DESIGNTIP **Understanding the psychology of color**

Have you ever wondered why some colors make you react a certain way? You might have noticed that some colors affect you differently than others. Color is such an important part of our lives, and in Photoshop, it's key. Specific colors are often used in print and Web pages to evoke the following responses:
- Blue tends to instill a feeling of safety and stability and is often used by financial services.
- Certain shades of green can generate a soft, calming feeling, while others suggest youthfulness and growth.
- Red commands attention and can be used as a call to action; it can also distract a reader's attention from other content.
- White evokes the feeling of purity and innocence, looks cool and fresh, and is often used to suggest luxury.
- Black conveys feelings of power and strength, but can also suggest darkness and negativity.

L*a*b Model

The L*a*b model is based on one luminance (lightness) component and two chromatic components (from green to red, and from blue to yellow). Using the L*a*b model has distinct advantages: you have the largest number of colors available to you and the greatest precision with which to create them. You can also create all the colors contained by other color models, which are limited in their respective color ranges. The L*a*b model is device-independent—the colors will not vary, regardless of the hardware. Use this model when working with photo CD images so that you can independently edit the luminance and color values.

HSB Model

Based on the human perception of color, the HSB (Hue, Saturation, Brightness) model has three fundamental characteristics: hue, saturation, and brightness. The color reflected from or transmitted through an object is called **hue**. Expressed as a degree (between 0° and 360°), each hue is identified by a color name (such as red or green). **Saturation** (or *chroma*) is the strength or purity of the color, representing the amount of gray in proportion to hue. Saturation is measured as a percentage from 0% (gray) to 100% (fully saturated). **Brightness** is the measurement of relative lightness or darkness of a color and is measured as a percentage from 0% (black) to 100% (white). Although you can use the HSB model to define a color on the Color palette or in the Color Picker dialog box, Photoshop does not offer HSB mode as a choice for creating or editing images.

RGB Mode

Photoshop uses color modes to determine how to display and print an image. Each mode is based on established models used in color reproduction. Most colors in the visible spectrum can be represented by mixing various proportions and intensities of red, green, and blue (RGB) colored light. RGB colors are additive colors. **Additive colors** are used for lighting, video, and computer monitors; color is created by light passing through red, green, and blue phosphors. When the values of red, green, and blue are zero, the result is black; when the values are all 255, the result is white. Photoshop assigns each component of the RGB mode an intensity value. Your colors can vary from monitor to monitor even if you are using the exact RGB values on different computers.

FIGURE 1
Photoshop color gamuts

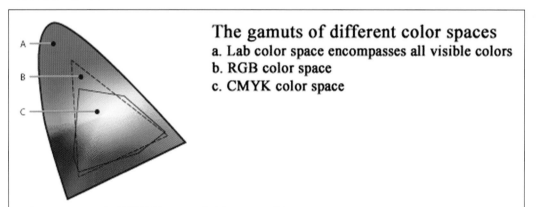

The gamuts of different color spaces
a. Lab color space encompasses all visible colors
b. RGB color space
c. CMYK color space

CMYK Mode

The light-absorbing quality of ink printed on paper is the basis of the CMYK (Cyan, Magenta, Yellow, Black) mode. Unlike the RGB mode—in which components are *combined* to create new colors—the CMYK mode is based on colors being partially *absorbed* as the ink hits the paper and being partially *reflected* back to your eyes. CMYK colors are **subtractive colors**—the *absence* of cyan, magenta, yellow, and black creates white. Subtractive (CMYK) and additive (RGB) colors are complementary colors; a pair from one model creates a color in the other. When combined, cyan, magenta, and yellow absorb all color and produce black. The CMYK mode—in which the lightest colors are assigned the highest percentages of ink colors—is used in four-color process printing. Converting an RGB image into a CMYK image produces a **color separation** (the commercial printing process of separating colors for use with

different inks). Note, however, that because your monitor uses RGB mode, you will not see the exact colors until you print the image, and even then the colors can vary depending on the printer and offset press.

Understanding the Bitmap and Grayscale Modes

In addition to the RGB and CMYK modes, Photoshop provides two specialized color modes: bitmap and grayscale. The **bitmap mode** uses black or white color values to represent image pixels, and is a good choice for images with subtle color gradations, such as photographs or painted images. The **grayscale mode** uses up to 256 shades of gray, assigning a brightness value from 0 (black) to 255 (white) to each pixel. Displayed colors can vary from monitor to monitor even if you use identical color settings on different computers.

Changing Foreground and Background Colors

In Photoshop, the **foreground color** is black by default and is used to paint, fill, and apply a border to a selection. The **background color** is white by default and is used to make **gradient fills** (gradual blends of multiple colors) and fill in areas of an image that have been erased. You can change foreground and background colors

using the Color palette, the Swatches palette, the Color Picker, or the Eyedropper Tool. One method of changing foreground and background colors is **sampling**, in which an existing color is used. You can restore the default colors by clicking the Default Foreground and Background Colors button on the Tools palette, shown in Figure 2. You can apply a color to the background of a layer using the Paint Bucket Tool. When you click an image with the Paint Bucket Tool, the current foreground color on the Tools palette fills the active layer.

FIGURE 2
Foreground and background color buttons

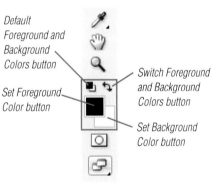

Default Foreground and Background Colors button

Set Foreground Color button

Switch Foreground and Background Colors button

Set Background Color button

FIGURE 3
Image with rulers displayed

FIGURE 4
Color Settings dialog box

Intent list arrow

Creating a rendering intent

The use of a **rendering intent** determines how colors are converted by a color management system. A **color management system** is used to keep colors looking consistent as they move between devices. Colors are defined and interpreted using a **profile**. You can create a rendering intent by clicking Edit on the menu bar, then clicking Color Settings. Click the More Options button in the Color Settings dialog box, click the Intent list arrow shown in Figure 4, then click one of the four options. Since a gamut is the range of color that a color system can display or print, the rendering intent is constantly evaluating the color gamut and deciding whether or not the colors need adjusting. So, colors that fall inside the destination gamut may not be changed, or they may be adjusted when translated to a smaller color gamut.

Set the default foreground and background colors

1. Start Photoshop, open PS 4-1.psd from the drive and folder where you save your Data Files, then save it as **Rooster**.

2. Click the **Default Foreground and Background Colors button** on the Tools palette.

   TIP If you accidently click the Set foreground color button, the Color Picker (Foreground Color) dialog box opens.

3. Change the status bar so the document sizes display, if necessary.

   TIP Document sizes will not display in the status bar if the image window is too small. Drag the lower-right corner of the image window to expand the window and display the menu button and document sizes.

4. Display the rulers in pixels (if necessary), then compare your screen to Figure 3.

   TIP You can right-click (Win) or [control]-click (Mac) one of the rulers to choose Pixels, Inches, Centimeters, Millimeters, Points, Picas, or Percent as a unit of measurement, instead of using the Rulers and Units Preferences dialog box.

You set the default foreground and background colors and displayed rulers in pixels.

Change the background color using the Color palette

1. Click the **Background layer** on the Layers palette.

2. Display the History palette, then click the **Color palette tab** [Color ×] (if it is not already selected).

3. Drag each color slider on the Color palette until you reach the values shown in Figure 5.

   The active color changes to the new color. Did you notice that this image is using the RGB mode?

   TIP You can also double-click each component's text box on the Color palette and type the color values.

4. Click the **Paint Bucket Tool** on the Tools palette.

   TIP If the Paint Bucket Tool is not visible on the Tools palette, click the Gradient Tool on the Tools palette, press and hold the mouse button until the list of hidden tools appears, then click the Paint Bucket Tool.

5. Click the image with the **Paint Bucket pointer**.

6. Drag the **Paint Bucket state** on the History palette onto the **Delete current state button**.

   TIP You can also undo the last action by clicking Edit on the menu bar, then clicking Undo Paint Bucket.

You set new values in the Color palette, used the Paint Bucket Tool to change the background to that color, then undid the change. You can change colors on the Color palette by dragging the sliders or by typing values in the color text boxes.

FIGURE 5
Color palette with new color

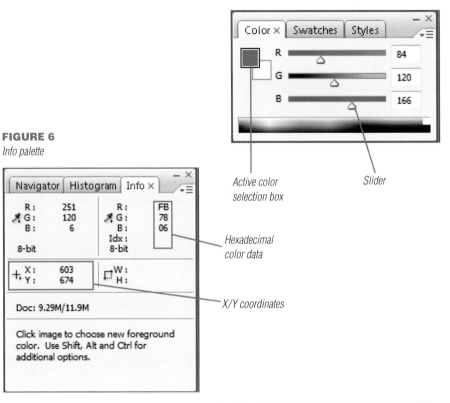

FIGURE 6
Info palette

Active color selection box

Slider

Hexadecimal color data

X/Y coordinates

Using ruler coordinates

Photoshop rulers run along the top and left sides of the document window. Each point on an image has a horizontal and vertical location. These two numbers, called X and Y coordinates, appear on the Info palette (which is located behind the Navigator palette) as shown in Figure 6. The X coordinate refers to the horizontal location, and the Y coordinate refers to the vertical location. You can use one or both sets of guides to identify coordinates of a location, such as a color you want to sample. If you have difficulty seeing the ruler markings, you can increase the size of the image; the greater the zoom factor, the more detailed the measurement hashes.

FIGURE 7

New foreground color applied to Background layer

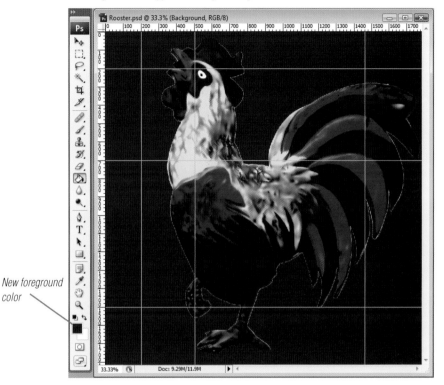

New foreground color

Change the background color using the Eyedropper Tool

1. Click the **Background layer** on the Layers palette.

2. Click the **Eyedropper Tool** 🖋️ on the Tools palette.

3. Click the **red part of the rooster's beak** in the image with the **Eyedropper pointer** 🖋️, using the Info palette and the blue guides to help ensure accuracy.

    The Set foreground color button displays the red color that you clicked (or sampled).

4. Click the **Paint Bucket Tool** 🪣 on the Tools palette.

5. Close the History palette, click the image, then compare your screen to Figure 7.

    TIP   Your color values on the Color palette might vary from the sample.

6. Save your work.

You used the Eyedropper Tool to sample a color as the foreground color, then used the Paint Bucket Tool to change the background color to the color you sampled. Using the Eyedropper Tool is a convenient way of sampling a color in any Photoshop image.

Using hexadecimal values in the Info palette

Colors can be expressed in a **hexadecimal value**, three pairs of letters or numbers that define the R, G, and B components of a color. The three pairs of letters/numbers are expressed in values from 00 (minimum luminance) to ff (maximum luminance). 00 represents the value of black, ffffff is white, and ff0000 is red. To view hexadecimal values in the Info palette, click the Info palette list arrow, then click Palette Options. Click Web Color from either the First Color Readout or Second Color Readout Mode list arrow, then click OK. This is just one more way you can exactly determine a specific color in an image.

USE THE COLOR PICKER AND
THE SWATCHES PALETTE

What You'll Do

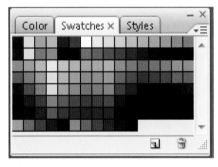

In this lesson, you'll use the Color Picker and the Swatches palette to select new colors, then you'll add a new color to the background and to the Swatches palette.

Making Selections from the Color Picker

Depending on the color model you are using, you can select colors using the **Color Picker**, a feature that lets you choose a color from a color spectrum or lets you numerically define a custom color. You can change colors in the Color Picker dialog box by using the following methods:

- Drag the sliders along the vertical color bar.
- Click inside the vertical color bar.
- Click a color in the Color field.
- Enter a value in any of the text boxes.

Figure 8 shows a color in the Color Picker dialog box. A circular marker indicates the active color. The color slider displays the range of color levels available for the active color component. The adjustments you make by dragging or clicking a new color are reflected in the text boxes; when you choose a new color, the previous color appears below the new color in the preview area.

Using the Swatches Palette

You can also change colors using the Swatches palette. The **Swatches palette** is a visual display of colors you can choose from, as shown in Figure 9. You can add your own colors to the palette by sampling a color from an image, and you can also delete colors. When you add a swatch to the Swatches palette, Photoshop assigns a default name that has a sequential number, or you can name the swatch whatever you like. Photoshop places new swatches in the first available space at the end of the palette. You can view swatch names by clicking the Swatches palette list arrow, then clicking Small List. You can restore the default Swatches palette by clicking the Swatches palette list arrow, clicking Reset Swatches, then clicking OK.

FIGURE 8

Color Picker dialog box and Swatches palette

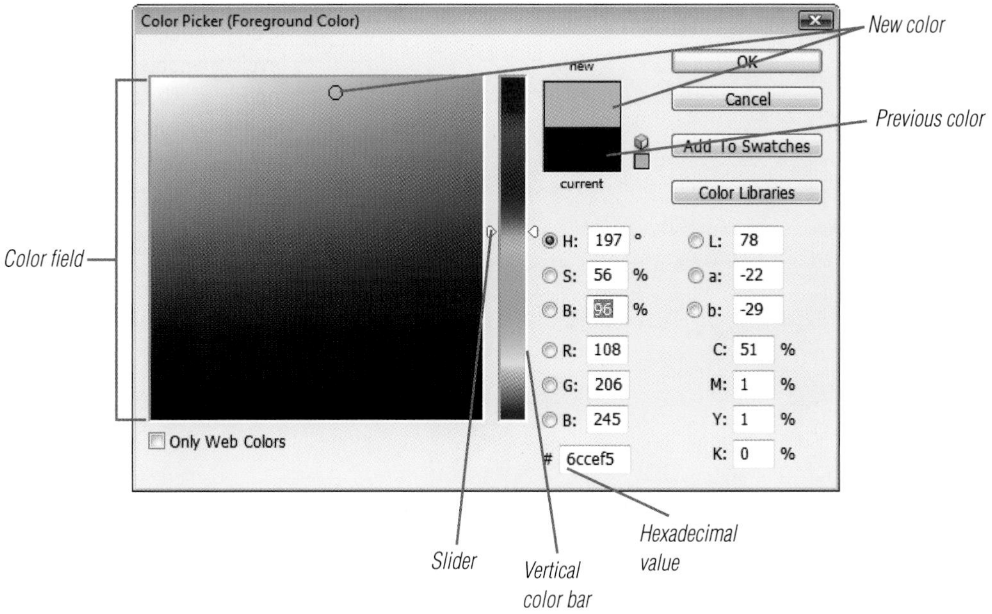

FIGURE 9

Color Picker dialog box and Swatches palette

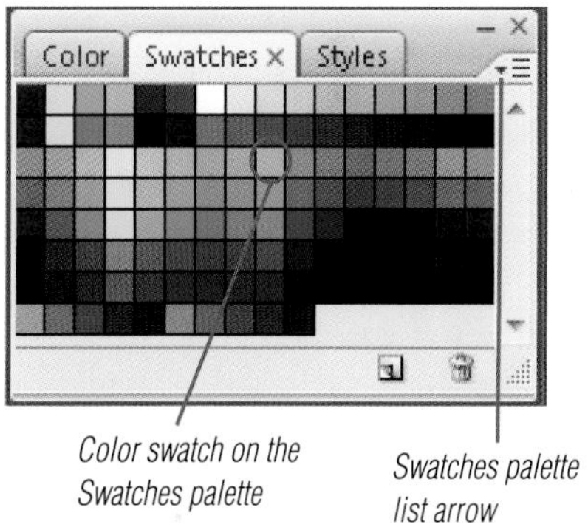

Select a color using the Color Picker dialog box

1. Click the **Set foreground color button** on the Tools palette, then verify that the H: option button is selected in the Color Picker dialog box.

2. Click the **R: option button**.

3. Click the **bottom-right corner** of the Color field (purple), as shown in Figure 10.

   TIP   If the Warning: out-of-gamut for printing indicator appears next to the color, then this color exceeds the printable range.

4. Click **OK**.

You opened the Color Picker dialog box, selected a different color palette, and then selected a new color.

Select a color using the Swatches palette

1. Click the **Swatches palette tab** 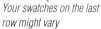.

2. Click the **second swatch from the left in the first row** (RGB Yellow), as shown in Figure 11.

   Did you notice that the foreground color on the Tools palette changed to a light, bright yellow?

3. Click the **Paint Bucket Tool** on the Tools palette (if it is not already selected).

4. Click the image with the **Paint Bucket pointer** , then compare your screen to Figure 12.

You opened the Swatches palette, selected a color, and then used the Paint Bucket Tool to change the background to that color.

FIGURE 10
Color Picker dialog box

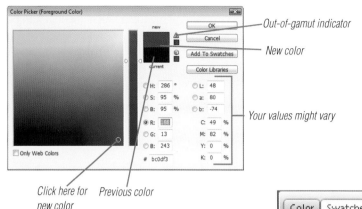

Out-of-gamut indicator

New color

Your values might vary

Click here for new color   Previous color

FIGURE 11
Swatches palette

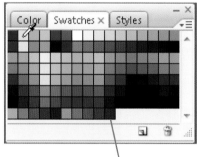

Your swatches on the last row might vary

FIGURE 12
New foreground color applied to Background layer

FIGURE 13

Swatch added to Swatches palette

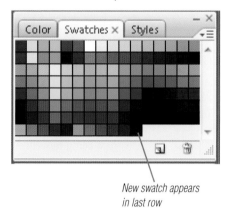

New swatch appears
in last row

1. Click the **Eyedropper Tool** 🖋 on the Tools palette.

2. Click **above and to the left of the rooster's eye** at coordinates **500 X/200 Y**.

3. Click the empty area to the right of the last swatch in the bottom row of the Swatches palette with the **Paint Bucket pointer** 🖐.

4. Type **Rooster eye surround** in the Name text box.

5. Click **OK** in the Color Swatch Name dialog box.

> TIP To delete a color from the Swatches palette, press [Alt] (Win) or [option] (Mac), position the pointer over a swatch, then click the swatch.

6. Save your work, then compare the new swatch on your Swatches palette to Figure 13.

You used the Eyedropper Tool to sample a color, and then added the color to the Swatches palette, and gave it a descriptive name. Adding swatches to the Swatches palette makes it easy to reuse frequently used colors.

Maintaining your focus

Adobe Photoshop is probably unlike any other program you've used before. In other programs, there's a central area on the screen where you focus your attention. In Photoshop, there's the workspace containing your document, but you've probably already figured out that if you don't have the correct layer selected in the Layer's palette, things won't quite work out as you expected. In addition, you have to make sure you've got the right tool selected in the Tools palette. You also need to keep an eye on the History palette. As you work on your image, it might feel a lot like negotiating a shopping mall parking lot on the day before Christmas: you've got to be looking in a lot of places at once.

PLACE A BORDER AROUND
AN IMAGE

What You'll Do

 In this lesson, you'll add a border to an image.

Emphasizing an Image

You can emphasize an image by placing a border around its edges. This process is called **stroking the edges**. The default color of the border is the current foreground color on the Tools palette. You can change the width, color, location, and blending mode of a border using the Stroke dialog box. The default stroke width is the setting last applied; you can apply a width from 1 to 16 pixels. The location option buttons in the dialog box determine where the border will be placed. If you want to change the location of the stroke, you must first delete the previously applied stroke, or Photoshop will apply the new border over the existing one.

Locking Transparent Pixels

As you modify layers, you can lock some properties to protect their contents. The ability to lock—or protect—elements within a layer is controlled from within the Layers palette, as shown in Figure 14. It's a good idea to lock transparent pixels when you add borders so that stray marks will

not be included in the stroke. You can lock the following layer properties:

- Transparency: Limits editing capabilities to areas in a layer that are opaque.
- Image: Makes it impossible to modify layer pixels using painting tools.
- Position: Prevents pixels within a layer from being moved.

QUICKTIP

You can lock transparency or image pixels only in a layer containing an image, not in one containing type.

FIGURE 14
Layer palette locking options

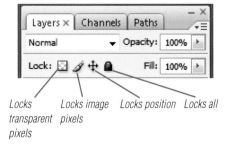

Locks transparent pixels   *Locks image pixels*   *Locks position*   *Locks all*

FIGURE 15
Locking transparent pixels

Lock transparent pixels button

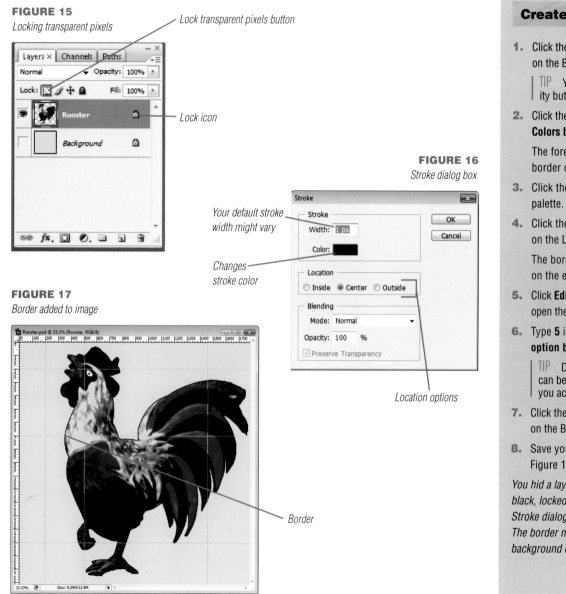

Lock icon

FIGURE 16
Stroke dialog box

Your default stroke
width might vary

Changes
stroke color

Location options

FIGURE 17
Border added to image

Border

Create a border

1. Click the **Indicates layer visibility button** 👁 on the Background layer on the Layers palette.

   TIP You can click the Indicates layer visibility button to hide distracting layers.

2. Click the **Default Foreground and Background Colors button** ⬛.

   The foreground color will become the default border color.

3. Click the **Rooster layer** on the Layers palette.

4. Click the **Lock transparent pixels button** ⊠ on the Layers palette. See Figure 15.

   The border will be applied only to the pixels on the edge of the rooster.

5. Click **Edit** on the menu bar, then click **Stroke** to open the Stroke dialog box. See Figure 16.

6. Type **5** in the Width text box, click the **Inside option button**, then click **OK**.

   TIP Determining the correct border location can be confusing. Try different settings until you achieve the look you want.

7. Click the **Indicates layer visibility button** ☐ on the Background layer on the Layers palette.

8. Save your work, then compare your image to Figure 17.

You hid a layer, changed the foreground color to black, locked transparent pixels, then used the Stroke dialog box to apply a border to the image. The border makes the image stand out against the background color.

BLEND COLORS USING THE
GRADIENT TOOL

What You'll Do

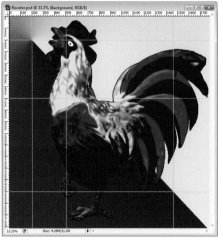

In this lesson, you'll create a gradient fill from a sampled color and a swatch, then apply it to the background.

Understanding Gradients

A **gradient fill**, or simply **gradient**, is a blend of colors used to fill a selection of a layer or an entire layer. A gradient's appearance is determined by its beginning and ending points, and its length, direction, and angle. Gradients allow you to create dramatic effects, using existing color combinations or your own colors. The Gradient picker, as shown in Figure 18, offers multi-color gradient fills and a few that use the current foreground or background colors on the Tools palette.

FIGURE 18
Gradient picker

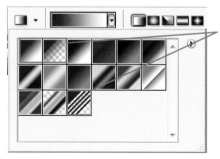

Gradient fills that use current foreground or background colors

Using the Gradient Tool

You use the Gradient Tool to create gradients in images. When you choose the Gradient Tool, five gradient styles become available on the options bar. These styles—Linear, Radial, Angle, Reflected, and Diamond—are shown in Figure 19. In each example, the gradient was drawn from 50 X/50 Y to 100 X/100 Y.

Customizing Gradients

Using the **gradient presets**—predesigned gradient fills that are displayed in the Gradient picker—is a great way to learn how to use gradients. But as you become more familiar with Photoshop, you might want to venture into the world of the unknown and create your own gradient designs. You can create your own designs by modifying an existing gradient using the Gradient Editor. You can open the Gradient Editor, shown in Figure 20, by clicking the selected gradient pattern that appears on the options bar. After it's open, you can use it to make the following modifications:

- Create a new gradient from an existing gradient.
- Modify an existing gradient.
- Add intermediate colors to a gradient.
- Create a blend between more than two colors.
- Adjust the opacity values.
- Determine the placement of the midpoint.

FIGURE 19
Sample gradients

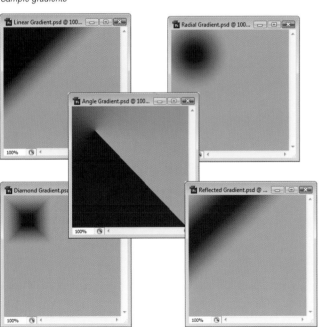

FIGURE 20
Gradient Editor dialog box

Drag slider to adjust opacity

Drag slider to adjust color

Adjust or delete colors and opacity values

Create a gradient from a sample color

1. Verify that the **Eyedropper Tool** 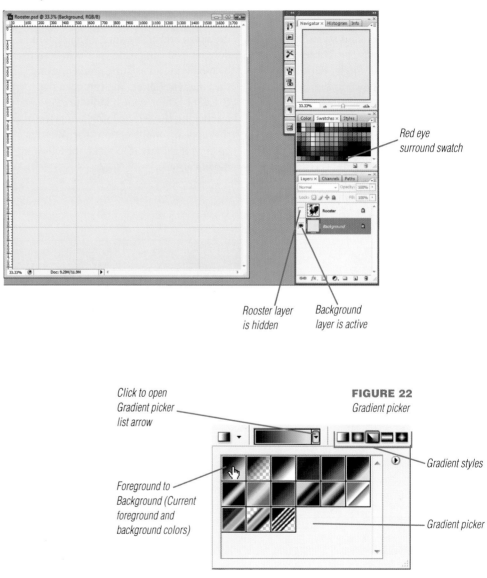 is selected.

2. Click the **yellow neck** in the image at coordinates **500 X/600 Y**.

   | TIP   To accurately select the coordinates, adjust the zoom factor as necessary.

3. Click the **Switch Foreground and Background Colors button** ↳ on the Tools palette.

4. Click **Rooster eye surround** on the Swatches palette (the new swatch you added) with the **Eyedropper pointer** .

5. Click the **Indicates layer visibility button** on the Rooster layer.

6. Click the **Background layer** on the Layers palette to make it active, as shown in Figure 21.

7. Click the **Paint Bucket Tool** on the Tools palette, then press and hold the mouse button until the list of hidden tools appears.

8. Click the **Gradient Tool** . on the Tools palette, then click the **Angle Gradient button** on the options bar (if it is not already selected).

9. Click the **Click to open Gradient picker list arrow** on the options bar, then click **Foreground to Background** (the first gradient fill in the first row), as shown in Figure 22.

You sampled a color on the image to set the background color, changed the foreground color using an existing swatch, selected the Gradient Tool, and then chose a gradient fill and style.

FIGURE 21
Rooster layer hidden

Red eye surround swatch

Rooster layer is hidden

Background layer is active

Click to open Gradient picker list arrow

FIGURE 22
Gradient picker

Gradient styles

Foreground to Background (Current foreground and background colors)

Gradient picker

FIGURE 23

Gradient fill applied to Background layer

1. Click the **Click to open Gradient picker list arrow** to close the Gradient picker.

   TIP You can also close the Gradient picker by pressing [Esc] (Win) or [esc] (Mac).

2. Drag the **Gradient pointer** -•- from **200 X/200 Y** to **1430 X/1500 Y** using the Info palette and the guides to help you create the gradient in the work area.

3. Click the **Indicates layer visibility button** on the Rooster layer.

   The Rooster layer appears against the new background, as shown in Figure 23.

   TIP It is a good practice to save your work early and often in the creation process, especially before making significant changes or printing.

4. Save your work.

You applied the gradient fill to the background. You can create dramatic effects using the gradient fill in combination with foreground and background colors.

ADD COLOR TO A
GRAYSCALE IMAGE

What You'll Do

 In this lesson, you'll convert an image to grayscale, change the color mode, then colorize a grayscale image using the Hue/Saturation dialog box.

Colorizing Options

Grayscale images can contain up to 256 shades of gray, assigning a brightness value from 0 (black) to 255 (white) to each pixel. Since the earliest days of photography, people have been tinting grayscale images with color to create a certain mood or emphasize an image in a way that purely realistic colors could not. To capture this effect in Photoshop, you convert an image to the Grayscale mode, then choose the color mode you want to work in before you continue. When you apply a color to a grayscale image, each pixel becomes a shade of that particular color instead of gray.

Converting Grayscale and Color Modes

When you convert a color image to grayscale, the light and dark values—called the **luminosity**—remain, while the color information is deleted. When you change from grayscale to a color mode, the foreground and background colors on the Tools palette change from black and white to the previously selected colors.

Converting a color image to black and white

Using the Black & White command, you can easily convert a color image to black and white. This feature lets you quickly make the color to black and white conversion while maintaining full control over how individual colors are converted. Tones can also be applied to the grayscale by applying color tones. To use this feature, click Image on the menu bar, point to Adjustments, then click Black & White. The Black & White command can also be applied as an Adjustment layer.

Colorizing a Grayscale Image

In order for a grayscale image to be colorized, you must change the color mode to one that accommodates color. After you change the color mode, and then adjust settings in the Hue/Saturation dialog box, Photoshop determines the colorization range based on the hue of the currently selected foreground color. If you want a different colorization range, you need to change the foreground color.

QUICKTIP

A duotone is a grayscale image that uses two custom ink colors. The final output is dramatically affected by both the order in which the inks are printed and the screen angles that you use.

Tweaking adjustments

Once you have made your color mode conversion to grayscale, you may want to make some adjustments. You can fine-tune the Brightness/Contrast, filters, and blending modes in a grayscale image.

FIGURE 24
Gradient Map dialog box

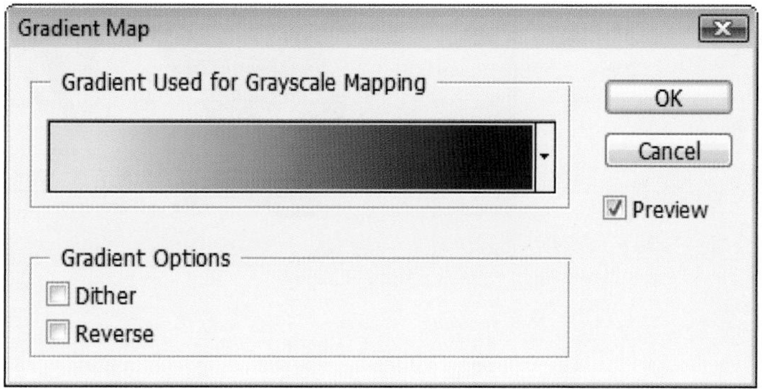

Applying a gradient effect

You can also use the Gradient Map to apply a colored gradient effect to a grayscale image. The Gradient Map uses gradient fills (the same ones displayed in the Gradient picker) to colorize the image, which can produce some stunning effects. You use the Gradient Map dialog box, shown in Figure 24, to apply a gradient effect to a grayscale image. You can access the Gradient Map dialog box using the Adjustments command on the Image menu.

Change the color mode

1. Open PS 4-2.psd from the drive and folder where you store your Data Files, save it as **Rooster Colorized**, then turn off the rulers if they are displayed.

2. Click **Image** on the menu bar, point to **Mode**, then click **Grayscale**.

3. Click **Flatten** in the warning box, then click **Discard**.

   The color mode of the image is changed to grayscale, and the image is flattened so there is only a single layer. All the color information in the image has been discarded.

4. Click **Image** on the menu bar, point to **Mode**, then click **RGB Color**.

   The color mode is changed back to RGB color, although there is still no color in the image. Compare your screen to Figure 25.

You converted the image to Grayscale, which discarded the existing color information. Then you changed the color mode to RGB color.

FIGURE 25
Image with RGB mode

Mode changed to RGB

Understanding the Hue/Saturation dialog box

The Hue/Saturation dialog box is an important tool in the world of color enhancement. Useful for both color and grayscale images, the saturation slider can be used to boost a range of colors. By clicking the Edit list arrow, you can isolate which colors (all, cyan, blue, magenta, red, yellow, or green) you want to modify. Using this tool requires patience and experimentation, but gives you great control over the colors in your image.

FIGURE 26
Hue/Saturation dialog box

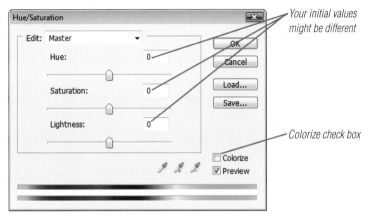

*Your initial values
might be different*

Colorize check box

FIGURE 27
Colorized image

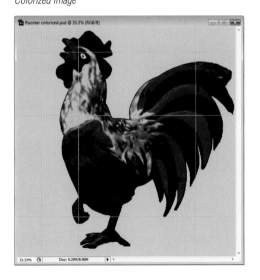

Colorize a grayscale image

1. Click **Image** on the menu bar, point to **Adjustments**, then click **Hue/Saturation** to open the Hue/Saturation dialog box, as shown in Figure 26.

2. Click the **Colorize check box** in the Hue/Saturation dialog box to add a check mark.

3. Drag the **Hue slider** until the text box displays **290**.

   TIP   You can also type values in the text boxes in the Hue/Saturation dialog box. Negative numbers must be preceded by a minus sign or a hyphen. Positive numbers can be preceded by an optional plus sign (+).

4. Drag the **Saturation slider** until the text box displays **40**.

5. Drag the **Lightness slider** until the text box displays **-15**.

6. Click **OK**.

7. Save your work, then compare your screen to Figure 27.

You colorized a grayscale image by adjusting settings in the Hue/Saturation dialog box.

Converting color images to grayscale
Like everything else in Photoshop, there is more than one way of converting a color image into one that is black & white. Changing the color mode to grayscale is the quickest method. You can also make this conversion through desaturation by clicking Image on the menu bar, pointing to Adjustments, then clicking Black & White, or Desaturate. Converting to Grayscale mode generally results in losing contrast, as does the desaturation method.

USE FILTERS, OPACITY, AND BLENDING MODES

What You'll Do

In this lesson, you'll adjust the brightness and contrast in the Chili Shop colorized image, apply a Sharpen filter, and adjust the opacity of the lines applied by the filter. You'll also adjust the color balance of the Chili Shop image.

Manipulating an Image

As you work in Photoshop, you might realize that some images have fundamental problems that need correcting, while others just need to be further enhanced. For example, you might need to adjust an image's contrast and sharpness, or you might want to colorize an otherwise dull image. You can use a variety of techniques to change the way an image looks. For example, you have learned how to use the Adjustments command on the Image menu to modify hue and saturation, but you can also use this command to adjust brightness and contrast, color balance, and a host of other visual effects.

Understanding Filters

Filters are Photoshop commands that can significantly alter an image's appearance. Experimenting with Photoshop's filters is a fun way to completely change the look of an image. For example, the Watercolor filter gives the illusion that your image was

Fixing blurry scanned images

An unfortunate result of scanning a picture is that the image can become blurry. You can fix this, however, using the Unsharp Mask filter. This filter both sharpens and smoothes the image by increasing the contrast along element edges. Here's how it works: the smoothing effect removes stray marks, and the sharpening effect emphasizes contrasting neighboring pixels. Most scanners come with their own Unsharp Masks built into the TWAIN driver, but using Photoshop, you have access to a more powerful version of this filter. You can use Photoshop's Unsharp Mask to control the sharpening process by adjusting key settings. In most cases, your scanner's Unsharp Mask might not give you this flexibility. Regardless of the technical aspects, the result is a sharper image. You can apply the Unsharp Mask by clicking Filter on the menu bar, pointing to Sharpen, then click Unsharp Mask.

painted using traditional watercolors. Sharpen filters can appear to add definition to the entire image, or just the edges. Compare the different Sharpen filters applied in Figure 28. The **Sharpen More filter** increases the contrast of adjacent pixels and can focus a blurry image. Be careful not to overuse sharpening tools (or any filter), because you can create high-contrast lines or add graininess in color or brightness.

Choosing Blending Modes

A **blending mode** controls how pixels are made either darker or lighter based on underlying colors. Photoshop provides a variety of blending modes, listed in Table 1, to combine the color of the pixels in the current layer with those in layer(s) beneath it. You can see a list of blending modes by clicking the Add a layer style button on the Layers palette.

Understanding Blending Mode Components

You should consider the following underlying colors when planning a blending mode: **base color**, which is the original color of the image; **blend color**, which is the color you apply with a paint or edit tool; and **resulting color**, which is the color that is created as a result of applying the blend color.

Softening Filter Effects

Opacity can soften the line that the filter creates, but it doesn't affect the opacity of the entire layer. After a filter has been applied, you can modify the opacity and apply a blending mode using the Layers palette or the Fade dialog box. You can open the Fade dialog box by clicking Edit on the menu bar, then clicking the Fade command.

Balancing Colors

As you adjust settings, such as hue and saturation, you might create unwanted imbalances in your image. You can adjust colors to correct or improve an image's appearance. For example, you can decrease a color by increasing the amount of its opposite color. You use the Color Balance dialog box to balance the color in an image.

FIGURE 28
Sharpen filters

Original image

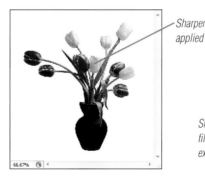
Sharpen filter applied

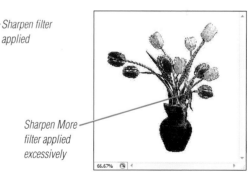
Sharpen More filter applied excessively

TABLE 1: Blending Modes

blending mode	description
Dissolve, Behind, and Clear modes	Dissolve mode creates a grainy, mottled appearance. The Behind mode paints on the transparent part of the layer—the lower the opacity, the grainier the image. The Clear mode paints individual pixels. All modes are available only when the Lock transparent pixels check box is *not* selected.
Multiply and Screen modes	Multiply mode creates semitransparent shadow effects. This mode assesses the information in each channel, then multiplies the value of the base color by the blend color. The resulting color is always *darker* than the base color. The Screen mode multiplies the value of the inverse of the blend and base colors. After it is applied, the resulting color is always *lighter* than the base color.
Overlay mode	Dark and light values (luminosity) are preserved, dark base colors are multiplied (darkened), and light areas are screened (lightened).
Soft Light and Hard Light modes	Soft Light lightens a light base color and darkens a dark base color. The Hard Light blending mode creates a similar effect, but provides greater contrast between the base and blend colors.
Color Dodge and Color Burn modes	Color Dodge mode brightens the base color to reflect the blend color. The Color Burn mode darkens the base color to reflect the blend color.
Darken and Lighten modes	Darken mode selects a new resulting color based on whichever color is darker—the base color or the blend color. The Lighten mode selects a new resulting color based on the lighter of the two colors.
Difference and Exclusion modes	The Difference mode subtracts the value of the blend color from the value of the base color, or vice versa, depending on which color has the greater brightness value. The Exclusion mode creates an effect similar to that of the Difference mode, but with less contrast between the blend and base colors.
Color and Luminosity modes	The Color mode creates a resulting color with the luminance of the base color, and the hue and saturation of the blend color. The Luminosity mode creates a resulting color with the hue and saturation of the base color, and the luminance of the blend color.
Hue and Saturation modes	The Hue mode creates a resulting color with the luminance of the base color and the hue of the blend color. The Saturation mode creates a resulting color with the luminance of the base color and the saturation of the blend color.

FIGURE 29

Brightness/Contrast dialog box

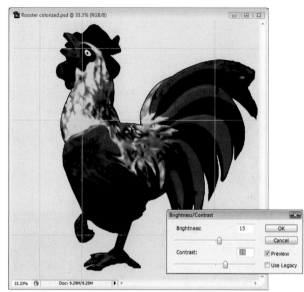

FIGURE 30

Shadow/Highlight dialog box

Adjust brightness and contrast

1. Click **Image** on the menu bar, point to **Adjustments**, then click **Brightness/Contrast** to open the Brightness/Contrast dialog box.

2. Drag the **Brightness slider** until **+15** appears in the Brightness text box.

3. Drag the **Contrast slider** until **+25** appears in the Contrast text box. Compare your screen to Figure 29.

4. Click **OK**.

You adjusted settings in the Brightness/Contrast dialog box. The image now looks much brighter, with a higher degree of contrast, which obscures some of the finer detail in the image.

Correcting shadows and highlights

The ability to correct shadows and highlights will delight photographers everywhere. This image correction feature (opened by clicking Image on the menu bar, pointing to Adjustments, then clicking Shadow/Highlight) lets you modify overall lighting and make subtle adjustments. Figure 30 shows the Shadow/Highlights dialog box with the Show More Options check box selected. Check out this one-stop shopping for shadow and highlight adjustments!

Work with a filter, a blending mode, and an opacity setting

1. Click **Filter** on the menu bar, point to **Sharpen**, then click **Sharpen More**.

   The border and other features of the image are intensified.

2. Click **Edit** on the menu bar, then click **Fade Sharpen More** to open the Fade dialog box, as shown in Figure 31.

3. Drag the **Opacity slider** until **45** appears in the Opacity text box.

   The opacity setting softened the lines applied by the Sharpen More filter.

4. Click the **Mode list arrow**, then click **Dissolve**.

   The Dissolve setting blends the surrounding pixels.

5. Click **OK**.

6. Save your work, then compare your image to Figure 32.

You applied the Sharpen More filter, then adjusted the opacity and changed the color mode in the Fade dialog box. The image looks crisper than before, with a greater level of detail.

FIGURE 31
Fade dialog box

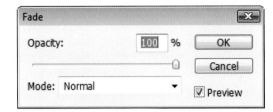

FIGURE 32
Image settings adjusted

FIGURE 33
Color Balance dialog box

FIGURE 34
Image with colors balanced

Adjust color balance

1. Switch to the Rooster image, with the Background layer active.

   The image you worked with earlier in this chapter becomes active.

2. Click **Image** on the menu bar, point to **Adjustments**, then click **Color Balance**.

3. Drag the **Cyan-Red slider** until **+70** appears in the first text box.

4. Drag the **Magenta-Green slider** until **–40** appears in the middle text box.

5. Drag the **Yellow-Blue slider** until **+35** appears in the last text box, as shown in Figure 33.

   Subtle changes were made in the color balance in the image.

6. Click **OK**.

7. Save your work, then compare your image to Figure 34.

You balanced the colors in the Chili Shop image by adjusting settings in the Color Balance dialog box.

MATCH COLORS

What You'll Do

 In this lesson, you'll make selections in source and target images, then use the Match Color command to replace the target color.

Finding the Right Color

If it hasn't happened already, at some point you'll be working on an image and wish you could grab a color from another image to use in this one. Just as you can use the Eyedropper Tool to sample any color in the current image for the foreground and background, you can sample a color from any other image to use in the current one. Perhaps the skin tones in one image look washed out: you can use the Match Color command to replace those tones with skin tone colors from another image. Or maybe the jacket color in one image would look better using a color in another image.

Using Selections to Match Colors

Remember that this is Photoshop, where everything is about layers and selections.

To replace a color in one image with one you've matched from another, you work with—you guessed it—layers and selections.

Suppose you've located the perfect color in another image. The image you are working with is the **target**, and that image that contains your perfect color is the **source**. By activating the layer on which the color lies in the source image, and making a selection around the color, you can have Photoshop match the color in the source and replace a color in the target. To accomplish this, you use the Match Color command, which is available through the Adjustments command on the Image menu.

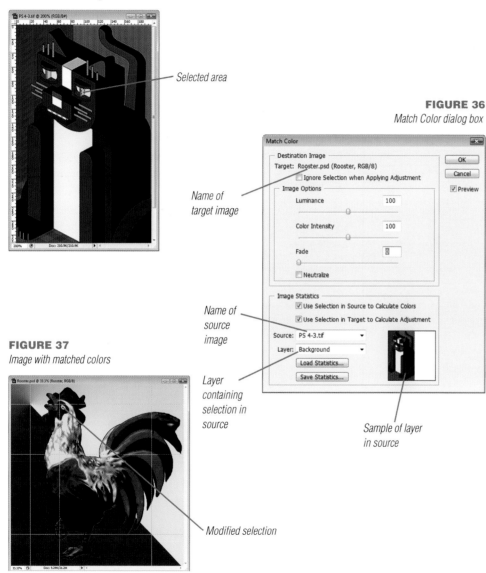

FIGURE 35
Selection in source image

Selected area

FIGURE 36
Match Color dialog box

Name of
target image

Name of
source
image

Layer
containing
selection in
source

Sample of layer
in source

FIGURE 37
Image with matched colors

Modified selection

1. Click the **Rooster layer** on the Layers palette, then zoom (once) into the eye of the rooster.

2. Click the **Magic Wand Tool** on the Tools palette.

3. Verify that the **Contiguous check box** on the options bar is selected, then set the **Tolerance** to **10**.

4. Click the image with the **Magic Wand pointer** on the white of the eye at approximately **550 X/210 Y**.

5. Open PS 4-3.tif from the drive and folder where you store your Data Files, zoom into the image if necessary, change the tolerance to **40** then click the **light green part of the cat's eye** (at **100 X/95 Y**) with the **Magic Wand pointer**. Compare your selection to Figure 35.

6. Activate the **Rooster image**, click **Image** on the menu bar, point to **Adjustments**, then click **Match Color**.

7. Click the **Source list arrow**, then click **PS 4-3.tif**. Compare your settings to Figure 36.

8. Click **OK**.

9. Deselect the selection, zoom out to **33.3%**, turn off the rulers, save your work, then compare your image to Figure 37.

10. Close all open images, then exit Photoshop.

You used the Match Color dialog box to replace a color in one image with a color from another image. The Match Color dialog box makes it easy to sample colors from other images, giving you even more options for incorporating color into an image.

Power User Shortcuts

to do this:	use this method:
Apply a sharpen filter	Filter ➢ Sharpen
Balance colors	Image ➢ Adjustments ➢ Color Balance
Change color mode	Image ➢ Mode
Choose a background color from the Swatches palette	[Ctrl]Color swatch (Win) ⌘ Color swatch (Mac)
Delete a swatch from the Swatches palette	[Alt], click swatch (Win) [option], click swatch (Mac)
Eyedropper Tool	⌕ or I
Fill with background color	[Shift][Backspace] (Win) ⌘ [delete] (Mac)
Fill with foreground color	[Alt][Backspace] (Win) option [delete] (Mac)
Gradient Tool	▦
Guide pointer	╫ or ╪
Hide a layer	👁

to do this:	use this method:
Hide or show rulers	[Ctrl][R] (Win) ⌘[R] (Mac)
Hide or show the Color Palette	[F6] (Win)
Lock transparent pixels check box on/off	/
Make Swatches palette active	Swatches ×
Paint Bucket Tool	◩ or G
Return background and foreground colors to default	◼ or D
Show a layer	▢
Show hidden Paint Bucket/ Gradient Tools	[Shift] G
Switch between open files	[Ctrl][Tab] (Win) [control tab] (Mac)
Switch Foreground and Background Colors	↰ or X

Key: Menu items are indicated by ➢ between the menu name and its command. Blue bold letters are shortcuts for selecting tools on the Tools palette.

Work with color to transform an image.

1. Start Photoshop.
2. Open PS 4-4.psd from the drive and folder where you store your Data Files, then save it as **Firetruck**.
3. Make sure the rulers appear in pixels, and that the default foreground and background colors display.
4. Use the Eyedropper Tool to sample the red color at 90 X/165 Y using the guides to help.
5. Use the Paint Bucket Tool to apply the new foreground color to the Background layer.
6. Undo your last step using either the Edit menu or the History palette.
7. Switch the foreground and background colors.
8. Save your work.

Use the Color Picker and the Swatches palette.

1. Use the Set foreground color button to open the Color Picker dialog box.
2. Click the R:, G:, and B: option buttons, one at a time. Note how the color palette changes.
3. With the B: option button selected, click the palette in the upper-left corner, then click OK.
4. Switch the foreground and background colors.
5. Add the foreground color (red) to the Swatches palette using a meaningful name of your choice.
6. Save your work.

Place a border around an image.

1. Make Layer 1 active (if it is not already active).
2. Revert to the default foreground and background colors.

3. Create a border by applying a 2-pixel outside stroke to the firetruck.
4. Save your work.

Blend colors using the Gradient Tool.

1. Change the foreground color to the fourth swatch from the right in the top row of the Swatches palette (35% Gray).
2. Switch foreground and background colors.
3. Use the new red swatch that you added previously as the foreground color.
4. Make the Background layer active.
5. Use the Gradient Tool, apply the Angle Gradient with its default settings, then using the guides to help, drag the pointer from 145 X/70 Y to 35 X/165 Y.
6. Save your work, and turn off the rulers display.

Add color to a grayscale image.

1. Open PS 4–5.psd, then save it as **Firetruck Colorized**.
2. Change the color mode to RGB Color.
3. Open the Hue/Saturation dialog box, then select the Colorize check box.
4. Drag the sliders so the text boxes show the following values: 175, 56, and –30, then click OK.
5. Save your work.

Use filters, opacity, and blending modes.

1. Use the Sharpen filter to sharpen the image.
2. Open the Fade Sharpen dialog box by using the Edit menu, change the opacity to 40%,

change the mode to Hard Light, then save your work.
3. Open the Color Balance dialog box.
4. Change the color level settings so the text boxes show the following values: +61, –15, and +20.
5. Turn off the rulers display if necessary.
6. Save your work.

Match colors.

1. Open PS 4-6.tif, then select the light green in the cat's eye.
2. Select the white areas of the fire truck in Firetruck.psd. (*Hint:* You can click on multiple areas using the Magic Wand Tool.)
3. Use the Match Color dialog box to change the white in Layer 1 of the Firetruck image to green (in the cat's eye). Compare your images to Figure 38.
4. Save your work.
5. Exit Photoshop.

FIGURE 38
Completed Skills Review

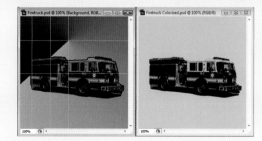

You are finally able to leave your current job and pursue your lifelong dream of opening a furniture repair and restoration business. While you're waiting for the laser stripper and refinisher to arrive, you start to work on a sign design.

1. Open PS 4-7.psd, substitte any missing fonts, then save it as **Furniture Wizard**.
2. Move the objects to any location to achieve a layout you think looks attractive and eye-catching.
3. Sample the blue pliers in the tool belt, then switch the foreground and background colors.
4. Sample the red tape measure in the tool belt.
5. Use any Gradient Tool to create an interesting effect on the Background layer.
6. Save the image, then compare your screen to the sample shown in Figure 39.

FIGURE 39
Completed Project Builder 1

You're painting the swing set at the PB&J Preschool, when you notice a staff member struggling to create a flyer for the school. Although the basic flyer is complete, it doesn't convey the high energy of the school. You offer to help, and soon find yourself in charge of creating an exciting background for the image.

1. Open PS 4-8.psd, update layers as needed, then save it as **Preschool**.
2. Apply a foreground color of your choice to the Background layer.
3. Add a new layer above the Background layer, then select a background color and apply a gradient you have not used before to the layer. (*Hint*: Remember that you can immediately undo a gradient that you don't want.)
4. Add the foreground and background colors to the Swatches palette.
5. Apply a Sharpen filter to the boy at blackboard layer and adjust the opacity of the filter.
6. Save your work.
7. Compare your screen to the sample shown in Figure 40.

FIGURE 40
Completed Project Builder 2

A local Top 40 morning radio show recently conducted a survey about chocolate, and discovered that only one in seven people knew about it health benefits. Now everyone is talking about chocolate. An interior designer wants to incorporate chocolates into her fall decorating theme, and has asked you to create a poster. You decide to highlight as many varieties as possible.

1. Open PS 4-9.psd, then save it as **Chocolate**.
2. If you choose, you can add any appropriate images that have been scanned or captured using a digital camera.
3. Activate the Background layer, then sample colors from the image for foreground and background colors. (*Hint*: Try to sample unusual colors, to widen your design horizons.)
4. Add the sampled colors to the Swatches palette.
5. Display the rulers, then move the existing guides to indicate the coordinates of the colors you sampled.
6. Create a gradient fill by using both foreground and background colors and the gradient style of your choice.
7. Defringe the Chocolate layer, if necessary.
8. Hide the rulers, save your work, then compare your image to the sample shown in Figure 41.

FIGURE 41
Completed Design Project

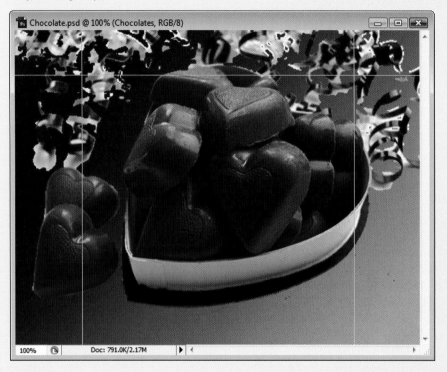

Depending on the size of your group, you can assign individual elements of the project to group members, or work collectively to create the finished product.

An educational toy and game store has hired your team to design a poster announcing this year's Most Unusual Hobby contest. After reviewing the photos from last year's awards ceremony, you decide to build a poster using the winner of the Handicrafts Award. You'll use your knowledge of Photoshop color modes to convert the color mode, adjust color in the image, and add an interesting background.

1. Open PS 4-10.psd, then save it as **Rubberband**.
2. Convert the image to Grayscale mode. (*Hint*: When Photoshop prompts you to flatten the layers, click Don't Flatten.)
3. Convert the image to RGB Color mode. (*Hint*: When Photoshop prompts you to flatten the layers, click Don't Flatten.)
4. Two or more people can colorize the image and adjust the Hue, Saturation, and Lightness settings as desired.
5. Adjust Brightness/Contrast settings as desired.
6. Adjust Color Balance settings as desired.
7. Two or more people can sample the image to create a new foreground color, then add a color of your choice as the background color.

8. Apply any two Sharpen filters and adjust the opacity for one of them.
9. Add a reflected gradient to the Background layer that follows the path of one of the main bands on the ball.

FIGURE 42
Completed Group Project

10. Save your work, then compare your image to the sample shown in Figure 42.
11. Be prepared to discuss the color-correcting methods you used and why you chose them.

5

PLACING TYPE IN
AN IMAGE

1. Learn about type and how it is created

2. Change spacing and adjust baseline shift

3. Use the Drop Shadow style

4. Apply anti-aliasing to type

5. Modify type with the Bevel and Emboss style

6. Apply special effects to type using filters

7. Create text on a path

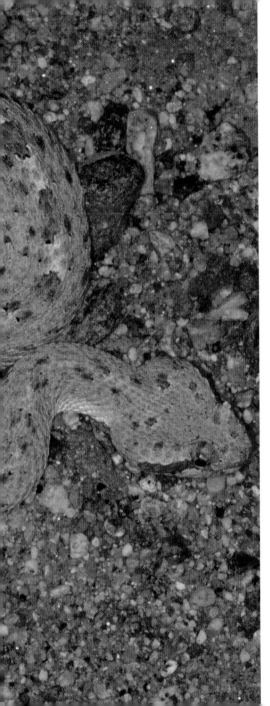

Learning About Type

Text plays an important design role when combined with images for posters, magazine and newspaper advertisements, and other graphics materials that need to communicate detailed information. In Photoshop, text is referred to as **type**. You can use type to express the ideas conveyed in a file's imagery or to deliver an additional message. You can manipulate type in many ways to reflect or reinforce the meaning behind an image. As in other programs, type has its own unique characteristics in Photoshop. For example, you can change its appearance by using different fonts (also called typefaces) and colors.

Understanding the Purpose of Type

Type is typically used along with imagery to deliver a message quickly and with flare. Because type is used sparingly (typically there's not a lot of room for it), its appearance is very important; color and imagery are often used to *complement* or *reinforce* the message within the text. Type should be limited, direct, and to the point. It should be large enough for easy reading, but should not overwhelm or distract from the central image. For example, a vibrant and daring advertisement should contain just enough type to interest the reader, without demanding too much reading.

Getting the Most Out of Type

Words can express an idea, but the appearance of the type is what drives the point home. After you decide on the content you want to use and create the type, you can experiment with its appearance by changing its **font** (characters with a similar appearance), size, and color. You can also apply special effects that make it stand out, or appear to pop off the page.

Tools You'll Use

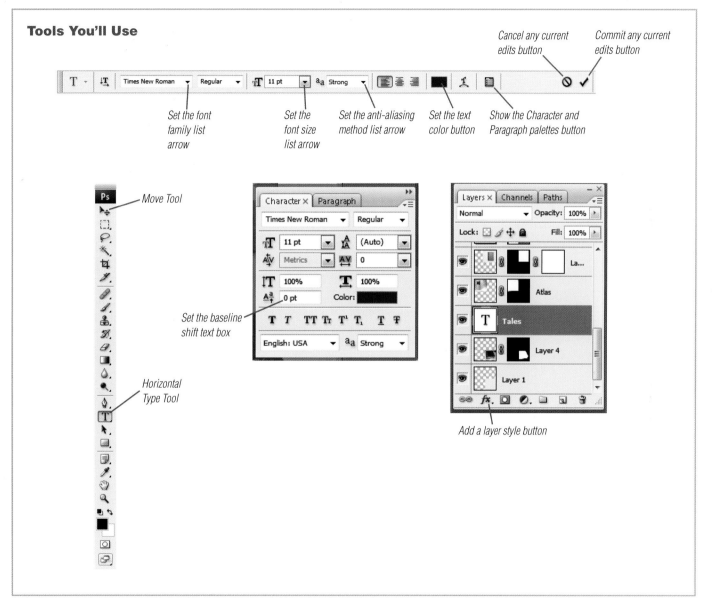

Cancel any current edits button

Commit any current edits button

Set the font family list arrow

Set the font size list arrow

Set the anti-aliasing method list arrow

Set the text color button

Show the Character and Paragraph palettes button

Move Tool

Horizontal Type Tool

Set the baseline shift text box

Add a layer style button

LEARN ABOUT TYPE AND
HOW IT IS CREATED

What You'll Do

Books.psd @ 66.7% (World Atlas, RGB/8#)

In this lesson, you'll create a type layer, then change the alignment, font family, size, and color of the type.

Introducing Type Types

Outline type is mathematically defined, which means that it can be scaled to any size without losing its sharp, smooth edges. Some programs, such as Adobe Illustrator, create outline type. **Bitmap type** is composed of pixels, and, like images, can develop jagged edges when enlarged. The type you create in Photoshop is initially outline type, but it is converted into bitmap type when you apply special filters. Using the type tools and the options bar, you can create horizontal or vertical type and modify font size and alignment. You use the Color Picker dialog box to change type color. When you create type in Photoshop, it is automatically placed on a new type layer on the Layers palette.

QUICKTIP

Keeping type on separate layers makes it much easier to modify and change positions within the image.

Getting to Know Font Families

Each **font family** represents a complete set of characters, letters, and symbols for a particular typeface. Font families are generally divided into three categories: serif, sans serif, and symbol. Characters in **serif fonts** have a tail, or stroke, at the end of some characters. These tails make it easier for the eye to recognize words. For this reason, serif fonts are generally used in text passages. **Sans serif fonts** do not have tails and are commonly used in headlines.

Symbol fonts are used to display unique characters (such as $, ÷, or ™). Table 1 lists commonly used serif and sans serif fonts. After you select the Horizontal Type Tool, you can change font families using the options bar.

Measuring Type Size

The size of each character within a font is measured in **points**. **PostScript**, a programming language that optimizes printed text and graphics, was introduced by Adobe in 1985. In PostScript measurement, one inch is equivalent to 72 points or six picas. Therefore, one pica is equivalent to 12 points. In traditional measurement, one inch is equivalent to 72.27 points. The default Photoshop type size is 12 points. In Photoshop, you have the option of using PostScript or traditional character measurement.

Acquiring Fonts

Your computer has many fonts installed on it, but no matter how many fonts you have, you probably can use more. Fonts can be purchased from private companies, individual designers, computer stores, catalog companies. Fonts are delivered on CD-ROM, DVDs, or over the Internet. Using your browser and your favorite search engine, you can locate Web sites that let you purchase or download fonts. Many Web sites offer specialty fonts, such as the Web site shown in Figure 1. Other Web sites offer these fonts free of charge or for a nominal fee.

TABLE 1: Commonly Used Serif and Sans Serif Fonts

serif fonts	sample	sans serif fonts	sample
Lucida Handwriting	*Adobe Photoshop*	Arial	Adobe Photoshop
Rockwell	Adobe Photoshop	Bauhaus	Adobe Photoshop
Times New Roman	Adobe Photoshop	Century Gothic	Adobe Photoshop

FIGURE 1
Font Web site

Courtesy of Betterfonts.com - http://betterfonts.com/

Create and modify type

1. Start Photoshop, open PS 5-1.psd from the drive and folder where you store your Data Files, update the text layers if necessary, then save the file as **Books**.

2. Display the document size in the status bar, and the rulers in pixels (if they are not already displayed).

   TIP You can quickly toggle the rulers on and off by pressing [Ctrl][R] (Win) or ⌘ [R] (Mac).

3. Click the **Default Foreground and Background Colors button** ▣ on the Tools palette.

4. Click the **Horizontal Type Tool** T. on the Tools palette.

5. Click the **Set the font family list arrow** on the options bar, click **Arial** (a sans-serif font), click the **Set the font style list arrow**, then click **Italic**.

   TIP If Arial is not available, make a reasonable substitution.

6. Click the **Center text button** ≡ on the options bar (if it is not already selected).

7. Click the **Set the font size list arrow** on the options bar, then click **24 pt** (if it is not already selected).

8. Click the image with the **Horizontal Type pointer** 〔T〕 in the center of the **brown area of the spine** just below the gold leaf at **160 X/130 Y**, then type **World**, press **[Shift] [Enter]** (Win) or **[shift][return]** (Mac), then type **Atlas**, as shown in Figure 2.

You created a type layer by using the Horizontal Type Tool on the Tools palette and modified the font family, alignment, and font size.

FIGURE 2
New type in image

New type

New type layer

Using the active layer palette background (Macintosh)
Icons used in Macintosh to identify type layers are similar to those found in Windows. In Macintosh, the active layer has the same Type and Layer style buttons. The active layer's background color is the same color as the Highlight Color. (In Windows, the active layer's background color is navy blue.)

FIGURE 3
Type with new color

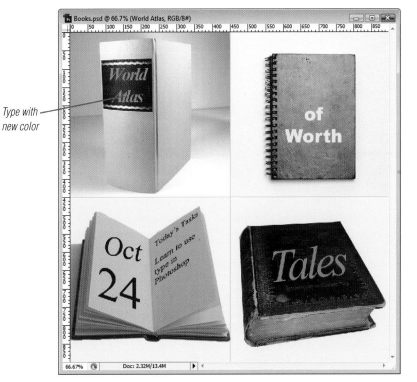

Type with
new color

1. Press **[Ctrl][A]** (Win) or ⌘ **[A]** (Mac) to select all the text.
2. Click the **Set the font family list arrow** on the options bar, scroll down, then click **Times New Roman**.

   TIP Click in the Set the font family text box and you can select a different font by typing the first few characters of the font name. Scroll through the fonts by clicking in the Set the font family text box, then pressing the [UpArrow] or [DownArrow].

3. Click the **Set the font style list arrow**, then click **Bold Italic**.
4. Click the **Set the text color button** ■ on the options bar.

   TIP Drag the Set text color dialog box out of the way if it blocks your view of the image.

   As you position the pointer over the image, the pointer automatically becomes an Eyedropper pointer.

5. Click the image with the **Eyedropper pointer** anywhere in the **letter "T"** in the book in the lower-right corner at approximately **600 X/610 Y**.

   The new color is now the active color in the Set text color dialog box.

6. Click **OK** in the Set text color dialog box.
7. Click the **Commit any current edits button** ✔ on the options bar.

   Clicking the Commit any current edits button accepts your changes and makes them permanent in the image.

8. Save your work, then compare your image to Figure 3.

You changed the font family, modified the color of the type by using an existing image color, and committed the current edits.

Using the Swatches palette to change type color

You can also use the Swatches palette to change type color. Select the type, then click a color on the Swatches palette. The new color that you click will appear in the Set foreground color button on the Tools palette and will be applied to type that is currently selected.

CHANGE SPACING AND
ADJUST BASELINE SHIFT

What You'll Do

 In this lesson, you'll adjust the spacing between characters and change the baseline of type.

Adjusting Spacing

Competition for readers on the visual landscape is fierce. To get and maintain an edge over other designers, Photoshop provides tools that let you make adjustments to your type, thereby making your type more distinctive. These adjustments might not be very dramatic, but they can influence readers in subtle ways. For example, type that is too small and difficult to read might make the reader impatient (at the very least), and he or she might not even look at the image (at the very worst). You can make finite adjustments, called **type spacing**, to the space between characters and between lines of type. Adjusting type spacing affects the ease with which words are read.

Understanding Character and Line Spacing

Fonts in desktop publishing and word processing programs use proportional spacing, whereas typewriters use monotype spacing. In **monotype spacing**, each character occupies the same amount of space. This means that wide characters such as "o" and "w" take up the same real estate on the page as narrow ones such as "i" and "l". In **proportional spacing**, each character can take up a different amount of space, depending on its width. **Kerning** controls the amount of space between characters and can affect several characters, a word, or an entire paragraph. **Tracking** inserts a *uniform* amount of space between selected characters. Figure 4 shows an example of type before and after it has been kerned.

The second line of text takes up less room and has less space between its characters, making it easier to read. You can also change the amount of space, called **leading**, between lines of type, to add or decrease the distance between lines of text.

Using the Character Palette

The **Character palette**, shown in Figure 5, helps you manually or automatically control type properties such as kerning, tracking, and leading. You open the Character palette from the options bar and the Dock.

Adjusting the Baseline Shift

Type rests on an invisible line called a **baseline**. Using the Character palette, you can adjust the **baseline shift**, the vertical distance that type moves from its baseline.

You can add interest to type by changing the baseline shift.

FIGURE 4
Kerned characters

FIGURE 5
Character palette

Kern characters

1. Click the **World Atlas type layer** on the Layers palette (if it is not already selected).

2. Click the **Horizontal Type Tool** T. on the Tools palette.

3. Click the **Toggle the Character and Paragraph palettes button** 🗔 on the options bar to open the Character palette.

   TIP You can close the Character palette by clicking the Collapse button in the upper-right corner of its title bar or by clicking the Character button. You can also open and close the Character palette by clicking the Character button on the vertical dock.

4. Click between "o" and "r" in the word "World."

   TIP You can drag the Character palette out of the way if it blocks your view.

5. Click the **Set the kerning between two characters list arrow** 🗚 -25 ▾ on the Character palette, then click **–25**.

   The spacing between the two characters decreases.

6. Click between "A" and "t" in the word "Atlas."

7. Click the **Set the kerning between two characters list arrow** 🗚 -25 ▾ , then click **–25**, as shown in Figure 6.

8. Click the **Commit any current edits button** ✔ on the options bar.

You modified the kerning between characters by using the Character palette.

FIGURE 6
Kerned type

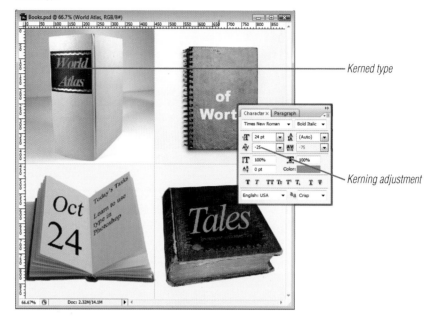

Kerned type

Kerning adjustment

Correcting spelling errors

Are you concerned that your gorgeous image will be ruined by misspelled words? Photoshop understands your pain and has included a spelling checker to make sure you are never plagued by incorrect spellings. If you want, the spelling checker will check the type on the current layer, or all the layers in the image. First, make sure the correct dictionary for your language is selected. English: USA is the default, but you can choose another language by clicking the Set the language on selected characters for hyphenation and spelling list arrow at the bottom of the Character palette. To check spelling, click Edit on the menu bar, then click Check Spelling. The spelling checker will automatically stop at each word not already appearing in the dictionary. One or more suggestions might be offered, which you can either accept or reject.

FIGURE 7
Select text color dialog box

Select text color:

new

OK

Cancel

New foreground color

Add To Swatches

current

Color Libraries

H: 355 °   L: 18

S: 61 %   a: 23

B: 29 %   b: 9

R: 75   C: 44 %

G: 29   M: 83 %

B: 33   Y: 69 %

4b1d21   K: 63 %

☐ Only Web Colors

*Selects the new
foreground color*

FIGURE 8
Type with baseline shifted

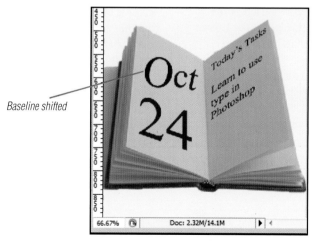

Baseline shifted

66.67%   Doc: 2.32M/14.1M

Shift the baseline

1. Double-click the **layer thumbnail** T on the Oct type layer, then use the **Horizontal Type Pointer** to select the "O".

2. Click the **Set the text color button** ■ on the options bar.

3. Click anywhere in the maroon area behind the World Atlas type, such as **210 X/180 Y**, compare your Select text color dialog box to Figure 7, then click **OK**.

4. Double-click **36** in the Set the font size text box on the Character palette, type **45**, double-click **0** in the Set the baseline shift text box on the Character palette, then type **−5**.

5. Click the **Commit any current edits button** ✔ on the options bar.

6. Click the **Toggle the Character and Paragraph palettes button** 🗐 on the options bar.

7. Save your work, then compare your screen to Figure 8.

You changed the type color, then adjusted the baseline of the first character in a word, to make the first character stand out.

USE THE DROP
SHADOW STYLE

What You'll Do

In this lesson, you'll apply the drop shadow style to a type layer, then modify drop shadow settings.

Adding Effects to Type

Layer styles (effects which can be applied to a type or image layer) can greatly enhance the appearance of type and improve its effectiveness. A type layer is indicated by the appearance of the T icon in the layer's thumbnail box. When a layer style is applied to any layer, the Indicates layer effects icon (*f*) appears in that layer when it is active. The Layers palette is a great source of information. You can see which effects have been applied to a layer by clicking the arrow to the left of the Indicates layer effects icon on the Layers palette if the layer is active or inactive. Figure 9 shows a layer that has two type layer styles applied to it. Layer styles are linked to the contents of a layer, which means that if a type layer is moved or modified, the layer's style will still be applied to the type.

Using the Drop Shadow

One method of placing emphasis on type is to add a drop shadow to it. A **drop shadow** creates an illusion that another colored layer of identical text is behind the selected type. The drop shadow default color is black, but it can be changed to another color using the Color Picker dialog box, or any of the other methods for changing color.

Applying a Style

You can apply a style, such as a drop shadow, to the active layer, by clicking Layer on the menu bar, pointing to Layer Style, then clicking a style. The settings

in the Layer Style dialog box are "sticky," meaning that they display the settings that you last used. An alternative method to using the menu bar is to select the layer that you want to apply the style to, click the Add a layer style button on the Layers palette, then click a style. Regardless of which method you use, the Layer Style dialog box opens. You use this dialog box to add all kinds of effects to type. Depending on which style you've chosen, the Layer Style dialog box displays options appropriate to that style.

QUICKTIP

You can apply styles to objects as well as to type.

Controlling a Drop Shadow

You can control many aspects of a drop shadow's appearance, including its angle, its distance behind the type, and the amount of blur it contains. The **angle** determines where the shadow falls relative to the text, and the **distance** determines how far the shadow falls from the text. The **spread** determines the width of the shadow

text, and the **size** determines the clarity of the shadow. Figure 10 shows samples of two different drop shadow effects. The first line of type uses the default background color (black), has an angle of 160 degrees, distance of 10 pixels, a spread of 0%, and a size of five pixels. The second line of type uses a purple background color, has an angle of 120 degrees, distance of 20 pixels, a spread of 10%, and a size of five pixels. As you modify the drop shadow, the preview window displays the changes.

FIGURE 9

Effects in a type layer

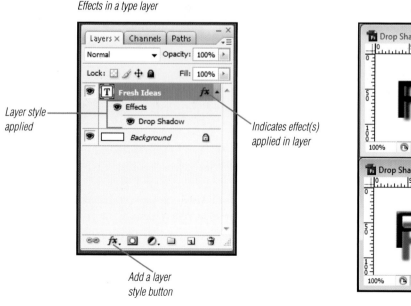

Layer style applied

Indicates effect(s) applied in layer

Add a layer style button

FIGURE 10

Sample drop shadows

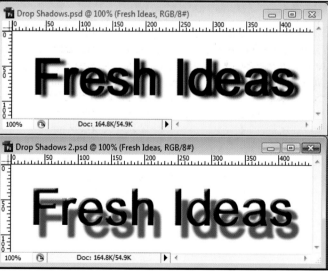

Add a drop shadow

1. Click the **layer thumbnail** on the Tales type layer.

2. Click the **Add a layer style button** *fx* on the Layers palette.

3. Click **Drop Shadow**.

4. Compare your Layer Style dialog box to Figure 11.

   The default drop shadow settings are applied to the type. Table 2 describes the drop shadow settings.

   TIP   You can also open the Layer Style dialog box by double-clicking a layer on the Layers palette.

You created a drop shadow by using the Add a layer style button on the Layers palette and the Layer Style dialog box.

FIGURE 11
Drop shadow settings

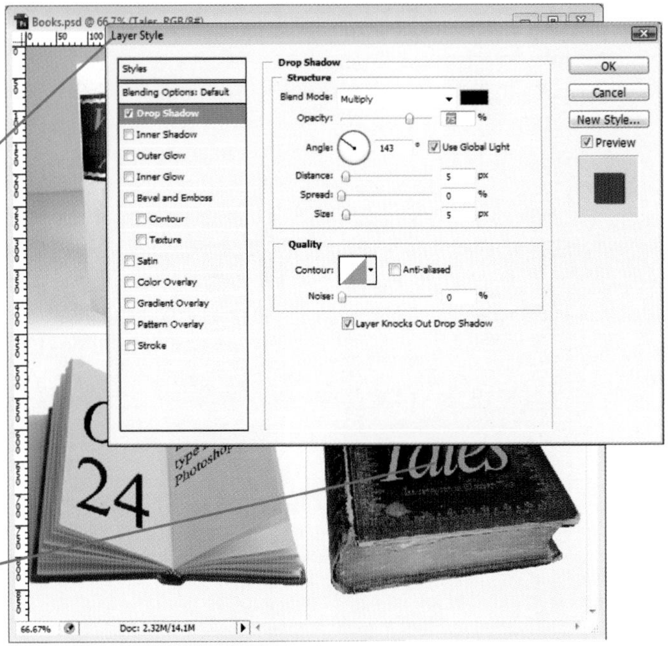

Layer Style dialog box positioned above modified type

Drop shadow applied to active type layer

TABLE 2: Drop Shadow Settings

setting	scale	explanation
Angle	0–360 degrees	At 0 degrees, the shadow appears on the baseline of the original text. At 90 degrees, the shadow appears directly below the original text.
Distance	0–30,000 pixels	A larger pixel size increases the distance from which the shadow text falls relative to the original text.
Spread	0–100%	A larger percentage increases the width of the shadow text.
Size	0–250 pixels	A larger pixel size increases the blur of the shadow text.

FIGURE 12
Layer Style dialog box

Angle text box

Distance text box

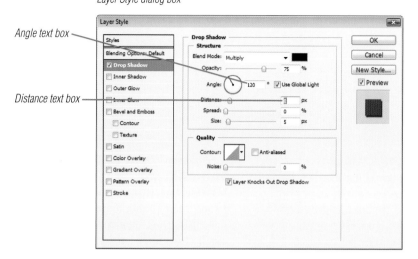

FIGURE 13
Drop shadow added to type layer

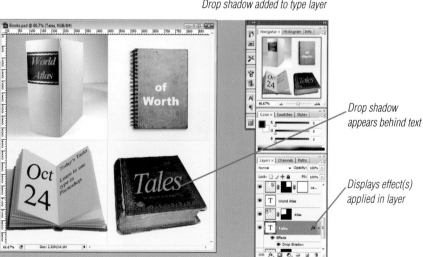

Drop shadow
appears behind text

Displays effect(s)
applied in layer

Modify drop shadow settings

1. Double-click the number in the Angle text box, then type **120**.

    Each style in the Layer Styles dialog box shows different options in the center section. These options are displayed as you click each style (in the Styles pane).

    TIP   You can also set the angle by dragging the dial slider in the Layer Style dialog box.

2. Double-click the number in the Distance text box, then type **8**. See Figure 12.

    TIP   You can create your own layer style in the Layer Style dialog box, by selecting style settings, clicking New Style, typing a new name or accepting the default, then clicking OK. The new style appears as a preset in the Styles list of the Layer Style dialog box.

3. Click **OK**, then compare your screen to Figure 13.

4. Click the **list arrow to the right of the Indicates layer effects icon** ▲ on the Tales layer to close the list.

5. Save your work.

You used the Layer Style dialog box to modify the settings for the drop shadow.

APPLY ANTI-ALIASING
TO TYPE

What You'll Do

In this lesson, you'll view the effects of the anti-aliasing feature, then use the History palette to return the type to its original state.

Eliminating the "Jaggies"

In the good old days of dot-matrix printers, jagged edges were obvious in many print ads. You can still see these jagged edges in designs produced on less sophisticated printers. To prevent the jagged edges (sometimes called "jaggies") that often accompany bitmap type, Photoshop offers an anti-aliasing feature. **Anti-aliasing** partially fills in pixel edges with additional colors, resulting in smooth-edge type and an increased number of colors in the image. Anti-aliasing is useful for improving the display of large type in print media; however, this can cause a file to become large.

Knowing When to Apply Anti-Aliasing

As a rule, type that has a point size greater than 12 should have some anti-aliasing method applied. Sometimes, smaller type sizes can become blurry or muddy when anti-aliasing is used. As part of the process, anti-aliasing adds intermediate colors to your image in an effort to reduce the jagged edges. As a designer, you need to weigh the following factors when determining if you should apply anti-aliasing: type size versus file size and image quality.

Understanding Anti-Aliasing

Anti-aliasing improves the display of type against the background. You can use five anti-aliasing methods: None, Sharp, Crisp, Strong, and Smooth. An example of each method is shown in Figure 14. The **None** setting applies no anti-aliasing, and can result in type that has jagged edges. The

Sharp setting displays type with the best possible resolution. The **Crisp** setting gives type more definition and makes type appear sharper. The **Strong** setting makes type appear heavier, much like the bold attribute. The **Smooth** setting gives type more rounded edges.

FIGURE 14
Anti-aliasing effects

Anti-aliasing method: None

Anti-aliasing method: Sharp

Anti-aliasing method: Crisp

Anti-aliasing method: Strong

Anti-aliasing method: Smooth

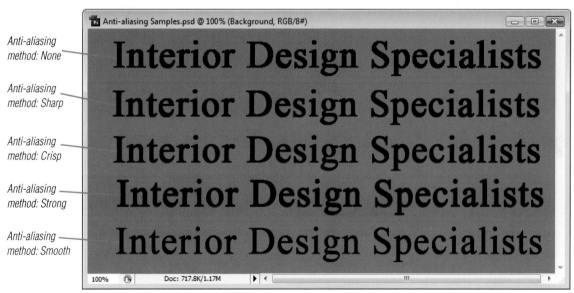

Apply anti-aliasing

1. Double-click the **layer thumbnail** on the Tales layer.

2. Click the **Set the anti-aliasing method list arrow** ᵃₐ Crisp ▾ on the options bar.

3. Click **Strong**, then compare your work to Figure 15.

4. Click the **Commit any current edits button** ✔ on the options bar.

You applied the Strong anti-aliasing setting to see how the setting affected the appearance of type.

FIGURE 15
Effect of Strong anti-aliasing

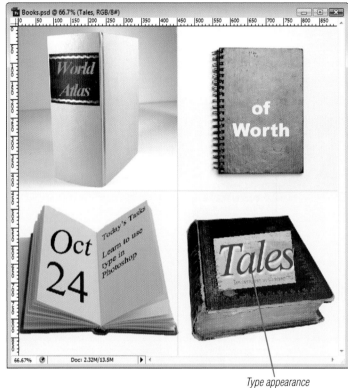

Type appearance altered

Different strokes for different folks

You're probably already aware that you can use different methods to achieve the same goals in Photoshop. For instance, if you want to see the type options bar, you can either double-click a type layer or single-click it, then click the Horizontal Type Tool. The method you use determines what you'll see in the History palette. Using the double-clicking method, a change in the anti-aliasing method will result in the following history state 'Edit Type Layer'. Using the single-clicking method to change to the anti-alias method to Crisp results in an 'Anti Alias Crisp' history state.

FIGURE 16

Deleting a state from the History palette

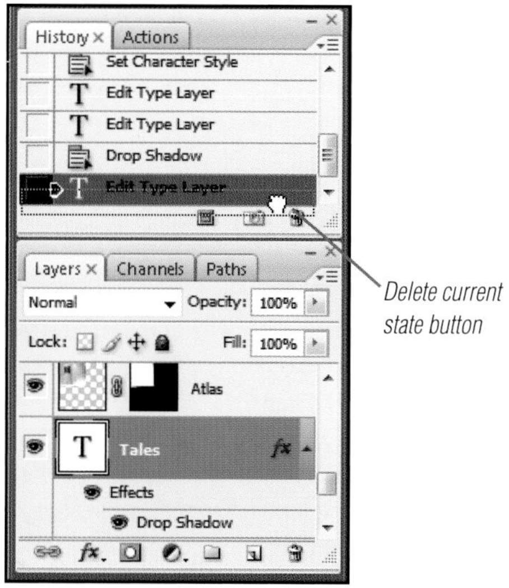

Delete current
state button

Undo anti-aliasing

1. Click **Window** on the menu bar, point to **Workspace**, then click **Legacy**.

   The palettes display in a format used by the previous version of Photoshop, allowing you to see the History palette.

2. Click the **Edit Type Layer state** listed at the bottom of the History palette, then drag it to the **Delete current state button** 🗑, as shown in Figure 16.

   > TIP   Various methods of undoing actions are reviewed in Table 3.

3. Save your work.

You deleted a state in the History palette to return the type to its original appearance. The History palette offers an easy way of undoing previous steps.

TABLE 3: Undoing Actions

method	description	keyboard shortcut
Undo	Edit ➢ Undo	[Ctrl][Z] (Win) ⌘ [Z] (Mac)
Step Backward	Click Edit on the menu bar, then click Step Backward	[Alt][Ctrl][Z] (Win) [option] ⌘ [Z] (Mac)
History palette	Drag state to the Delete current state button on the History palette	[Alt] 🗑 (Win) [option] 🗑 (Mac)

MODIFY TYPE WITH THE
BEVEL AND EMBOSS STYLE

What You'll Do

In this lesson, you'll apply the Bevel and Emboss style, then modify the Bevel and Emboss settings.

Using the Bevel and Emboss Style

You use the Bevel and Emboss style to add combinations of shadows and highlights to a layer and make type appear to have dimension and shine. You can use the Layer menu or the Layers palette to apply the Bevel and Emboss style to the active layer. Like all Layer styles, the Bevel and Emboss style is linked to the type layer that it is applied to.

Understanding Bevel and Emboss Settings

You can use two categories of Bevel and Emboss settings: structure and shading. **Structure** determines the size and physical properties of the object, and **shading** determines the lighting effects. Figure 17 contains several variations of Bevel and Emboss structure settings. The shading used in the Bevel and Emboss style determines how and where light is projected on

Filling type with imagery

You can use the imagery from a layer in one file as the fill pattern for another image's type layer. To create this effect, open a multi-layer file that contains the imagery you want to use (the source), then open the file that contains the type you want to fill (the target). In the source file, activate the layer containing the imagery you want to use, use the Select menu to select all, then use the Edit menu to copy the selection. In the target file, press [Ctrl] (Win) or ⌘ (Mac) while clicking the type layer to which the imagery will be applied, then click Paste Into on the Edit menu. The imagery will appear within the type.

the type. You can control a variety of settings, including the angle, altitude, and gloss contour, to create a unique appearance. The **Angle** setting determines where the shadow falls relative to the text, and the **Altitude** setting affects the amount of visible dimension. For example, an altitude of 0 degrees looks flat, while a setting of 90 degrees has a more three-dimensional appearance. The **Gloss Contour** setting determines the pattern with which light is reflected, and the **Highlight Mode** and **Shadow Mode** settings determine how pigments are combined. When the Use Global Light check box is selected, *all the type* in the image will be affected by your changes.

FIGURE 17
Bevel and Emboss style samples

Add the Bevel and Emboss style with the Layer menu

1. Click the **of Worth layer** on the Layers palette.

2. Click **Layer** on the menu bar, point to **Layer Style**, click **Bevel and Emboss,** then click **Bevel and Emboss** in the Styles column (if it is not already selected).

3. Review the Layer Style dialog box shown in Figure 18, then move the Layer Style dialog box (if necessary), so you can see the "of Worth" type.

You applied the Bevel and Emboss style by using the Layer menu. This gave the text a more three-dimensional look.

FIGURE 18
Layer Style dialog box

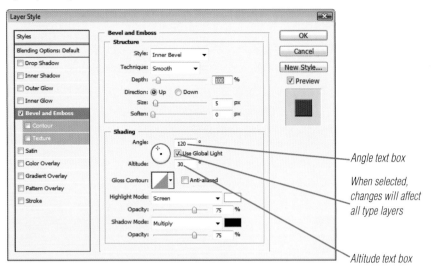

Angle text box

When selected, changes will affect all type layers

Altitude text box

Warping type

You can add dimension and style to your type by using the Warp Text feature. After you select the type layer you want to warp, click the Horizontal Type Tool on the Tools palette. Click the Create warped text button on the options bar to open the Warp Text dialog box. If a warning box opens telling you that your request cannot be completed because the type layer uses a faux bold style, click the Toggle the Character and Paragraph palettes button on the options bar, click the Character palette list arrow, click Faux Bold to deselect it, then click the Create warped text button again. You can click the Style list arrow to select from 15 available styles. After you select a style, you can modify its appearance by dragging the Bend, Horizontal Distortion, and Vertical Distortion sliders.

TABLE 4: Bevel and Emboss Structure Settings

sample	style	technique	direction	size	soften
1	Inner Bevel	Smooth	Up	5	1
2	Outer Bevel	Chisel Hard	Up	5	8
3	Emboss	Smooth	Down	10	3
4	Pillow Emboss	Chisel Soft	Up	10	3

FIGURE 19

Bevel and Emboss style applied to type

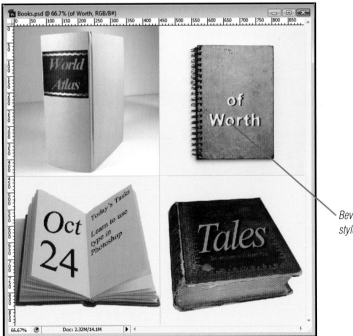

Bevel and Emboss
style applied to layer

Modify Bevel and Emboss settings

1. Double-click the number in the Angle text box, then type **163**.

   Some of the Bevel and Emboss settings are listed in Table 4.

   You can use the Layer Style dialog box to change the structure by adjusting style, technique, direction, size, and soften settings.

2. Double-click the **Altitude text box**, then type **20**.

3. Click **OK**, then compare your type to Figure 19.

4. Save your work.

You modified the default settings for the Bevel and Emboss style. Experimenting with different settings is crucial to achieve the effect you want.

APPLY SPECIAL EFFECTS TO
TYPE USING FILTERS

What You'll Do

 In this lesson, you'll rasterize a type layer, then apply a filter to it to change its appearance.

Understanding Filters

Like an image layer, a type layer can have one or more filters applied to it to achieve special effects and make your text look unique. Some filter dialog boxes have preview windows that let you see the results of the particular filter before it is applied to the layer. Other filters must be applied to the layer before you can see the results. Before a filter can be applied to a type layer, the type layer must first be **rasterized**, or converted to an image layer. After it is rasterized, the type characters *can no longer be edited* because it is composed of pixels, just like artwork. When a type layer is rasterized, the T icon in the layer thumbnail becomes an image thumbnail while the Effects icons remain on the type layer.

Creating Special Effects

Filters enable you to apply a variety of special effects to type, as shown in Figure 20. Notice that none of the original type layers on the Layers palette in Figure 20 display

the T icon in the layer thumbnail because the layers have all been rasterized.

QUICKTIP

Because you cannot edit type after it has been rasterized, you should save your original type by making a copy of the layer *before* you rasterize it, then hide it from view.

Producing Distortions

Distort filters let you create waves or curves in type. Some of the types of distortions you can produce include Glass, Pinch, Ripple, Shear, Spherize, Twirl, Wave, and Zigzag. These effects are sometimes used as the basis of a corporate logo. The Twirl dialog box, shown in Figure 21, lets you determine the amount of twirl effect you want to apply. By dragging the Angle slider, you control how much twirl effect is added to a layer. Most filter dialog boxes have Zoom In and Zoom Out buttons that make it easy to see the effects of the filter.

Placing Type in an Image   Chapter 5

Using Textures and Relief

Many filters let you create the appearance of textures and **relief** (the height of ridges within an object). One of the Stylize filters, Wind, applies lines throughout the type, making it appear shredded. The Wind dialog box, shown in Figure 22, lets you determine the kind of wind and its direction. The Texture filter lets you choose the type of texture you want to apply to a layer: Brick, Burlap, Canvas, or Sandstone.

Blurring Imagery

The Gaussian Blur filter softens the appearance of type by blurring its edge pixels. You can control the amount of blur applied to the type by entering high or low values in the Gaussian Blur dialog box. The higher the blur value, the blurrier the effect.

QUICKTIP

Be careful: too much blur applied to type can make it unreadable.

FIGURE 20
Sample filters applied to type

Colored pencil filter

Fresco filter

Gaussian blur filter

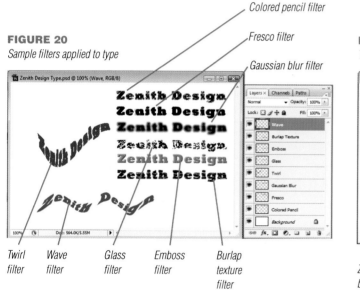

Twirl filter

Wave filter

Glass filter

Emboss filter

Burlap texture filter

FIGURE 21
Twirl dialog box

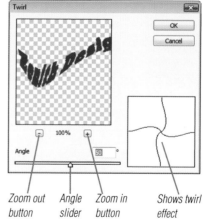

Zoom out button

Angle slider

Zoom in button

Shows twirl effect

FIGURE 22
Wind dialog box

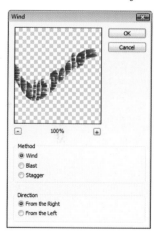

Rasterize a type layer

1. Click the **Learn to use type in Photoshop** layer on the Layers palette.

2. Click **Filter** on the menu bar, point to **Sharpen**, then click **Unsharp Mask**.

3. Click **OK** to rasterize the type and close the warning box shown in Figure 23.

   TIP   You can also rasterize a type layer by clicking Layer on the menu bar, pointing to Rasterize, then clicking Type.

   The Unsharp Mask dialog box opens.

You rasterized a type layer in preparation for filter application.

FIGURE 23
Warning box

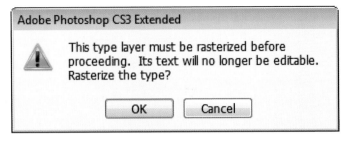

DESIGNTIP   Using multiple filters

Sometimes, adding one filter doesn't achieve the effect you had in mind. You can use multiple filters to create a unique effect. Before you try your hand at filters, though, it's a good idea to make a copy of the original layer. That way, if things don't turn out as you planned, you can always start over. You don't even have to write down which filters you used, because you can always look at the History palette to see which filters you applied.

FIGURE 24
Unsharp Mask dialog box

Slider

FIGURE 25
Type with Gaussian blur filter

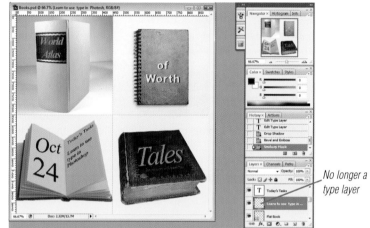

No longer a
type layer

Modify filter settings

1. Drag the default background patterns in the preview window of the dialog box to position the type so it is visible.

2. Drag the sliders in the Unsharp Mask dialog box until **250** appears in the Amount text box, **6** appears in the Radius pixels text box, and **85** appears in the Threshold levels text box, as shown in Figure 24.

3. Click **OK**.

4. Save your work. Compare your modified type to Figure 25.

You modified the Unsharp Mask filter settings to modify the appearance of the layer.

Creating a neon glow

Want to create a really cool effect that takes absolutely no time at all, and works on both type and objects? You can create a neon glow that appears to surround an object. You can apply the Neon Glow filter (one of the Artistic filters) to any flattened image. This effect works best by starting with any imagery—either type or objects—that has a solid color background. Flatten the image so there's only a Background layer. Click the Magic Wand Tool on the Tools palette, then click the solid color (in the background). Click Filter on the menu bar, point to Artistic, then click Neon Glow. Adjust the glow size, the glow brightness, and color, if you wish, then click OK. (An example of this technique is used in the Design Project at the end of this chapter.)

CREATE TEXT
ON A PATH

What You'll Do

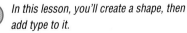

In this lesson, you'll create a shape, then add type to it.

Understanding Text on a Path

Although it is possible to create some cool type effects by adding layer styles such as bevel, emboss, and drop shadow, you can also create some awesome warped text. Suppose you want type to conform to a shape, such as an oval or a free-form you've drawn? No problem—just create the shape and add the text!

Creating Text on a Path

You start by creating a shape using one of the Photoshop shape tools on the Tools palette, and then adding type to that shape (which is called a path). Add type to a shape by clicking the Horizontal Type Tool. When the pointer nears the path, you'll see that it changes to the Type Tool pointer. Click the path when the Type Tool pointer displays and begin typing. You can change fonts, font sizes, add styles, and any other interesting effects you've learned to apply with type. As you will see, the type is on a path!

QUICKTIP

Don't worry when you see the outline of the path on the screen. The path won't print, only the type will.

FIGURE 26
Type on a path

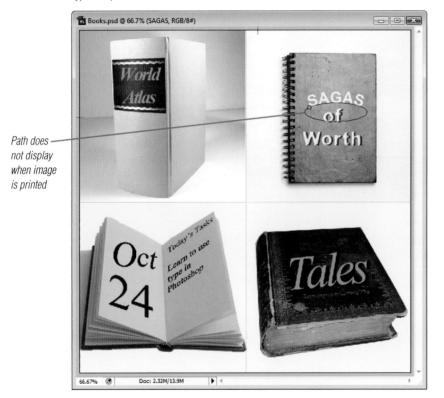

Path does
not display
when image
is printed

1. Click the **Rectangle Tool** on the Tools palette.

2. Click the **Ellipse Tool** on the options bar.

3. Click the **Paths button** on the options bar.

4. Drag the **Paths pointer** to encircle the word "of" from **610 X/190 Y** to **780 X/240 Y**.

5. Click the **Horizontal Type Tool** on the Tools palette.

6. Change the font to **Arial**, use the Bold font style, set the font size to **20** pt, then verify that the **Left align text button** is selected.

   TIP You can change to any point size by typing the number in the Set the font text box.

7. Click the **Horizontal Type pointer** at approximately **620 X/205 Y** on the left edge of the ellipse.

8. Change the font color by sampling the **white of Worth type,** turn on the Caps Lock, then type **SAGAS.**

9. Commit any current edits, then turn off the Caps Lock.

10. Hide the rulers, reset the palette locations, and save your work. Compare your image to Figure 26.

11. Close the Books.psd file and exit Photoshop.

You created a path using a shape tool, then added type to it.

Power User Shortcuts

to do this:	use this method:
Apply anti-alias method	ᵃₐ Crisp ▼
Apply Bevel and Emboss style	*fx.*, Bevel and Emboss
Apply blur filter to type	Filter ➤ Blur ➤ Gaussian Blur
Apply Drop Shadow style	*fx.*, Drop Shadow
Cancel any current edits	⊘
Change font family	Times New Roman ▼
Change font size	₸ 11 pt ▼
Change type color	■
Close type effects	▽
Commit current edits	✔
Display/hide rulers	[Ctrl][R] (Win) or ⌘[R] (Mac)
Erase a History state	Select state, drag to 🗑

to do this:	use this method:
Horizontal Type Tool	T. or T
Kern characters	A͟v -25 ▼
Move Tool	►⊕ or V
Open Character palette	▤
Save image changes	[Ctrl][S] (Win) or ⌘[S] (Mac)
See type effects (active layer)	▶
See type effects (inactive layer)	▶
Select all text	[Ctrl][A] (Win) or ⌘[A] (Mac)
Shift baseline of type	₸T 100%
Warp type	⫨

Key: Menu items are indicated by ➤ between the menu name and its command. Blue bold letters are shortcuts for selecting tools on the Tools palette.

Learn about type and how it is created.

1. Open PS 5-2.psd from the drive and folder where you store your Data Files, then save it as **ZD-Logo**.
2. Display the rulers with pixels.
3. Use the Horizontal Type Tool to create a type layer that starts at 45 X/95 Y.
4. Use a black 35 pt Lucida Sans font or substitute another font.
5. Type **Zenith**.
6. Use the Horizontal Type Tool and a 16 pt type size to create a type layer at 70 X/180 Y, then type **unique and uncompromising**.
7. Save your work.

Change spacing and adjust baseline shift.

1. Use the Horizontal Type Tool to create a new type layer at 205 X/95 Y.
2. Use a 35 pt Myriad font.
3. Type **Design**.
4. Select the Design type.
5. Change the type color to the color used in the lower-left background.
6. Change the type size of the Z and D to 50 pts.
7. Adjust the baseline shift of the Z and D to –5.
8. Save your work.

Use the Drop Shadow style.

1. Activate the Zenith type layer.
2. Apply the Drop Shadow style.
3. In the Layer Style dialog box, set the angle to 150°, then close the Layer Style dialog box.
4. Save your work.

Apply anti-aliasing to type.

1. Activate the Zenith type layer.
2. Change the Anti-Alias method to Smooth.
3. Save your work.

Modify type with the Bevel and Emboss style.

1. Activate the Design type layer.
2. Apply the Bevel and Emboss style.
3. In the Layer Style dialog box, set the style to Inner Bevel.
4. Set the angle to 150° and the altitude to 30°.
5. Close the Layer Style dialog box.
6. Activate the Zenith type layer.
7. Apply the Bevel and Emboss style.
8. Set the style to Inner Bevel.
9. Verify that the angle is set to 150° and the altitude is set to 30°.
10. Close the Layer Style dialog box.
11. Save your work.

Apply special effects to type using filters.

1. Apply a 1.0 pixel Gaussian Blur effect to the "unique and uncompromising" layer.
2. Save your work.

Create text on a path.

1. Use the Ellipse Tool to draw an ellipse from approximately 200 X/120 Y to 370 X/185 Y.
2. Click the line with the Horizontal Type Tool at 210 X/130 Y.
3. Type **Founded in 2002** using the second color swatch in the first row of the Swatches palette (RGB Yellow), in a 16 pt Arial font.
4. Change the anti-aliasing method to Crisp.
5. Change the opacity of the type on the path to 45%.
6. Turn off the ruler display.
7. Save your work, then compare your image to Figure 27.

FIGURE 27
Completed Skills Review Project

A local flower shop, Beautiful Blooms, asks you to design its color advertisement for the trade magazine, *Florists United*. You have already started on the image, and need to add some type.

1. Open PS 5-3.psd, then save it as **Beautiful Blooms Ad**.
2. Click the Horizontal Type Tool, then type **Beautiful Blooms** using a 55 pt Impact font in black.
3. Create a catchy phrase of your choice, using a 24 pt Verdana font.
4. Apply a drop shadow style to the name of the flower shop using the following settings: Multiply blend mode, 75% Opacity, 120%, 5 pixel distance, 0° spread, and 5 pixel size.
5. Apply a Bevel and Emboss style to the catch phrase using the following settings: Inner Bevel style, Smooth technique, 100% depth, Up direction, 5 pixel size, 0 pixel soften, 120° angle, 30° altitude, and using global light.
6. Compare your image to the sample in Figure 28.
7. Save your work.

FIGURE 28
Sample Project Builder 1

You are a junior art director for an advertising agency. You have been working on an ad that promotes milk and milk products. You have started the project, but still have a few details to finish up before it is complete.

1. Open PS 5-4.psd, then save it as **Milk Promotion**.
2. Create a shape using any shape tool, then use the shape as a text path and type a snappy phrase of your choosing on the shape.
3. Change the font color to any shade of red found in the Swatches palette.
4. Use a 24 pt Arial font in the style and color of your choice for the catch phrase type layer. (If necessary, substitute another font.)
5. Create a Bevel and Emboss style on the type layer, setting the angle to 100° and the altitude to 30°.
6. Compare your image to the sample in Figure 29.
7. Save your work.

FIGURE 29
Sample Project Builder 2

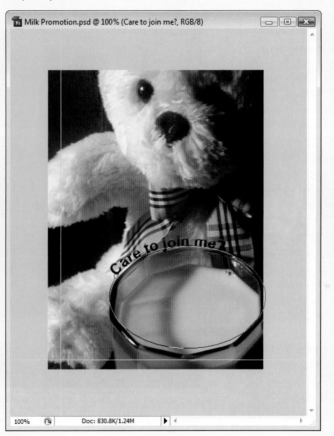

You are a freelance designer. A local clothing store, Attitude, is expanding and has hired you to work on an advertisement. You have already created the file, and inserted the necessary type layers. Before you proceed, you decide to explore the Internet to find information on using type to create an effective design.

1. Connect to the Internet and use your browser to find information about typography. (Make a record of the site you found so you can use it for future reference, if necessary.)
2. Find information about using type as an effective design element.
3. Open PS 5-5.psd, update the layers if necessary, then save the file as **Attitude**.
4. Modify the existing type by changing fonts, font colors, and font sizes.
5. Edit the type, if necessary, to make it shorter and clearer.
6. Rearrange the position of the type to create an effective design.
7. Add a Bevel and Emboss style using your choice of settings, then compare your image to the sample in Figure 30. (The fonts Mistral and Trebuchet MS are used in this image. Make substitutions if you don't have these fonts on your computer.)
8. Save your work.

FIGURE 30
Sample Design Project

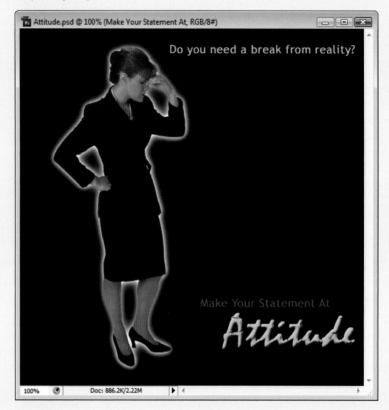

Depending on the size of your group, you can assign individual elements of the project to group members, or work collectively to create the finished product.

You have been hired by your community to create an advertising campaign that promotes tourism. Assemble a team and decide what aspect of the community you want to emphasize. Locate appropriate imagery (already existing on your hard drive, on the Web, your own creation, or using a scanner), then add type to create a meaningful Photoshop image.

1. Create an image with the dimensions 550 pixels × 550 pixels.
2. Save this file as **Community Promotion**.
3. Work together to locate imagery that exists on your hard drive, or from a digital camera or a scanner.
4. Add at least two layers of type in the image, using multiple font sizes. (Use any fonts available on your computer. You can use multiple fonts if you want.)
5. Add a Bevel and Emboss style to at least one type layer, and add a drop shadow to at least one layer. (*Hint*: You can add both effects to the same layer.)
6. Position type layers to create an effective design.
7. Compare your image to the sample in Figure 31.
8. Save your work.

FIGURE 31
Sample Group Project

Community Promotion.psd @ 33.3% (Find yourself , RGB/8)

Find yourself in beautiful Maui, Hawaii

33.33%   Doc: 8.03M/8.81M

chapter 1

GETTING STARTED
WITH ILLUSTRATOR

1. Create a new document

2. Explore the Illustrator window

3. Create basic shapes

4. Apply fill and stroke colors to objects

5. Select, move, and align objects

6. Transform objects

7. Make direct selections

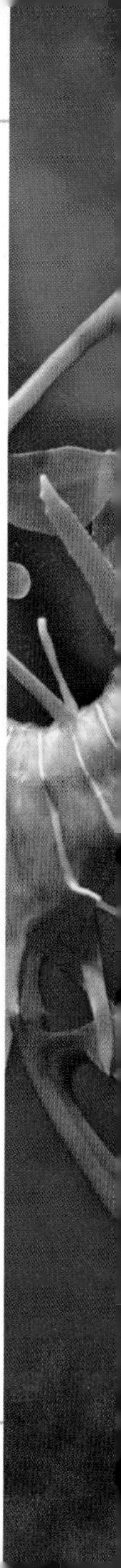

GETTING STARTED
WITH ILLUSTRATOR

Getting to Know Illustrator

Adobe Illustrator CS3 is a professional illustration software application created by Adobe Systems Incorporated. If this name is familiar to you, it's because Adobe is a leading producer of graphics software for the personal computer. Along with Illustrator, Adobe produces an entire suite of applications, including InDesign, Acrobat, Type Manager, Dreamweaver, and, of course, the revolutionary and award-winning Photoshop.

With Illustrator, you can create everything from simple graphics, icons, and text to complex and multilayered illustrations, all of which can be used within a page layout, in a multimedia presentation, or on the Web.

Adobe Illustrator offers dozens of essential tools. Using them in combination with various menu commands, you have the potential to create any illustration that your imagination can dream up. With experience, you will find that your ability to create complex graphics rests on your ability to master simple, basic operations.

Tools You'll Use

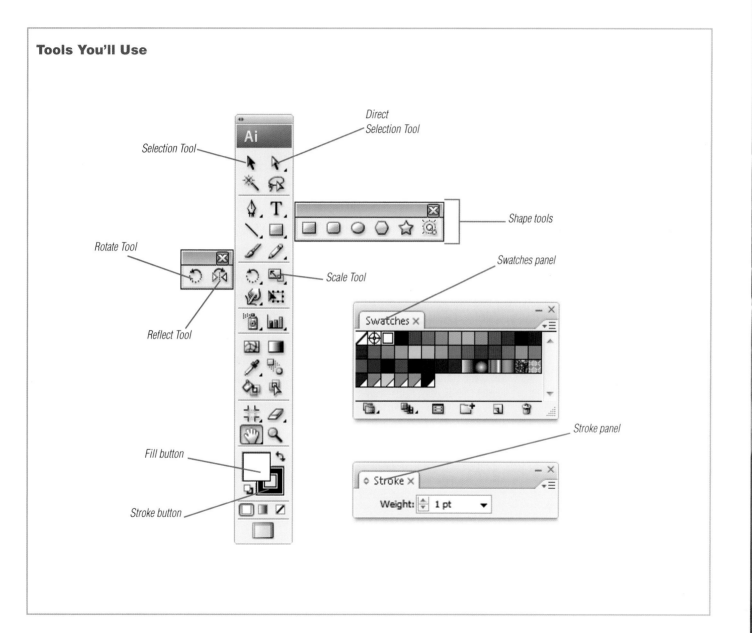

Selection Tool

Direct Selection Tool

Shape tools

Rotate Tool

Scale Tool

Swatches panel

Reflect Tool

Fill button

Stroke panel

Stroke button

CREATE A
NEW DOCUMENT

What You'll Do

In this lesson, you will start Adobe Illustrator and create a new document.

Creating a New Document

When you are ready to create a new document in Illustrator, you begin in the New Document dialog box. In the New document dialog box, you specify the name of the document, which will appear in the title bar of the new file. You also use this dialog box to specify the document size—the width and height of the finished document. In addition, you can choose the page orientation, landscape or portrait, and the unit of measure you would like the rulers to display. Some designers like to work with inches; others prefer points or picas. Finally, you can choose the appropriate color mode to work in based on the type of document you are creating.

Choosing Color Modes and Document Size

Generally, CMYK Color (Cyan, Magenta, Yellow, and Black) is the color mode used for print projects, and RGB Color (Red, Green, and Blue) is the color mode used for projects that will appear on a screen, such as a monitor, a television or on the Web. The

---

Understanding native file types

The "native" Illustrator file format is noted as an .ai suffix. Native Illustrator files can be opened and placed by other Adobe software packages, most notably Photoshop and InDesign. If you want to save an Illustrator file for use in QuarkXPress, save the file as an Illustrator EPS (Encapsulated PostScript). QuarkXPress does not recognize nor does it import Illustrator files in the native .ai format.

New Document Profile menu in the New Document dialog box allows you to specify the type of document you need. You can choose Print, Web, Mobile and Devices, Video and Film, as well as Basic CMYK or Basic RGB. The dialog box options available depend on which profile you choose. For example, if you choose Mobile and Devices, the Color Mode changes to RGB, the unit of measure changes to pixels, and the Device Central button appears in the dialog box. This button launches Adobe Device Central which allows you to preview how your document will appear on a specific device or mobile phone. If you choose Print, the dialog box will offer all of the appropriate settings for a document that you intend to print.

Another method for specifying the color mode is to click the expand button to the left of the word Advanced, click the Color Mode list arrow, then choose RGB or CMYK.

Once a document is created, you may change color mode settings by clicking File on the menu bar, pointing to Document Color Mode, then clicking CMYK Color or RGB Color. In addition, once a document is created, you can alter the current settings, such as the page size, in the Document Setup dialog box. The Document Setup command is on the File menu.

Choosing a Unit of Measure

Precision is often a key to good design, and many designers choose points and picas as units of measure. A point is $\frac{1}{72}$ of an inch. A pica is 12 points, or $\frac{1}{6}$ of an inch. Defining your artboard in points and picas versus inches is a matter of personal preference. As a designer, you're probably familiar with points and picas, but would you really refer to a letter-size page as 612×792 points? On the other hand, when working in inches, using measurements such as $\frac{29}{32}$ of

an inch would also be a bit ridiculous. Working with a combination of the two is the best bet; many designers work in points for text, rules, and strokes, but they define the page itself in inches.

To set your preferences for units of measure, click Edit on the menu bar, point to **Preferences,** then click Units & Display Performance. Click the General, Stroke, and Type list arrows to choose your preferred unit of measure. The General setting determines the units of measurement for the page and objects on the page.

You'll certainly want to measure your strokes and type in points. Imagine setting type in ¾" Garamond!

QUICKTIP
If you are using a Macintosh, you will find the Preferences command on the Illustrator menu.

Using the Illustrator Options dialog box

Let's say that you have a friend, a co-worker, or a client that you want to send an Illustrator CS3 file to, but you find out that he or she never upgraded to CS3, and therefore cannot open a CS3 file. No problem: Adobe Illustrator CS3 makes it easy to save files that previous versions of Illustrator can open. Simply click the Save As command on the File menu. In the Save As dialog box, choose Adobe Illustrator(*.AI), then click Save. The Illustrator Options dialog box opens. Click the Versions list arrow, then choose the format you need. CS Formats include CS3, CS2, and CS. Legacy Formats include Illustrator 3, 8, 9, 10, and Japanese Illustrator 3.

Create a new document (Windows)

1. Click the **Start button** 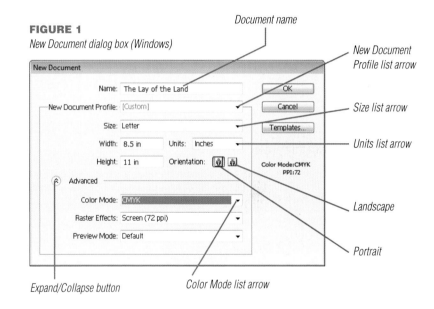 on the taskbar, point to **All Programs**, click **Adobe Design Premium CS3** (or the name of your Adobe suite), then click **Adobe Illustrator CS3**.

2. Click **File** on the menu bar, then click **New**.

3. Type **The Lay of the Land** in the New Document dialog box.

   TIP   Note that you have *named* the file in the New Document dialog box, but you have not yet *saved* it.

4. Click the **Size list arrow** to view the available sizes, then click **Letter**, if necessary.

5. Click the **Units list arrow**, then click **Inches**, if necessary.

   The size of your artboard will be 8.5" × 11".

6. Click the **left icon** next to Orientation (Portrait as opposed to Landscape) as the page orientation.

7. Click the **Expand button** to the left of the word Advanced, click the **Color Mode list arrow**, then click **CMYK**.

   Your New Document dialog box should resemble Figure 1.

8. Click **OK** to create a new document with these settings.

9. Click **File** on the menu bar, then click **Close**.

You started Illustrator in Windows, then created a new document.

FIGURE 1
New Document dialog box (Windows)

Document name

New Document Profile list arrow

Size list arrow

Units list arrow

Landscape

Portrait

Expand/Collapse button

Color Mode list arrow

FIGURE 2

New Document dialog box (Macintosh)

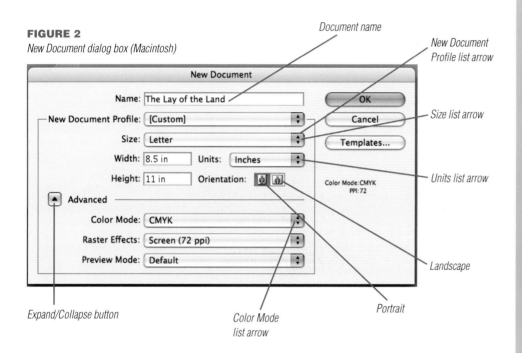

Document name

New Document Profile list arrow

Size list arrow

Units list arrow

Landscape

Portrait

Color Mode list arrow

Expand/Collapse button

1. Double-click the **hard drive icon**, then navigate to and double-click the **Adobe Illustrator CS3 folder**.

2. Double-click the **Adobe Illustrator CS3 program icon**.

3. Click **File** on the menu bar, then click **New**.

4. Type **The Lay of the Land** in the New Document dialog box, as shown in Figure 2.

   TIP Note that you have *named* the file in the New Document dialog box, but you have not yet *saved* it.

5. Click the **Size list arrow** to view the available sizes, then click **Letter**.

6. Click the **Units list arrow**, then click **Inches**, if necessary.

   The size of your artboard will be 8.5" × 11".

7. Click the **left icon** next to Orientation (Portrait as opposed to Landscape) as the page orientation.

8. Click the **Expand button** to the left of the word Advanced, click the **Color Mode list arrow**, then click **CMYK**.

   Your New Document window should resemble Figure 2.

9. Click **OK** to create a new document with these settings.

10. Click **File** on the menu bar, then click **Close**.

You started Illustrator in Macintosh, then created a new document.

EXPLORE THE ILLUSTRATOR WINDOW

What You'll Do

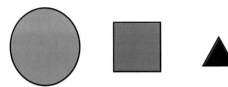

▶ In this lesson, you will learn about the key architecture of the Illustrator window and practice some basic Illustrator skills.

Touring the Illustrator Window

Let's take a few quick minutes to get the lay of the land. It all starts here. If you want to get really good at Illustrator, it's critical that you understand the workspace and learn to how to manage it. Nothing will slow down your work—and dull your creativity—like wrestling with the application. Moving around the window should become second nature.

The Illustrator window includes the artboard, scratch area, tools, and panels, all of which are described below. Figure 3 shows some of the more commonly used panels.

The **title bar** contains the name of your document, magnification level, and color mode; it also contains the Minimize, Maximize, and Close buttons.

The **menu bar** includes all of the Illustrator menus. If a menu item leads to a submenu, a black triangle will be positioned to the right. If a menu item requires you to enter information into a dialog box, it is followed by an ellipsis.

The **artboard** is the area, bound by a solid line, in which you create your artwork; the size of the artboard can be set as large as 227" × 227".

The **scratch area** is the area outside the artboard where you can store objects before placing them on the artboard; objects on the scratch area will not print.

The **Tools panel** contains tools that let you create, select, and manipulate objects in Illustrator. A tiny black triangle beside a tool indicates "hidden" tools behind that tool. Press and hold a tool to expose the panel of hidden tools behind it. Click the Tearoff tab (the tiny black triangle next to the last tool in the panel) to create a floating toolbar.

QUICKTIP

Click the tiny double arrows at the top left corner of the Tools panel to toggle between a two-column and a single-column Tools panel.

The **Zoom text box** in the lower-left corner of the Illustrator window displays the current magnification level. To the right of the Zoom text box is the Zoom menu, which you access by clicking the Zoom list arrow. The Zoom menu lets you choose another magnification level to work in.

FIGURE 3

Illustrator window

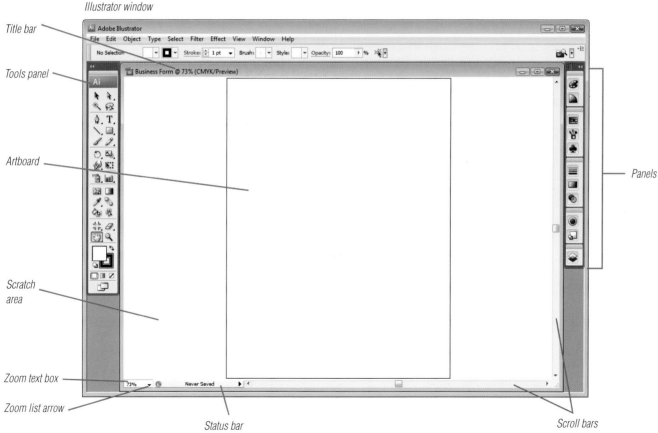

Title bar

Tools panel

Artboard

Scratch area

Zoom text box

Zoom list arrow

Panels

Status bar

Scroll bars

The **status bar** contains a list arrow menu from which you can choose a status line with information about the current tool, the date and time, the number of undo operations, or the document color profile.

Scroll bars run along the bottom and right sides of the window; dragging the scroll boxes, clicking in a scroll bar, or clicking the scroll arrows changes the portion of the document displayed in the Illustrator window.

Panels are windows containing features for modifying and manipulating Illustrator objects. Panels are arranged in groups on the right side of the workspace. Each group is represented by a button. Simply click a button to expand a panel group. To expand all panel groups, click the Expand

Dock button at the top of the panels window. To resize the panels section of the workspace, drag the three horizontal lines to the left of the Expand Dock button.

Panels are grouped by function. For example, if you click the Gradient button, you'll see that the Gradient panel is grouped with the Stroke and Transparency panels. If you drag the top of the panel group, all panels in the group move together. You can separate panels from their group by simply dragging the panel name tab to a new location. You can also merge two panels together by dragging a panel name tab into a new group.

Docking panels allows you to arrange multiple panels or panel groups vertically. Like grouped panels, docked panels move together. To dock a panel or a

panel group to another panel group, drag one of the panel name tabs in the group to the bottom edge of another panel then release when the bottom edge is highlighted.

Not all panels are represented by a button in the Illustrator workspace, however, all panels can be accessed using the Window menu.

QUICKTIP
You can temporarily hide all open panels and the Tools panel by pressing [Tab]. Press [Tab] again to show the panels and the Tools panel.

QUICKTIP
You can restore the default arrangement of panels by clicking Window on the menu bar, pointing to Workspace, then clicking [Basic].

Using Quick Keys in Illustrator

Along with the various tools in the Tools panel, the commands on the menu bar are essential for performing both basic and complex operations in Illustrator. Many of the menu commands execute operations that you will use over and over again. For that reason, it is a smart idea to memorize the quick keys associated with the basic menu commands. When a quick key is available, it is listed beside the command in the menu.

Many make the mistake of associating quick keys with speed. True, using quick keys will speed up your work, but the real benefit of them is that they help your work flow with fewer disruptions. Leaving your keyboard, moving your mouse, and clicking on a menu command all disrupt the essential flow of your work. Quick keys allow you to quickly execute a command without taking your hands off the keyboard or your eyes off the monitor.

Quick keys are not for 'power users' only; anybody working in Illustrator can use them beneficially. Make learning quick keys a fun part of your work; test yourself along the way. They are so intuitively assigned that you may even find yourself guessing correctly!

In Illustrator, the best place to start memorizing quick keys is with commands on the File, Edit, and Object menus, especially for Open, Close, Save,

Copy, Paste, Paste in Front, Paste in Back, Bring to Front, Send to Back, Hide, Show All, Lock, and Unlock All. When you have mastered those commands, keep going. Memorize the keys you use often, and know when to stop. There's no need to memorize the quick key for Clear Guides, unless you find yourself doing it often. Table 1 and Table 2 list essential quick keys for Windows and Macintosh.

QUICKTIP

Illustrator automatically positions crop marks at the artboard size that you choose. Although the crop marks may be turned on or off, Illustrator regards your artboard size as your trim size.

QUICKTIP

The imageable area is the area inside the dotted line on the artboard, which is intended to represent the portion of the page that a default printer can print. Most designers find this dotted line annoying and irrelevant. If it appears on your artboard, hide it by clicking Hide Page Tiling on the View menu.

Adobe Bridge

Adobe Bridge is a stand-alone software package that ships with the Adobe Creative Suite 3 software package. Bridge, as it is referred to, is a file browser that allows you to locate, browse, and organize files more easily. It also allows you to categorize your files using labels and/or ratings. Using the Sort command on the View menu, you can sort your files in a variety of ways, including, By Date created, By File size, and By Resolution. You can also choose numerous ways to view your files, such as thumbnails, details, or a slideshow. In Bridge, you can assign keywords and metadata to each file, and then search for assets with common metadata attributes, such as files that call for a certain font or a specific Pantone color. You can even embed additional metadata into an asset in Bridge—without opening the file itself. To do so, simply select the file in Bridge, click File on the menu bar, then click File Info. On the left side of the dialog box are many categories such as Camera Data 1, Camera Data 2, and so on. However, if you click the Description category, you can enter custom information about the file, such as the title, author, description, and keywords. This information will then appear in the Metadata and Keywords panels in the Bridge window. To access Bridge, click File on the menu bar, then click Browse. Adobe Bridge may be the perfect tool to help you organize your design projects.

TABLE 1: Essential Illustrator Quick Keys (Windows)

command	Windows	command	Windows
Outline	[Ctrl][Y]	Deselect	[Ctrl][Shift][A]
Preview	[Ctrl][Y]	Cut	[Ctrl][X]
Fit in Window	[Ctrl][0]	Copy	[Ctrl][C]
Zoom In	[Ctrl][+]	Paste	[Ctrl][V]
Zoom Out	[Ctrl][-]	Paste in Front	[Ctrl][F]
Access Hand Tool	[Spacebar]	Paste in Back	[Ctrl][B]
Access the Zoom In Tool	[Ctrl][Spacebar]	Undo	[Ctrl][Z]
Access the Zoom Out Tool	[Ctrl][Spacebar][Alt]	Redo	[Ctrl][Shift][Z]
Select All	[Ctrl][A]		

TABLE 2: Essential Illustrator Quick Keys (Macintosh)

command	Macintosh	command	Macintosh
Outline	⌘[Y]	Deselect	⌘[Shift][A]
Preview	⌘[Y]	Cut	⌘[X]
Fit in Window	⌘[0]	Copy	⌘[C]
Zoom In	⌘[+]	Paste	⌘[V]
Zoom Out	⌘[-]	Paste in Front	⌘[F]
Access Hand Tool	[Spacebar]	Paste in Back	⌘[B]
Access the Zoom In Tool	⌘[Spacebar]	Undo	⌘[Z]
Access the Zoom Out Tool	⌘[Spacebar][option]	Redo	⌘[Shift][Z]
Select All	⌘[A]		

Navigate the Illustrator artboard

1. Click **File** on the menu bar, click **Open**, navigate to the drive and folder where your Data Files are stored, click **AI 1-1.ai,** then click **Open**.

2. Click **File** on the menu bar, click **Save As**, type **Window Workout** in the File name text box (Win) or the Save As text box (Mac), navigate to the drive and folder where your Data Files are stored, click **Save**, then click **OK** to close the Illustrator Options dialog box.

3. Click **View** on the menu bar, note the quick key for Outline, then click **Outline**.

   As shown in Figure 4, outline mode shows the skeleton of your work—the lines and curves that you have drawn. Outline mode can be useful for making very specific selections.

4. Click **View** on the menu bar, note the quick key for Preview, then click **Preview**.

   Preview mode shows your work complete with the colors and styles you used.

5. Toggle between Outline and Preview modes using the quick key, then return to Preview mode.

6. Click the **Zoom Tool** 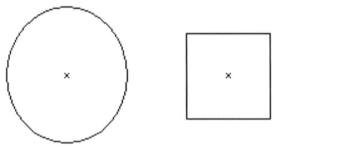 in the Tools panel, then click the **circle** four times.

7. Click the **Selection Tool** in the Tools panel.

8. Click **View** on the menu bar, then click **Fit in Window**.

(continued)

ILLUSTRATOR 1-14

FIGURE 4
Viewing the document in outline mode

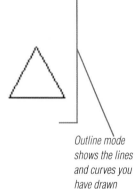

Outline mode shows the lines and curves you have drawn

FIGURE 5
Moving the artboard with the Hand Tool

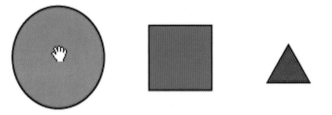

Exploring the Adobe Illustrator CS3 Welcome Screen

When you start Adobe Illustrator CS3 for the first time, the Welcome Screen appears. The Welcome Screen includes a list of recently opened items on the left and new document templates on the right, such as Web Document and Mobile and Devices Document. The From Template link leads you to pre-designed templates. Templates can really help you jump-start a project if you're running out of time or need some creative guidance. Templates are categorized into two categories: Basic and Inspiration. Within those categories are many more. For example, in the Basic category, you'll find more categories, such as Artist, Event Planning, and Environmental. Within those folders are the actual templates, such as Business Card, Post Card, or DVD Menu. If you've already installed CS3 and the Welcome Screen doesn't open when you launch the application, fear not! Simply click Help on the menu bar, then click Welcome Screen. If you do not want the Welcome Screen to appear each time, simply click the Don't show again check box in the Welcome Screen dialog box.

9. Click **View** on the menu bar, note the quick keys for Zoom In and Zoom Out, then release the menu.

10. Use the quick key to zoom in to 200%.

> TIP The current magnification level appears in the title bar and the Zoom text box in the lower-left corner.

11. Use the quick key to zoom out to 66.67%.

12. Press and hold **[Spacebar]**, notice that the pointer changes to the Hand Tool, then click and drag the **artboard** with the Hand Tool, as shown in Figure 5.

The Hand Tool allows you to move the artboard in the window; it's a great alternative to using the scroll arrows. Always press [Spacebar] to access the Hand Tool, so as not to interrupt the flow of your work.

You opened an Illustrator document, saved it with a new name, and used menu commands and the Zoom Tool to change the view size of the artboard. You then used the Hand Tool to move the artboard around.

Work with objects

1. Click **Select** on the menu bar, then click **All**.

2. Click **View** on the menu bar, then click **Show Bounding Box**, if necessary.

   The bounding box is a box with eight hollow white squares that appears around an object or objects when selected.

   | TIP   If you see Hide Bounding Box on the View menu, the bounding box is already showing.

3. Click **View** on the menu bar, then click **Hide Bounding Box**.

4. Click **Select** on the menu bar, then click **Deselect**.

5. Click the **Selection Tool** in the Tools panel, then move each shape—one at a time—to the bottom of the page.

6. Click **Edit** on the menu bar, then click **Undo Move**.

   The last object you moved returns to its original position, as shown in Figure 6.

7. Undo your last two steps.

8. Click **Edit** on the menu bar, then click **Redo Move**.

9. Redo your last two steps.

10. Click the **artboard** to deselect, click the **red triangle**, click **Edit** on the menu bar, then click **Copy**.

11. Click **Edit** on the menu bar, then click **Paste**.

(continued)

FIGURE 6
Undoing your last step

The last object you moved returns to its original position

FIGURE 7

Copying and pasting the triangle

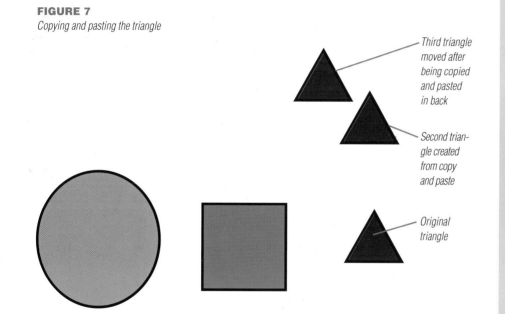

Third triangle moved after being copied and pasted in back

Second triangle created from copy and paste

Original triangle

12. Copy the new triangle, click **Edit** on the menu bar, then click **Paste in Back**.

The Paste in Front and Paste in Back commands paste the copied object from the clipboard in front or in back of a selected object. If you select an object, copy it, and then choose Paste in Front; the copy will be pasted above the original in exactly the same location.

13. Move the top red triangle to expose the copied triangle pasted behind it, as shown in Figure 7.

14. Save your work, then close Window Workout.

You moved objects on the artboard and used the Undo and Redo commands on the Edit menu. You selected and copied objects, then applied the Paste in Back command to position a copy precisely in back of its original.

CREATE BASIC SHAPES

What You'll Do

In this lesson, you will examine the differences between bitmap and vector graphics. Then you will use the Rectangle Tool to examine Illustrator's various options for creating simple vector graphics.

Getting Ready to Draw

Are you eager to start drawing? Do you want to create complex shapes, special effects, and original art? Perhaps you are a self-taught user of Adobe Illustrator, and your main interest is to graduate to advanced techniques and add a few of those cool special effects to your skill set. Good for you! Enthusiasm is priceless, and no book can teach it. So maintain that enthusiasm for this first exercise, where you'll start by creating a square. That's right . . . a square.

Consider for a moment that Mozart's sublime opera Don Giovanni is based primarily on eight notes, or that the great American novel can be reduced to 26 letters. Illustrator's foundation is basic geometric shapes, so let's start at square one . . . with one square.

Don't rush. As you work, keep in mind that the lessons you will learn here are the foundation of every great illustration.

Understanding Bitmap Images and Vector Graphics

Computer graphics fall into two main categories—bitmap images and vector graphics. To create effective artwork, you need to understand some basic concepts about the two.

Bitmap images are created using a square or rectangular grid of colored squares called **pixels**. Because pixels (a contraction of "picture elements") can render subtle gradations of tone, they are the most common medium for continuous-tone images—what you perceive as a photograph. All scanned images are composed of pixels. All "digital" images are composed of pixels. Adobe Photoshop is the leading graphics application for working with digital "photos." Figure 8 shows an example of a bitmap image. The number of pixels in a given inch is referred to as the image's **resolution**. To be effective, pixels must be small enough to create an image with the illusion of continuous tone. Thus, bitmap images are termed **resolution-dependent**.

The important thing to remember about bitmap images is that any magnification—resizing the image to be bigger—essentially means that fewer pixels are available per inch (the same number of pixels is now spread out over a larger area). This decrease in resolution will have a negative impact on the quality of the image. The greater the magnification, the greater the negative impact.

Graphics that you create in Adobe Illustrator are vector graphics. **Vector graphics** are created with lines and curves and are defined by mathematical objects called vectors. Vectors use geometric characteristics to define the object. Vector graphics consist of **anchor points** and **line segments**, together referred to as **paths**.

For example, if you use Illustrator to render a person's face, the software will identify the iris of the eye using the mathematical definition of a circle with a specific radius and a specific location in respect to other graphics. It will then fill that circle with the color you have specified. Figure 9 shows an example of a vector graphic.

Computer graphics rely on vectors to render bold graphics that must retain clean, crisp lines when scaled to various sizes. Vectors are often used to create logos or "line art," and they are the best choice for typographical work, especially small and italic type.

As mathematical objects, vector graphics can be scaled to any size. Because they are not created with pixels, there is no inherent resolution. Thus, vector graphics are termed **resolution-independent**. This means that any graphic that you create in Illustrator can be output to fit on a postage stamp or on a billboard!

FIGURE 8

Bitmap graphics

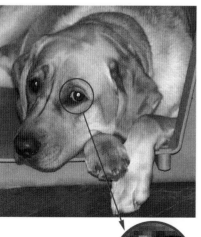

FIGURE 9

Vector graphics

Use the Rectangle Tool

1. Click **File** on the menu bar, click **New**, create a new document that is 8" wide by 8" in height, name the file **Basic Shapes**, then click **OK**.

2. Click **File** on the menu bar, click **Save As**, navigate to the drive and folder where your Data Files are stored, click **Save,** then click **OK** to close the Illustrator Options dialog box.

3. Click **View** on the menu bar, then click **Hide Page Tiling**, if necessary.

4. Click the **Swap Fill and Stroke button** 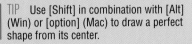 in the Tools panel to reverse the default colors.

   Your fill color should now be black and your stroke color white. The **fill color** is the inside color of an object. The **stroke color** is the color of the object's border or frame.

5. Click the **Rectangle Tool** in the Tools panel.

6. Click and drag the **Rectangle Tool pointer** on the artboard, then release the mouse to make a rectangle of any size.

7. Press and hold **[Shift]** while you create a second rectangle.

   Pressing and holding [Shift] while you create a rectangle constrains the shape to a perfect square, as shown in Figure 10.

8. Create a third rectangle drawn from its center point by pressing and holding **[Alt]** (Win) or **[option]** (Mac) as you drag the **Rectangle Tool pointer**.

   TIP Use [Shift] in combination with [Alt] (Win) or [option] (Mac) to draw a perfect shape from its center.

You created a freeform rectangle, then you created a perfect square. Finally you drew a square from its center point.

FIGURE 10
Creating a rectangle and a square

Square created by pressing [Shift] while creating a rectangle

FIGURE 11

Rectangle dialog box

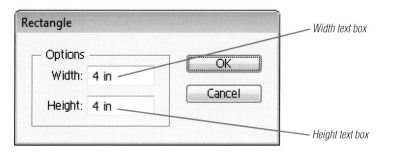

Width text box

Height text box

1. Click **Select** on the menu bar, then click **All** to select all of the objects.

2. Click **Edit** on the menu bar, then click **Cut** to remove the objects from the artboard.

3. Click anywhere on the artboard.

   When a shape tool is selected, clicking once on the artboard opens a dialog box, which allows you to enter precise information for creating the object. In this case, it opens the Rectangle dialog box.

4. Type **4** in the Width text box, type **4** in the Height text box, as shown in Figure 11, then click **OK**.

5. Save your work.

Using the Rectangle Tool, you clicked the artboard, which opened the Rectangle dialog box. You entered a specific width and height to create a perfect 4" square.

APPLY FILL AND STROKE
COLORS TO OBJECTS

What You'll Do

▶ *In this lesson you will use the Swatches panel to add a color fill to an object and apply a stroke as a border. Then you will use the Stroke panel to change the size of the default stroke.*

Activating the Fill or Stroke

The Fill and Stroke buttons are at the bottom of the Tools panel. To apply a fill or stroke color to an object, you must first activate the appropriate button. You activate either button by clicking it, which moves it in front of the other. When the Fill button is in front of the Stroke

button, the fill is activated, as shown in Figure 12. The Stroke button is activated when it is in front of the Fill button.

As you work, you will often switch back and forth, activating the fill and the stroke. Rather than using your mouse to activate the fill or the stroke each time, simply press [X] to switch between the two modes.

FIGURE 12
Fill and Stroke buttons

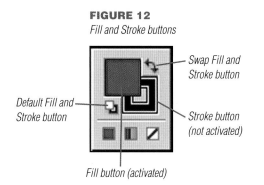

Swap Fill and
Stroke button

Default Fill and
Stroke button

Stroke button
(not activated)

Fill button (activated)

Getting Started with Illustrator

Applying Color with the Swatches Panel

The Swatches panel as shown in Figure 13, is central to color management in the application and a simple resource for applying fills and strokes to objects.

The panel has 48 preset colors, along with gradients and patterns. The swatch with the red line through it is called [None] and used as a fill for a "hollow" object. Any object without a stroke will always have [None] as its stroke color.

When an object is selected, clicking a swatch in the panel will apply that color as a fill or a stroke, depending on which of the two is activated in the Tools panel. You can also drag and drop swatches onto unselected objects. Dragging a swatch to an unselected object will change the color of its fill or stroke, depending upon which of the two is activated.

FIGURE 13
Swatches panel

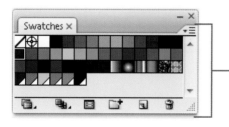

Forty-eight pre-set colors, gradients and patterns

Apply fill and stroke colors

1. Verify that the new square is still selected.

2. Click the **Swatches button**  to open the Swatches panel.

   Your Swatches panel may already be available.

3. Click any blue swatch in the Swatches panel to fill the square.

   Note that the Fill button in the Tools panel is now also blue.

   > TIP When you position your pointer over a color swatch in the Swatches panel, a tooltip appears that shows the name of that swatch.

4. Click the **Selection Tool** , then click anywhere on the artboard to deselect the blue square.

5. Drag and drop a **yellow swatch** onto the blue square.

   The fill color changes to yellow because the Fill button is activated in the Tools panel. Your colors may vary from the colors shown in the figures.

6. Press **[X]** to activate the Stroke button in the Tools panel.

7. Drag and drop the **red swatch** in the Swatches panel onto the yellow square.

   As shown in Figure 14, a red stroke is added to the square because the Stroke button is activated in the Tools panel.

8. Click the **Stroke button** ≡ to display the Stroke panel.

   Your Stroke panel may already be available.

   (continued)

FIGURE 14
Red stroke is added to the yellow square

FIGURE 15

Yellow square without a stroke

9. Select the square, click the **Weight list arrow** in the Stroke panel, then click **8 pt**.

   TIP Illustrator positions a stroke equally inside and outside an object. Thus, an 8 pt stroke is rendered with 4 pts inside the object and 4 pts outside.

10. Click **[None]** ◸ in the Swatches panel to remove the stroke from the square.

    Your screen should resemble Figure 15.

11. Save your work.

You filled the square with blue by clicking a blue swatch in the Swatches panel. You then changed the fill and stroke colors to yellow and red by dragging and dropping swatches onto the square. You used the Stroke panel to increase the weight of the stroke, then removed the stroke by choosing [None] from the Swatches panel.

SELECT, MOVE, AND
ALIGN OBJECTS

What You'll Do

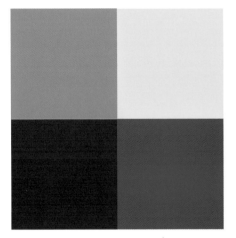

▶ *In this lesson, you will use the Selection Tool in combination with Smart Guides to move, copy, and align four squares.*

Selecting and Moving Objects

When it comes to accuracy, consider that Illustrator can move objects incrementally by fractions of a point—which itself is a tiny fraction of an inch! That level of precision is key when moving and positioning objects.

Before you can move or modify an Illustrator object, you must identify it by selecting it with a selection tool, menu item, or command key. When working with simple illustrations that contain few objects, selecting is usually simple, but it can become very tricky in complex illustrations, especially those containing a large number of small objects positioned closely together.

Two very basic ways to move objects are by clicking and dragging or by using the arrow keys, which by default move a selected item in 1-pt increments. Pressing [Shift] when dragging an

object constrains the movement to the horizontal, the vertical, and 45° diagonals. Pressing [Alt] (Win) or [option] (Mac) when dragging an object creates a copy of the object.

Grouping Objects

Many of the illustrations you create will be composed of a number of small objects. Once you have established the relationships among those objects, grouping them allows you to select them all with one click of the Selection Tool and then move or modify them simultaneously. To group objects, click them, click Object on the menu bar, then click Group.

Making a Marquee Selection with the Selection Tool

By now, you're familiar with using the Selection Tool to select objects. You can also use the Selection Tool to create a marquee selection, a dotted rectangle that

disappears as soon as you release the mouse. Any object that the marquee touches before you release the mouse will be selected. Marquee selections are very useful for both quick selections and precise selections. Practice, and make this part of your skill set.

Working with Smart Guides

Smart Guides are temporary guides that can be turned on and off on the View menu. Smart Guides help you move and align objects in relation to other objects or in relation to the artboard. With Smart Guides turned on, you will see words, called Smart Guides, that identify visible or invisible objects, page boundaries, intersections, anchor points, paths, and center points as you move your mouse along the objects on the artboard. When you move an object, Smart Guides give you a visual reference for precise alignment, as shown in Figure 16. For example, if you want to align two squares exactly side by side, Smart Guides will signal you when the two items come into contact, using the word "intersect."

FIGURE 16
Using Smart Guides

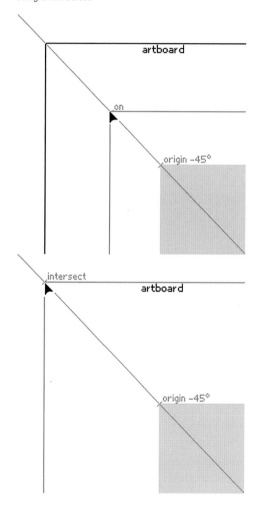

Select and move an object using Smart Guides

1. Click **View** on the menu bar, then click **Fit in Window**.

2. Click **View** on the menu bar, then verify that both Smart Guides and Snap to Point are checked by verifying that there is a check mark to the left of each menu item.

    TIP If you do not see a check mark next to Smart Guides or Snap to Point, click View on the menu bar, then click each item, one at a time, to turn these two features on.

    Snap to Point automatically aligns anchor points when they get close together. When dragging an object, you'll see it "snap" to align itself with a nearby object (or guide).

3. Click the **Selection Tool** in the Tools panel, then click the **yellow square**.

4. Identify the anchor points, paths, and center point, as shown in Figure 17.

5. Move the Selection Tool pointer over the anchor points, over the paths that connect the points, and over the center point.

6. Position the pointer over the top-left anchor point, click and drag so that the anchor point aligns with the top-left corner of the art-board, as shown in Figure 18, then release the mouse.

    The Smart Guide changes from "anchor" to "intersect" when the two corners are aligned.

You used the Selection Tool in combination with Smart Guides to position an object exactly at the top-left corner of the artboard.

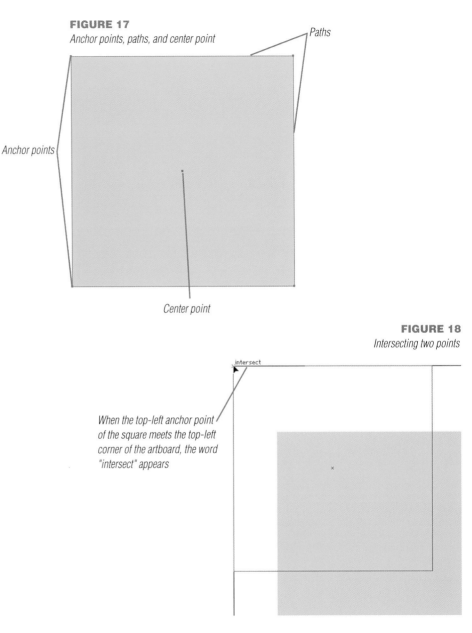

FIGURE 17
Anchor points, paths, and center point

Paths

Anchor points

Center point

FIGURE 18
Intersecting two points

intersect

When the top-left anchor point of the square meets the top-left corner of the artboard, the word "intersect" appears

Getting Started with Illustrator

FIGURE 19
Duplicating the square

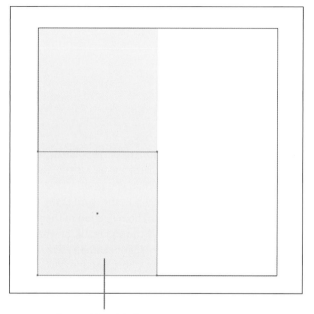

A copy of the original square

FIGURE 20
Four squares created using drag and drop

Duplicate objects using drag and drop

1. Click the **top-left anchor point**, press and hold **[Shift][Alt]** (Win) or **[Shift][option]** (Mac), drag straight down until the top-left anchor point touches the bottom-left anchor point (the "intersect" Smart Guide will appear), then release the mouse.

   When moving an object, pressing and holding [Shift] constrains the movement vertically, horizontally, or on 45° diagonals. Pressing [Alt] (Win) or [option] (Mac) while dragging an object creates a copy of the object, as shown in Figure 19.

   > TIP   When you press [Alt] (Win) or [option] (Mac) while dragging an object, the pointer becomes a double-arrow pointer. When two anchor points are directly on top of each other, the Selection Tool pointer turns from black to white.

2. With the bottom square still selected, press and hold **[Shift]**, then click the **top square** to select both items.

3. Click the **top-left anchor point** of the top square, press and hold **[Shift][Alt]** (Win) or **[Shift][option]** (Mac), drag to the right until the top-left anchor point touches the top-right anchor point, then release the mouse.

4. Change the fill color of each square to match the colors shown in Figure 20.

5. Save your work.

You moved and duplicated the yellow square using [Shift] to constrain the movement and [Alt] (Win) or [option] (Mac) to duplicate or "drag and drop" copies of the square.

TRANSFORM OBJECTS

What You'll Do

 In this lesson, you will scale, rotate, and reflect objects, using the basic transform tools. You will also create a star and a triangle.

Transforming Objects

The Scale, Rotate, and Reflect Tools are the fundamental transform tools. As their names make clear, the Scale and Rotate Tools resize and rotate objects, respectively. Double-click a transform tool to open the tool's dialog box. When you use the tool's dialog box, the objects are transformed from their centerpoints. This can be a useful choice, because the object's position essentially doesn't change on the artboard or in relation to other objects.

Use the Reflect Tool to "flip" an object over an imaginary axis. The best way to understand the Reflect Tool is to imagine

positioning a mirror perpendicular to a sheet of paper with a word written on it. The angle at which you position the mirror in relation to the word is the reflection axis. The reflection of the word in the mirror is the end result of what the Reflect Tool does. For example, text reflected across a horizontal axis would appear upside down and inverted. Text reflected across a vertical axis would appear to be inverted and running backwards, as shown in Figure 21.

You can transform an object using the desired tool or its dialog box. Each transform tool has a dialog box where you can

enter precise numbers to execute the transformation on a selected object. You can access a tool's dialog box by double-clicking the tool. Click the Copy button in the dialog box to create a transformed copy of the selected object. Figure 22 shows the Scale dialog box.

Repeating Transformations

One of the most powerful commands relating to the transform tools is Transform Again, found on the Object menu. Unfortunately, it is a command often overlooked by new users. Whenever you transform an object, selecting Transform Again repeats the transformation. For example, if you scale a circle 50%, the Transform Again command will scale the circle 50% again.

The power of the command comes in combination with copying transformations. For example, if you rotate a square 10° and copy it at the same time, the Transform Again command will create a second square, rotated another 10° from the first copy. Applying Transform Again repeatedly is very handy for creating complex geometric shapes from basic objects.

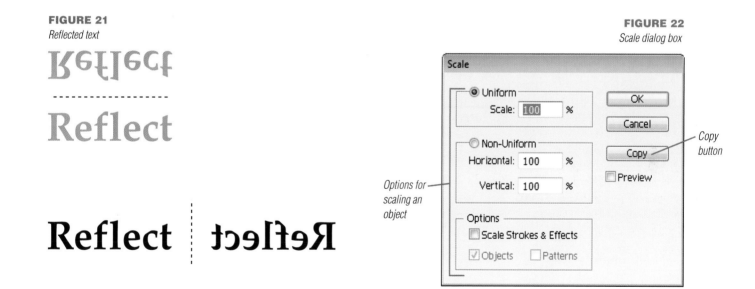

FIGURE 21
Reflected text

FIGURE 22
Scale dialog box

Options for scaling an object

Copy button

Use the Scale and Rotate Tools

1. Select the **green square**, double-click the **Scale Tool** , type **50** in the Scale text box, then click **OK**.

2. Click **Edit** on the menu bar, then click **Undo Scale**.

   TIP You can also undo your last step by pressing [Ctrl][Z] (Win) or ⌘ [Z] (Mac).

3. Double-click the **Scale Tool** again, type **50** in the Scale text box, then click **Copy**.

   The transformation is executed from the center point; the center points of the original and the copy are aligned.

4. Fill the new square created in Step 3 with blue.

5. Double-click the **Rotate Tool** , type **45** in the Angle text box, click **OK**, then click the **Selection Tool** .

6. Apply a 22 pt, yellow stroke to the rotated square, deselect, then compare your screen to Figure 23.

You used the Scale Tool to create a 50% copy of the square, then filled the copy with blue. You rotated the copy 45°. You then applied a 22 pt, yellow stroke.

FIGURE 23
Scaling and rotating a square

FIGURE 24

Using the Transform Again command

1. Click the **Ellipse Tool** in the Tools panel.

    TIP To access the Ellipse Tool, press and hold the Rectangle Tool until a toolbar of shape tools appears, then click the Ellipse Tool.

2. Click the **artboard**, type **3** in the Width text box and **.5** in the Height text box, then click **OK**.

3. Change the fill color to [None], the stroke color to blue, and the stroke weight to 3 pt.

4. Click the **Selection Tool**, click the **center point** of the ellipse, then drag it to the center point of the yellow square. (*Hint*: The center Smart Guide appears when the two centers meet.)

5. Double-click the **Rotate Tool**, type **45** in the Angle text box, then click **Copy**.

6. Click **Object** on the menu bar, point to **Transform**, then click **Transform Again**.

    TIP You can also access the Transform Again command by pressing [Ctrl][D] (Win) or [⌘][D] (Mac).

7. Repeat Step 6 to create a fourth ellipse using the Transform Again command.

    Your screen should resemble Figure 24.

8. Select the four ellipses, click **Object** on the menu bar, then click **Group**.

You created an ellipse, filled and stroked it, and aligned it with the yellow square. You then created a copy rotated at 45°. With the second copy still selected, you used the Transform Again command twice, thus creating two more rotated copies. You then grouped the four ellipses.

Create a star and a triangle, and use the Reflect Tool

1. Select the **Star Tool** ☆, then click any-where on the artboard.

   The Star Tool is hidden beneath the current shape tool.

2. Type **1** in the Radius 1 text box, type **5** in the Radius 2 text box, type **5** in the Points text box, as shown in Figure 25, then click **OK**.

   A star has two radii; the first is from the center to the outer point, and the second is from the center to the inner point. The **radius** is a measurement from the center point of the star to either point.

3. Double-click the **Scale Tool** ⬚, type **25** in the Scale text box, then click **OK**.

   When you create a star using the Star dialog box, the star is drawn upside down.

4. Fill the star with white, then apply a 5 pt blue stroke to it.

5. Click the **Selection Tool** ▸, then move the star so that it is completely within the red square.

6. Double-click the **Reflect Tool** ⬚, click the **Horizontal option button**, as shown in Figure 26, then click **OK**.

   The star "flips" over an imaginary horizontal axis.

   TIP   The Reflect Tool is hidden beneath the Rotate Tool.

   (continued)

FIGURE 25
Star dialog box

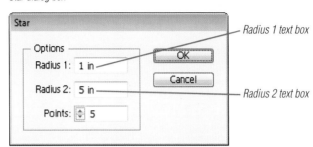

Radius 1 text box

Radius 2 text box

FIGURE 26
Reflect dialog box

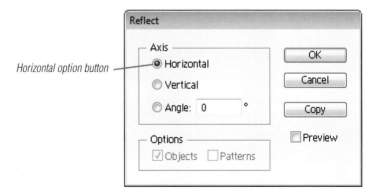

Horizontal option button

FIGURE 27
Reflecting the star horizontally

FIGURE 28
The finished project

Selecting

The Select menu offers some powerful selection commands under the Same submenu. There you have commands to select by the same fill, stroke, fill and stroke, stroke color, and stroke weight. You can even select objects with the same opacity and blending mode applied. When it comes to selecting multiple objects, using the Select menu is much faster than Shift-clicking!

7. Use the Selection Tool or the arrow keys on your keyboard to position the star roughly in the center of the red square.

   Your work should resemble Figure 27.

   > TIP Arrow keys move a selected item in 1 pt increments, known as the Keyboard Increment. You can change this amount by clicking Edit (Win) or Illustrator (Mac) on the menu bar, pointing to Preferences, clicking General, then typing a new value in the Keyboard Increment text box.

8. Click the **Polygon Tool** in the Tools panel.

   The Polygon Tool is hidden beneath the current shape tool in the Tools panel.

9. Click anywhere on the blue square.
10. Type **1.5** in the Radius text box, type **3** in the Sides text box, then click **OK**.
11. Fill the triangle with red.
12. Change the stroke color to yellow and the stroke weight to 22 pt.
13. Position the triangle so that it is centered within the blue square.

    Your completed project should resemble Figure 28.

14. Save your work, then close Basic Shapes.

You used the shape tools to create a star and a triangle and used the Reflect Tool to "flip" the star over an imaginary horizontal axis.

MAKE DIRECT SELECTIONS

What You'll Do

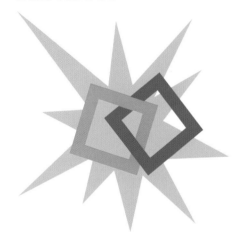

In this lesson, you will use the Direct Selection Tool and a combination of menu commands, such as Add Anchor Points and Paste in Front, to convert existing shapes into new designs.

Using the Direct Selection Tool

The Direct Selection Tool selects individual anchor points or single paths of an object. Using [Shift], you can select multiple anchor points or multiple paths. You can also select multiple points or paths by dragging a direct selection marquee. The tool also selects individual objects within a group, which can be very useful for modifying just one object in a complex group. Figure 29 demonstrates the Direct Selection Tool selecting one piece of a grouped object.

Clicking the center of an object with the Direct Selection Tool selects the entire object. Clicking the edge selects the path only. You will know you have made this direct selection successfully if the anchor points on the object all appear white. A white anchor point is not selected.

The Direct Selection Tool gives you the power to distort simple objects such as squares and circles into unique shapes. Don't underestimate its significance. While the Selection Tool is no more than a means to an end for selecting and moving objects, the Direct Selection Tool is in itself a drawing tool. You will use it over and over again to modify and perfect your artwork.

Adding Anchor Points

As you distort basic shapes with the Direct Selection Tool, you will often find that to create more complex shapes, you will need additional anchor points to work with.

The Add Anchor Points command creates new anchor points without distorting the object. To add anchor points to an object, click the Object menu, point to Path, then click Add Anchor Points. The new points are automatically positioned exactly between the original anchor points. You can create as many additional points as you wish to use.

Turning Objects into Guides

Guides are one of Illustrator's many features that help you to work with precision. Any object you create can be turned into a guide. With the object selected, click the View menu, point to Guides, then click Make Guides. Guides can be locked or unlocked in

the same location. It is a good idea to work with locked guides so that they don't interfere with your artwork. Unlock guides only when you want to select them or delete them.

When an object is turned into a guide, it loses its attributes, such as its fill, stroke, and stroke weight. However, Illustrator remembers the original attributes for each

guide. To transform a guide back to its original object, first unlock, then select the guide. Click the View menu, point to Guides, then click Release Guides.

FIGURE 29
Using the Direct Selection Tool

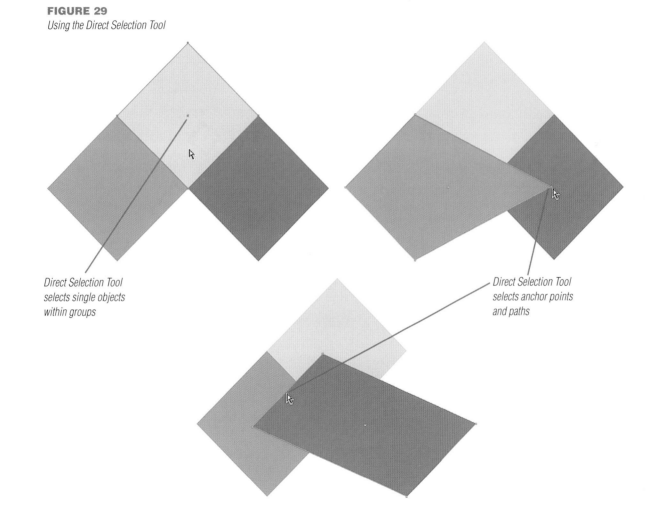

Direct Selection Tool selects single objects within groups

Direct Selection Tool selects anchor points and paths

Make guides and direct selections

1. Open AI 1-2.ai, then save it as **Direct Selections**.

   TIP Each time you save a Data File, click OK to close the Illustrator Options dialog box.

2. Click **View** on the menu bar, then click **Smart Guides** to turn this feature off.

3. Select the **green polygon**.

4. Click **View** on the menu bar, point to **Guides**, then click **Make Guides**.

   The polygon is converted to a guide.

   TIP If you do not see the polygon-shaped guide, click View on the menu bar, point to Guides, then click Show Guides.

5. Convert the purple starburst to a guide.

6. Click **View** on the menu bar, point to **Guides**, verify that there is a check mark to the left of Lock Guides, then release the mouse.

7. Click the **Direct Selection Tool**, then click the edge of the red square.

   The four anchor points turn white, as shown in Figure 30.

8. Click and drag the anchor points to the four corners of the guide to distort the square.

   Your work should resemble Figure 31.

You converted two objects into guides. You then used the Direct Selection Tool to create a new shape from a square by moving anchor points independently.

FIGURE 30
Red square selected with the Direct Selection Tool

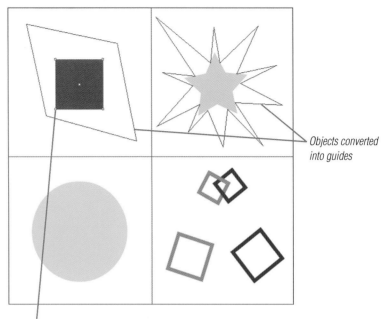

Objects converted into guides

Anchor points are hollow

FIGURE 31
Red square distorted

Getting Started with Illustrator

FIGURE 32
Star selected with Direct Selection Tool

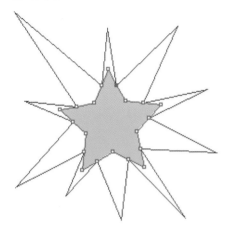

FIGURE 33
Completed starburst

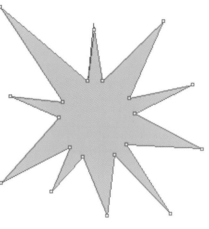

Add anchor points

1. Using the **Direct Selection Tool** ![tool] click the center of the light blue star, and note the anchor points used to define the shape.

2. Click **Object** on the menu bar, point to **Path**, then click **Add Anchor Points**.

3. Click the **artboard** to deselect the star, then click the edge of the star.

   All the anchor points turn white and are available to be selected independently, as shown in Figure 32.

4. Move the top anchor point on the star to align with the top point of the guide that you made earlier.

5. Working clockwise, move every other anchor point outward to align with the guide, creating a ten-point starburst.

   Your work should resemble Figure 33.

6. Select and move any of the inner anchor points to modify the starburst to your liking.

You used the Add Anchor Points command and the Direct Selection Tool to create an original ten-point starburst from a generic five-point star.

Making a direct selection marquee

When you create a marquee selection with the Selection Tool, any object the marquee touches is selected in its entirety. You can also use the Direct Selection Tool to create selection marquees. A Direct Selection Tool marquee selects only the anchor points and the paths that it touches. A Direct Selection Tool marquee is very useful for selecting multiple points or paths in one step.

Select paths

1. Click the edge of the yellow circle with the Direct Selection Tool [icon].

   The yellow circle is comprised of four anchor points and four line segments, as shown in Figure 34. Clicking the edge selects one of the four segments.

2. Copy the segment.

3. Click **Edit** on the menu bar, then click **Paste in Front**.

   A copy is pasted directly on top of the selected segment.

4. Change the fill color to [None].

5. Change the stroke color to dark blue and the stroke weight to 14 pt.

6. Moving clockwise, repeat Steps 1, 2, 3, and 4 for the next three line segments, choosing different colors for each.

   Your finished circle should resemble Figure 35.

You selected individual segments of a circle, copied them, and then pasted them in front. You then created a special effect by stroking the four new segments with different colors.

FIGURE 34
Viewing the path of the circle

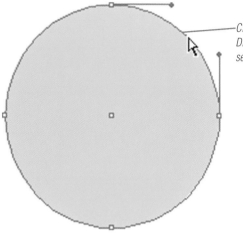

Clicking the edge of an object with the Direct Selection Tool selects one line segment of the entire path

FIGURE 35
Completed circle

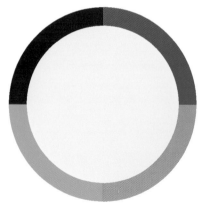

FIGURE 36

Completed linked squares

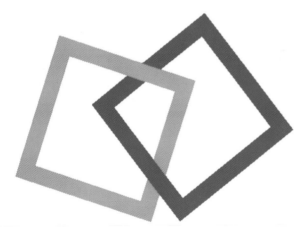

right column:

Create a simple special effect utilizing a direct selection

1. Click the Selection Tool , then overlap the large orange and blue squares so that they resemble the small orange and blue squares, then deselect.

2. Click the Direct Selection Tool , then select the top path of the orange square.

3. Copy the path.

4. Select the intersecting path on the blue square.

5. Paste in front, then save your work.

   Your work should resemble Figure 36.

6. Close the document.

   TIP   Remember this technique; it's one you'll probably use over and over again when you create artwork in Illustrator.

You learned a classic Illustrator trick. Selecting only a path, you copied it and pasted it in front of an intersecting object to create the illusion that the two objects were linked.

Lesson 7   Make Direct Selections

ILLUSTRATOR 1-41

Start Illustrator and create a new document.

1. Create a new document and name it **Flag**.
2. Make the size of the document 6" × 4".
3. Select Inches for the type of units, and CMYK Color for the color mode, then click OK.
4. Click File on the menu bar, click Save As, navigate to the drive and folder where you store your Data Files, then click Save.
5. Click View on the menu bar, then click Hide Page Tiling, if necessary.
6. Create a circle at the center of the artboard.
7. Click the Selection Tool.

Explore the Illustrator window.

1. Click View on the menu bar, then click Outline.
2. Click View on the menu bar, then click Preview.
3. Click View on the menu bar, then click Zoom In.
4. Click View on the menu bar, then click Zoom Out.
5. Press and hold [Spacebar] to access the Hand Tool, then move the artboard.
6. Click View on the menu bar, then click Fit in Window.
7. Select the circle, click Edit on the menu bar, then click Copy.

8. Click Edit on the menu bar, then click Paste in Front.
9. Move the new circle to the bottom of the artboard.
10. Click Edit on the menu bar, then click Undo Move.
11. Click Edit on the menu bar, then click Redo Move.
12. Click Select on the menu bar, then click All.
13. Click Select on the menu bar, then click Deselect.
14. Select all of the objects, click Edit on the menu bar, then click Cut.
15. Save your work.

Create basic shapes and apply fill and stroke colors.

1. Set the Fill and Stroke buttons in the Tools panel to black and [None], respectively.
2. Create a rectangle that is 3" × 1".
3. Show the Swatches panel, if necessary.
4. Fill the rectangle with a light yellow.

Select, move, and align objects.

1. Click View on the menu bar, then click Smart Guides, if necessary.
2. Move the rectangle so that its top-left anchor point intersects with the top-left corner of the artboard.
3. Click the top-left anchor point, press and hold [Shift][Alt] (Win) or [Shift][option] (Mac), drag straight down until the top-left anchor point touches the bottom-left anchor

point (the "intersect" Smart Guide appears), then release the mouse.
4. Click Object on the menu bar, point to Transform, then click Transform Again.
5. Repeat Step 4.
6. Change the fill color of the second and fourth rectangles to a darker yellow.
7. Save your work.

Transform objects.

1. Select the four rectangles.
2. Double-click the Reflect Tool, click the Horizontal option button, then click Copy. The four rectangles are copied on top of the original rectangles.
3. Move the four new rectangles to the right so that they align with the right side of the artboard.
4. Click the Rectangle Tool, click the artboard, and create a square that is .75" × .75".
5. Apply a 1-point black stroke to the square and no fill.
6. Click the Selection Tool, click the edge of the square, then position it at the center of the artboard.
7. Use the Rotate dialog box to create a copy of the square rotated at 10°.
8. Apply the Transform Again command seven times.
9. Save your work.

Make direct selections.

1. Use [Shift] to select each of the nine black squares.
2. Click Object on the menu bar, then click Group.
3. Scale the group of squares 200%.
4. Create a 3.75" × 3.75" circle, fill it with orange, add a 1-point black stroke, then position it at the center of the artboard.
5. Cut the circle from the artboard, click the group of black squares, click Edit on the menu bar, then click Paste in Back.
6. Adjust the location of the circle, as needed.
7. Click Object on the menu bar, point to Path, then click Add Anchor Points.
8. Deselect the circle by clicking anywhere on the artboard.
9. Click the Direct Selection Tool, then click the edge of the circle.
10. One at a time, move each of the four new anchor points to the center of the circle.
11. Switch to the Selection Tool, then select the orange-filled shape.
12. Double-click the Rotate Tool, type **22** in the Angle text box, then click Copy.
13. Apply the Transform Again command two times.
14. Save your work, then compare your illustration to Figure 37.
15. Close the Flag document.

FIGURE 37
Completed Skills Review

The lady who owns the breakfast shop that you frequent knows that you are a designer and asks for your help. Her nephew has designed a sign for her store window, but she confides in you that she doesn't like it. She thinks that it's "boring" and "flat." She wants to redesign the sign with something that is "original" and feels "more like a starburst."

1. Open AI 1-3.ai, then save it as **Window Sign**.
2. Click the Direct Selection Tool, then click the edge of the star.
3. Move two of the outer anchor points of the star farther from its center.
4. Move four of the inner points toward the center.
5. Select the entire star.
6. Reflect a copy of the star across the horizontal axis.
7. Fill the new star with an orange swatch and reposition it to your liking.
8. Group the two stars.
9. Copy the group, then paste in back.
10. Fill the copies with black.
11. Using your arrow keys, move the black copies five points to the right and five points down.

12. Select only the orange star using the Direct Selection Tool.
13. Copy the orange star, then paste in back.
14. Fill the new copy with black.
15. Rotate the black copy 8°.

FIGURE 38
Completed Project Builder 1

16. Apply a yellow fill to the orange star, then apply a 1-point black stroke to both yellow stars.
17. Save your work, then compare your illustration to Figure 38.
18. Close Window Sign.

Iris Vision Labs has contracted with your design firm to bid on a design for their logo. Researching the company, you learn that they are a biotech firm whose mission is to develop cures for genetic blindness and vision problems. You decide to build your design around the idea of an iris.

1. Create a new document that is 6" × 6".
2. Save the document as **Iris Vision Design**.
3. Create an ellipse that is 1" wide × 4" in height, and position it at the center of the artboard.
4. Fill the ellipse with [None], and add a 1-point blue stroke.
5. Create a copy of the ellipse rotated at 15°.
6. Apply the Transform Again command 10 times.
7. Select all and group the ellipses.
8. Create a copy of the group rotated at 5°.
9. Apply a red stroke to the new group.
10. Transform again.
11. Apply a bright blue stroke to the new group.
12. Select all.
13. Rotate a copy of the ellipses 2.5°.
14. Create a circle that is 2" × 2".
15. Fill the circle with a shade of gray.
16. Remove the stroke from the circle.
17. Position the gray-filled circle in the center of the ellipses.

18. Cut the circle.
19. Select all.
20. Paste in back.

FIGURE 39
Completed Project Builder 2

21. Save your work, then compare your illustration to Figure 39.
22. Close Iris Vision Design.

The owner of Emerald Design Studios has hired you to design an original logo for her new company. She's a beginner with Illustrator, but she's created a simple illustration of what she has in mind. She tells you to create something "more sophisticated." The only other information that she offers about her company is that they plan to specialize in precise, geometric design.

1. Open AI 1-4.ai, then save it as **Emerald Logo**.
2. Select all four diamonds and group them.
3. Select the group of diamonds on the artboard, then create a 75% copy.
4. Use the Transform Again command five times.
5. Use Smart Guides or Outline mode to help you identify each of the seven groups.
6. Rotate one of the groups 75°.
7. Select two other groups of your choice and repeat the last transformation, using the Transform Again command.
8. Apply a dark green stroke to all groups. Figure 40 shows one possible result of multiple transformations. Your illustration may differ.
9. Save your work, then close Emerald Logo.

FIGURE 40
Completed Design Project

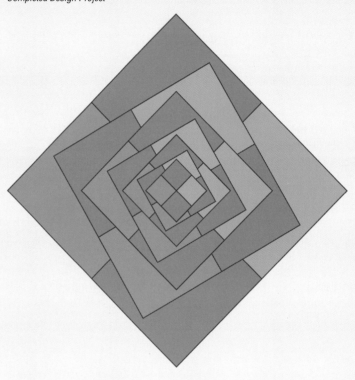

You attend a design school, and you're part of a team that is responsible for the artwork placed throughout the common areas of the school. One of the most admired professors brings you a file that he created in Illustrator, admitting that he's a beginner. Your team opens the file and notices that the file is poorly built—everything is misaligned and uneven. After consulting with the professor, your team decides that the file needs to be rebuilt from scratch.

1. Open AI 1-5.ai, then save it as **Rings**.
2. Distribute copies of the file to the members of your group.
3. Discuss with the group the areas of the file that are misaligned and poorly constructed.
4. Assign one member the task of pulling apart the file, object by object, to see how the effect was achieved.
5. Have the group create a "game plan" for reproducing the artwork with precision. Where's the best place to start? What's the best methodology for recreating the professor's design?
6. Have a group discussion about the art itself. If the professor is open to new ideas, how would the group suggest that the design could be improved?

7. Have one member work on the original Illustrator file.
8. Work as a group to rebuild the file, using precise methods.

9. Save your work, then compare your illustration to Figure 41.
10. Close the Rings document.

FIGURE 41
Completed Group Project

CREATING TEXT AND
GRADIENTS

1. Create and format text

2. Flow text into an object

3. Position text on a path

4. Create colors and gradients

5. Apply colors and gradients to text

6. Adjust a gradient and create a drop shadow

chapter **2** CREATING TEXT AND
GRADIENTS

Working with Text

When it comes to creating compelling and
dramatic display text, no other software
package offers the graphic sophistication
that you'll find with Adobe Illustrator. You
can quickly change fonts, font size, leading, and other text attributes in the
Character panel. You can make tracking
and kerning measurements with a level of
precision that would satisfy even the most
meticulous typographer. For the designer,
Illustrator is the preeminent choice for
typography. Powerful type tools offer the
ability to fill objects with text, position text
on lines—curved or straight—and set type
vertically, one letter on top of the next.
Once the text is positioned, the Create
Outlines command changes the fonts to
vector graphics that you can manipulate
as you would any other object. For

example, you can apply a gradient fill to
letter outlines for stunning effects.

Creating and Applying
Gradient Fills

A **gradient** is a graduated blend between
two or more colors used to fill an object
or multiple objects. Illustrator's sophistication for creating gradients and its ease
of use for applying them to objects are a
dream come true for today's designers.
You can create linear or radial gradients
between multiple colors, then control the
way they fill an object. Moreover, a single
gradient can be used to fill multiple
objects simultaneously! The unique gradient fills that you create can be saved
with descriptive names, then imported
into other Illustrator documents to be
used again.

Tools You'll Use

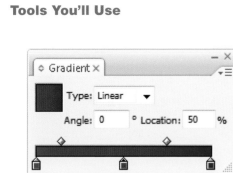

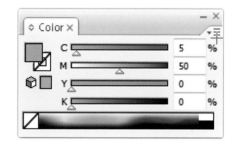

| Charac | ◇ Paragraph × | enType |

| ◇ Character × | agraph | enType |

Times New Roman

Regular

T	47 pt		A/IA	(56.4 pt
AV	Auto		AV	0
T	100%		IT	100%
Aa	-21 pt		T	0°

Language: English: USA

Type tools

CREATE AND
FORMAT TEXT

What You'll Do

Creating Type

You can create text anywhere on the artboard simply by selecting the Type Tool then clicking the artboard to start typing. You can enter text horizontally or vertically. The ability to type vertically is rather unusual; most text-based applications don't offer this option.

Text generated by the Type Tool is positioned on a path called the **baseline**. You can select text simply by clicking anywhere on the text. This feature is a preference that you can turn on or off: Click Edit on the menu bar, point to Preferences, click Type, then remove the check mark in the Type Object Selection by Path Only check box, if necessary. When this feature is checked, you must click the baseline to select text.

Formatting Text

The Character and Paragraph panels neatly contain all of the classic commands for formatting text. Use the Character panel to modify text attributes such as font and type size, tracking, and kerning. You can adjust the **leading**, which is the vertical space between baselines, or apply a horizontal or vertical scale, which compresses or expands selected type. The Paragraph panel applies itself to more global concerns, such as text alignment, paragraph indents, and vertical spaces between paragraphs. Figure 1 shows examples of formatting that you can apply to text.

Tracking and kerning are essential (and often overlooked) typographic operations. **Tracking** inserts uniform spaces between characters to affect the width of selected words or entire blocks of text. **Kerning** is used to affect the space between any two characters; it is particularly useful for improving the appearance of headlines and other display text. Positive tracking or kerning values move characters farther apart; negative values move them closer together.

Illustrator can track and kern type down to $1/1000$ of a standard em space. The width of an em space is dependent on the current type size. In a 1-point font, the em space is 1 point. In a 10-point font, the em space is 10 points. With kerning units that are $1/1000$ of an em, Illustrator can manipulate a 10-point font at increments of $1/1000$ of 1 point! Figure 2 shows examples of kerning and tracking values.

Hiding Objects

Two factors contribute to difficulty in selecting text and other objects: the number of objects in the document and proximity of objects. Multiple objects positioned closely together can make selections difficult and impede productivity.

Hiding an object is one simple solution. Hidden objects are safe; they won't be deleted from the document when you quit.

Also, they won't print. Just don't forget that they're there!

The Hide Selection command is under the Object menu, as is Show All, which reveals all hidden objects. When hidden objects are revealed, they are all selected; you can use this to your advantage. Simply press [Shift] as you click to deselect the object you want to see, then hide the remaining objects.

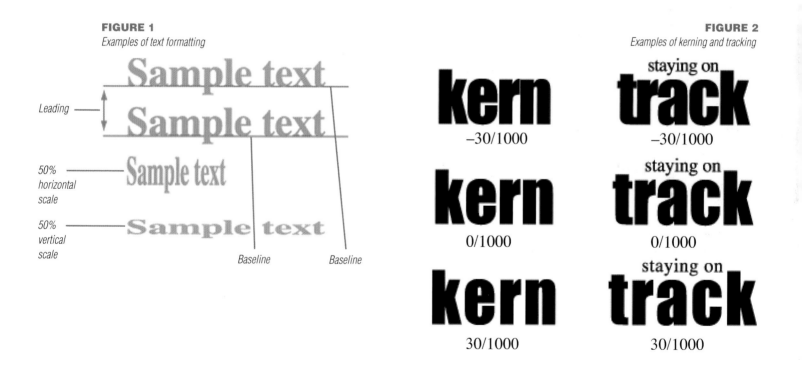

FIGURE 1
Examples of text formatting

Leading

50% horizontal scale

50% vertical scale

Baseline   Baseline

FIGURE 2
Examples of kerning and tracking

kern −30/1000

kern 0/1000

kern 30/1000

staying on track −30/1000

staying on track 0/1000

staying on track 30/1000

Create text

1. Open AI 2-1.ai, then save it as **Berry Symposium**.

2. Click **View** on the menu bar, then click **Hide Bounding Box**, if necessary.

3. Click the **Type Tool** T., then click anywhere on the artboard.

4. Type **BERRY** using all capital letters.

   TIP By default, new text is generated with a black fill and no stroke.

5. Click the **Selection Tool** ▶, then drag the **text** to the center of the artboard.

   TIP Hide Smart Guides, if necessary.

6. Click **Window** on the menu bar, point to **Type**, then click **Character** to show the Character panel.

7. Click the **Character panel list arrow**, then click **Show Options** to view the entire panel as shown in Figure 3.

You used the Type Tool to create the word BERRY, showed the Character panel then expanded the view of the Character panel.

FIGURE 3
Character panel

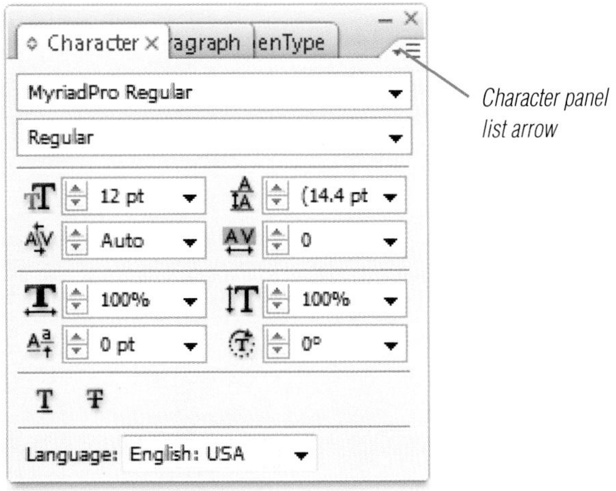

Character panel list arrow

Typography, the art of designing letterforms, has a long and rich history that extends back to the Middle Ages. With the advent of desktop publishing in the mid-1980s, many conventional typographers and typesetters declared "the death of typography." Cooler minds have since prevailed. The personal computer and software such as Adobe Illustrator have made vast libraries of typefaces available as never before. Imagine the days when the typewriter ruled—its single typeface and two point sizes the standard for literally millions of documents—and you get a sense of the typographic revolution that has occurred in the last 20 years.

Many designers are so eager to tackle the "artwork" that they often overlook the type design in an illustration. Tracking and kerning—the manipulation of space between words and letters—are essential elements to good type design and are often woefully ignored.

Illustrator's precise tracking and kerning abilities are of no use if they are ignored. One good way of maintaining awareness of your tracking and kerning duties is to take note of others' oversights. Make it a point to notice tracking and kerning—or lack thereof—when you look at magazines, or posters, or especially billboards. You'll be amazed at what you'll see.

Creating Text and Gradients

FIGURE 4
Character panel

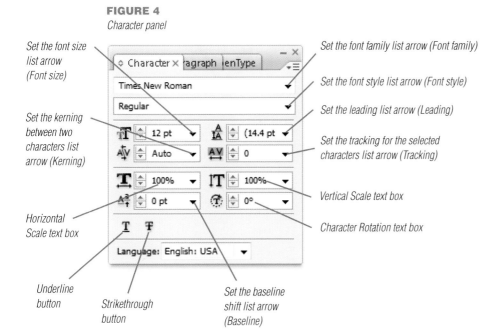

Set the font size list arrow (Font size)

Set the kerning between two characters list arrow (Kerning)

Horizontal Scale text box

Underline button

Strikethrough button

Set the font family list arrow (Font family)

Set the font style list arrow (Font style)

Set the leading list arrow (Leading)

Set the tracking for the selected characters list arrow (Tracking)

Vertical Scale text box

Character Rotation text box

Set the baseline shift list arrow (Baseline)

Format text

1. Click the **Font family** (Win) or **Font menu** (Mac) **list arrow**, then click **Times New Roman PS MT**, or a similar font, as shown in Figure 4.

   TIP   Figure 4 shows the full name of each setting in the Character panel. The steps in this chapter refer to the shorter name provided in parentheses.

2. Click the **Font size text box**, type **150**, then press **[Enter]** (Win) or **[return]** (Mac).

3. Click the **Horizontal Scale text box**, type **90**, then press **[Enter]** (Win) or **[return]** (Mac).

4. Deselect all.

5. Compare your text to Figure 5.

You used the Character panel to modify the font, the font size, and the horizontal scaling of the word BERRY.

FIGURE 5
Formatted text

BERRY

Track and kern text

1. Select the text, if necessary.

2. Using the Character panel, click the **Tracking text box**, then type **-30**.

   TIP Click the Character panel list arrow, then click Show Options, if necessary.

3. Click the **Type Tool** T., then click the cursor between the B and the E.

4. Using the Character panel, click the **up and down arrows** in the Kerning text box to experiment with higher and lower kerning values, then change the kerning value to -40.

5. Using Figure 6 as a guide, change the kerning to -20, 0, and -120 between the next three letter pairs.

6. Click the **Selection Tool** ▶, click the **Paragraph panel name tab**, then click the **Align center button** ≡, as shown in Figure 7.

   When text is center-aligned, its anchor point doubles as its center point, which is handy for aligning it with other objects.

   TIP If you do not see the Paragraph panel, click Window on the menu bar, point to Type, then click Paragraph.

7. Click **Object** on the menu bar, point to **Hide**, then click **Selection**.

You used the Character panel to change the tracking of the word BERRY, then you entered different kerning values to affect the spacing between the four letter pairs. You center-aligned the text, then hid the text.

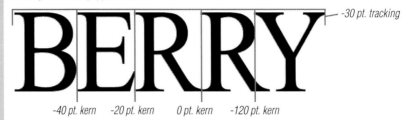

FIGURE 6
Kerning and tracking applied to text

-30 pt. tracking

-40 pt. kern   -20 pt. kern   0 pt. kern   -120 pt. kern

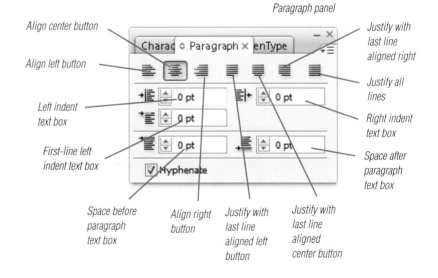

FIGURE 7
Paragraph panel

Align center button

Align left button

Left indent text box

First-line left indent text box

Justify with last line aligned right

Justify all lines

Right indent text box

Space after paragraph text box

Space before paragraph text box

Align right button

Justify with last line aligned left button

Justify with last line aligned center button

FIGURE 8
Vertical text

B
E
R
R
Y

Using the Glyphs panel

The Glyphs panel contains various type characters that aren't necessarily available on your keyboard. Examples of these characters include trademarks, copyright marks, accented letters, and numbers expressed as fractions. Click Window on the menu bar, point to Type, then click Glyphs to display the Glyphs panel. To access a glyph, click the Type Tool, click the artboard as you would to type any character, then double-click the glyph in the Glyph panel that you wish to use.

Create vertical type

1. Click the **Vertical Type Tool** |T , then click anywhere on the artboard.

   TIP   The Vertical Type Tool is hidden beneath the Type Tool.

2. Type the word **BERRY** using all capital letters.

   TIP   The type tools retain the formatting attributes that were previously chosen.

3. Click the **Selection Tool** , select the text, then move it to the center of the artboard.

   TIP   When any tool other than the Selection Tool is selected in the Tools panel you can press [Ctrl] (Win) or ⌘ (Mac) to switch to the Selection Tool. When you release [Ctrl] (Win) or ⌘ (Mac), the last chosen tool will be active again.

4. Using the Character panel, change the font size to 84 pt.

5. Change the tracking value to -160.

6. Set both the horizontal and vertical scales to 100%, then deselect the text.

   Your screen should resemble Figure 8.

7. Delete the vertical text, then save your work.

You used the Vertical Type Tool to create a vertical alternative to the first word you typed. You adjusted the tracking and kerning to better suit a vertical orientation, and then deleted the text.

FLOW TEXT INTO
AN OBJECT

What You'll Do

```
                    rasp
                 straw blue
               cran straw tea
             straw checker cran
           blue boysen black tea straw
        blue boysen checker cran tea rasp
       boysen blue black straw tea boysen
   checker cran rasp boysen blue black rasp straw
 blue black straw tea boysen checker cran rasp straw
  blue tea black rasp straw blue black straw tea
   boysen checker cran rasp straw blue black
     rasp straw blue cran straw tea straw
        checker cran  straw boysen
           black tea  straw blue
              boysen checker
                cran tea
                  rasp
```

In this lesson, you will use the Area Type Tool to flow text into an object.

Filling an Object with Text

Using the Area Type Tool and the Vertical Area Type Tool, you can flow text into any shape you can create, from circles to birds to bumblebees! Text in an object can be formatted as usual. You can change fonts, font size, alignment, etc., and the text will be reflowed in the object as you format it.

When text is flowed into an object, you can manipulate the object as you would any other object. Apply fills and strokes and transformations; use the Rotate Tool, or the Scale or Reflect Tools. You can even use the Direct Selection Tool to distort the shape. Best of all, you can apply those operations to the text or to the text object independently! Figure 9 shows an example of an object, in this case a star, filled with text.

QUICKTIP

You can underline text and strike through text using the Underline and Strikethrough buttons on the Character panel.

Locking Objects

Working in tandem with the Hide command, the Lock Selection command on the Object menu allows you to exempt an object from selections and affix its position on the artboard. The Lock Selection command is useful simply as a device to protect objects from accidental modifications.

Locked objects can be selected only after they are unlocked by choosing the Unlock All command on the Object menu. The Unlock All command unlocks every locked object on the artboard. When locked objects are unlocked, they are all selected. Simply press [Shift] while you click to deselect the object you want to work with, and relock the remaining objects.

Using Rulers, Guides, and the Grid

Illustrator has two built-in rulers that run along the top and left side of the document window. You can create ruler guides and place them on the artboard by positioning the mouse pointer in the top or left ruler, then dragging the mouse pointer onto the artboard. As you drag, you'll see a guide emerge and when you release the mouse pointer, the guide will be positioned at that point. To view rulers, click View on the menu bar, then click Show Rulers. You can lock guides and hide guides temporarily as you work in Illustrator. Click View on the menu bar,

point to Guides and you will see all of the Guide menu commands.

Another tool for aligning objects on the artboard is to use the grid. Grid settings are defined in the Guides & Grid section of the Preferences dialog box. You can choose a color and style for the grid, choose the distance between gridlines and how many subdivisions between gridlines. To hide and show the grid, click View on the menu bar, then click Hide Grid or Show Grid.

Making Guides

Guides are one of Illustrator's many features that help you to work with precision. You can select any object and make it into a guide with the Make Guides command on the View menu. You can also create guides by clicking and dragging the mouse pointer from each ruler to the artboard.

FIGURE 9
An object filled with text

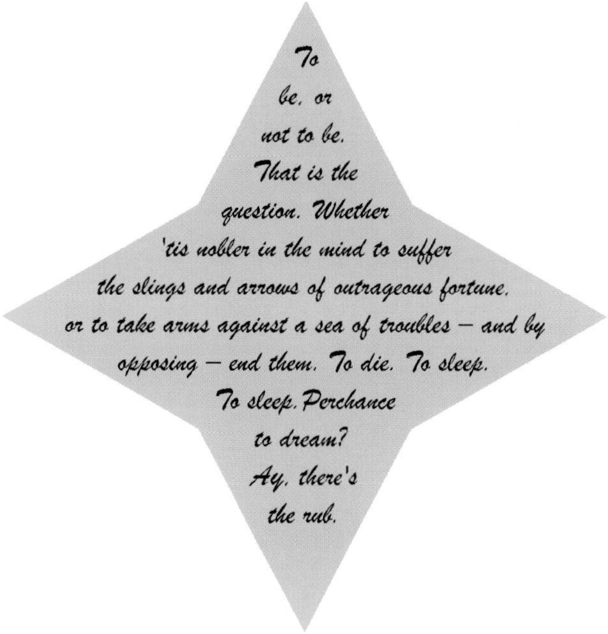

To be, or not to be. That is the question. Whether 'tis nobler in the mind to suffer the slings and arrows of outrageous fortune, or to take arms against a sea of troubles — and by opposing — end them. To die. To sleep. To sleep. Perchance to dream? Ay, there's the rub.

Fill an object with text

1. Open AI 2-2.ai, then save it as **Diamond Text**.

2. Select the yellow square, double-click the **Rotate Tool** ⟳, type **45** in the Angle text box, then click **OK**.

3. Click the **Area Type Tool** ⬚, then click the block of text.

   TIP The Area Type Tool is hidden beneath the current type tool.

4. Click **Select** on the menu bar, then click **All**.

   TIP When you click a type tool cursor on text and apply the Select All command, all the text is selected—not the object that contains the text, and not any other text or objects on the page.

5. Copy the text.

6. Click the **Selection Tool** ▶, select the yellow square, then change the font size to 12 using the Character panel.

   TIP When you are working with a Type Tool, you can press [Ctrl] (Win) or ⌘ (Mac) to access the Selection Tool temporarily and remain in Area Type Tool mode.

7. Click the **Area Type Tool** ⬚, if necessary, then click the edge of the yellow square.

   A flashing cursor appears, and the square loses its fill color, as shown in Figure 10.

8. Paste the copied text into the square.

   Your work should resemble Figure 11.

You rotated the yellow square, then filled it with text by first copying text from another object, then clicking the edge of the square with the Area Type Tool before you pasted the text into the square.

FIGURE 10
Applying the Area Type Tool

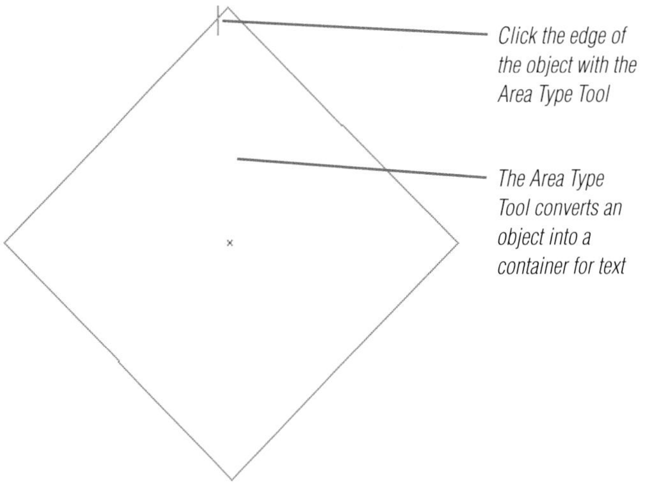

Click the edge of the object with the Area Type Tool

The Area Type Tool converts an object into a container for text

FIGURE 11
Text pasted into an object

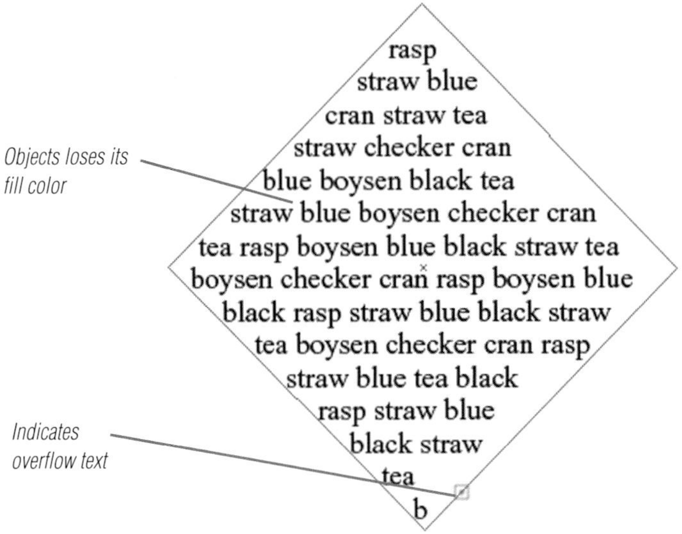

Objects loses its fill color

rasp
straw blue
cran straw tea
straw checker cran
blue boysen black tea
straw blue boysen checker cran
tea rasp boysen blue black straw tea
boysen checker cran rasp boysen blue
black rasp straw blue black straw
tea boysen checker cran rasp
straw blue tea black
rasp straw blue
black straw
tea
b

Indicates overflow text

Creating Text and Gradients

FIGURE 12

Centered text in an object

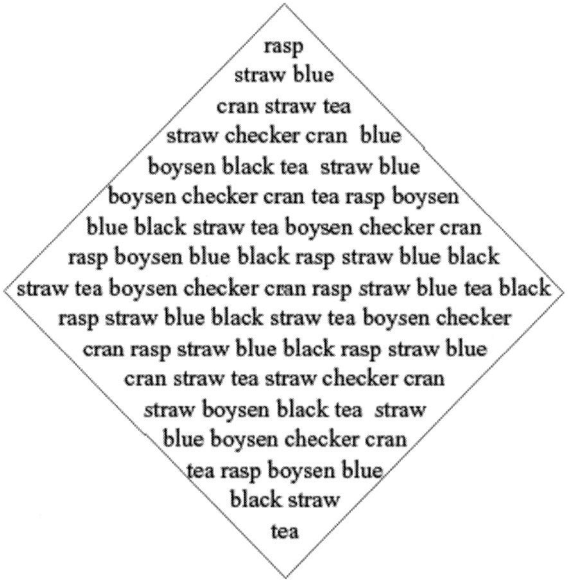

```
                    rasp
                 straw blue
               cran straw tea
            straw checker cran  blue
          boysen black tea  straw blue
        boysen checker cran tea rasp boysen
      blue black straw tea boysen checker cran
    rasp boysen blue black rasp straw blue black
  straw tea boysen checker cran rasp straw blue tea black
    rasp straw blue black straw tea boysen checker
      cran rasp straw blue black rasp straw blue
        cran straw tea straw checker cran
          straw boysen black tea  straw
            blue boysen checker cran
               tea rasp boysen blue
                 black straw
                    tea
```

Using Character and Paragraph Styles

A **style** is a group of formatting attributes, such as font, font size, color, and tracking, that is applied to text. You use the Character Styles panel to create and apply styles for individual words or characters, such as a footnote. You use the Paragraph Styles panel to apply a style to a paragraph. Paragraph styles include formatting options such as indents and drop caps. Using styles saves you time, and it keeps your work consistent. If you create styles for an Illustrator document, the styles are saved with the document and are available to be loaded for use in other documents.

Format text in an object

1. Select all of the text in the rotated square.

2. Click the **Align center button** ≡ in the Paragraph panel.

   | TIP   When filling an object other than a square or a rectangle with text, centering the text is often the best solution.

3. Click the **Character panel name tab** next to the Paragraph panel name tab, then change the font size to 9 pt.

4. Click the **Leading text box**, type **11**, click the **artboard** to deselect the text, then compare your work to Figure 12.

   It's OK if the line breaks in your document differ from the text in the figure.

5. Click the **Selection Tool** ▶, then click the **diamond-shaped text**.

   Both the text and the object that contains the text are selected.

6. Copy the text object.

   Both the text and the object are copied.

7. Click **Window** on the menu bar, then click **Berry Symposium** at the bottom of the menu.

   | TIP   All open Illustrator documents are listed at the bottom of the Window menu

8. Paste the text object into the Berry Symposium document.

You used the Paragraph and Character panels to format text in the object. You used the Selection Tool to select the text object, and then you copied and pasted it into the Berry Symposium document.

Make guides and use the Lock command

1. Click **View** on the menu bar, then click **Show Rulers**, if necessary.

2. Using Figure 13 as a reference, position your pointer in the top horizontal ruler, click and drag the pointer straight down to the 5" mark on the vertical ruler, then release the mouse to create a guide.

   TIP You may need to move the Tools panel out of the way to see the vertical ruler.

3. Position a vertical guide at the 5" mark on the horizontal ruler.

   TIP To change the color or style of guides, click Edit (Win) or Illustrator (Mac) on the menu bar, point to Preferences, then click Guides & Grid. The Guides & Grid Preferences dialog box is shown in Figure 14.

4. Click **View** on the menu bar, point to **Guides**, then verify that Lock Guides is checked.

5. Click the **Selection Tool** , if necessary.

(continued)

FIGURE 13
Making guides

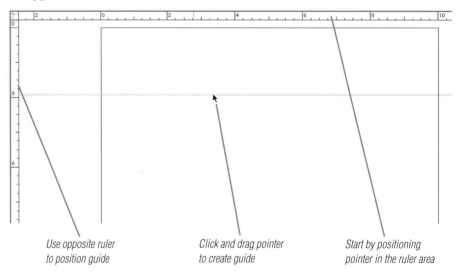

Use opposite ruler to position guide

Click and drag pointer to create guide

Start by positioning pointer in the ruler area

Creating Text and Gradients

FIGURE 14

Guides & Grid Preferences settings

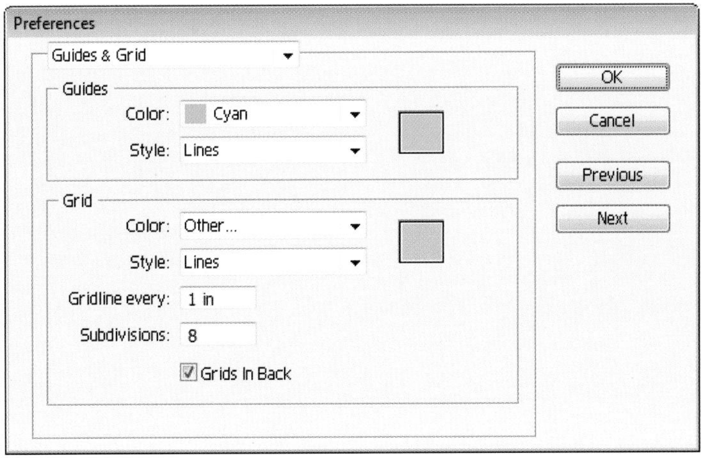

6. Select the text object, then align the center point of the text object with the intersection of the guides.

> TIP Use the arrow keys on your keypad to nudge the selection right, left, up, or down.

7. Click **Object** on the menu bar, point to **Lock**, then click **Selection**.

> TIP Locking objects is standard practice. You can also lock a selection by first selecting an object, then pressing [Ctrl][2] (Win) or ⌘ [2] (Mac). Make it a point to remember the quick key.

8. Save your work.

You created a horizontal and a vertical guide that intersect at the center of the artboard. You then aligned the center of the diamond text object with the intersection of the guides, and locked the diamond text object.

POSITION TEXT
ON A PATH

What You'll Do

three rivers

```
           rasp
         straw blue
       cran straw tea
      straw checker cran
    blue boysen black tea  straw
  blue boysen checker cran tea rasp
  boysen blue black straw tea boysen
checker cran rasp boysen blue black rasp straw
blue black straw tea boysen checker cran rasp straw
  blue tea black rasp straw blue black straw tea
  boysen checker cran rasp straw blue black
    rasp straw blue cran straw tea straw
      checker cran  straw boysen
        black tea  straw blue
         boysen checker
           cran tea
             rasp
```

symposium

In this lesson, you will explore the many options for positioning text on a path.

Using the Path Type Tools

Using the Type on a Path Tool or the Vertical Type on a Path Tool, you can type along a straight or curved path. This is the most compelling of Illustrator's text effects, and it opens up a world of possibilities for the designer and typographer.

You can move text along a path to position it where you want. You can "flip" the text to make it run in the opposite direction—on the opposite side of the path. You can also change the baseline shift to modify the distance of the text's baseline in relation to the path. A positive value "floats" the text above the path, and a negative value moves the text below the path. You can modify text on a path in the same way you would modify any other text element. Figure 15 shows an example of text on a path, whereas Figure 16 shows an example of text flipped across a path.

FIGURE 15
Text on a path

FIGURE 16
Text flipped across a path

Text flowed along a sharply curved path often presents kerning challenges

Flow text on a path

1. Click the **Ellipse Tool** , press **[Alt]** (Win) or **[option]** (Mac), then click the center of the artboard.

   Pressing [Alt] (Win) or [option] (Mac) while you click a shape tool on the artboard ensures that the center of the shape will be drawn from the point that you clicked.

2. Enter **2.9** in for the width and the height of the circle in the Ellipse dialog box, then click **OK**.

3. Click the **Type on a Path Tool** , then click anywhere on the edge of the circle.

   TIP The Type on a Path Tool may be hidden beneath the current type tool.

   A flashing cursor appears, and the circle loses its fill color.

4. Type **three rivers** in lowercase, using Times New Roman PS MT for the font.

   TIP If you do not have Times New Roman PS MT, substitute a similar font.

5. Click the **Selection Tool** to select the text by its baseline, then change the font size to 47 pt.

   You will see three brackets—one at the beginning of the path, one at the end of the path, and one at the midpoint between the two brackets. These brackets allow you to move text along a path.

   TIP Text flowed on a circle will often require kerning, especially when it is set at a large point size.

6. Compare your screen to Figure 17.

You created a 2.9" circle from its center, then typed along the circle's path using the Type on a Path Tool. You changed the font and font size using the Character panel.

FIGURE 17
Text on a circular path

Center bracket

Start and end brackets (overlapped because a circle path begins and ends at the same point)

Creating Text and Gradients

FIGURE 18

Moving text on a path

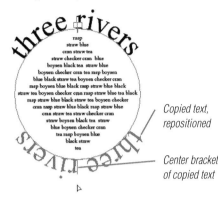

Copied text, repositioned

Center bracket of copied text

FIGURE 19

Flipping text across a path

Center bracket of copied text

FIGURE 20

Modifying a baseline shift

Baseline shift

FIGURE 21

Flipped text positioned below the path

Move text along a path

1. Click **View** on the menu bar, point to **Guides**, then click **Hide Guides**.

2. Using the Selection Tool ▸, drag the **center bracket** until the text is centered at the top of the circle.

3. Click **Edit** on the menu bar, click **Copy**, click **Edit** on the menu bar, then click **Paste in Front**.

4. Drag the **center bracket** of the copied text clockwise to move the copied text to the position shown in Figure 18.

5. Drag the **center bracket** of the copied text straight up to flip the text across the path, as shown in Figure 19.

   TIP   Enlarge your view of the artboard if you have trouble dragging the bracket.

6. Click the **Baseline text box** in the Character panel, type **-21**, as shown in Figure 20, then press **[Enter]** (Win) or **[return]** (Mac).

7. Click the **Type Tool** T, highlight **three rivers** at the bottom of the circle, then type **symposium**.

8. Click the **Selection Tool** ▸, then drag the **center bracket** to center the text at the bottom of the circle, if necessary.

9. Lock the two text objects, save your work, then compare your image to Figure 21.

You moved and copied text along a path, flipped its direction, changed the baseline shift, then locked both text objects.

CREATE COLORS AND
GRADIENTS

What You'll Do

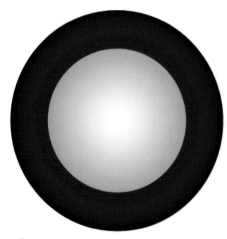

In this lesson, you will use the Color panel, the Gradient panel, and the Swatches panel to create, name, and save colors and gradients.

Using the Gradient Panel

A **gradient** is a graduated blend between colors. The Gradient panel is the command center for creating and adjusting gradients. In the panel you will see a slider that represents the gradient you are creating or working with. The slider has at least two colors. The leftmost color is the starting color, and the rightmost color is the ending color.

The colors used in a gradient are represented in the Gradient panel by small house-shaped icons called **stops**. The Gradient panel shown in Figure 22 shows a two-color gradient.

The point at which two colors meet in equal measure is called the **midpoint** of the gradient. The midpoint is represented by the diamond above the slider, which is called the Gradient Slider. The midpoint does not necessarily need to be positioned evenly between the starting and ending colors. You can change the look of a gradient by moving the Gradient Slider to change the location of the midpoint.

The Swatches panel contains standard gradients that come with the software. To create your own original gradients, start by clicking an object filled with an existing gradient. You can then modify that existing gradient in the Gradient panel. You can change either or both the beginning and ending colors. You can change the location of the midpoint. You can also add additional colors into the gradient, or remove existing colors.

QUICKTIP

As you work to perfect a gradient, you can see how your changes will affect the gradient automatically, by filling an object with the gradient that you are working on. As you make changes in the Gradient panel, the changes will be reflected in the object.

You can define a gradient as linear or radial. A linear gradient can be positioned left to right, up and down, or on any angle. You can change the angle of the gradient by entering a new value in the Angle text box in the Gradient panel.

Think of a radial gradient as a series of concentric circles. With a radial gradient, the starting color appears at the center of the gradient. The blend radiates out to the ending color. By definition, a radial gradient has no angle ascribed to it.

Using the Color Panel

The Color panel, as shown in Figure 23, is where you move sliders to mix new colors for fills, strokes, and gradients. You can also use the panel to adjust the color in a filled object. The panel has five color modes: CMYK, RGB, Grayscale, HSB, and Web Safe RGB. The panel will default to CMYK or RGB, depending on the color mode you choose when creating a new document. Grayscale mode allows you to create shades of gray in percentages of black. If you select a filled object and choose the HSB mode, you can adjust its basic color (hue), the intensity of the color (saturation), and the range of the color from light to dark (brightness). If you are designing illustrations for the Internet, you might consider using Web Safe RGB mode to create colors that are in accordance with colors defined in HTML.

Rather than use the sliders, you can also type values directly into the text boxes. For example, in CMYK mode, a standard red color is composed of 100% Magenta and 100% Yellow. The notation for this callout would be 100M/100Y. Note that you don't list the zero values for Cyan (C) and Black (K). In RGB mode (0-255), a standard orange color would be noted as 255R/128G.

Adding Colors and Gradients to the Swatches Panel

Once you have defined a color or a gradient to your liking, it's a smart idea to save it by dragging it into the Swatches panel. Once a color or gradient is moved into the Swatches panel, you can name it by double-clicking it, then typing a name in the Swatch Options dialog box. You can't, however, modify it. For example, if you click a saved gradient and adjust it in the Gradient panel, you can apply the new gradient to an object, but the original gradient in the Swatches panel remains unaffected. You can save the new gradient to the Swatches panel for future use.

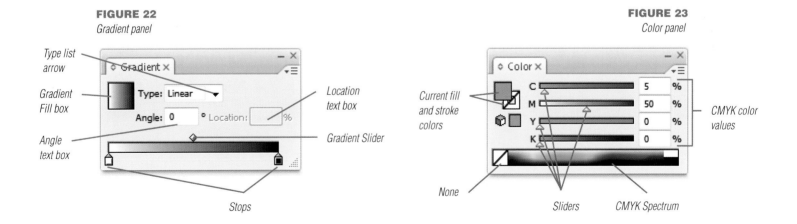

FIGURE 22
Gradient panel

Type list arrow
Gradient Fill box
Angle text box
Stops
Location text box
Gradient Slider

FIGURE 23
Color panel

Current fill and stroke colors
None
Sliders
CMYK Spectrum
CMYK color values

Create a gradient and a color

1. Show the guides.

2. Create a 4" circle at the center of the art-board, then apply a yellow fill to the circle.

   The most recently drawn object is automatically placed above the other objects on the artboard.

3. Hide the guides, click **Window** on the menu bar, then click **Gradient** to select it, if necessary.

4. Click **Window** on the menu bar, then click **Color** to select it, if necessary.

5. Click the **Blended Rainbow swatch** in the Swatches panel.

   The yellow fill changes to the Blended Rainbow fill.

6. Click the **Gradient panel list arrow**, then click **Show Options**, if necessary.

7. Click the **yellow stop** on the Gradient Slider, and drag it straight down off the panel to delete it.

8. Delete all the stops except for the first and last stops.

   | TIP   The changes you make to the Gradient Slider are reflected in the circle.

9. Click the bottom edge of the Gradient Slider to add a new color stop, then drag the stop along the slider until you see 50% in the Location text box in the Gradient panel as shown in Figure 24.

10. Drag each Gradient Slider to the 50% mark in the Location text box.

11. Verify that the new stop is selected, press and hold **[Alt]** (Win) or **[option]** (Mac), click **Squash** in the Swatches panel, then com-pare your circle to Figure 25.

(continued)

FIGURE 24
Adding and deleting stops

Location text box

Gradient Sliders

Click bottom edge of slider to add a new stop

Drag stop along the slider to position it at a new location

FIGURE 25
The color Squash is added to the gradient

Creating Text and Gradients

FIGURE 26
Black starting and ending colors

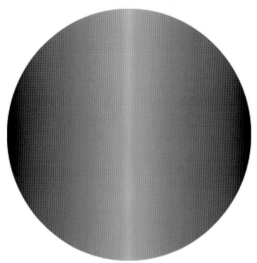

FIGURE 27
Changing the location of the midpoint of two colors

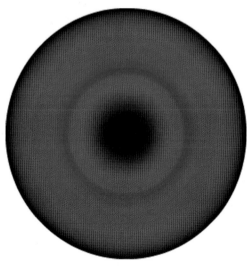

You must select a stop in order to change its color.

> TIP   If you don't press [Alt] (Win) or [option] (Mac), as you choose a swatch for your gradient, you will change the selected object's fill to a solid color.

11. Click the **first stop** on the Gradient Slider, press **[Alt]** (Win) or **[option]** (Mac), then click **Black** on the Swatches panel.

12. Repeat Step 11 to apply Black to the third stop, then compare your circle to Figure 26.

13. Click the **Squash stop** to select it, then drag each slider in the Color panel until the new CMYK values are 5C/95M/95Y/3K.

> TIP   Expand the view of the Color panel, if necessary.

14. Click the **Type list arrow** in the Gradient panel, then click **Radial**.

15. Click the **diamond** at the top of the Gradient Slider between the first two stops, then drag it to the 87% location on the slider.

16. Compare your circle to Figure 27.

You applied the Blended Rainbow gradient to the yellow circle. You created a new gradient by deleting the four intermediary stops and adding a new stop to the gradient. You changed the gradient from linear to radial, then adjusted the midpoint of the blend between the starting color and the red intermediate color.

Add gradients and colors to the Swatches panel

1. Double-click the **Scale Tool** 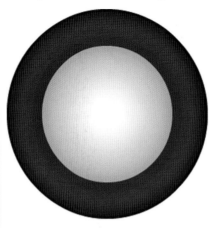, type **65** in the Scale text box, then click **Copy**.

2. Keeping the smaller circle selected, delete the red stop on the Gradient Slider in the Gradient panel.

3. Change the first stop starting color to White and the ending stop to 0C/40M/50Y/0K.

   | TIP   Press [Alt] (Win) or [option] (Mac).

   When a stop is selected on the Gradient Slider, the color of that stop appears in the Gradient Stop Color box in the Color panel.

4. Position the midpoint on the Gradient Slider at 65%.

   Your screen should resemble Figure 28.

5. Drag the **Gradient Fill box** from the Gradient panel to the Swatches panel, as shown in Figure 29.

6. Double-click **New Gradient Swatch 1** (the gradient you just added) in the Swatches panel to open the Swatch Options dialog box.

7. Type **Pinky** in the Swatch Name text box, then click **OK**.

8. Click the **last color stop** on the Gradient Slider.

(continued)

FIGURE 28
A radial gradient with white as the starting color

FIGURE 29
Adding a gradient to the Swatches panel

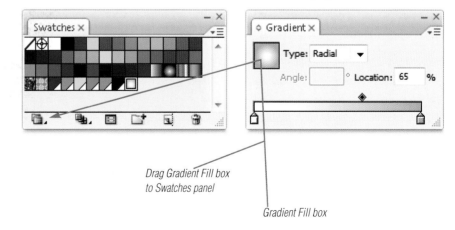

Drag Gradient Fill box to Swatches panel

Gradient Fill box

FIGURE 30

Adding a gradient to the Swatches panel

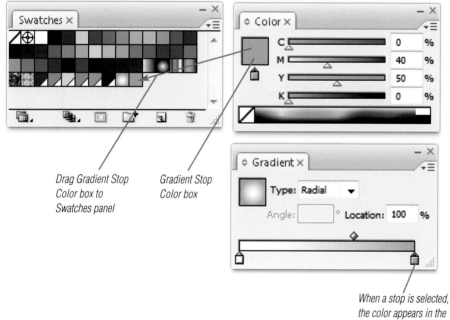

Drag Gradient Stop
Color box to
Swatches panel

Gradient Stop
Color box

When a stop is selected,
the color appears in the
Gradient Stop Color box
in the Color panel

9. Drag the **Gradient Stop Color box** from the Color panel to the Swatches panel to add this color to the Swatches panel, as shown in Figure 30.

10. Click the **Selection Tool**.

11. Click the **artboard** to deselect the smaller circle.

12. Name the new color swatch **Pinky Ending**, then click **OK**.

13. Click the **large circle**, drag the **Gradient Fill box** in the Gradient panel to the Swatches panel, then name the new gradient **Crimson Gradient**.

14. Save your work.

You used the Gradient panel to create a new gradient. You added the gradient fills from the two circles to the Swatches panel and gave them descriptive names. You added a color named Pinky Ending to the Swatches panel then created a new gradient called Crimson Gradient.

APPLY COLORS AND
GRADIENTS TO TEXT

What You'll Do

▶ *In this lesson, you will apply colors to text, convert text into objects, and fill the objects with a gradient.*

Applying Fills and Strokes to Text

Regardless of the fill and stroke colors shown in the Tools panel new text is generated by default with a black fill and no stroke. To change the color of text, you must either select the text by highlighting it with a type tool, or switch to a selection tool. When you switch to a selection tool, the text is selected as a single object (a blue baseline and anchor point are revealed). Any color changes you make will affect the text globally. If you want to change the fill or the stroke of an individual character, you must select that character with a type tool.

Converting Text to Outlines

About the only thing you can't do to Illustrator text is fill it with a gradient. To create the effect, you first need to convert the text into objects. You can do this by selecting the text, then using the Create Outlines command on the Type menu. The letterforms, or outlines, become standard Illustrator objects with anchor points and

Working with the stacking order

The stacking order defines how objects will be displayed when they overlap. Illustrator stacks each object. Beginning with the first object, each successive object you create overlaps the previously drawn objects. You can change the stacking order by moving objects forward and backward through the stack, one object at a time. You can also move an object to the very top or the very bottom of the stack with one command. Grouped objects are stacked together behind the top object in the group. If you group two objects that are separated in the stack, the objects in between will be positioned behind the new group.

paths able to be modified like any other object—and able to be filled with a gradient. Figure 31 shows an example of text converted to outlines.

Create Outlines is a powerful feature. Beyond allowing you to fill text with a gradient, it makes it possible to create a document with text and without fonts. This can save you time in document management when sending files to your printer, and will circumvent potential problems with missing fonts or font conflicts.

Once text is converted to outlines, you can no longer change the typeface. Also, the type loses its font information, including sizing "hints" that optimize letter shape at different sizes. Therefore, if you plan to scale type, change its font size in the Character panel before converting to outlines.

FIGURE 31
Text converted to outlines

Apply color to text

1. Select the two circles, click **Object** on the menu bar, point to **Arrange**, then click **Send to Back**.

   The two circles move behind the locked text objects.

2. Click **Object** on the menu bar, then click **Unlock All**.

   The three text objects you created and locked are now unlocked and selected.

3. Apply the Pinky Ending color as a fill for the three unlocked text objects.

4. Deselect all, then lock the diamond text object.

   Your work should resemble Figure 32.

   You unlocked the three text objects, filled them with the Pinky Ending color, then locked the diamond text object.

FIGURE 32
Text with a new fill color

Importing a swatch library

Swatches and gradients that you create are saved with the document they were created in. You can, however, import swatches from one document into another. Click Window on the menu bar, point to Swatch Libraries, then click Other Library. A dialog box opens allowing you to choose the document whose swatches you want to import. Click Open, and that document's Swatches panel will appear in your current document. When you import a Swatches panel, the panel automatically appears with the name of the document from which it came. The imported Swatches panel is not editable—you cannot add new swatches to it or delete existing ones from it.

FIGURE 33
Outlines filled with a gradient

Each outline is filled
with the gradient

1. Show the guides.
2. Click **Object** on the menu bar, then click **Show All**.
3. Select the **BERRY** text, click **Object** on the menu bar, point to **Arrange**, then click **Bring to Front**.
4. Click **Type** on the menu bar, then click **Create Outlines**.
5. Apply the Steel gradient in the Swatches panel to fill the text outlines, then deselect the outlines.
6. Using Figure 33 as a guide, position the BERRY text outlines so that they are centered within the entire illustration, then hide the guides.
7. Save your work.

You showed the BERRY text, moved it to the front, converted it to outlines, then filled the outlines with a gradient.

ADJUST A GRADIENT AND
CREATE A DROP SHADOW

What You'll Do

In this lesson, you will use the Gradient Tool to modify how the gradient fills the outlines. You will then explore the effectiveness of a simple drop shadow as a design element.

Using the Gradient Tool

The Gradient Tool is used to manipulate gradient fills that are already applied to objects; it affects only the way a gradient fills an object. To use the tool, you first select an object with a gradient fill. You then drag the Gradient Tool over the object. For both linear and radial gradients, where you begin dragging and where you end dragging determine the length of the blend from starting to ending color. For linear gradients, the angle that you drag in determines the angle at which the blend fills the object. If you apply the same gradient to multiple objects, you can select all the objects and use the Gradient Tool to extend a single gradient across all of them.

If you select and fill multiple objects with a gradient, each object is filled with the entire length of the gradient, from beginning color to ending color.

When you convert text to outlines and apply a gradient fill, the gradient automatically fills each letter independently. In

other words, if you fill a five-letter word with a rainbow gradient, each of the five letters will contain the entire spectrum of colors in the gradient. To extend the gradient across all the letters, drag the Gradient Tool from the left edge of the word to the right edge. Figure 34 shows examples of different angles and lengths of a gradient fill created with the Gradient Tool.

Adding a Drop Shadow

Applying a shadow behind text is an effective design tool to distinguish the text from other objects and add dimension to the illustration. To apply a drop shadow to text, copy the text, then paste the copy behind it. Fill the copy with a darker color, then use the keyboard arrows to move it so that it is offset from the original text. See Figure 35.

QUICKTIP

When adding subtle design effects to objects, you may want to work without seeing the anchor points and paths on selected items. You can hide them by using the Hide Edges command on the View menu. Hiding edges allows you to work on an object without the distraction of the points and paths.

FIGURE 34
Using the Gradient Tool

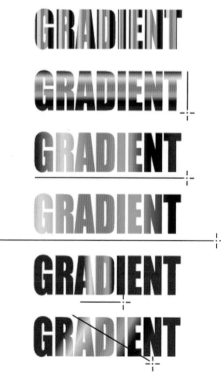

FIGURE 35
Drop shadow created using the Paste in Back command

Use the Gradient Tool

1. Select the **BERRY text outlines**, if necessary.

2. Click the **Gradient Tool** 🔲, then position the pointer at the top of the B.

3. Drag straight down to the bottom of the B, then release the mouse.

   Your work should resemble Figure 36.

   > TIP Pressing and holding [Shift] while you drag the Gradient Tool pointer allows you to drag in a perfectly straight line.

4. Switch to the **Selection Tool** ▶, then click the large circle filled with the Crimson Gradient fill behind the text.

5. In the Gradient panel, reposition the red center color stop so that the value in the Location text box reads 82%.

   The red stop in the blend is now positioned behind the three rivers and symposium text, as shown in Figure 37.

You used the Gradient Tool to flow the gradient from top to bottom in the word BERRY. You adjusted the red stop in the Gradient panel to move the red highlight behind the three rivers and symposium text.

FIGURE 36
Gradient Tool applied top to bottom

FIGURE 37
A highlight behind the text

Red stop in a
radial gradient

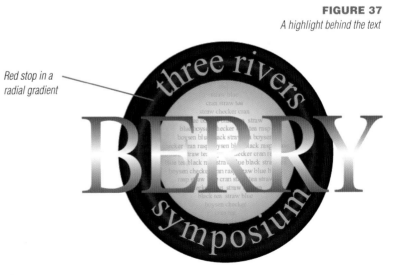

FIGURE 38
Drop shadow with a 3 pt offset

FIGURE 39
Drop shadows add dimension

Drop shadow added
to symposium

FIGURE 40
The finished illustration

1. Select the word **BERRY**.

2. Apply a 1 pt Black stroke to the outlines.

3. Copy the word, then paste in back.

4. Change the fill of the copied object to Black.

   | TIP   Even though you can't see the copy of the text in back, it is still selected.

5. Press ↓ three times and ← three times to move the copied text 3 pts down and 3 pts to the left, as shown in Figure 38.

6. Copy the word symposium, then paste in back.

7. Change the fill of the copied text to Black.

   | TIP   Since the copy is still selected, you only need to click Black in the Swatches panel.

8. Using the arrow keys, move the copied text 2 pts down and 2 pts to the left, as shown in Figure 39.

9. Apply the same drop shadow to the three rivers text.

   | TIP   You might find it easier to select the three rivers text if you first lock the symposium text and the symposium shadow text.

10. Unlock all, select everything on the artboard, then rotate the illustration 15°.

11. Click the **Selection Tool** ▶, then click the **artboard** to deselect all.

   Your work should resemble Figure 40.

12. Save your work, then close and save each document.

You applied a black stroke to the display text and then pasted a copy behind. You filled the copy with black, then offset the copy to create a drop shadow effect. You then applied a drop shadow to symposium and three rivers. Finally, you rotated the entire illustration.

Create and format text.

1. Open AI 2-3.ai, then save it as **Restaurant Logo.**
2. Using a bold font, type **NOW OPEN** on two lines, using all capital letters. (*Hint*: The font used in Figure 41 is Impact.)
3. Change the font size to 29 pt and the leading to 25 pt.
4. Change the baseline shift to 0.
5. Change the alignment to center and the horizontal scale to 75%.
6. Position the text in the center of the white circle.
7. Hide the text.
8. Save your work.

Flow text into an object.

1. Copy the beige circle.
2. Paste the copy in front of it.
3. Click the Type Tool, then select all of the green text at the bottom of the artboard, with the Type Tool.
4. Copy the green text.
5. Click the Selection Tool, then click the top beige circle.
6. Click the Area Type Tool, click the edge of the top beige circle, then paste.
7. Center-align the text in the circle.
8. Change the baseline shift to -4 pts.
9. Fill the selected text with the same fill color as the beige circle (50% Orange).
10. In the Color panel, drag the Magenta slider to 40% to darken the text.
11. Hide the text.
12. Save your work.

Position text on a path.

1. Select the dark gray circle.
2. Click the Type on a Path Tool, then click the top of the circle.
3. Using a bold font, type **THE HOLE-IN-ONE** in all capital letters across the top of the circle. (*Hint*: The font in Figure 41 is Techno Regular. If your type appears at the bottom of the circle, drag the start or end bracket to position the type at the top of the circle. Zoom in so that you can clearly see the brackets. If you move the circle instead of the type, undo your last step and try again.)
4. Change the font size to 34 pt and the fill color to white. (*Hint*: You may need to use a smaller font size, depending on the font you choose.)
5. Click the Selection Tool, click Edit on the menu bar, click Copy, click Edit on the menu bar, click Paste in Front, then move the center bracket clockwise to position the copied text across the bottom of the circle.
6. Highlight the copied text, then type **RESTAURANT & BAR** with the Type Tool.
7. Drag the RESTAURANT & BAR text across the path to flip its direction.
8. Apply a negative baseline shift to move the text below the path. (*Hint*: The baseline shift used in Figure 41 is -27 pts.)
9. Copy both text objects, then paste them in back.
10. Fill the back copies of the text with black, then move them 2 pts up and 2 pts to the right.
11. Save your work.

Create and apply gradient fills to objects.

1. Apply the White, Black Radial gradient to the small white circle.
2. Change the ending color stop on the Gradient panel to Smoke. (*Hint*: Press [Alt] (Win) or [option] (Mac) while you select Smoke from the Swatches panel.)
3. Save the new gradient in the Swatches panel.
4. Name it **Golf Ball**.
5. Fill the large green circle with the Golf Ball gradient.
6. Change the starting color stop to Pure Yellow.
7. Change the ending color stop to Little Sprout Green.

8. Move the midpoint of the two colors to the 80% location on the Gradient Slider.
9. Save the new gradient as **The Rough**.
10. Save your work.

Adjust a gradient and create a drop shadow.

1. Click Object on the menu bar, then click Show All.
2. Deselect all by clicking the artboard.
3. Select NOW OPEN and convert the text to outlines. (*Hint*: Use the Type menu.)
4. Fill the text with the White, Black gradient.
5. Change the starting color stop to black.
6. Create an intermediary white color stop at the 50% mark on the Gradient Slider.
7. Drag the Gradient Tool starting at the top of the word NOW to the bottom of the word OPEN.
8. Change the middle color stop of the gradient to Latte.
9. Save the new gradient as **Flash**.
10. Deselect the text.
11. Delete the green text from the bottom of the artboard.
12. Convert the remaining text objects into outlines.
13. Select all, then lock all objects.
14. Save your work, compare your illustration to Figure 41, then close Restaurant Logo.

FIGURE 41
Completed Skills Review

Creating Text and Gradients

An eccentric California real-estate mogul hires your design firm to "create an identity" for La Mirage, his development of high-tech executive condominiums in Palm Springs. Since he's curious about what you'll come up with on your own, the only creative direction he'll give you is to tell you that the concept is "a desert oasis."

1. Create a new 6" × 6" CMYK Color document, then save it as **Desert Oasis**.
2. Using a bold font and 80 pt for a font size, type **LA MIRAGE** in all capitals. (*Hint*: The font shown in Figure 42 is Impact.)
3. Change the horizontal scale to 80%.
4. Change the baseline shift to 0.
5. Apply a -100 kerning value between the two words.
6. Convert the text to outlines, then click the Linear Gradient 1 gradient in the Swatches panel.
7. Using the Color panel, change the first color stop to 66M/100Y/10K (*Hint*: Press and hold [Alt] (Win) or [option] (Mac) when creating the new color.)
8. Create an intermediary color stop that is 25M/100Y.
9. Position the intermediary color stop at 70% on the slider.
10. Save the gradient in the Swatches panel, and name it **Desert Sun**.
11. Drag the Gradient Tool from the exact top to the exact bottom of the text.

12. Create a rectangle around the text and fill it with the Desert Sun gradient.
13. Drag the Gradient Tool from the bottom to the top of the rectangle.
14. Send the rectangle to the back of the stack.

FIGURE 42
Completed Project Builder 1

15. Apply a 1-point black stroke to LA MIRAGE.
16. Type the tagline: **a desert oasis** in 14 pt lowercase letters.
17. Apply a tracking value of 500 or more to the tagline, then convert it to outlines.
18. Save your work, then close Desert Oasis.

Creating Text and Gradients

Your friend owns Loon's Balloons. She stops by your studio with a display ad that she's put together for a local magazine and asks if you can make all the elements work together better. Her only direction is that the balloon must remain pink, the same color as her logo.

1. Open AI 2-4.ai, then save it as **Balloons**.
2. Save the pink fill on the balloon to the Swatches panel, and name it **Hot Pink**.
3. Fill the balloon shape with the White, Black Radial gradient from the Swatches panel.
4. Change the black stop on the Gradient Slider to Hot Pink.
5. Using the Gradient Tool, change the highlight point on the balloon shape so that it is no longer centered in the balloon shape.
6. Copy the balloon, then paste it in front.
7. Click the Selection Tool on the block of text that says "specializing in etc.", then cut the text.
8. Click the top balloon with the Selection Tool, then switch to the Area Type Tool.
9. Click the top edge of the top balloon, then paste.
10. Center the text and apply a -4 baseline shift.
11. Adjust the layout of the text as necessary. (*Hint*: You can force a line of text to the next line by clicking before the first word in the line you want to move, then pressing [Shift][Enter] (Win) or [Shift][return] (Mac).)

12. Move the headline LOON'S BALLOONS so that each word is on a different side of the balloon string.

FIGURE 43
Completed Project Builder 2

13. Apply a 320 kerning value between the two words.
14. Save your work, compare your screen to Figure 43, then close Balloons.

You work in the marketing department of a major movie studio, where you design movie posters and newspaper campaigns. You are respected for your proficiency with typography. Your boss asks you to come up with a "teaser" campaign for the movie *Vanishing Point*, a spy thriller. The campaign will run on billboards in 10 major cities and will feature only the movie title, nothing else.

1. Create a new 6" × 6" CMYK Color document, then save it as **Vanish.**
2. Type **VANISHING POINT**, using 100 pt and a bold font. (*Hint*: The font used in Figure 44 is Impact.)
3. Change the horizontal scale to 55%.
4. Convert the text to outlines.
5. In the Swatches panel, click the Linear Gradient 1 gradient.
6. Drag the Gradient Tool from the exact bottom to the exact top of the letters.
7. Copy the letters, then paste them in front.
8. Fill the copied letters in front with white.
9. Using your arrow keys, move the white letters 2 pts to the left and 8 pts up.
10. Save your work, then compare your text with Figure 44.
11. Close Vanish.

FIGURE 44
Completed Design Project

Firehouse Chili Pepper Company, a local specialty food manufacturer, has hired your team to design a label for its new line of hot sauces. Since this is a new product line, they have no existing materials for your team to start from.

1. Create a new 6" × 6" CMYK Color document, then save it as **Firehouse Chili**.
2. Assign two team members to search the Internet to get design ideas. They should use keywords such as chili, pepper, hot sauce, barbecue, and salsa. What have other designers created to convey these concepts? Is there a broad range of ideas, or are they all pretty much different versions of the same idea? If so, can your group think of something original that works?
3. Assign two other members to go to the grocery store and return with some samples of other products in this niche. Be sure they purchase both products that you've heard of before and products you've never heard of before. Are the known products' design concepts better than the unknown products'? Have the group discuss any correlation between the successful products and better design, if it is evident.
4. Two other team members should be in charge of typographic research and should work closely with the design team. Again, have the group discuss whether it sees a variety of typefaces used in relation with this concept, or whether they are all pretty much the same.
5. While everyone else is researching, the design team should begin brainstorming and sketching out ideas. Although there are no existing materials, the product line's name is very evocative. The team should create design ideas that spring from the concepts of "firehouse" and "chili pepper," as well as from more broad-based concepts such as salsa, Mexico, and fire.

FIGURE 45
Completed Group Project

6. Use the skills that you learned in this chapter to create the label. (*Hint*: Fill text outlines with a gradient that conveys "hot." Use reds, oranges, and blacks. Use a bold font for the text so that the gradient will be clearly visible. Position the stops on the slider so that the "hot" colors are prominent in the letterforms.)
7. Save your work, then compare your results with Figure 45.
8. Close Firehouse Chili.

Creating Text and Gradients

chapter

3

DRAWING AND COMPOSING
AN ILLUSTRATION

1. Draw straight lines

2. Draw curved lines

3. Draw elements of an illustration

4. Apply attributes to objects

5. Assemble an illustration

6. Stroke objects for artistic effect

7. Use Live Trace and the Live Paint Bucket Tool

Drawing in Illustrator

You can create any shape using the Pen Tool, which is why it's often called "the drawing tool." More precisely, the pen is a tool for drawing straight lines, curved lines, polygons, and irregularly shaped objects. It is, however, no *more* of a drawing tool than the shape tools—it's just more versatile.

The challenges of the Pen Tool are finite and able to be grasped with no more than 30 minutes' study. As with many aspects of graphic design (and of life!), mastery comes with practice. So make it a point to learn Pen Tool techniques. Don't get frustrated. And use the Pen Tool often, even if it's just to play around making odd shapes.

To master Illustrator, you must master the Pen Tool.

All artists learn techniques for using tools—brushes, chalk, palette knives, etc.

Once learned, those techniques become second nature—subconscious and unique to the artist. Ask yourself, was Van Gogh's mastery of the palette knife a triumph of his hands or of his imagination?

When you draw, you aren't conscious of how you're holding the crayon or how much pressure you're applying to the paper. Much the same goes for Illustrator's Pen Tool. When you are comfortable and confident, you will find yourself effectively translating design ideas from your imagination straight to the artboard—without even thinking about the tool!

When you work with the Pen Tool, you'll want complete control over your artboard. Using the Zoom Tool and the New View feature, you can create custom views of areas of your artboard, making it easy to jump to specific elements of your illustration for editing purposes.

Tools You'll Use

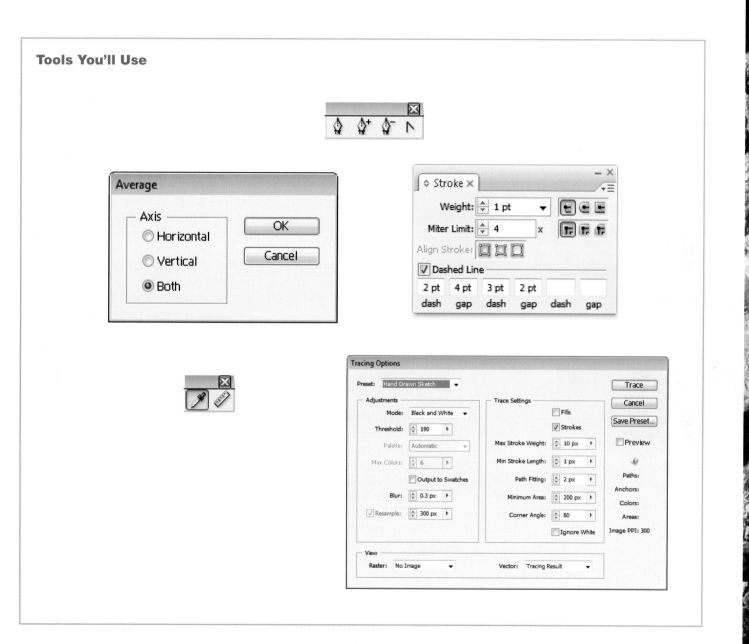

DRAW STRAIGHT LINES

What You'll Do

In this lesson, you will create three new views, then explore basic techniques for using the Pen Tool as you prepare to draw a complex illustration.

Viewing Objects on the Artboard

If you are drawing on paper and you want to see your work up close, you move your nose closer to the paper. Computers offer more effective options. As you have already seen, the Zoom Tool is used to enlarge areas of the artboard for easier viewing. When you are working with the Pen Tool, your view of the board becomes more critical, as anchor points are tiny, and you will often move them in 1 point increments.

Instead of clicking the Zoom Tool to enlarge an area, you can click and drag it over the area you want to zoom in on, creating a **marquee**, a rectangular, dotted line that surrounds the area you drag over. When you release the Zoom Tool, the marquee disappears, and whatever was in the marquee is magnified as much as possible while still fitting in the window.

The New View command allows you to save any view of the artboard. Let's say you zoom in on an object. You can save that view and give it a descriptive name, using the New View command. The name of the view is then listed at the bottom of the View menu, so you can return to it at any time by selecting it. Saving views is an effective way to increase your productivity.

Drawing Straight Segments with the Pen Tool

You can use the Pen Tool to make lines, also known as paths; you can also use it to create a closed shape such as a triangle or a pentagon. When you click the Pen Tool to make anchor points on the artboard, straight segments are automatically placed between the points. When the endpoints of two straight segments are united by a point that point is called a **corner point**. Figure 1 shows a simple path drawn with five anchor points and four segments.

Perfection is an unnecessary goal when you are using the Pen Tool. Anchor points and segments can be moved and repositioned. New points can be added and deleted. Use the Pen Tool to create the general shape that you have in your mind. Once the object is complete, use the Direct Selection Tool to perfect—or tweak—the points and segments. "Tweaking" a finished object—making small, specific improvements—is always part of the drawing process.

Aligning and Joining Anchor Points

Often, you will want to align anchor points precisely. For example, if you have drawn a diamond-shaped object with the Pen Tool, you may want to align the top and bottom points on the same vertical axis and then align the left and right points on the same horizontal axis to perfect the shape.

The **Average** command is a simple and effective choice for aligning points. With two or more points selected, you can use the Average command to align them on the horizontal axis, on the vertical axis, or on both the horizontal and vertical axes. Two points aligned on both the horizontal and vertical axes are positioned one on top of the other.

Why is the command named Average? The name is appropriate, because when the command moves two points to line them up on a given axis, that axis is positioned at the average distance between the two points. Thus, each moves the same distance.

The **Join** command unites two anchor points. When two points are positioned in different locations on the artboard, the Join command creates a segment between them. When two points are aligned on both the horizontal and vertical axes and are joined, the two points become one.

You will often use the Average and Join commands in tandem. Figure 2 shows two pairs of points that have each been aligned on the horizontal axis, then joined with the Join command.

FIGURE 1

Elements of a path composed of straight segments

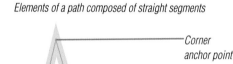

Corner anchor point

Ending anchor point

Starting anchor point

Segment

Corner anchor points

FIGURE 2

Join command unites open points

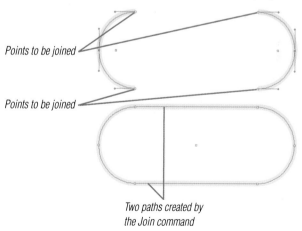

Points to be joined

Points to be joined

Two paths created by the Join command

Create new views

1. Open AI 3-1.ai, then save it as **Straight Lines**.

2. Click the **Zoom Tool** 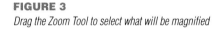, then position it at the upper-left corner of the artboard.

3. Click and drag a **selection box** that encompasses the entire yellow section, as shown in Figure 3.

   The area within the selection box is now magnified.

4. Click **View** on the menu bar, then click **New View**.

5. Name the new view **yellow**, then click **OK**.

6. Press and hold **[Spacebar]** to access the Hand Tool, then drag the **artboard** upward until you have a view of the entire pink area.

7. Create a new view of the pink area, and name it **pink**.

   TIP If you need to adjust your view, you can quickly switch to a view of the entire artboard by pressing [Ctrl][0] (Win) or [⌘][0] (Mac), then create a new selection box with the Zoom Tool.

8. Create a new view of the green area, named **mint**.

9. Click **View** on the menu bar, then click **yellow** at the bottom of the menu.

   The Illustrator window changes to the yellow view.

   TIP You can change the name of a view by clicking View on the menu bar, then clicking Edit Views.

You used the Zoom Tool to magnify an area of the artboard. You then named and saved the new view of the artboard. You named and saved two other views.

FIGURE 3
Drag the Zoom Tool to select what will be magnified

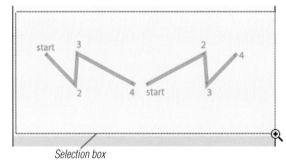

Selection box

FIGURE 4
Four anchor points and three segments

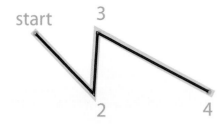

FIGURE 5
Click the path with the Pen Tool to add a new point

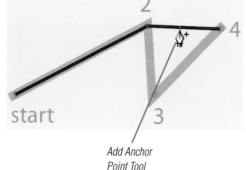

Add Anchor
Point Tool

FIGURE 6
Move an anchor point with the Direct Selection Tool

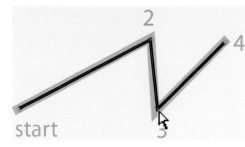

1. Verify that you are still in the yellow view, then click the **Pen Tool** ✎.

2. Set the fill color to [None], the stroke color to Black, and the stroke weight to 1 pt.

3. Using Figure 4 as a reference, click **position 1 (start)**.

4. Click **position 2**, then notice the segment that is automatically drawn between the two anchor points.

5. Click **position 3**, then click **position 4**.

   TIP If you become disconnected from the current path you are drawing, undo your last step, then click the last anchor point with the Pen Tool and continue.

6. Press **[Ctrl]** (Win) or ⌘ (Mac) to switch to the Selection Tool ▶, then click the artboard to stop drawing the path and to deselect it.

   You need to deselect one path before you can start drawing a new one.

7. Click **position 1 (start)** on the next path, then click **position 2**.

8. Skip over position 3 and click **position 4**.

9. Using Figure 5 as a guide, position the Pen Tool anywhere on the segment between points 2 and 4, then click to add a new anchor point.

   TIP When the Pen Tool is positioned over a selected path, the Add Anchor Point Tool appears.

10. Click the **Direct Selection Tool** ▶, then drag the **new anchor point** to position 3, as shown in Figure 6.

Using the Pen Tool, you created two straight paths.

Close a path and align the anchor points

1. Click **View** on the menu bar, then click **pink**.

2. Click the **Pen Tool** [🖊], click the **start/end position** at the top of the polygon, then click **positions 2 through 6**.

3. Position the Pen Tool over the first point you created, then click to close the path, as shown in Figure 7.

4. Switch to the **Direct Selection Tool** [▶], click **point 3**, press and hold **[Shift]**, then click **point 6**.

   TIP Use the [Shift] key to select multiple points.

   Anchor points that are selected appear as solid blue squares; anchor points that are not selected are white or hollow squares.

5. Click **Object** on the menu bar, point to **Path**, then click **Average**.

6. Click the **Horizontal option button** in the Average dialog box, then click **OK**.

   The two selected anchor points align on the horizontal axis, as shown in Figure 8.

7. Select both the start/end point and point 4.

8. Use the Average command to align the points on the vertical axis.

9. Select both point 2 and point 5, then use the Average command to align the points on both axes, as shown in Figure 9.

You drew a closed path, then used the Average command to align three sets of points. You aligned the first set on the horizontal axis, the second on the vertical axis. You aligned the third set of points on both axes, which positioned them one on top of the other.

FIGURE 7
Close a path at its starting point

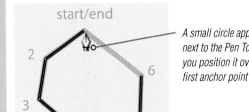

A small circle appears next to the Pen Tool when you position it over the first anchor point

FIGURE 8
Two points aligned on the horizontal axis

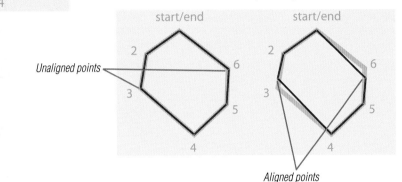

Unaligned points

Aligned points

FIGURE 9
Averaging two points on both the horizontal and vertical axes

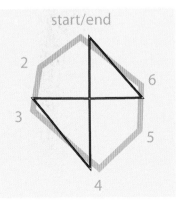

FIGURE 10

Cutting points also deletes the segments attached to them

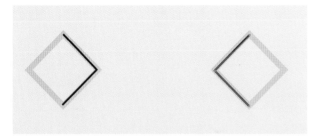

FIGURE 11

Join command unites two distant points with a straight segment

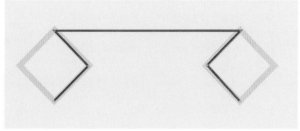

FIGURE 12

Joining the two open anchor points on an open path closes the path

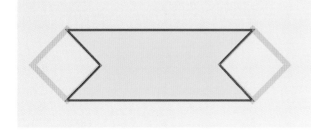

Join anchor points

1. Switch to the mint view of the artboard.

2. Use the Pen Tool ✎ to trace the two diamond shapes.

   > TIP   Remember to deselect the first diamond path with the Selection Tool before you begin tracing the second diamond.

3. Click the **left anchor point** of the first diamond with the Direct Selection Tool ▶, click **Edit** on the menu bar, then click **Cut**.

   Cutting points also deletes the segments attached to them.

4. Cut the right point on the second diamond.

   Your work should resemble Figure 10.

5. Select the top point on each path.

6. Click **Object** on the menu bar, point to **Path**, then click **Join**.

   The points are joined by a straight segment, as shown in Figure 11.

   > TIP   The similarity of the quick keys for Average and Join makes them easy to work with in tandem.

7. Join the two bottom points.

8. Apply a yellow fill to the object, then save your work.

   Your work should resemble Figure 12.

9. Close the Straight Lines document.

You drew two closed paths. You cut a point from each path, which deleted the points and the segments attached to them, creating two open paths. You used the Join command, which drew a new segment between the two top points and the two bottom points on each path. You then applied a yellow fill to the new object.

DRAW CURVED LINES

What You'll Do

In this lesson, you will use the Pen Tool to draw and define curved paths, and learn techniques to draw lines that abruptly change direction.

Defining Properties of Curved Lines

When you click to create anchor points with the Pen Tool, the points are connected by straight segments. You can "draw" a curved path between two anchor points by *clicking and dragging* the Pen Tool to create the points, instead of just clicking. Anchor points created by clicking and dragging the Pen Tool are known as **smooth points**.

When you use the Direct Selection Tool to select a point connected to a curved segment, you will expose the point's **direction lines**, as shown in Figure 13. The angle and length of the direction lines determine the arc of the curved segment. Direction lines are editable. You can click

and drag the **direction points**, or handles, at the end of the direction lines to reshape the curve. Direction lines function only to define curves and do not appear when you print your document.

A smooth point always has two direction lines that move together as a unit. The two curved segments attached to the smooth point are both defined by the direction lines. When you manipulate the direction lines on a smooth point, you change the curve of both segments attached to the point, always maintaining a *smooth* transition through the anchor point.

QUICKTIP

You can change the appearance of anchors and handles in the Selection & Anchor Display section of the Preferences dialog box.

When two paths are joined at a corner point, the two paths can be manipulated independently. A corner point can join two straight segments, one straight segment and one curved segment, or two curved segments. That corner point would have zero, one, or two direction lines, respectively. Figure 14 shows examples of smooth points and corner points.

FIGURE 13
Direction lines define a curve

FIGURE 14
Smooth points and corner points

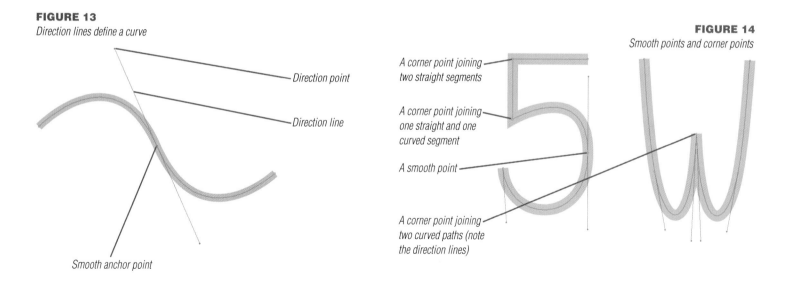

Direction point

Direction line

Smooth anchor point

A corner point joining two straight segments

A corner point joining one straight and one curved segment

A smooth point

A corner point joining two curved paths (note the direction lines)

When a corner point joins one or two curved segments, the direction lines are unrelated and are often referred to as "broken." When you manipulate one, the other doesn't move.

Converting Anchor Points

The Convert Anchor Point Tool changes corner points to smooth points and smooth points to corner points.

To convert a corner point to a smooth point, you click and drag the Convert Anchor Point Tool on the anchor point to *pull out* direction lines. See Figure 15.

The Convert Anchor Point Tool works two ways to convert a smooth point to a corner point, and both are very useful when drawing.

FIGURE 15
Converting a corner point to a smooth point

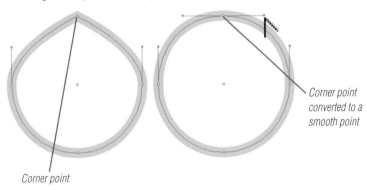

Corner point

Corner point converted to a smooth point

Drawing and Composing an Illustration

When you click directly on a smooth point with the Convert Anchor Point Tool, the direction lines disappear. The two attached segments lose whatever curve defined them and become straight segments, as shown in Figure 16.

You can also use the Convert Anchor Point Tool on one of the two direction lines of a smooth point. The tool "breaks" the direction lines and allows you to move one independently of the other. The smooth point is converted to a corner point that now joins two unrelated curved segments.

Once the direction lines are broken, they remain broken. You can manipulate them independently with the Direct Selection Tool; you no longer need the Convert Anchor Point Tool to do so.

FIGURE 16
Converting smooth points to corner points

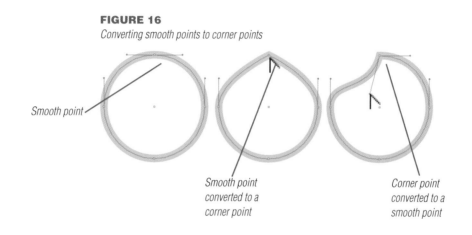

Smooth point

Smooth point
converted to a
corner point

Corner point
converted to a
smooth point

Toggling between the Pen Tool and the selection tools
Drawing points and selecting points go hand in hand, and you will often switch back and forth between the Pen Tool and one of the selection tools. Clicking from one tool to the other in the Tools panel is unnecessary and will impede your productivity. To master the Pen Tool, you *must* incorporate the keyboard command for "toggling" between the Pen Tool and the selection tools. With the Pen Tool selected, press [Ctrl] (Win) or ⌘ (Mac), which will switch the Pen Tool to the Selection Tool or the Direct Selection Tool, depending on which tool you used last.

Draw and edit a curved line

1. Open AI 3-2.ai, then save it as **Curved Lines 1**.
2. Click the **Pen Tool** ✎, then position it over the first point position on the line.
3. Click and drag upward until the pointer is at the center of the purple star.
4. Position the Pen Tool over the second point position.
5. Click and drag down to the red star.
6. Using the same method, trace the remainder of the blue line, as shown in Figure 17.
7. Click the **Direct Selection Tool** ▶.
8. Select the second anchor point.
9. Click and drag the **direction handle** of the *top* direction line to the second purple star, as shown in Figure 18.

   The move changes the shape of *both* segments attached to the anchor point.
10. Select the third anchor point.
11. Drag the **bottom direction handle** to the second red star, as shown in Figure 19.
12. Manipulate the direction lines to restore the curves to their appearance in Figure 17.
13. Save your work, then close the Curved Lines 1 document.

You traced a curved line by making smooth points with the Pen Tool. You used the Direct Selection Tool to manipulate the direction lines of the smooth points and adjust the curves. You then used the direction lines to restore the line to its original curves.

FIGURE 17
Smooth points draw continuous curves

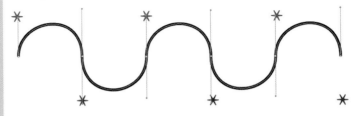

FIGURE 18
Moving one direction line changes two curves

Click the Direct Selection Tool on any smooth point to expose its direction lines

FIGURE 19
Round curves are distorted by moving direction lines

Drawing and Composing an Illustration

FIGURE 20

Smooth points are converted to corner points

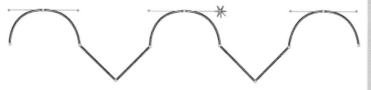

FIGURE 21

Smooth points restored from corner points

Convert anchor points

1. Open AI 3-3.ai, then save it as **Curved Lines 2**.
2. Click **View** on the menu bar, then click **View #1**.
3. Click the **Direct Selection Tool** any-where on the black line.

    Six anchor points become visible.
4. Click **Object** on the menu bar, point to **Path**, then click **Add Anchor Points**.

    Five anchor points are added that do not change the shape of the line.
5. Click the **Convert Anchor Point Tool**, then click each of the five new anchor points.

    > TIP   The Convert Anchor Point Tool is hidden beneath the Pen Tool.

    The smooth points are converted to corner points, as shown in Figure 20.
6. Click the six original anchor points with the Convert Anchor Point Tool.
7. Starting from the left side of the line, posi-tion the Convert Anchor Point Tool over the sixth anchor point.
8. Click and drag the **anchor point** to the purple star.

    The corner point is converted to a smooth point.
9. Using Figure 21 as a guide, convert the cor-ner points to the left and right of the new curve.

You added five new anchor points to the line, then used the Convert Anchor Point Tool to convert all 11 points from smooth to corner points. You then used the Convert Anchor Point Tool to convert three corner points to smooth points.

Draw a line with curved and straight segments

1. Click **View** on the menu bar, then click **View #2**.

2. Click the **Pen Tool** 🖊, position it over the first point position, then click and drag down to the green star.

3. Position the Pen Tool over the second point position, then click and drag up to the purple star, as shown in the top section of Figure 22.

4. Click the **second anchor point**.

   The direction line you dragged is deleted, as shown in the lower section of Figure 22.

5. Click the **third point position** to create the third anchor point.

6. Position the Pen Tool over the third anchor point, then click and drag a direction line up to the green star.

7. Position the Pen Tool over the **fourth point position**, then click and drag down to the purple star.

8. Click the **fourth anchor point**.

9. Position the Pen Tool over the fifth position, then click.

10. While the Pen Tool is still positioned over the fifth anchor point, click and drag a direction line down to the green star.

11. Finish tracing the line, then deselect the path.

You traced a line that has three curves joined by two straight segments. You used the technique of clicking the previous smooth point to convert it to a corner point, allowing you to change the direction of the path.

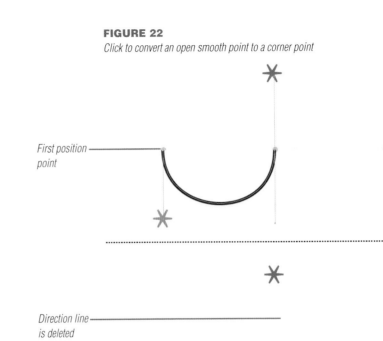

FIGURE 22
Click to convert an open smooth point to a corner point

First position point

Direction line is deleted

Clicking the last smooth point you drew converts it to a corner point

FIGURE 23

Use the Convert Anchor Point Tool to "break" the direction lines and redirect the path

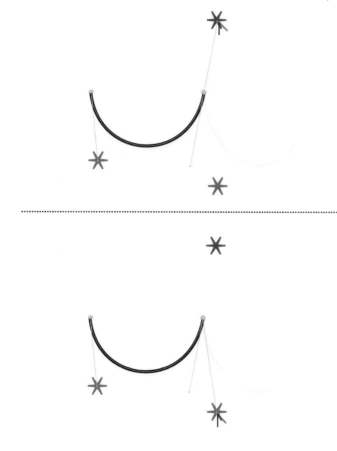

Reverse direction while drawing

1. Click **View** on the menu bar, then click **View #3**.

2. Click the **Pen Tool** position it over the first point position, then click and drag down to the purple star.

3. Position the Pen Tool over the second point position, then click and drag up to the red star, as shown in the top section of Figure 23.

4. Press and hold **[Alt]** (Win) or **[option]** (Mac) to switch to the Convert Anchor Point Tool , then click and drag the **direction handle** on the red star down to the second purple star, as shown in the lower section of Figure 23.

   TIP Press [Alt] (Win) or [option] (Mac) to toggle between the Pen and the Convert Anchor Point Tools.

5. Release [Alt] (Win) or [option] (Mac), then continue to trace the line using the same method.

   TIP If you switch between the PenTool and the Convert Anchor Point Tool using the Tools panel, instead of using [Alt] (Win) or [option] (Mac), you will disconnect from the current path.

6. Save your work, then close the Curved Lines 2 document.

You used the Convert Anchor Point Tool to "break" the direction lines of a smooth point, converting it to a corner point in the process. You used the redirected direction line to define the next curve in the sequence.

DRAW ELEMENTS OF
AN ILLUSTRATION

What You'll Do

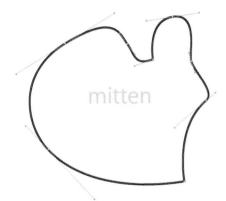

In this lesson, you will draw 14 elements of an illustration. By tracing previously drawn elements, you will develop a sense of where to place anchor points when drawing a real-world illustration.

Starting an Illustration

Getting started with drawing an illustration is often the hardest part. Sometimes the illustration will be an image of a well-known object or a supplied sketch or a picture. At other times, the illustration to be created will exist only in your imagination. In either case, the challenge is the same: How do you translate the concept from its source to the Illustrator artboard?

Drawing from Scratch

Drawing from scratch means that you start with a new Illustrator document and create the illustration, using only the Illustrator tools. This approach is common, especially when the goal is to draw familiar items such as a daisy, a fish, or the sun, for example.

Illustrator's shape tools (such as the Ellipse Tool) combined with the transform tools (such as the Rotate Tool) make the program very powerful for creating geometric designs from scratch. The Undo and Redo commands allow you to experiment, and

you will often find yourself surprised by the design you end up with!

Typographic illustrations—even complex ones—are often created from scratch.

Many talented illustrators and designers are able to create complex graphics off the cuff. It can be an astounding experience to watch an illustrator start with a blank artboard and, with no reference material, produce sophisticated graphics—graphics with attitude and expression and emotion, with unexpected shapes and subtle relationships between objects.

Tracing a Scanned Image

Using the Place command, it is easy to import a scanned image into Illustrator. For complex illustrations—especially those of people or objects with delicate relationships, such as maps or blueprints—many designers find it easier to scan a sketch or a photo and import it into Illustrator as a guide or a point of reference.

Tracing a scanned image is not "cheating." An original drawing is an original drawing, whether it is first created on a computer or on a piece of paper. Rather than being a negative, the ability to use a computer to render a sketch is a fine example of the revolutionary techniques that illustration software has brought to the art of drawing. Figure 24 shows an illustration created from scratch in Illustrator, and Figure 25 shows a scanned sketch that will be the basis for the illustration you will create throughout this chapter.

FIGURE 24
An illustration created from scratch

FIGURE 25
Place a scanned sketch in Illustrator, and you can trace it or use it as a visual reference

SUSAN'S DANCE STUDIO

Draw a closed path using smooth points

1. Open AI 3-4.ai, then save it as **Snowball Parts**.

2. Click **View** on the menu bar, then click **Arm**.

3. Verify that the fill color is set to [None] and the stroke color is set to Black.

4. Click the **Pen Tool** ✎ , position it over point 1, then click and drag a **direction line** to the green star on the right side of the 1.

5. Go to position 2, then click and drag a **direction line** to the next green star.

   TIP Watch the blue preview of the new segment fall into place as you drag the Pen Tool. This will help you understand when to stop dragging the direction line.

6. Using the same method, continue to draw points 3 through 6, then compare your screen to Figure 26.

7. Position the Pen Tool over point 1.

8. Press and hold **[Alt]** (Win) or **[option]** (Mac), then click and drag to position the ending segment and close the path.

You drew a curved path. To close the path, you used a corner point, which allowed you to position the ending segment without affecting the starting segment.

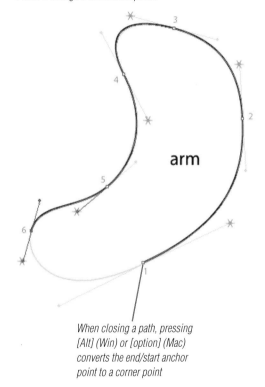

FIGURE 26
Points 1 through 6 are smooth points

arm

When closing a path, pressing
[Alt] (Win) or [option] (Mac)
converts the end/start anchor
point to a corner point

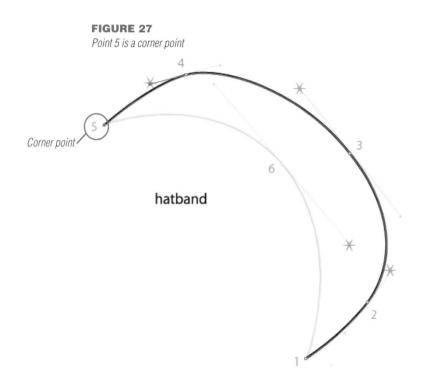

FIGURE 27
Point 5 is a corner point

Corner point

hatband

Begin and end a path with a corner point

1. Click **View** on the menu bar, then click **Hatband**.

2. Verify that the fill color is set to [None] and the stroke color is set to Black.

3. Click the **Pen Tool** ⬧ , then click **position 1** to create a corner point.

4. Draw the next two curved segments for positions 2 and 3, using the green stars as guides.

5. Position the Pen Tool over position 4, then click and drag to the green star.

6. Click **position 5** to create a corner point, as shown in Figure 27.

7. Position the Pen Tool over position 6, then click and drag to the green star.

8. Click **position 1** to close the path with a corner point.

9. Click the **Selection Tool** ▶ , then deselect the path.

You began a path with a corner point. When it was time to close the path, you simply clicked the starting point. Since the point was created without direction lines, there were no direction lines to contend with when closing the path.

Redirect a path while drawing

1. Click **View** on the menu bar, then click **Nose**.

    The Nose view includes the nose, mouth, eyebrow, and teeth.

2. Click the **Pen Tool** 🖊, then click **point 1** on the nose to start the path with a corner point.

3. Create smooth points at positions 2 and 3.

    The direction of the nose that you are tracing abruptly changes at point 3.

4. Press and hold **[Alt]** (Win) or **[option]** (Mac) to switch to the Convert Anchor Point Tool 🖊, then move the top direction handle of point 3 down to the red star, as shown in Figure 28.

5. Release [Alt] (Win) or [option] (Mac) to switch back to the Pen Tool, click and drag **position 4** to finish drawing the path, click the Selection Tool ▶, then deselect the path.

    The nose element, as shown in Figure 29, is an open path.

Tracing the nose, you encountered an abrupt change in direction, followed by a curve. You used the Convert Anchor Point Tool to redirect the direction lines on point 3, simultaneously converting point 3 from smooth to corner and defining the shape of the curved segment that follows.

FIGURE 28
Use the Convert Anchor Point Tool to redirect the path

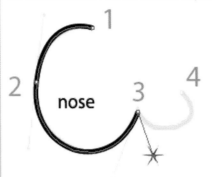

FIGURE 29
Nose element is an open path

Drawing and Composing an Illustration

FIGURE 30

Use a scanned sketch as a reference or for tracing

1. Click **View** on the menu bar, then click **Fit in Window**.

2. Click **File** on the menu bar, then click **Place**.

3. Navigate to the drive and folder where your Data Files are stored.

4. Click **Snowball Sketch.tif**, then click **Place**.

   A scan of the Snowball Sketch illustration is placed in a bounding box at the center of the artboard.

5. Use the Scale Tool ⬚ to scale the placed file 115%.

   | TIP You can apply all of the transform tools to placed files.

6. Click the **Selection Tool** ▶, move the placed file into the scratch area, then lock it.

7. Draw the remaining elements of the illustration, referring to the sketch in the scratch area or to Figure 30 for help.

   | TIP The mouth, eyebrow, and teeth are located in the Nose view.

8. Save your work after you complete each element.

You placed a file of a scanned sketch to use as a reference guide. You scaled the object, dragged it to the scratch area, locked it, then drew the remaining elements of the illustration.

APPLY ATTRIBUTES
TO OBJECTS

What You'll Do

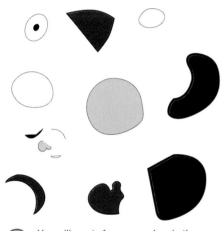

You will create four new colors in the Color panel and apply each to one of the illustration elements. Using the Eyedropper Tool, you will paint the remaining items quickly and easily.

Using the Eyedropper Tool

Illustrator uses the word **attributes** to refer to that which has been applied to an object that affects its appearance. Typographic attributes, for example, would include font, leading, horizontal scale, etc. Artistic attributes include the fill color, stroke color, and stroke weight.

The Eyedropper Tool is handy for applying *all* of an object's attributes to another object. Its icon is particularly apt: The Eyedropper Tool "picks up" an object's attributes, such as fill color, stroke color, and stroke weight.

QUICKTIP
You can think of the Eyedropper Tool as taking a sample of an object's attributes.

The Eyedropper Tool is particularly useful when you want to apply one object's attrib-utes to another. For example, if you have appplied a blue fill with a 3.5 pt orange stroke to an object, you can easily apply those attributes to new or already-existing objects. Simply select the object that you want to format, then click the formatted object with the Eyedropper Tool.

This is a simple example, but don't under-estimate the power of the Eyedropper Tool. As you explore more of Illustrator, you will find that you are able to apply a variety of increasingly complex attributes to objects. The more – and more complex – the attrib-utes, the more the Eyedropper Tool reveals its usefulness.

You can also use the Eyedropper Tool to copy type formatting and effects between text elements. This can be especially useful when designing display type for headlines.

Adding a Fill to an Open Path

You can think of the letter O as an example of a closed path and the letter U as an example of an open path. Although it seems a bit strange, you are able to add a fill to an open path just as you would to a closed path. The program draws an imaginary straight line between the endpoints of an open path to define where the fill ends. Figure 31 shows an open path in the shape of a U with a red fill. Note where the fill ends. For the most part, avoid applying fills to open paths. Though Illustrator will apply the fill, an open path's primary role is to feature a stroke. Any effect that you can create by filling an open path you can also create with a more effective method by filling a closed path.

FIGURE 31

A fill color applied to an open path

Apply new attributes to open and closed paths

1. Verify that nothing is selected on the artboard.

2. Create a royal blue color in the Color panel.

3. Fill the arm with the royal blue color, then change its stroke weight to 6 pt.

   TIP Use the views at the bottom of the View menu to see and select each element you need to work with. The mouth, eyebrow, and teeth are located in the Nose view.

4. Deselect the arm, then create a deep red color in the Color panel.

5. Fill the hatband with the deep red color, then change its stroke weight to 3 pt.

6. Deselect the hatband, then create a flesh-toned color in the Color panel that is 20% magenta and 56% yellow.

7. Fill the head with the flesh tone; don't change the stroke weight.

8. Fill the pompom with White; don't change the stroke weight.

9. Fill the mouth with Black; don't change the stroke weight.

10. Compare your work with Figure 32.

You applied new attributes to five closed paths by creating three new colors, using them as fills, then changing the stroke weight on two of the objects.

FIGURE 32
New attributes applied to five elements

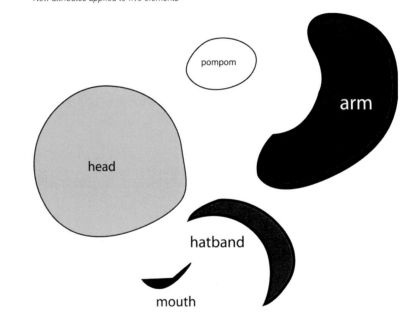

FIGURE 33

Use the Eyedropper Tool to apply the attributes of one object to another . . . with one click!

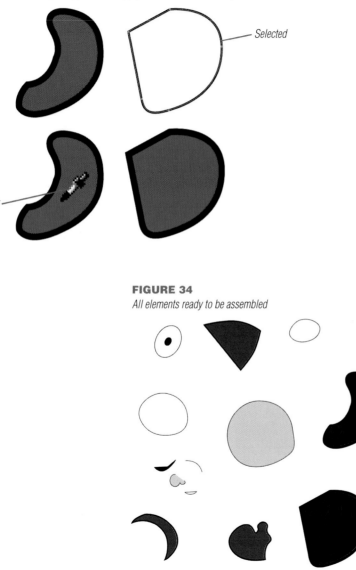

Selected

Click

FIGURE 34

All elements ready to be assembled

1. Select the torso.
2. Click the **Eyedropper Tool** 🖊, then click the **blue arm**.

   As shown in Figure 33, the torso takes on the same fill and stroke attributes as the arm.
3. Switch to the Selection Tool 🔺, select the hat, click the **Eyedropper Tool** 🖊 then click the **hatband**.
4. Using any method you like, fill and stroke the remaining objects using the colors shown in Figure 34.

You applied the same attributes from one object to another by first selecting the object you wanted to apply the attributes to, then clicking the object with the desired attributes, using the Eyedropper Tool.

ASSEMBLE AN
ILLUSTRATION

What You'll Do

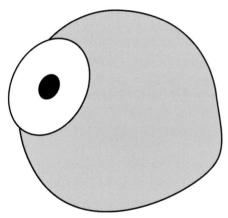

In this lesson, you will arrange the elements that you drew in Lesson 4 to create a composed illustration.

Assembling an Illustration

Illustrator's basic stacking order design is sophisticated enough to compose any illustration. Assembling an illustration with multiple objects will test your fluency with the stacking order commands: Bring to Front, Send to Back, Bring Forward, Send Backward, Paste in Front, Paste in Back, Group, Lock, Unlock All, Hide, and Show All. The sequence in which you draw the elements determines the stacking order (newer elements are in front of older ones), so you'll almost certainly need to adjust the stacking order when assembling the elements. Locking and hiding placed elements will help you to protect the elements when they are positioned correctly.

FIGURE 35
Eye positioned on the head

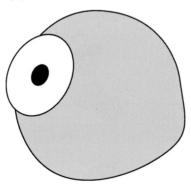

FIGURE 36
Second eye is a copy of the first

FIGURE 37

Nose pasted in front of the left eye

The nose behind
the left eye

The nose in front
of the left eye

FIGURE 38

Eyebrow positioned over the right eye

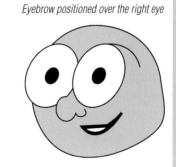

FIGURE 39

All elements in position

Assemble the illustration

1. Select and copy all the elements on the artboard.

2. Create a new CMYK Color document that is 9" × 9", then save it as **Snowball Assembled**.

3. Paste the copied elements into the Snowball Assembled document.

4. Deselect all objects, select the head, click **Object** on the menu bar, point to **Arrange**, then click **Send to Back**.

5. Group the eye and the iris, then position the eye on the head as shown in Figure 35.

6. Click the **eye**, press **[Alt]** (Win) or **[option]** (Mac), then drag to create a copy of it, as shown in Figure 36.

7. Position the nose on the face, cut the nose, select the left eye, then paste in front.

   The nose is pasted in the same position, but now it is in front of the eye, as shown in Figure 37.

8. Select the teeth, then bring them to the front.

9. Position the teeth over the mouth, then group them.

10. Position the mouth and the teeth on the head, and the eyebrow over the right eye, as shown in Figure 38.

11. Finish assembling the illustration, using Figure 39 as a guide, then save your work.

   TIP Use the Object menu and the Arrange menu command to change the stacking order of objects, as necessary.

You assembled the illustration, utilizing various commands to change the stacking order of the individual elements.

Lesson 5   Assemble an Illustration

ILLUSTRATOR 3-29

STROKE OBJECTS FOR
ARTISTIC EFFECT

What You'll Do

In this lesson, you will experiment with strokes of varying weight and attributes, using options in the Stroke panel. You will then apply pseudo-strokes to all of the objects to create dramatic stroke effects.

Defining Joins and Caps

In addition to applying a stroke weight, you use the Stroke panel to define other stroke attributes, including joins and caps, and whether a stroke is solid or dashed. Figure 40 shows the Dashed Line utility in the Stroke panel.

Caps are applied to the ends of stroked paths. The Stroke panel offers three choices: Butt Cap, Round Cap, and Projecting Cap. Choose Butt Cap for squared ends and Round Cap for rounded ends. Generally, round caps are more appealing to the eye.

The projecting cap applies a squared edge that extends the anchor point at a distance that is one-half the weight of the stroke. With a projecting cap, the weight of the stroke is equal in all directions around the line. The projecting cap is useful when you align two anchor points at a right angle, as shown in Figure 41.

FIGURE 40
Stroke panel

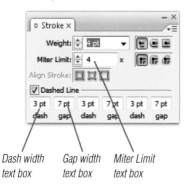

Dash width text box   Gap width text box   Miter Limit text box

FIGURE 41
Projecting caps are useful when segments meet at right angles

Two segments with butt caps   *Two segments with projecting caps*

When two stroked paths form a corner point, **joins** define the appearance of the corner. The default is a miter join, which produces stroked lines with pointed corners. The round join produces stroked lines with rounded corners, and the bevel join produces stroked lines with squared corners. The greater the weight of the stroke, the more apparent the join will be, as shown in Figure 42.

Defining the Miter Limit

The miter limit determines when a miter join will be squared off to a beveled edge. The miter is the length of the point, from the inside to the outside. The length of the miter is not the same as the stroke weight. When two stroked paths are at an acute angle, the length of the miter will greatly exceed the weight of the stroke, which results in an extreme point that can be very distracting.

QUICKTIP
You can align a stroke to the center, inside, or outside of a path using the Align Stroke buttons on the Stroke panel.

The default miter limit is 4, which means that when the length of the miter reaches 4 times the stroke weight, the program will automatically square it off to a beveled edge. Generally, you will find the default miter limit satisfactory, but remain conscious of it when you draw objects with acute angles, such as stars and triangles. Figure 43 shows the impact of a miter limit on a stroked star with acute angles.

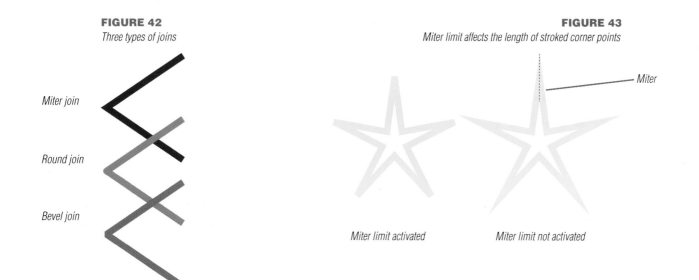

FIGURE 42
Three types of joins

Miter join

Round join

Bevel join

FIGURE 43
Miter limit affects the length of stroked corner points

Miter

Miter limit activated   Miter limit not activated

Creating a Dashed Stroke

A dashed stroke is like any other stroked path in Illustrator, except that its stroke has been broken up into a sequence of dashes separated by gaps. The Stroke panel offers you the freedom to customize dashed or dotted lines; enter the lengths of the dashes and the gaps between them in the six dash and gap text boxes. You can create a maximum of three different sizes of dashes separated by three different sizes of gaps. The pattern you establish will be repeated across the length of the stroke.

When creating dashed strokes, remain conscious of the cap choice in the Stroke panel. Butt caps create familiar square dashes, and round caps create rounded dashes. Creating a dotted line requires round caps. Figure 44 shows two dashed lines using the same pattern but with different caps applied.

Creating Pseudo-Stroke Effects

Strokes around objects—especially black strokes—often contribute much to an illustration in terms of contrast, dimension, and dramatic effect. To that end, you may find the Stroke panel to be limited.

Sometimes, the most effective stroke is no stroke at all. A classic technique that designers have used since the early versions of Illustrator is the "pseudo-stroke," or false stroke. Basically, you place a black-filled copy behind an illustration element, then distort the black element with the Direct Selection Tool so that it "peeks" out from behind the element in varying degrees.

This technique, as shown in Figure 45, is relatively simple to execute and can be used for dramatic effect in an illustration.

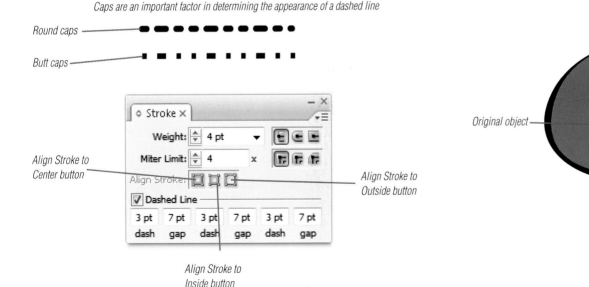

FIGURE 44

Caps are an important factor in determining the appearance of a dashed line

Round caps

Butt caps

Align Stroke to Center button

Align Stroke to Outside button

Align Stroke to Inside button

FIGURE 45

The "pseudo-stroke" effect

Original object

Black copy pasted in back and distorted

FIGURE 46

Bevel joins applied to paths

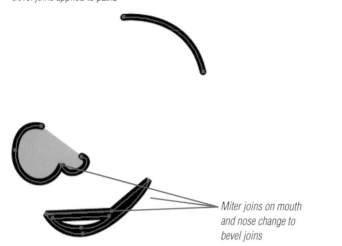

Miter joins on mouth
and nose change to
bevel joins

FIGURE 47

Round joins applied to paths

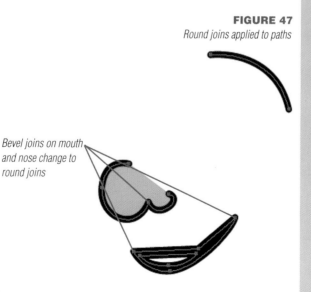

Bevel joins on mouth
and nose change to
round joins

Modify stroke attributes

1. Select the eyebrow, the nose, and the mouth.

2. Click **Select** on the menu bar, then click **Inverse**.

   The selected items are now deselected, and the deselected items are selected.

3. Hide the selected items.

4. Select all, then change the stroke weight to 3 pt.

5. Click the **Stroke panel list arrow**, click **Show Options** if necessary, then click the **Round Cap button** [icon].

   The caps on open paths are rounded.

6. Click the **Bevel Join button** [icon].

   The miter joins on the mouth and nose change to a bevel join, as shown in Figure 46.

7. Click the **Round Join button** [icon].

   The bevel joins on the mouth and nose change to round joins, as shown in Figure 47.

8. Remove the stroke from the teeth.

   TIP Use the Direct Selection Tool to select the teeth, since they are grouped to the mouth.

You hid elements so you could focus on the eyebrow, nose, and mouth. You applied round caps to the open paths and round joins to the corner points.

Create a dashed stroke

1. Show all objects, then select all.

2. Deselect the snowball, then hide the selected items.

   The snowball should be the only element showing.

3. Select the snowball, then change the stroke weight to 4 pt.

4. Click the **Dashed Line check box** in the Stroke panel.

5. Experiment with different dash and gap sizes.

6. Toggle between butt and round caps.

   The dashes change from rectangles to ovals.

7. Enter 1 pt dashes and 4 pt gaps.

8. Click the **Round Cap button** 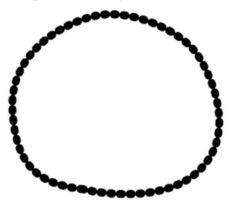, compare your snowball to the one shown in Figure 48, then show all of the objects that are currently hidden.

You applied a dashed stroke to the snowball object and noted how a change in caps affected the dashes.

FIGURE 48
Creating a dashed stroke using the Stroke panel

Drawing and Composing an Illustration

FIGURE 49

A black copy peeking out beneath the front object

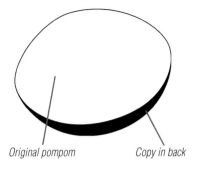

Original pompom   Copy in back

FIGURE 51

Completed illustration

FIGURE 50

Pompom with the pseudo-stroke effect

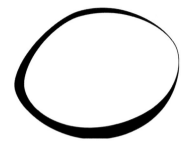

Create pseudo-strokes

1. Copy the pompom, then paste in back.

2. Apply a black fill to the copy.

   TIP The copy is still selected behind the original white pompom, making it easy to apply the black fill.

3. Click the **white pompom**, then remove the stroke.

4. Lock the white pompom.

5. Using the Direct Selection Tool [▶], select the bottom anchor point on the black copy.

6. Use the arrow keys to move the anchor point 5 pts down, away from the white pompom, using Figure 49 as a reference.

   The black copy is increasingly revealed as its size is increased beneath the locked white pompom.

7. Move the left anchor point 4 pts to the left.

8. Move the top anchor point 2 pts up, then deselect.

   Your work should resemble Figure 50.

9. Using the same methods, and Figure 51 as a reference, create distorted black copies behind all the remaining elements except the torso, the mouth, and the eyebrow.

10. Save your work, then close Snowball Assembled.

You created black copies behind each element, then distorted them, using the Direct Selection Tool and the arrow keys, to create the illusion of uneven black strokes around the object.

USE LIVE TRACE AND THE
LIVE PAINT BUCKET TOOL

What You'll Do

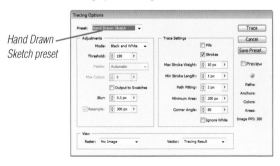

In this lesson, you will use the Live Trace and Live Paint features.

Introducing Live Trace

Have you ever roughed out a sketch on paper, only to have to recreate it from scratch on your computer? Or, have you ever wished that you could convert a scanned photograph into editable vector graphics to use as the basis of an illustration? With Live Trace, you can have Illustrator trace a graphic for you.

Live Trace offers a number of built-in tracing presets that help you fine-tune your tracing results from the start. Additional presets, such as Hand Drawn Sketch, Comic Art, and Detailed Illustration, help create even extra special effects.

So what is the "live" in Live Trace, you ask? The live aspects of Live Trace occur in the Tracing Options dialog box, shown in Figure 52. Here, you can click the Preset list arrow to choose which type of preset you want to use to trace the bitmap (in the figure, Hand Drawn Sketch is the chosen

FIGURE 52
Tracing Options dialog box

Hand Drawn Sketch preset

preset). To see the resulting artwork before you close the dialog box, click the Preview check box. You can also continue to manipulate the graphic by changing the many settings in the Adjustments and Trace Settings sections of the dialog box. Illustrator will continually retrace the graphic to preview the final effect. That's the live part of Live Trace!

Tracing a Line-Art Sketch

Figure 53 shows a magic marker sketch of a dog that has been scanned into Photoshop and placed in Illustrator. Figure 54 shows the artwork after it has been traced using the default Live Trace settings. Not much difference,

you say? Well, that's a good thing, a testament to how accurately Live Trace does its job.

As you were undoubtedly taught years ago, appearances can be deceiving. Though the artwork in 53 and 54 appears similar, they couldn't be more different, because the artwork in 54 is a vector graphic that has been traced from the bitmap graphic shown in 54.

Expanding a Traced Graphic

When a bitmap image is selected in Illustrator, the Live Trace button becomes available on the Control panel. After Live

Trace has been executed, the Expand button becomes available in the Control panel. In order to select and modify the paths and points that make up the new vector graphic, you must first click the Expand button. Once done, the illustration is able to be selected and modified, as shown in Figure 55.

QUICKTIP

Figure 55 shows the artwork in Outline mode so that you can better see the paths and points.

FIGURE 55
Expanded traced graphic, in Outline mode

FIGURE 54
Traced graphic

FIGURE 53
Bitmap graphic placed in Illustrator

Tracing a Photograph

You use Live Trace to trace a bitmap photo the same way you trace a sketch. With photographic images, however, the settings in the Tracing Options dialog box can be used to create some very interesting illustration effects.

Figure 56 shows a scanned photograph that has been placed in Illustrator. Clicking the Live Trace button instructs Illustrator to trace the photo using the default Black & White setting. The result is shown in Figure 57.

QUICKTIP

The default Black & White setting is 128 Threshold.

The resulting graphic is not the only result possible—not by a long shot. Rather than use the default setting, you can click the Tracing presets and options list arrow on the Control panel and choose from a variety of styles, such as Comic Art or Technical Drawing. The Tracing presets and options list arrow is also available in the Tracing Options dialog box.

FIGURE 56
Scanned photograph placed in Illustrator

FIGURE 57
Photograph traced at default Black & White setting

Introducing Live Paint

Adobe is touting the Live Paint Bucket Tool as being "revolutionary," and it's not an overstatement. The Live Paint Bucket Tool breaks all the fundamental rules of Illustrator, and creates some new ones. For that reason, when you are working with the Live Paint Bucket Tool, it's a good idea to think of yourself as working in Live Paint *mode*, because Illustrator will function differently with this tool than it will with any other.

Essentially, the Live Paint Bucket Tool is designed to make painting easier and more intuitive. It does this by changing the basic rules of Illustrator objects. In Live Paint mode, the concept of layers no longer applies—selected objects are all on the same level. The Live Paint Bucket Tool uses two new Illustrator object types called regions and edges. Regions and edges are comparable to fills and strokes, but they are "live." As shown in Figure 58, where two regions overlap, a third region is created and can be painted with its own color. Where two edges overlap, a third edge is created. It too can be painted its own color.

Adobe likes to say that Live Paint is intuitive—something that looks like it should be able to be filled with its own color can indeed be filled with its own color. As long as you have the Live Paint Bucket Tool selected, selected objects can be filled using the new rules of Live Paint mode. Once you leave Live Paint mode, the paint that you have applied to the graphic remains part of the illustration.

FIGURE 58
Identifying regions and edges in an illustration

Edge

Region

Edge with new
color applied

Region with new
color applied

Live Painting Regions

To paint objects with the Live Paint Bucket Tool, you must first select the objects you wish to paint. Figure 59 shows three selected rectangles that overlap each other. The selection marks show various shapes created by the overlapping. As stated earlier, these overlapping areas or shapes are called regions. To fill the regions, click the Live Paint Bucket Tool, click a color in the Swatches panel, then click a region that you want to fill. As shown in Figure 60, when you position the Live Paint Bucket Tool pointer over a region,

that region is highlighted. Click the Live Paint Bucket Tool and the region is filled, as shown in Figure 61.

As shown in Figure 62, each region can be filled with new colors. But that's not all that the Live Paint Bucket Tool has to offer. The "live" part of Live Paint is that these regions are now part of a **live paint group**, and they maintain a dynamic relationship with each other. This means that when any of the objects is moved, the overlapping area changes shape—and fill—accordingly. For

example, in Figure 63, the tall thin rectangle has been moved to the left—note how the overlapping regions have been redrawn and how their fills have updated with the move.

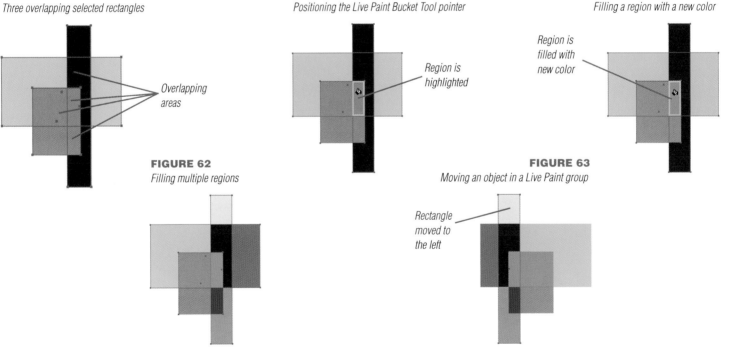

FIGURE 59
Three overlapping selected rectangles

Overlapping areas

FIGURE 60
Positioning the Live Paint Bucket Tool pointer

Region is highlighted

FIGURE 61
Filling a region with a new color

Region is filled with new color

FIGURE 62
Filling multiple regions

FIGURE 63
Moving an object in a Live Paint group

Rectangle moved to the left

Drawing and Composing an Illustration

Painting Virtual Regions

The intuitive aspect of Live Paint mode goes one step further with virtual regions. Figure 64 shows six Illustrator paths. Each has a 1-point black stroke and no fill—and each is selected. With the Live Paint Bucket Tool, the regions that are created by the intersection of the paths are able to be filled—as though they were objects. Figure 65 shows four regions that have been filled with the Live Paint Bucket Tool.

In this case, as in the case of the overlapping rectangles, the dynamic relationship is maintained. Figure 66 shows the same six regions having been moved, and the filled regions have been redrawn and their fills updated.

FIGURE 64
Six paths

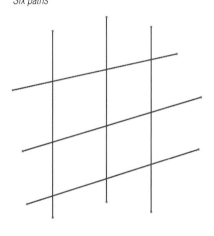

FIGURE 65
Four regions between paths filled

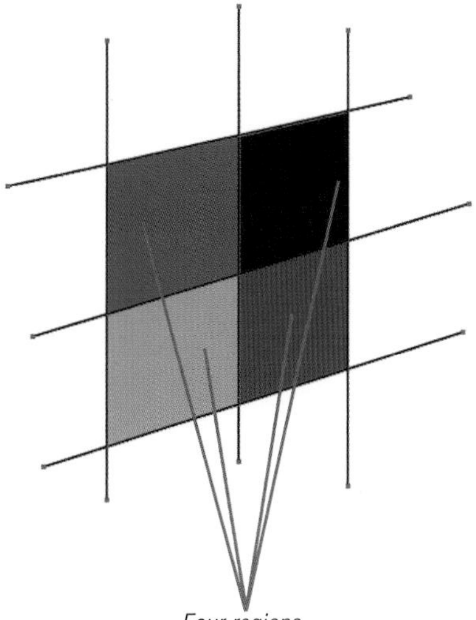

Four regions

FIGURE 66
Moving paths in a live paint group

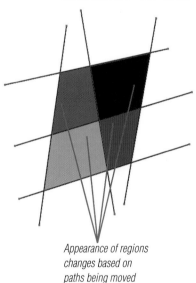

Appearance of regions changes based on paths being moved

Inserting an Object into a Live Paint Group

New objects can be inserted into a live paint group. To do so, switch to the Selection Tool, then double-click inside any of the regions of the group. As shown in Figure 67, a gray rectangle appears around the group, indicating that you are in **insertion mode**. Once in insertion mode, you can then add an object or objects to the group.

As shown in Figure 68, another tall rectangle has been added to the group. It can now be painted with the Live Paint Bucket Tool as part of the live paint group. Once you've added all that you want to the live paint group, exit insertion mode by double-clicking the Selection Tool outside of the live paint group.

FIGURE 67

Viewing the art in insertion mode

FIGURE 68

Adding an object to the live paint group

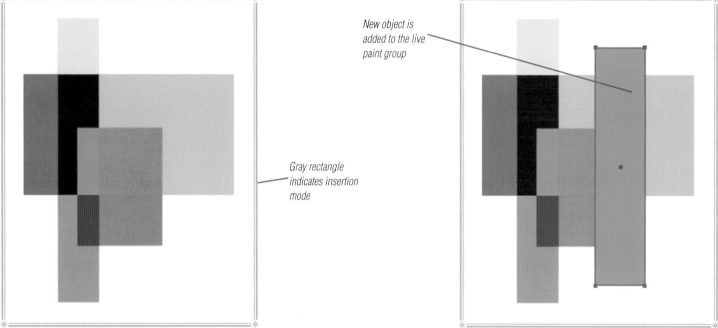

Gray rectangle indicates insertion mode

New object is added to the live paint group

Expanding a Live Paint Group

When you deselect a live paint group, the deselected group does not change its appearance. Additionally, you have the option of using the Expand command to release the Live Paint group into its component regions. Simply select the live paint group, then click the Expand button on the Control panel. Each region will be converted to an ordinary Illustrator object.

Live Painting Edges

In Live Paint mode, if regions are akin to fills, then edges are akin to strokes. With the Live Paint Bucket Tool, you can paint edges as well as regions.

Figure 69 shows two overlapping objects, each with a 6-point stroke. To paint edges (strokes), double-click the Live Paint Bucket Tool, then click the Paint Strokes check box in the Live Paint Bucket Options dialog box, as shown in Figure 70.

When you position the Live Paint Bucket Tool over an edge, its icon changes to a paint brush icon. The edge is highlighted and able to be painted as though it were its own object, as shown in 71.

FIGURE 69
Two overlapping rectangles

FIGURE 70
Specifying the Live Paint Bucket Tool to paint strokes (edges)

FIGURE 71
Painting edges

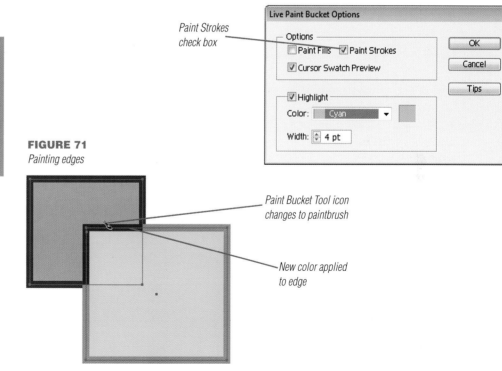

Paint Strokes check box

Paint Bucket Tool icon changes to paintbrush

New color applied to edge

Use Live Trace to trace a sketch

1. Open AI 3-5.ai, then save it as **Live Trace Sketch**.

   The file contains a placed marker sketch that was scanned in Photoshop.

2. Click **Window** on the menu bar, then click **Control**, if necessary.

3. Click the **Selection Tool** ▶ then click the **placed graphic**.

   When the placed graphic is selected, the Live Trace button on the Control panel becomes visible.

4. Click the **Live Trace button** on the Control panel.

5. Click the **Expand button** on the Control panel.

   As shown in Figure 72, the traced graphic is expanded into vector objects.

6. Deselect all, then using the Direct Selection Tool ▶, select and fill the illustration with whatever colors you like.

   Figure 73 shows one example.

7. Save your work, then close the Live Trace Sketch document.

You used the default settings of the Live Trace utility to convert a placed sketch into Illustrator objects.

FIGURE 72
Expanding the traced graphic

FIGURE 73
One example of the painted illustration

Drawing and Composing an Illustration

FIGURE 74
Photo traced with default Black and White

FIGURE 75
Comparing a Black and White trace using different threshold values

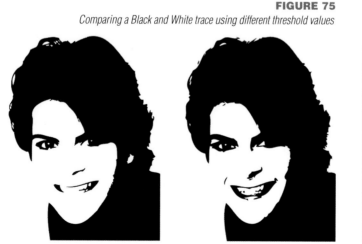

1. Open AI 3-6.ai, then save it as **Live Trace Photo.ai**.

   The file contains three copies of a placed photo that was scanned in Photoshop.

2. Zoom in on the top photo, click the **Selection Tool** ▸ , click the **top photo,** then click the **Live Trace button** on the Control panel.

   Using default black and white settings, Live Trace creates the trace shown in Figure 74.

3. Deselect the image, then zoom in on the middle photo.

4. Click the **Selection Tool** ▸ click the **middle photo**, click the **Tracing presets and options list arrow** to the right of the Live Trace button, then click **Tracing Options**.

5. Click the **Preview check box**, if necessary, to place a check mark.

6. In the Adjustments section, click the **arrow** to the right of current Threshold value, then drag the **Threshold slider** until the Threshold value reads 200.

   Live Trace redraws the graphic.

7. Drag the **Threshold slider** until the Threshold value reads 160, wait for Live Trace to redraw the graphic, then click **Trace**.

8. Drag the **middle graphic** to the right of the top graphic, then compare the two graphics to Figure 75.

9. Deselect all, zoom in on the bottom photo, select it, click the **Tracing presets and options list arrow**, then click **Color 6**.

Color 6 is a tracing preset.

10. Click the **Expand button** in the Control panel, then deselect all.

11. Click the **Direct Selection Tool** ▸, then select and fill the objects that make up the illustration.

Figure 76 shows one example.

12. Save your work, then close the Live Trace Photo.

You used Live Trace to trace a photo three different ways. First, you simply clicked the Live Trace button, which executed the Default preset. Next, you opened the Trace Options dialog box and specified the threshold value for the Black and White trace. Finally, you traced with the Color 6 preset.

FIGURE 76
Applying fills to the traced photo

Drawing and Composing an Illustration

FIGURE 77

Painting the region that is the overlap between two circles

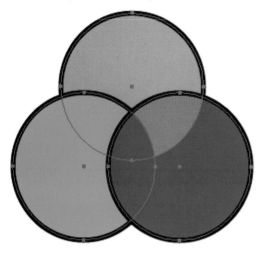

Use the Live Paint Bucket Tool

1. Open AI 3-7.ai, then save it as **Live Paint Circles.**

2. Fill the top circle with red, fill the left circle with green, then fill the right circle with blue.

3. Select all, then double-click the **Live Paint Bucket Tool** 🪣 to open its options dialog box, verify that both the Paint Fills and Paint Strokes check boxes are checked, then click **OK.**

4. Click any of the orange swatches in the Swatches panel.

   Note that because you are in Live Paint mode, none of the selected objects changes to orange when you click the orange swatch.

5. Position the Live Paint Bucket Tool pointer 🪣 over the red fill of the red circle, then click.

6. Click any pink swatch in the Swatches panel, position the Live Paint Bucket Tool pointer 🪣 over the area where the orange circle overlaps the blue circle, then click.

   As shown in Figure 77, the region of overlap between the two circles is filled with pink.

7. Using any colors you like, fill all seven regions so that your artwork resembles Figure 78.

8. Change the Stroke button on the Tools panel to any purple, position the Live Paint Bucket Tool pointer 🪣 over any of the black strokes in the artwork, then click.

FIGURE 78

Viewing seven painted regions

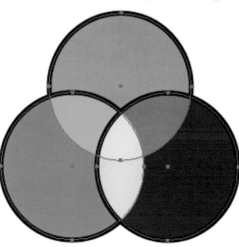

When positioned over a stroke, the Live Paint Bucket Tool pointer changes to a paintbrush icon.

9. Using any color you like, change the color of all twelve edges then deselect all so that your artwork resembles Figure 79.

10. Click the **Direct Selection Tool** ▶, then, without pulling them apart, move the circles in different directions so that your artwork resembles Figure 80.

The components of the live paint group maintain a dynamic relationship.

11. Select all, click **Expand** on the Control panel, deselect all, then pull out all of the regions so that your artwork resembles Figure 81.

The illustration has been expanded into multiple objects.

12. Save your work, then close the Live Paint Circles document.

You used the Live Paint Bucket Tool to fill various regions and edges of three overlapping circles. You then moved various components of the live paint group, noting that they maintain a dynamic relationship. Finally, you expanded the live paint group, which changed your original circles into multiple objects.

FIGURE 79
Viewing twelve painted edges

FIGURE 80
Exploring the dynamic relationship between regions in a live paint group

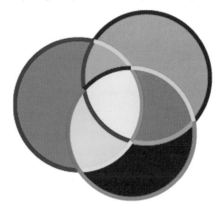

FIGURE 81
Dissecting the expanded live paint group

Drawing and Composing an Illustration

FIGURE 82
Using the Live Paint Selection Tool

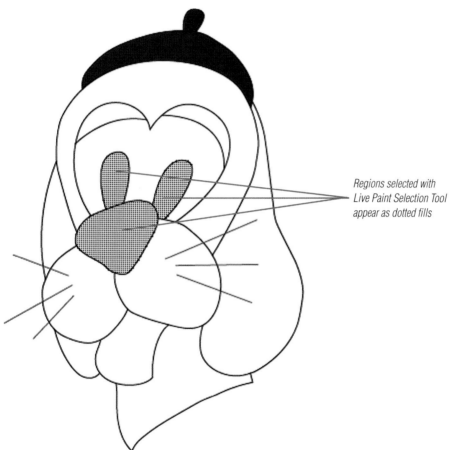

Regions selected with
Live Paint Selection Tool
appear as dotted fills

Use the Live Paint Bucket Tool to paint an illustration

1. Open AI 3-8.ai, then save it as **Live Paint Dog.**

2. Click the **Selection Tool** ，then click the different colored strokes so that you understand how the illustration has been drawn.

   The illustration has been created with a series of open paths. The only closed path is the nose.

3. Select all, then change the stroke of all the paths to Black.

4. Click the **Live Paint Bucket Tool** ，then click a **red swatch** in the Swatches panel.

   Note that because you are in Live Paint mode, none of the selected objects changes to red when you click the red swatch.

5. Fill the hat and the knot at the top of the hat with red, then click **Black** in the Swatches panel.

6. Click the **Live Paint Selection Tool** ，click the **nose,** press and hold **[Shift],** click the **left eye,** then click the **right eye.**

   Your illustration should resemble Figure 82.

   > TIP When you select multiple areas with the Live Paint Selection Tool, the areas are filled with a dot pattern until you apply a color.

7. Click **Black** in the Swatches panel.

8. Using the same method, select both eyelids, then fill them with a lavender swatch.

9. Click the **Live Paint Bucket Tool** , click a **yellow swatch** in the Swatches panel, then paint the illustration so that your illustration resembles Figure 83.

   Note the small areas between the whiskers that must be painted yellow.

10. Using the Live Paint Bucket Tool , paint the right jowl light brown, paint the left jowl a darker brown, then paint the tongue pink.

11. Click the **Stroke button** in the Tools panel to activate the stroke, then click a **gray swatch** in the Swatches panel.

12. Double-click the **Live Paint Bucket Tool** , click the **Paint Stroke check box** in the Live Paint Bucket Options dialog box if it is not already checked, then click **OK**.

FIGURE 83

Painting the yellow regions

Drawing and Composing an Illustration

FIGURE 84
Viewing the finished artwork

13. Paint the edges that draw the whiskers.

   TIP   You will need to click 14 times to paint the six whiskers.

14. Deselect, compare your work to Figure 84, save your work, then close the Live Paint Dog document.

You used the Live Paint Bucket Tool to fill regions created by the intersection of a collection of open paths. You also used the tool to paint edges.

Lesson 7   Use Live Trace and the Live Paint Bucket Tool

Draw straight lines.

1. Open AI 3-9.ai, then save it as **Mighty Montag**.
2. Place the Montag Sketch.tif from the drive and folder where your Data Files are stored into the Montag document.
3. Position the sketch in the center of the artboard, then lock it.
4. Set the fill color to [None] and the stroke to 1 pt black.
5. Use the Pen Tool to create a four-sided polygon for the neck. (*Hint*: Refer to Figure 53 as a guide.)
6. Draw six whiskers.
7. Save your work.

Draw curved lines.

1. Using the Pen Tool, draw an oval for the eye.
2. Draw a crescent moon shape for the eyelid.
3. Draw an oval for the iris.
4. Save your work.

Draw elements of an illustration.

1. Trace the left ear.
2. Trace the hat.
3. Trace the nose.
4. Trace the left jowl.
5. Trace the right jowl.
6. Trace the tongue.
7. Trace the right ear.
8. Trace the head.
9. Save your work.

Apply attributes to objects.

1. Unlock the placed sketch and hide it.
2. Fill the hat with a red swatch.
3. Fill the right ear with 9C/18M/62Y.
4. Fill the nose with black.
5. Fill the eye with white.
6. Fill the tongue with salmon.
7. Using Figure 85 as a guide, use the colors in the Swatches panel to finish the illustration.
8. Save your work.

Assemble an illustration.

1. Send the neck to the back of the stacking order, then lock it.
2. Send the head to the back, then lock it.
3. Send the left ear to the back, then lock it.
4. Bring the hat to the front.
5. Bring the right ear to the front.
6. Select the whiskers, group them, then bring them to the front.
7. Select the tongue, then cut it.
8. Select the right jowl, then apply the Paste in Back command.
9. Bring the nose to the front.
10. Select the eye, the eyelid, and the iris, then group them.
11. Drag and drop a copy of the eye group. (*Hint*: Press and hold [Alt] (Win) or [option] (Mac) as you drag the eye group.)
12. Select the right jowl.
13. In the Color panel add 10% K to darken the jowl.
14. Use the Color panel to change the fills on other objects to your liking.
15. Save your work.

Stroke objects for artistic effect.

1. Make the caps on the whiskers round.
2. Change the whiskers' stroke weight to .5 pt.
3. Unlock all.
4. Select the neck and change the joins to round.
5. Apply pseudo-strokes to the illustration. (*Hint*: Copy and paste the elements behind themselves, fill them with black, lock the top objects, then use the Direct Selection Tool to select anchor points on the black-filled copies. Use the arrow keys on the keyboard to move the anchor points. The black copies will peek out from behind the elements in front.)
6. Click Object on the menu bar, then click Unlock All.
7. Delete the Montag Sketch file behind your illustration.
8. Save your work, compare your illustration to Figure 85, then close Mighty Montag.

FIGURE 85
Completed Skills Review

Drawing and Composing an Illustration

The owner of The Blue Peppermill Restaurant has hired your design firm to take over all of their marketing and advertising, saying they need to expand their efforts. You request all of their existing materials—slides, prints, digital files, brochures, business cards, etc. Upon examination, you realize that they have no vector graphic version of their logo. Deciding that this is an indispensable element for future design and production, you scan in a photo of their signature peppermill, trace it, and apply a blue fill to it.

1. Create a new 6" × 6" CMYK Color document, then save it as **Peppermill**.
2. Place the Peppermill.tif file into the Peppermill Vector document. (*Hint*: The Peppermill.tif file is in the Chapter 3 Data Files folder.)
3. Scale the placed image 150%, then lock it.
4. Set your fill color to [None], and your stroke to 2 pt black.
5. Using the Zoom Tool, create a selection box around the round element at the top of the peppermill to zoom in on it.
6. Using the Pen Tool, trace the peppermill, then fill it with a blue swatch.
7. When you finish tracing, tweak the path if necessary, then save your work.

8. Unlock the placed image and cut it from the document.

FIGURE 86
Completed Project Builder 1

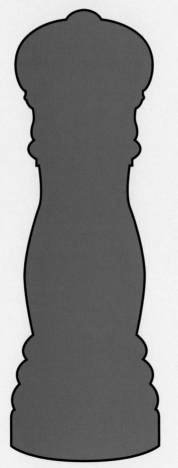

9. Save your work, compare your illustration to Figure 86, then close Peppermill.

Drawing and Composing an Illustration

Bostonchefs.com, your client of three years, contacts you with bad news. They have accidentally deleted their Illustrator "chef logo" from the backup server. They need the vector graphic to produce many of their materials. Their first designer has all the original files, but he has retired to a small island in the Caribbean and cannot be contacted. They want to know if there's anything you can do to recreate the vector graphic.

1. Connect to the Internet, then go to www.bostonchefs.com.
2. Right-click (Win) or [control] click (Mac) the logo of the chef, click Save Picture As (Win) or Save to the Desktop (Mac), then save it in your Chapter 3 Solution Files folder, keeping the same name.
3. Create a new 6" × 6" CMYK Color document, then save it as **Boston chefs.**
4. Place the chef logo file into the document and lock it.
5. Zoom in on the chef logo so that you are at a comfortable view for tracing. (*Hint*: Use the Zoom Tool to create a selection box around the logo.)
6. Set your fill color to [None] and your stroke to 1 pt red.
7. Use the Ellipse Tool to trace the head.

8. Use the Pen Tool to trace the hat and the perimeter of the body.
9. Trace the two triangles that define the chef's inner arms.
10. Unlock the placed image and cut it from the document.
11. Fill the head, the hat, and the body with White.

FIGURE 87
Completed Project Builder 2

12. Fill the triangles with a shade of blue.
13. Remove the strokes from the objects.
14. Create a rectangle that encompasses the chef objects, then fill it with the same shade of blue.
15. Send the rectangle to the back of the stacking order.
16. Save your work, compare your illustration to Figure 87, then close Boston chefs.

Drawing and Composing an Illustration

Your design firm is contacted by a company called Stratagem with a request for a proposal. They manufacture molds for plastic products. The terms of the request are as follows: You are to submit a design for the shape of the bottle for a new dishwashing liquid. You are to submit a single image that shows a black line defining the shape. The line art should also include the nozzle. The size of the bottle is immaterial. The design is to be "sophisticated, so as to be in visual harmony with the modern home kitchen." The name of the product is "Sleek."

1. Go to the grocery store and purchase bottles of dishwashing liquid whose shape you find interesting.
2. Use the purchases for ideas and inspiration.
3. Sketch your idea for the bottle's shape on a piece of paper.
4. Scan the sketch and save it as a TIFF file.
5. Create a new Illustrator document, then save it as **Sleek Design**.
6. Place the scan in the document, then lock it.
7. Trace your sketch, using the Pen Tool.
8. When you are done tracing, delete the sketch from the document.
9. Tweak the line to define the shape to your specifications.
10. Use the Average dialog box to align points to perfect the shape.
11. Save your work, compare your illustration to Figure 88, then close Sleek Design.

FIGURE 88
Completed Design Project

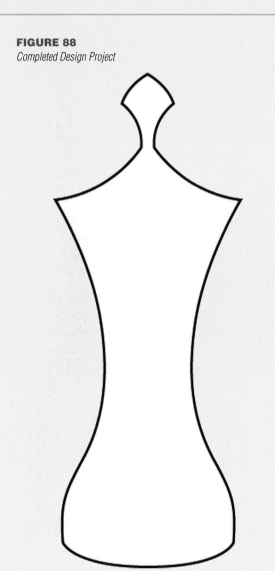

Drawing and Composing an Illustration

You teach a class on digital graphics to junior designers. To stimulate a discussion on shape and design theory, you show the 20-minute "Dawn of Man" sequence of the classic sci-fi movie *2001: A Space Odyssey*.

Note: The central point of this exercise—a group discussion of shapes and their role in the history of mankind—can be had with or without screening *2001: A Space Odyssey*. Should you choose to not show the film, simply omit questions 1 and 2. Rephrase Question 8 so that individuals are instructed to draw any abstract shape from their own imaginations.

The sequence begins millions of years ago with a group of apes, presumably on the African plains. One day, *impossibly*, a tall, black, perfectly rectangular slab appears out of nowhere on the landscape. At first the apes are afraid of it, afraid to touch it. Eventually, they accept its presence.

Later, one ape looks upon a femur bone from a dead animal. With a dawning understanding, he uses the bone as a tool, first to kill for food, and then to kill another ape from an enemy group. Victorious in battle, the ape hurls the bone into the air. The camera follows it up, up, up, and—in one of the most famous cuts in film history—the image switches from the white bone in the sky to the similar shape of a white spaceship floating in space.

1. Have everyone in the group share his or her feelings upon first seeing the "monolith" (the black rectangular slab). What percentage of the group was frightened? Does the group sense that the monolith is good, evil, or neutral?
2. Discuss the sudden appearance of the straight-edged, right-angled monolith against the landscape. What words describe the shapes of the landscape in contrast to the monolith?
3. Have the group debate a central question: Do perfect shapes exist in nature, or are they created entirely out of the imagination of human beings?
4. If perfect shapes exist—if they are *real*—can you name one example? If they are not real, how is it that humankind has proven so many concepts in mathematics that are based on shapes, such as the Pythagorean theorem?
5. What advancements and achievements of humankind have their basis in peoples' ability to conceive of abstract shapes?
6. Can it be said legitimately that the ability to conceive abstract shapes is an essential factor that distinguishes humankind from all the other species on the planet?
7. Create a new document, then save it as **Shape**.
8. Give the members of the group 10 minutes to draw, in Adobe Illustrator, any shape that they remember from the opening sequence, *except* the monolith. When the group has finished, take a count: How many rendered a shape based on the bone?
9. Save your work, compare your results to Figure 89, then close Shape.

FIGURE 89
Completed Group Project

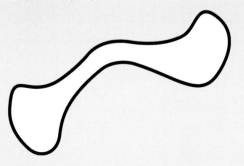

chapter

4

TRANSFORMING AND
DISTORTING OBJECTS

1. Transform objects

2. Offset and outline paths

3. Create compound paths

4. Work with the Pathfinder panel

5. Create clipping masks

4 TRANSFORMING AND
DISTORTING OBJECTS

Putting It All Together

Think about a conventional toolbox. You've got a hammer, nails, a few different types of screwdrivers, screws, nuts, bolts, a wrench, and probably some type of measuring device. That set of tools could be used to build anything from a birdhouse to a dollhouse to a townhouse to the White House.

A carpenter uses tools in conjunction with one another to create something, and that something is defined far less by the tools than by the imagination of the carpenter. But even the most ambitious imagination is tempered by the demands of knowing which tool to use, and when.

Illustrator offers a number of sophisticated transform "tools" in the Tools panel, and the metaphor is apt. Each "tool" provides a basic function: a rotation, a scale, a precise

move, a precise offset, or a reflection. It is you, the designer, who uses those tools in combination with each other, with menu commands, and with other features, to realize your vision. And like the carpenter's, your imagination will be tempered by your ability to choose the right tool at the right time.

This is one of the most exciting aspects of working in Illustrator. After you learn the basics, there's no map, no blueprint for building an illustration. It's your skills, your experience, your smarts, and your ingenuity that lead you toward your goal. No other designer will use Illustrator's tools quite the same way you do. People who appreciate digital imagery understand this salient point: Although the tools are the same for everyone, the result is *personal*. It's *original*.

Tools You'll Use

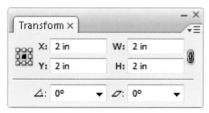

Shear Tool

Rotate Tool *Reflect Tool*

TRANSFORM
OBJECTS

What You'll Do

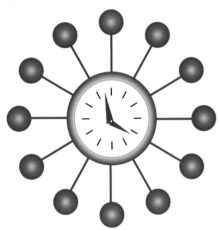

In this lesson, you will explore options for transforming objects with the transform tools.

Defining the Transform Tools

When you change an object's size, shape, or position on the artboard, Illustrator defines that operation as a transformation. Transforming objects is a fundamental operation in Illustrator, one you will perform countless times.

Because transformations are so essential, Illustrator provides a number of methods for doing them. As you gain experience, you will naturally adopt the method that you find most comfortable or logical.

The Tools panel contains five transform tools: the Rotate, Scale, Reflect, Shear, and Free Transform Tools. The essential functions of the Rotate and Scale Tools are self-explanatory. The Reflect Tool "flips" an object across an imagined axis, usually the horizontal or the vertical axis. However, you can define any diagonal as the axis for a reflection. In Figure 1, the illustration has been flipped to create the illusion of a reflection in a mirror.

QUICKTIP

The Reflect Tool comes in very handy when you are drawing or tracing a symmetrical object, like a spoon. Simply draw or trace half of the drawing, then create a flipped copy—a mirror image. Join the two halves, and you have a perfectly symmetrical shape . . . in half the time!

The Shear Tool slants—or skews—an object on an axis that you specify. By definition, the Shear Tool distorts an object. Of the five transform tools, you will probably use the Shear Tool the least, although it is useful for creating a cast shadow or the illusion of depth.

Finally, the Free Transform Tool offers you the ability to perform quick transformations and distort objects in perspective.

Defining the Point of Origin

All transformations are executed in relation to a fixed point; in Illustrator, that point is called the **point of origin**. For each transform tool, the default point of

origin is the selected object's center point. However, you can change that point to another point on the object or to a point elsewhere on the artboard. For example, when a majorette twirls a baton, that baton is essentially rotating on its own center. By contrast, the petals of a daisy rotate around a central point that is not positioned on any of the petals themselves, as shown in Figure 2.

There are four basic methods for making transformations with the transform tools. First, select an object, then do one of the following:

■ Click a transform tool, then click and drag anywhere on the artboard. The object will be transformed using its center point as the default point of origin.

■ Double-click the transform tool, which opens the tool's dialog box. Enter the values by which you want to execute the transformation, then click OK. You may also click Copy to create a transformed copy of the selected object. The point of origin for the transformation will be the center point of the selected object.

■ Click a transform tool, then click the artboard. Where you click the artboard defines the point of origin for the transformation. Click and drag anywhere on the artboard, and the selected object will be transformed from the point of origin that you clicked.

■ Click a transform tool, Press [Alt] (Win) or [option] (Mac), then click the artboard. The tool's dialog box opens, allowing you to enter precise values for the transformation. When you click OK or Copy, the selected object will be transformed from the point of origin that you clicked.

QUICKTIP

If you transform an object from its center point, then select another object and apply the Transform Again command, the point of origin has not been redefined, and the second object will be transformed from the center point of the first object.

FIGURE 1

The Reflect Tool flips an image horizontally or vertically

FIGURE 2

All transformations are executed from a point of origin

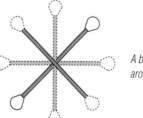

A baton rotating around its own center

Petals of a daisy rotate around a central point

Working with the Transform Again Command

An essential command related to transformations is Transform Again. Whenever you execute a transformation, such as scale or rotate, you can repeat the transformation quickly by using the Transform Again command. This is also true for moving an object. Using the Transform Again command will move an object the same distance and angle entered in the last step. The quickest way to use the Transform Again command is to press [Ctrl][D] (Win) or ⌘[D] (Mac). To remember this quick key command, think D for *duplicate*.

A fine example of the usefulness of the Transform Again command is its ability to make transforming in small increments easy. For example, let's say you have created an object to be used in an illustration, but you haven't decided how large the object should be. Simply scale the object by a small percentage—say 5%—then press the quick key for Transform Again repeatedly until you are happy with the results. The object gradually gets bigger, and you can choose the size that pleases your eye. If you transform again too many times, and the object gets too big, simply undo repeatedly to decrease the object's size in the same small increments.

Using the Transform Each Command

The Transform Each command allows you to transform multiple objects individually, as shown in Figure 3. The Transform Each dialog box offers options to move, scale, rotate, or reflect an object, among others. All of them will affect an object independent of the other selected objects.

Without the Transform Each command, applying a transformation to multiple objects simultaneously will often yield an undesired effect. This happens because the selected objects are transformed as a group—in relation to a single point of origin—and are repositioned on the artboard.

FIGURE 3
Multiple objects rotated individually

Before   *After*

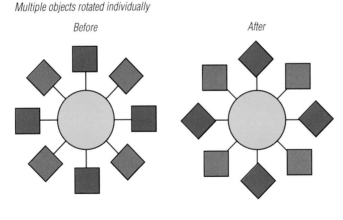

The eight squares are rotated on their own center points

Using the Free Transform Tool

The Free Transform Tool applies an eight-handled bounding box to a selected image. You can move those handles to scale and shear the object. You can click and drag outside the object to rotate the object.

With the Free Transform Tool, transformations always use the selected object's center point as the point of origin. In general, the role of the Free Transform Tool is to make quick, inexact transformations. However, the tool has a powerful, hidden ability. Moving the handles in conjunction with certain keyboard commands allows you to distort the object or distort the object in perspective, as shown in Figure 4. Press and hold [Shift][Ctrl] (Win) or [Shift]⌘ (Mac) to distort the image. Press and hold [Shift][Alt][Ctrl] (Win) while dragging to distort in perspective. On a Macintosh, press and hold [Shift][option]⌘ to execute the same transformation.

Using the Transform Panel

The Transform panel displays information about the size, orientation, and location of one or more selected objects. You can type new values directly into the Transform panel to modify selected objects. All values in the panel refer to the bounding boxes of the objects, whether the bounding box is visible or not. You can also identify—in the Transform panel—the reference point on the bounding box from which the object will be transformed. To reflect an object vertically or horizontally using the Transform panel, click the Transform panel list arrow, then choose the appropriate menu item, as shown in Figure 5.

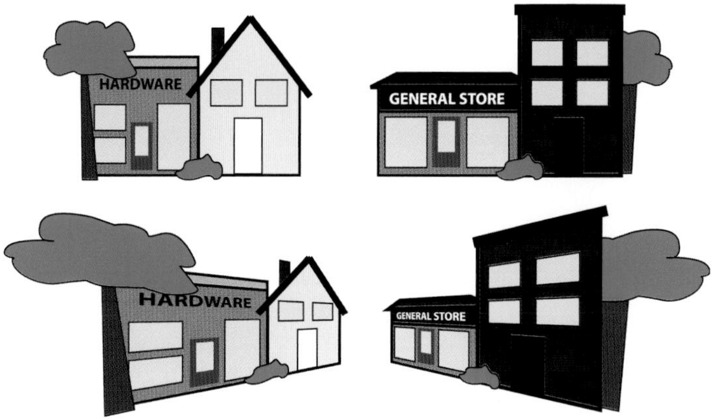

FIGURE 5

Transform panel

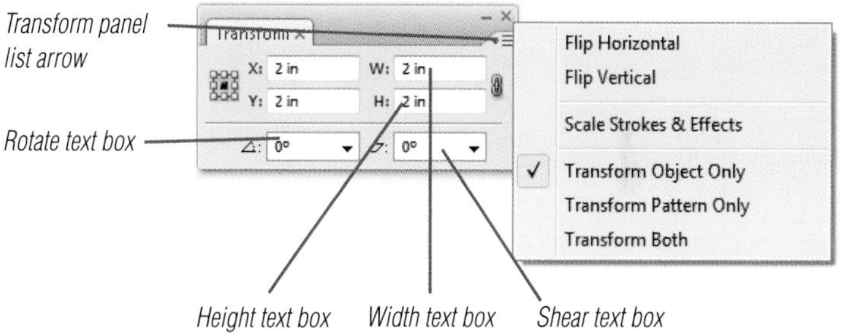

Transform panel list arrow

Rotate text box

Flip Horizontal
Flip Vertical
Scale Strokes & Effects
✓ Transform Object Only
Transform Pattern Only
Transform Both

Height text box   Width text box   Shear text box

Rotate an object around a defined point

1. Open AI 4-1.ai, then save it as **Mod Clock**.

2. Click the **Selection Tool** , click the **brown line**, then click the **Rotate Tool** .

3. Press and hold **[Alt]** (Win) or **[option]** (Mac), then click the **bottom anchor point** of the line to set the point of origin for the rotation.

   With a transform tool selected, pressing [Alt] (Win) or [option] (Mac) and clicking the artboard defines the point of origin and opens the tool's dialog box.

4. Enter **30** in the Angle text box, then click **Copy**.

5. Press **[Ctrl][D]** (Win) or [D] (Mac) ten times so that your screen resembles Figure 6.

   [Ctrl][D] (Win) or [D] (Mac) is the quick key for the Transform Again command.

6. Select all twelve lines, group them, send them to the back, then hide them.

7. Select the small orange circle, click **View** on the menu bar, then click **Outline**.

(continued)

FIGURE 6
Twelve paths rotated at a point

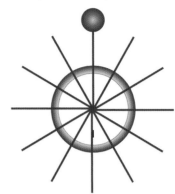

X and Y coordinates

The X and Y coordinates of an object indicate the object's horizontal (X) and vertical (Y) locations on the artboard. These numbers, which appear in the Transform panel, represent the horizontal and vertical distance from the bottom-left corner of the artboard. The current X and Y coordinates also depend on the specified reference point. Nine reference points are listed to the left of the X and Y Value text boxes in the Transform panel. Reference points are those points of a selected object that represent the four corners of the object's bounding box, the horizontal and vertical centers of the bounding box, and the center point of the bounding box. (You do not need to have the bounding box option turned on to view any of the reference point coordinates.)

FIGURE 7

Twelve circles rotated around a central point of origin

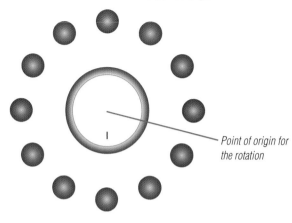

Point of origin for
the rotation

FIGURE 8

Completed illustration

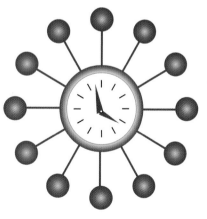

8. Click the **Rotate Tool**, press and hold
   [Alt] (Win) or **[option]** (Mac), then click the
   center point of the larger circle to set the
   point of origin for the next rotation.

   The small circle will rotate around the
   center point of the larger circle.

   > TIP   Outline mode is especially useful for
   > rotations; center points are visible and easy
   > to target as points of origin.

9. Enter **30** if necessary, click **Copy**, apply the
   Transform Again command ten times, then
   switch to Preview mode.

   Your screen should resemble Figure 7.

10. Select the small black vertical dash, then
    transform again eleven times.

    The dash is also rotated around the center
    point of the larger circle, since a new point
    of origin has not been set.

11. Unlock the hands in the scratch area, then
    move them onto the clock face.

12. Show all, then deselect all to reveal the
    twelve segments, as shown in Figure 8.

13. Save your work, then close the Mod Clock
    document.

*You selected a point on the brown line, then
rotated eleven copies of the object around that
point. Second, you defined the point of origin for a
rotation by clicking the center point of the larger
circle, then rotated eleven copies of the smaller
circle and the dash around that point.*

Use the Shear Tool

1. Open AI 4-2.ai, then save it as **Shear**.

2. Select all, copy, paste in front, then fill the copy with the swatch named Graphite.

3. Click the **Shear Tool** ▯⧄.

   | TIP The Shear Tool is hidden behind the Scale Tool.

4. Press and hold **[Alt]** (Win) or **[option]** (Mac), then click the **bottom-right anchor point** of the letter R to set the origin point of the shear and open the Shear dialog box.

5. Enter **45** in the Shear Angle text box, verify that the Horizontal option button is checked, then click **OK**.

   Your screen should resemble Figure 9.

6. Click the **Scale Tool** ▱.

7. Press **[Alt]** (Win) or **[option]** (Mac), then click any bottom anchor point or segment on the sheared objects to set the point of origin for the scale and open the Scale dialog box.

8. Click the **Non-Uniform option button**, enter **100** in the Horizontal text box, enter **50** in the Vertical text box, then click **OK**.

9. Send the sheared objects to the back.

10. Apply a 1 pt black stroke to the orange letters, deselect, then compare your screen to Figure 10.

11. Save your work, then close the Shear document.

You created a shadow effect using the Shear Tool.

FIGURE 9
Letterforms sheared on a 45° axis

The objects are sheared on a 45° angle in relation to a horizontal axis

FIGURE 10
Shearing is useful for creating a cast-shadow effect

The shadow is "cast" from the letters in the foreground

FIGURE 11
Use the Reflect Tool for illustrations that demand exact symmetry

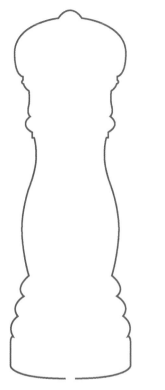

Use the Reflect Tool

1. Open AI 4-3.ai, then save it as **Reflect**.
2. Select all, then zoom in on the top anchor point.
3. Click the **Reflect Tool** ⬚.

   The Reflect Tool is hidden behind the Rotate Tool.
4. Press **[Alt]** (Win) or **[option]** (Mac), then click the **top anchor point** to set the point of origin for the reflection.
5. Click the **Vertical option button**, then click **Copy**.

   A copy is positioned, reflected across the axis that you defined, as shown in Figure 11.
6. Deselect all, then click the **Direct Selection Tool** ⬚.
7. Using Figure 12 as a guide, drag a selection box around the top two anchor points to select them.
8. Click **Object** on the menu bar, point to **Path**, click **Average**, click the **Both option button**, then click **OK**.
9. Click **Object** on the menu bar, point to **Path**, click **Join**, click the **Smooth option button**, then click **OK**.
10. Select the bottom two anchor points, average them on both axes, then join them in a smooth point to close the path.
11. Save your work, then close the Reflect document.

You created a reflected copy of a path, then averaged and joined two pairs of open points.

FIGURE 12
Selecting two anchor points with the Direct Selection Tool

Selection box

Selected anchor points

OFFSET AND
OUTLINE PATHS

What You'll Do

In this lesson, you will use the Offset Path command to create concentric squares and the Outline Stroke command to convert a stroked path into a closed path.

Using the Offset Path Command

Simply put, the Offset Path command creates a copy of a selected path set off by a specified distance. The Offset Path command is useful when working with closed paths—making concentric shapes or making many copies of a path at a regular distance from the original.

Figure 13 shows two sets of concentric circles. By definition, the word **concentric** refers to objects that share the same centerpoint, as the circles in both sets do. The set on the left was made with the Scale Tool, applying an 85% scale and copy to the outer circle, then repeating the transformation ten times. Note that with each successive copy, the distance from the copy to the previous circle decreases. The set on the right was made by offsetting the outside circle -.125", then applying the same offset to each successive copy. Note the different effect.

When you offset a closed path, a positive value creates a larger copy outside the original; a negative value creates a smaller copy inside the original.

Using the Outline Stroke Command

The Outline Stroke command converts a stroked path into a closed path that is the same width as the original stroked path.

This operation is useful if you want to apply a gradient to a stroke. It is also a useful design tool, allowing you to modify the outline of an object more than if it were just a stroke. Also, it is often easier to create an object with a single heavy stroke—for example the letter S—and then convert it to a closed path than it would be to try to draw a closed path directly, as shown in Figure 14.

FIGURE 13

Two sets of concentric circles

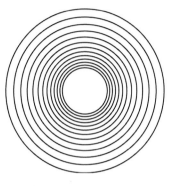

Concentric circles produced by the Scale Tool

Concentric circles produced by the Offset Path command

FIGURE 14

The Outline Stroke command converts a stroked path to a closed object

Offset a path

1. Open AI 4-4.ai, then save it as **Squares**.

2. Select the square.

3. Click **Object** on the menu bar, point to **Path**, then click **Offset Path**.

4. Enter **-.125** in the Offset text box, then click **OK**.

   | TIP Be sure that your Units preference is set to Inches in the General section of the Units & Display Performance Preferences.

   A negative value reduces the area of a closed path; a positive value increases the area.

5. Apply the Offset Path command four more times, using the same value.

   | TIP The Transform Again command does not apply to the Offset Path command because it is not one of the transform tools.

6. Deselect all, save your work, compare your screen to Figure 15, then close the Squares document.

You used the Offset Path command to create concentric squares.

FIGURE 15
Concentric squares created with the Offset Path command

FIGURE 16

The Outline Stroke command converts any stroked path into a closed path

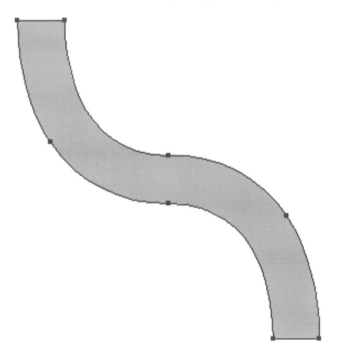

1. Open AI 4-5.ai, then save it as **Outlined Stroke**.

2. Select the path, then change the weight to 36 pt.

3. Click **Object** on the menu bar, point to **Path**, then click **Outline Stroke**.

   The full weight of the stroke is converted to a closed path, as shown in Figure 16.

4. Save your work, then close the Outlined Stroke document.

You applied a heavy weight to a stroked path, then converted the stroke to a closed path, using the Outline Stroke command.

CREATE COMPOUND
PATHS

What You'll Do

 In this lesson, you will explore the role of compound paths for practical use and for artistic effects.

Defining a Compound Path

Practically speaking, you make a compound path to create a "hole" or "holes" in an object. As shown in Figure 17, if you were drawing the letter "D," you would need to create a hole in the outlined shape, through which you could see the background. To do so, select the object in back (in this case, the black outline that defines the letter) and the object in front (the yellow object that defines the hole) and apply the Make Compound Path command. When compounded, a "hole" appears where the two objects overlap.

The overlapping object still exists, however. It is simply *functioning* as a transparent hole in conjunction with the object behind it. If you move the front object independently, as shown in Figure 18, it yields an interesting result. Designers have seized upon this effect and have run with it, creating complex and eye-catching graphics, which Illustrator calls compound shapes.

It is important to understand that when two or more objects are compounded, Illustrator defines them as *one* object. This sounds strange at first, but the concept is

as familiar to you as the letter D. You identify the letter D as one object. Although it is drawn with two paths—one defining the outside edge, the other defining the inside edge—it is nevertheless a single object.

Compound paths function as groups. You can select and manipulate an individual element with the Direct Selection Tool, but you cannot change its appearance attributes independently. Compound paths can

be released and returned to their original component objects by applying the Release Compound Path command.

FIGURE 17
The letter D is an example of a compound path

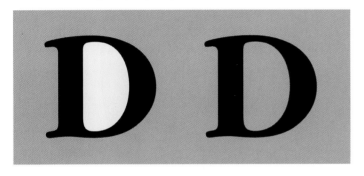

FIGURE 18
Manipulating compound paths can yield interesting effects

Create compound paths

1. Open AI 4-6.ai, then save it as **Simple Compound**.

2. Cut the red circle in the middle of the illustration, then undo the cut.

   The red circle creates the illusion that there's a hole in the life-preserver ring.

3. Select the red background object, then change its fill to the Ocean Blue gradient in the Swatches panel.

   The illusion is lost; the red circle no longer appears as a hole in the life preserver.

4. Select both the white "life preserver" circle and the red circle in the center.

5. Click **Object** on the menu bar, point to **Compound Path**, then click **Make**.

   As shown in Figure 19, the two circles are compounded, with the top circle functioning as a "hole" in the larger circle behind it.

6. Move the background object left and right, and up and down behind the circles.

   The repositioned background remains visible through the compounded circles.

7. Deselect all, save your work, then close the Simple Compound document.

You selected two concentric circles and made them into one compound path, which allowed you to see through to the gradient behind the circles.

FIGURE 19
A compound path creates the effect of a hole where two or more objects overlap

FIGURE 20

A simple compound path

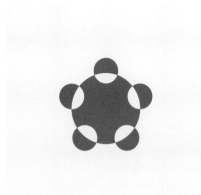

FIGURE 21

A more complex compound path

Each of the five small circles is scaled, using its own center point as the point of origin

FIGURE 22

Simple compound paths can yield stunning visual effects

Create special effects with compound paths

1. Open AI 4-7.ai, then save it as **Compound Path Effects**.

2. Select all.

   The light blue square is locked and does not become part of the selection.

3. Click **Object** on the menu bar, point to **Compound Path**, then click **Make**.

4. Deselect, click the **Direct Selection Tool**, then click the **edge** of the large blue circle.

5. Click the **center point** of the circle, then scale the circle 50% so that your work resembles Figure 20.

6. Click **Select** on the menu bar, then click **Inverse**.

7. Click **Object** on the menu bar, point to **Transform**, then click **Transform Each**.

8. Enter **225** in the Horizontal and Vertical text boxes in the Scale section of the Transform Each dialog box, click **OK,** then deselect all.

   Your work should resemble Figure 21.

9. Using the Direct Selection Tool, click the edge of the center circle, click its center point to select the entire circle, then scale the circle 120%.

10. Apply the Transform Again command twice, then compare your screen to Figure 22.

11. Deselect all, save your work, then close Compound Path Effects.

You made a compound path out of five small circles and one large circle. You then manipulated the size and location of the individual circles to create interesting designs.

WORK WITH THE
PATHFINDER PANEL

What You'll Do

 In this lesson, you will use pathfinders to create compound shapes from simple shapes.

Defining a Compound Shape

Like a compound path, a **compound shape** is two or more paths that are combined in such a way that "holes" appear wherever paths overlap.

The term compound shape is used to distinguish a complex compound path from a simple one. Compound shapes generally assume an artistic rather than a practical role. To achieve the effect, compound shapes tend to be composed of multiple objects. You can think of a compound shape as an illustration composed of multiple compound paths.

Understanding Essential Pathfinder Filters

The **pathfinders** are a group of preset operations that help you combine paths in a variety of ways. Pathfinders are very useful operations for creating complex or irregular shapes from basic shapes. In some cases, the pathfinders will be a means to an end in creating an object; in others, the operation they provide will be the end result you want to achieve.

Illustrator offers ten pathfinders. Pathfinders can be applied to overlapping objects using the Effect menu or the Pathfinder panel. For the purposes of drawing and creating new objects, the following five pathfinders are essential; compare each with Figure 23.

- **Add to shape area**: Converts two or more overlapping objects into a single, merged object.
- **Subtract from shape area**: Where objects overlap, deletes the frontmost object(s) from the backmost object in a selection of overlapped objects.
- **Intersect shape areas**: Creates a single, merged object from the area where two or more objects overlap.

- **Minus Back**: The opposite of Subtract; deletes the backmost object(s) from the frontmost object in a selection of overlapped objects.
- **Divide**: Divides an object into its component filled faces. Illustrator defines a "face" as an area undivided by a line segment.

FIGURE 23
Five essential pathfinders

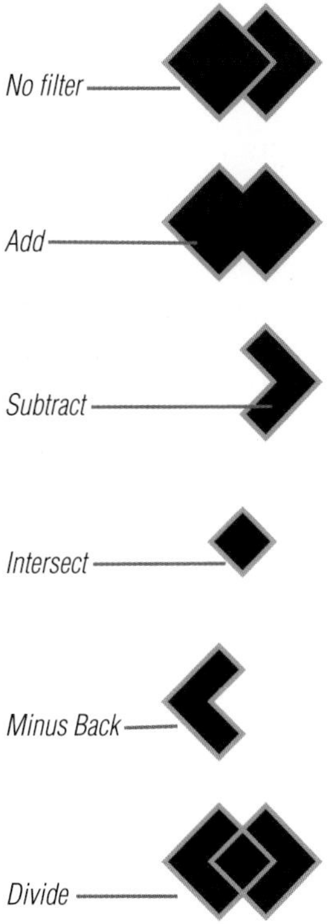

No filter ——————

Add ——————

Subtract ——————

Intersect ——————

Minus Back ——————

Divide ——————

Using the Pathfinder Panel

The Pathfinder panel contains ten buttons for applying pathfinders and for creating compound shapes, as shown in Figure 24. As you learned earlier, a compound shape is a complex compound path. You can create a compound shape by overlapping two or more objects, then clicking one of the four shape mode buttons in the top row of the Pathfinder panel, or clicking the Pathfinder panel list arrow, then clicking Make Compound Shape. The four shape mode buttons are Add to shape area (Add), Subtract from shape area (Subtract), Intersect shape areas (Intersect), and Exclude overlapping shape areas (Exclude). When you apply a shape mode button, the two overlapping objects are combined into one object with the same formatting as the topmost object in the group before the shape mode button was applied. After applying a shape mode button, the original objects in the compound shape can be selected and formatted using the Direct Selection Tool. Another way to create a compound shape is to click the Expand button in the Pathfinder panel, or press [Alt] (Win) or [option] (Mac) when you click a shape mode button. Doing so results in a compound shape whose original objects can no longer be selected with the Direct Selection Tool. It is instead one complete path.

FIGURE 24
Pathfinder panel

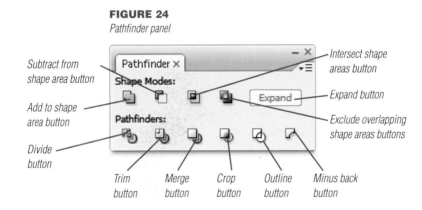

Subtract from shape area button

Add to shape area button

Divide button

Intersect shape areas button

Expand button

Exclude overlapping shape areas buttons

Trim button

Merge button

Crop button

Outline button

Minus back button

Applying Shape Modes

Figure 25 shows a square overlapped by a circle.

If you apply the Subtract shape mode button, the resulting object is a compound shape, as shown in Figure 26. Notice the circle is not deleted; it is functioning as a hole or a "knockout" wherever it overlaps the square. The relationship is dynamic: You can move the circle independently with the Direct Selection Tool to change its

effect on the square and the resulting visual effect.

If you took the same two overlapping shapes shown in Figure 25, but this time pressed [Alt] (Win) or [option] (Mac) when applying the Subtract shape mode button, the overlapped area is deleted from the square. The circle, too, is deleted, as shown in Figure 27. The result is a simple reshaped object.

Pressing [Alt] (Win) or [option] (Mac) when applying a shade mode is an essential

factor that distinguishes applying a shape mode with and without expanding. When shape modes are applied to objects, the resulting compound shape can be manipulated endlessly. When they are expanded, the result is final.

Figure 28 shows a group of objects converted into a compound shape using the Make Compound Shape command in the Pathfinder panel.

FIGURE 25
Two overlapping objects

FIGURE 26
The effect of applying the Subtract shape mode button

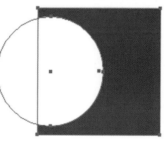

FIGURE 27
The effect of expanding a compound shape using the Subtract shape mode button

FIGURE 28
A compound shape

Apply the Add shape mode

1. Open AI 4-8.ai, then save it as **Heart Parts**.

2. Click **Window** on the menu bar, then click **Pathfinder**, if necessary.

3. Select both circles, press and hold **[Alt]** (Win) or **[option]** (Mac), then click the **Add to shape area button** 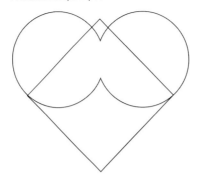 in the Pathfinder panel.

   The two objects are united. For brevity's sake, Add to shape area will be referred to as Add.

4. Move the diamond shape up so that it overlaps the united circles, as shown in Figure 29.

5. Click the **Delete Anchor Point Tool** , then delete the top anchor point of the diamond.

6. Select all, press and hold **[Alt]** (Win) or **[option]** (Mac), then click the **Add button** so that your screen resembles Figure 30.

7. Remove the black stroke, then apply a red fill to the new object.

8. Draw a rectangle that covers the "hole" in the heart, then fill it with black, as shown in Figure 31.

9. Select all, press **[Alt]** (Win) or **[option]** (Mac), then click the **Add button** .

10. Double-click the **Scale Tool** , then apply a non-uniform scale of 90% on the horizontal axis and 100% on the vertical axis.

You created a single heart-shaped object from two circles and a diamond shape using the Add button.

FIGURE 29
A diamond shape in position

FIGURE 30
The diamond shape and the object behind it are united

FIGURE 31
A heart shape created by applying the Add shape mode to three objects

FIGURE 32
Circle overlaps the square

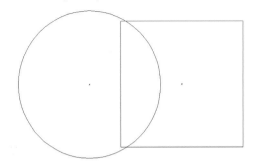

FIGURE 33
Right circle is a reflected copy of the left one

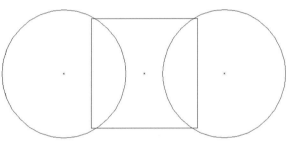

FIGURE 34
The final shape, with all elements united

Apply the Subtract shape mode

1. Rotate the black heart shape 180°, then hide it.

2. Create a square that is 1.5" × 1.5" without a fill color and with a 1 pt black stroke.

3. Create a circle that is 1.75" in width and height.

4. Switch to Outline mode.

5. Move the circle so that it overlaps the square, as shown in Figure 32.

6. Verify that the circle is still selected, click the **Reflect Tool**, press **[Alt]** (Win) or **[option]** (Mac), then click the **center point** of the square.

7. Click the **Vertical option button**, then click **Copy** so that your work resembles Figure 33.

8. Select all, press **[Alt]** (Win) or **[option]** (Mac), then click the **Subtract from shape area button** in the Pathfinder panel.

9. Switch to Preview mode, then apply a black fill to the new object.

10. Show all, then overlap the new shape with the black heart shape to make a spade shape.

11. Select all, click the **Add shape mode button** then deselect.

Your work should resemble Figure 34.

You overlapped a square with two circles, then applied the Subtract shape mode, expanding the compound shape, to delete the overlapped areas from the square. You used the Add shape mode button to unite the new shape with a heart-shaped object to create a spade shape.

Apply the Intersect shape mode

1. Click the **Star Tool** , then click the **artboard**.

2. Enter **1** in the Radius 1 text box, **3** in the Radius 2 text box, and **8** in the Points text box, then click **OK**.

3. Apply a yellow fill to the star and remove any stroke, if necessary.

4. Use the Align panel to align the center points of the two objects, so that they resemble Figure 35.

5. Copy the black spade, then paste in front.

   Two black spades are now behind the yellow star; the top one is selected.

6. Press and hold **[Shift]**, then click to add the star to the selection.

7. Click the **Intersect shape areas button** in the Pathfinder panel.

   The intersection of the star and the copied spade is now a single closed path. Your work should resemble Figure 36.

8. Save your work, then close Heart Parts.

You created a star and then created a copy of the black spade-shaped object. You used the Intersect shape mode button to capture the intersection of the two objects as a new object.

FIGURE 35
Use the Align panel to align objects precisely

FIGURE 36
Yellow shape is the intersection of the star and the spade

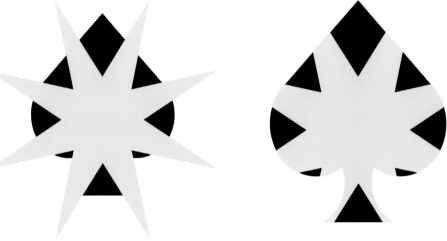

Working with the Align panel

The Align panel offers a quick and simple solution for aligning selected objects along the axis you specify. Along the vertical axis, you can align selected objects by their rightmost point, leftmost point, or center point. On the horizontal axis, you can align objects by their topmost point, center point, or bottommost point. You can also use the panel to distribute objects evenly along a horizontal or vertical axis. In contrasting the Align panel with the Average command, think of the Average command as a method for aligning anchor points and the Align panel as a method for aligning entire objects.

When you align and distribute objects, you have the choice of aligning them to the artboard or to the crop area. If you want to align or distribute objects using a crop area, you must first define the crop area using the crop Area Tool on the Tools panel. The next step is to choose Align to Crop Area, which is a button found on the Align panel or on the Control panel. (If you see the Align to Artboard button, click the list arrow next to it, then click Align to Crop Area.) Finally, choose the alignment setting you need in the Align panel. For example, if you want to vertically distribute the center points of three squares relative to the crop area, first create the crop area, select the squares, click the Align to Crop Area button on the Align or Control panel, then click the Vertical Distribute Center button on the Align panel.

Transforming and Distorting Objects

FIGURE 37
Blue star is divided into twelve objects by the Divide pathfinder

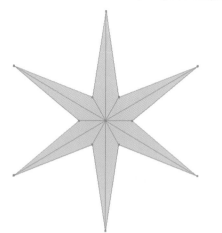

Apply the Divide pathfinder

1. Open AI 4-9.ai, then save it as **Divide**.

2. Select the red line, then double-click the **Rotate Tool** ⟳.

3. Enter **30** in the Angle text box, then click **Copy**.

4. Repeat the transformation four times.

5. Select all, then click the **Divide button** ▦ in the Pathfinder panel.

   The blue star is divided into twelve separate objects, as defined by the red lines, which have been deleted. See Figure 37.

6. Deselect, click the **Direct Selection Tool** ▸, select the left half of the top point, press **[Shift]**, then select every other object, for a total of six objects.

7. Apply an orange fill to the selected objects.

8. Select the inverse, then apply a yellow fill so that your work resembles Figure 38.

9. Save your work, then close the Divide document.

You used six lines to define a score pattern, then used those lines and the Divide pathfinder to break the star into twelve separate objects.

FIGURE 38
Divide pathfinder is useful for adding dimension

Create compound shapes using the Pathfinder panel

1. Open AI 4-10.ai, then save it as **Compound Shapes**.

2. Click **View** on the menu bar, then click **Yellow**.

3. Select the two yellow circles, then click the **Exclude overlapping shape areas button** 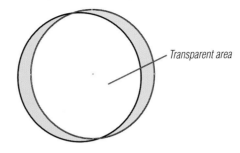 in the Pathfinder panel.

   The area that the top object overlaps becomes transparent.

4. Deselect, click the **Direct Selection Tool** , then move either circle to change the shape and size of the filled areas.

   Figure 39 shows one effect that can be achieved.

5. Select **Green** from the View menu, select the two green circles, then click the **Intersect shape areas button** in the Pathfinder panel.

   The area not overlapped by the top circle becomes transparent.

6. Deselect, then use the Direct Selection Tool to move either circle to change the shape and size of the filled area.

   Figure 40 shows one effect that can be achieved.

7. Save your work, then close the Compound Shapes document.

You applied shape modes to two pairs of circles, then moved the circles to create different shapes and effects.

FIGURE 39
An example of the Exclude shape mode

Transparent area

FIGURE 40
An example of the Intersect shape mode

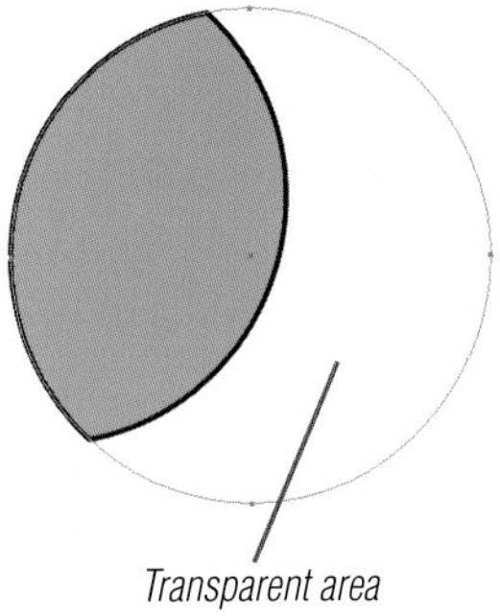

Transparent area

FIGURE 41
A compound shape

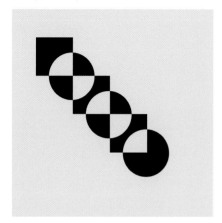

FIGURE 42
A compound shape

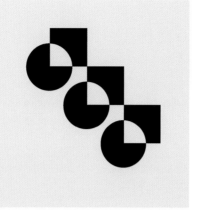

FIGURE 43
A compound shape

FIGURE 44
A compound shape

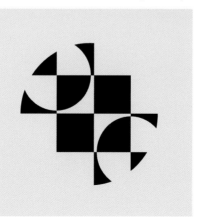

Create special effects with compound shapes

1. Open AI 4-11.ai, then save it as **Compound Shape Effects**.
2. Select all, then click the **Exclude overlapping shape areas button** 🔲 in the Pathfinder panel.

   Your work should resemble Figure 41.
3. Deselect all, click the **Direct Selection Tool** ▶, select the three squares, then move them to the right, as shown in Figure 42.
4. Drag and drop a copy of the three squares, as shown in Figure 43.

   TIP   Use [Shift][Alt] (Win) or [Shift] [option] (Mac) to drag and drop a copy at a 45-degree angle or in straight lines vertically or horizontally.
5. Scale each circle 150% using the Transform Each command.
6. Scale the center circle 200%, then bring it to the front of the stacking order.
7. Click the **Intersect shape areas button** 🔲 in the Pathfinder panel.

   Figure 44 shows the results of the intersection. Your final illustration may vary slightly.

   TIP   The topmost object affects all the objects behind it in a compound shape.
8. Save your work, then close Compound Shape Effects.

You made three squares and three circles into a compound shape by excluding overlapping shape areas. You then manipulated the size and location of individual elements to create different effects. Finally, you enlarged a circle, brought it to the front, then changed its mode to Intersect. Only the objects that were overlapped by the circle remained visible.

CREATE CLIPPING MASKS

What You'll Do

In this lesson, you will explore the role of clipping masks for practical use and for artistic effects.

Defining a Clipping Mask

As with compound paths, clipping masks are used to yield a practical result. And as with compound paths, that practical result can be manipulated to create interesting graphic effects.

Practically speaking, you use a clipping mask as a "window" through which you view some or all of the objects behind the mask in the stacking order. When you select any two or more objects and apply the Make Clipping Mask command, the *top object* becomes the mask and the object behind it becomes "masked." You will be able to see only the parts of the masked object that are visible *through* the mask, as shown in Figure 45. The mask crops the object behind it.

Using Multiple Objects as a Clipping Mask

When multiple objects are selected and the Make Clipping Mask command is applied, the top object becomes the mask. Since every object has its own position in the stacking order, it stands to reason that there can be only one top object.

If you want to use multiple objects as a mask, you can do so by first making them into a compound path. Illustrator regards compound paths as a single object. Therefore, a compound path containing multiple objects can be used as a single mask.

Creating Masked Effects

Special effects with clipping masks are, quite simply, fun! You can position as many objects as you like behind the mask, and position them in such a way that the mask crops them in visually interesting (and eye-popping!) ways. See Figure 46 for an example.

FIGURE 45
Clipping mask crops the object behind it

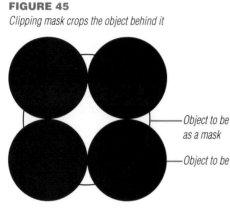

—Object to be used as a mask

—Object to be masked

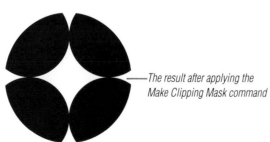

—The result after applying the Make Clipping Mask command

FIGURE 46
Masks can be used for stunning visual effects

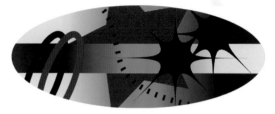

Create a clipping mask

1. Open AI 4-12.ai, then save it as **Simple Masks**.

2. Click **View** on the menu bar, then click **Mask 1**.

3. Move the rectangle so that it overlaps the gold spheres, as shown in Figure 47.

4. Apply the Bring to Front command to verify that the rectangle is in front of all the spheres.

5. Select the seven spheres and the rectangle.

6. Click **Object** on the menu bar, point to **Clipping Mask**, then click **Make**.

7. Deselect, then compare your screen to Figure 48.

8. Click **View** on the menu bar, then click **Mask 2**.

9. Select the three circles, then move them over the "gumballs."

   The three circles are a compound path.

10. Select the group of gumballs and the three circles, then apply the Make Clipping Mask command.

11. Deselect, click **Select** on the menu bar, point to **Object**, then click **Clipping Masks**.

12. Apply a 1 pt black stroke to the masks.

    Your work should resemble Figure 49.

13. Save your work, then close the Simple Masks document.

You used a rectangle as a clipping mask. Then, you used three circles to mask a group of small spheres, and applied a black stroke to the mask.

FIGURE 47
Masking objects must be in front of objects to be masked

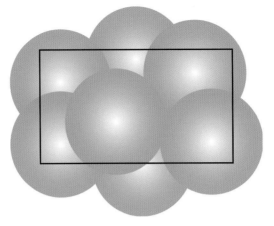

FIGURE 48
The rectangle masks the gold spheres

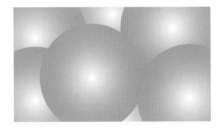

FIGURE 49
A compound path used as a mask

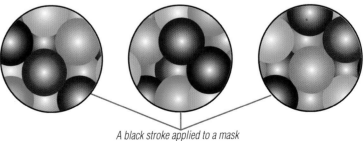

A black stroke applied to a mask

Transforming and Distorting Objects

FIGURE 50
Lining up the letter g

FIGURE 51
Positioning the magnifying glass

The two objects that make up the magnifying glass are not grouped

FIGURE 52
A fill and stroke are applied to a mask

The mask

By default, a fill is positioned behind the masked elements, and the stroke is in front of the mask

FIGURE 53
Large text is masked by the magnifying glass

When a fill is applied to a mask, the fill is positioned behind all the objects that are masked

As the mask moves, different areas of the large text become visible, creating the illusion of a magnifying glass moving over a word

Apply a fill to a clipping mask

1. Open AI 4-13.ai, then save it as **Magnify**.
2. Move the large outlined text over the small outlined text so that the *g*s align as shown in Figure 50.
3. Select the smaller text, then hide it.
4. Select the magnifying glass and the handle, then drag them over the letter *g*, as shown in Figure 51.
5. Deselect all, select only the circle and the text, click **Object** on the menu bar, point to **Clipping Mask**, then click **Make**.

   The circle is the masking object.
6. Deselect, click **Select** on the menu bar, point to **Object**, then click **Clipping Masks**.
7. Use the Swatches panel to apply a light blue fill and a gray stroke to the mask.
8. Change the weight of the stroke to 8 pt, so that your work resembles Figure 52.
9. Show all, deselect, then compare your screen to Figure 53.
10. Select the mask only, press and hold **[Shift]**, then click the **magnifying glass handle.**
11. Press the **arrow keys** to move the magnifying glass.
12. Save your work, then close the Magnify document.

You used the circle in the illustration as a clipping mask in combination with the large text. You added a fill and a stroke to the mask, creating the illusion that the small text is magnified in the magnifying glass.

Use text as a clipping mask

1. Open AI 4-14.ai, then save it as **Mask Effects**.
2. Select the four letters that make the word MASK.

   The word MASK was converted to outlines and ungrouped.
3. Make the four letters into a compound path.
4. Select the compound path and the rectangle behind it.
5. Apply the Make Clipping Mask command, then deselect.
6. Save your work, then compare your text to Figure 54.

You converted outlines to a compound path, then used the compound path as a mask.

FIGURE 54
Outlined text used as a mask

FIGURE 55

Curvy object in position to be masked by the letters

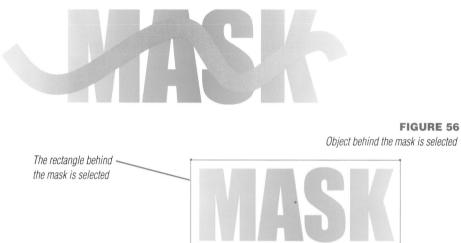

FIGURE 56

Object behind the mask is selected

The rectangle behind
the mask is selected

FIGURE 57

Curvy object is masked by the letters

FIGURE 58

Pasting multiple objects behind a mask yields interesting effects

Use a clipping mask for special effects

1. Position the curvy object with the gradient fill over the mask, as shown in Figure 55.

2. Cut the curvy object.

3. Use the **Direct Selection Tool** to select the original rectangle behind the mask.

   TIP Click slightly above the mask until you see the rectangle selected, as shown in Figure 56.

4. Paste in front, then deselect so that your screen resembles Figure 57.

   The object is pasted in front of the masked rectangle and behind the mask.

5. Click the **Selection Tool**, select the purple dotted line, position it over the letter K, then cut the purple dotted line.

6. Select the mask (rectangle) with the Direct Selection Tool, click **Edit** on the menu bar, then click **Paste in Front**.

7. Using the same technique, mask the other objects on the artboard in any way that you choose.

   When finished, your mask should contain all of the objects, as shown in Figure 58.

   TIP Add a stroke to the mask if desired.

8. Save and close Mask Effects.

You created visual effects by pasting objects behind a mask.

Transform objects.

1. Open AI 4-15.ai, then save it as **Transform Skills.**
2. Select "DIVIDE."
3. Scale the text objects non-uniformly: Horizontal = 110% and Vertical = 120%.
4. Rotate the text objects 7°.
5. Shear the text objects 25° on the horizontal axis.
6. Save your work.

Offset and outline paths.

1. Ungroup the text outlines.
2. Using the Offset Path command, offset each letter -.05".
3. Save your work.

Work with the Pathfinder panel.

1. Select all.
2. Apply the Divide pathfinder.

3. Fill the divided elements with different colors, using the Direct Selection Tool.
4. Select all, then apply a 2-point white stroke. Figure 59 is an example of the effect. (*Hint*: Enlarge the view of your document window, if necessary.)
5. Save your work, compare your image to Figure 59, then close the Transform Skills document.

FIGURE 59
Completed Skills Review, Part 1

Create compound paths.

1. Open AI 4-16.ai, then save it as **Compounded**.
2. Select all, then click the Exclude overlapping shape areas button.
3. Deselect, then click the center of the small square with the Direct Selection Tool.
4. Rotate a copy of the small square 45°.
5. Save your work, compare your image to Figure 60, then close the Compounded document.

FIGURE 60

Completed Skills Review, Part 2

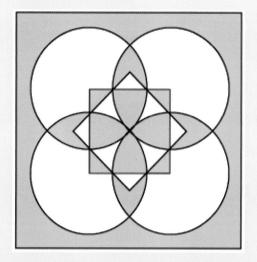

You are entering a contest to design a new stamp. You have decided to use a picture of Mona Lisa, which you have placed in an Illustrator document. You have positioned text over the image. Now, to complete the effect, you want to mimic the perforated edges of a stamp.

1. Open AI 4-.17.ai, then save it as **Mona Lisa**.
2. Select all the circles, then make them into a compound path.
3. Add the rectangle to the selection.
4. Apply the Subtract from shape area button then deselect all.
5. Save your work, compare your image to Figure 61, then close Mona Lisa.

FIGURE 61
Completed Project Builder 1

Transforming and Distorting Objects

You're contracted to design the logo for Wired Gifts, an online gift site. Your concept is of a geometric red bow. You feel that your idea will simultaneously convey the concepts of gifts and technology.

1. Open AI 4-18.ai, then save it as **Wired**.
2. Switch to Outline mode.
3. Select the small square, click the Rotate Tool, press and hold [Alt] (Win) or [option] (Mac), then click the center of the large square.
4. Type **15** in the Angle text box, then click Copy.
5. Repeat the transformation 22 times.
6. Delete the large square at the center.
7. Switch to Preview mode.
8. Select all, then fill all the squares with Caribbean Blue.
9. Apply the Divide pathfinder to the selection.
10. Fill the objects with the Red Bow gradient.
11. Delete the object in the center of the bow. (*Hint*: Use the Direct Selection Tool to select the object.)
12. Select all, then remove the black stroke from the objects.
13. Save your work, compare your illustration with Figure 62, then close Wired.

FIGURE 62
Completed Project Builder 2

You are a fabric designer for a line of men's clothing. The line is known for its conservative patterns and styles. You are asked to supervise a team that will design new patterns for men's ties. You will present your recommended new patterns using Illustrator.

FIGURE 63
Completed Design Project

1. Create a new CMYK Color document and name it **New Tie.**
2. Create a square, rotate it 45°, then reshape it using the Direct Selection Tool by dragging the top anchor point straight up to create the shape of a tie.
3. Use a square and the Subtract from shape area button to square off the top of the diamond.
4. Draw a second polygon to represent the tie's knot.
5. Lock the two polygons.
6. Create a small circle, then copy it using the Move dialog box to create a polka dot pattern that exceeds the perimeter of both polygons.
7. Unlock the polygons, then bring them to the front.
8. Create a compound path out of the two polygons.
9. Select all, then use the polygons to mask the polka-dot pattern.
10. Apply a fill to the mask, save your work, compare your image to Figure 63, then close the New Tie document.

You are the design department manager for a toy company, and your team's next project will be to design a dartboard that will be part of a package of "Safe Games" for kids. The target market is boys and girls ages six to adult. Your team will design only the board, not the darts.

1. Create a new CMYK Color document and name it **Dartboard**.
2. Have part of the group search the Internet for pictures of dartboards.
3. Have two members research the sport of throwing darts. What are the official dimensions of a dartboard? Is there an official design? Are there official colors?
4. The other team members should discuss which colors should be used for the board, keeping in mind that the sales department plans to position it as a toy for both girls and boys.
5. The team should also discuss whether they will use alternate colors even if the research team learns the official colors for a dartboard.
6. Using the skills you learned in this chapter, work together to design a dartboard, using Figure 64 as a guide.
7. Save your work, compare your image to Figure 64, then close Dartboard.

FIGURE 64
Completed Group Project

Transforming and Distorting Objects

chapter

5

WORKING WITH
LAYERS

1. Create and modify layers

2. Manipulate layered artwork

3. Work with layered artwork

4. Create a clipping set

Designing with Layers

When you're creating complex artwork, keeping track of all the items on the artboard can become quite a challenge. Small items hide behind larger items, and it may become difficult to find them, select them, and work with them. The Layers panel solves this problem. Using the Layers panel, you organize your work by placing objects or groups of objects on separate layers. Artwork on layers can be manipulated and modified independently from artwork on other layers. The Layers panel also provides effective options to select, hide, lock, and change the appearance of your work. In addition, layers are an effective solution for storing multiple versions of your work in one file.

Tools You'll Use

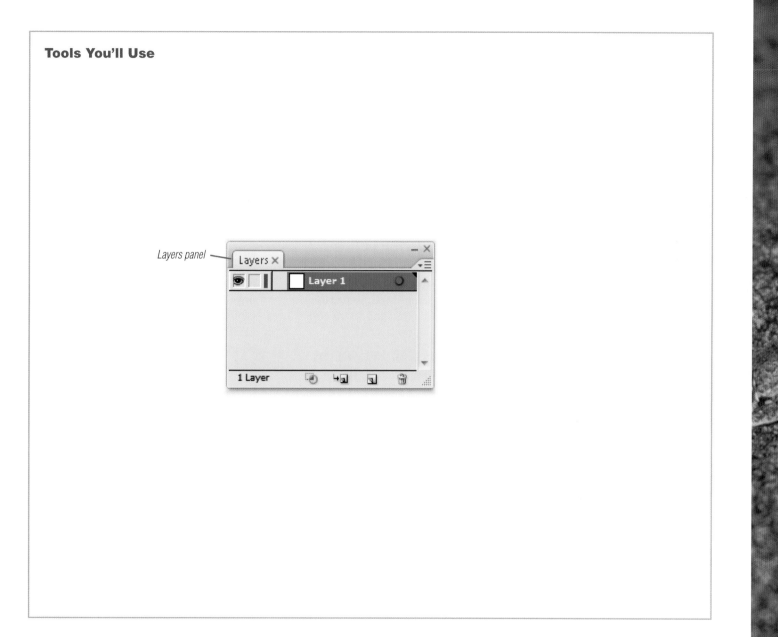

Layers panel

Layers ×

Layer 1

1 Layer

CREATE AND
MODIFY LAYERS

What You'll Do

In this lesson, you will create new layers and explore options in the Layers panel for viewing, locking, hiding, and selecting layers and layered artwork.

Creating Layers and Sublayers

Layers are a smart solution for organizing and managing a complex illustration. For example, if you were drawing a map of your home state, you might put all the interstate freeways on one layer, the local freeways on a second layer, secondary roads on a third layer, and all the text elements on a fourth layer.

As the name suggests, the Layers panel consists of a series of layers. The number of layers that a document can have is limited only by your computer's memory. By default, every Illustrator document is created with one layer, called Layer 1. As you work, you can create new layers and move objects into them, thereby segregating and organizing your work. The first object that is placed on Layer 1 is placed on a sublayer called <Path>. Each additional object placed on the same layer is placed on a separate <Path> sublayer.

Importing an Adobe Photoshop file with layers

When you use the Open command to import a layered Photoshop file into Illustrator CS3, you have the option to open that file with its layers intact. In the Photoshop Import Options dialog box that appears, click the Convert Photoshop layers to objects option button, then click OK. Display the Illustrator Layers panel and you will see that Illustrator has preserved as much of the Photoshop layer structure as possible.

Each layer has a thumbnail, or miniature picture of the objects on that layer, to the left of the layer name. Thumbnails display the artwork that is positioned on all of the sublayers in the layer. You can change the size of the rows in the Layers panel by choosing a new size in the Layer Panel Options dialog box. Click the Layers panel list arrow, then click Panel Options. Layers and sublayers can also be given descriptive names to help identify their contents.

The stacking order of objects on the artboard corresponds to the hierarchy of layers in the Layers panel. Artwork in the top layer is at the front of the stacking order, while artwork in the bottom layer is in the back. The hierarchy of sublayers corresponds to the stacking order of the objects within a single layer.

Illustrator offers two basic ways to create new layers and sublayers. You can click the New Layer or New Sublayer command in the Layers panel menu, or you can click the Create New Layer or Create New Sublayer button in the Layers panel. Figure 1 shows a simple illustration and its corresponding layers in the Layers panel.

Duplicating Layers

In addition to creating new layers, you can duplicate existing layers by clicking the Duplicate command in the Layers panel menu, or by dragging a layer or sublayer onto the Create New Layer button in the Layers panel. When you duplicate a layer, all of the artwork on the layer is duplicated as well. Note the difference between this and copying and pasting artwork. When you copy and paste artwork, the copied artwork is pasted on the same layer.

FIGURE 1
Layers panel

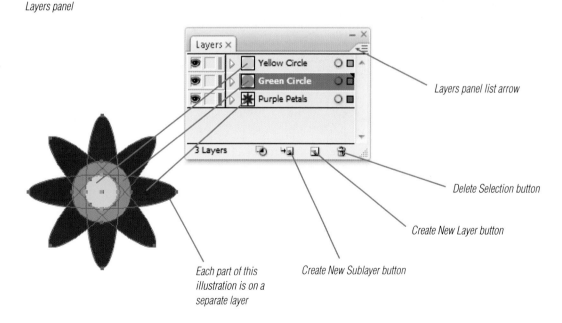

Layers panel list arrow

Delete Selection button

Create New Layer button

Create New Sublayer button

Each part of this illustration is on a separate layer

Setting Layer Options

The Layer Options dialog box offers a wealth of options for working with layered artwork, many of which are not available to you unless you are working with layers. You can name a layer, and you can also set a selection color for the layer. When an object is selected, its selection marks will be the same color as specified for the layer, making it easy to differentiate layers of artwork on the artboard.

Also in the Layer Options dialog box are options for locking, unlocking, showing, and hiding artwork on the layer. When you lock a layer, all the objects on the layer are locked and protected. When the Show check box is checked, all the artwork that is contained in the layer is displayed on the artboard. When the Show check box is not checked, the artwork is hidden.

The Preview option displays all the artwork on a layer in Preview mode. When the Preview option is not activated, the artwork is displayed in Outline mode. Thus, with layers, some elements on the artboard can be in Preview mode, while others are in Outline mode.

The Print option allows you to choose whether or not to print a layer. This feature is useful for printing different versions of the same illustration. The Dim Images to option reduces the intensity of bitmap images that are placed on the artboard. Dimming a bitmap often makes it easier to trace an image.

Use the Template option when you want to use the artwork on a layer as the basis for a new illustration—for example, if you want to trace the artwork. By default, a template layer is locked and cannot be printed.

Buttons in the Layers panel represent ways to lock, unlock, hide, and show artwork on each layer, making it unnecessary to use the Layer Options dialog box to activate these functions. The Toggles Visibility button (the eye) lets you hide and show layers, and the Toggles Lock button (the padlock) lets you lock and unlock layers.

Selecting Artwork on Layers and Sublayers

When you select an object on the artboard, its layer is selected (highlighted) in the Layers panel, and the Indicates Selected Art button appears, as shown in Figure 2. Selecting a layer or sublayer in the Layers panel does not select the artwork on that layer.

Changes that you make to layers in the Layers panel affect the artwork on those layers. For example, if you delete a layer, the artwork on the layer will be deleted. The artwork on a layer will be duplicated if the layer is duplicated. Changing a layer's position in the layers hierarchy will move the artwork forward or backward in the stacking order.

Duplicating the artwork on the artboard does not duplicate the layer that the artwork is on. If you delete all the artwork on a layer, you are left with an empty layer. *A layer is never automatically created, copied, or deleted, regardless of what you do to the artwork on the layer.*

The same is *not* true for sublayers. If you delete or copy artwork that is on a sublayer, the *sublayer* is deleted or copied, respectively.

Selecting All Artwork on a Layer

The Select All command makes it easy to select every object on the artboard in one step. At times, however, you will want to select every object on a layer or sublayer, not every object on the artboard. To select all the artwork on a single layer or sublayer, select the Click to target, drag to move appearance button to the left of the Indicates Selected Art button, shown in Figure 2, or [Alt] (Win) or [option] (Mac) click the layer. All objects on that layer will become selected on the artboard.

FIGURE 2
The chair on the artboard and in the Layers panel

Selection marks for chair are red, the Chair layer's assigned color

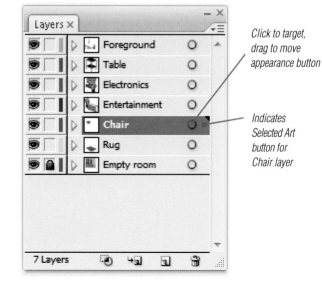

Click to target, drag to move appearance button

Indicates Selected Art button for Chair layer

Create a new layer

1. Open AI 5-1.ai, then save it as **Living Room**.

2. Open AI 5-2.ai, then save it as **Showroom**.

   You will work with two documents during this lesson.

3. Click the **Selection Tool** ▶, select the chair, then copy it.

4. Click **Window** on the menu bar, then click **Living Room**.

   | TIP   Using the Window menu is an easy way to switch between open documents.

5. Click the **Layers button** ◆ to open the Layers panel.

   The Layers panel shows two layers. The Empty room layer contains the artwork you see on the artboard. The objects on the Foreground layer are hidden.

6. Click the **Create New Layer button** 🖫 in the Layers panel.

   A new layer named Layer 3 appears above the Foreground layer.

7. Click **Edit** on the menu bar, then click **Paste**.

   The chair artwork is pasted into Layer 3.

8. Position the chair on the artboard as shown in Figure 3.

You created a new layer using the Create New Layer button in the Layers panel, then pasted an object into that new layer.

FIGURE 3
Chair positioned on its own layer

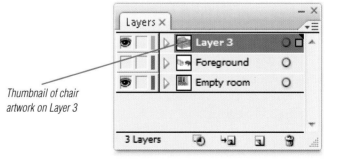

Thumbnail of chair artwork on Layer 3

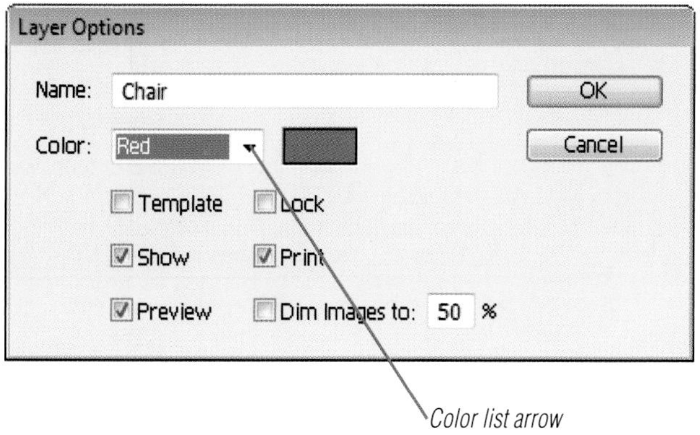

Name a layer and change a layer's selection color

1. Double-click **Layer 3**.
2. Name the layer **Chair**, then click **OK**.

   The Layers panel reflects the name change.
3. Double-click the **Chair layer**.
4. Click the **Color list arrow**, click **Red**, as shown in Figure 4, then click **OK**.

   Note that the selection marks on the chair are now red, reflecting the new selection color for the Chair layer.
5. Deselect the chair.

You used the Layer Options dialog box to rename Layer 3 and assign it a new selection color.

FIGURE 4
Layer Options dialog box

Color list arrow

Select items on a layer and lock a layer

1. Click the **chair** with the Selection Tool ▶.

   Note that the Indicates Selected Art button appears when the chair is selected, as shown in Figure 5.

   > TIP The Indicates Selected Art button is the same color as its layer.

2. Deselect the chair.

   The Indicates Selected Art button disappears.

3. Press **[Alt]** (Win) or **[option]** (Mac), then click the **Chair layer** in the Layers panel.

   The chair artwork is selected.

4. Click either of the two mauve walls in the illustration.

   When an object is selected on the artboard, the layer on which the selected object is placed is highlighted in the Layers panel.

5. Double-click the **Empty room layer**, click the **Lock check box**, then click **OK**.

   The Toggles Lock button 🔒 appears on the Empty room layer, indicating that all the objects on the Empty room layer are locked. See Figure 6.

You noted the relationship between a selected item and its corresponding layer in the Layers panel. You activated the Indicates Selected Art button and selected the artwork on the Chair layer. You then locked the Foreground layer.

FIGURE 5
Indicates Selected Art button identifies the layer of a selected object

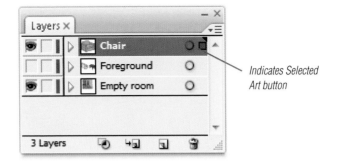

Indicates Selected Art button

FIGURE 6
Toggles Lock button identifies a locked layer

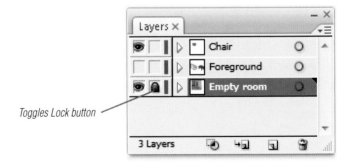

Toggles Lock button

FIGURE 7
Foreground layer is locked and hidden

The absence of the
Toggles Visibility
button indicates
that this layer is hidden

The Toggles Lock
button indicates that
this layer is locked

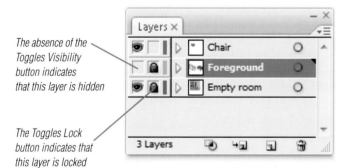

1. Double-click the **Foreground layer**.

2. Click the **Color list arrow**, then click **Grass Green**.

3. Click the **Show check box**, then click **OK**.

   The objects on the Foreground layer become visible, and the Toggles Visibility button appears on the Foreground layer.

4. Click the **Toggles Visibility button** on the Foreground layer to hide the objects.

5. Click the **Toggles Visibility button** (in its off state) on the Foreground layer to show the objects.

   TIP The Toggles Visibility and Toggles Lock buttons appear as empty gray squares in their off state.

6. Click the **Toggles Lock button** (in its off state) on the Foreground layer.

   The **Toggles Lock button** appears.

7. Click the **Toggles Visibility button** on the Foreground layer to hide the objects.

   Your Layers panel should resemble Figure 7.

8. Save your work.

You used the Toggles Visibility button in the Layers panel to toggle between showing and hiding the artwork on two layers. You also locked the Foreground layer.

MANIPULATE LAYERED
ARTWORK

What You'll Do

In this lesson, you will learn methods for manipulating layers to change the display of layered artwork. You will change the order of layers in the panel, merge layers, work with sublayers, and move objects between layers.

Changing the Order of Layers and Sublayers

The hierarchy of the layers in the Layers panel determines how objects on the artboard overlap. All the objects on a given layer are behind the objects on the layer above it and in front of the objects on the layer beneath it. Multiple objects within a given layer overlap according to their stacking order and can be repositioned with the standard stacking order commands.

To change the position of a layer or sublayer in the hierarchy, simply drag it up or down in the panel. Small black triangles and a heavy horizontal line identify where the layer will be repositioned, as shown in Figure 8. When you reposition a layer, its sublayers move with it.

Merging Layers

When you have positioned artwork to your liking using multiple layers and sublayers, you will often want to consolidate those layers to simplify the panel. First, you must select the layers that you want to merge. Press [Ctrl] (Win) or ⌘ (Mac) to select multiple layers. Once you have selected the layers that you want to merge, apply the Merge Selected command in the Layers panel menu. When you merge layers, all the artwork from one or more layers moves onto the layer that was last selected before the merge.

Be careful not to confuse merging layers with condensing layers. Condensing layers is simply the process of dragging one layer into another. The repositioned layer becomes a sublayer of the layer it was dragged into.

Defining Sublayers

Whenever you have one or more objects on a layer, you by definition have **sublayers**. For example, if you draw a circle and a square on Layer 1, it will automatically have two sublayers—one for the square, one for the circle. The layer is the sum total of its sublayers.

As soon as the first object is placed on a layer, a triangle appears to the left of the layer name, indicating that the layer contains sublayers. Click the triangle to expand the layer and see the sublayers, then click it again to collapse the layer and hide the sublayers.

Working with Sublayers

When you place grouped artwork into a layer, a sublayer is automatically created with the name <Group>. A triangle appears on the <Group> sublayer, which, when clicked, exposes the sublayers—one for every object in the group, as shown in Figure 9.

Dragging Objects Between Layers

Sublayers are the easiest objects to move between layers: You can simply drag and drop a sublayer from one layer to another.

You can drag artwork from one layer to another by dragging the Indicates Selected Art button. Select the artwork on the artboard that you want to move; the layer is selected, and the Indicates Selected Art button appears. Drag the button to the destination layer or sublayer, as shown in Figure 10. If you drag the Indicates Selected Art button to a layer, the artwork becomes the top sublayer in the layer. If you drag the Indicates Selected Art button to a

sublayer, the artwork is grouped with the object already on the sublayer.

If you don't feel comfortable dragging artwork between layers, you have two other options for moving objects between layers. You can simply cut and paste artwork from one layer to another by selecting the object that you want to move, cutting it from the artboard, selecting the layer you wish to place it on, then pasting. You can also use the Send to Current Layer command. Select the artwork you want to move, click the name of the destination layer to make it the active layer, click Object on the menu bar, point to Arrange, then click Send to Current Layer.

FIGURE 9

A <Group> sublayer

FIGURE 8

Changing the order of layers

Moving a layer in the Layers panel

Each object in a group is placed on its own sublayer

FIGURE 10

Dragging a sublayer to another layer

Drag the Indicates Selected Art button to another layer

Change the hierarchy of layers

1. Use the Window menu to switch to the Showroom document, copy the rug, then return to the Living Room document.

2. Press **[Ctrl]** (Win) or ⌘ (Mac), then click the **Create New Layer button** 🖫 in the Layers panel.

   Pressing [Ctrl] (Win) or ⌘ (Mac) creates a new layer at the top of the layer list.

3. Click **Edit** on the menu bar, then click **Paste**.

   The rug is pasted into the new layer because it is the active—or "targeted"—layer.

4. Name the new layer **Rug**, then position the rug artwork with a corner of it hanging slightly off the artboard, as shown in Figure 11.

5. Click and drag the **Rug layer** and position it below the Chair layer until you see a double black line with small triangles beneath the Chair layer, as shown in Figure 12, then release the mouse.

   The rug artwork is now positioned below the chair artwork.

You created a new layer at the top of the Layers panel. You pasted artwork into that layer, then moved the layer below another layer in the hierarchy so that the artwork on the two layers overlapped properly on the artboard.

FIGURE 11
The Rug layer is at the top of the layers hierarchy

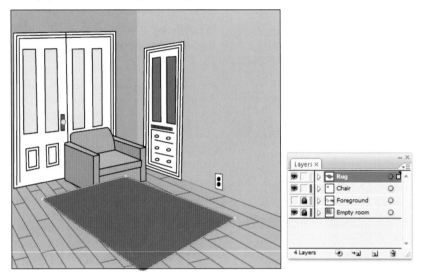

FIGURE 12
Changing the hierarchy of layers

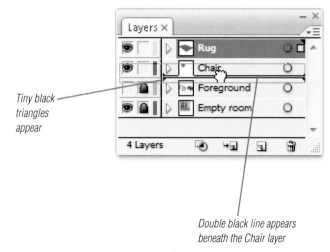

Tiny black triangles appear

Double black line appears beneath the Chair layer

Working with Layers

FIGURE 13

Sculpture artwork positioned on top of the end table

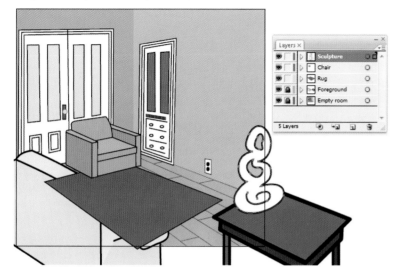

FIGURE 14

Foreground and Sculpture layers merged

Merged layer

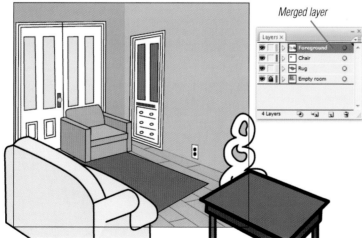

Merge layers

1. Switch to the Showroom document, copy the sculpture, then return to the Living Room document.

2. Press **[Ctrl]** (Win) or ⌘ (Mac), then click the **Create New Layer button** .

3. Paste the sculpture into the new layer, then name the layer **Sculpture**.

4. Show the Foreground layer, then position the sculpture artwork on the brown end table, as shown in Figure 13.

5. Deselect the sculpture, then drag the **Foreground layer** above the Sculpture layer in the Layers panel.

6. Unlock the Foreground layer.

7. Click the **Sculpture layer** to select it, press **[Ctrl]** (Win) or ⌘ (Mac), then click the **Foreground layer**.

   When merging layers, the last layer selected becomes the merged layer.

8. Click the **Layers panel list arrow**, then click **Merge Selected**.

   The objects from both layers are merged into the Foreground layer; the Sculpture layer is deleted.

   | TIP   Layers must be showing and unlocked in order to be merged.

9. Compare your screen to Figure 14.

   Don't worry that your sculpture is temporarily behind the table.

You merged the Sculpture and the Foreground layers.

Work with sublayers

1. Expand the Foreground layer by clicking the **triangle** ▷ to the left of the layer.

   Three sublayers, all named <Group>, are revealed.

2. Expand the sofa <Group> sublayer by clicking the **triangle** ▷ to the left of it.

   The five paths that compose the sofa are revealed.

3. Select the sofa artwork on the artboard.

   The Indicates Selected Art buttons appear for each of the selected paths, as shown in Figure 15.

4. Click the **triangle** ▽ to the left of the sofa <Group> sublayer to collapse it, then deselect the sofa.

5. Double-click the **sofa <Group> sublayer**, name it **Sofa**, then click **OK**.

6. Name the sculpture sublayer **Sculpture**, then name the end table sublayer **End Table**.

7. Move the Sculpture sublayer above the End Table sublayer so that your Layers panel resembles Figure 16.

   Notice that the sculpture artwork is on top of the end table.

8. Click the **triangle** ▽ to the left of the Foreground layer to hide the three sublayers.

9. Hide the Foreground layer.

You viewed sublayers in the Foreground layer. You then renamed the three sublayers in the Foreground layer and rearranged the order of the Sculpture and the End Table sublayers.

FIGURE 15

Each path in the sofa <Group> sublayer is selected

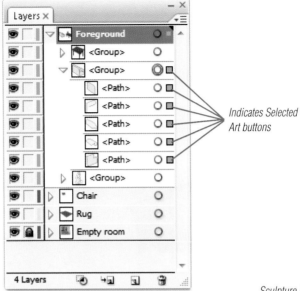

Indicates Selected
Art buttons

FIGURE 16

Sculpture layer moved above the End Table sublayer

FIGURE 17

Cabinet and plant are on the same layer

FIGURE 18

Moving the Plant 2 sublayer

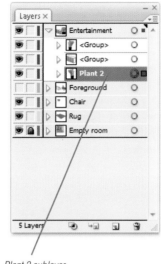

Plant 2 sublayer

FIGURE 19

The reflected copy of the plant in position

The new plant is positioned
behind the cabinet

FIGURE 20

The reflected copy of the plant, scaled and pruned

Create new sublayers

1. Switch to the Showroom document, copy the cabinet, then return to the Living Room document.

2. Press **[Ctrl]** (Win) or ⌘ (Mac), then click the **Create New Layer button** 🔲.

3. Name the new layer **Entertainment**, select Violet as the layer color, then click **OK**.

4. Paste the cabinet artwork into the new layer.

5. Copy the plant from the Showroom document, then paste the plant artwork into the Entertainment layer.

6. Position the cabinet artwork and the plant artwork as shown in Figure 17.

7. Deselect all, expand the Entertainment layer, then select the plant artwork on the artboard.

8. Double-click the **Reflect Tool** 🔘, click the **Vertical option button**, then click **Copy**.

   The reflected copy of the plant is placed on a new sublayer above the original plant sublayer.

9. Rename the new sublayer **Plant 2**.

10. Move the Plant 2 sublayer to the bottom of the Entertainment sublayer hierarchy, as shown in Figure 18.

11. Click the **Selection Tool** ▶, then move the new plant artwork into the position shown in Figure 19.

12. Scale the new plant artwork 85%, delete or move some leaves on it so that it's not an obvious copy of the original plant, then compare your screen to Figure 20.

You created and moved new sublayers.

Move objects between layers

1. Switch to the Showroom document, copy the electronics images, then return to the Living Room document.

2. Create a new layer at the top of the hierarchy, name it **Electronics**, choose Magenta as its color, then click **OK**.

3. Paste the electronics on the Electronics layer, then position the electronics artwork on the cabinet.

   The plant on the right needs to be positioned in front of the electronics for the visual to be realistic.

4. Name the top sublayer in the Entertainment layer **Plant 1**, then select the Plant 1 artwork on the artboard.

   The Indicates Selected Art button appears in the Plant 1 sublayer.

5. Drag the **Indicates Selected Art button** from the Plant 1 sublayer to the Electronics layer, as shown in Figure 21.

   The Plant 1 sublayer moves into the Electronics layer. The Plant 1 sublayer automatically becomes the top sublayer in the Electronics layer.

6. Switch to the Showroom document, copy the Matisse, return to the Living Room document, then create a new layer at the top of the hierarchy, named **Matisse**.

7. Paste the Matisse artwork into the new layer, then position it as shown in Figure 22.

   (continued)

FIGURE 21
Moving a sublayer from one layer to another

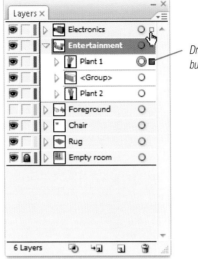

Drag the Indicates Selected Art button to the Electronics layer

FIGURE 22
The Matisse in position on its own layer

Working with Layers

FIGURE 23

Moving the Matisse layer into the Electronics layer

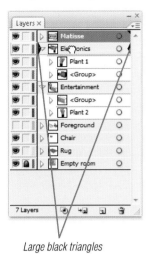

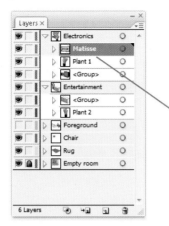

The Matisse layer becomes a
sublayer of the Electronics layer

Large black triangles

8. Drag the Matisse layer on top of the
   Electronics layer.

   Two large, black triangles appear on the
   Electronics layer when the Matisse layer is
   on top of it, as shown in Figure 23. The
   Matisse layer is moved into the Electronics
   layer as the topmost sublayer.

9. Create new layers for the lamp and the table,
   copy and paste the lamp and table artwork
   from the Showroom document to the new
   layers, then position the artwork so that your
   illustration resembles Figure 24.

10. Save your work.

*You created a new layer named Electronics,
dragged the Plant 1 sublayer into the Electronics
layer by dragging its Indicates Selected Art button
to the Electronics layer. You then moved the
Matisse layer into the Electronics layer by dragging it on top of the Electronics layer and created
new layers for the table and the lamp.*

FIGURE 24

The lamp and table in position

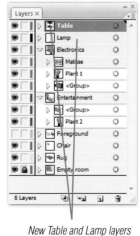

New Table and Lamp layers

WORK WITH LAYERED
ARTWORK

What You'll Do

In this lesson, you will explore options for managing your work using the Layers panel.

Using the View Buttons in the Layers Panel

The view options available in the Layers panel make working with layers a smart choice for complex illustrations. The options are targeted: You can apply specific viewing options to each layer in the document. Without layers, your options for viewing your work are limited to the Hide and Show All commands on the Object menu.

The Toggles Visibility button makes it easy to quickly change what can be seen on the artboard. Clicking this button once hides all the artwork on a layer, and the button disappears. Clicking the empty gray square where the button was shows all of the artwork on the layer, and the button reappears. Pressing [Alt] (Win) or [option] (Mac) and clicking the button once shows all layers; clicking a second time hides all layers except for the layer you clicked.

Pressing [Ctrl] (Win) or ⌘ (Mac) and clicking the button toggles between Outline and Preview modes; all the artwork on the layer will switch between outlined and filled objects. Pressing [Alt][Ctrl] (Win) or [option] ⌘ (Mac) and clicking the button switches all other layers between Outline and Preview modes.

Locating an Object in the Layers Panel

With complex illustrations, layers and sublayers tend to multiply—so much so that you will often find it easiest to work with collapsed layers, those in which you hide the sublayers. Sometimes it can be difficult to identify an object's layer or sublayer, especially if there are multiple copies of the object in the illustration. The Locate Object command offers a simple solution. Select an object on the artboard, click the Layers panel list arrow, then click Locate Object. The layers expand, revealing their sublayers, and the selected object's layer or sublayer is selected.

Reversing the Order of Layers

Another option that the Layers panel offers for managing your artwork is the ability to reverse the order of layers. Select the layers whose order you want to reverse. Press [Shift] to select multiple contiguous (those next to each other in the panel) layers. Press [Ctrl] (Win) or [⌘] (Mac) to select multiple noncontiguous layers. Click the Layers panel list arrow, then click Reverse Order.

Making Layers Nonprintable

The ability to choose whether or not the artwork on a specific layer will print is a useful function, especially during the middle stages of producing an illustration. For example, you could print just the text elements and give them to a copy editor for proofing. You could print just the elements of the illustration that are ready to be shown to the client, holding back the elements that still need work.

Another value of the print option is the ability to print different versions of a document. Let's say you're working on the design of a poster for a client, and you've finalized the artwork but you're still undecided about the typeface for the headline, after narrowing down the choices to five typefaces. You could create five layers, one for the headline formatted in each typeface. Then you would print the illustration five times, each time printing only one of the five different headline layers. This is a smart and simple way to produce comps quickly.

Explore view options in the Layers panel

1. Collapse the Electronics and Entertainment layers, then hide them.

2. Press and hold **[Alt]** (Win) or **[option]** (Mac), then click the **Toggles Visibility button**  on the Chair layer.

   All of the layers are displayed.

3. Using the same keyboard commands, click the **Toggles Visibility button** on the Chair layer again.

   All layers, except for the Chair layer, are hidden.

4. Using the same keyboard commands, click the **Toggles Visibility button** on the Chair layer again so that all of the layers are displayed.

5. Move the Foreground layer to the top of the hierarchy.

6. Press **[Ctrl]** (Win) or ⌘ (Mac), then click the **Toggles Visibility button** on the Chair layer.

   The artwork on the Chair layer switches to Outline mode.

7. Using the same keyboard commands, click the **Toggles Visibility button** on the Chair layer again.

8. Press **[Alt][Ctrl]** (Win) or **[option]** ⌘ (Mac), then click the same **Toggles Visibility button**.

   The artwork on every layer, except for the Chair layer, switches to Outline mode, as shown in Figure 25.

9. Using the same keyboard commands, click the **Toggles Visibility button** again.

You learned keyboard commands to explore view options in the Layers panel.

FIGURE 25
The Chair layer shown in Preview mode and all other layers shown in Outline mode

FIGURE 26
Duplicating the Lamp layer

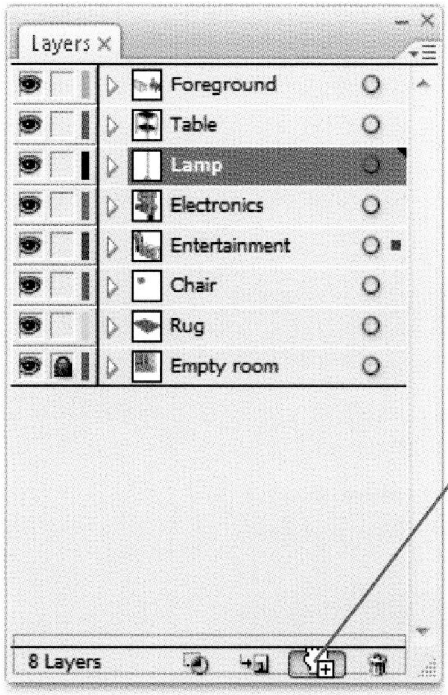

To duplicate a layer and its
contents, drag it on top of the
Create New Layer button

FIGURE 27
Positioning the second lamp

Locate, duplicate, and delete layers

1. Select the Plant 2 artwork on the artboard.

2. Click the **Layers panel list arrow**, then click **Locate Object**.

   The Entertainment layer expands, as does the Plant 2 sublayer.

   > TIP The Locate Object command is useful when you are working with collapsed layers or with many layers and sublayers.

3. Collapse the Entertainment layer.

4. Select the Lamp layer, then drag it on top of the Create New Layer button 🔲 , as shown in Figure 26.

   The Lamp layer and its contents are duplicated onto a new layer that is created above the original lamp layer. The copied lamp artwork is positioned directly on top of the original lamp artwork.

5. Position the duplicated lamp artwork on the artboard, as shown in Figure 27.

6. Drag the **Lamp copy layer** to the Delete Selection button 🗑 in the Layers panel.

You used the Locate Object command to identify a selected object's position in the Layers panel. You duplicated a layer, then deleted it.

Dim placed images

1. Hide all layers, then create a new layer at the top of the hierarchy, named **Photo**.

2. Click **File** on the menu bar, then click **Place**.

3. Navigate to the drive and folder where your Data Files are stored, click **Living Room Original.tif**, then click **Place**.

   The source for the illustration is placed on its own layer.

4. Align the photo with the top-left corner of the artboard, as shown in Figure 28.

5. Double-click the **Photo layer**, click the **Dim Images to check box**, type **50** in the Dim Images to text box, then click **OK**.

   The placed image is less vivid.

   | TIP   Dimming a placed image is useful for tracing.

You created a new layer, placed a photo on the new layer, then used the Layer Options dialog box to dim the photo 50%.

FIGURE 28
The source of the illustration, placed on its own layer

FIGURE 29
Using a layer for a message to the printer

Printer: Use photo for reference if necessary. Thank you!
Call me at 555-1234 if any problems.

1. Create a new layer at the top of the hierarchy, named **Message**.

2. Using any font you like, type a message for the printer, as shown in Figure 29.

3. Convert the message text to outlines. Double-click the **Message layer**, remove the check mark from the Print check box, then click **OK**.

   The Message layer will not print to any output device.

   | TIP   When a layer is set to not print, its name is italicized in the Layers panel.

4. Make the Photo layer nonprintable.

5. Hide the Message and Photo layers.

6. Make all the other layers visible.

7. Save your work.

You created a new layer called Message, typed a message for the printer, then designated the Message and Photo layers as nonprintable. You then displayed all of the layers except for the Message and Photo layers.

CREATE A
CLIPPING SET

What You'll Do

In this lesson, you will create a clipping mask on a sublayer that will mask the other sublayers in the layer.

Working with Clipping Sets

Adobe uses the terms "clipping mask" and "clipping path" interchangeably. The term **clipping set** is used to distinguish clipping paths used in layers from clipping paths used to mask nonlayered artwork. There's no difference; it's just terminology. Essentially, the term "clipping set" refers to the clipping mask *and* the masked sublayers as a unit.

The following rules apply to clipping sets:
- The clipping mask and the objects to be masked must be in the same layer.
- You cannot use a sublayer as a clipping mask, unless it is a <Group> sublayer. However, the top sublayer in a layer becomes the clipping mask if you first select the layer that the sublayer is in, then create the clipping mask.

- The top object in the clipping set becomes the mask for every object below it in the layer.
- A <Group> sublayer can be a clipping set. The top object in the group will function as the mask.
- Dotted lines between sublayers indicate that they are included in a clipping set.

Flattening Artwork

When you apply the Flatten Artwork command, all visible objects in the artwork are consolidated in a single layer. Before applying the command, select the layer into which you want to consolidate the artwork. If you have a layer that is hidden, you will be asked whether to make the artwork visible so that it can be flattened into the layer, or whether to delete the layer and the artwork on it.

Working with Layers

FIGURE 30
The new <Path> sublayer

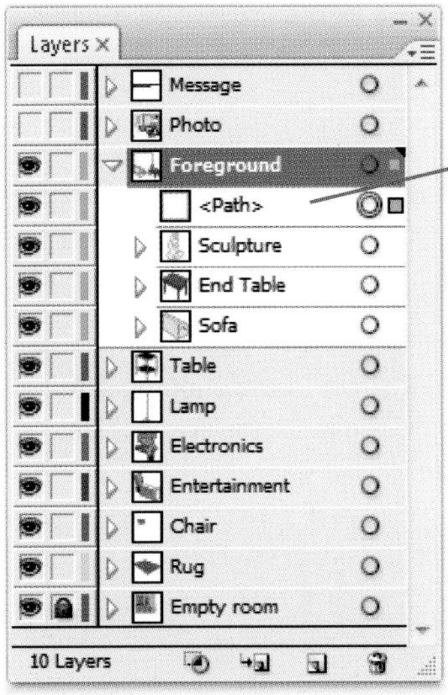

*The rectangle is placed on a
new sublayer called <Path>,
on top of the other sublayers
in the Foreground layer*

FIGURE 31
Clipping path masks only the objects on its own layer

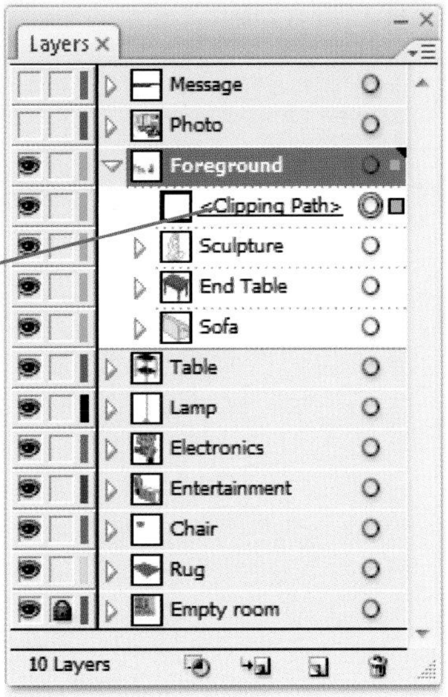

Clipping path

Create clipping sets

1. Select the Foreground layer, click the **Rectangle Tool** , then create a rectangle that is 6.5" × 6".

2. Position the rectangle so that it aligns exactly with the edges of the artboard.

3. Apply a black stroke to the rectangle and no fill color.

4. Expand the Foreground layer.

   The rectangle, identified as <Path>, is at the top of the sublayers, as shown in Figure 30.

5. Click the **Make/Release Clipping Mask button** in the Layers panel.

   Any path on the Foreground layer that is positioned off the artboard is masked. The part of the rug that extends beyond the artboard is not masked, because it is not in the same layer as the clipping path. The lamp, too, extends beyond the artboard and is not masked, as shown in Figure 31.

You created a rectangle, then used it as a clipping path to mask the sublayers below it in its layer.

Copy a clipping mask and flatten artwork

1. Click the **<Clipping Path> layer** to select it.

2. Click **Edit** on the menu bar, click **Copy**, click **Edit** on the menu bar again, then click **Paste in Front**.

   A new sublayer named <Path> is created. The rectangle on the <Clipping Path> sublayer is duplicated on the new <Path> sublayer and can be used to mask other layers.

3. Drag the **Indicates Selected Art button** on the <Path> sublayer down to the Rug layer, as shown in Figure 32.

4. Expand the Rug layer to see the new <Path> sublayer, select the Rug layer, then click the **Make/Release Clipping Mask button** .

   Compare your Layers panel to Figure 33. The <Path> sublayer becomes the <Clipping Path> sublayer, and the rectangle on the <Clipping Path> sublayer is used to mask the rug on the artboard.

   (continued)

FIGURE 32

Moving the copy of the rectangle to the Rug layer

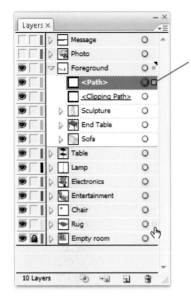

Drag the Indicates Selected Art button to the Rug layer

FIGURE 33

Using the duplicate rectangle to mask the rug

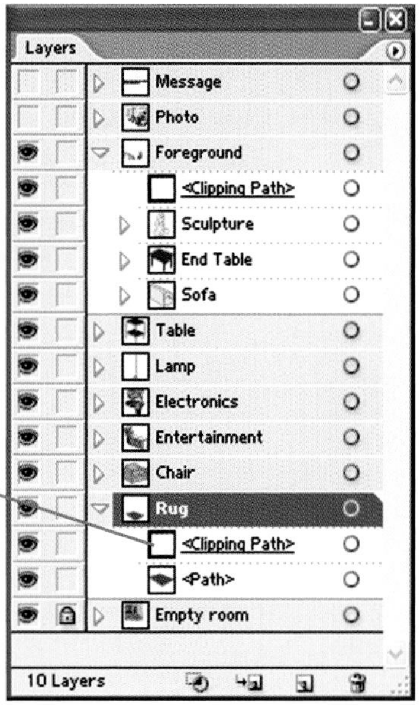

The <Path> sublayer becomes the <Clipping Path> sublayer, and the rectangle on the <Clipping Path> sublayer is used to mask the rug on the artboard

FIGURE 34
Completed illustration

5. Select the lamp artwork on the artboard, drag the **Indicates Selected Art button** on the Lamp layer to the Sculpture sublayer of the Foreground layer, then deselect all.

   The lamp artwork moves to the Sculpture sublayer and is therefore masked. Deselect the lamp and your illustration should resemble Figure 34.

   > TIP When you drag the Indicates Selected Art button from one layer to another, the selected artwork moves to the new layer, but the layer does not move.

6. Select the empty Lamp layer, then click the **Delete Selection button** ⬚ in the Layers panel.

7. Click **File** on the menu bar, then click **Save**.

8. Select the Foreground layer, click the **Layers panel list arrow**, click **Flatten Artwork**, then click **Yes** when you are asked whether or not you want to discard the hidden art on the hidden layers.

9. Click **File** on the menu bar, click **Save As**, then save the file as **Living Room Flat**.

   Note that we saved the flattened version as a separate file and saved the original Livingroom.ai file with all layers intact. Whenever you flatten a layered document, always save the flattened version as a copy so that you can preserve your original layered file.

You made a copy of the rectangle, moved the copied rectangle to the Rug layer, then made it into a clipping path to mask the rug artwork. You then moved the lamp artwork into the Sculpture sub-layer, which masked the lamp. You deleted the empty Lamp layer and flattened all of the artwork on the Foreground layer.

SKILLS REVIEW

Create and modify layers.

1. Open AI 5-3.ai, then save it as **Gary**.
2. Create a new layer at the top of the layer hierarchy, named **Text**.
3. Create a new layer at the top of the hierarchy, named **Gary Garlic**.
4. Rename Layer 2 **Body Parts**.
5. Save your work.

Manipulate layered artwork.

1. Move the garlic artwork into the Gary Garlic layer.
2. Move the three text groups into the Text layer.
3. Merge the Background layer with the Box Shapes layer so that the Box Shapes layer is the name of the resulting merged layer. (*Hint*: Click the Background layer, press [Ctrl] (Win) or ⌘ (Mac), click the Box Shapes layer, click the Layers panel list arrow, then click Merge Selected.)
4. Move the Body Parts layer to the top of the layer hierarchy.
5. Save your work.

Work with layered artwork.

1. View each layer separately to identify the artwork on each.
2. Using Figure 35 as a guide, assemble Gary Garlic.
3. Merge the Gary Garlic and Body Parts layers so that the resulting merged layer will be named Body Parts.
4. Select all the artwork on the Body Parts layer, then group the artwork.
5. Save your work.

Create a clipping set.

1. Select the Box Shapes layer.
2. Create a rectangle that is 5" wide by 8" in height.
3. Position the rectangle so that it is centered on the artboard.
4. Apply the Make Clipping Mask command.
5. Reposition the masked elements (text and box parts) so that your illustration resembles Figure 35.
6. Save your work, then close Gary.

FIGURE 35
Completed Skills Review

You are designing an outdoor sign for Xanadu Haircutters, a salon that recently opened in your town. You are pleased with your concept of using scissors to represent the X in Xanadu, and decide to design the logo with different typefaces so that the client will feel she has some input into the final design.

1. Open AI 5-4.ai, then save it as **Xanadu**.
2. Create a new layer, then move the ANADU headline into that layer.
3. Make four duplicates of the new layer.
4. Change the typeface on four of the layers, for a total of five versions of the logo type.
5. Rename each type layer, using the name of the typeface you chose.
6. Rename Layer 1 Xanadu Art.
7. View the Xanadu Art layer five times, each time with one of the typeface layers, so that you can see five versions of the logo.
8. Save your work, compare your illustration with Figure 36, then close Xanadu.

FIGURE 36
Completed Project Builder 1

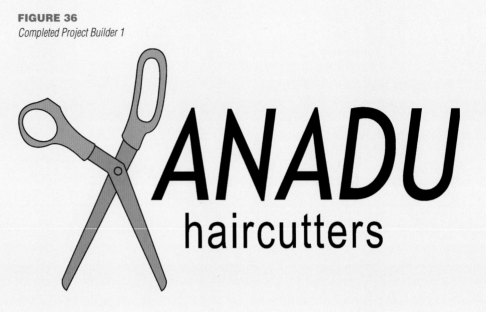

Working with Layers

You are the Creative Director for a Los Angeles design firm that specializes in identity packages for television networks. One of your most important projects this week is delivering the first round of comps for a new cable channel, Milty TV. Your art directors have come up with two concepts—one dark, one light. You decide to bring each to the client with two options for typography, for a total of four comps.

1. Open AI 5-5.ai, then save it as **Milty Cable**.
2. Select the four pieces of artwork at the top of the artboard, then group them.
3. Group the four pieces of artwork at the bottom of the artboard, then cut them.
4. Create a new layer, name it **Orange**, then paste the artwork.
5. Position the orange artwork exactly on top of the blue artwork on the artboard so that it is covered.
6. Rename Layer 1 **Blue**, then duplicate the layer and name it **Blue Two**.
7. Duplicate the Orange layer, then name it **Orange Two**.
8. Deselect all, use the Direct Selection Tool to select the large M, change its typeface to Algerian, then hide the two Orange layers. (*Hint*: If you do not have Algerian as a typeface, choose another one.)

9. Select the Blue Two layer, change the M to Algerian, then hide it.

10. View each of the four layers separately.
11. Save your work, compare your illustration to Figure 37, then close Milty Cable.

FIGURE 37
Completed Project Builder 2

You are a freelance designer, working out of your house. The owner of the town's largest plumbing company, Straight Flush, has hired you to redesign his logo. He gives you an Illustrator file with a design created by his son. You study the logo, then decide that it lacks cohesion and focus.

1. Open **AI 5-6.ai**, then save it as **Straight Flush**.
2. Group the elements of each playing card together.
3. Create four new layers.
4. Move each card to the layer with the corresponding number in the layer name.
5. Select all the layers, click the Layers panel list arrow, then click Reverse Order.
6. Reposition the cards on each layer so that they are in order, directly behind the ace.
7. Adjust the layout of the cards to your liking to create a new layout for the logo.
8. Save your work, compare your illustration with Figure 38, then close Straight Flush.

FIGURE 38
Completed Design Project

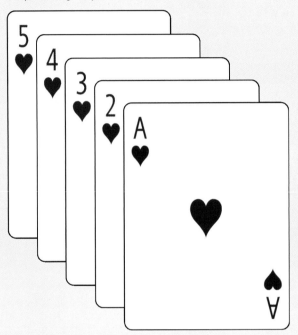

You are a fabric designer for a line of men's clothing. You are asked to supervise a team that will design new patterns for men's ties. Now that you have studied working with layers, how would you approach building a file that shows three patterns for a tie?

1. Open AI 5-7.ai, then save it as **Tie Pattern**.
2. Have one group member select objects in the document while the group watches.
3. Have the group discuss how each tie illustration has been created.
4. Have the group discuss how the document would be more practical if built with layers. How many masks would be required to show the three patterns?
   How many layers would be required?
5. Have the group redesign the document with layers so that the three patterns are all in one clipping set with one tie shape functioning as the mask.
6. Save your work, compare your Layers panel, with Figure 39, then close Tie Pattern.

FIGURE 39
Completed Group Project

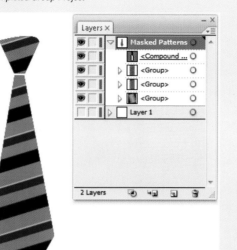

Read the following information carefully.

Find out from your instructor the location where you will store your files.

- To complete many of the chapters in this book, you need to use the Data Files on the CD at the back of this book.

- All of the Data Files are organized in folders named after the chapter in which they are used. For instance, all Chapter 1 Data Files are stored in the chapter_1 folder. You should leave all the Data Files in these folders; do not move any Data File out of the folder in which it is originally stored.

- Your instructor will tell you whether you will be working from the CD or copying the files to a drive on your computer or on a server. Your instructor will also tell you where you will store the files you create and modify.

Copy and organize your Data Files.

- Use the Data Files List to organize your files to a USB storage device, network folder, hard drive, or other storage device.

- If you are working from the CD, you should store the files you modify or create in each chapter in the chapter folder.

Find and keep track of your Data Files and completed files.

- Use the **Data File Supplied** column to make sure you have the files you need before starting the chapter or exercise indicated in the **Chapter** column.

- Use the **Student Creates File** column to determine the filename you use when saving your new file for the exercise.

- The **Used** in column tells you where a file is used in a chapter.

DESIGN COLLECTION 1

Adobe InDesign CS3

Chapter	Data File Supplied	Student Creates File	Used In
1	ID 1-1.indd		Lesson 1, 2, 3, & 4
	ID 1-2.indd		Skills Review
	None	Student creates file, explores interface, no solution file	Project Builder 1
	ID 1-3.indd		Project Builder 2
	None	Student uses Web site, no solution file	Design Project
	ID 1-4.indd		Group Project
2	ID 2-1.indd		Lesson 1 & 2
	ID 2-2.indd		Lesson 3
	ID 2-3.indd		Lesson 4
	ID 2-4.indd		Skills Review
	ID 2-5.indd		Skills Review
	ID 2-6.indd		Skills Review
	ID 2-7.indd		Project Builder 1
	ID 2-8.indd		Project Builder 2
	ID 2-9.indd		Design Project
	ID 2-10.indd		Group Project
3	None	Setup	Lessons 1, 2, 3, 4, 5, & 6
	None	Skills Review	Skills Review
	ID 3-1.indd		Project Builder 1
	ID 3-2.indd		Project Builder 2
	ID 3-3.indd		Design Project
	ID 3-4.indd		Group Project
4	ID 4-1.indd		Lesson 1
	ID 4-2.indd		Lesson 1
	ID 4-3.indd		Lesson 2
	ID 4-4.indd		Lesson 2
	ID 4-5.indd		Lesson 3

Chapter	Data File Supplied	Student Creates File	Used In
	ID 4-6.indd		Lesson 4
	ID 4-7.indd		Skills Review
	ID 4-8.indd		Skills Review
	ID 4-9.indd		Project Builder 1
	ID 4-10.indd		Project Builder 2
	ID 4-11.indd		Design Project
	ID 4-12.indd		Group Project
5	ID 5-1.indd		Lessons 1, 2, & 3
	ID 5-2.indd		Lesson 4
	ID 5-3.indd		Skills Review
	ID 5-4.indd		Skills Review
	ID 5-5.indd		Project Builder 1
	ID 5-6.indd		Project Builder 2
	ID 5-7.indd		Design Project
	ID 5-8.indd		Group Project

Adobe Photoshop CS3

Chapter	Data File Supplied	Student Creates File	Used in
1	PS 1-1.psd PS 1-2.tif		Lessons 2–8
		Review.psd	Skills Review
	PS 1-3.psd		Skills Review
	PS 1-4.psd		Project Builder 2
		Critique-1.psd Critique-2.psd	Design Project
2	PS 2-1.psd PS 2-2.psd		Lessons 1–4
	PS 2-3.psd PS 2-4.psd		Skills Review
	PS 2-5.psd PS 2-6.psd		Project Builder 1
	PS 2-7.psd PS 2-8.psd		Project Builder 2
	PS 2-9.psd PS 2-10.psd		Design Project
	PS 2-11.psd		Group Project
3	PS 3-1.psd PS 3-2.psd PS 3-3.psd PS 3-4.psd PS 3-5.psd PS 3-6.psd		Lessons 1–4
	PS 3-7.psd PS 3-8.tif PS 3-9.tif PS 3-10.tif		Skills Review
	PS 3-11.psd		Project Builder 1
	PS 3-12.psd		Project Builder 2
		Sample Compositing.psd	Design Project
	PS 3-13.psd		Group Project

Chapter	Data File Supplied	Student Creates File	Used in
4	PS 4-1.psd		Lessons 1–4, 6-7
	PS 4-2.psd		Lessons 5–6
	PS 4-3.tif		Lesson 7
	PS 4-4.psd		Skills Review
	PS 4-5.psd		
	PS 4-6.tif		
	PS 4-7.psd		Project Builder 1
	PS 4-8.psd		Project Builder 2
	PS 4-9.psd		Design Project
	PS 4-10.psd		Group Project
5	PS 5-1.psd		Lessons 1–7
	PS 5-2.psd		Skills Review
	PS 5-3.psd		Project Builder 1
	PS 5-4.psd		Project Builder 2
	PS 5-5.psd		Design Project
		Community Promotion.psd	Group Project

Adobe Illustrator CS3

Chapter	Data File Supplied	Student Creates File	Used in
1		The Lay of the Land	L1
	AI 1-1.ai		L2
		Basic Shapes	L3–L6
	AI 1-2.ai		L7
		Flag	Skills Review
	AI 1-3.ai		Project Builder 1
		Iris Vision Design	Project Builder 2
	AI 1-4.ai		Design Project
	AI 1-5.ai		Group Project
2	AI 2-1.ai		L1–L6
	AI 2-2.ai		L2
	AI 2-3.ai		Skills Review
		Desert Oasis	Project Builder 1
	AI 2-4.ai		Project Builder 2
		Vanish	Design Project
		Firehouse Chili	Group Project
3	AI 3-1.ai		L1
	AI 3-2.ai		L2
	AI 3-3.ai		L2
	AI 3-4.ai		L3–L4
	AI 3-5.ai		L7
	AI 3-6.ai		L7
	AI 3-7.ai		L7
	AI 3-8.ai		L7
		Snowball Assembled	L5–L6
	AI 3-9.ai		Skills Review
		Peppermill	Project Builder 1
		Boston chefs	Project Builder 2
		Sleek Design	Design Project
		Shape	Group Project

Chapter	Data File Supplied	Student Creates File	Used in
4	AI 4-1.ai		L1
	AI 4-2.ai		L1
	AI 4-3.ai		L1
	AI 4-4.ai		L2
	AI 4-5.ai		L2
	AI 4-6.ai		L3
	AI 4-7.ai		L3
	AI 4-8.ai		L4
	AI 4-9.ai		L4
	AI 4-10.ai		L4
	AI 4-11.ai		L4
	AI 4-12.ai		L5
	AI 4-13.ai		L5
	AI 4-14.ai		L5
	AI 4-15.ai		Skills Review
	AI 4-16.ai		Skills Review
	AI 4-17.ai		Project Builder 1
	AI 4-18.ai		Project Builder 2
		New Tie	Design Project
		Dartboard	Group Project
5	AI 5-1.ai		L1–L4
	AI 5-2.ai		L1–L4
	AI 5-3.ai		Skills Review
	AI 5-4.ai		Project Builder 1
	AI 5-5.ai		Project Builder 2
	AI 5-6.ai		Design Project
	AI 5-7.ai		Group Project

Action
A series of tasks that you record and save to play back later as a single command.

Additive colors
A color system in which, when the values of R, G, and B are 0, the result is black; when the values are all 255, the result is white.

Adobe Bridge
A sophisticated, stand-alone file browser, tightly integrated with the CS3 applications. The main role of Bridge is to help you locate, browse and organize files—also called "assets"—more easily.

Adobe ImageReady
A program included with Photoshop that you can use to create buttons, rollovers, and animations.

Aligning
Positioning objects in specific relationship to each other on a given axis.

Altitude
A Bevel and Emboss setting that affects the amount of visible dimension.

Angle
In the Layer Style dialog box, the setting that determines where a drop shadow falls relative to the text.

Anti-aliasing
Partially fills in pixel edges, resulting in smooth-edge type. This feature lets your type maintain its crisp appearance and is especially useful for large type.

Attributes
Formatting which has been applied to an object that affects its appearance.

Background color
Used to make gradient fills and to fill in areas of an image that have been erased. The default background color is white.

Balance colors
Process of adding and subtracting colors from those already existing in a layer.

Base color
The original color of an image.

Baseline
An invisible line on which type rests.

Baseline grid
A grid of page guides that typographers use to keep consistent leading from baseline to baseline in a text block.

Baseline shift
The distance type appears from its original position.

Bevel
The angle that one surface makes with another when they are not at right angles.

Bevel join
Produces stroked lines with squared corners.

Bitmap
A geometric arrangement of different color dots on a rectangular grid.

Bitmap graphics
Images that are created by pixels in a program like Photoshop. Every digital image and scanned graphic is a bitmap graphic.

Bitmap images
Graphics created using a grid of colored squares called pixels.

Bitmap mode
Uses black or white color values to represent image pixels; a good choice for images with subtle color gradations, such as photographs or painted images.

Bitmap type
Type that may develop jagged edges when enlarged.

Blend
A series of intermediate objects and colors between two or more selected objects.

Blend color
The color applied to the base color when a blending mode is applied to a layer.

Blend Step
Controls how smoothly shading appears on an object's surface and is most visible in the transition from the highlight areas to the diffusely lit areas.

Blending mode
Affects the layer's underlying pixels or base color. Used to darken or lighten colors, depending on the colors in use. Also, preset filters that control how colors blend when two objects overlap.

Bounding box
A rectangle with handles that appears around an object or type and can be used to change dimensions, also called a *transform controls box*.

Bridge
See Adobe Bridge.

Brightness
The measurement of relative lightness or darkness of a color (measured as a percentage from 0% [black] to 100% [white]).

Butt caps
Squared ends of a stroked path.

Camera Raw
Allows you to use digital data directly from a digital camera.

Caps
Define the appearance of end points when a stroke is added to a path. The Stroke panel offers three types of caps: butt, round, and projecting.

Cell
A rectangle at the intersection of a table row and column.

Character palette
Helps you control type properties. The Toggle the Character and Paragraph palette button is located on the options bar when you select a Type tool.

Clipboard
Temporary storage area, provided by your operating system, for cut and copied data.

Clipping mask (Clipping group)
A group of two or more contiguous layers linked for the purposes of masking. Effect used to display the image or pattern from one layer into the shape of another layer. The area of a clipping mask crops objects behind it in the stacking order.

Clipping path
A graphic you draw in Photoshop that out-lines the areas of the image you want to show when the file is placed in a layout program like InDesign.

Clipping set
Term used to distinguish clipping paths used in layers from clipping paths used to mask non-layered artwork.

CMYK
Cyan, Magenta, Yellow, and Black; four inks essential to professional printing.

CMYK image
An image using the CMYK color system, containing at least four channels (one each for cyan, magenta, yellow, and black).

Color gamut
Refers to the range of colors that can be printed or displayed within a given color model.

Color mode
Used to determine how to display and print an image. Each mode is based on established models used in color repro-duction. Also an Illustrator setting deter-mining the color model of a document: RGB or CMYK.

Color Picker
A feature that lets you choose a color from a color spectrum.

Color Range command
Used to select a particular color contained in an existing image.

Color separation
Result of converting an RGB image into a CMYK image; the commercial printing process of separating colors for use with different inks.

Color tools
Circle icons in the Live Color dialog box which represent the colors for the loaded harmony rule.

Column break
A typographic command that forces text to the next column.

Columns
Vertical page guides often used to define the width of text frames and body copy. Also, in a table , the vertical arrangement of cells.

Composite channel
The top channel on the Channels palette that is a combination of all the default channels.

Compositing
Combining images from sources such as other Photoshop images, royalty-free images, pictures taken from digital cameras, and scanned artwork.

Compound shape

A term used to distinguish a complex compound path from a simple one. Compound shapes generally assume an artistic rather than a practical role.

Contiguous

Items that are next to one another.

Compound paths

Two or more closed paths joined using the Compound Path command to create one complete path. You create compound paths when you want to use one object to cut a hole in another object. In other words, when compound paths overlap, the overlapped area becomes a negative space.

Corner point

An anchor point joining two straight segments, one straight segment, and one curved segment, or two curved segments.

Crisp

Anti-aliasing setting that gives type more definition and makes it appear sharper.

Crop

To exclude part of an image. Cropping hides areas of an image without losing resolution quality.

Crop marks

Guide lines that define the trim size. Or page notations that indicate where trimming will occur. They can be printed at the corners, center of each edge, or both.

Dashed strokes

Created and formatted using the Stroke panel, strokes that consist of a series of dashes and gaps.

Defringe command

Replaces fringe pixels with the colors of other nearby pixels.

Deselect

A command that removes the marquee from an area, so it is no longer selected.

Destination

A location that is displayed after a user clicks a hyperlink.

Digital camera

A camera that captures images on electronic media (rather than film). Its images are in a standard digital format and can be downloaded for computer use.

Digital image

A picture in electronic form. It may be referred to as a file, document, picture, or image.

Direction handle

The round blue circle at the top of the direction line.

Direction lines

Two lines attached to a smooth point or an anchor point. Direction lines determine the arc of the curved path, depending on their direction and length.

Distance

Determines how far a shadow falls from the text. This setting is used by the Drop Shadow and Bevel and Emboss styles.

Distort filters

Create three-dimensional or other reshaping effects. Some of the types of distortions you can produce include Glass, Pinch, Ripple, Shear, Spherize, Twirl, Wave, and ZigZag.

Distributing

Positioning objects on a page so that they are spaced evenly in relation to one another.

Dock

A collection of palettes or buttons surrounded by a dark gray bar. The arrows in the dock are used to maximize and minmize the palettes.

'Drag & drop' a copy

Pressing [Alt] (Win) or [option] (Mac) when moving an object; creates a copy of the object.

Drop cap

A design element in which the first letter or letters of a paragraph are increased in size to create a visual effect.

Drop shadow

A soft-edged graphic behind another graphic that appears as though it is the shadow of the graphic DTD. Also a style that adds what looks like a colored layer of identical text behind the selected type. The default shadow color is black.

Drop Zone

A blue outline area that indicates where a palette can be moved.

Dynamic preview

An Indesign feature in which the entirety of a placed graphic—even areas outside a

graphics frame—can be seen as the graphic is being moved.

Effect
A type of appearance attribute which alters an object's appearance without altering the object itself.

Em space
A type of white space inserted into a text box. The width of an em space is equivalent to that of the lowercase letter m in the current typeface and type size.

En space
A type of white space inserted into a text box. The width of an en space is equivalent to that of the lowercase letter n in the current typeface and type size.

Ending color
The last color in a gradient.

Eraser Tool
Has the opposite function of a brush in that it eliminates pixels on a layer.

Extract feature
Used to isolate a foreground object from its background.

Facing pages
Two pages in a layout that face each other, as in an open magazine, book, or newspaper.

Fade options
Brush settings that determine how and when brushes fade toward the end of their strokes.

Fastening point
An anchor within the marquee. When the marquee pointer reaches the initial fastening point, a small circle appears on the pointer, indicating that you have reached the starting point.

Feather
A method used to control the softness of a selection's edges by blurring the area between the selection and the surrounding pixels.

Fill
A color you apply that fills an object.

Filter Gallery
A feature that lets you see the effects of each filter before applying it.

Filters
Used to alter the look of an image and give it a special, customized appearance by applying special effects, such as distortions, changes in lighting, and blurring.

Flatten Artwork
Consolidating all layers in a document into a single layer.

Flattening
Merges all visible layers into one layer, named the Background layer, and deletes all hidden layers, greatly reducing file size.

Font
Characters with a similar appearance.

Font family
Represents a complete set of characters, letters, and symbols for a particular typeface. Font families are generally divided into three categories: serif, sans serif, and symbol.

Foreground color
Used to paint, fill, and stroke selections. The default foreground color is black.

Fuzziness
Similar to tolerance, in that the lower the value, the closer the color pixels must be to be selected.

Gamut
The range of displayed colors in a color model.

GIF
A standard file format for compressing images by lowering the number of colors available to the file.

Gloss Contour
A Bevel and Emboss setting that determines the pattern with which light is reflected.

Glyphs
Alternate versions of type characters; usually used for symbols like trademarks, etc.

Gradient / Gradient Fill
A graduated blend between two or more colors used to fill an object or multiple objects. A gradient's appearance is determined by its beginning and ending points. Photoshop contains five gradient fill styles.

Gradient presets
Predesigned gradient fills that are displayed in the Gradient picker.

Graphic
In an InDesign document, refers to a bitmap or vector image.

Graphics frames
Boxes in which you place imported artwork.

Grayscale image
Can contain up to 256 shades of gray. Pixels can have brightness values from 0 (black) to white (255).

Grayscale mode
Uses up to 256 shades of gray, assigning a brightness value from 0 (black) to 255 (white) to each pixel.

Guides
Horizontal or vertical lines that you position on a page. As their name suggests, guides are used to help guide you in aligning objects on the page.

Gutter
The space between two columns.

Handles
Small boxes that appear along the perimeter of a selected object and are used to change the size of an image.

Hard return
See Paragraph return.

Harmony Rule
Sets of complimentary colors in the Color Guide, which work well together and help you choose colors for your illustration.

Highlight Mode
A Bevel and Emboss setting that determines how pigments are combined.

Highlights
The light areas of a graphic.

History palette
Contains a record of each action performed during a Photoshop session. Up to 1000 levels of Undo are available through the History palette (20 levels by default).

Hotspot
Area within an object that is assigned a URL. This area can then be clicked to jump to the associated Web address.

Hue
The color reflected from/transmitted through an object and expressed as a degree (between 0° and 360°). Each hue is identified by a color name (such as red or green). Also the name of a color, or its identity on a standard color wheel.

Imageable area
The area inside the dotted line on the artboard which represents the portion of the page that a standard printer can print.

Image-editing program
Used to manipulate graphic images that can be reproduced by professional printers using full-color processes.

Intellectual property
An image or idea that is owned and retained by legal control.

Isolation Mode
A mode in which you work in Illustrator. In isolation mode, the selected group appears in full color, while all the remaining objects on the art board are dimmed and unable to be selected.

Joins
Define the appearance of a corner point when a path has a stroke applied to it. There are three types of joins: miter, round, and bevel.

JPEG
A standard file format for compressing continuous tone images, gradients, and blends.

Kerning
The A long-standing process of increasing or decreasing space between a pair of characters.

Keyboard increment
The distance that a single press of an arrow key moves a selected item; editable as a preference.

Keyboard shortcuts
Combinations of keys that can be used to work faster and more efficiently.

Landscape orientation
An image with the long edge of the paper at the top and bottom.

Layer (Photoshop)
A section within an image on which objects can be stored. The advantage: Individual effects can be isolated and manipulated without affecting the rest of the image. The disadvantage: Layers can increase the size of your file.

Layers
A solution for organizing and managing a complex illustration by segregating artwork.

Layer comp
A variation on the arrangement and visibility of existing layers within an image; an organizational tool.

Layer group
An organizing tool you use to group layers on the Layers palette.

Layers palette
Displays all the layers within an active image. You can use the Layers palette to create, delete, merge, copy, or reposition layers.

Layer style
An effect that can be applied to a type or image layer.

Layer thumbnail
Contains a miniature picture of the layer's content, and appears to the left of the layer name on the Layers palette.

Leading
The amount of vertical space between lines of type.

Libraries
Files you create that appear as a panel in your InDesign document. You can use this "library panel" to organize and store graphics that you use most often. Also called Object Libraries.

Lighten Only option
Replaces dark pixels with light pixels.

Linear gradient
A gradient which can fill an object from left to right, top to bottom, or on any angle. Also a series of straight lines that gradate from one color to another (or through multiple colors).

List mode
The default display of actions in which all action detail can be viewed.

Live paint group
A live paint group is created when the Live Paint Bucket Tool is applied to selected objects. All of the resulting regions and edges are part of the live paint group and share a dynamic relationship.

Local changes
Changes made to master items on a document page but not on the master page.

Logo
A distinctive image used to identify a company, project, or organization. You can create a logo by combining symbols, shapes, colors, and text.

Luminosity
The remaining light and dark values that result when a color image is converted to grayscale.

Magic Eraser Tool
Used to erase areas in an image that have similar-colored pixels.

Magic Wand Tool
Used to choose pixels that are similar to the ones where you first click in an image.

Margins
Page guides that define the interior borders of a document.

Marquee
A series of dotted lines indicating a selected area that can be edited or dragged into another image.

Mask
A feature that lets you protect or modify a particular area; created using a marquee.

Master items
All objects on the master page that function as a place where objects on the document pages are to be positioned.

Master pages
Templates that you create for a page layout or for the layout of an entire publication.

Match Color command
Allows you to replace one color with another.

Menu bar

At the top of the InDesign, Photoshop, and Illustrator windows; a bar which includes all of the application's menus.

Merging layers

Process of combining multiple image layers into one layer.

Miter join

Produces stroked lines with pointed corners.

Miter limit

Determines when a Miter join will be squared off to a beveled edge.

Mode

Represents the amount of color data that can be stored in a given file format, and determines the color model used to display and print an image.

Model

Determines how pigments combine to produce resulting colors; determined by the color mode.

Monitor calibration

A process that displays printed colors accurately on your monitor.

Monotype spacing

Spacing in which each character occupies the same amount of space.

Named color

Any color that you create in the New Color Swatch dialog box.

Nested styles

Paragraph styles that contain two or more character styles. In other words, two or more character styles are "nested" within the paragraph style.

Noise filters

Used to add or remove pixels with randomly distributed color levels.

None

Anti-aliasing setting that applies no anti-aliasing, resulting in jagged edges.

Normal blend mode

The default blending mode.

Object Styles

Named sets of formatting properties that can be applied to graphic objects or text frames.

Offset

The distance an object is moved or copied.

Offset path

A command that creates a copy of a selected path repositioned at a specified distance.

Opacity

Determines the percentage of transparency. Whereas a layer with 100% opacity will obstruct objects in the layers beneath it, a layer with 1% opacity will appear nearly transparent.

Options bar

Displays the settings for the active tool. The options bar is located directly under the menu bar but can be moved anywhere in the workspace for easier access.

Orientation

Direction an image appears on the page: portrait or landscape.

Outline stroke

A command that converts a stroked path into a closed path that is the same width as the original stroked path.

Outline type

Type that is mathematically defined and can be scaled to any size without its edges losing their smooth appearance.

Outlined text

A command that changes text in a document to standard vector graphics.

Outport

A small box in the lower right corner of a text frame that you click to flow text from that frame to another.

Page size

See Trim Size.

Palette well

An area where you can assemble palettes for quick access.

Palettes (Photoshop)

Floating windows that can be moved and are used to modify objects. Palettes contain named tabs, which can be separated and moved to another group. Each palette contains a menu that can be viewed by

clicking the list arrow in its upper-right corner.

Panels

Floating windows that can be moved and are used to modify objects. Panels contain named tabs, which can be separated and moved to another group. Each panel contains a menu that can be viewed by clicking the list arrow in its upper-right corner.

Paragraph

A word, a line of text, or a block of text that is followed by a paragraph return.

Paragraph return

Inserted into the text formatting by pressing [Enter] (Win) or [return] (Mac). Also called a hard return.

Pasteboard

The area surrounding the document.

Pathfinders

Preset operations that combine paths in a variety of ways; useful for creating complex or irregular shapes from basic shapes.

Pica

12 points, or $\frac{1}{6}$ of an inch.

Pixel

Each dot in a bitmapped image that represents a color or shade.

Placeholder

The frame created for text or graphics on a master page.

Point

A unit used to measure page elements; equal to $\frac{1}{72}$ of an inch.

Point (Photoshop)

Unit of measurement for font sizes. Traditionally, 1 inch is equivalent to 72.27 points. The default Photoshop type size is 12 points.

Point of origin

The point from which an object is transformed; by default, the center point of an object, unless another point is specified.

Portrait orientation

An image or page with the short edge of the paper at the top and bottom.

PostScript

A programming language created by Adobe that optimizes printed text and graphics.

Preferences

Used to control the Photoshop environment using your specifications.

Process colors

Colors you create (and eventually print) by mixing varying percentages of cyan, magenta, yellow, and black (CMYK) inks.

Process inks

Cyan, Magenta, Yellow, and Black ink; the fundamental inks used in printing.

Process tints

Colors that can be printed by mixing varying percentages of CMYK inks.

Projecting cap

Produces a squared edge that extends the anchor point of a stroked path by a distance that is ½ the weight of the stroke.

Proportional spacing

The text spacing in which each character takes up a different amount of space, based on its width.

Pull quote

A typographical design solution in which text is used at a larger point size and positioned prominently on the page.

Radial gradient

A series of concentric circles. With a radial gradient, the starting color appears at the center of the gradient, then radiates out to the ending color.

Rasterize

Converts a type layer to an image layer.

Rasterized shape

A shape that is converted into a bitmapped object. It cannot be moved or copied and has a much smaller file size.

Region

Similar to a fill, a region is a new shape or area created by the overlap of Illustrator objects. Regions are created when the Live Paint Bucket Tool is applied.

Relief

The height of ridges within an object.

Rendering intent

The way in which a color-management system handles color conversion from one color space to another.

Resize Image Wizard
Feature that helps you change an image's size for different output.

Resolution
The number of pixels in a given inch of a bitmap graphic.

Resolution independent
Refers to a graphic which can be scaled with no impact on image quality. Graphics professionals refer to vector graphics as being resolution independent because they are not made of pixels and therefore have no resolution issues.

Resulting color
The outcome of the blend color applied to the base color.

Revolve
Another method that Illustrator CS3 provides for applying a 3D effect to a 2D object by "sweeping" a path in a circular direction around the Y axis of the object.

RGB
Red, Green and Blue; the additive primary colors of light.

RGB image
Image that contains three color channels (one each for red, green, and blue).

Round cap
Produces a stroked path with rounded ends.

Round join
Produces stroked lines with rounded corners.

Rulers
Onscreen markers that help you precisely measure and position an object. Rulers can be displayed using the View menu.

Rules
Lines on the page used as design elements or to underline text.

Sampling
A method of changing foreground and background colors by copying existing colors from an image.

Sans serif fonts
Fonts that do not have tails or strokes at the end of characters; commonly used in headlines.

Saturation
The intensity of a hue, or the strength or purity of the color, representing the amount of gray in proportion to hue (measured as a percentage from 0% [gray], to 100% [fully saturated]), Also known as *chroma*.

Save As
A command that lets you create a copy of the open file using a new name.

Scale
A transformation in which an object changes size.

Scanner
An electronic device that converts print material into an electronic file.

Scratch area
The area outside the artboard where objects may be stored for future use; objects on the scratch area will not print.

Sections
Pages in a document where page numbering changes.

Selection
An area in an image that is surrounded by a selection marquee.

Serif fonts
Fonts that have a tail, or stroke, at the end of some characters. These tails make it easier for the eye to recognize words; therefore, serif fonts are generally used in text passages.

Shading
Bevel and Emboss setting that determines lighting effects.

Shadow Mode
Bevel and Emboss setting that determines how pigments are combined.

Sharp
Anti-aliasing setting that displays type with the best possible resolution.

Sharpen More filter
Increases the contrast of adjacent pixels and can focus blurry images.

Size
Determines the clarity of a drop shadow.

Smart guides (Illustrator)
Non-printing words that appear on the artboard and identify visible or invisible objects, page boundaries, intersections, anchor points, etc.

Smart Guides (Photoshop)
A feature that displays vertical or horizontal guides that appear automatically when you draw a shape or move an object.

Smooth
Anti-aliasing setting that gives type more rounded edges.

Smooth points
Anchor points created by clicking and dragging the Pen Tool; the path continues uninterrupted through the anchor point.

Snap to point
Automatically aligns points when they get close together.

Snippet
A snippet is an XML file with an .inds file extension that contains complete representation of document elements, including all formatting tags and document structure.

Soft return
In typography, using the Shift key in addition to the Return key to move text onto the following line without creating a new paragraph.

Source
The image containing the color that will be matched.

Splash screen
A window that displays information about the software you are using.

Spot colors
Non-process inks that are manufactured by companies. Spot colors are special pre-mixed inks that are printed separately from process inks.

Spread
Determines the width of drop shadow text.

Spreads
See Facing pages.

Stacking order
The hierarchy of objects on the artboard or in a file, from frontmost to backmost.

Starting and Ending colors
The first and last colors in a gradient.

State
An entry on the History palette, or the appearance of a rollover on the Rollover palette in ImageReady.

Status bar (Illustrator)
A utility on the artboard that contains a list arrow menu from which you can choose a status line with information about the current tool, the date and time, the amount of free memory, or the number of undo operations.

Status bar (Photoshop)
The area located at the bottom of the program window (Win) or the image window (Mac) that displays information such as the file size of the active window and a description of the active tool.

Step and Repeat
A dialog box in which you can specify the number and offset value of copies of a selected object.

Stroke
A color applied to the outline of an object.

Stroke weight
The thickness of a stroke; usually measured in points.

Stroking the edges
The process of making a selection or layer stand out by formatting it with a border.

Strong
Anti-aliasing setting that makes type appear heavier, much like the bold attribute.

Structure
A Bevel and Emboss setting that determines the size and physical properties of the object.

Style
A group of formatting attributes that can be applied to text or objects.

Style (Photoshop)
Eighteen predesigned styles that can be applied to buttons.

Stylize filters
Used to produce a painted or impressionistic effect.

Subtractive colors
A color system in which the full combination of cyan, magenta, and yellow absorb all color and produce black.

Swatches palette (Photoshop)
Contains available colors that can be selected for use as a foreground or background color. You can also add your own colors to the Swatches palette.

Swatches panel
Contains available colors that can be selected for use as a foreground or background color. You can also add your own colors to the Swatches panel.

Symbol fonts
Used to display unique characters (such as $, ÷, or ™).

Target
When sampling a color, the image that will receive the matched color.

Target layer
The layer selected in the Layers panel.

Targeting
Clicking a layer in the Layers panel to select it.

Text frames
Drawn with the Type Tool, boxes in which you type or place text.

Text insets
In a text frame, the distance the text is from the frame edge.

Texture filters
Used to give the appearance of depth or substance.

Threading
A term used to describe linking text from one text frame to another.

Thumbnail
Contains a miniature picture of the layer's content, appears to the left of the layer name, and can be turned on or off.

Title bar (Illustrator)
At the top of the Illustrator window; contains the name of the document, magnification level, and color mode.

Title bar (Photoshop)
Displays the program name and filename of the open image. The title bar also contains buttons for minimizing, maximizing, and closing the image.

Tolerance
The range of pixels that determines which pixels will be selected. The lower the tolerance, the closer the color is to the selection. The setting can have a value from 0–255.

Tonal values
Numeric values of an individual color that can be used to duplicate a color. Also called color levels.

Tools panel (Illustrator)
A panel containing Illustrator tools for creating, selecting, and manipulating objects in Illustrator.

Tools palette (Photoshop)
Contains tools for frequently used commands. On the face of a tool is a graphic representation of its function. Place the pointer over each button to display a ScreenTip, which tells you the name or function of that button.

Tracking
The insertion of a uniform amount of space between characters.

Transform
The act of moving, scaling, skewing, or rotating an object. Also to change the shape, size, perspective, or rotation of an object or objects on a layer.

Transform box
A rectangle that surrounds an image and contains handles that can be used to change dimensions. Also called a bounding box.

Trim size
The size to which a printed document will be cut—or trimmed—when it clears the printing press.

Tweaking
Making small, specific improvements to artwork or typography.

Twirl filter
Applies a circular effect.

Type
Text, or a layer containing text. Each character is measured in points. In PostScript measurement, 1 inch is equivalent to 72 points. In traditional measurement, 1 inch is equivalent to 72.27 points.

Type area select
An Illustrator preference which allows the user to select text simply by clicking anywhere on the text.

Type spacing
Adjustments you can make to the space between characters and between lines of type.

Unnamed colors
Any colors you create that aren't saved to the Swatches panel.

URL
Uniform Resource Locator, a Web address.

Variation
A group of swatches loaded by the Color Guide panel when you select an object on the artboard and then choose a harmony rule.

Vector graphics
Resolution-independent graphics created with lines, curves, and fills.

Version Cue
A file versioning and management feature of the Adobe Creative Suite.

Vignette
A feature in which the border of a picture or portrait fades into the surrounding color at its edges.

Vignette effect
A feature that uses feathering to fade a marquee shape.

Warping type
A feature that lets you create distortions that conform to a variety of shapes.

Web-safe colors
The 216 colors that can be displayed on the Web without dithering.

Workspace
The entire window, from the menu bar at the top of the window, to the status bar at the bottom border of the program window. Also the arrangement of windows and palettes on your monitor.

Zero point
Often at the top left corner of the document; the point from which the location of all objects on the page is measured.

Zoom text box
A utility in the lower-left corner of the Illustrator window that displays the current magnification level.

active layer, inserting layers beneath, PHOTOSHOP 2-10
Add a layer style button, PHOTOSHOP 5-3
Add Anchor Point Tool, INDESIGN 4-29
additive colors, PHOTOSHOP 4-5—4-6
Add shape mode, ILLUSTRATOR 4-24
Add to shape area pathfinder, ILLUSTRATOR 4-21, ILLUSTRATOR 4-22
administrative functions, Version Cue, PHOTOSHOP 1-15
Adobe Bridge. See Bridge
Adobe Design Premium Creative Design Suite 3, PHOTOSHOP 1-2
Adobe Dreamweaver CS3, PHOTOSHOP 1-5
Adobe Help Viewer, INDESIGN 1-22—1-23
Adobe Illustrator CS3, overview, ILLUSTRATOR 1-2—1-3
Adobe Photoshop. See Photoshop
Adobe Stock Photos, PHOTOSHOP 1-15
Adobe Web site, PHOTOSHOP 1-36
aligning
    anchor points, ILLUSTRATOR 3-5, ILLUSTRATOR 3-8
    objects, INDESIGN 4-7, INDESIGN 4-12
Align panel, ILLUSTRATOR 4-26
Altitude setting, Bevel and Emboss style, PHOTOSHOP 5-21
anchor(s), changing appearance, ILLUSTRATOR 3-11
anchor points, ILLUSTRATOR 1-19
    aligning, ILLUSTRATOR 3-5, ILLUSTRATOR 3-8
    converting, ILLUSTRATOR 3-12—3-13, ILLUSTRATOR 3-15
    direct selections, ILLUSTRATOR 1-36, ILLUSTRATOR 1-39
    hiding, ILLUSTRATOR 2-31
    joining, ILLUSTRATOR 3-5, ILLUSTRATOR 3-9
angle, drop shadows, PHOTOSHOP 5-13, PHOTOSHOP 5-14
Angle setting, Bevel and Emboss style, PHOTOSHOP 5-21
anti-aliasing, PHOTOSHOP 5-16—5-19
    applying, PHOTOSHOP 5-18, PHOTOSHOP 5-30

undoing, PHOTOSHOP 5-19
    when to apply, PHOTOSHOP 5-16
Anti-alias setting, Magnetic Lasso Tool, PHOTOSHOP 3-11
Apply Color button, INDESIGN 5-13
Apply Gradient buttons, INDESIGN 5-13
applying color, INDESIGN 5-12—5-23
    black shadow text, INDESIGN 5-16, INDESIGN 5-21—5-22
    Color Picker, INDESIGN 5-18
    modifying and deleting swatches, INDESIGN 5-16—5-17, INDESIGN 5-23
    to objects, INDESIGN 5-12—5-13, INDESIGN 5-18—5-19
    paper swatches, INDESIGN 5-14
    to text, INDESIGN 5-15, INDESIGN 5-20
Apply Master dialog box, INDESIGN 3-33
Apply None button, INDESIGN 5-13
Arrange commands, INDESIGN 4-18—4-19
artboard, ILLUSTRATOR 1-8, ILLUSTRATOR 1-9
    navigating, ILLUSTRATOR 1-14—1-15
    viewing objects, ILLUSTRATOR 3-4, ILLUSTRATOR 3-6
artwork, selecting on layers, INDESIGN 4-16
.arw files, PHOTOSHOP 1-5
attributes
    applying to objects, ILLUSTRATOR 3-24—3-27
    copying with Eyedropper Tool, ILLUSTRATOR 3-27
    strokes, modifying, ILLUSTRATOR 3-33
Autocorrect feature, INDESIGN 2-29
autoflow text, INDESIGN 4-38—4-39, INDESIGN 4-41—4-42
automatic page numbering, INDESIGN 3-19—3-20, INDESIGN 3-26
Average command, ILLUSTRATOR 3-5

background color, PHOTOSHOP 4-6
    changing using Color palette, PHOTOSHOP 4-8
    changing using Eyedropper Tool, PHOTOSHOP 4-9
    choosing from Swatches palette, PHOTOSHOP 4-32
    default. See default background color
    fill with, PHOTOSHOP 4-32
    switching between foreground color and, PHOTOSHOP 4-32
Background Eraser Tool, PHOTOSHOP 2-13
Background layer, PHOTOSHOP 2-4, PHOTOSHOP 2-5
    converting image layers to, PHOTOSHOP 2-6, PHOTOSHOP 2-7
    converting to image layer, PHOTOSHOP 2-6
    new, from existing layer, PHOTOSHOP 2-22
balancing colors, PHOTOSHOP 4-25, PHOTOSHOP 4-29, PHOTOSHOP 4-32
base color, PHOTOSHOP 4-25
baseline, ILLUSTRATOR 2-4
    shifting, PHOTOSHOP 5-30
    text, INDESIGN 2-4
    type, PHOTOSHOP 5-9
baseline grids, text boxes, INDESIGN 3-13
Behind mode, PHOTOSHOP 4-26
Bevel and Emboss style, PHOTOSHOP 5-20—5-23
    adding with Layer menu, PHOTOSHOP 5-22
    applying, PHOTOSHOP 5-30
    settings, PHOTOSHOP 5-20—5-21, PHOTOSHOP 5-23
bevel joins, ILLUSTRATOR 3-31
bitmap(s), PHOTOSHOP 4-2
bitmap graphics, ILLUSTRATOR 1-18—1-19, INDESIGN 4-24
    resolution, PHOTOSHOP 4-2
bitmap mode, PHOTOSHOP 4-6
bitmap type, PHOTOSHOP 5-4
black shadow text, INDESIGN 5-16, INDESIGN 5-21—5-22

Black & White command,
PHOTOSHOP 4-20
blend color, PHOTOSHOP 4-25
blending modes, PHOTOSHOP 2-8,
PHOTOSHOP 4-25, PHOTOSHOP 4-26,
PHOTOSHOP 4-28
components, PHOTOSHOP 4-25
blur, fixing blurry images,
PHOTOSHOP 4-24
.BMP files, PHOTOSHOP 1-5
borders, PHOTOSHOP 4-14—4-15
bounding box(es), INDESIGN 4-26
Bridge, ILLUSTRATOR 1-12
closing, PHOTOSHOP 1-10
finding files, PHOTOSHOP
1-9—1-10
opening, PHOTOSHOP 1-9,
PHOTOSHOP 1-38
sorting files, PHOTOSHOP 1-13
uses, PHOTOSHOP 1-10,
PHOTOSHOP 1-15
brightness, PHOTOSHOP 4-5
adjusting, PHOTOSHOP 4-27
Brightness/Contrast dialog box,
PHOTOSHOP 4-27
bulleted lists, INDESIGN 2-15
Burlap texture filter, PHOTOSHOP 5-25

Camera Raw images, formats,
PHOTOSHOP 1-5
Cancel any current edits button,
PHOTOSHOP 5-3, PHOTOSHOP 5-30
caps, ILLUSTRATOR 3-30
.CDR files, PHOTOSHOP 1-5
center point, ILLUSTRATOR 1-33
character(s), inserting white space
between, INDESIGN 3-20,
INDESIGN 3-26—3-27
Character palette, PHOTOSHOP 5-9
opening, PHOTOSHOP 5-30
Character panel, INDESIGN 1-6,
INDESIGN 1-7
formatting text, INDESIGN 2-4,
INDESIGN 2-8
scaling text, INDESIGN 2-6

character styles, ILLUSTRATOR 2-13,
INDESIGN 2-20, INDESIGN 2-22—2-23
applying, INDESIGN 2-23
creating, INDESIGN 2-22—2-23
importing, INDESIGN 2-20
Character Styles panel, INDESIGN 2-20,
INDESIGN 2-21
Check Spelling dialog box, INDESIGN 2-27
chroma, PHOTOSHOP 4-5
circles, concentric, ILLUSTRATOR 4-12
Clear mode, PHOTOSHOP 4-26
clipping groups. See clipping masks;
clipping sets
clipping masks, ILLUSTRATOR
4-30—4-35. See also clipping sets
applying fills, ILLUSTRATOR 4-33
creating, ILLUSTRATOR 4-32
creating masked effects,
ILLUSTRATOR 4-31
defining, ILLUSTRATOR 4-30
multiple objects as, ILLUSTRATOR 4-31
special effects, ILLUSTRATOR 4-35
text as, ILLUSTRATOR 4-34
clipping path(s), INDESIGN 4-28—4-29
clipping sets, ILLUSTRATOR
5-26—5-29. See also clipping masks
copying, ILLUSTRATOR 5-28—5-29
creating, ILLUSTRATOR 5-27
definition, ILLUSTRATOR 5-26
flattening artwork, ILLUSTRATOR
5-26, ILLUSTRATOR 5-28—5-29
closed paths
adding attributes, ILLUSTRATOR 3-26
converting stroked path to,
ILLUSTRATOR 4-13,
ILLUSTRATOR 4-15
drawing using smooth points,
ILLUSTRATOR 3-20
closing
Bridge, PHOTOSHOP 1-10
files, PHOTOSHOP 1-36, PHOTOSHOP
1-37, PHOTOSHOP 1-38
paths, ILLUSTRATOR 3-8
CMYK inks, INDESIGN 5-4
CMYK mode, ILLUSTRATOR 1-4—1-5,
ILLUSTRATOR 2-21, PHOTOSHOP 4-6

color(s), INDESIGN 5-1—5-43,
PHOTOSHOP 4-1—4-37
adding to Swatches palette,
PHOTOSHOP 4-13
adding to Swatches panel,
ILLUSTRATOR 2-21,
ILLUSTRATOR 2-24—2-25
additive, PHOTOSHOP 4-5—4-6
applying to text, ILLUSTRATOR
2-26—2-29
applying with Swatches panel,
ILLUSTRATOR 1-23
background. See background color
balancing, PHOTOSHOP 4-25,
PHOTOSHOP 4-29, PHOTOSHOP 4-32
base, PHOTOSHOP 4-25
blend, PHOTOSHOP 4-25
blending using Gradient Tool,
PHOTOSHOP 4-16—4-19
columns, INDESIGN 3-7,
INDESIGN 3-15
creating, ILLUSTRATOR 2-21,
ILLUSTRATOR 2-22—2-23
fill, ILLUSTRATOR 1-20,
ILLUSTRATOR 1-22—1-25
foreground. See foreground color
guides, INDESIGN 3-7, INDESIGN 3-15
layers, INDESIGN 4-16, PHOTOSHOP
2-17, PHOTOSHOP 2-22
margins, INDESIGN 3-7,
INDESIGN 3-15
matching, PHOTOSHOP 4-30—4-31
models, PHOTOSHOP 4-2,
PHOTOSHOP 4-4—4-5
modes, ILLUSTRATOR 1-4—1-5,
ILLUSTRATOR 2-21, PHOTOSHOP
4-2, PHOTOSHOP 4-5—4-6,
PHOTOSHOP 4-22,
PHOTOSHOP 4-32
printing images, PHOTOSHOP 1-33
psychology, PHOTOSHOP 4-4
resulting, PHOTOSHOP 4-25
sample, creating gradients,
PHOTOSHOP 4-18
selections based on, PHOTOSHOP
3-16—3-18, PHOTOSHOP 3-24

selections in layers, changing, layers, ILLUSTRATOR 5-9
spot, INDESIGN 5-24—5-29
stroke, ILLUSTRATOR 1-22, ILLUSTRATOR 1-24—1-25
subtractive, PHOTOSHOP 4-6
type, PHOTOSHOP 5-7, PHOTOSHOP 5-30
Color Balance dialog box, PHOTOSHOP 4-29
Color Burn mode, PHOTOSHOP 4-26
Color Dodge mode, PHOTOSHOP 4-26
Colored Pencil filter, PHOTOSHOP 5-25
color images, converting grayscale and color modes, PHOTOSHOP 4-20
colorizing grayscale images, PHOTOSHOP 4-21—4-23
Color list arrow, PHOTOSHOP 2-3
color mode(s), ILLUSTRATOR 1-4—1-5, ILLUSTRATOR 2-21, PHOTOSHOP 4-2, PHOTOSHOP 4-5—4-6, PHOTOSHOP 4-26
changing, PHOTOSHOP 4-22, PHOTOSHOP 4-32
color models, PHOTOSHOP 4-2, PHOTOSHOP 4-4—4-5
Color palette
changing background color, PHOTOSHOP 4-8
displaying, PHOTOSHOP 4-32
hiding, PHOTOSHOP 4-32
Color panel, ILLUSTRATOR 2-21, INDESIGN 5-6, INDESIGN 5-10—5-11
Fill and Stroke buttons, INDESIGN 5-12, INDESIGN 5-13
Color Picker, INDESIGN 5-18
Color Picker dialog box, PHOTOSHOP 4-10, PHOTOSHOP 4-11, PHOTOSHOP 4-12
color range(s), selecting, PHOTOSHOP 2-22
Color Range command, PHOTOSHOP 2-12—2-13, PHOTOSHOP 2-14, PHOTOSHOP 3-17
Color Range dialog box, PHOTOSHOP 2-14, PHOTOSHOP 3-18

color separation, PHOTOSHOP 4-6
Color Settings dialog box, PHOTOSHOP 4-7
column breaks, text frames, INDESIGN 4-39—4-40, INDESIGN 4-43—4-44
Command bar, INDESIGN 1-20
Commit any current edits button, PHOTOSHOP 5-3, PHOTOSHOP 5-30
compound paths, ILLUSTRATOR 4-16—4-19
creating, ILLUSTRATOR 4-18
defining, ILLUSTRATOR 4-16—4-17
special effects, ILLUSTRATOR 4-19
compound shapes
creating, ILLUSTRATOR 4-28
defining, ILLUSTRATOR 4-20
special effects, ILLUSTRATOR 4-29
concentric circles, ILLUSTRATOR 4-12
Content panel, Adobe Bridge, PHOTOSHOP 1-9
Contents link, Help system, PHOTOSHOP 1-28, PHOTOSHOP 1-29
Contour setting, Bevel and Emboss style, PHOTOSHOP 5-21
contrast, adjusting, PHOTOSHOP 4-27
Control panel, INDESIGN 3-8
Convert Anchor Point Tool, ILLUSTRATOR 3-12—3-13, ILLUSTRATOR 3-15
coordinates, ILLUSTRATOR 4-8
copying. *See also* duplicating
attributes with Eyedropper Tool, ILLUSTRATOR 3-27
clipping sets, ILLUSTRATOR 5-28—5-29
selections, PHOTOSHOP 3-7, PHOTOSHOP 3-24
corner points, ILLUSTRATOR 3-4, ILLUSTRATOR 3-11—3-12
beginning and ending paths with, ILLUSTRATOR 3-21
converting, ILLUSTRATOR 3-12—3-13
correcting text automatically, INDESIGN 2-29
Create Outlines command, ILLUSTRATOR 2-26—2-27, ILLUSTRATOR 2-29
Creative Suite, PHOTOSHOP 1-2
.cr2 files, PHOTOSHOP 1-5

Crisp setting, anti-aliasing, PHOTOSHOP 5-17
cropping images, PHOTOSHOP 2-12
Crop Tool, PHOTOSHOP 2-13
.crw files, PHOTOSHOP 1-5
CS3 Welcome Screen, ILLUSTRATOR 1-15
curved lines, ILLUSTRATOR 3-10—3-17
converting anchor points, ILLUSTRATOR 3-12—3-13, ILLUSTRATOR 3-15
drawing, ILLUSTRATOR 3-14
drawing lines with curves and straight segments, ILLUSTRATOR 3-16
editing, ILLUSTRATOR 3-14
properties, ILLUSTRATOR 3-10—3-12
reshaping, ILLUSTRATOR 3-11
reversing direction while drawing, ILLUSTRATOR 3-17
customizing
gradients, PHOTOSHOP 4-17
How-To's, PHOTOSHOP 1-31
opening files, PHOTOSHOP 1-8
Photoshop window, PHOTOSHOP 1-18, PHOTOSHOP 1-23
custom workspaces, INDESIGN 1-21
cutting selections, PHOTOSHOP 3-24
Clipboard, PHOTOSHOP 3-7

Darken mode, PHOTOSHOP 4-26
dashed strokes, ILLUSTRATOR 3-32, ILLUSTRATOR 3-34
data merge, INDESIGN 2-22
.dcr files, PHOTOSHOP 1-5
default background color
returning to, PHOTOSHOP 4-32
setting, PHOTOSHOP 4-7
Default Fill and Stroke button, INDESIGN 5-12—5-13, INDESIGN 5-19
Default Foreground and Background Colors button, PHOTOSHOP 4-6
default foreground color
returning to, PHOTOSHOP 4-32
setting, PHOTOSHOP 4-7
Defringe command, PHOTOSHOP 2-13, PHOTOSHOP 2-15

defringing selections, PHOTOSHOP 2-22
Delete Anchor Point Tool, INDESIGN 4-29
Delete current state button,
    PHOTOSHOP 2-3
Delete Swatch dialog box,
    INDESIGN 5-17, INDESIGN 5-23
deleting
    layers, ILLUSTRATOR 5-23,
        PHOTOSHOP 2-9, PHOTOSHOP
        2-11, PHOTOSHOP 2-22
    selections, PHOTOSHOP 3-7
    states, PHOTOSHOP 1-27
    swatches, INDESIGN 5-16—5-17,
        INDESIGN 5-23
deselecting, selections, PHOTOSHOP 3-5,
    PHOTOSHOP 3-7, PHOTOSHOP 3-9
detaching master items, INDESIGN 3-42
device(s), resolution, PHOTOSHOP 1-29
Difference mode, PHOTOSHOP 4-26
digital cameras, PHOTOSHOP 1-37
    Camera Raw images. See Camera Raw
        images
digital images, PHOTOSHOP 1-2. See also
    file(s); graphics; image(s)
dimming placed images,
    ILLUSTRATOR 5-24
direction lines, ILLUSTRATOR 3-10—3-11
direction points, ILLUSTRATOR 3-11
direct selection(s), ILLUSTRATOR
    1-36—1-41
    anchor points, ILLUSTRATOR 1-36,
        ILLUSTRATOR 1-39
    guides, ILLUSTRATOR 1-36—1-38
    selecting paths, ILLUSTRATOR 1-40
    selection marquees, ILLUSTRATOR 1-39
    special effects using,
        ILLUSTRATOR 1-41
Direct Selection Tool, ILLUSTRATOR 1-3,
    ILLUSTRATOR 1-36—1-41,
    INDESIGN 1-8
    Selection Tool versus,
        INDESIGN 4-25—4-26
    tweaking objects, ILLUSTRATOR 3-5
displaying. See also viewing
    Color Palette, PHOTOSHOP 4-32
    Gradient Tool, PHOTOSHOP 4-32

layers, PHOTOSHOP 1-25, PHOTOSHOP
    1-26, PHOTOSHOP 4-32
panels, ILLUSTRATOR 1-10
rulers, PHOTOSHOP 2-6, PHOTOSHOP
    4-32, PHOTOSHOP 5-30
Dissolve mode, PHOTOSHOP 4-26
distance, drop shadows, PHOTOSHOP
    5-13, PHOTOSHOP 5-14
Distort filters, PHOTOSHOP 5-24
distributing objects, INDESIGN 4-7,
    INDESIGN 4-8, INDESIGN 4-13
Divide pathfinder, ILLUSTRATOR 4-21,
    ILLUSTRATOR 4-22, ILLUSTRATOR 4-27
.dng files, PHOTOSHOP 1-5
dock(s), PHOTOSHOP 1-17
docking panels, ILLUSTRATOR 1-10,
    INDESIGN 1-7
document(s). See also file(s); graphics;
    image(s)
    choosing size, ILLUSTRATOR 1-5
    flattening, INDESIGN 4-16
    new, creating, ILLUSTRATOR 1-4—1-7
document views, INDESIGN 1-10—1-15
    Hand Tool, INDESIGN 1-11—1-12,
        INDESIGN 1-13—1-14
    multiple, INDESIGN 1-12
    Zoom Tool, INDESIGN 1-10—1-11,
        INDESIGN 1-13—1-14
drag and drop method, INDESIGN 2-28
    applying color to objects,
        INDESIGN 5-12, INDESIGN 5-18
    duplicating objects, ILLUSTRATOR 1-29
dragging
    layers, INDESIGN 4-16,
        PHOTOSHOP 1-38
    objects between layers,
        ILLUSTRATOR 5-13,
        ILLUSTRATOR 5-18—5-19
drawing, ILLUSTRATOR 3-1—3-51
    curved lines, ILLUSTRATOR
        3-10—3-17, ILLUSTRATOR 3-14
    lines with curved and straight
        segments, ILLUSTRATOR 3-16
    overview, ILLUSTRATOR 3-2
    reversing direction while drawing,
        ILLUSTRATOR 3-17

straight lines, ILLUSTRATOR 3-4—3-9
stroke objects, ILLUSTRATOR
    3-30—3-35
tools, ILLUSTRATOR 3-3
Dreamweaver CS3, PHOTOSHOP 1-5
drop caps, INDESIGN 2-14, INDESIGN 2-19
drop shadows, ILLUSTRATOR 2-31,
    ILLUSTRATOR 2-33,
    PHOTOSHOP 5-12—5-15
    adding, PHOTOSHOP 5-14,
        PHOTOSHOP 5-30
    settings, PHOTOSHOP 5-13,
        PHOTOSHOP 5-14—5-15
drop zones, PHOTOSHOP 1-18
duotones, PHOTOSHOP 4-21
Duplicate Layer dialog box, INDESIGN 5-21
duplicating. See also copying
    layers, ILLUSTRATOR 5-5,
        ILLUSTRATOR 5-23, INDESIGN 4-15,
        PHOTOSHOP 2-16
    objects, ILLUSTRATOR 1-29
dynamic preview, INDESIGN 4-27
dynamic spell checking, INDESIGN 2-29

E

edge(s), painting in Live Paint mode,
    ILLUSTRATOR 3-43
Edge Contrast setting, Magnetic Lasso Tool,
    PHOTOSHOP 3-11
editing
    curved lines, ILLUSTRATOR 3-14
    text. See editing text
editing text, INDESIGN 2-26—2-29
    Drag and Drop method,
        INDESIGN 2-28
    Find/Change command,
        INDESIGN 2-26, INDESIGN 2-28
    spell checking, INDESIGN
        2-26—2-27, INDESIGN 2-29
Elliptical Marquee Tool, PHOTOSHOP 2-13,
    PHOTOSHOP 3-5, PHOTOSHOP 3-24
Emboss filter, PHOTOSHOP 5-25
em dashes, INDESIGN 3-20—3-21
em space, INDESIGN 3-20
en dashes, INDESIGN 3-20—3-21
ending color, gradients, INDESIGN 5-30

endpoints, 11-2. *See* clipping masks
en space, INDESIGN 3-20
.EPS files, PHOTOSHOP 1-5
Eraser Tool, PHOTOSHOP 2-13
.erf files, PHOTOSHOP 1-5
error correction. *See also* anti-aliasing;
    imperfections, correcting
        selections, PHOTOSHOP 3-5
        spelling errors, PHOTOSHOP 5-10
ethical issues, altering images,
    PHOTOSHOP 1-22
Exclusion mode, PHOTOSHOP 4-26
exiting Photoshop, PHOTOSHOP 1-36,
    PHOTOSHOP 1-37, PHOTOSHOP 1-38
expanding traced graphics,
    ILLUSTRATOR 3-37
exporting layers to Photoshop,
    ILLUSTRATOR 5-21
extending gradients across multiple
    objects, INDESIGN 5-36—5-37
Extract command, PHOTOSHOP 2-12
Eyedropper Tool, ILLUSTRATOR 3-24,
    ILLUSTRATOR 3-27, INDESIGN 1-8,
    PHOTOSHOP 4-3, PHOTOSHOP 4-32
        changing background color,
            PHOTOSHOP 4-9

facing pages, INDESIGN 3-4
Fade dialog box, PHOTOSHOP 4-25,
    PHOTOSHOP 4-28
fastening points, PHOTOSHOP 3-4
Favorites tab, Adobe Bridge,
    PHOTOSHOP 1-14
feathering, PHOTOSHOP 3-22—3-23
Feather setting, Magnetic Lasso Tool,
    PHOTOSHOP 3-11
fields, data merge, INDESIGN 2-22
file(s)
        closing, PHOTOSHOP 1-36,
            PHOTOSHOP 1-37, PHOTOSHOP 1-38
        finding, PHOTOSHOP 1-9—1-10
        flattening, PHOTOSHOP 1-4
        new, creating, PHOTOSHOP 1-38
        opening, INDESIGN 1-22. *See* opening
            files

saving. *See* saving files
sorting using Adobe Bridge,
    PHOTOSHOP 1-13
switching between, PHOTOSHOP 4-32
file formats
    changing, PHOTOSHOP 1-12
    "native," ILLUSTRATOR 1-4
    supported in Photoshop,
        PHOTOSHOP 1-5
File Info dialog box, PHOTOSHOP 1-9
File menu, opening files,
    PHOTOSHOP 1-11
fill(s), INDESIGN 4-4—4-5, INDESIGN 4-9
    adding to open paths, ILLUSTRATOR
        3-25—3-26
    applying to text, ILLUSTRATOR 2-26,
        ILLUSTRATOR 2-29
    clipping masks, ILLUSTRATOR 4-33
Fill and Stroke buttons, INDESIGN 5-12,
    INDESIGN 5-13, INDESIGN 5-15
Fill button, ILLUSTRATOR 1-3,
    ILLUSTRATOR 1-22,
    ILLUSTRATOR 1-24—1-25,
    INDESIGN 4-5
fill color, ILLUSTRATOR 1-20,
    ILLUSTRATOR 1-22—1-25
filter(s), PHOTOSHOP 4-24—4-25,
    PHOTOSHOP 4-28. *See also specific
    filters*
        applied to type. *See* filters applied to
            type
        sharpen, PHOTOSHOP 4-32
        softening filter effects,
            PHOTOSHOP 4-25
Filter panel, Adobe Bridge,
    PHOTOSHOP 1-9
filters applied to type,
    PHOTOSHOP 5-24—5-27
        blurring, PHOTOSHOP 5-25
        distortions, PHOTOSHOP 5-24
        modifying settings, PHOTOSHOP 5-27
        multiple filters, PHOTOSHOP 5-26
        neon glow, PHOTOSHOP 5-27
        rasterizing, PHOTOSHOP 5-24,
            PHOTOSHOP 5-26
        relief, PHOTOSHOP 5-25

special effects, PHOTOSHOP 5-24,
    PHOTOSHOP 5-25
textures, PHOTOSHOP 5-25
Find/Change command, INDESIGN 2-26,
    INDESIGN 2-28
Find/Change dialog box, INDESIGN 2-27
finding objects in Layers panel,
    ILLUSTRATOR 5-21,
    ILLUSTRATOR 5-23
Fitting commands, INDESIGN 4-28
flattening
    artwork, ILLUSTRATOR 5-26,
        ILLUSTRATOR 5-28—5-29
    documents, INDESIGN 4-16
    files, PHOTOSHOP 1-4
    images, PHOTOSHOP 2-17,
        PHOTOSHOP 2-21, PHOTOSHOP 2-22
flaws. *See* imperfections, correcting
flipping
    images, PHOTOSHOP 3-24
    selections, PHOTOSHOP 3-20
flowing
    text into objects, ILLUSTRATOR 2-10,
        ILLUSTRATOR 2-12
    text on paths, ILLUSTRATOR
        2-16—2-19
focus, maintaining, PHOTOSHOP 4-13
Folders palette in Adobe Bridge, opening
    files, PHOTOSHOP 1-11
Folders tab, Adobe Bridge,
    PHOTOSHOP 1-14
font(s), PHOTOSHOP 5-2
    acquiring, PHOTOSHOP 5-5
    sans serif, PHOTOSHOP 5-4,
        PHOTOSHOP 5-5
    serif, PHOTOSHOP 5-4,
        PHOTOSHOP 5-5
    symbol, PHOTOSHOP 5-5
font families, PHOTOSHOP 5-4—5-5
    changing, PHOTOSHOP 5-30
font size, changing, PHOTOSHOP 5-30
footnote(s)
    formatting, INDESIGN 2-11
    inserting automatically,
        INDESIGN 2-10
footnote text, INDESIGN 2-10

foreground color, PHOTOSHOP 4-6
    default. *See* default foreground color
    fill with, PHOTOSHOP 4-32
    switching between background color
        and, PHOTOSHOP 4-32
formatting
    footnotes, INDESIGN 2-11
    paragraphs. *See* formatting paragraphs
    text. *See* formatting text
Formatting affects container button,
    INDESIGN 5-15
Formatting affects text button,
    INDESIGN 5-15
formatting paragraphs,
    INDESIGN 2-12—2-19
    drop caps, INDESIGN 2-14,
        INDESIGN 2-19
    hard returns, INDESIGN 2-15
    indenting, INDESIGN 2-18
    Paragraph panel, INDESIGN
        2-12—2-14, INDESIGN 2-16
    paragraph returns, INDESIGN 2-15,
        INDESIGN 2-17
    soft returns, INDESIGN 2-15,
        INDESIGN 2-19
formatting text, ILLUSTRATOR 2-4—2-5,
    ILLUSTRATOR 2-7, INDESIGN 2-4—2-11
    Character panel, INDESIGN 2-4,
        INDESIGN 2-8
    kerning, INDESIGN 2-6—2-7,
        INDESIGN 2-9—2-10
    leading, INDESIGN 2-4—2-5
    in objects, ILLUSTRATOR 2-13
    scaling text horizontally and vertically,
        INDESIGN 2-6
    selecting text, INDESIGN 2-5
    subscript characters, INDESIGN 2-7
    superscript characters, INDESIGN 2-7,
        INDESIGN 2-10
    tracking, INDESIGN 2-6—2-7,
        INDESIGN 2-9—2-10
    underlining text, INDESIGN 2-7,
        INDESIGN 2-11
frames, INDESIGN 4-1—4-53
    aligning objects, INDESIGN 4-7,
        INDESIGN 4-12

distributing objects, INDESIGN 4-7,
    INDESIGN 4-8, INDESIGN 4-13
fills and strokes, INDESIGN 4-4—4-5,
    INDESIGN 4-9
stacking order, INDESIGN 4-14,
    INDESIGN 4-18—4-18
Step and Repeat command, INDESIGN
    4-6, INDESIGN 4-10—4-11
Free Transform Tool, ILLUSTRATOR 4-4,
    ILLUSTRATOR 4-7
Frequency setting, Magnetic Lasso Tool,
    PHOTOSHOP 3-11
Fresco filter, PHOTOSHOP 5-25
Full Screen Mode, PHOTOSHOP 1-20
fuzziness setting, Color Range command,
    PHOTOSHOP 3-17

gamut, PHOTOSHOP 4-4
Gaussian Blur filter, PHOTOSHOP 5-25,
    PHOTOSHOP 5-30
Getting Started section, PHOTOSHOP 1-28
GIF animations, turning graphics into,
    PHOTOSHOP 1-5
.GIF files, PHOTOSHOP 1-5
Glass filter, PHOTOSHOP 5-25
Gloss setting, Bevel and Emboss style,
    PHOTOSHOP 5-21
glyphs, INDESIGN 2-21
Glyphs panel, ILLUSTRATOR 2-9
gradient(s), ILLUSTRATOR 2-2,
    ILLUSTRATOR 2-20—2-25,
    INDESIGN 5-30—5-37
    adding to Swatches panel,
        ILLUSTRATOR 2-21, ILLUSTRATOR
        2-24—2-25
    adjusting, ILLUSTRATOR 2-30—2-31,
        ILLUSTRATOR 2-32
    applying, INDESIGN 5-32,
        INDESIGN 5-35—5-36
    applying to text, ILLUSTRATOR
        2-26—2-29
    creating, ILLUSTRATOR 2-20—2-21,
        ILLUSTRATOR 2-22—2-23,
        INDESIGN 5-30—5-31,
        INDESIGN 5-33—5-34

ending color, INDESIGN 5-30
extending across multiple objects,
    INDESIGN 5-36—5-37
Gradient Swatch Tool,
    INDESIGN 5-35—5-37
linear, ILLUSTRATOR 2-20,
    INDESIGN 5-30, INDESIGN 5-31
midpoint, ILLUSTRATOR 2-20
modifying using Gradient panel,
    INDESIGN 5-32, INDESIGN
    5-36—5-37
radial, ILLUSTRATOR 2-20—2-21,
    INDESIGN 5-30, INDESIGN 5-31,
    INDESIGN 5-34—5-35
starting color, INDESIGN 5-30
swatches, INDESIGN 5-33—5-35
Gradient Editor dialog box,
    PHOTOSHOP 4-17
Gradient Feather Tool, INDESIGN 5-32
gradient fills (gradients), PHOTOSHOP
    4-6, PHOTOSHOP 4-16—4-19
    applying, PHOTOSHOP 4-19
    creating from sample color,
        PHOTOSHOP 4-18
    customizing, PHOTOSHOP 4-17
    grayscale images, PHOTOSHOP 4-21
Gradient Map dialog box,
    PHOTOSHOP 4-21
Gradient panel, ILLUSTRATOR 2-20—2-21
    Illustrator window, ILLUSTRATOR 1-10
    modifying gradient fills, INDESIGN 5-32
Gradient picker, PHOTOSHOP 4-3,
    PHOTOSHOP 4-16, PHOTOSHOP 4-18
gradient presets, PHOTOSHOP 4-17
Gradient Ramp, INDESIGN 5-30
Gradient styles, PHOTOSHOP 4-3
gradient swatch(es)
    applying, INDESIGN 5-35—5-36
    linear gradients, INDESIGN 5-33—5-34
    radial gradients, INDESIGN 5-34—5-35
Gradient Swatch Tool, INDESIGN 1-8,
    INDESIGN 5-32
    applying swatches,
        INDESIGN 5-35—5-36
    extending gradients across multiple
        objects, INDESIGN 5-36—5-37

INDEX

Gradient Tool, ILLUSTRATOR 2-30—2-31, ILLUSTRATOR 2-32, PHOTOSHOP 4-3, PHOTOSHOP 4-17, PHOTOSHOP 4-32
    displaying, PHOTOSHOP 4-32
graphics. *See also* image(s)
    bitmap. *See* bitmap graphics
    graphics frames versus, INDESIGN 4-25
    importing with spot colors, INDESIGN 5-25, INDESIGN 5-27—5-29
    moving within graphics frames, INDESIGN 4-27, INDESIGN 4-31—4-32
    multiple, placing, INDESIGN 4-33
    resizing, INDESIGN 4-27, INDESIGN 4-33—4-34
graphics frames, INDESIGN 3-6, INDESIGN 4-24—4-37
    Fitting commands, INDESIGN 4-28
    graphic versus, INDESIGN 4-25
    moving graphics within, INDESIGN 4-27, INDESIGN 4-31—4-32
    placing graphics in documents, INDESIGN 4-24, INDESIGN 4-30—4-31, INDESIGN 4-33
    resizing graphics, INDESIGN 4-27, INDESIGN 4-33—4-34
    Selection Tool versus Direct Selection Tool, INDESIGN 4-25—4-26
    wrapping text around graphics, INDESIGN 4-28—4-29, INDESIGN 4-35—4-37
grayscale images, PHOTOSHOP 4-20—4-23
    colorizing, PHOTOSHOP 4-21—4-23
    converting color images to, PHOTOSHOP 4-23
    converting grayscale and color modes, PHOTOSHOP 4-20
    duotones, PHOTOSHOP 4-21
    gradient fills, PHOTOSHOP 4-21
Grayscale mode, ILLUSTRATOR 2-21
grayscale mode, PHOTOSHOP 4-6
grid, ILLUSTRATOR 2-11
grouping
    objects, ILLUSTRATOR 1-26
    panels, ILLUSTRATOR 1-10

growing selections, PHOTOSHOP 3-24
guide(s), ILLUSTRATOR 2-11, INDESIGN 3-6—3-8, INDESIGN 3-15, PHOTOSHOP 2-5, PHOTOSHOP 3-6
    adding to master pages, INDESIGN 3-12—3-13
    color, INDESIGN 3-7, INDESIGN 3-15
    creating, INDESIGN 3-6—3-7
    direct selections, ILLUSTRATOR 1-36—1-38
    locked and unlocked, ILLUSTRATOR 1-37
    making, ILLUSTRATOR 2-11, ILLUSTRATOR 2-14
    turning objects into guides, ILLUSTRATOR 1-36—1-38
Guide pointer, PHOTOSHOP 4-32

handles, PHOTOSHOP 3-17
    changing appearance, ILLUSTRATOR 3-11
    direction lines, ILLUSTRATOR 3-11
Hand Tool, INDESIGN 1-11—1-12, INDESIGN 1-13—1-14
Hard Light mode, PHOTOSHOP 4-26
hard returns, INDESIGN 2-15
hardware requirements
    Macintosh platform, PHOTOSHOP 1-7
    Windows platform, PHOTOSHOP 1-6
Healing Brush Tool, PHOTOSHOP 3-17, PHOTOSHOP 3-20, PHOTOSHOP 3-21
    options, PHOTOSHOP 3-21
Help, INDESIGN 1-22—1-23
Help system, PHOTOSHOP 1-28—1-31
    Contents link, PHOTOSHOP 1-28, PHOTOSHOP 1-29
    How-To feature, PHOTOSHOP 1-30, PHOTOSHOP 1-31
    Index link, PHOTOSHOP 1-28, PHOTOSHOP 1-30
    opening, PHOTOSHOP 1-38
    Search feature, PHOTOSHOP 1-28, PHOTOSHOP 1-31
hexadecimal values, Info palette, PHOTOSHOP 4-9

Hide Edges command, ILLUSTRATOR 2-31
Hide Selection command, ILLUSTRATOR 2-5
hiding
    anchor points, ILLUSTRATOR 2-31
    Color Palette, PHOTOSHOP 4-32
    layers, ILLUSTRATOR 5-11, PHOTOSHOP 1-25, PHOTOSHOP 1-26, PHOTOSHOP 1-38, PHOTOSHOP 4-32
    objects, ILLUSTRATOR 2-5
    palettes, PHOTOSHOP 1-22
    panels, ILLUSTRATOR 1-10
    rulers, PHOTOSHOP 2-6, PHOTOSHOP 2-22, PHOTOSHOP 4-32, PHOTOSHOP 5-30
hierarchy. *See* order
highlight(s), correcting, PHOTOSHOP 4-27
Highlight Mode setting, Bevel and Emboss style, PHOTOSHOP 5-21
History palette, PHOTOSHOP 1-5, PHOTOSHOP 1-25
    deleting states, PHOTOSHOP 1-27, PHOTOSHOP 5-19, PHOTOSHOP 5-30
    hidden, showing, PHOTOSHOP 1-38
    methods for accessing, PHOTOSHOP 5-18
Horizontal Type Tool, PHOTOSHOP 5-3, PHOTOSHOP 5-30
    text on a path, PHOTOSHOP 5-28—5-29
How-To feature, Help system, PHOTOSHOP 1-30, PHOTOSHOP 1-31
HSB mode, ILLUSTRATOR 2-21
HSB model, PHOTOSHOP 4-5
hue, PHOTOSHOP 4-5
Hue mode, PHOTOSHOP 4-26
Hue/Saturation dialog box, PHOTOSHOP 4-22, PHOTOSHOP 4-23

illustrations, ILLUSTRATOR 3-18—3-51
    applying attributes to objects, ILLUSTRATOR 3-24—3-27
    assembling, ILLUSTRATOR 3-28—3-29
    drawing from scratch, ILLUSTRATOR 3-18

elements, ILLUSTRATOR
3-18—3-23
Live Paint. *See* Live Paint; live paint
groups
Live Trace. *See* Live Trace
starting, ILLUSTRATOR 3-18
tracing scanned images,
ILLUSTRATOR 3-18—3-19
Illustrator CS3, overview, ILLUSTRATOR
1-2—1-3
Illustrator window, ILLUSTRATOR
1-8—1-17
elements, ILLUSTRATOR 1-8—1-10
navigating, ILLUSTRATOR 1-14—1-15
quick keys, ILLUSTRATOR 1-11—1-13
working with objects, ILLUSTRATOR
1-16—1-17
image(s). *See also* graphics; illustration(s)
color, converting grayscale and color
modes, PHOTOSHOP 4-20
cropping, PHOTOSHOP 2-12
emphasizing by stroking the edges,
PHOTOSHOP 4-14
ethical implications of altering,
PHOTOSHOP 1-22
flattening, PHOTOSHOP 2-17,
PHOTOSHOP 2-21,
PHOTOSHOP 2-22
flipping, PHOTOSHOP 3-24
grayscale. *See* grayscale images
magnifying. *See* magnifying images
resizing, PHOTOSHOP 1-23
resolution, PHOTOSHOP 1-29
scanning, PHOTOSHOP 1-37
selecting, PHOTOSHOP 1-9—1-10
selections, PHOTOSHOP 2-2
sources, PHOTOSHOP 1-2
turning into GIF animations,
PHOTOSHOP 1-5
image-editing programs, PHOTOSHOP 1-4.
See also Photoshop
image layers, PHOTOSHOP 2-4
imperfections, correcting. *See also*
anti-aliasing
blurry images, PHOTOSHOP 4-24
eliminating red eye, PHOTOSHOP 3-20

Healing Brush Tool, PHOTOSHOP 3-17,
PHOTOSHOP 3-20, PHOTOSHOP 3-21
importing
Adobe Photoshop files with layers,
ILLUSTRATOR 5-4
character styles, INDESIGN 2-20
graphics with spot colors, INDESIGN
5-25, INDESIGN 5-27—5-29
paragraph styles, INDESIGN 2-20
scanned images, ILLUSTRATOR 3-18,
ILLUSTRATOR 3-23
swatches from other documents,
ILLUSTRATOR 2-28
indenting paragraphs, INDESIGN 2-18
InDesign, opening Illustrator files,
ILLUSTRATOR 1-4
Index link, Help system, PHOTOSHOP 1-28,
PHOTOSHOP 1-30
Indicates current drawing layer icon,
INDESIGN 4-16
Indicates selected items button,
INDESIGN 4-16
Info palette, PHOTOSHOP 4-8
hexadecimal values, PHOTOSHOP 4-9
Info panel, INDESIGN 3-8
information overload, PHOTOSHOP 1-16
in ports, text frames, INDESIGN 3-38
insertion mode, ILLUSTRATOR 3-42
Intersect shape areas pathfinder,
ILLUSTRATOR 4-21, ILLUSTRATOR 4-22
Intersect shape mode,
ILLUSTRATOR 4-26

"jaggies," eliminating. *See* anti-aliasing
join(s), ILLUSTRATOR 3-31
bevel, ILLUSTRATOR 3-31
miter, ILLUSTRATOR 3-31
round, ILLUSTRATOR 3-31
Join command, ILLUSTRATOR 3-5
joining anchor points, ILLUSTRATOR
3-5, ILLUSTRATOR 3-9
.JPE files, PHOTOSHOP 1-5
.JPEG files, PHOTOSHOP 1-5
.JPG files, PHOTOSHOP 1-5
.kdc files, PHOTOSHOP 1-5

kerning, ILLUSTRATOR 2-4, ILLUSTRATOR
2-5, ILLUSTRATOR 2-6, ILLUSTRATOR
2-8, INDESIGN 2-6—2-7, INDESIGN
2-9—2-10, PHOTOSHOP 5-8,
PHOTOSHOP 5-9, PHOTOSHOP 5-10,
PHOTOSHOP 5-30
keyboard shortcuts, PHOTOSHOP 1-18
applying color, INDESIGN 5-12
learning, PHOTOSHOP 1-19
Keyboard Shortcuts and Menus dialog box,
PHOTOSHOP 1-18
Keywords palette, Adobe Bridge,
PHOTOSHOP 1-9

L*a*b* model, PHOTOSHOP 4-5
landscape orientation, PHOTOSHOP 1-32
language, selecting for dictionary,
INDESIGN 2-27
Lasso Tool, PHOTOSHOP 1-38,
PHOTOSHOP 2-13, PHOTOSHOP 3-5,
PHOTOSHOP 3-24
lasso tool(s), PHOTOSHOP 1-3
hidden, showing, PHOTOSHOP 1-38
layer(s), ILLUSTRATOR 5-1—5-29,
INDESIGN 4-14—4-23, PHOTOSHOP
1-24, PHOTOSHOP 2-1—2-27
adding color, PHOTOSHOP 2-17
adding to images, PHOTOSHOP 2-8,
PHOTOSHOP 2-10
adding using Layers palette,
PHOTOSHOP 2-11
Background. *See* Background layer
changing order, ILLUSTRATOR 5-12,
ILLUSTRATOR 5-14,
ILLUSTRATOR 5-21
changing order in Layers panel,
INDESIGN 4-22—4-23
changing selection color,
ILLUSTRATOR 5-9
color, INDESIGN 4-16,
PHOTOSHOP 2-22
converting, PHOTOSHOP 2-6,
PHOTOSHOP 2-7
creating, ILLUSTRATOR 5-4—5-5,
ILLUSTRATOR 5-8, INDESIGN 4-19

defringing contents, PHOTOSHOP 2-13,
PHOTOSHOP 2-15
deleting, ILLUSTRATOR 5-23,
PHOTOSHOP 2-9, PHOTOSHOP 2-11,
PHOTOSHOP 2-22
designing with, ILLUSTRATOR 5-2
displaying, PHOTOSHOP 1-25,
PHOTOSHOP 1-26, PHOTOSHOP 4-32
dragging, INDESIGN 4-16,
PHOTOSHOP 1-38
duplicating, ILLUSTRATOR 5-5,
ILLUSTRATOR 5-23, INDESIGN 4-15,
PHOTOSHOP 2-16
exporting to Photoshop,
ILLUSTRATOR 5-21
groups, PHOTOSHOP 2-16—2-17
hiding, PHOTOSHOP 1-25, PHOTOSHOP
1-26, PHOTOSHOP 1-38,
PHOTOSHOP 4-32
image, PHOTOSHOP 2-4
importance, PHOTOSHOP 2-2
importing Adobe Photoshop files with,
ILLUSTRATOR 5-4
inserting beneath active layer,
PHOTOSHOP 2-10
Layers panel. See Layers panel
locking, ILLUSTRATOR 5-10
making nonprintable, ILLUSTRATOR
5-21, ILLUSTRATOR 5-25
merging, ILLUSTRATOR 5-12,
ILLUSTRATOR 5-15, PHOTOSHOP 2-8
merging contents, INDESIGN 4-16
modifying images, PHOTOSHOP 2-2
moving, PHOTOSHOP 1-27
moving objects between,
ILLUSTRATOR 5-13, ILLUSTRATOR
5-18—5-19
naming, ILLUSTRATOR 5-9,
PHOTOSHOP 2-9
new, INDESIGN 4-19, PHOTOSHOP 2-22
opacity, PHOTOSHOP 2-2,
PHOTOSHOP 2-22
order, INDESIGN 4-16, INDESIGN
4-17, PHOTOSHOP 2-5
organizing, PHOTOSHOP 2-5,
PHOTOSHOP 2-16—2-17

positioning objects on, INDESIGN
4-20—4-21
rasterizing, PHOTOSHOP 2-8
renaming, PHOTOSHOP 2-20,
PHOTOSHOP 2-22
selecting artwork, INDESIGN 4-17
selecting items, ILLUSTRATOR 5-7,
ILLUSTRATOR 5-10
selecting objects behind other objects,
INDESIGN 4-17
setting options, ILLUSTRATOR 5-6
showing, PHOTOSHOP 1-38
showing/hiding, ILLUSTRATOR 5-11
stacking order, ILLUSTRATOR 5-5
sublayers. See sublayers
targeting, INDESIGN 4-16
thumbnails, PHOTOSHOP 2-4
types, PHOTOSHOP 2-4—2-5
layer comps, PHOTOSHOP 2-18
creating, PHOTOSHOP 2-20,
PHOTOSHOP 2-22
updating, PHOTOSHOP 2-22
Layer Comps palette, PHOTOSHOP 2-20
layer groups, PHOTOSHOP 2-16
creating, PHOTOSHOP 2-16—2-17,
PHOTOSHOP 2-19, PHOTOSHOP 2-22
moving layers to, PHOTOSHOP 2-19
Layer menu
adding Bevel and Emboss styles,
PHOTOSHOP 5-22
adding layers, PHOTOSHOP 2-10
Layer Options dialog box,
ILLUSTRATOR 5-6
Layers palette, PHOTOSHOP 1-24—1-25,
PHOTOSHOP 2-4
adding layers, PHOTOSHOP 2-11
displaying layers, PHOTOSHOP 1-25,
PHOTOSHOP 1-26
hiding layers, PHOTOSHOP 1-25,
PHOTOSHOP 1-26
locking options, PHOTOSHOP 4-14
moving layers, PHOTOSHOP 1-27
Layers panel, INDESIGN 4-15,
INDESIGN 4-19
changing order of layers, INDESIGN
4-22—4-23

creating new layers, INDESIGN 4-19
locating objects, ILLUSTRATOR 5-21,
ILLUSTRATOR 5-23
view buttons, ILLUSTRATOR 5-20,
ILLUSTRATOR 5-22
layer style(s), PHOTOSHOP 5-12
applying, PHOTOSHOP 5-12—5-13,
PHOTOSHOP 5-14
Layer Style dialog box,
PHOTOSHOP 5-13, PHOTOSHOP 5-15,
PHOTOSHOP 5-22
layer thumbnail, PHOTOSHOP 2-4
leading, ILLUSTRATOR 2-4, INDESIGN
2-4—2-5, PHOTOSHOP 5-9
Lighten mode, PHOTOSHOP 4-26
line(s). See curved lines; straight lines
linear gradients, ILLUSTRATOR 2-20,
INDESIGN 5-30, INDESIGN 5-31
line-art sketches, tracing, ILLUSTRATOR
3-37, ILLUSTRATOR 3-44
line segments, ILLUSTRATOR 1-19
Links dialog box, responding to,
INDESIGN 1-8
lists
bulleted, INDESIGN 2-15
numbered, INDESIGN 2-15
Live Paint, ILLUSTRATOR 3-39—3-43,
ILLUSTRATOR 3-47—3-51
groups. See live paint groups
painting edges, ILLUSTRATOR 3-43
regions, ILLUSTRATOR 3-40
virtual regions, ILLUSTRATOR 3-41
Live Paint Bucket Tool, ILLUSTRATOR
3-47—3-51
live paint groups, ILLUSTRATOR 3-40
expanding, ILLUSTRATOR 3-43
inserting objects, ILLUSTRATOR 3-42
selecting multiple regions,
ILLUSTRATOR 3-40
Live Trace, ILLUSTRATOR 3-36—3-38,
ILLUSTRATOR 3-44—3-46
expanding traced graphics,
ILLUSTRATOR 3-37
tracing line-art sketches,
ILLUSTRATOR 3-37
tracing photos, ILLUSTRATOR 3-38

loading selections, PHOTOSHOP 3-9
locked guides, ILLUSTRATOR 1-37
locking
    layers, ILLUSTRATOR 5-10
    objects, ILLUSTRATOR 2-11,
        ILLUSTRATOR 2-14—2-15
    transparent pixels, PHOTOSHOP 4-14,
        PHOTOSHOP 4-15
Lock Selection command, ILLUSTRATOR
    2-11, ILLUSTRATOR 2-14—2-15
logos, PHOTOSHOP 1-4
luminosity, PHOTOSHOP 4-20
Luminosity mode, PHOTOSHOP 4-26

Macintosh platform, PHOTOSHOP 1-2
    hardware requirements,
        PHOTOSHOP 1-7
    right-clicking, PHOTOSHOP 2-11
    starting Photoshop, PHOTOSHOP 1-5,
        PHOTOSHOP 1-7
Magic Eraser Tool, PHOTOSHOP 2-13
Magic Wand Tool, PHOTOSHOP 2-13,
    PHOTOSHOP 3-16, PHOTOSHOP 3-19,
    PHOTOSHOP 3-24
    neon glow, PHOTOSHOP 5-27
    options, PHOTOSHOP 3-17
    settings, PHOTOSHOP 3-19
Magnetic Lasso Tool, PHOTOSHOP 2-13,
    PHOTOSHOP 3-5, PHOTOSHOP 3-10,
    PHOTOSHOP 3-24
    settings, PHOTOSHOP 3-11
magnification, Zoom Tool, INDESIGN
    1-10—1-11, INDESIGN 1-13—1-14
magnifying images
    Navigator palette, PHOTOSHOP 1-34
    Zoom Tool, PHOTOSHOP 1-32,
        PHOTOSHOP 1-34
Make Guides command,
    ILLUSTRATOR 2-11
margins, INDESIGN 3-4, INDESIGN 3-5,
    INDESIGN 3-7, INDESIGN 3-15
    color, INDESIGN 3-7, INDESIGN 3-15
marquee(s), ILLUSTRATOR 3-4,
    PHOTOSHOP 2-12, PHOTOSHOP 3-4,
    PHOTOSHOP 3-12—3-15

moving, PHOTOSHOP 3-13,
    PHOTOSHOP 3-14,
    PHOTOSHOP 3-24
    Quick Selection Tool, PHOTOSHOP
        3-13, PHOTOSHOP 3-15
    resizing, PHOTOSHOP 3-12,
        PHOTOSHOP 3-14
marquee selections
    Direct Selection Tool,
        ILLUSTRATOR 1-39
    Selection Tool, ILLUSTRATOR
        1-26—1-27
marquee tools, PHOTOSHOP 2-12,
    PHOTOSHOP 2-13
masks, PHOTOSHOP 3-22
    clipping. *See* clipping masks;
        clipping sets
    creating vignettes, PHOTOSHOP 3-22,
        PHOTOSHOP 3-23
master items, INDESIGN 3-6, INDESIGN
    3-28—3-29
    detaching, INDESIGN 3-42
    overriding on document pages,
        INDESIGN 3-42, INDESIGN 3-43
master pages, INDESIGN 3-5—3-6,
    INDESIGN 3-11—3-13, INDESIGN
    3-18—3-31
    adding guides, INDESIGN 3-12—3-13
    applying to document pages,
        INDESIGN 3-32—3-35
    automatic page numbering,
        INDESIGN 3-19—3-20,
        INDESIGN 3-26
    based on another master page,
        INDESIGN 3-21, INDESIGN
        3-30—3-31
    em dashes and en dashes,
        INDESIGN 3-20—3-21
    inserting white space between
        characters, INDESIGN 3-20,
        INDESIGN 3-26—3-27
    loading, INDESIGN 3-19
    master items, INDESIGN 3-6,
        INDESIGN 3-28—3-29
    modifying, INDESIGN 3-11,
        INDESIGN 3-42—3-45

new, creating, INDESIGN 3-18,
    INDESIGN 3-22—3-23
    renaming, INDESIGN 3-11
    text frames, INDESIGN 3-24—3-25
    viewing thumbnails, INDESIGN 3-16
Match Color dialog box, PHOTOSHOP 4-31
matching colors, PHOTOSHOP 4-30—4-31
measurement units, ILLUSTRATOR 1-5
menu bar
    Illustrator window, ILLUSTRATOR 1-8
    Photoshop window, PHOTOSHOP
        1-16, PHOTOSHOP 1-17
merged documents, data merge,
    INDESIGN 2-22
merging
    contents of layers, INDESIGN 4-16
    layers, ILLUSTRATOR 5-12,
        ILLUSTRATOR 5-15, PHOTOSHOP 2-8
Metadata palette, Adobe Bridge,
    PHOTOSHOP 1-9
midpoint, of gradient, ILLUSTRATOR 2-20
Minus back pathfinder, ILLUSTRATOR
    4-21, ILLUSTRATOR 4-22
misspellings, correcting, PHOTOSHOP 5-10
miter joins, ILLUSTRATOR 3-31
miter limit, ILLUSTRATOR 3-31
modifying selections,
    PHOTOSHOP 3-20—3-21
monitors, resolution, PHOTOSHOP 1-29
monotype spacing, PHOTOSHOP 5-8
mouse, right-clicking,
    PHOTOSHOP 2-11
Move Pages command, INDESIGN 3-28
Move Tool, PHOTOSHOP 2-22,
    PHOTOSHOP 3-24, PHOTOSHOP 5-3,
    PHOTOSHOP 5-30
    moving selections, PHOTOSHOP 3-6,
        PHOTOSHOP 3-8
    temporarily changing other tools into,
        PHOTOSHOP 3-6
moving. *See also* navigating
    graphics within graphics frames,
        INDESIGN 4-27,
        INDESIGN 4-31—4-32
    layers to layer groups,
        PHOTOSHOP 2-19

INDEX

marquees, PHOTOSHOP 3-13,
PHOTOSHOP 3-14, PHOTOSHOP 3-24
objects. *See* moving objects
selections, PHOTOSHOP 2-13,
PHOTOSHOP 2-15, PHOTOSHOP
3-6, PHOTOSHOP 3-7, PHOTOSHOP
3-8, PHOTOSHOP 3-11
text on paths, ILLUSTRATOR 2-19
moving objects, ILLUSTRATOR 1-26,
ILLUSTRATOR 1-27—1-28
between layers, ILLUSTRATOR 5-13,
ILLUSTRATOR 5-18—5-19
.mrw files, PHOTOSHOP 1-5
multiple document views, INDESIGN 1-12
multiple objects
as clipping masks, ILLUSTRATOR 4-31
extending gradients across,
INDESIGN 5-36—5-37
Multiply mode, PHOTOSHOP 4-26

Named colors, process colors,
INDESIGN 5-4
naming layers, ILLUSTRATOR 5-9,
PHOTOSHOP 2-9
navigating, INDESIGN 1-16—1-21
artboard, ILLUSTRATOR 1-14—1-15
Navigator panel, INDESIGN 1-18,
INDESIGN 1-20—1-21
to pages in documents, INDESIGN
1-16—1-17, INDESIGN 1-19—1-20
Navigator palette, PHOTOSHOP 1-34
Navigator panel, INDESIGN 1-18,
INDESIGN 1-20—1-21
.nef files, PHOTOSHOP 1-5
neon glow, PHOTOSHOP 5-27
New Color Swatch db, INDESIGN 5-5
New Dialog box, INDESIGN 3-10
New dialog box, PHOTOSHOP 1-5
new document(s), creating,
INDESIGN 3-4—3-17
columns, INDESIGN 3-5,
INDESIGN 3-7, INDESIGN 3-15
Control panel, INDESIGN 3-8
guides, INDESIGN 3-6—3-8,
INDESIGN 3-15

margins, INDESIGN 3-4, INDESIGN 3-5,
INDESIGN 3-7, INDESIGN 3-15
master pages, INDESIGN 3-5—3-6,
INDESIGN 3-11—3-13
placeholder text frames, INDESIGN 3-14
Transform panel, INDESIGN 3-9,
INDESIGN 3-16—3-17
New Document dialog box, ILLUSTRATOR
1-4, ILLUSTRATOR 1-5, ILLUSTRATOR
1-6, ILLUSTRATOR 1-7, INDESIGN
3-4gutter3-5
New Gradient Swatch box, INDESIGN
5-30, INDESIGN 5-31, INDESIGN 5-33,
INDESIGN 5-34, INDESIGN 5-35
New Group dialog box, PHOTOSHOP 2-19
New Layer Comp dialog box, PHOTOSHOP
2-18, PHOTOSHOP 2-20
New Master dialog box, INDESIGN 3-22
New Section dialog box, INDESIGN 3-46
New Window command, PHOTOSHOP 1-33
Next Page Number command,
INDESIGN 4-40
None fills, INDESIGN 5-14
None setting, anti-aliasing,
PHOTOSHOP 5-17
numbered lists, INDESIGN 2-15

Objects
applying attributes, ILLUSTRATOR
3-24—3-27
applying color, INDESIGN 5-12—5-13,
INDESIGN 5-18—5-19
dragging between layers,
ILLUSTRATOR 5-13, ILLUSTRATOR
5-18—5-19
duplicating, ILLUSTRATOR 1-29
filling with text, ILLUSTRATOR 2-10,
ILLUSTRATOR 2-12
formatting text in, ILLUSTRATOR 2-13
grouping, ILLUSTRATOR 1-26
hiding, ILLUSTRATOR 2-5
inserting into live paint groups,
ILLUSTRATOR 3-42
locking, ILLUSTRATOR 2-11,
ILLUSTRATOR 2-14—2-15

moving, ILLUSTRATOR 1-26,
ILLUSTRATOR 1-27—1-28
multiple, extending gradients across,
INDESIGN 5-36—5-37
selecting. *See* selecting objects
stacking order, ILLUSTRATOR 2-26
transforming. *See* transforming
objects
turning into guides,
ILLUSTRATOR 1-36—1-38
tweaking, ILLUSTRATOR 3-5
working with, ILLUSTRATOR
1-16—1-17
Offset Path command, ILLUSTRATOR
4-12, ILLUSTRATOR 4-14
offset value, Step and Repeat command,
INDESIGN 4-6
opacity, PHOTOSHOP 2-2,
PHOTOSHOP 4-28
layers, PHOTOSHOP 2-22
Opacity list arrow, PHOTOSHOP 2-3
Open As command, PHOTOSHOP 1-8
Open dialog box, PHOTOSHOP 1-11
opening
Bridge, PHOTOSHOP 1-38
files. *See* opening files
Help system, PHOTOSHOP 1-38
Preferences dialog box,
PHOTOSHOP 1-38
opening files, INDESIGN 1-22,
PHOTOSHOP 1-8, PHOTOSHOP 1-38
customizing, PHOTOSHOP 1-8
File menu, PHOTOSHOP 1-11
Folders palette in Adobe Bridge,
PHOTOSHOP 1-11
thumbnails, PHOTOSHOP 1-10
open paths, adding attributes,
ILLUSTRATOR 3-25—3-26
options bar, PHOTOSHOP 1-3
Photoshop window,
PHOTOSHOP 1-17
showing, PHOTOSHOP 1-38
Options dialog box, ILLUSTRATOR 1-5
order, stacking, INDESIGN 4-14,
INDESIGN 4-18—4-29
layers, ILLUSTRATOR 5-5

order of layers, INDESIGN 4-16, INDESIGN
4-17, INDESIGN 4-22—4-23,
PHOTOSHOP 2-5
changing, ILLUSTRATOR 5-12,
ILLUSTRATOR 5-14,
ILLUSTRATOR 5-21
stacking, ILLUSTRATOR 5-5
.orf files, PHOTOSHOP 1-5
orientation, paper, PHOTOSHOP 1-32
Outline Stroke command, ILLUSTRATOR
4-13, ILLUSTRATOR 4-15
outline type, PHOTOSHOP 5-4
out ports, text frames, INDESIGN 3-38
Overlay mode, PHOTOSHOP 4-26
overriding master items on document
pages, INDESIGN 3-42, INDESIGN 3-43
overset text, INDESIGN 3-38

page(s)
applying master pages to document
pages, INDESIGN 3-32—3-35
facing, INDESIGN 3-4
placing text on, INDESIGN
3-36—3-37, INDESIGN 3-40
zero point, INDESIGN 3-7
page continuation notations, INDESIGN
4-40, INDESIGN 4-44—4-45
page numbering, automatic, INDESIGN
3-19—3-20, INDESIGN 3-26
Page Setup command, PHOTOSHOP 1-38
Page Setup dialog box, PHOTOSHOP
1-32, PHOTOSHOP 1-35
Pages panel, INDESIGN 1-17,
INDESIGN 3-5
page trim, INDESIGN 3-4
Paint Bucket Tool, PHOTOSHOP 4-32
displaying, PHOTOSHOP 4-32
palette(s). See also specific palettes
hiding, PHOTOSHOP 1-22
open, showing, PHOTOSHOP 1-38
Photoshop window, PHOTOSHOP
1-17—1-18
resetting to default location,
PHOTOSHOP 1-18
showing, PHOTOSHOP 1-22

panel(s), INDESIGN 1-6—1-7, INDESIGN
1-9. See also palette(s)
docking, ILLUSTRATOR 1-10,
INDESIGN 1-7
grouped, INDESIGN 1-7
grouping, ILLUSTRATOR 1-10
hiding/unhiding, ILLUSTRATOR 1-10
Illustrator window, ILLUSTRATOR 1-9,
ILLUSTRATOR 1-10
ungrouping, INDESIGN 1-7
Panel Options command, INDESIGN 1-17
Paper fills, INDESIGN 5-14
paper orientation, PHOTOSHOP 1-32
paper swatches, INDESIGN 5-14
Paragraph panel, INDESIGN 1-7, INDESIGN
2-12—2-14, INDESIGN 2-16
paragraph returns, INDESIGN 2-15,
INDESIGN 2-17
paragraph styles, ILLUSTRATOR 2-13,
INDESIGN 2-20, INDESIGN 2-23—2-24
applying, INDESIGN 2-35
creating, INDESIGN 2-24
importing, INDESIGN 2-20
Paragraph Styles panel, INDESIGN 2-20,
INDESIGN 2-21
pasteboard, INDESIGN 1-4—1-5
pasting
selections, PHOTOSHOP 3-7,
PHOTOSHOP 3-24
text without formatting, INDESIGN 2-4
path(s), ILLUSTRATOR 1-19
beginning and ending with corner
points, ILLUSTRATOR 3-21
closed. See closed paths
closing, ILLUSTRATOR 3-8
compound. See compound paths
drawing with Pen Tool, ILLUSTRATOR
3-4—3-5
offsetting, ILLUSTRATOR 4-12,
ILLUSTRATOR 4-14
open, adding attributes, ILLUSTRATOR
3-26
positioning text along, ILLUSTRATOR
2-16—2-19
redirecting while drawing,
ILLUSTRATOR 3-22

selecting, ILLUSTRATOR 1-40
stroked, converting to closed path,
ILLUSTRATOR 4-13, ILLUSTRATOR
4-15
pathfinder(s), ILLUSTRATOR 4-20—4-29
Pathfinder panel, ILLUSTRATOR
4-22—4-29
applying shape modes,
ILLUSTRATOR 4-23—4-26
creating compound shapes,
ILLUSTRATOR 4-28
Divide pathfinder, ILLUSTRATOR 4-27
.PCX files, PHOTOSHOP 1-5
PDF presentation(s), creating using Bridge,
PHOTOSHOP 1-10
PDF Presentation server-based,
PHOTOSHOP 1-10
.pef files, PHOTOSHOP 1-5
Pencil Tool, INDESIGN 1-8
Pen Tool, ILLUSTRATOR 3-2,
ILLUSTRATOR 3-3, INDESIGN 1-8
drawing curved lines, ILLUSTRATOR
3-10, ILLUSTRATOR 3-14
drawing straight segments,
ILLUSTRATOR 3-4—3-5
toggling between selection tools and,
ILLUSTRATOR 3-13
photos, tracing, ILLUSTRATOR 3-38,
ILLUSTRATOR 3-45—3-46
Photoshop
choosing version, PHOTOSHOP 1-33
exiting, PHOTOSHOP 1-36,
PHOTOSHOP 1-37,
PHOTOSHOP 1-38
exporting layers to,
ILLUSTRATOR 5-21
features, PHOTOSHOP 1-4—1-5
file formats supported, PHOTOSHOP 1-5
importing files with layers,
ILLUSTRATOR 5-4
opening Illustrator files,
ILLUSTRATOR 1-4
starting in Windows, PHOTOSHOP
1-5, PHOTOSHOP 1-6
starting with Macintosh, PHOTOSHOP
1-5, PHOTOSHOP 1-7

Photoshop window, PHOTOSHOP
1-16—1-23
customizing, PHOTOSHOP 1-18,
PHOTOSHOP 1-23
tool shortcut keys, PHOTOSHOP 1-19
workspace, PHOTOSHOP 1-16
picas, ILLUSTRATOR 1-5
picture(s). *See* file(s); graphics;
illustrations; image(s)
pixels, ILLUSTRATOR 1-18—1-19,
PHOTOSHOP 1-4, PHOTOSHOP 4-2
transparent, locking, PHOTOSHOP 4-
14, PHOTOSHOP 4-15
Place command, PHOTOSHOP 2-14
importing scanned images,
ILLUSTRATOR 3-18,
ILLUSTRATOR 3-23
placeholder(s), automatic page
numbering, INDESIGN 3-19—3-20,
INDESIGN 3-26
placeholder text, text frames,
INDESIGN 3-14
placing text, INDESIGN 3-36—3-37,
INDESIGN 3-40
platforms, PHOTOSHOP 1-2
point(s), ILLUSTRATOR 1-5,
PHOTOSHOP 5-5
point of origin, ILLUSTRATOR 4-4—
ILLUSTRATOR 4-5, INDESIGN 3-9
Polygonal Lasso Tool, PHOTOSHOP 2-13,
PHOTOSHOP 3-5, PHOTOSHOP 3-24
Polygon Tool, ILLUSTRATOR 1-35
portrait orientation, PHOTOSHOP 1-32
positioning objects,
INDESIGN 3-7—3-8
on layers, INDESIGN 4-20—4-21
PostScript, PHOTOSHOP 5-5
preferences, PHOTOSHOP 1-8
resetting to default settings,
PHOTOSHOP 1-38
Preferences command, ILLUSTRATOR 1-5
Preferences dialog box, PHOTOSHOP 1-8,
PHOTOSHOP 1-24
opening, PHOTOSHOP 1-38
Units & Increments section,
INDESIGN 2-8

Preview option, Layer Options dialog box,
ILLUSTRATOR 5-6
Print command, PHOTOSHOP 1-32
Print File command, PHOTOSHOP 1-38
printing images, PHOTOSHOP 1-32—1-33
color, PHOTOSHOP 1-33
modifying print settings,
PHOTOSHOP 1-35
Proof Setup, PHOTOSHOP 1-35
Print One Copy command,
PHOTOSHOP 1-32
Print option, Layer Options dialog box,
ILLUSTRATOR 5-6
process colors, INDESIGN 5-4—5-11
Color panel, INDESIGN 5-10—5-11
named colors, INDESIGN 5-4
tints, INDESIGN 5-4—5-5
tint swatches, INDESIGN 5-6,
INDESIGN 5-8—5-9
unnamed, INDESIGN 5-6—5-7,
INDESIGN 5-11
process inks, INDESIGN 5-4
Proof Setups
creating, PHOTOSHOP 1-35
saving, PHOTOSHOP 1-35
proportional spacing, PHOTOSHOP 5-8
.PSD files, PHOTOSHOP 1-5
pseudo-stroke effects, ILLUSTRATOR
3-32, ILLUSTRATOR 3-35
.ptx files, PHOTOSHOP 1-5
pull quotes, INDESIGN 2-13,
INDESIGN 2-18

Quark XPress, opening Illustrator files,
ILLUSTRATOR 1-4
Quick Apply, INDESIGN 2-24
quick keys, ILLUSTRATOR 1-11—1-13
Quick Selection Tool, PHOTOSHOP 3-13,
PHOTOSHOP 3-15, PHOTOSHOP 3-24

radial gradients, ILLUSTRATOR 2-20—2-21,
INDESIGN 5-30, INDESIGN 5-31,
INDESIGN 5-34—5-35
radius, ILLUSTRATOR 1-34

.raf files, PHOTOSHOP 1-5
rasterizing
layers, PHOTOSHOP 2-8
type, PHOTOSHOP 5-24,
PHOTOSHOP 5-26
raw data. *See* Camera Raw images
raw formats, PHOTOSHOP 1-5
records, data merge, INDESIGN 2-22
Rectangle dialog box, ILLUSTRATOR 1-21
Rectangle Frame Tool, INDESIGN 1-8
Rectangle Tool, ILLUSTRATOR 1-20,
INDESIGN 1-8
Rectangular Marquee Tool,
PHOTOSHOP 2-13, PHOTOSHOP 3-5,
PHOTOSHOP 3-7
red eye, eliminating, PHOTOSHOP 3-20
Red Eye Tool, PHOTOSHOP 3-20
redirecting paths while drawing,
ILLUSTRATOR 3-22
Redo command, ILLUSTRATOR 1-16
redoing actions, PHOTOSHOP 1-5
reference numbers, footnotes,
INDESIGN 2-10
Reflect Tool, ILLUSTRATOR 1-3,
ILLUSTRATOR 1-34—1-35,
ILLUSTRATOR 4-4, ILLUSTRATOR 4-11
reflow text, INDESIGN 4-42—4-43
regions, Live Paint, ILLUSTRATOR 3-40
multiple, selecting in live paint groups,
ILLUSTRATOR 3-40
virtual, painting, ILLUSTRATOR 3-41
relief, filters, PHOTOSHOP 5-25
Remember Palette Locations dialog box,
PHOTOSHOP 1-24
renaming layers, PHOTOSHOP 2-20,
PHOTOSHOP 2-22
rendering intents, PHOTOSHOP 4-7
repeating transformations, ILLUSTRATOR
1-31, ILLUSTRATOR 1-33,
ILLUSTRATOR 4-6
resizing
graphics, INDESIGN 4-27, INDESIGN
4-33—4-34
images, PHOTOSHOP 1-23
marquees, PHOTOSHOP 3-12,
PHOTOSHOP 3-14

resolution, ILLUSTRATOR 1-18
  bitmapped images, PHOTOSHOP 4-2
  monitor, image, and device,
    comparison, PHOTOSHOP 1-29
resolution-dependent images,
  ILLUSTRATOR 1-18
resolution-independent images,
  ILLUSTRATOR 1-19
resulting color, PHOTOSHOP 4-25
returns
  hard, INDESIGN 2-15
  paragraph, INDESIGN 2-15,
    INDESIGN 2-17
  soft, INDESIGN 2-15, INDESIGN 2-19
reversing
  direction, while drawing,
    ILLUSTRATOR 3-17
  order of layers, ILLUSTRATOR 5-21
RGB mode, ILLUSTRATOR 1-4—1-5,
  ILLUSTRATOR 2-21, PHOTOSHOP
  4-5—4-6
right-clicking, PHOTOSHOP 2-11
Rotate Tool, ILLUSTRATOR 1-3,
  ILLUSTRATOR 1-32, ILLUSTRATOR
  4-4, ILLUSTRATOR 4-8—4-9
rotating objects, around defined point,
  ILLUSTRATOR 4-8—4-9
round joins, ILLUSTRATOR 3-31
rule(s), INDESIGN 2-7, INDESIGN 2-11
ruler(s), ILLUSTRATOR 2-11
  displaying, PHOTOSHOP 2-6,
    PHOTOSHOP 5-30
  hiding, PHOTOSHOP 2-6,
    PHOTOSHOP 2-22, PHOTOSHOP
    4-32, PHOTOSHOP 5-30
  Photoshop window, PHOTOSHOP 1-18
  showing, PHOTOSHOP 2-22,
    PHOTOSHOP 4-32
  units of measurement, PHOTOSHOP
    2-6, PHOTOSHOP 2-22
ruler coordinates, PHOTOSHOP 4-8

sampling, PHOTOSHOP 4-6
sans serif fonts, PHOTOSHOP 5-4,
  PHOTOSHOP 5-5

saturation, PHOTOSHOP 4-5
Saturation mode, PHOTOSHOP 4-26
Save As command, PHOTOSHOP 1-12,
  PHOTOSHOP 1-38
  Save command versus,
    PHOTOSHOP 1-10
Save As dialog box, PHOTOSHOP 1-12,
  PHOTOSHOP 2-21
Save command, Save As command versus,
  PHOTOSHOP 1-10
Save Selection dialog box,
  PHOTOSHOP 3-9
Save Workspace dialog box,
  PHOTOSHOP 1-23
saving
  files, PHOTOSHOP 1-10, PHOTOSHOP
    1-12, PHOTOSHOP 1-38
  image changes, PHOTOSHOP 5-30
  Proof Setups, PHOTOSHOP 1-35
  selections, PHOTOSHOP 3-9
Scale dialog box, ILLUSTRATOR 1-31
Scale Tool, ILLUSTRATOR 1-3,
  ILLUSTRATOR 1-32, ILLUSTRATOR
  4-4, INDESIGN 1-8
scaling
  graphics, INDESIGN 4-27,
    INDESIGN 4-33—4-34
  text, horizontally and vertically,
    INDESIGN 2-6
scanned images
  blurry, fixing, PHOTOSHOP 4-24
  importing, ILLUSTRATOR 3-18,
    ILLUSTRATOR 3-23
  tracing, ILLUSTRATOR 3-18—3-19
scanning images, PHOTOSHOP 1-37
scratch area, ILLUSTRATOR 1-8,
  ILLUSTRATOR 1-9
Screen mode, PHOTOSHOP 4-26
Search feature, Help system, PHOTOSHOP
  1-28, PHOTOSHOP 1-31
sections, creating, INDESIGN 3-46,
  INDESIGN 3-48—3-49
selecting
  all objects, PHOTOSHOP 3-24
  all text, PHOTOSHOP 5-30
  artwork on layers, INDESIGN 4-17

color as basis, PHOTOSHOP
  3-16—3-19, PHOTOSHOP 3-24
color range, PHOTOSHOP 2-22
direct selections. See direct
  selection(s)
images, PHOTOSHOP 1-9—1-10
items in layers, ILLUSTRATOR 5-7,
  ILLUSTRATOR 5-10
language for dictionary,
  INDESIGN 2-27
Magic Wand Tool, PHOTOSHOP 3-24
objects. See selecting objects
paths, ILLUSTRATOR 1-40
Quick Selection Tool, PHOTOSHOP
  3-13, PHOTOSHOP 3-15,
  PHOTOSHOP 3-24
reselecting deselected objects,
  PHOTOSHOP 3-24
Select menu, ILLUSTRATOR 1-35
by shape. See selecting by shape
text, INDESIGN 2-5
tools, INDESIGN 1-6,
  PHOTOSHOP 1-19—1-20
selecting by shape, PHOTOSHOP
  3-4—3-11
  guides, PHOTOSHOP 3-6
  placing selections, PHOTOSHOP 3-6,
    PHOTOSHOP 3-8, PHOTOSHOP 3-11
  selection tools, PHOTOSHOP 3-5
selecting objects, ILLUSTRATOR 1-26
  marquee selections, ILLUSTRATOR
    1-26—1-27
  objects behind other objects,
    INDESIGN 4-17
  Smart Guides, ILLUSTRATOR
    1-27—1-28
selection(s), PHOTOSHOP 2-2,
  PHOTOSHOP 3-1—3-29. See also
  marquee(s)
  adding and subtracting from,
    PHOTOSHOP 3-13
  adding from one image to another,
    PHOTOSHOP 2-12—2-15
  color as basis, PHOTOSHOP 3-16—3-18
  combining images, PHOTOSHOP 3-2
  complex, moving, PHOTOSHOP 3-11

copying, PHOTOSHOP 3-7,
PHOTOSHOP 3-24
correcting errors, PHOTOSHOP 3-5
creating, PHOTOSHOP 3-7,
PHOTOSHOP 3-10
cutting, PHOTOSHOP 3-7,
PHOTOSHOP 3-24
defringing, PHOTOSHOP 2-22
deleting, PHOTOSHOP 3-7
deselecting, PHOTOSHOP 3-5,
PHOTOSHOP 3-7, PHOTOSHOP 3-9
flipping, PHOTOSHOP 3-20
growing, PHOTOSHOP 3-24
loading, PHOTOSHOP 3-9
Magic Wand Tool, PHOTOSHOP 3-16,
PHOTOSHOP 3-19
making, PHOTOSHOP 2-13
matching colors, PHOTOSHOP
4-30—4-31
modifying, PHOTOSHOP 3-20—3-21
modifying marquees. See marquee(s)
moving, PHOTOSHOP 2-13,
PHOTOSHOP 2-15, PHOTOSHOP 3-7
pasting, PHOTOSHOP 3-7,
PHOTOSHOP 3-24
saving, PHOTOSHOP 3-9
selecting by shape. See selecting by
shape
selecting with color, PHOTOSHOP
3-16—3-19, PHOTOSHOP 3-24
selection tools, PHOTOSHOP 3-2,
PHOTOSHOP 3-3
vignette effects, PHOTOSHOP
3-22—3-23, PHOTOSHOP 3-24
selection marquees, direct selections,
ILLUSTRATOR 1-39
Selection Tool, ILLUSTRATOR 1-3
Direct Selection Tool versus,
INDESIGN 4-25—4-26
marquee selections, ILLUSTRATOR
1-26—1-27
selection tools, PHOTOSHOP 2-12,
PHOTOSHOP 2-13, PHOTOSHOP 3-5
choosing, PHOTOSHOP 3-16
toggling between Pen Tool and,
ILLUSTRATOR 3-13

Select menu, ILLUSTRATOR 1-35
Select text color dialog box,
PHOTOSHOP 5-11
semi-autoflowing text, INDESIGN 4-38
serif fonts, PHOTOSHOP 5-4,
PHOTOSHOP 5-5
Set Background Color button,
PHOTOSHOP 4-6
Set Foreground Color button,
PHOTOSHOP 4-6
Set the anti-aliasing method list arrow,
PHOTOSHOP 5-3
Set the baseline shift text box,
PHOTOSHOP 5-3
Set the font family list, PHOTOSHOP 5-3
Set the font size list arrow,
PHOTOSHOP 5-3
Set the text color button, PHOTOSHOP 5-3
Shading setting, Bevel and Emboss style,
PHOTOSHOP 5-20
shadow(s), correcting, PHOTOSHOP 4-27
Shadow/Highlight dialog box,
PHOTOSHOP 4-27
Shadow Mode setting, Bevel and Emboss
style, PHOTOSHOP 5-21
shape(s), compound. See compound
shapes
shape modes, applying, ILLUSTRATOR
4-23—4-26
Shape tools, ILLUSTRATOR 1-3
Sharpen filters, PHOTOSHOP 4-3,
PHOTOSHOP 4-32
Sharpen More filter, PHOTOSHOP 4-25
Sharp setting, anti-aliasing,
PHOTOSHOP 5-17
Shear Tool, ILLUSTRATOR 4-4,
ILLUSTRATOR 4-10
shortcut keys, INDESIGN 1-6,
PHOTOSHOP 1-18
learning, PHOTOSHOP 1-19
showing
hidden lasso tools, PHOTOSHOP 1-38
History palette, PHOTOSHOP 1-38
layers, ILLUSTRATOR 5-11,
PHOTOSHOP 1-38
open palettes, PHOTOSHOP 1-38

options bar, PHOTOSHOP 1-38
palettes, PHOTOSHOP 1-22
rulers, PHOTOSHOP 2-22
Swatches palette, PHOTOSHOP 1-38
Tools palette, PHOTOSHOP 1-38
Show the Character and Paragraph palettes
button, PHOTOSHOP 5-3
Single Column Marquee Tool, PHOTOSHOP
2-13, PHOTOSHOP 3-5, PHOTOSHOP 3-24
Single Row Marquee Tool, PHOTOSHOP 2-13,
PHOTOSHOP 3-5, PHOTOSHOP 3-24
size
drop shadows, PHOTOSHOP 5-13,
PHOTOSHOP 5-14
resizing graphics, INDESIGN 4-27,
INDESIGN 4-33—4-34
text, scaling horizontally and vertically,
INDESIGN 2-6
sketches, line-art, tracing, ILLUSTRATOR
3-37, ILLUSTRATOR 3-44
Smart Guides, ILLUSTRATOR 1-27—1-28,
PHOTOSHOP 3-8
smooth points, ILLUSTRATOR 3-10,
ILLUSTRATOR 3-11
converting, ILLUSTRATOR 3-12—3-13
drawing closed paths using,
ILLUSTRATOR 3-20
Smooth setting, anti-aliasing,
PHOTOSHOP 5-17
Soft Light mode, PHOTOSHOP 4-26
soft returns, INDESIGN 2-15,
INDESIGN 2-19
sorting files, Adobe Bridge,
PHOTOSHOP 1-13
sources, matching colors,
PHOTOSHOP 4-30
Space symbol, INDESIGN 2-18
spacing
kerning, ILLUSTRATOR 2-4,
ILLUSTRATOR 2-5, ILLUSTRATOR
2-6, ILLUSTRATOR 2-8
between paragraphs, INDESIGN 2-17
tracking, ILLUSTRATOR 2-4,
ILLUSTRATOR 2-5, ILLUSTRATOR
2-6, ILLUSTRATOR 2-8
type. See type spacing

special effects
 clipping masks, ILLUSTRATOR 4-35
 compound paths, ILLUSTRATOR 4-19
 compound shapes, ILLUSTRATOR 4-29
 direct selections, ILLUSTRATOR 1-41
 type, PHOTOSHOP 5-24,
  PHOTOSHOP 5-25
spell checking, INDESIGN 2-26—2-27,
 INDESIGN 2-29
 automatic, INDESIGN 2-29
 dynamic, INDESIGN 2-29
spelling errors, correcting,
 PHOTOSHOP 5-10
spot colors, INDESIGN 5-24—5-29
 creating, INDESIGN 5-25
 importing graphics, INDESIGN 5-25,
  INDESIGN 5-27—5-29
 names, INDESIGN 5-24—5-25
 swatches, INDESIGN 5-26
Spot Healing Brush Tool, PHOTOSHOP
 3-22—3-23
spread(s), INDESIGN 1-16
 drop shadows, PHOTOSHOP 5-13,
  PHOTOSHOP 5-14
.srf files, PHOTOSHOP 1-5
stacking order, ILLUSTRATOR 2-26,
 INDESIGN 4-14, INDESIGN
 4-18—4-19
 layers, ILLUSTRATOR 5-5
starting color, gradients, INDESIGN 5-30
starting Photoshop
 Macintosh, PHOTOSHOP 1-5,
  PHOTOSHOP 1-7
 Windows, PHOTOSHOP 1-5,
  PHOTOSHOP 1-6
Star Tool,
 ILLUSTRATOR 1-34
states, deleting, PHOTOSHOP 1-27,
 PHOTOSHOP 5-19, PHOTOSHOP 5-30
status bar
 Illustrator window, ILLUSTRATOR 1-9,
  ILLUSTRATOR 1-10
 Photoshop window, PHOTOSHOP 1-17,
  PHOTOSHOP 1-18
Step and Repeat command, INDESIGN 4-6,
 INDESIGN 4-10—4-11

Step and Repeat dialog box, INDESIGN 4-6
Step Backward command, PHOTOSHOP
 5-19
stops, Gradient panel, ILLUSTRATOR 2-20
Story Editor, INDESIGN 4-39
straight lines, ILLUSTRATOR 3-4—3-9
 aligning anchor points, ILLUSTRATOR
  3-5, ILLUSTRATOR 3-8
 creating new views, ILLUSTRATOR 3-6
 drawing lines with curves and straight
  segments, ILLUSTRATOR 3-16
 drawing with Pen Tool, ILLUSTRATOR
  3-4—3-5
 joining anchor points, ILLUSTRATOR
  3-5, ILLUSTRATOR 3-9
striking through text, ILLUSTRATOR 2-10
stroke(s), ILLUSTRATOR 3-30—3-35
 applying to text, ILLUSTRATOR 2-26
 caps, ILLUSTRATOR 3-30
 dashed, ILLUSTRATOR 3-32,
  ILLUSTRATOR 3-34
 frames, INDESIGN 4-4—4-5,
  INDESIGN 4-9
 joins, ILLUSTRATOR 3-31
 miter limit, ILLUSTRATOR 3-31
 modifying attributes,
  ILLUSTRATOR 3-33
 pseudo-stroke effects, ILLUSTRATOR
  3-32, ILLUSTRATOR 3-35
Stroke button, ILLUSTRATOR 1-3,
 ILLUSTRATOR 1-22, ILLUSTRATOR
 1-24—1-25, INDESIGN 4-5
stroke color, ILLUSTRATOR 1-20,
 ILLUSTRATOR 1-22—1-25
Stroke dialog box, PHOTOSHOP 4-15
stroked paths, converting to closed path,
 ILLUSTRATOR 4-13, ILLUSTRATOR
 4-15
Stroke panel, ILLUSTRATOR 1-3
stroke weight, INDESIGN 4-4
stroking edges, PHOTOSHOP 4-14
Strong setting, anti-aliasing,
 PHOTOSHOP 5-17
Structure settings, Bevel and
 Emboss style, PHOTOSHOP 5-20,
  PHOTOSHOP 5-23

styles, INDESIGN 2-20—2-25
 character, ILLUSTRATOR 2-13,
  INDESIGN 2-20, INDESIGN
  2-22—2-23
 paragraph, ILLUSTRATOR 2-13,
  INDESIGN 2-20, INDESIGN
  2-23—2-24
sublayers, ILLUSTRATOR 5-4—5-5
 changing order, ILLUSTRATOR 5-12,
  ILLUSTRATOR 5-14
 creating, ILLUSTRATOR 5-4—5-5,
  ILLUSTRATOR 5-17
 definition, ILLUSTRATOR 5-12—5-13
subscript characters, INDESIGN 2-7
Subtract from shape area pathfinder,
 ILLUSTRATOR 4-21, ILLUSTRATOR 4-22
subtractive colors, PHOTOSHOP 4-6
Subtract shape mode, ILLUSTRATOR 4-25
superscript characters, INDESIGN 2-7,
 INDESIGN 2-10
Swap Fill and Stroke button,
 INDESIGN 5-13
Swap Fill button, INDESIGN 5-19
swatches
 importing from other documents,
  ILLUSTRATOR 2-28
 process colors, deleting, INDESIGN
  5-16—5-17, INDESIGN 5-23
 process colors, modifying, INDESIGN
  5-16, INDESIGN 5-23
 spot colors, INDESIGN 5-26
Swatches palette, PHOTOSHOP 4-11,
 PHOTOSHOP 4-12—4-13
 adding colors, PHOTOSHOP 4-13
 changing type color, PHOTOSHOP 5-7
 choosing background colors,
  PHOTOSHOP 4-32
 showing, PHOTOSHOP 1-38
Swatches palette list arrow,
 PHOTOSHOP 4-3
Swatches panel, ILLUSTRATOR 1-3,
 ILLUSTRATOR 2-20, INDESIGN 4-5,
 INDESIGN 5-5
 adding colors and gradients,
  ILLUSTRATOR 2-21, ILLUSTRATOR
  2-24—2-25

adding gradients and colors, ILLUSTRATOR 2-24—2-25
applying color, ILLUSTRATOR 1-23
Fill and Stroke buttons, INDESIGN 5-12, INDESIGN 5-13
tint swatches, INDESIGN 5-6
unnamed colors, INDESIGN 5-7
Swatch Options dialog box, INDESIGN 5-16, INDESIGN 5-17
Switch Foreground and Background Colors button, PHOTOSHOP 4-3, PHOTOSHOP 4-6
switching
    foreground and background colors, PHOTOSHOP 4-32
    between open files, PHOTOSHOP 4-32
symbol fonts, PHOTOSHOP 5-5

target(s), matching colors, PHOTOSHOP 4-30
target documents, data merge, INDESIGN 2-22
targeting layers, INDESIGN 4-16
target layers, INDESIGN 4-16
Template option, Layer Options dialog box, ILLUSTRATOR 5-6
text, INDESIGN 2-1—2-37. *See also* type
    applying color, INDESIGN 5-15, INDESIGN 5-20
    applying colors and gradients, ILLUSTRATOR 2-26—2-29
    autoflow, INDESIGN 4-38—4-39, INDESIGN 4-41—4-42
    baseline, INDESIGN 2-4
    black shadow, INDESIGN 5-16, INDESIGN 5-21—5-22
    as clipping mask, ILLUSTRATOR 4-34
    converting to outlines, ILLUSTRATOR 2-26—2-27, ILLUSTRATOR 2-29
    creating, ILLUSTRATOR 2-4, ILLUSTRATOR 2-6
    drop shadows, ILLUSTRATOR 2-31, ILLUSTRATOR 2-33
    filling objects with, ILLUSTRATOR 2-10, ILLUSTRATOR 2-12

footnotes, INDESIGN 2-10
formatting, ILLUSTRATOR 2-4—2-5, ILLUSTRATOR 2-7
overset, INDESIGN 3-38
pasting without formatting, INDESIGN 2-4
placeholder, text frames, INDESIGN 3-14
placing, INDESIGN 3-36—3-37, INDESIGN 3-40
positioning on paths, ILLUSTRATOR 2-16—2-19
reflow, INDESIGN 4-42—4-43
semi-autoflowing, INDESIGN 4-38
striking through, ILLUSTRATOR 2-10
threading, INDESIGN 3-38—3-39, INDESIGN 3-41
underlining, ILLUSTRATOR 2-10
wrapping around a frame, INDESIGN 3-47, INDESIGN 3-49
wrapping around graphics, INDESIGN 4-28—4-29, INDESIGN 4-35—4-37
text boxes, baseline grids, INDESIGN 3-13
text columns, INDESIGN 3-4, INDESIGN 3-5, INDESIGN 3-7, INDESIGN 3-15
    color, INDESIGN 3-7, INDESIGN 3-15
text frames, INDESIGN 3-6, INDESIGN 4-38—4-46
    autoflowing text, INDESIGN 4-38—4-39, INDESIGN 4-41—4-42
    column breaks, INDESIGN 4-39—4-40, INDESIGN 4-43—4-44
    master pages, INDESIGN 3-24—3-25
    out ports, INDESIGN 3-38
    page continuation notations, INDESIGN 4-40, INDESIGN 4-44—4-45
    placeholder text, INDESIGN 3-14
    in ports, INDESIGN 3-38
    reflow text, INDESIGN 4-42—4-43
    semi-autoflowing text, INDESIGN 4-38
    transforming, INDESIGN 3-16—3-17
Texture filter, PHOTOSHOP 5-25
thumbnails
    layer, PHOTOSHOP 2-4
    master pages, INDESIGN 3-16

opening files, PHOTOSHOP 1-10
    viewing, PHOTOSHOP 1-10
.TIFF files, PHOTOSHOP 1-5
.TIF files, PHOTOSHOP 1-5
tint(s), process colors, INDESIGN 5-4—5-5
tint swatches, process colors, INDESIGN 5-6, INDESIGN 5-8—5-9
title bar
    Illustrator window, ILLUSTRATOR 1-8, ILLUSTRATOR 1-9
    Photoshop window, PHOTOSHOP 1-16, PHOTOSHOP 1-17
Toggles lock button, Layers panel, INDESIGN 4-15
Toggles Visibility button, ILLUSTRATOR 5-20, ILLUSTRATOR 5-22
    Layers panel, INDESIGN 4-15
tool(s). *See also specific tools and types of tools*
    adding to Tool Preset picker, PHOTOSHOP 1-21
    selecting, INDESIGN 1-6, PHOTOSHOP 1-19—1-20
toolbar, INDESIGN 1-5—1-6, INDESIGN 1-8
tool preset(s), modifying, PHOTOSHOP 1-21
Tool Preset picker, PHOTOSHOP 1-20
    adding tools, PHOTOSHOP 1-21
Tools palette, PHOTOSHOP 1-3, PHOTOSHOP 1-16—1-17, PHOTOSHOP 1-16—1-18
    shortcut keys, PHOTOSHOP 1-18
    showing, PHOTOSHOP 1-38
Tools panel, Illustrator window, ILLUSTRATOR 1-9
tooltips, INDESIGN 1-6
tracing
    expanding traced graphics, ILLUSTRATOR 3-37
    line-art sketches, ILLUSTRATOR 3-37, ILLUSTRATOR 3-44
    photos, ILLUSTRATOR 3-38, ILLUSTRATOR 3-45—3-46

tracking, ILLUSTRATOR 2-4, ILLUSTRATOR 2-5, ILLUSTRATOR 2-6, ILLUSTRATOR 2-8, INDESIGN 2-6—2-7, INDESIGN 2-9—2-10, PHOTOSHOP 5-8
Transform Again command, ILLUSTRATOR 1-31, ILLUSTRATOR 1-33, ILLUSTRATOR 4-6, INDESIGN 3-12
Transform Each command, ILLUSTRATOR 4-6
transforming objects, ILLUSTRATOR 1-30—1-35, ILLUSTRATOR 4-4—4-11
    defining point of origin, ILLUSTRATOR 4-4—4-5
    Free Transform Tool, ILLUSTRATOR 4-4, ILLUSTRATOR 4-7
    multiple objects, ILLUSTRATOR 4-6
    Reflect Tool, ILLUSTRATOR 1-34—1-35, ILLUSTRATOR 4-4, ILLUSTRATOR 4-11
    repeating transformations, ILLUSTRATOR 1-31, ILLUSTRATOR 1-33, ILLUSTRATOR 4-6
    Rotate Tool, ILLUSTRATOR 4-4, ILLUSTRATOR 4-8—4-9
    Scale and Rotate Tools, ILLUSTRATOR 1-32
    Shear Tool, ILLUSTRATOR 4-4, ILLUSTRATOR 4-10
    tools, ILLUSTRATOR 4-4
    Transform panel, ILLUSTRATOR 4-7
Transform panel, ILLUSTRATOR 4-7, INDESIGN 1-7, INDESIGN 3-7—3-8, INDESIGN 3-9, INDESIGN 3-16—3-17
    scaling graphics, INDESIGN 4-27
Transform/Scale command, scaling graphics, INDESIGN 4-27
trim size, INDESIGN 3-4
tweaking objects, Direct Selection Tool, ILLUSTRATOR 3-5
Twirl dialog box, PHOTOSHOP 5-25
Twirl filters, PHOTOSHOP 5-25
type, PHOTOSHOP 1-5, PHOTOSHOP 5-1—5-35. See also text
    anti-aliasing, PHOTOSHOP 5-16—5-19
    baseline, PHOTOSHOP 5-9

Bevel and Emboss style. See Bevel and Emboss style
    bitmap, PHOTOSHOP 5-4
    closing type effects, PHOTOSHOP 5-30
    color, PHOTOSHOP 5-7, PHOTOSHOP 5-30
    creating, PHOTOSHOP 5-6
    drop shadows. See drop shadows
    filling with imagery, PHOTOSHOP 5-20
    filters. See filters applied to type
    font. See font(s)
    measuring size, PHOTOSHOP 5-5
    modifying, PHOTOSHOP 5-6
    outline, PHOTOSHOP 5-4
    purpose, PHOTOSHOP 5-2
    seeing effects (inactive layer), PHOTOSHOP 5-30
    selecting all text, PHOTOSHOP 5-30
    shifting baseline, PHOTOSHOP 5-30
    text on a path, PHOTOSHOP 5-28—5-29
    vertical, ILLUSTRATOR 2-9
    warping, PHOTOSHOP 5-22, PHOTOSHOP 5-30
type layers, PHOTOSHOP 2-4
Type on a Path Tool, ILLUSTRATOR 2-16
type spacing, PHOTOSHOP 5-8—5-11
    adjusting, PHOTOSHOP 5-8
    baseline shift, PHOTOSHOP 5-9, PHOTOSHOP 5-11
    kerning, PHOTOSHOP 5-8, PHOTOSHOP 5-9, PHOTOSHOP 5-10, PHOTOSHOP 5-30
    monotype, PHOTOSHOP 5-8
    proportional, PHOTOSHOP 5-8
Type Tool, INDESIGN 1-8, INDESIGN 5-15
Type tool(s), ILLUSTRATOR 2-2, ILLUSTRATOR 2-3
typography, ILLUSTRATOR 2-6

underlining text, ILLUSTRATOR 2-10, INDESIGN 2-7, INDESIGN 2-11
Undo command, ILLUSTRATOR 1-16
undoing
    actions, PHOTOSHOP 1-5
    anti-aliasing, PHOTOSHOP 5-19

ungrouping panels, INDESIGN 1-7
unhiding panels, ILLUSTRATOR 1-10
units of measurement, rulers, PHOTOSHOP 2-6, PHOTOSHOP 2-22
unlocked guides, ILLUSTRATOR 1-37
unnamed colors, INDESIGN 5-6—5-7, INDESIGN 5-11
Unsharp Mask dialog box, PHOTOSHOP 5-27
Unsharp Mask filter, PHOTOSHOP 4-24
updating layer comps, PHOTOSHOP 2-22

vector graphics, ILLUSTRATOR 1-19
version, Photoshop, PHOTOSHOP 1-33
Version Cue, PHOTOSHOP 1-14—1-15
    administrative functions, PHOTOSHOP 1-15
    workspaces, PHOTOSHOP 1-14
vertical type, ILLUSTRATOR 2-9
Vertical Type on a Path Tool, ILLUSTRATOR 2-16
view(s)
    Bridge, PHOTOSHOP 1-10
    multiple, of same image, PHOTOSHOP 1-33
    reducing, PHOTOSHOP 1-32, PHOTOSHOP 1-34
View Box, INDESIGN 1-18, INDESIGN 1-21
view buttons, Layers panel, ILLUSTRATOR 5-20, ILLUSTRATOR 5-22
viewing. See also displaying
    Full Screen Mode, PHOTOSHOP 1-20
    thumbnails, PHOTOSHOP 1-10
vignette(s), PHOTOSHOP 3-22—3-23
    creating, PHOTOSHOP 3-22—3-23
vignette effects, PHOTOSHOP 3-22—3-23, PHOTOSHOP 3-24

warping, type. See warping type
warping type, PHOTOSHOP 5-22, PHOTOSHOP 5-30
Warp Text feature, PHOTOSHOP 5-22
Wave filter, PHOTOSHOP 5-25

Web documents, Camera Raw images. *See* Camera Raw images
Web Safe RGB mode, ILLUSTRATOR 2-21
Welcome Screen, ILLUSTRATOR 1-15
white space, inserting between characters, INDESIGN 3-20, INDESIGN 3-26—3-27
Width setting, Magnetic Lasso Tool, PHOTOSHOP 3-11
Wind dialog box, PHOTOSHOP 5-25
windows, new, creating, INDESIGN 1-14—1-15
Windows platform, PHOTOSHOP 1-2
    hardware requirements, PHOTOSHOP 1-6
    starting Photoshop, PHOTOSHOP 1-5, PHOTOSHOP 1-6

workspaces, INDESIGN 1-4—1-9
    creating, PHOTOSHOP 1-38
    custom, INDESIGN 1-21
    modifying display, PHOTOSHOP 1-38
    Photoshop window, PHOTOSHOP 1-16
    Version Cue, PHOTOSHOP 1-14
wrapping text
    around frames, INDESIGN 3-47, INDESIGN 3-49
    around graphics, INDESIGN 4-28—4-29, INDESIGN 4-35—4-37

X coordinates, ILLUSTRATOR 4-8
.x3f files, PHOTOSHOP 1-5
Y coordinates, ILLUSTRATOR 4-8

zero point, INDESIGN 3-7
zooming in, PHOTOSHOP 1-38
zooming out, PHOTOSHOP 1-38
Zoom Slider, INDESIGN 1-18, INDESIGN 1-20
Zoom text box, Illustrator window, ILLUSTRATOR 1-9
Zoom Tool, ILLUSTRATOR 3-4, ILLUSTRATOR 3-6, INDESIGN 1-10—1-11, INDESIGN 1-13—1-14, PHOTOSHOP 1-3, PHOTOSHOP 1-32, PHOTOSHOP 1-34, PHOTOSHOP 1-38

INDEX

Design Chapter Opener Art Credits